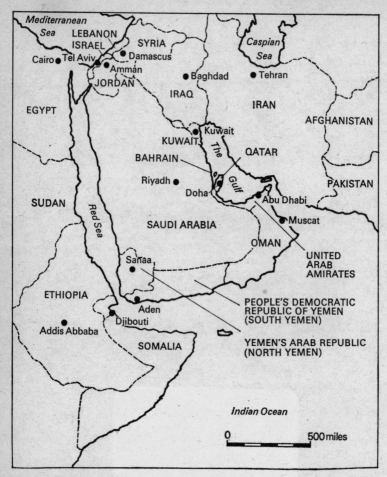

Map 1 The Arabian Peninsula – Political

Arabia Without Sultans

A Political Survey of Instability in the Arab World

Fred Halliday

Vintage Books

A Division of Random House
New York

VINTAGE BOOKS EDITION April 1975
FIRST EDITION

Copyright © 1974 by Fred Halliday
Introduction for U.S. edition Copyright © 1975 by
Fred Halliday

Library of Congress Cataloging in Publication Data

Halliday, Fred.
  Arabia without sultans.

  Includes bibliographical references.
  1. Arabia—Politics and government. I. Title.
DS227.H25 1975   953'.05   74-29336
ISBN 0-394-71529-2

Acknowledgements

Thanks are due to Her Majesty's
Stationery Office for permission to
reproduce *Muscat and Oman*, Treaty
Series No. 28, 1958, Cmnd. 507.

The plates are derived as follows:
1, 2, 3, 4, 5 Associated Press; 8 United
Press International; 9 *Daily Telegraph*;
12 the author.

Author's Preface

Three aspects of this book require some explanation – its approach, its emphasis and its relevance.

My intention is to provide a comprehensive analysis of the contemporary Arabian peninsula, by presenting and interpreting information that has, till now, been dispersed or inaccessible. The whole world has heard of Arabia – of Mecca, the desert, the bedouin and now of oil – but there has been little understanding of the internal politics and social structure of the region.[1]

This is vividly illustrated by the standard presentation of the oil crisis. In this conventional account, millionaire 'Arabs' are 'blackmailing' the helpless consumer nations. It is misleading, in two important ways. First, because this version, in talking of 'Arabs' and 'sheikhs', ignores the fact that there are sharp social divisions within these Arab states. There are sheikhs and kings in Arabia – but there are also workers, nomads and peasants. The spectacular rise in oil revenues has benefited the ruling classes of these countries; as for the oppressed inhabitants of this Arabia their rulers are now stronger than ever before, and more able to crush all opposition.[2] Those who complain only about the fate of the car-owners of the advanced capitalist countries should remember the more brutal fate reserved for the working classes of Arabia by the local tyrants and the oil companies.

The second distortion in the conventional picture is that, while it ignores real divisions within Arabian society, it exaggerates the difference between the rulers of the oil states and the major capitalist states. The ruling classes of the Middle East owe their present strength, and in some cases their very existence, to decades of support from the capitalist West. Today they are more powerful and are in a position to demand a higher price for, and greater

5

control over, the oil in their countries. This is only 'blackmail' in the sense that all capitalist business is blackmail – i.e. marketing products at the highest price the market will bear. The enriched tyrants of the peninsula and Iran are certainly intent on maximizing their profits; but they have no intention of weakening world capitalism as a whole, and are competitors, rather than enemies, of the interests now dominating the US, Europe and Japan. Beneath the disputes over the terms of partnership, there lies a sharing of interest.

It is because of this anti-capitalist approach that the book adopts its specific emphasis. Special attention has been paid to the revolutionary movements of North Yemen, South Yemen and Oman. These are the most heavily populated states of Arabia, and the ones which have not seen wide-scale exploitation of oil. It is precisely here, away from the centres of oil, that the social contradictions of Arabian society have been even more fiercely felt, and it is here that an alternative to capitalist development has been tried. Very little is known in the world about these conflicts: the Yemen civil war died in obscurity; the word 'Aden' has disappeared from the world's horizons since the British withdrawal of 1967; and the war in Oman has always been stifled by the censors of Whitehall. It is this approach too which has led me to include a chapter on Iran. Although lying outside the peninsula, this state plays a dominant role in peninsular politics and the future of the region cannot be conceived of apart from it.

The revolutionary wars that have been raging in Arabia since 1962 form the hidden face of the energy crisis, and it is this relation that defines the relevance of the book. Internationalist solidarity always includes a *political* element, of helping those who need support, and an *instructive* element, of learning from the study of other struggles. But it is founded on the *material sharing of interests* that unites the oppressed of different countries, just as the rulers of these countries share common interests which underlie their own competition. The chauvinist convention of talking about 'the Arabs' and 'us' is an ideological way of creating a false division in order to conceal a real one – the real one being that *within* 'us' and *within* 'the Arabs', between oppressors and oppressed. My hope is that this book will help to destroy the ideology and replace it with a more accurate understanding.

It will be obvious to any reader that this book distils an experience that goes far beyond that of the writer; and many people have helped me write it. It is not the official position of any movement, and so far as I know no individual or party shares all the views it puts forward. It is an account, by an outside observer, of a revolutionary process that I have tried to report and understand. I have a special debt of thanks to Fawwaz Trabulsi, without whom the project would never have begun, and to the members of the Gulf Committee, who encouraged and tolerated me for several years. I would also like to thank those people who read parts of the manuscript and helped me to improve it: Perry Anderson, Anthony Barnett, Jon Halliday, Judith Herrin, Helen Lackner, Maxine Molyneux, Roger Owen, Bill Warren and Ken Whittingham. Many comrades from the region under discussion – Iranians, Arabs and Kurds – have also helped me, but must for obvious reasons remain unnamed. Finally, I would like to thank the members of P F L O A G, who on two occasions welcomed me to Dhofar and spent many hours discussing their activities. I hope this book will contribute to the success of their enterprise, and to the liberation for which they and many others are fighting.

Fred Halliday

Contents

Contents

Part Two   North Yemen

Part Three   South Yemen

Contents

Part One
Peninsular Politics

Introduction

During the summer and autumn of 1973, as the oil crisis built up and exploded into the Arab embargo, a series of rumors suggested that the United States was planning to invade Arabia. To protect its access to oil, Washington was contemplating another Suez, possibly even another Vietnam. Senator J. W. Fulbright began speculation in May by evoking 'an ominous possible scenario for the years just ahead,' in which the U.S. government 'may come to the conclusion that military action is required to secure the oil resources of the Middle East, to secure our exposed jugular.' He added, 'There is no question of our ability forcibly to take over the oil-producing states of the Middle East. They are militarily insignificant.' Although Fulbright later announced that he had been assured officially that no such move was envisaged, speculation revived in August when eight thousand U.S. marines went on maneuvers in California's Mojave Desert: the battle plan for Alkali Canyon 73 specified that the marines were being sent in to save a Pro-Western desert state, Argos, from being overrun by the Communist-backed state of Yarmonia. The conclusion drawn by observers and participants was not surprising. 'The Pentagon has a computer plan for the invasion of every civilized country in the world,' Colonel Jerry O'Leary told reporters. 'The Middle East is the obvious powder keg, and we'd be fools if we didn't prepare'.[1]

In October, when the Arab–Israeli war broke out, ships of the U.S. Sixth Fleet converged on the Eastern Mediterranean, while those of the Seventh Fleet moved westward across the Indian Ocean to probe the mouth of the Red Sea, a strategically important strait which Arab forces were blocking to Israel-bound

17

shipping. At one point in the crisis, U.S. forces throughout the world went on the alert – allegedly for fear of a Russian intervention to save Egypt from an Israeli advance. But while these moves appeared to be supporting Israel against its Arab opponents in the war, other voices were raised when the oil embargo took effect to suggest a direct attack on the producer countries themselves. *The Economist*, a well-informed London weekly prone to airmailing strident advice to a putative White House readership, mused about the division of the world's states into 'lions' and 'gazelles':

The Saudis and the Kuwaitis know they are gazelles, all right. Their governments also know that in the last resort they are dependent on American help to protect them against the coups that could overthrow them. The growl that the lion might emit to the gazelle could at first just be a suggestion that this protection might be withdrawn; then it might be elevated into a hint that coups might be support on a different side (especially as nominally left-wing Arab politicians are often most especially venal) long before anybody would talk of another Suez operation 1956-style (although, in a western world that was really starved of oil, a Suez operation could be immensely popular).[2]

At least one Washington official appeared to concur with this: speaking on January 6, 1974, U.S. Secretary of Defense John Schlesinger warned the oil states against using their power 'to paralyze the industrialized world,' and the invasion rumors appearing in the press appeared to have some Pentagon inspiration. The response of two Arab producer states, Saudi Arabia and Kuwait, was to announce that they had mined their oil-fields: a U.S. invasion would result in the oil being blown up, causing the largest non-nuclear explosion in history. The well fires might never be put out, a huge black cloud would rise up from the Gulf and drift slowly across Asia, killing tens of thousands with sulphur dioxide as the world, energyless, ground to a halt beneath.

The Arab states gained prestige from these rumors: no one could now accuse them of being clients of the United States. Yet no invasion took place, and it seemed to many that none had ever been possible. The Saudis are long-standing allies of the

U.S.: although by mid-1973 relations were, as King Feisal said, 'difficult' because of a deep disagreement over Israel, the Saudis were and are no enemies of private enterprise. Fifty-seven years after the Russian Revolution they still refuse to recognize a single Communist country; thousands of political opponents lie unheard in Saudi jails; and Feisal has used his oil revenues to chase every opponent, left-wing or not, in the entire Middle Eastern and 'Muslim' world. Indeed, when the October war began the Saudis tried to insulate the United States from any damaging effects. Saudi Foreign Minister Omar Saqqaf flew to Washington and stood on the White House lawn lauding his host, who had dropped four million tons of explosives on Vietnam, as a man of peace. Despite some fears that the Saudis would pass on advanced military equipment to the belligerent Arab states, Feisal sent only a token infantry force to the battle zone. And while before the war the Saudis had talked tough about using the oil weapon, they proved reluctant to act once the fighting began. The war began on October 6; the Arab oil ministers did not even meet until the seventeenth. Then they did nothing, and it was only at the very end of the month, when Nixon requested $2.2 billion in emergency aid for Israel, that the Saudis agreed to impose an embargo on the U.S.; even then, Sheikh Yamani, the Saudi oil minister, attended the Kuwait meeting of Arab oil ministers only under strong pressure from his non-Saudi colleagues.

Not that the oil embargo was all that the U.S. or the Saudis made it out to be. Some oil allegedly being sent to Europe was diverted to the U.S., transhipped across Europe, or routed via Caribbean refineries to the East Coast. Total pre-embargo U.S. oil imports from the Arab world ran at around 1.7 million barrels per day (mbd) – about 27 per cent of U.S. imports and about 10 per cent of U.S. consumption. In January 1974, at the height of the embargo, an estimated 700,000 barrels per day of Arab oil were entering the U.S.; at the Saudi end, government officials claimed that oil production for January 1974 had fallen by 15 per cent on the previous September's levels, whereas tanker sailings from the Saudi port of Ras Tanura fell by less than 2 per cent –

a clear indication that the Saudis were lying about the amount by which they were cutting their oil. Some of this concealed production as well as some of the oil officially allocated elsewhere was getting through to the U.S. market.[3]

Throughout the crisis the Saudis worked hard to cushion the U.S.: in January 1974 the Saudis persuaded the OPEC (Organization of Petroleum Exporting Countries) states to freeze oil prices for three months; in March they had the freeze extended for another three months; and in June, when all oil companies had announced record profits, the Saudis asked for the price of oil to be *reduced*. In the face of other OPEC states' demands for a higher oil price the Saudis managed to hold the increase to a derisory 4 per cent.

The Saudis also knew that the oil restrictions, while to some extent hitting the U.S. consumer, also strengthened the position of the major U.S. oil companies. Restrictions on supply allowed the major American companies to squeeze out independent distributors. OPEC price rises empowered the oil industry to raise their prices, and in particular to upvalue stocks purchased at the old, lower price. Record company profits in the final quarter of 1973 and the first of 1974 confirmed these benefits, and it was not long before the embargo on the U.S. was lifted altogether. By early February Saudi Oil Minister Yamani was promising an end soon and the ban was finally lifted in late March; but under U.S. pressure, the ban was kept on Holland, the other embargoed country, in order to remind the truculent states of Western Europe *which* capitalist country was still number one. As the Algerians pointed out, in refusing to go along with this selective lifting, the Saudis were acting within the international economy as the agents of the U.S.[4]

The oil embargo was, of course, lifted long before any of the original conditions for its being ended had been met. Not an inch of Palestinian land had been returned, but U.S.–Saudi relations had gone beyond this 'difficult' phase. A series of military deals followed: $850 million were to be spent on U.S. equipment for the Saudi navy; $335 million on re-equipping the Saudi National Guard with armored cars, 105 mm. howitzers and anti-tank weapons; and $270 million on air defense missiles designed 'to protect the holy places,' according to Saudi Minister of Defense and Aviation Amir Sultan[5]. Most important of all was a long-term economic and military agreement estimated at $3 billion, under which the U.S. would 'assist' the Saudis to transform their economy and armed forces. Meanwhile, oil production rose from a daily 8.5 mbd before the embargo to 11.5 mbd in mid-1974, and in June, Nixon visited the Saudi town of Jiddah to consecrate the new arrangements.

Estimation of how serious that 'invasion' threat ever was involves distinguishing three different scenarios under which U.S. forces could debouch into the area. All three have held for some years past and will continue to operate for the rest of the century: they are therefore not merely of historical interest. The first possible scenario is to protect Israel in the event that an Arab victory appears likely: during both the 1967 and 1973 wars, U.S. naval and land forces in Europe and the Mediterranean were mobilized for such an eventuality, and in 1973 a massive airlift took U.S. supplies to airfields near the Israeli front line in the Sinai peninsula. Under a second scenario, U.S. forces could go into an Arab state to save it from being overrun by a more anti-imperialist rival: U.S. troops were sent into Lebanon in 1958, allegedly to prevent Syria from taking it over; in 1963 the U.S. air force went into Saudi Arabia to counter Egyptian air attacks from neighboring North Yemen; and in 1970 U.S. troops in Europe went on the alert in case the Jordanian army should be overrun by the Syrian tanks which half-heartedly invaded northern Jordan during King Hussein's attack on the Palestinian resistance – the 'black September.' The Alkali Canyon 73 maneuvers were supposedly for such an eventuality. A third kind of intervention would be in the event of an internal crisis in one of the Arab states – either a left-wing coup or a seizure of U.S. assets such as to provoke American intervention. Interventions of this third kind are less visible: direct interference in the internal politics of a country tends to take place through local agents (as in Iran in 1953, or in Cuba in 1961), and where U.S. forces do go in, the invasion is sometimes disguised as being

21

necessary because of an external threat. Both the Lebanese and Jordanian cases *were* ones in which the predominant threat to American interests came from within the country, but where an external force provided the legitimization.

While these three kinds of invasion are distinct, they overlap in the obvious sense that the U.S. troops will depart from the same bases and the ships of the same fleets will be involved. And it is possible that had the U.S. invaded Saudi Arabia or Libya in 1973 some kind of 'external threat' or local ally would have been produced to legitimize the invasion. There is, however, an absence of evidence to prove that an invasion was definitely considered: five different hypotheses about the invasion 'threat' suggest themselves.

(1) It was a fraud, part of a U.S.–Saudi understanding, to give the Saudis a nationalist reputation and thereby enable them to exert greater restraint on other Arab states, just as the American authorities were pretending to be hurt by an oil embargo that was weaker than officially described. Such an understanding between Washington and Riyadh could have been tacit or explicit.

(2) The 'plans' were real enough, but only reflected standard contingency preparations. Any government has such plans; their existence at any time does not necessarily mean they are being considered as immediate policy alternatives.

(3) The intention was to deter radical Arab states – Libya or Iraq – and possible like minded conspirators in Saudi Arabia from trying to go further than the Saudis were doing.

(4) There was a division of opinion within the U.S. government between the diplomatic sector (Kissinger plus the State Department) and the military sector (Schlesinger plus the Pentagon). The 'war plans' reflected the policy of the latter.

(5) The Washington authorities as a whole genuinely did believe that there might be a need to attack the existing Saudi and Kuwaiti regimes – allies have fallen out before. The invasion menaces were a way of letting it be known that if the embargo was maintained for a long time with damaging international effect, military pressure would be exerted (this being *The Econo-*

mist's advice). Daniel Ellesberg has pointed out that the threat of force is integral to both the foreign policies and the personalities of Nixon and Kissinger: they may have been considering a re-run of the Christmas bombing,[6] à la North Vietnam 1972.

No final answer to the invasion question is possible until more evidence is available, and some pairs of hypotheses could be true at the same time. Whatever the reality, they indicate the importance which at least some people in Washington attach to keeping access to raw materials, and to the high price which maintaining such an access can command. Any analysis of the question should, however, avoid the temptation of fighting tomorrow's campaign through the stereotype of yesterday's. A seizure of the Saudi wells would not be a Suez: the troops could not quickly be withdrawn, and the cost in destroyed installations and lost oil supplies would be far greater than the closure of the Suez Canal. Nor would it be a Vietnam: in one sense it would be less serious, since no war of such a protracted and bloody kind could be fought in the underpopulated and barren Arabian desert. On the other hand, the political situation would be more acute: there might be no Diem and no Thieu to legitimize invasion, and the need for oil would be an even greater incentive to annex the area outright than any raw material or strategic interest in Indochina.

In another sense, though, the very question is misguided. It is not a matter of whether the U.S. will intervene and fight a war in Arabia for control of oil: *the U.S. has been involved and fighting for oil for the past fifteen years – by proxy, in a campaign more covert and strategically more important than any war in Indochina or Latin America*. This is the hidden truth behind the invasion debate: the U.S. has already invaded. The whole world has now heard of the covert U.S. campaigns in Laos and Cambodia, but few know of the eight-year U.S. support, via Saudi Arabia, for the royalist counterrevolutionaries in North Yemen. Everyone has heard of the Bay of Pigs invasion of Cuba in 1961 but not of its Arabian counterpart – the September 1972 attack on South Yemen, when thousands of right-wing exiles and their tribal allies hurled themselves against the boundaries of the beleaguered anti-imperialist republic. No one has yet made photostats of the Washington memos detailing support for this invasion, nor documented the U.S. arms shipment and training advice for the thousands of other exiles harassing South Yemen from the Saudi Arabian desert.[7] Most striking of all is the thundering silence that followed the invasion of Arabia that *did* take place during the 1973 oil crisis; on December 20 of that year, around 10,000 Iranian troops were sent into Oman to crush the guerrilla forces fighting in that country's Dhofar province. This was the invasion to protect oil from a revolutionary threat about which so much had been heard, but it was concealed in part because attention was focused the wrong way – on the troop carriers flying from American bases in Turkey and Germany. And lest anyone think that 10,000 troops is a small number, they should remember that the total population of Dhofar is at most 250,000 – i.e., one sixtieth the population of South Vietnam. And sixty times 10,000 is 600,000, the number of U.S. troops committed to battle at the height of *that* counterrevolutionary invasion.

Fighting by proxy is, of course, the key to the Nixon Doctrine, as exemplified in Vietnamization. In Indochina, Thai troops have been used to play the role once filled by GIs; in Latin America, Brazil has upheld or instigated military regimes in Uruguay, Bolivia and Chile. In the Gulf area, the two states chosen are Iran and Saudi Arabia, today the two largest U.S. arms clients in the world. In a limited sense, there is nothing new in this policy of a major imperialist country delegating repressive functions. Throughout the period of their empire, the British used 'native troops' to garrison their dominions and fight 'dirty' wars for them. Much of the most brutal counter-revolutionary fighting in the Napoleonic wars and elsewhere was done by Irish troops. And Indian forces not only were used to garrison the subcontinent but were also deployed internationally against revolutionary movements in Russia (1919–20), Greece (1944–45) and Vietnam (1945).[8] The Kennedy-MacNamara limited war strategy in the early 1960s was centred on training Third World armies to counter internal subversion, while the U.S. military provided advice and technique. American troops were to be sent in only when all else failed. In this sense the massive commitment of ground troops to Vietnam was an exception, and 'Vietnamization', the allegedly *new* policy, is a return to an older style.

The difference between what is now called 'sub-imperialism' and these earlier British and U.S. strategies lies not so much in the military as in the political and economic spheres: Brazil, Iran, even Thailand are more politically independent and economically more autonomous than were either the colonies of the British Empire or the shaky neocolonial states of the early 1960s. In the military sphere the relationship's core has been well described by Nixon's first-term Defense Secretary, Melvin Laird: 'Each partner does its share and contributes what it best can to the common effort. In the majority of cases, this means indigenous manpower organized into properly equipped and well-trained armed forces with the help of materiel, training, technology and specialized skills furnished by the United States.'[9] This is exactly what has happened in Arabia. Although the U.S. has provided military assistance to Saudi Arabia since the 1940s, this has taken on new dimensions in the past decade and especially since the oil boom began in the late 1960s. Saudi Arabia, however, is not the only state to be involved. In 1971 Kuwait was made eligible for military sales, and in 1973 the five remaining capitalist states in Arabia – North Yemen, Oman, Bahrain, Qatar, the United Arab Amirates – were also included. Following visits by a U.S. military mission to Kuwait in 1972 and in 1973 the Kuwaitis announced plans to purchase $500 million worth of arms from the United States. In Bahrain the United States maintains a naval position at al-Jufair and the Bahraini Defense Minister, Sheikh Hamad bin Isa, has spent a year training in a course at Fort Leavenworth. In Oman the U.S. presence has been more low-key and front-line commitments have been left to the British and Iranians; but behind this apparent disinterest, the United States has taken up position in the Sultanate. Following a secret meeting in London in 1971 between Sultan Qabus and CIA representatives, millions of dollars in covert U.S. military aid were 'laundered' through Saudi Arabia. In early 1972 a private American fishing fleet began operations off the Omani coast, and Washington officials admitted that this fleet carried electronic surveillance equipment on behalf of the Pentagon[10]. No doubt, too, U.S. reconnaissance satellites provide useful information to the Sultan's forces on guerrilla movements in the Dhofar mountains. In North Yemen, finally, the United States has provided some military aid, but the army is still Russian-equipped and some spare parts have come from supplies captured from Egypt in the 1967 war, moved from Israel to Iran, and then provided by Iran to North Yemen.

The principles followed in all cases are those laid down by Laird: insofar as is possible the active personnel have been local; not only has this avoided the political problems involved in sending in U.S. or British ground troops but it has also accorded with the increased strength of the oil-producing states.

In Iran the policy has gone furthest of all, and Iran today is the strongest power in the whole Gulf area. Inside the country the SAVAK, modeled along American police and FBI lines, has been an efficient repressor of all opposition – a torturing and crushing device as efficient as its fellow organizations in South Vietnam and Brazil. Between 1950 and 1972 Iran received $837 million in U.S. military aid, a high amount for the time. Beginning in 1965 and up to the end of fiscal 1973 Iran purchased around $3.7 billion in more equipment – a sharp rise which turned Iran into the gendarme of the region. Not content with crushing his own people, the Shah has gone on to menace his neighbors, and in a meaningful extension of its counterrevolutionary role Iran has come to the aid of the United States in Indochina. Iran, along with Taiwan and South Korea, sent F–5A jets to bolster Saigon's defenses in November 1972, and when the hesitant Canadians dropped out of the four-power international observation team the Iranians stepped in to partner the Indonesians as the United State's representatives: in a macabre conjunction the Shah and Suharto, twin pillars of the Asian counterrevolution, have joined forces to serve their patron on the battlefield of Vietnam.

Table 1
Official US Military Relations with Gulf States to 1973

Date	Iran	Saudi Arabia	Kuwait/Lower Gulf States
1942	U.S. forces sent to Iran under Persian Gulf Command in December.		
1943	U.S. military advisory mission with Iranian Gendarmerie signed Nov. 27.	U.S. mission arrives in July to determine Saudi requirements for military equipment and training.	
1944		First U.S. military training mission arrives in April.	
1946		Dhahran Airfield completed	
1947	U.S. grants Iran a £25,000,000 credit agreement signed Oct. 6 to establish U.S. military advisory mission.		
1950	Mutual Defense Assistance (grant aid) Agreement signed May 23.		
1951		Dhahran Air Base agreement and Mutual Defense Assistance Agreement signed June 18.	
1953		Agreement to establish U.S. military mission signed June 27.	
1955	Iran joins Baghdad Pact (now CENTO) on Oct. 11.	Saudis purchase in August first U.S. tanks and subsequently reject Soviet arms offer.	

27

Date	Iran	Saudi Arabia	Kuwait/Lower Gulf States
1957		Dhahran Air Base renewed in February in exchange for continued military assistance. Training starts for Saudi Air Force and first F-86 jets delivered.	
1959	United States–Iran Defense Co-operation Agreement signed.		
1963		U.S. Air Force interceptors temporarily stationed at Dhahran as deterrent after Egyptian planes bomb 3 Saudi towns in January. Saudis initiate discussions for acquisition of modern air defense system.	
1964	U.S. military sales program inaugurated.		
1965		Agreement signed June 5 for U.S. Corps of Engineers to supervise the construction of military facilities. Initial sales contract for C-130 aircraft signed in September. Letter of intent signed with Raytheon in December for the Hawk Air Defense system and British Lightnings.	

Date	Iran	Saudi Arabia	Kuwait/Lower Gulf States
1966	United States agrees to sell Iran F–4 aircraft.	Signature of Saudi Arabian mobility program (vehicles, training in maintenance, logistics).	
1968	(British announce decision to withdraw from the Gulf by 1971). First F-4 delivered to Iran	United States conducts initial survey of Saudi naval expansion requirements.	
1969	U.S. grant aid for equipment ended.	Attacks on Saudi border posts by South Yemeni troops repulsed by Saudi forces in November-December.	
1971	Export-Import Bank provides credit assistance for Iran's military purchases.	Letters of offer for F–5 aircraft signed in July and September. Request for help in National Guard modernization received in September.	Kuwait made eligible for foreign military sales in January.
1972	U.S. residual grant aid program for training terminated.	Agreement on naval modernization program signed in February.	U.S. mission visits Kuwait in February to conduct defense survey.
1973		Agreement to arm and train National Guard units concluded in April. Saudi outpost hit by South Yemeni aircraft on, Mar. 22. Offer in principle to sell a limited number of F–4 aircraft made in May.	Lower Gulf States, Oman, and Yemen made eligible for foreign military sales in January. Border skirmish with Iraq occurs on Mar. 20. U.S. team visits Kuwait in April to offer military program based essentially on earlier survey.

Source: *New Perspectives on the Persian Gulf*, U.S. Government Printing Office 1973, p.16.

This flow of arms to the Gulf has involved not only the reinforcement of 'stability' in the area, but also a boost to American exports and to American arms firms, who – along with their British and French counterparts – have taken full advantage of the opportunity.

The volume of this expenditure raised certain questions in the U.S. Congress, especially when in mid-1973 the Saudis, Kuwaitis and Iranians started to request F–4 Phantom jets. Assistant Secretary of State for Near Eastern and South Asian Affairs Joseph J. Sisco justified the sale of Phantoms to Saudi Arabia on the grounds that there existed a threat to this country:

. . . as the states in the Gulf and the peninsula have taken on more responsibilities for their economic destiny, they, too, have become increasingly aware of threats they see to their security and of the need to improve their defensive capacity. These concerns have intensified as a result of the conflict between South and North Yemen last September, the continuing insurrection in Oman's Dhofar province which has its base of support in South Yemen, the arrest in recent months in the United Arab Emirates, Bahrain and Oman of a number of members of the subversive South Yemeni-supported Popular Front for the Liberation of Oman and the Arab Gulf (PFLOAG), the increasing supply of Soviet arms equipment, and technicians to South Yemen and to Iraq, the March 20 border skirmish between Iraq and Kuwait, and the March 22 attack by South Yemeni aircraft on a Saudi border outpost.

One of the principal U.S. policies in the Gulf since the British announced in 1968 their intention to end their protective treaty relationships there has been to encourage friendly states in the area to assume increasing responsibility for collective security in the region. In the Gulf, this has been shared primarily by Iran and Saudi Arabia . . . Elsewhere in the peninsula Saudi Arabia now bears the primary responsibility.[11]

In further elaboration Sisco stressed the danger of Soviet influence in the area, and argued that the Israelis need not fear the Saudi weapons. The Saudis were, he said, 'looking south, not north'. Under questioning, a number of problems arose. First, it appeared that the volume of U.S. arms sales to the region was between five and six times that of Soviet sales; moreover, that while the range

Table 2

US Arms Firms Officially Active in Iran and Saudi Arabia 1973

Currently, there are approximately 30 U.S. firms with defense-related contracts operating in Iran utilizing about 900 civilian employees in-country. The number of contractor personnel is expected to increase in the year ahead as some programs, now in their early stages, take on momentum. In Saudi Arabia, the comparable figures are 5 firms with about 700 civilians. In both countries, the firms are providing a wide spectrum of assistance to the military services of the two countries primarily related to instruction, training, and maintenance concerning the equipment purchased from the United States.

Firms operating in this fashion include the following, among others:

In Iran: Boeing
Raytheon
Bowen-McLaughlin-York
Control Data Corp.
I.T. & T.
Hughes Aircraft
Iran Aircraft
Lockheed Aircraft Corp.
Northrop
Bell Helicopter
Motorola, Inc.
Stanwick Corp.
General Electric
Westinghouse
Philco-Ford
McDonnell Douglas
Computer Sciences

In Saudi Arabia: Lockheed
Raytheon
Bendix
AVCO
Northrop (and subsidiaries)

Source: *New Perspectives on the Persian Gulf*, U.S. Government Printing Office 1973, p. 57.

of the Phantom is 1,000 miles, that of the Mig-21 (the plane the Russians supplied to South Yemen and Iraq) is 400 miles: this means that the Saudis would be able to bomb Aden and Baghdad, while neither the South Yemenis nor the Iraqis could reach Saudi cities or the main Saudi oilfields. Other, even more relevant qualifications were not brought up at all. The 'March 20 border incident' appeared to be all too convenient for the Saudis, as it provided justification for their arms request, and indeed this clash had been provoked not by South Yemen but by Saudi Arabia in order to produce a sense of crisis in the region – a Tonkin Gulf incident in the heart of the Arabian desert. Nor did anyone question Sisco's version of the September 1972 inter-Yemeni war, which was a deliberate attempt by U.S.-supported forces to topple the Aden government. It is true that the PDRY (People's Democratic Republic of Yemen), and PFLOAG (People's Front for the Liberation of Oman and the Arabian Gulf), present a threat to the regimes of the Gulf; this is because of the political character of these regimes. It is also true that the Soviet Union supports the PDRY and PFLOAG; but the Soviet Union did not create the conditions in which the Arabian revolutionaries are fighting – these were created by the United States, Britain and their local allies. Moreover, it is absurd to think that the PDRY could constitute any military threat to the Saudis: in this respect, as in the others detailed here, Sisco's picture was a distortion designed to justify arms supplies to the aggressive Riyadh regime.

The U.S. buildup in Arabia and the Gulf has, therefore, ominous similarities to U.S. policies in other regions where 'incidents' and 'foreign threats' are being used to justify a massive counterrevolutionary intervention. The reason for all this concern is oil. But the precise economic relationships involved in oil have been changing, and this, along with the partial British withdrawal from the area and the growing power of local states, has contributed to the new American approach. Until 1972 American firms controlled about 70 per cent of Gulf production, but exported very little of this directly to the United States. The American firms sold their Gulf oil in third countries –

Table 3

1972 Imports by Gulf Countries from United States, Western Europe, and Japan, and Market Shares (In millions of dollars)

Importing countries	World	United States		4 major European suppliers[1]		Japan	
		Amount	Percent	Amount	Percent	Amount	Percent
Saudi Arabia	1,397	346	25	[2]445	34	265	19
Kuwait	797	104	13	218	27	128	16
Iraq[3]	843	26	3	[2]313	37	35	4
United Arab Emirates	514	70	14	[4]159	31	98	19
Oman	185	7	4	144	78	8	4
Bahrain	[5]231	30	13	69	30	34	15
Qatar	138	14	10	58	42	17	12
Iran	2,555	425	17	[6]1,125	44	358	14

[1] Figures relate to imports from the United Kingdom, West Germany, France and Italy except as noted.

[2] Includes industralized Western Europe, i.e., Austria, Belgium, Denmark, France, West Germany, Italy, Netherlands, Norway, Sweden, Switzerland, and United Kingdom.

[3] Source is the IMF Direction of Trade.

[4] Includes Switzerland in addition to United Kingdom, West Germany, France, and Italy.

[5] Imports exclude crude petroleum from Saudi Arabia. These amounted to $147,000,0000 in 1972; their inclusion would lower all market shares shown above proportionately but does not distort the relative market positions shown.

[6] Includes United Kingdom, West Germany, France, Italy, Netherlands, Belgium, and Switzerland.

Source: *New Perspectives on the Persian Gulf*, U.S. Government Printing Office, p. 179.

Europe, Japan, the Third World – and then repatriated part of the profit to the United States, where the oil industry was less profitable. Little of the profit needed to be reinvested in the Middle East: for example, between 1948 and 1960 only $1.3 billion out of total receipts of $28.4 billion were reinvested, while $12.8 billion were repatriated[12]. In 1972 it was estimated that $2 billion were earned by American firms from oil operations in the Middle East and North Africa, this representing an 80 per cent return on net assets.

The other major interest, prior to 1972, was trade. Between 1967 and 1972 the United States exported approximately $1.5 billion per annum to the Gulf states, and there was an average surplus in the United State's favor of $0.5 billion each year.

This situation altered in 1972, when the United States began for the first time to require significant imports of crude oil. This new U.S. dependence is the material and real core of the energy crisis and it is this which has provoked sharper divisions among the imperialist countries and has made *guaranteed access* to oil more important than low prices and juridical ownership. Because of the greater need and the greater competition, the oil-producing states have been able to push up the price and alster the terms on which oil is exported.

The United States began to import oil in 1949. But although imported oil was cheaper than domestic oil, the major companies restricted imports and in 1959 they had imports legally held to 12.8 per cent of total consumption. This restriction held throughout the 1960s, when a series of protectionist measures looted an estimated $3.5 billion a year from American purchasers. Then in the late 1960s the importation of oil increased slightly and in 1970 the import quotas were raised for the first time. U.S. imports of oil rose from 2.8 mbd in 1968 to 4.7 in 1972, and in April 1973 import restrictions were abolished altogether.

Projections of U.S. energy requirements for the last quarter of the century show that the dependence on imported oil is bound to increase: this is certainly so in the period 1975–1985, and this trend will only be checked or reversed if emergency measures are taken at once to boost alternative supplies for the 1990s.

34

Table 4
US Oil Imports by Region of Origin

	1968		1972	
	Thousand barrels per day	Percent	Thousand barrels per day	Percent
Canada	470	16.7	1,085	22.9
Carribean	1,580	56.2	2,270	47.9
Middle East	270	9.6	475	10.0
North Africa	155	5.5	230	4.9
West Africa	15	.5	265	5.6
Western Europe	120	4.3	160	3.4
Other	200	7.1	255	5.4
Total	2,810	100.0	4,740	100.0

Source; *energy and Foreign Policy*, U.S. Government Printing Office 1974, p. 12.

Total U.S. energy consumption in 1972 was the equivalent of 35 mbd of oil and is expected to rise to 80 or 100 mbd by the year 2000. Within this the oil component was around 17 mbd in 1972, and is expected to hit 40 or more mbd at the end of the century. U.S. domestic production is expected, on the other hand, to stagnate between 10 and 15 mbd, leaving a massive gap which only imports can fill: the likely picture is that by 1985 the United States will need to import 60 percent of its petroleum, and that 40 percent of this will come from the Middle East, mainly Saudi Arabia. The reason for the dependence on the Middle East is simply that it has two-thirds of all known reserves, and has the greatest capacity for expansion.

A number of different arguments can be used to counter this prediction. The oil companies claim that if restrictions are lifted on U.S. production, the import dependence can then be lessened. In November 1973 Nixon proclaimed Project Independence, under which the United States would become self-sufficient in energy by 1980. Moreover, there are many Americans who think that the whole energy crisis is a fraud, dreamed up by the oil companies to boost profits and strangle competition. Out of this melee, three solid arguments can be extracted: first, that U.S. energy needs will not rise so much: secondly, that alternative sources of energy will lessen the importance of oil; and thirdly, that oil production outside of the Middle East will be able to meet U.S. demand.

First, energy demand. Energy demand rises faster than GNP for a number of reasons: the poor get richer and want the same domestic appliances as the rich; employers want to increase worker productivity, so they install more machinery per employee; leisure activities expand as incomes rise; and young couples, the highest per capita energy consumers, form a preponderant part of the American population. There has been speculation about replacing the car by mass transit; this is possible, but these systems take ten years to build, so every such system operative by 1985 has already been scheduled. Alternatively there are ways of cutting energy consumption by restricting its use: all cars could be limited to 40 horsepower; no plane could be allowed to fly unless 85 percent full; all leisure consumption – second homes, snowmobiles, speedboats – could be banned; all buildings could be properly insulated. But the result of all these together would be to hold energy consumption to about 80 mbd by 2000.

The second objection concerns the availability of energy other than petroleum. Six candidates have been brought forward: gas, coal, shale oil, nuclear energy, geothermal energy and solar energy. Gas and coal are traditional sources of energy and exist in large quantities in the United States; the 3,000 trillion cubic feet of gas estimated to exist in 1973 were reckoned to be enough for eleven years, and the 1.5 trillion tons of coal were enough for five hundred years. Coal is therefore a possible candidate; but the major technological requirement is mass coal gasification, and given the present state of knowledge this is unlikely to be available in any significant degree before the 1990s.

This leaves the four 'new' energy sources; here the question is also one of the time needed to develop a new technology of extraction. In 1973 the 47 operative nuclear reactors provided less than 1 percent of the United States' energy needs, and the leadtime on building a reactor is seven to nine years. As with the rapid transit systems, every reactor that will be in operation in 1985 has already been scheduled; and nuclear energy will not provide more than 10 or 15 percent of total energy needs. The state of the other three candidates is even more primitive: in 1973–74 whereas $561 million were being spent on nuclear research, only $12 million were being spent on solar energy research, $5 million on shale oil and $4 million on geothermal energy research.[13] By contrast $2.5 billion were spent on the Skylab Project alone, and the primitive state of these energy alternatives confirms the disparity. Shale oil was the great chimera behind Nixon's Project Independence: there are enormous reserves in the Rockies and initial optimists spoke of 23 mbd by the mid-1980s. Then the problems were noted. First, only 6 to 7 percent of the material dug up is usable, so there are enormous extraction and waste-disposal problems. Secondly, large quantities of water are needed to wash and process the shale by the standard surface-extraction process: even if all the water used at present in

Wyoming, Utah and Colorado were diverted to shale production, the maximum production would be 5 mbd. Finally: the environment. Extraction of the shale would involve ripping open large expanses of the Rockies, a practice that many in the United States will oppose. Later post-'Independence' projections reduced the prediction to 1 mbd by 1985, and the first experimental station at Parachute Creek, Colorado, had a planned output of fifty thousand barrels per day. Solar energy and geothermal energy are certainly candidates for the post-2000 era, but the technology is too limited at the moment for mass consumption to be feasible in the final quarter of the century.

The third possible objection to the 'Middle East dependency' thesis is that oil can be found elsewhere in sufficient quantities. For a start, there is more U.S. oil – both 'lower 48' and Alaskan. Lower 48 production could be increased somewhat, but at a cost in environmental disruption: permitting wide-scale offshore drilling on the East and West coasts. However, estimates suggest that the potential increase would not be that great, or cheap. Alaskan oil, when it finally comes onstream, will be at a modest 2 mbd, and maximum production in the mid-1980s is scheduled to be 4 mbd. There is, of course, oil elsewhere, but not in adequate quantities. Maximum production of the Athabasca tar sands in Canada is reckoned to be 3 mbd; Venezuelan production has leveled off; Indonesian production is unlikely to go beyond 2 mbd; Africa and Indochina have reserves for which there is intense competition, but their production is modest in comparison with that of the Middle East. As for Russia and China, they are both self-sufficient in oil, but neither appears able or willing to export in large quantities. So the United States is left with the Middle East, on which it will become more dependent as Europe becomes able to supply a part of its increase from the new sources in the North Sea.

It is because of this almost inevitable dependence that the United States has consolidated its relations: Washington wants to ensure that the Saudi government has no reason to quarrel with it and also to provide the Saudis with the assistance they need to repress their enemies, internal and external. An added reason is that the American authorities are eager to funnel back into the United States the Saudi and Kuwaiti monies that these states do not want to spend at the moment.[14] This developing U.S.-Saudi alliance is, moreover, part of a general rightward shift in the Arab world from which the United States has benefited. In the 1950s and 1960s Egypt was the leader of anti-imperialism in the Arab world: although limited by the class interests of the new bourgeoisie created in Egypt by the government's industrialization and administrative expansion, this Nasserite anti-imperialism played an important part in the peninsula and helped to encourage the revolutionary movements in North Yemen, South Yemen and Oman.[15] Following the 1967 defeat by Israel, Nasser abandoned this militant foreign policy and began to encourage the private sector in Egyptian agriculture and industry. Anwar es-Sadat, who became president on Nasser's death in October 1970, accelerated this process and consolidated a new relationship with Saudi Arabia, the country that had once been Nasser's main enemy. The war of 1973, perceived in Arab eyes as a victory, did not reverse the tendency begun by the 1967 defeat: it intensified it, appearing to legitimize Egypt's rightward shift at home and abroad. Saudi money, and Saudi-supported emphasis on 'traditional' Islamic values, have helped to shape the character of Sadat's Egypt, and when Nixon was given an ecstatic welcome in Egypt in June 1974 the Saudi press cited this as proof of Egypt having rejected the policies of the previous two decades. Diplomatic and economic ties were reopened with the United States, and the country which had once confusedly but militantly pioneered Arab nationalism now extended its embrace to Henry Kissinger and Richard Nixon.

Three issues remain to trouble the smooth development of the new U.S.-Arab relationship. The first is Israel. The Arab oil producers are capable of clashing with the United States until there is a definitive settlement of the Palestinian question. For the Arab states, this means until the Palestinian people regain sovereignty over at least part of their lost lands. The Saudis and the other states are not opposed to American imperialism in general: they happily shipped oil to the U.S. war machine in Indochina, and one can only speculate as to what would have happened had they chosen to exert a *total* and *unified* blockade of the advanced capitalist countries during the American bombing of North Vietnam in December 1972. But no such gesture of internationalism was possible, and the brutal exploitation of the African oil-importing states through the price rises is eloquent testimony of the rapacious character of the Saudi and Kuwaiti rulers. They have no desire to weaken American capitalism; they are not even as grasping as the Iranians who pressed for a rise in oil prices in 1974 while the Saudis wanted the price to be lowered. Saudi militancy over Israel is based on three factors: a religious obsession about 'the holy places' of Jerusalem; a displaced solidarity with the Palestinians – displaced in that the population of Saudi Arabia and the Arab world support the Palestinians and thereby force the governments to play along; and, thirdly, a realization that the conflict with Israel provides a means whereby the oil-rich countries can gain diplomatic influence in those states along the front line. For these three reasons the Saudis are concerned about Palestine and a failure to resolve the question of Israel poses a long-term threat for the American position in the Arab Middle East.

The second problem concerns U.S. relations with its junior imperialist rivals. While it is a common assumption in the United States that American imperialism enjoys unquestioned predominance within world capitalism, this view, somewhat narcissistic, in both its triumphant and condemnatory forms, ignores the competition which the United States faces from its European and Japanese rivals. The Arab Middle East has for a century been the scene of sharp inter-imperialist contradictions, partly at least because the threat of 'communism' has been less. In all four Arab-Israeli wars (1948, 1956, 1967, 1973) the United States has supported a position different from that of either France or Britain – i.e. there has never been a common imperialist stand on this question.[16] In 1973 the differences were evident: the Europeans and the Japanese were more dependent on Arab oil supplies and therefore went further toward placating the Arab states. Britain, France, Japan and West Germany all tried to arrange bilateral state-to-state deals to ensure access to oil. The United States condemned these deals as 'breaking ranks', and the disunity was celebrated at the February 1974 Washington conference of oil-importing states, which broke down because the other countries would not form a common front with the United States. The competition for Arab oil revenues, and for privileged access to oil supplies, is certain to exacerbate inter-imperialist rivalries that have already been aggravated by the trade disputes and currency crises of the late 1960s and early 1970s.

The third major challenge to the new alliance comes from the peoples of the Arab world themselves. And it is their history that forms the content of this book. The Algerian people fought an eight-year war which finally expelled the French and established an independent state. Since 1967 the Palestinians have, despite setbacks, forced much of the world to recognize their right to self-determination. In the Arabian peninsula there has been war in one country or another, since 1962; and it is this process of radicalization and revolt in the least-known part of the Middle East that threatens imperialist access to oil. Neither the enrichment of the Saudi regime nor the capitulations of Egypt have aided the liberation of the Arab peoples, but the changes have produced a movement that is more original and more rooted in the people than any before. An oil-hungry America, already brooding uneasily over its foreign entanglements, is now tied to an insurgent Arabia.

June 1974

Notes

1. See 'In Rommel's Shadow: Jungle-Weary Machines Go to "War," Stress Desert Combat,' *The National Observer*, August 25, 1973; and Barry Rubin in *M E R I P* Report No. 22. The periodical *M E R I P* (*Middle East Research and Information Project*), P.O. Box 48, Cambridge, Mass. 02138, is the best English-language source of analysis on the area.

2. *The Economist*, November 17, 1973.

3. 'The Oil Embargo,' *M E R I P* Report, No. 28.

4. *Le Monde*, June 4, 1974, carried a lucid editorial 'L'Arabie Américaine,' uncovering the U.S.–Saudi connection.

5. *BBC Summary of World Broadcasts*, Part 4, April 10, 1974; henceforth *SWB*.

6. *Rolling Stone*, November 8, 1973.

7. Documents captured by PDRY forces during the 1972 war included one set of instructions from the Saudi Ministry of the Interior to tribal leaders in North Yemen: the invasion plans were stated to be authorized by a committee, which included Saudi government nominees and an unnamed 'American Military Adviser.' Another document, broadcast by Libyan radio in 1974 (*SWB*, April 30, 1974), was a letter from Feisal's expert on North Yemen affairs and brother-in-law, Kamal Adham, to the North Yemeni President al-Iryani. This explained how 'our American friends' supported the call for Yemeni unity in the belief that it would serve to isolate the PDRY; now that the PDRY was calling for unity, the Saudis were against it. It is worth noting that officially inspired Washington journalism on the CIA in the 1973–4 period more than once stressed that the Gulf and Arabia had become one of that agency's top priorities. The appointment of former CIA chief Helms as U.S. Ambassador to Tehran and the moving of U.S. intelligence headquarters for the Middle East from Nicosia, Cyprus, to Tehran in or around 1973 were further indications of a substantial and deep concentration of emphasis.

8. See *The British in Vietnam*, by George Rosie, for details of how Britain launched the anti-communist war in Indochina *after* the defeat of Japan and *before* the French were strong enough to retake control.

9. Quoted in *Open Secret: The Kissinger–Nixon Doctrine in Asia*, ed. Virginia Brodie and Mark Selden, p. 103.

10. 'Who Runs the Sultan of Oman?' *Economist Foreign Report*, February 3, 1972, gives details of the laundering operation. See also p. 297 of the present volume.

11. *New Perspectives on the Persian Gulf*, U.S. Government Printing Office, 1973, pp. 2–3.

12. *MERIP* Reports Nos. 20 and 21. 'Middle East Oil and the Energy Crisis,' by Joe Stork, gives extensive background to this question.

13. *Energy and Foreign Policy*, U.S. Government Printing Office, 1974, p. 31.

14. Details of Arab capital flows to different capitalist countries are hard to come by. Some Arab money has been invested in U.S. real estate (especially in Florida) and the size of the Wall Street market is bound in time to give U.S. capitalism a significant hold on this surplus cash.

15. The key political organization in this influence was the Movement of Arab Nationalists (MAN) which originated in Palestinian exile circles in 1948 and later spread its branches throughout the Arab world. It acted as a covert Nasserite political party at the pan-Arab level, though it was not allowed to operate in Egypt itself. It dissolved in the mid-1960s, and

some of its branches emerged as independent radicalized organizations: they include the N L F of South Yemen, the P F L P (Popular Front for the Liberation of Palestine) among the Palestinians, P F L O A G (People's Front for the Liberation of Oman and the Arabian Gulf) and other smaller groups in North Yemen, the Gulf and Lebanon.

16. The situation in 1948 was that Britain and France leant toward the Arabs, whereas the U.S. supported Israel. In 1956 the British and French fought with Israel, while the U.S. at least formally disapproved. In 1967 the U.S. and Britain supported Israel, while France affected a 'pro-Arab' stance. In 1973 the U.S. backed Israel, while Britain and France tried to placate the Arab states.

Chapter One
Society and History in the
Arabian Peninsula

The Economy of Arabia and the Structure of Tribes

The revolutionary movement that swept the Arabian peninsula in the 1960s emerged from a society of the most static and impoverished kind. The peninsula, known to Arabs as *al-Jazira* (the peninsula) and only to non-Arabs as 'Arabia', had only a relative unity; it was split by geographical, social and historical divisions, and the operations of imperialism had increased political distinctions between its different parts.[1] At no time in its history, except for a few years at the beginning of the Islamic era, had it been united under a single power. Yet despite these disunifying factors Arabia had a definable cohesion, derived both from geographical unity and from economic links that had existed for millennia and had been strengthened in the twentieth century. Whatever its variations, the peninsula possessed a general system that had operated along constant lines from the first millennium B.C. to the middle of the twentieth century.

The most prominent feature of the Arabian peninsula is known to every outsider: the area is predominantly barren with little water or cultivable land. It has always been populated sparsely, and even in the mid twentieth century t has a population of under twelve million for an area of over one million square miles. This gives it a population density of around 10–11 per square mile, one of the lowest in the world. The amount of cultivated land is minimal: in Saudi Arabia, the largest state, around 0·2 per cent of the land is cultivated; in South Yemen it rises to 0·5 per cent; in Oman it rises to possibly 1 per cent and in North Yemen it reaches its highest proportion, at around 5 per cent. There is regular rainfall in only a few minor parts of the peninsula. In the mountains of Yemen, Dhofar and Oman the monsoon comes in from the Indian Ocean and provides a regular down-

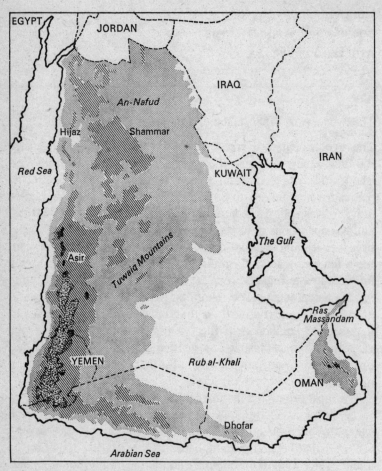

Map 2 The Arabian Peninsula – Physical

pour; but in the whole of Arabia not one river flows all the year from its source to the sea.

Arabia is not in the main a land of sandy deserts. Parts of the area known to outsiders as the 'Empty Quarter' are of this classic romantic kind of desert; and most of the peninsula is barren. But the most common kind of desert is hard steppe-like land, often stony, but capable of supporting a transient plant life when occasional rains fall.

The peninsula rises sharply in the west along the Red Sea coast and then slopes gradually eastwards towards the coast of the Gulf.[2] Parts of North Yemen, Dhofar and Oman are mountainous, and the smaller Shammar, Tuwaiq and Hijaz ranges rise in the middle and north of the peninsula. Most inhabitants are not, as commonly supposed, pastoral nomads. Although up to 40 per cent of them are nomadic bedouin, and they certainly predominate in most of the land area, 50 per cent of the population are settled people, concentrated in the fertile areas and along the coast. The majority are peasants and fishermen, not herders of camels and goats. There are also a number of towns, both on the coast and in the interior. Some were previously agricultural centres, in fertile parts of Yemen and Oman and in the oases of the desert, and including towns such as Medina, Sanaa, Shibam and Nizwa. Others were trading and transit centres dependent on the fluctuations of a particular market; these included Mecca, Aden, Muscat and Kuwait.

Historically the peninsula had a subsistence economy; but a commercial sector existed that markedly influenced the general social condition. In the areas where nomadic pastoralism dominated, mainly in the north, the bedouin lived off their camels, which provided food, clothing, housing materials and transport. The camels fed off the permanent vegetation of oases and off the greenery that sprung up in the desert after occasional rains. In the settled southern part of the peninsula and in the agricultural oases peasants grew cereals and dates. Throughout most areas irrigation systems conserved what water there was. Only in the tropical mountains of Dhofar was there enough rain for crops to be grown without irrigation, and there, for social reasons, the population remained predominantly nomadic. Both nomadic and settled peoples practised trade, of which there were three distinct varieties. The first was intra-peninsular exchange between different economic sectors; nomads traded animal products (milk, skins, etc.) for peasant crops and for products of the small artisanal community in the towns. Fishermen traded their catch for the produce of the other sectors. The second kind of trade involved the exchange of peninsular products for imported goods. The most important exported product used to be incense, grown in the South Yemeni hills and above all in Dhofar. It was transported, via a caravan route, up the western peninsula along the Red Sea to the Mediterranean, and was also exported by sea to India. In the eighteenth century North Yemen exported large quantities of coffee, via the port of Mocha, to Europe and North America. In return for these exports the peninsula purchased gold and the manufactured products of the countries to the north. The third form of exchange was the entrepot trade; lying between India, China and Africa on the south-east and south-west and the Mediterranean and Mesopotamia (modern Iraq) on the north, both the peninsula and its adjacent waterways were used for this purpose. Although this trade did not originate in the peninsula it benefited Arabia considerably, and the caravan route that transferred incense north from south Arabia was also dependent for its prosperity on this entrepot trade. The fate of the entrepot ports in both the Gulf and the Red Sea, most notably Aden and Muscat, was therefore affected by the state of trade at either end of this route. Growth in Egypt meant expansion in Aden; crisis in Mesopotamia meant decline in Muscat and in other Gulf ports. Economic dependence on the countries to the north was greater and more lasting than any political relationship.

The predominant form of social organization was the tribe. This was a kinship unit, formally based on real or imagined descent from a common ancestor through the male line.[3] Marriage was usually within the tribe, and women from other tribes, sometimes married for reasons of dynastic alliance, were assumed into the tribe of the man they married. The tribe was the unit that constituted economic, military and political activity, in settled communities as among nomads. Both in the sedentary peasant societies of Yemen and Oman, and in merchant towns such as Aden, Bahrain and Kuwait, the tribe remained the constitutive form of social organization. In many cases transition to sedentarization and, later, contact with the more developed outside world actually served to reinforce, rather than weaken, tribal ties.

The leader of the tribe was the sheikh (literally 'old man'). He had two main duties: to arbitrate within the tribe between conflicting factions and to represent the tribe and lead it in dealings with external forces, whether in peace or in war. The sheikh was formally chosen by the council of leading tribal figures, known as the *majles*, and his position was liable to be challenged if he did not perform his duties in the way that the more powerful members of the tribe wanted. In practice the position of sheikh was often reserved for members of specific families within the tribe and could be passed from father to son; once appointed, a sheikh could use this power to eliminate any challenge. The assertion made by some romantic writers that the tribe was in any meaningful sense a 'democratic' institution is inaccurate. An important aspect of Arabian life, especially among the nomads, is that the economy of the people was so near subsistence that there was no significant surplus for anyone with power to appropriate. In this sense the sheikh was no richer than his fellow tribesmen. But power within the tribe was always reserved for the more influential minority of male family leaders, and their powers of arbitration included powers of economic management. Elder male members of a tribe also had the power to fix bride-prices and to arrange marriages; this too gave them control of one of the key means of allotting and transferring wealth within tribal society. In the settled and merchant communities, where division of labour and surpluses were more articulated, the position of sheikh carried definite economic advantages.

Because of the relatively undeveloped economic system, property took correspondingly simple forms. In even the most arrested nomadic societies individual families possessed their own

49

movable objects – tents, cooking utensils, clothes – and in nearly all cases it was the family, not the tribe, that owned animals. 'Land ownership' varied with economic activity: in nomadic areas tribes as a whole had by tradition the rights to certain grazing areas and to particular sources of water. Though the exclusive 'property' of specific tribes, these were not worked on in any way. Similarly, in settled areas, agricultural land was the domain of specific tribes, with the difference that here individual ownership was found. In North Yemen and in Oman, as well as in the oases of central Arabia, the most common form of agrarian labour was share-cropping; the owners of the land, who could be sheikhs, or small merchants,[4] or simply richer peasants, would get other labourers to work on their lands in return for a percentage of the crop. In the coastal towns boat-owners would hire fishers and pearl divers in return for their receiving a share of the catch. In both the agrarian and maritime areas small individual operators, individual peasants or fishermen, were common.

In former tribal society some animals may have been owned collectively, and there certainly was collective tribal appropriation of water and grazing rights. There is no evidence of full collective ownership of animals; and there is every indication that even in the most 'primitive' tribes power was unequally distributed, first as between men and women, and secondly as between more and less powerful male leaders within the tribe. In the centuries after the founding of Islam there arose numerous utopian communist sects inside the Moslem community who called for collective ownership of land and other property and who, like the analogous movements inside medieval Christianity, were accused of many apparently unorthodox practices. These movements spread to parts of the Arabian peninsula and traces of them are said to survive; but whatever the truth of this, their 'communism' would be quite distinct from the primitive tribal communism that allegedly existed in early Arabian society.[5]

Relations between tribes were regulated by a set of conventions which controlled and constantly reaccentuated inter-tribal conflicts. The basic forms of inter-tribal relations were alliances and feuds. Allied tribes formed confederations – *hilf*, plural *ahlaf*

– which agreed not to fight, or agreed to join in a common campaign; but these were usually without any accepted dominant leader and altered rapidly. In both North Yemen and the interior of Oman there existed long-standing confederations; yet even here membership of such groups varied. Most conflicts were between sub-sections and did not involve all the members of the confederation at any one time. Inter-tribal feuding was a dominant feature of the area and one which prevented the emergence of larger political units or of economic cooperation. It locked individuals into the tribe, since it was incumbent on a tribe to avenge a wrong done to any member of the tribe; and an individual without a tribe was, conversely, helpless.

Because of the prevalence of feuding, every tribesman, whether nomad or peasant, was also a warrior. Feuding was partly provoked by the scarcity of water, food and animals, which encouraged constant theft. The pillaging of caravans, or at least the exaction of tolls, formed a major part of the livelihood of many tribes. Yet feuding was also an integral and autonomous part of the system of the peninsula, and continued irrespective of scarcity of resources.[6] While usually less common in settled societies, feuding did itself prevent sedentarization. A tribe with its wealth located in an arable crop was more vulnerable to attack than one which could move and split up its wealth. As an ideological consequence, many tribes felt it dishonourable to practise agriculture.

Stratification operated both within and between tribes. The growth of social inequalities accompanying sedentarization in turn encouraged differences between members of tribes in power, wealth and ownership of the means of production. From the most primitive nomadic societies onwards some families were more privileged than others, either by having more camels or by traditionally greater influence within the tribe. Outside intervention encouraged this influence; by bribing a sheikh to get his tribe's loyalty, an outside power gave the sheikh the means (gold coin, guns) to increase his domination over the members of this tribe. The major social consequence of the Yemeni civil war of 1962–70 was the strengthening of sheikhs in this way; the advent of new money and of capitalism to North Yemen actually reinforced pre-capitalist relations.

Tribes were traditionally graded according to the stronger and weaker, the richer and the poorer, those who carried arms and those who did not. The share-croppers who worked in settled areas were frequently from lower tribes rather than from the same tribe as the landowner. At either end of the social scale there were minorities who were outside the tribal system altogether. At the top end in Yemen and elsewhere arbitrators and often landowners formed the Sada. This caste claimed direct descent from Mohammad but was not considered a tribe like other kinship groups. At the bottom of the social scale in Yemen and in Oman were domestic slaves, often imported from Africa, and outcast groups who performed specific jobs. In Yemen the *akhdam* – probably descendants of Ethiopian immigrants – were menial artisans in the towns and were considered even lower than slaves. In Oman a group called the *afaris*, of indeterminate but apparently non-Arab descent, were traditionally employed as keepers of irrigation systems when tribes left their oases for seasonal wanderings.

Peninsular society was marked by great poverty and an inability to develop. Both the nomads of the deserts and the sedentary societies of Yemen and the Omani interior were stagnant, and trapped individuals in a system from which there was no escape. In so far as it helped weaken these systems the advent of capitalism was a progressive development. This was not because in itself it was the best possible, but because it introduced some improvements; and, although it substituted one form of oppression for another, it also provided a means for the peoples of Arabia independently to develop their society and break out of the arrested structures of the past three thousand years.

The Peninsula and the Islamic World

From the earliest known period the Arabian peninsula comprised a settled southern part and a nomadic north. Early history mainly concerns the settled civilizations of the south.[7] The fertile soil and annual rains of Yemen made agriculture possible; and the prosperity of the region's pre-Islamic kingdoms rested on centralized direction of agriculture and control of the incense crop. The Minaeans (*c.* 1500 B.C.–900 B.C.), the Sabaeans (*c.* 900 B.C.–115 B.C.) and the Himyarites (*c.* 115 B.C.–A.D. 525) are the most notable of these kingdoms, some of which extended over the whole of present North Yemen, South Yemen and Dhofar. The crux of this system was reputed to be the dam at Marib in northern Yemen, allegedly constructed in the seventh century B.C. and which functioned until the second century A.D. The decline of the south Arabian kingdom is associated with the 'bursting' of the Marib dam, though this may be a convenient myth for explaining a more general decline caused by shifting trade routes and political decay.

Numerous inscriptions, religious or related to the irrigation system, are to be found in the south Arabian area and give an idea of the civilization that flourished there. Through the incense trade Yemen had contact with the classical civilizations around the Mediterranean and the 'Queen of Sheba' (Sheba = Sabaea) is reported in the Bible to have visited Solomon in Jerusalem. The Romans knew Yemen as 'happy Arabia' (*Arabia Felix*) to distinguish it from 'stony Arabia' (*Arabia Petrea*) that lay to the north. In 24 B.C. they even launched an unsuccessful attack on it led by Allius Gallus, prefect of Egypt under Caesar Augustus. After the fall of Jerusalem in A.D. 70 many Jews emigrated to Yemen and Judaism was the official religion in the last days of the Himyaritic kingdom.[8]

The Himyarites fell in A.D. 525 to an Abyssinian invasion which imposed Christianity on the area. This defeat marked the end of the south Arabian civilizations. The decline had set in long before that with the 'bursting' of the Marib dam and there had been a series of migrations from the Yemeni area to Oman and northwards into the more nomadic zones. The nomads of the north had contact both with the settled south and with the agrarian communities of the Fertile Crescent and Egypt; and the trade route ran from south Arabia through the nomadic areas. Several political entities had briefly existed on the border of the

Roman and Iranian empires in the first centuries of the Christian epoch; and military and political events in these northern states had an effect on the nomads to the south. For most of this time the Arabian interior was under no unified rule and the states that did spring up were limited by the powers in the north. In the sixth and seventh centuries, however, the Iranian and Byzantine empires grew weaker in the northern border areas of the peninsula, and the Arabian tribes launched themselves northwards on a victorious campaign.

The origins of this great expansion lay in the towns of Mecca and Medina, which were situated in western Arabia on the trade route. Mecca was a trading town without any agricultural community; Medina was situated in an oasis. The emergence of Islam was generated by several interrelated factors – by the influx of migrant tribes from the decaying southern civilization, by the growth of social differentiation in Mecca and Medina and by ideological conflicts between Jews, Christians and Arab pagans in the trading towns. Mohammad, born in Mecca in A.D. 570, was expelled from Mecca because his new beliefs threatened the tolerant religious atmosphere of Mecca, on which rested its commercial prosperity. He was able to settle, however, at Medina, where rival tribal factions accepted him as an arbitrator in their disputes and subsequently became converts to his new religion.[9]

As a religious belief, Islam was generated and consolidated in towns – in Medina and in Mecca. Only later did it spread to the desert people who provided its expansionist dynamic with military backing for the conquests of the mid seventh century. Within a few decades of the flight of Mohammad to Medina (A.D. 622), the Arab armies had captured the whole peninsula, Iran, parts of the Byzantine empire and all of North Africa and Spain. But though these conquests diffused the Islamic religion and the Arabic language over a vast area, they had surprisingly small political effect in the region of their origin. From the beginning the Islamic capital was outside the peninsula; although Mecca remained a centre of pilgrimage, the political capitals of the Moslem world – Damascus, Baghdad, Cairo and Istanbul – lay in the agrarian states to the north; and the cities and tribes of the peninsula soon broke any strong ties of allegiance to the imperial centres.[10]

From the eighth to the nineteenth centuries outside influence on and control of the peninsula was inconsistent. Although the early Arab empires of the Ummayads (up to 750) and the Abbasids (750–1258) tried to conquer and tax parts of the peninsula, they had little success, and as the Abbasid empire weakened in the ninth and tenth centuries Arabian autonomy was correspondingly confirmed. The last major Moslem empire was that of the Ottoman Turks, who captured Constantinople in 1453 and occupied Egypt in 1517. They sent armies to Yemen and to Mecca and imposed an exploitative administration which lasted for over a century until their empire began to weaken. In the eighteenth century a revitalized Iranian state attacked across the Gulf and briefly ruled the coast of Oman. In the nineteenth century a temporarily revived Turkish empire tried once again to exert control on the Hijaz and Yemen, and the Turks were only finally expelled in the First World War. Neither the economy nor the social organization of the peninsula were lastingly affected by these incursions.

The Impact of Imperialism

All the Islamic empires that had tried to rule Arabia had been based on pre-capitalist modes of production. These extracted surplus wealth without necessarily transforming the socio-economic order. Capitalism is unique among social formations in that over time it necessarily pervades and dominates the societies with which it comes into contact. In its extension from Europe and later from North America throughout the world it has only been successfully resisted by those societies that have tried to abolish it by socialist revolution. No pre-capitalist society has been able to hold out in the end against the capitalist onslaught.

Capitalism in the Arabian peninsula has gone through four phases of escalating intensity. In the first phase, from around 1500 to 1800, the impact of European capitalism was confined economically to trade and geographically to the ports of the Gulf and the Red Sea. In the second phase, from 1800 to the end of the Second World War, Britain carried out annexation that left the economic and social structures of the peninsula relatively unaltered. In the third phase, which began after 1945 with the rise of the Gulf oil industry and the expansion of the port of Aden, capitalist socio-economic relations made a major impact on the peninsula; at the same time direct political ties characteristic of the previous epoch began to be modified. By the beginning of the 1970s a fourth phase had begun: the growth of the oil industry had transformed the economic and political structure of the peninsula; the local ruling classes, enriched and encouraged, had acquired substantial economic and political importance within the world capitalist system.

In the first two phases capitalism saw the peninsula as marginal to its main strategic and economic interests, and had no intrinsic reason for changing the structure of Arabian society. In the decades after 1800 British control was established over a vast swathe of coastal territory running from Aden in the south-west, through Muscat at the north-eastern tip of the peninsula and up the coast of the Gulf. By the 1870s the British dominated two thirds of the peninsula's coast. British policy in Arabia was governed by the desire to protect India, and this dictated a policy of retardation of the peninsula's socio-economic life. Precisely because Arabia was a buffer, it was essential for the British to keep a firm grip on it.[11]

The general model of this form of colonialism was as follows. Local tribal leaders were patronized by the supply of money and weapons; if they resisted, these gifts were withheld and they were attacked. As a consequence, the policy of formally preserving the existing system became one of arresting certain changes and of encouraging others. None of the more conventional indices of colonial economic exploitation were found: there was no extraction of raw materials or growing of commercial crops, no settling of significant numbers of European settlers, no opening of lucrative but weak markets. Political and economic influences from outside were excluded. On the other hand, certain leaders became stronger, and divisions between tribes and between different regions were strengthened. For example, the pre-existing divisions between North and South Yemen, and between the interior of Oman and the coast of Oman (the so-called 'Trucial States'), were accentuated and given a new solidity. The very policy of preventing change produced its own results, and, with the intense impact of change after 1945, the uneven and arrested society of the peninsula was to wreak an unexpected revenge on the forces that had dominated it till then.

Notes

1. There is no universally clear criterion for what constitutes the northern boundary of the peninsula, and the Arabian desert stretches up into parts of what are now Iraq and Jordan. In this book what is understood by 'the peninsula' has been extended to the northern boundaries of the present Saudi state.

2. In this book the term 'the Gulf' is used, rather than 'the Persian Gulf' or 'the Arabian Gulf'. The question of nomenclature has been exploited by chauvinists in Iran and in Arab countries for their own diversionary purposes. The inhabitants are Arabs on one side and Iranians on the other. At the moment political power on land and sea belongs to the people of neither shore.

3. Little systematic anthropological work has been done on the peninsula, and few travel works contain even a glimmer of a general description. This absence has both reflected and reinforced the prevalent mystique about Arabia.

4. The merchant communities existed exclusively in towns; in the country-side usury and trade were controlled by sheikhs and landowners. Land owned by merchants was in the vicinity of towns. The power of the merchants was always less than that of the landowners and sheikhs, except in the strongest trading towns such as, at different times, Mecca and Kuwait.

5. Unconfirmed reports of communist tribes survive in Arabia; during the author's visit to South Yemen in 1970 he was told of a tribe in the Yafai area who 'worshipped no God except equality', see also p. 11 n.5.

6. See Louise E. Sweet, 'Camel Raiding of North Arabian Beduin: A Mechanism of Ecological Adaptation', *Peoples and Cultures of the Middle East*, Vol. 1, New York, 1970.

7. See Brian Doe, *South Arabia*, London, 1971, for an illustrated account of this society.

8. Two kinds of Jewish community existed in Arabia until the twentieth century. In commercial towns – such as Aden and Bahrain – there were

Jewish merchants and artisans. In the Yemeni countryside there existed a socially quite distinct phenomenon – Jewish peasant communities. Most of both kinds of community emigrated to Israel after 1948; but in the 1960s travellers to North Yemen reported that at least some of the peasant communities remained.

9. There exists a large literature on the origins of Islam. W. Montgomery Watt, *Mohammed at Mecca*, Oxford, 1953, gives a materialist account of the formation of Islam, seen in its Meccan context; while Barbara Aswad locates it in a wider context in 'Social and Ecological Aspects in the Formation of Islam' in Sweet, op. cit., Vol. 1. Maxime Rodinson, *Mohammad*, London, 1971, gives a general materialist account of the period and of Mohammad's life.

10. No account of Middle Eastern society can avoid the fact that Islam has permeated it so thoroughly that all political and social conflicts take a religious form to a degree found less frequently in other societies. In their brief exchange of letters in 1853 on the question of the origins of Islam Marx and Engels tried to grapple with the origins of Islam both as social phenomenon and religion. As Marx asked: 'Why does the history of the east *appear* as a history of religions?' Marx and Engels, *Werke*, Berlin, 1963, Vol. 28, p. 251. Marx and Engels ascribed the rise of Islam to the collapse of the south Arabian civilizations and the decline in the Red Sea and west Arabian trade routes in favour of the Gulf. See ibid., pp. 252, 259.

11. The eighteenth and nineteenth centuries saw the arrival of the first western explorers. The early history of exploration is told in D.G. Hogarth, *The Penetration of Arabia*, London, 1905.

Chapter Two
Saudi Arabia:
Bonanza and Repression

The Origins of the Saudi State

The partial withdrawal of British imperialism from the Arabian peninsula and the great increase in oil revenues paid to Arabian governments led to the rise of newly strengthened states eager to advance their own interests and to exploit their collaboration with the west and Japan. Of these by far the most important is Saudi Arabia, which by the early 1970s had become the dominant power in the peninsula. Although it had less than a half of the peninsula's twelve million inhabitants, the Saudi state covered four fifths – 927,000 square miles – of Arabia. This gave it common borders with every other peninsular state and with Jordan and Iraq to the north, and a nodal position in relation to the whole region. In addition to this geographical significance, Saudi Arabia contained an estimated quarter of the world's known oil reserves and was capable of supplying nearly half of US petroleum needs by 1980. The potential dependence of the world's most powerful capitalist nation on Saudi Arabia for economic survival guaranteed a particular western interest. At the same time, enriched by oil and encouraged by the capitalist world, Saudi Arabia adopted an aggressive and interventionist foreign policy in the Arabian peninsula and in the Middle East as a whole. After centuries of confusion an expansionist state had been founded in central Arabia after the First World War and had been converted, in an unique process of assimilation, into the guardian of capitalist concerns.[1]

The modern Saudi state has its origins in the conflicts of the eighteenth century, when the northern peninsula was temporarily united, by a coalition of tribes led by the Saudi tribe from Najd in eastern Arabia. This coalition produced, for the first time since Mohammad, a force capable of imposing a single authority on the whole area. No adequate social explanation of this movement has yet been produced: its ideology was expressed through the teachings of a militant preacher named Mohammad Ibn Abd al-Wahhab (*c*.1703–*c*.1792), whose version of Islam, Wahhabism, called for the purification of religion. In particular, it stressed the 'oneness' of God, opposing the worship of holy places and excessive veneration of Mohammad; and on the other hand, it called for the firm practice of Islamic legal punishments, including the stoning of adulterous women, public beheadings and amputations. Under the banner of this 'pure' Islam the Saudi-led tribes conquered a large part of the peninsula in the eighteenth and early nineteenth centuries and were only limited by the two outside powers then encroaching on the area: Britain, reaching out from India, was gaining power in a vast L-shaped block running from Bahrain in the Gulf to Aden in South Yemen, and the Ottoman Turks, enjoying a temporary revival, were reaffirming their position in the north-west of the peninsula.[2]

Wahhabi expansionism was blocked and then reversed in the nineteenth century by a series of campaigns launched by powers to the north and north-east: armies from Egypt (at that time under Mohammad Ali) and from the Ottoman empire drove the Wahhabis out of western Arabia, and the Hijaz, site of Mecca and Medina, was annexed to the Ottoman empire. The Saudi-led tribes, confined to their eastern Arabian terrain, were even there replaced by a rival tribe, the Rashid. However, in 1902 a new Saudi counter-attack began: under the leadership of Abdel Aziz Ibn Saud they recaptured Riyadh, the capital of Najd, and soon held the two provinces of eastern Arabia, Najd and al-Hasa, in their power. During the First World War, the British state paid them a monthly subsidy of £5,000 in order to induce them not to attack westwards; for a time the Saudis respected this. In the west the British had formed a separate alliance with the ruler of the Hijaz, the Hashemite Sharif Hussein of Mecca.[3] This former dependant of the Ottoman empire was hoping to use the occasion of the war to throw off Turkish rule and set himself up as ruler of the Arab areas of the Ottoman empire. But although the Sharif and his sons were able to acquire certain portions of the empire (Iraq, Jordan and temporarily Syria) they lost their position in Arabia itself. When the war ended and British protection declined, the Saudis attacked again: by 1925 they had conquered the western provinces of Asir and Hijaz, and driven the Hashemites into exile. In 1926 Abdel Aziz Ibn Saud crowned himself King of the Hijaz, and in 1932 he announced that the whole of his territory had been united under a new name, Saudi Arabia.[4]

This new state covered a larger area than had been united since the seventh century. Wahhabism, by cohering previously divided tribes, could even be said to have played a progressive role without which any future liberation would have been impossible. In one single respect, its forced sedentarization of certain tribes, it also attacked the nomadic structure of peninsular society. But the state was founded on the most backward ideology: unity of religion and loyalty to one family, making Saudi Arabia the only state in the world that was titled as the property of a single dynasty. Moreover tribal divisions were not abolished, but were manipulated by the regime. Power was held in the hands of the leading male members of the Saudi family. On its own this regime was an unstable anachronism: it required outside support to survive. Oil and U S imperialism fulfilled this function.

U S Imperialism: A R A M C O and Military Aid

The Saudi state consolidated itself in the late 1920s and early 1930s: internal opposition from tribes was crushed in 1930 and, after border clashes with British-occupied Jordan and Iraq in the north and with North Yemen in the south-west, the Wahhabi state entertained peaceful relations with its neighbours. The British recognized the government in 1927 and after initial opposition relations with Arab states went slowly forward. Formal relations with Egypt were established in 1936 and even the remnants of the Hashemite family came to accept the Saudi state. Wahhabism's positive mission expired after it had unified the country and imposed its coercive peace on the feuding tribes. From then on it settled into an increasingly negative role, and in this it received the active support of a new-found ally, the US. In 1933 Ibn Saud had to face a severe financial crisis because his main source of income, taxation of the *hajj* (Moslim pilgrimage), had been undermined by the world slump; for £50,000 in gold he gave an oil concession to Standard Oil of California. Socal later merged with three other US firms (Esso, Texaco, Mobil) to form the Arabian American Oil Company – ARAMCO. This began exploration in eastern Arabia and in 1938 production of Saudi Arabian oil commenced.

This oil concession established ties between a major US company and the Saudi state; the Second World War brought the US government into action as well. Because the *hajj* was stopped again, this time by the Second World War, and because Saudi oil production fell for the same reason, Ibn Saud was in need of $10 million a year to run the country. Socal decided to get the money from the US government: it wrote to Roosevelt asking him to provide Saudi Arabia with funds. 'We believe that unless this is done, and soon, this independent kingdom, and perhaps with it the entire Arab World, will be thrown into chaos,' they said.[5] Roosevelt's main assistant, Harry Hopkins, urged that money be provided although it was hard to 'call that outfit a "democracy"', but at first the US government balked. In 1941 and 1942 it was the British who provided the money, paying $5 million and $12 million respectively out of money the US had loaned to them.

It was the Americans who had arranged for the British to pay the money; but once the subsidy had been paid the US oil companies realized that the British would use this in order to expand their influence into Saudi Arabia and get a share of the oil riches awaiting them. The Americans feared that the British were already carrying out oil exploration under the guise of curbing locusts. So, in 1943, Washington decided that 'the defense of Saudi Arabia is vital to the defense of the United States' and lend-lease aid was provided: a US military mission arrived to train Ibn Saud's army and the USAF began construction of an airfield at Dhahran, near the oil-wells, which was to give the US a position independent of the British bases at Cairo and Abadan;

this base became the largest US air position between Germany and Japan, and the one nearest Soviet industrial installations. Although never used in combat it upheld a link in US global communications during the Cold War period. While the base was being constructed, in February 1945, Roosevelt and King Ibn Saud met aboard a US warship in the Red Sea, and in March Saudi Arabia declared war on the Axis Powers. In the immediate aftermath of the war Saudi–US relations were placed in question by the public debate in the USA on the need for 'Arab oil', prefiguring the panic on the 'energy crisis'.[6] But despite protests, ARAMCO and US government intervention in Saudi Arabia continued without hindrance.

By 1947 King Ibn Saud had received an estimated $100 million in US aid. In 1950 ARAMCO finished construction of a $200 million pipeline from its wells in eastern Arabia to the Mediterranean. Tapline, as it was called, had been originally thought of by the US navy who wanted to get supplies of oil for its Sixth Fleet operating in the Mediterranean. In 1951 ARAMCO at a cost of $160 million built a prestige railway for King Ibn Saud on a 360-mile run from the Gulf port of Dammam to the Saudi capital Riyadh. Around this time ARAMCO was also giving legal and logistical support to the Saudi government's clashes with the Sultan of Oman over possession of the oasis at Buraimi. US government support continued alongside ARAMCO's: in 1951 Saudi Arabia was included in the Point Four technical assistance programme and under a treaty between the two governments the US was allowed to maintain the Dhahran base for another five years.

During Congressional hearings in 1974, George McGhee, a former Assistant Secretary of State, revealed another way in which the US government had supported the Saudi state in these early years: on orders from the National Security Council, the US tax authorities allowed ARAMCO to deduct from their US taxes all moneys paid to the Saudi government. Between 1950 and 1951 ARAMCO's US taxes fell from $30 million to $5 million, while its payments to the Saudi government rose from $44 million to $110 million. The purpose of this change was to

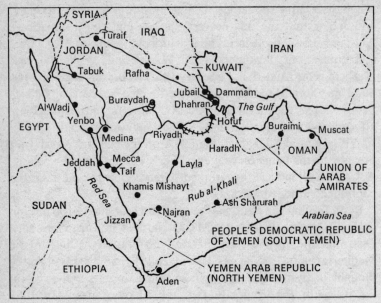

Map 3 Saudi Arabia

stabilize the situation in the Middle East. According to a Senate sub-committee, the two lawyers who drafted this arrangement, H. Chapman Rose and Kenneth Gemmill, later became tax lawyers for Richard Nixon.

In 1953 Abdel Aziz Ibn Saud died, and he was succeeded by his son Saud. US – Saudi relations then entered a temporary storm. The Saudi government tried to acquire some independence, and signed an agreement with Greek ship owner Onassis under which Onassis was to build a 500,000-ton tanker fleet for Saudi Arabia to transport all oil not transported by ARAMCO's existing tankers; as ARAMCO was barred from replacing old ships this would have led to a steady increase in Saudi control of the transport of their crude. ARAMCO fought back and was fully supported by the US administration: 'Our government . . . rose in horror at such a thought,' later stated George Wadsworth, the US ambassador to Saudi Arabia.[7] ARAMCO took the case to court and won; and the US government developed a sudden investigative interest in some of Onassis's US trading deals. The project was blocked.

In the mid 1950s Nasserism was in the ascendant in the Middle East, and the Saudi leadership, while maintaining their long-term orientation, decided to adopt an apparently anti-imperialist position. In August 1954 Saudi Arabia told the US to stop providing technical aid under the 1951 agreement on the grounds that the £1·7 million allocated was too small in comparison with what the US was giving to Israel. Then, swinging to the right, the Saudis announced in August 1955 that they had 'rejected' an offer of Soviet weapons and had decided to purchase eighteen US tanks under the 1951 Dhahran agreement. Then when the Dhahran agreement expired in June 1956, the Saudis only renewed it in one month phases and US–Saudi relations appeared to have deteriorated once again.

This period of superficial conflict was brought to an end when King Saud visited the US in February 1957 in the aftermath of the November 1956 attack on Egypt by Britain, France and Israel. During the Suez crisis the US had postured as a friend of Arab nationalism and had tried to gain credit from disowning its belligerent junior allies. The overall motivation of this policy was the fear that the Soviet Union would use the situation to increase its influence in the Middle East and in response the U S evolved the 'Eisenhower Doctrine'. On 1 January 1957 Eisenhower announced that: 'The existing vacuum in the Middle East must be filled by the United States before it is filled by Russia.' On 5 January the President spoke to Congress urging that the U S increase its economic and military aid to the area. Congress then held hearings on this proposal at which the U S ambassador to Saudi Arabia defended the Saudi regime. King Saud, he said, is 'a good king ... who has the welfare of his people primarily in mind'. One problem that the U S press had highlighted was the prevalence of the slave trade in Saudi Arabia. U S Ambassador Wadsworth felt that the extent of this had been exaggerated.[8]

When King Saud arrived in Washington he was given special treatment.

Early in 1957 the Arabian despot was ardently courted by the American Government in order to secure a renewal of the base agreement. The United States delegate at the United Nations Economic and Social Council, obviously reluctant to offend Arabian desert chieftains, refused to go along with stronger antislavery conventions backed by most nations. President Eisenhower took the unusual step of greeting King Saud in person at the Washington airport, a courtesy he had extended to no other head of state up to that time. Oil leaders as well as State Department officials met with the king during the negotiations. A forma White House dinner included as guests the top executives of the Arabian American Oil Company, its four parent companies, and related banking interests. Asked why his colleagues received such special consideration in working out these matters of American foreign policy, President Rathbone of Jersey Standard replied: 'I presume because they are the ones that have the principal interests.'[9]

All went well on the trip and King Saud agreed to renew the Dhahran lease for another five years, in return for continued U S military support. The 15,000-man Saudi army was to be doubled and equipped with U S arms, artillery and jet fighter planes;

an air force and navy were to be established as well. In 1958 Saudi Arabia got a $25 million Foreign Assistance Act grant from the US. But having secured its military interests the US encountered another problem: the incompetence of King Saud. Despite a steady rise in income the country had become heavily indebted as Saud spent money lavishly on luxury projects. There was no budget, no accounting and no regular government. One item alone, the al-Nassariyah palace at Riyadh, cost $25 million and by 1958 consumption was exceeding revenue by 25 per cent. This critical situation in Saudi Arabia coincided with the merger of Egypt and Syria into the United Arab Republic in February 1958, a development that strengthened the appeal of Nasserism and weakened Saudi influence along its northern boundaries.[10] Under heavy US pressure and the equally important coercion by more modern-minded sections of the ruling family executive power was taken from King Saud and handed to his younger brother Amir Feisal.

Feisal, born in 1905, was a more efficient and cautious ruler than his sibling and he was able to re-establish financial balance in the government. Although he was favoured by US support his position was at first insecure and in 1960 Saud staged a comeback. He toured the country to win support from tribal leaders who had been hit by Feisal's financial cuts, and opportunistically allied himself with a group of reformers within the ruling family. These reformers included Prince Talal, who called for a constitution and elections, and Abdullah Ibn Hamud Tariqi, the first ever Saudi Minister of Petroleum and Mineral Resources. In December 1960 Saud announced that he had become Prime Minister, Feisal was dismissed, and the country lurched to the left under the divided leadership of Saud and the reformers.

The most coherent position was that of Tariqi, who called for Saudi control not only of production but of transportation and marketing and who expounded a hard anti-imperialist line on oil. He pointed out that as a result of cuts in the price of crude oil in 1958–9 Saudi Arabia had lost $35 million, Kuwait $46 million, Iran $27 million and Iraq $24 million. The weakness of the reformers in Saudi Arabia was that they represented a small group at the top of the state machine without any mass base, any political organization or any foreign support capable of resisting A R A M C O and the U S government. In addition King Saud was an unreliable ally in any confrontation. In 1961–2 Feisal and the U S were able to regain ground: Saud was ill and departed to the U S for treatment, Talal fled into exile, and in March 1962 Feisal returned to power. Tariqi was at once dismissed and his place as Saudi Arabia's second Minister of Petroleum and Mineral Resources was taken by Harvard-educated Sheikh Ahmad Zaki Yamani.

Feisal's position was further strengthened in the autumn of 1962 when the revolution in North Yemen brought a political threat and Egyptian troops to the south-west borders of the kingdom. Feisal then became undisputed head of government and brought three of his own most able brothers into power with him: Khalid, who came to head the crack White army, Fahd, who became Minister of the Interior, and Sultan, who became Minister of Defence. A number of minimal reforms followed: slavery was declared 'abolished', although it in fact continued; in October 1963 a local government reform law divided the country into five provinces and set up advisory councils in each under the guidance of the governor;[11] education was expanded, and the power of the religious police was slightly relaxed. Saud tried to fight back, perhaps out of personal hostility and perhaps out of opposition to Feisal's intervention in North Yemen, but he had no success. In March 1964 he demanded that full executive powers be returned to him and tried to mobilize the Royal Guard to support his bid; but Feisal had full control of the armed forces and Saud's attempt failed. Full powers were now formally assigned to Feisal by the princes of the royal family and by the religious leaders of the country. In November 1964 the final blow came when Feisal took the title of King for himself and Saud was dispatched to exile.[12]

The Military Consolidation

With Feisal firmly in command, Saudi Arabia and the US were able to consolidate the relationship that had been developing since the first ARAMCO concession of 1933. Unlike other US clients in the third world Saudi Arabia was not in need of financial aid: it had enough money from the oil revenues provided by ARAMCO, and the US government was willing to encourage greater Saudi revenues as large-scale capitalist development benefited imperialism. There was enough for both partners, and careful spending by Feisal strengthened the Saudi regime and ensured long-term US access to the oil supplies which lay under the Saudi deserts. It was therefore a form of dependent relationship different economically and politically from that which the US had with its neo-colonial dependencies in Latin America and the Far East. The US interest lay in a rapid economic development of the country provided it ensured 'stability', and they were dealing with a regime which had some political autonomy. It is mistaken to see Saudi Arabia as just a US colony with the appearance of independence. The wealth of Saudi Arabia and the political character of the ruling family enabled it to forge an alliance with the US in which its ruling class wielded a degree of real power consonant with the preservation of US interests.

The two key items in the post-1964 consolidation of Saudi Arabia were the building up of the armed forces and the capitalist development of the economy. The Saudi army had gone through several phases. Originally Ibn Saud had relied on a force of Wahhabi militants, the *ikhwan* (brothers), whom he had used to conquer eastern and western Arabia between 1902 and 1926. The *ikhwan*, however, refused to accept the territorial limits set by Ibn Saud and took to attacking northwards into Jordan and Iraq; in 1930 Ibn Saud, using motorized transport provided by the British, was able to crush the *ikhwan* in desert battle. In the subsequent period Saudi Arabia had two armies: a regular army used mainly for border duty, and a crack White army, drawn from special pro-Saudi tribes (mainly in the Shammar area) and used for internal repression. In addition to these two armies there was a Royal Guard, used for protecting the members of the royal family. Ibn Saud used the long-standing principle whereby tribal leaders had the duty of ensuring order and providing him with troops in return for his recognizing them and guaranteeing to respect their tribal autonomy.[13]

During the Second World War small British and US military missions worked with the Saudi armies and in 1947 the British trained up the 10,000-man White army on the lines they had used in Jordan to train the Arab Legion (now the Jordanian army). But in 1951 when Britain and Saudi Arabia clashed over the Sultanate of Oman the US took over full control and set up a Saudi military academy at Riyadh, in addition to helping to found the Saudi navy and air force. Between 1951 and 1957 an Egyptian military mission also trained in Saudi Arabia and the US considered this a threat to their monopoly; in the end Saudi-Egyptian hostility ended the arrangement and the Saudi security forces maintained vigilance to prevent Nasserite ideas from permeating the armed forces.

This fear of Nasserism, and US alarm, were confirmed when the revolution broke out in North Yemen in 1962 and an eight-year civil war began. At first the US tried to block the spread of Nasserism by recognizing the new Yemeni Arab Repub ic; but the Saudis opposed this and from the start poured arms and money into Yemen to bolster the Yemeni royalists. Prince Khalid deployed the White Guard along the North Yemeni border, at Jizan and Najran, and in January 1963 Saudi-Egyptian fighting broke out. Nine Saudi air force pilots defected to the YAR in opposition to their government's policies and Egyptian planes bombed Saudi border positions from which arms were being sent into royalist areas. The US, which had initially tried to restrain Saudi Arabia, soon switched policies. In March 1963 US planes and warships were sent to bolster Saudi aggression, in operation 'Hard Surface', and Ellsworth Bunker was flown to Riyadh to reassure the regime (see p153.).

Under King Saud's 1957 agreement with Eisenhower the US had remained in the Dhahran base until 1962 and had then

withdrawn. Yet as a result of the North Yemen revolution the
US was back in Saudi Arabia less than a year later with a
permanent military combat force alongside its military training
mission. The Nasserite threat to Saudi Arabia and the growth
of the revolutionary movement elsewhere in the peninsula
led to the decision by Feisal and the US to build Saudi Arabia up
into being a massive military force capable not only of crushing any
internal threat but of intervening throughout the neighbouring
states. Saudi defence expenditure from the middle 1960s reflected
this decision. Defence expenditure rose from 243 million rials
in 1961, and 414 million in 1963, to 925 million rials in 1970
and 1,138 million in 1971 (100 ríals = £9·30 or $24·15). This
absolute increase in defence expenditure also represented a
relative increase in defence expenditure as a percentage of the
total budget, since it rose from 14·1 per cent in 1961, to 18·9
per cent in 1965, to a proposed 21·3 per cent for the overall period
1970–74. In 1971 Saudi defence expenditure at $383 million
represented 8·9 per cent of GNP and a per capita expenditure
of $53: outside of twelve advanced industrial nations this was
a higher per capita figure than for any state except Israel and
Singapore.[14]

British Intervention

One of the first consequences of the revolution and civil war in
North Yemen was that Saudi Arabia re-established diplomatic
relations with Britain. These had been broken off in 1956,
after Suez, but the revolution in North Yemen posed a threat
to the British position in South Yemen, where an attempt was
being made to fabricate a federation of Aden and the hinterland
states. Saudi Arabia and the British therefore shared a common
interest in crushing the new Yemeni Arab Republic. In 1963 a
British military mission returned to train the White army. It
was renamed the National Guard (*al-Haras al-Watani*) but continued to be recruited and deployed on the old principles. In 1964
the Royal Guard and the regular army were merged in a further
tightening. The British and the US then set about providing

71

the Saudis with an 'air defence system'. After trial flights in Saudi Arabia and considerable inter-imperialist rivalry a joint US – UK deal was announced late in 1965. Under it Britain won the then largest military export deal in its history: it totalled £120 million. The British Aircraft Corporation was to provide forty Lightning jets, twenty-five Jet Provosts, and air-to-air missiles. Associated Electrical Industries provided an advance radar system. Airwork Services Ltd provided around 1,000 training personnel. A US firm, Raytheon, provided a Hawk missile system worth £20 million.[15]

This deal had two important aspects. The first was that despite appearances it did not reflect a weakening of the US position in Saudi Arabia. The US had competed for the fighter contract with its F-104, but the Saudi purchase of British exports was a means of paying the British back for their purchase of the US F-111 at that time. The British Minister of Defence, Denis Healey, made this clear: 'We agreed when we made the F-111A deal that we would include the Saudi purchase arrangements, which had not then been concluded, in that part of the offset arrangements which related to sales to third countries.'[16] The other important side of the 1965 deal was that it in effect provided British pilots for the Saudi air force in the period in between the signing of the deal and the availability of the Saudi-trained pilots themselves. The Saudis had few pilots of their own, and the whole of the air force had been grounded in 1962 when some pilots had defected to Egypt. After 1965 Saudi pilots were trained at the RAF base at Coltishall, Norfolk, England, and although the British personnel working on the Saudi installations were officially civilians they were all ex-RAF personnel and the degree of independence from the British government was unclear.[17] In 1968 when the Lightnings themselves were actually delivered *serving* RAF pilots ferried the aircraft to Saudi Arabia.[18] This relationship was further confirmed in the deals reached in 1966 and 1967. When the US failed to speed up delivery of the Hawk missiles the British rushed in planes under the rubric 'Operation Magic Carpet', designed to provide an interim air defence system. Six Hunter jets, seven Lightnings, thirty-seven refurbished

Thunderbird missiles and radar were provided; by July 1966 'ex'-RAF pilots recruited by Airwork Services Ltd were flying patrols along the Yemeni border from a special new base at Khamis Mishayt. British denials that their government was officially involved were unconvincing.[19]

When Egyptian troops withdrew from North Yemen in 1967 the most obvious threat to Saudi Arabia was removed; yet this Egyptian withdrawal, following on the Israeli victory in June of that year, led to Saudi Arabia being confirmed as the unchallenged dominating power in the peninsula. As a consequence, the Saudi military build-up, far from slowing down, continued to increase. In 1969–70 the Saudis purchased twenty-five British Aircraft Corporation Strikemaster jets and in 1970 the British negotiated a further £20-million air-defence contract.[20] In July 1971 it was announced that for £146 million the US was to provide two squadrons of F-5 fighters.[21] France managed to enter this Anglo-Saxon market, selling AMX-30 amphibious tanks and Pakistani pilots were also brought in to fly British aircraft under the original 1965 deal. In 1972 certain changes were made: the Saudis let it be known that they were dissatisfied with the Lightnings and that they considered Airwork to be performing the ground work inadequately. US personnel began to be recruited by ITT, Lockheed and Northrop to replace the disgraced ex-RAF personnel. In May 1973, however, the British won a new spectacular £250 million deal, the largest export order ever placed in Britain. Under it the British Aircraft Corporation were to replace the Lightnings by Strikemasters and were to move in about 2,000 'civilian' British personnel to work on another air-defence system.[22] At the same time Washington sources reported that the US was planning to sell the Saudis F-4 Phantom jets.

The list of major and minor contracts represented a huge, successful manoeuvre by western capital as a whole: it funnelled back to Europe and North America up to £1,000 million in the period of 1965–71 thus diverting up to one third of all the revenues paid to Saudi Arabia in that period. Equally importantly it gave the Saudi regime a military machine of massive power whose aim

73

was the aggressive maintenance of Saudi predominance in the peninsula and the long-term guarantee of the 'stability' of the regime. By 1972 Saudi Arabia had a regular army of 36,000 men heavily armed by the U S and with a 191-man U S military mission advising it.[23] The air force had around 3,500 men and seventy-two combat aircraft – others were still under order and several had crashed in training after delivery. There was also a small navy, of around 1,000, based at Dammam. These were the forces for external aggression. The internal repression was maintained by the 10,000 men of the National Guard, backed by a much larger apparatus of police, spies and paramilitary tribal forces.

Economic Transformation

The internal consolidation carried through after 1962 by Feisal rested above all on the military and the police. Economic change was slower. Apart from the wealth of oil, the overwhelming fact about the Saudi economy was that under a million acres were cultivated, i.e., 0·2 per cent of the country, and non-agricultural production was minimal. Most of the land was government-

Table 5
Saudi Arabian Labour Force in 1970

Nomads	145,000
Agriculture	331,000
Petroleum	15,000
Mining	14,000
Manufacturing	52,000
Construction	142,000
Public utilities	12,000
Commerce	130,000
Transport and communication	62,000
Services	138,000
Public sector	138,000
Total	1,200,000

Source: Central Planning Organization.

owned, and had been confiscated by Ibn Saud in the 1920s. On it worked share-croppers who were the employees of tenants, who in their turn leased the land from the government. In over half of the rest of the country pasturing of some kind prevailed; there were an estimated 1 million (single-humped) camels and 4 million sheep and goats in Saudi Arabia in the 1960s. Agriculture and pasturing still provided the livelihood of half of the population, while providing only 8 per cent of GNP.

The petroleum industry remained relatively isolated from the rest of the economy and it only affected the country through the government's decision to distribute oil revenues. Until the 1960s very little was done in this respect – much was wasted on luxury projects and a lot more was deployed abroad. Even though Feisal spent more money on guns than Saud had on palaces and cars, the rise in oil revenues in the 1960s and 1970s enabled even the most wasteful regime to initiate development of some kind.

Table 6

Saudi Arabian Oil Revenues (in $ millions)

1964	523·2
1965	662·2
1966	789·7
1967	909·1
1968	926·8
1969	949·0
1970	1,149·7
1971	1,949·9
1972	2,779·3
1973	4,915
1974*	19,400
1975*	22,150/23,500
1980*	36,300/50,550

Source: Saudi Arabian Monetary Agency, Statistical Survey, December 1972, *The Times*, 30 January 1974.
*estimate

Since oil provided over 50 per cent of GNP and 87 per cent of government revenues it was clear the economic diversification was a major priority. In 1962 a national oil company, Petromin, began operations and by the early 1970s it had set up a fertilizer plant, a steel mill and a refinery. Agricultural productivity and the area of cultivated land were steadily increased; dams for power and water were built; and a network of roads was laid, with the declared aim being to have 8,400 miles of paved road by 1975. Alleged spending on education rose from 12·8 million rials in 1953–4 to 664·7 million in 1970. Yet in 1970 only 700 girls and only 10,000 boys were receiving secondary education. In 1970 the first five-year plan was announced: with an investment of £4,000 million (41,314 million rials) it aimed to raise GDP by 9·8 per cent per annum and set itself three main aims: to diversify the economy and lessen dependence on oil; to increase employment; and to bring about a more equal distribution of wealth.

The function of this development strategy was to stabilize Saudi society and to transform its structure so that it could play its role in the world economy. If estimated Saudi oil production in 1980 would be 20 million barrels a day, this would mean that Saudi Arabia could have provided 80 per cent of the total projected consumption needs of either Europe or North America, and it was with the USA that its economic advance was most closely tied. In 1970 18 per cent of Saudi Arabia's imports came from the USA while only 4 per cent of its oil exports went there; its main export markets were Europe (60 per cent) and Japan, with a quarter of its exports going out via Tapline and the rest through tankers loaded in the Gulf.[24] But projected US needs made it clear that ARAMCO would be raising production and the possible Saudi rise of 12 million barrels a day corresponded precisely to the projected increase in US import needs. Once the US dependence on Saudi oil became clear, in 1970–71, further negotiations took place. In May 1971 King Feisal visited the USA where it was reported that the main outlines of a future supply system were worked out. In November 1972 Saudi oil minister Ahmad Zaki Yamani headed the oil-producing nations team that introduced 'participation' in the Arab states of the Gulf. Under this scheme local governments were to obtain an immediate 20 per cent share in local operations; this was to rise to 25 per cent in 1975, by 5 per cent in each successive year and in 1983 local participation was to reach 51 per cent.

In 1973, however, the Saudis called a halt to negotiations; in July Feisal began to protest strongly about continued U S support for Israel, and during the October war they cut production by 12·2 per cent, imposing a complete embargo on shipments to the U S. Following the price rises of this period, and the abandonment of 'participation' in neighbouring Kuwait and Qatar, it seemed likely that the Saudis would also negotiate immediate majority or full ownership of A R A M C O. But the Saudis had no intention of harming the U S economy; they actively countered the more aggressive policies of their partners (see p. 84) and were concerned merely to secure a better position for themselves within the world economy.

Crushing the Saudi People

This regime so essential to the U S was marked by a policy of internal repression which combined the most virulent tribal tyranny with the most advanced repressive techniques imported from abroad. The ruling Saudi family held all power in its hands, at times recruiting individuals from other important families to assist in handling the new problems they faced. An example of such a recruit was oil minister Yamani. Officially, however, no concessions were made: there was no legal opposition, no trades union organization, no constitution, no elections. The Saudi clique had the double and unequivocal role of crushing all internal challenges and of policing as much of the Middle East as it could in the interests of pro-imperialist 'stability'. Both the oil consortium and the U S government did all they could to keep the Saudi regime in power, intervening only to urge reforms that would strengthen their clients. As the official U S government handbook on the country inanely put it: 'the company (A R A M C O) has carefully eschewed political activity or any actions which would give the appearance of exerting influence with the government. Its relations with the government have been generally good, inasmuch as it believes that a strong, stable government is essential to the long-term interests of ARAMCO.'[25]

The establishment of the Saudi regime in the 1920s was accompanied by a series of clashes with old rivals and former supporters which culminated in the defeat of the *ikhwan* in 1930. Ibn Saud appears to have been able to control the traditional kind of Arabian opposition and it was not until after the Second World War that the development of the oil economy and the spread of nationalism throughout the Arab world gave rise to a new kind of opposition movement. There have been several different strands within the new opposition. There were groups from within the ruling family, either conservatives who opposed the minimal modernization being carried out, or reformers such as Amir Talal who wanted more political changes. Outside the ruling family but still within the state structure were intellectuals educated abroad who were nationalists and wanted to challenge the ruling family's autocratic position; Abdullah Tariqi, who tried to limit ARAMCO's power around 1960, and the different conspiracies in the air force and army, represented this trend. Finally there was a working-class revolutionary trend, which led strikes in the oil-producing areas and also carried out a number of urban guerrilla actions in the 1960s. None of these forces was able to overthrow the regime, but all reflected tensions within the country which the Saudi rulers were only able to control by continued repression.

The first working-class revolt came in October 1953 when 13,000 workers in the oil-fields around Dammam went on strike; the government sent in troops, and hundreds of workers were arrested. But the workers held out for three weeks and the oil-fields were paralysed. As a result there was a certain improvement in welfare conditions: pay was increased, and shorter working hours allowed. No union organization was permitted. In June 1956 when King Saud was visiting Dhahran the workers demonstrated against him: the army went in, many strikers were arrested and foreign workers were deported. A royal decree was issued under which strikes and work stoppages were banned. This brutal attack on the working class by the Saudi government was directly supported by A R A M C O whose American employees helped the Saudi military to pick out the strike leaders.

In the 1960s there were further outbreaks. The North Yemeni revolution of September 1962 found a strong echo in the Saudi armed forces: the air force had to be grounded when nine pilots defected to the Nasserites, and U S planes had to be brought in to provide a substitute air defence. There were mass arrests and deportations among the Yemeni migrant workers in Saudi Arabia many of whom were sympathetic to the YAR. In the early part of 1963 as Egyptian planes were bombing Saudi border posts the U A R also dropped arms to supposedly resisting groups inside Saudi Arabia. The next three years saw less apparent Egyptian encouragement to the Saudi opposition, perhaps because of Nasser's desire to reach some agreement with King Feisal.

The next big wave of resistance broke out only at the end of 1966. This time a nationalist organization operating out of North Yemen, the Arabian Peninsula People's Union (A P P U), announced that it was launching an armed struggle. It claimed to represent all classes of Saudi society: 'we, who include soldiers, officers, doctors, engineers, writers, civil servants, merchants, and workers are everywhere. We are the people.'[26] In up to thirty bomb explosions between November 1966 and February 1967 the A P P U claimed to have blown up parts of the Tapline pipeline, the U S military headquarters at the Zahrat ash-Sharq Hotel in Riyadh, the public security building in Dammam, parts of two royal palaces, and part of the biggest Saudi air base at Khamis Mishayt, near the North Yemeni border. Despite these successes, the Saudi and U S security forces were able to counter-attack, and in March 1967 seventeen people were publicly executed in Riyadh for their participation in the A P P U armed struggle. According to Jiddah radio the militants were 'Egyptian-trained Yemenis' who wanted 'to make us renounce Islam and follow Lenin instead of Mohammad'.[27] This appeared to end the A P P U's armed campaign for the time being; hundreds of Yemeni were deported and there were no more reports of bomb explosions. When Saudi Arabia and Egypt realigned their policies in the aftermath of the June 1967 war and when the counter-revolution triumphed in North Yemen, the APPU lost its main base and its main supporter.

The Contemporary Opposition

Despite Nasserism's capitulation to Saudi Arabia in 1967, an opposition continued within Saudi society and on occasion news of political resistance has filtered through to the outside world.[28] In September 1969 the APPU announced in Beirut that 136 people had been arrested in the previous June. They included the commander of the Dhahran air base, Colonel Daoud al-Roumieh and the military commander of the Dhahran area, Said Omari, whom the APPU reported had died under torture. The aims of the opposition had been the declaration of the 'Republic of the Arabian Peninsula' which would have supported the Arab movement for 'socialism, liberty, unity and democracy'. Later it appeared that there had been at least two distinct conspiracies: one was led by civilian reformers who had previously been associated with Amir Talal and included members of notable Hejazi families with a long history of hostility to the Saudi family; the other group included young officers in the army and air force. Some of the latter had been recalled from training in Norfolk, England on the excuse that their relatives had 'fallen ill', and on their return had reportedly been executed. In a further report later in September 1969 the APPU gave details of a second military conspiracy which had included the military attachés in London and Karachi and the former military commander of the Mecca region. Up to 2,000 people in all were arrested in the 1969 security clampdown.[29]

In May 1970 there was a further wave of arrests in the eastern province when a reported thirty people, including the dean of the petroleum college, were thrown into prison. After that, muffled accounts of arrests and torture continued to come out. The level of terror and isolation brought to bear by the Saudi regime is such that information on what is happening is extremely hard to come by. Minister of the Interior Amir Fahd was reported to have said in 1971 that 'the internal situation in Saudi Arabia is perfect'.[30] Many foreign apologists of the regime said the same thing. Reginald Maudling, a British politician with business contacts in Saudi Arabia, certainly seemed to share Amir Fahd's view. 'Security, internal and external, is a problem; but in what country is it not? Certainly the government have clear ideas on how to handle it.'[31]

The opposition faced many acute difficulties. One was certainly the ferocity and efficiency of the repressive apparatus. A second problem was the social character of the country: population centres were dispersed and the government had a great advantage in being able to isolate different areas while moving its forces quickly from place to place. An added problem was that up to half of the country, the nomadic and agricultural populations, was kept in ignorance by the regime and encouraged to remain trapped in their traditional universe. Political work among them was extremely difficult. In 1973 the opposition appeared to fall into distinct groups, corresponding to political distinctions prevalent elsewhere in the Arab world. The National Liberation Front, founded in 1956, was the nearest equivalent to a Saudi Communist party, following a line sympathetic to the Soviet Union, and enjoying good relations with similar groups elsewhere in the Middle East. The Nasserist Arabian Peninsula People's Union, responsible for considerable opposition in the late 1960s, was believed to be influential in the army and among tribes in the northern Shammar region, who were historically opposed to the Saudis. The third main group were the Popular Democratic Party, formed in 1970 by the fusion of two groups of radical nationalists, one a group of former Ba'athis and the other a group of former Nasserites. The Popular Democratic Party stated that it was guided by Marxism-Leninism and called for the liberation of Saudi Arabia through a protracted people's war. In 1973 it was estimated by Saudi exiles that about 2,000 political prisoners lay in Feisal's jails.

Foreign Policy

In more than any other country in the world religion was a tool used by the regime to mystify and terrorize the population. Religious beliefs were still strong among the rural population, and the origins of the Wahhabi state made religion one of the cornerstones of the regime's hold on the country. The Saudi state has the added benefit of being in control of the holy cities of Mecca and Medina, to which by the early 1970s up to a million pilgrims were coming at the end of Ramadan.[32] Religion pervaded every aspect of Saudi life: religious police, *motawwahs*, terrorized the population and enforced the observance of prayer and the seclusion of women; political prisoners were forced to read the Koran for many hours a day; the Saudi authorities paraded themselves as the defenders of Islam and attacked all their enemies for being the enemies of God.

The use of religion also determined the ideological expression of Saudi foreign policy. By a quick sleight of hand the original trans-tribal universalism of the Wahhabis was turned into an aggressive policy of foreign intervention, with US imperialism providing material guidelines and the Koran the ideological justification. Saudi Arabia had only a fragmented and intermittent foreign policy in its first decades; but faced with the threat of Nasserism in the 1960s it launched itself on the world as a violent exponent of pro-western policies. When the Jiddah agreement between Nasser and Feisal on North Yemen had broken down – i.e. in the autumn of 1965 – Feisal raised the call for an Islamic Pact and toured Moslem countries to drum up support. Just to make sure that the aim of all this was clear to the world he escalated the royalist campaign in North Yemen, forcing Egypt to send in more troops which Feisal could then point to as agents of communist aggression. All this went down well in Washington, where a more virulent foreign outlook was taking shape in the aftermath of the full-scale entry of US troops into Vietnam. Feisal soon got support from predictable allies: the Shah of Iran, King Hussein of Jordan, King Hassan of Morocco and the reactionary Moslem states of the Asian subcontinent – Pakistan,

Malaya and Indonesia. The rapprochement with Egypt after 1967 did not stop him and in 1969 a full-blown Islamic Summit Conference was held in Morocco under the patronage of Kings Feisal and Hassan. In 1970 after a meeting of Islamic foreign ministers in Jiddah an Islamic Secretariat was established and the British client Malayan ex-premier Tunku Abdul Rahman was appointed secretary-general. The Second Islamic Summit Conference, held at Lahore in February 1974, was the occasion for further confirmation of Saudi influence.

This corrupt alliance went hand in hand with a more active Saudi role in Arab politics which the defeat of Egypt in 1967 and the British withdrawal from the peninsula in the late 1960s encouraged. Saudi Arabia, with growing US backing, saw itself as the leader of the Arab world and the guarantor of 'stability' in the Middle East as a whole and in the Gulf in particular. It poured money into Egypt, Jordan and Lebanon both as government-to-government grants and as private capital flows. With its neighbours it pursued a clear modernized version of the old Wahhabi expansionism: it continued to dominate North Yemen through supplies of arms and finance to its client tribes and in September 1972 organized an attack on the revolutionary South; it refused to recognize South Yemen and armed and trained counter-revolutionary exiles; albeit with some misgivings, it gave military aid to the Sultan of Oman. It exercised a firm if indirect influence on the smaller Arab states of the Gulf. Bahrain depended on Saudi oil for its economic livelihood; and Qatar was tied to Saudi Arabia by Wahhabism and family ties. Kuwait, although financially self-sufficient, was also grateful for Saudi military support as in the 1973 confrontation with Iraq when Riyadh promised to assist Kuwait if Iraq attacked. All of these coastal states knew that Saudi forces could intervene in the event of any revolutionary movement seizing power.

The one major topic of dispute between Saudi Arabia and the advanced capitalist countries is the question of Israel; the changes in oil policy do involve contradictions, but they are ones that form part of all inter-capitalist competition, and are found with regimes that are equally counter-revolutionary – such as that in

Iran. The Saudi position on Israel is dominated more by religious obsession about the 'Islamic' character of Jerusalem than by solidarity with the Palestinian people;[33] but since the 1967 war, Saudi Arabia has given increased backing to the Palestinian resistance and to the Arab states confronting Israel. The Egyptian –Syrian decision to go to war in October 1973 would have been impossible without the knowledge that Saudi diplomatic and economic backing was available.

The US has historically tried to back both Israel and the conservative Arab states, without being able to impose a solution. Until 1973 this ambiguous policy worked reasonably well, partly because the US at times made pro-Arab gestures (as in 1956), partly because the Arab states were too weak to challenge the pro-Israeli tendency of Washington's approach. But in 1973 the contradiction came to a head: in June of that year the US Senate tried to block the supply of Phantom jets to Saudi Arabia, and of other military aid to Kuwait. US government officials argued that these jets were needed because of the revolutionary threat in South Yemen and Iraq; their critics pointed out that what could be used against these radical states could also be used against Israel.[34] At the same time, King Feisal suspended discussion of oil output increases with ARAMCO, in protest at US favouring of Israel and US refusal to pressure the Israeli government.

Saudi policy during the October war and the oil crisis followed a consistent line: they wanted to exert maximum diplomatic pressure on Washington. Even the war itself was conceived of as a means of drawing US attention to the problems of the area – it was limited in its aims. The Saudis at first opposed any acts hostile to the US; a few days after the war began, Saudi Foreign Minister Omar Saqqaf stood with Nixon on the White House lawn, lauding the murderer of Vietnam as a 'man of peace'. The Saudis tried to avoid attending any meetings of the Arab oil producers which discussed oil cuts, and only agreed to suspend shipments to the US when Nixon asked Congress for $2·2 billion in emergency aid to Israel. Following the November ceasefire, Saudi oil minister Yamani toured western capitals, reassuring them of Saudi concern and Saudi determination not to inflict permanent damage on the advanced capitalist economies. In early 1974 the Saudis fought and won on two issues of direct concern to the west: Yamani got the oil producers to freeze their prices for six months – against the pressure of Iran – and in March the oil embargo was lifted, on Saudi and Egyptian urging, as a token of 'Arab good-will'.

Saudi policy, which in the western press was seen as part of some evil 'blackmail' of the advanced capitalist economies, was in fact a policy of trying to improve the Saudi economic position within the international market, and simultaneously of trying to fend off the more militant oil-producing states. The common identity of Saudi and imperialist concerns was shown by a number of incidents during the 1973 crisis. Throughout the period discussions continued with the US on the supplying of Phantoms, and in June of 1974 a $3,000 million bilateral technical and economic agreement between the two countries was announced. Britain, which during the October war had over 600 'civilian' air-force personnel in Saudi Arabia, also maintained good relations: Prime Minister Heath sent a special envoy, Lord Aldington, to Riyadh in December to see King Feisal, to 'use the argument, which is certain to appeal to the King, that any prolonged oil squeeze will, by weakening the west, strengthen communism'.[35] The Saudis agreed to treat Britain as a favoured country, and both increased their oil supplies and guaranteed not to weaken sterling by withdrawing their London deposits. The French were equally welcome: Foreign Minister Jobert visited Riyadh in January, and signed a series of bilateral economic and military agreements.

Had the Saudis been convinced anti-imperialists they could have used their economic power both to cause serious damage to the advanced capitalist economies and to give support to governments all over the world who were in need of financial support in establishing their independence – to the governments of South Yemen, Cuba, North Vietnam. As it was, they had no such intentions. As Sheikh Yamani himself put it: 'We are very much concerned with the economy of the whole world and we don't want in any way to destroy it.'[36] The Saudi role in the crisis of 1973 confirmed this.

Another difficulty imperialism faced was that Iran was a far more capable and efficient guardian of western interests in the Gulf than Saudi Arabia could conceivably prove to be: its population was several times larger, its armed forces three times larger, and its level of efficiency and powers of intervention greater. Yet it was impossible to grant Iran a unique role in this respect for two reasons: first, because the western dependence on Saudi oil was far greater than on Iranian, and the consequent risks involved in slighting the Saudis larger; secondly, because Iran's powers of intervention in the Arab states were limited by the fact that any major intervention would provide a large nationalist opposition throughout the Arab world. The division of repressive function seemed to be as follows: Iran had clearly appropriated to itself the task of patrolling the strategic waters of the Gulf and the approaches in the Indian Ocean, and had annexed several islands in the Gulf to this end. Moreover, Iranian money and covert Iranian military missions operated in certain Arabian peninsula states – Oman and North Yemen. But the dominant power, politically and militarily, on the Arabian peninsula itself remained Saudi Arabia and would continue to do so.

Potential Contradictions

Imperialism's relationship to Saudi Arabia could encounter a number of problems, which could be divided into two categories: increased contradictions between the regime as at present constituted and the west; and new contradictions arising from a change of regime inside Saudi Arabia itself. Under the first category fell the possibilities of a clash with other pro-western regimes in the area. While there existed diplomatic disputes with the Union of Arab Amirates and with the Sultanate of Oman these were extremely unlikely to prove explosive. The conflict with Iran was certainly more substantial and more deep-rooted, but neither side stood to gain from such a clash; occasional bursts of chauvinism will probably prove the limit to this contradiction.

The possibility of internal change in Saudi Arabia opens other perspectives. Change would be certain when Feisal retired or died: there might have been disputes within the ruling family, but even so it was probable that one of the leading Saudi family ministers would take his place and continue the prevailing policies. Neither the emergence of a radical anti-imperialist wing within the Saudi royal family nor a protracted inter-familial struggle such as to weaken the regime as a whole were likely. A second possibility was certainly that of the military seizing power, ousting the royal family and imposing some kind of Arab nationalism on the country. There may well have been Saudi Nassers or Gaddafis and the precise ideological complexion of such plotters was unknown; however it is essential to underline that the Saudi ruling clique was quite distinct from that which ruled in Egypt to 1952, in Iraq to 1958 or in Libya to 1969. They are far more diverse, better organized and far richer and Feisal has deliberately purged the most enfeebled elements. They have consistently organized the armed forces so as to disperse and divide them, in addition to riddling them with spies. Constant purges of the armed forces since 1962 have also weakened the opposition. Any such coup would, of course, deal a crippling blow to imperialism and is certainly a prospect that the west is frightened of. The Shah of Iran in an interview expressed concern at this prospect: 'Heaven forbid', he said, 'It's always a danger, I must admit.'[37] Yet surface appearances showed little sign of such an eventuality. The vicious regime established by the Saudis fifty years before has received a new lease of life from the material needs of the advanced industrial nations.

Notes

1. Information on Saudi Arabia is rare and unreliable. Estimates of the population, for example, range from three to eight million; official reluctance to carry out a census probably reflects the fear that the smaller figure will prove accurate. A collection of data and a bibliography can be found

in the *Area Handbook for Saudi Arabia* published for the U S government by the American University, Washington D C, in their Foreign Area Studies series.

2. For a historical overview of Wahhabism see George Rentz, 'The Wahhabis in Saudi Arabia', *The Arabian Peninsula*, ed. Derek Hopwood, London, 1972.

3. This was the revolt in which T. E. Lawrence, 'Lawrence of Arabia', participated. As a result of the Hashemites' activity one prince, Abdullah, was given the throne of the newly created half-state of Transjordan, and another, Feisal, was given the throne of the new state of Iraq. The former's grandson Hussein still rules in Jordan; the latter's progeny were ousted and executed in the Baghdad republican rising of 1958. The dispute about Lawrence and the 'Arab Revolt' is made up of two distinct issues. One is the question of how the British deceived the Hashemites about their plans and then used them to hold down the Arab world after the First World War. The other is the question of Lawrence's personality and its relation to the pathology of the British imperialist imagination in general. Both are interesting, but they have nothing to do with each other. For Lawrence's own account see his *Seven Pillars of Wisdom*, London, 1926; for an excellent demystification of the whole affair see Phillip Knightley and Colin Simpson, *The Secret Lives of Lawrence of Arabia*, London, 1969.

4. In the 1920s the Bolsheviks considered Ibn Saud to be a progressive anti-imperialist force, and the U S S R established diplomatic relations with him as early as 1926. These lapsed in the 1930s and Saudi Arabia then refused diplomatic relations with all communist countries.

5. Harvey O'Connor, *World Crisis in Oil*, London, 1962, p. 327. O'Connor gives an excellent analysis of this period. For a detailed account of how the U S ran the British out of Saudi Arabia see Gabriel Kolko, *The Politics of War*, London, 1969, pp. 294–313.

6. On the relation between 'Arab oil' and the Palestine question in this period see Joyce and Gabriel Kolko, *The Limits of Power: The World and United States Foreign Policy*, 1945–54, New York, 1972, pp. 403–27.

7. Robert Engler, *The Politics of Oil*, Chicago, 1967, p. 180.

8. ibid., p. 254.

9. ibid., p. 255.

10. On the background to this and Saudi Arabia's attitude to the Fertile Crescent see Patrick Seale, *The Struggle for Syria*, London, 1965.

11. The five provinces were: Central (Najd), Eastern (al-Hasa), Western (Hijaz), Southern (Asir) and Northern Frontier.

12. Feisal himself denied playing any role, for or against, in the final deposition of Saud, a position he illustrated with the bedouin proverb: 'If I spit in the air, I dirty my moustache; if I spit on the ground, I dirty my beard' (*Le Monde*, 7 November 1964). Saud went to Egypt and broadcast pro-Nasser speeches over Radio Cairo. In 1967 he stated that he had been ousted because a squadron of US jets based at Dhahran had intervened

at the decisive moment and had frightened the Royal Guard into submission. He died in Athens in 1969.

13. On the origins and development of the Saudi army see J. C. Hurewitz, *Middle East Politics: the Military Dimension*, London, 1969, Chapter 13, 'Saudi Arabia: the Peninsula under Najdi Rule'.

14. Figures taken from *The Military Balance 1972–1973*, International Institute for Strategic Studies, London, 1972.

15. *The Arms Trade with the Third World*, Stockholm International Peace Research Institute, Stockholm, 1971, pp. 560–65, 848–9.

16. ibid., p. 563. Under the same offset agreement U K aeronautical exports to the U S rose from $80 million in 1965 to $160 million in 1966. Considerable quantities of British weapons were sent to Vietnam under this deal.

17. Airwork Services Ltd have been playing a parallel role in the Sultanate of Oman where ex-R A F personnel 'assist' the Sultan's air force in their war against the people of Dhofar, the Sultanate's southern province. Here the personnel work in what is officially an R A F base, at Salala. See pp. 356 ff.

18. *English Electric (BAC) Lightning in Royal Air Force and Foreign Service*, Aircam Aviation Series, No. 37, Reading, 1972, pp. 13–14.

19. The man credited with being mainly responsible for arranging the 1965–6 deal was Geoffrey Edwards, an independent salesman and ex-R A F pilot (*Sunday Telegraph*, 26 June 1966). Edwards was a close friend of Colonel David Stirling, the man who helped organize the covert supply of British military personnel to the royalists in North Yemen and was involved in a later attempt to oust Libyan ruler Gaddafi. See p. 161. In 1971 a High Court action was taken out against Edwards by a Colonel Richard Lonsdale of St Lawrence, Jersey, alleging that they had reached an agreement in 1963, under which Lonsdale was to get 10 per cent commission on all arms sales made by Edwards to Saudi Arabia, and 8 per cent on all sales to Jordan, Syria and the Trucial States. Lonsdale stated that he had received only one payment of £40,000 on a £77 million Saudi contract. He named eight separate deals, totalling £313 million and referred to five others which he did not specify on which he also claimed his commission (*Observer*, 10 October 1971).

20. *The Times*, 8 July 1970.

21. *Daily Telegraph*, 13 July 1971.

22. *The Times*, 11 April 1973.

23. *The Military Balance 1972–1973*, p. 34; U S Department of Defense press release, 13 August 1971, gave the U S military mission as 141 on 1 July 1971.

24. In 1970 10·8 per cent of Saudi oil went to Italy, 7·6 per cent to the U K, 9·1 per cent to Holland, 4·2 per cent to Spain, 6·3 per cent to France and 2·1 per cent to West Germany. Tapline became an unreliable means of exporting after 1969 when it was blown up on several occasions by Palestinian guerrillas.

25. *Area Handbook for Saudi Arabia*, p. 4.

26. *BBC Summary of World Broadcasts*, 13 April 1967.

27. ibid., 7 March 1967.

28. After the June War Radio Cairo ceased anti-Saudi broadcasts; before the war the programme for Saudi Arabia, entitled 'Enemies of God', had been broadcast daily over *Voice of the Arabs*. Normal transmissions were suspended during the war and when regular schedules restarted on 15 June 1967 'Enemies of God' had disappeared, for ever.

29. *Le Monde*, 6 September, 7–8 September, 26 September 1969.

30. *The Times* special supplement on Saudi Arabia, 29 November 1971.

31. 'Opportunities Await British Trade', *The Times*, 9 May 1967. Maudling records that he had visited Saudi Arabia on several occasions as a director of the merchant bank Kleinwort Benson. Another enterprise in which Maudling was involved was the architectural business of J. G. L. Poulson, two of whose associate firms, J. G. L. Poulson Associates and Inter-planning Design, had been operating in Saudi Arabia.

32. In 1969–70 there were officially 406,205 pilgrims from outside Saudi Arabia and roughly the same number from within. Of the foreign pilgrims, 56,600 came from Turkey, 54,700 from North Yemen, 28,600 from Pakistan, 15,100 from Iran, 24,900 from Iraq, 20,500 from Sudan, 16,000 from India, 22,400 from Syria, 24,200 from Nigeria and 13,500 from Libya. Figures for other countries were not available. By 1970 50 per cent of the pilgrims arrived by air.

33. The bigoted character of Feisal's thinking on Palestine can be gauged from the speech he gave to the Mecca pilgrims in December 1973:

'Today, we regret to say, we hear voices in the world alleging that the Jews have the right to exist in the Holy Lands, in Jerusalem, despite the fact that it is common knowledge that the Jews have no relationship with Jerusalem, nor do they have any holy places there . . . The Almighty God has said that they have been cursed through his prophets . . . It is our duty, our brothers, to move today, to move to save our holy places and to drive out our enemies, and to be against all the doctrines founded by the Zionists – the corrupt doctrines, the atheist communist doctrines which seek to deny the existence of God and to deviate from Faith and from our religion of Islam . . .' SWB 1 January 1974.

34. See 'New Perspectives on the Persian Gulf', Hearings Before the Subcommittee on the Near East and South Asia of the Committee on Foreign Affairs, House of Representatives, Washington, 1973. These hearings are also interesting in that they show for the first time official US alarm at the developments in South Yemen and Oman.

35. *The Times*, 12 December 1973.

36. *Financial Times*, 28 January 1974.

37. *Newsweek*, 21 May 1973.

Part Two
North Yemen

Chapter Three
The Imamate and Its Contradictions

The Historical Origins of the Imamate

Until the revolution of 1962 North Yemen was one of the most isolated and static countries in the world. This state had never been forced to allow any capitalist enterprise to operate freely within its boundaries and its commercial ties with the outside world were slight. Yet North Yemen was situated near the British colony of Aden and to the west of the oil-rich kingdom of Saudi Arabia; and from this it acquired a strategic position of some importance. While it was tranquil it provided a safe flank for its neighbours; when it was in turmoil its internal conflicts affected political conditions in the states near by and drew these states into greater involvement. On 26 September 1962, after decades of seclusion, a nationalist and anti-imperialist revolution overthrew the reigning Imam al-Badr and proclaimed North Yemen the Yemen Arab Republic (YAR).

Within a week fighting had broken out between the protagonists of the deposed but still living Imam and the supporters of the new republic. With outside forces supporting the two local forces North Yemen became for a time the epicentre of political contradiction in Arabia. Because of the close interrelationship of North and South Yemen, two halves of a divided country, the explosion in the North led inexorably to struggle in the South. The battle for the YAR became not merely the struggle of the new republic against its traditionalist enemies, but the struggle of all nationalist and anti-imperialist forces in the peninsula against the leading imperialist client in the area – Saudi Arabia – and, through her, against Britain and the United States, the leading imperialist powers in the world.

North Yemen is the most densely populated country in the

peninsula, with an area of 75,000 square miles and a population estimated at four million.[1] Its fertile soil and annual tropical rains enable it to sustain a settled agrarian population and in pre-Islamic times the then undivided Yemen was the site of a number of prosperous centralized societies. After the last of the Yemeni agrarian states, the Himyaritic, fell in A.D. 525, and after occupations by the Persians and the Abyssinians, Yemen was occupied in A.D. 631 by the Arab armies of Islam. The new religion was quickly assimilated but so were its splits, and in the next two centuries Yemen came to be divided between the two major sects that grew out of the clashes of early Islam: the Sunni and the Shia.[2] The Sunni supported non-hereditary elected caliphs as the leaders of Islam and became the dominant trend within Arab Islam as a whole. The Shia tended to represent groups who for ethnic (i.e. non-Arab) or social or geographical reasons were more peripheral; they suffered defeat by the Sunni armies in Iraq. The Shia traced leadership of Islam through the descendants of Mohammad and his son-in-law Ali; and one of Ali's followers, Zeid, gave his name to a particular brand of Shi'ism called Zeidism. The Zeidis were driven out of Iraq in A.D. 870 and some fled to the mountains of Yemen where they settled and where they converted the tribes to their particular version of Islam. The leader of the Zeidis was known as the Imam who was chosen by the alleged descendants of Mohammad known as the Sada (singular Seyyid). The Imam was supposed to lead his people in prayer and in war and to govern through mediating different factions; and, while in practice all sorts of pressures including descent were invoked, the theory was that any male Seyyid could be elected Imam.

While Zeidism dominated the tribes of the northern and eastern mountains, the other part of the population, in the coastal plain – the Tihama – and in the cities of Sanaa and Taiz, were followers of Sunni doctrines. Their particular brand of Sunnism was known as Shafeism and they recognized whatever secular rulers were dominant – distant caliphs, local monarchs or individual tribal leaders. For centuries this Zeidi–Shafei division constituted the ideological level at which Yemeni politics was fought out; but while the religious division had its own intrinsic dynamic it corresponded to social and economic divisions: the mountain tribes had poorer lands and often relied on raiding the Shafei towns and coastal areas. The religious difference also expressed the conflict between the tribal leaders in the two areas who competed in a constantly changing pattern of alliances for dominance or marginal advantage over each other and for the seizure of the small agrarian and trade surplus.

Traditionally North Yemen as now constituted was split into a Zeidi area in the north, centred on the town of Sadaa, and a Shafei area centred on the Tihama plain; in the thirteenth century the Rassuli dynasty (*c*.1232–*c*.1454) established control over an area that stretched from the present Tihama through Aden to what is now Dhofar. The Rassulis fell in the fifteenth century and another unifier appeared a hundred years later in the shape of the Turkish Ottomans who captured Taiz in 1545; they conquered the Yemeni plains and Aden but were never able decisively to subjugate the mountains. The Turks departed in 1636; and on their departure the Zeidi Imam came out of the northern mountains, captured Sanaa and unified the mountains and the plain into a single state. With his capital at Sanaa the Imam's power extended to Aden, until in 1728 his subordinate in Lahej, near Aden, revolted and broke away. This was the origin of the division between North and South Yemen that was reinforced by the differential impact of imperialism, by the different class structures produced, and which has continued to this day.

The Imam maintained control over the rest of his kingdom, and strengthened his economic position by developing the export of coffee to Europe via the Red Sea port of Mocha. But imperialism closed in. In the nineteenth century the Arabian peninsula was invaded by the armies of Mohammad Ali, ruler of Egypt; and this in turn led the British in 1839 to occupy Aden and the neighbouring province of Lahej on the peninsula's south-eastern tip. The British and other maritime European nations had since the sixteenth century been nibbling at the edges of the peninsula, in the Red Sea, along the southern coast and in the Gulf; and this occupation of Aden was the culmination of a history of sporadic encroachment which confirmed the division between Yemen's North and South.

Mohammad Ali's invasion in 1849 was followed by the Ottoman Turks, who in 1871 captured Sanaa. As during their first occupation three centuries before the Turks tried to contain rather than conquer the Zeidi tribes of the north; but they had to deal with a new expansive Zeidi family, the Hamid ad-Din, whose leader, Mohammad bin Yahya, was 'elected' Imam in 1891. The Turks took several years to contain an offensive launched by Imam Mohammad, and on the latter's death in 1904 they faced a second offensive launched by the new Imam Mohammad's son, Yahya. Imam Yahya drove the Turks out of Sanaa, and although they later recaptured it they were forced to come to terms with Yahya in 1911. Under the Treaty of Da'an, they recognized him as the head of the Zeidi community with the right to collect taxes, appoint administrators and judges and receive an annual subsidy from the Ottoman court. In effect this treaty divided Yemen into its old Zeidi–Shafei areas, with the Imam in the mountains and the Turks ruling the Shafei on the plain. When the Turks were defeated in the First World War and had to withdraw from North Yemen and Arabia altogether the Imam was in a position to reconquer the Shafei areas and unite both parts of the area into the modern unit of North Yemen.

Economy and Society: A Pre-Capitalist Enclave

After the unification of 1918 North Yemen was ruled by the Zeidi Imams up to the revolution of 1962. It was in this period that the Imamate both consolidated its hold and created the conditions for its own collapse. Imam Yahya (ruled 1904–48) and Imam Ahmad (ruled 1948–62) built up their position through two policies: by strengthening key social relations underneath themselves and by excluding as much as possible foreign influences that might challenge these relations. The isolation of North Yemen was not a haphazard or aberrant policy of the Imams; it served directly to conserve their position. Only when contact with the outside world was likely to strengthen them (e.g. through buying

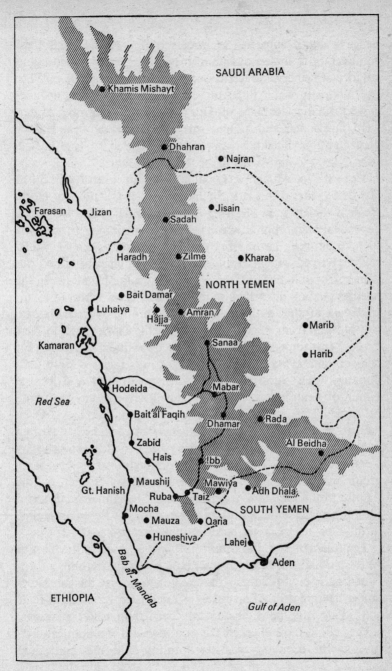

Map 4   North Yemen

he gave added subsidies to leaders of the Hashed and Bakil confederations to consolidate their loyalty, thereby upsetting the balance of bribery and terror on which Ahmad had relied. When the Imam returned in fit health at the end of the summer he made a wild attempt to undo al-Badr's changes. Reforming leaders were imprisoned, and Ahmad executed the sheikh of the Hashed confederation, Sheikh al-Ahmar, who refused to give back a subsidy paid to him earlier in the year by al-Badr.

Nevertheless Ahmad was unable to regain control; and in the last three years of his rule the multiple contradictions of North Yemeni society grew sharper. Ahmad himself was a sick man, dependent on morphine, which he tried to encourage his courtiers to take as well; he had fits of hallucination, when he would retire, charged with morphine, to a special chamber fitted out with coloured lights and toys where he would play alone. In the northern mountains tribal opposition had been increased by his treatment of Sheikh al-Ahmar; and his brother, Prince Hassan, was plotting from the distant safety of the Plaza Hotel in New York. Most importantly, a Nasserite opposition was calling for democratic and economic reforms and was released from temporizing when Ahmad broke with Egypt in 1961 and left the Union of Arab States, to which he had never in any real sense belonged. This schism reached a crisis in December when Ahmad read over the radio an anti-socialist poem he had written denouncing Nasser.[18] In reply Cairo radio broadcast speeches by Yemeni exiles from the Yemeni Union (*al-Ittihad al-Yamani*), a group including Free Yemenis and nationalists such as the Ba'athi Mohsen al-Aini, together with a Shafei merchant Abdul Rahman al-Beidhani, who was linked with the Egyptian regime through his marriage to the sister of Anwar es-Sadat.

The Imamate could not survive. It was exposed to the blast of Arab nationalism, beseiged internally by several groups of opponents and unable either to contain or to resolve the contradiction it had created. Ahmad was too sick to govern and al-Badr had no decisive power base; and, even if in better positions, neither could have checked the tide. Beneath the political convulsions the economy was deteriorating. The merchants had small minifundista peasants were forced in bad years to borrow at rates of up to 200 per cent or more, pledging their future crops as repayments for the loan. Without any alternative source of credit the peasant was often permanently in debt and discouraged from raising his output since a large percentage of his output would go to the landowner or tax collector to whom he owed past borrowings. This set of entrapping relations was of course by no means specific to North Yemen.

A further means of extracting the surplus was by ferocious taxation. The basic tax was *zakat*, originally a religious due paid by all Moslems as a form of alms, but since the Imam was both religious and secular ruler the *zakat* was taken into his treasury. The minimal rate was 10 per cent for all crops with the tax collector able to take a further 'commission' which he fixed at will. As there was no cadastral survey and as crops were measured on sight the estimations of tax were very imprecise and open to bribery and coercion of different kinds, with the peasant giving the tax collector a bribe to stop him from taking even more in tax. Animals were also taxed at a fixed rate per head. The officials themselves were of various kinds. One account listed the *mokhammen*, who assessed the crop before the harvest was brought in; the *kashshaf*, who came round during the harvest; the *moqasseb*, who fixed the taxes on irrigated land; and the *morshed*, a religious taxman, who travelled the country raising funds for the Imam's defence of the Moslem religion.[7] Peasants were expected to make certain annual presents to the landlords of honey and ghee, and to house and feed government officials and soldiers free of charge as a form of *corvée*. Families who had relatives abroad and received remittances from them could also expect to be pressured by local officials who knew they had extra cash.

On average the tax collector took 25 per cent of the crop, and after all other levies were exacted the peasant was left with 20 per cent of his produce. In 1968 a peasant committee at Qabita near Taiz produced a list of the taxes they had had to pay during the Imam's rule: *zakat*, a percentage of the crop; *futra*, a head tax; a land tax on irrigated land; an animal tax on sheep and goats; a tax on the income of more prosperous peasants;

a tax for road construction; and bribes to assessors, soldiers, sheikhs and village headmen.[8] Inhabitants of Shafei areas also had to pay a tax exempting them from service in the army, which they were discouraged from joining anyway – a practice similar to the virtually compulsory exemption tax – the *bedel* – paid by Christians in the European provinces of the old Ottoman empire.

The crops can be divided into two kinds: those for local consumption, i.e. for subsistence, and those grown for markets elsewhere in North Yemen or abroad. Cereals (millet, wheat, maize), some vegetables (beans, peas, potatoes) and certain fruits made up the first category; the basic North Yemeni diet was of cereals. Meat was consumed only on special occasions and rice was imported. The main crops grown for export were coffee, cotton and *qat*, a local narcotic. Historically coffee had been North Yemen's main export, but from 1945 onwards its production fell – from 12,000 tons per year to 5,000 tons in 1962. The production of coffee tended to be carried out in the mountains in small properties with around 100 coffee trees. When it was carried out on big estates the terms for share-cropping were particularly heavy, with up to two thirds of the crop going to the owner. The price of coffee was also dependent on the world market, and its export was in the hands of merchant favourites of the Imam. Under Imam Ahmad one merchant named al-Jabaly acquired an almost total monopoly over the export of coffee; he was not capable of, nor interested in, expanding its export. The only export crop that did expand under the Imam was cotton, which the British had introduced into South Yemen, and which was grown from 1951 onwards, in response to a rise in world demand.

The growing of coffee and of all other foods was displaced by the increased production under the Imams of *qat*, a drug that plays a significant part in North and South Yemeni culture. It was originally brought to Yemen in the fifteenth century and its growth and use are confined to Ethiopia and the Yemeni areas of the Arabian peninsula. It is a small shrub and its bitter leaves when chewed for quite a while (half an hour or more) stimulate the chewer and give a sense of well-being. Different areas produce different qualities; and the finest *qat* is believed to be Taizi. It is best when fresh and cut early in the morning for chewing that afternoon. It is not hallucinogenic, but gives a gentle stimulation. Chewing often lasts for several hours and the mouth of the *qat*-taker is after a time filled with a ball of green sludge or slime which he sustains and rolls around. The effect wears off once chewing stops but the drug leaves a sense of mild depression and in the long run allegedly affects sexual potency.

Qat's social role is felt in a number of ways. The chewing of the leaves is the centre of the male Yemeni day; as one Yemeni writer has put it: 'from the afternoon to sunset all activity ceases and the Yemenis are plunged into an ecstatic torpor'.[9] Chewers claim that *qat*, by stimulating, helps the chewer to work and to concentrate, but the social nexus within which the chewing takes place is one of enforced and routinized lethargy as groups of men lie around chatting from two to eight. In this way *qat*, by blocking off the whole of every afternoon with institutionalized idleness, i.e. unemployment, greatly contributes to Yemen's problems. But under the Imams, *qat*, produced for domestic consumption, also undermined the country, by displacing the growing of coffee and thus undercutting the little export earning Yemen received. For the peasant himself it was a special bane, since however meagre his income he would spend a sizeable portion of his earnings on *qat* rather than on food for himself and his family or on tools for production. While it was obviously in part a reflection of the misery of life under the Imams the prevalence of *qat* also contributed in its turn to this misery and to the deterioration of the North Yemeni economy.[10]

While *qat* came to dominate rural production and undercut export earnings the cities remained relatively static, housing 10–15 per cent of the population in Sanaa, Taiz and the port of Hodeida. These were not the result of any industrialization: North Yemen did not have a single modern factory; and a textile factory built in 1957 was prevented from starting production by the merchants who depended on the import of cotton goods. Merchants and artisans formed the main economically active sections of the cities; and most of the merchants were Shafeis depending on foreign trade and on lending money to the Imam. Imamic confiscations and high taxes discouraged these merchants, who were therefore reluctant to invest capital in Yemen and exported it where possible. In the period of Imam Ahmad escalating taxation, and special privileges extended to the favourite al-Jabaly, produced a merchant opposition movement based among exiles in Aden and in such other expatriate communities as the Yemeni communities in East Africa and in Tiger Bay, Cardiff. There were also small shopkeepers and tradesmen in the cities, but there was no capitalism-based urban proletariat nor was there a large unemployed lumpenproletariat of migrant peasants like that found in the cities of Latin America or Asia. The cities held the administration, and the small commercial sector, absentee landlords and Sada; as in many other pre-capitalist societies a small bourgeoisie existed as a minority capitalist sector within a larger pre-capitalist formation without in any way inducing a change in that formation towards the capitalist mode.

North Yemen remained isolated from world politics and economies both because the ruling Imams wanted to keep the world out and because capitalism had no strong economic or strategic reason for wanting to intrude. Foreign trade reflected this relation and in particular showed how North Yemen differed from those other poor countries that had a colonial relation to the capitalist world. In 1961 North Yemen's exports were valued at $8·2 million (out of a GNP of $300 million), with coffee making up to 49 per cent of them and cotton 19 per cent.[11] Imports totalled $17 million, of which 29 per cent was food, 7 per cent tobacco and 17 per cent textiles. North Yemen was not, as colonial countries tend to do, exporting primary products and importing manufactured goods. She was exporting primary products in order to *import* other primary products. There was no foreign capital invested in North Yemen and no foreign control of North Yemeni production except through purchase from abroad; and this foreign trade represented a marginal element in North Yemen's total production. The deficit in its foreign trade was filled partly by remittances from Yemenis abroad and partly by aid cajoled out of the Soviet Union and Egypt which went to reinforce rather than alter North Yemen's enclave position.

The absence of financial institutions and of most essential public structures also reflected this pre-capitalist formation. The only bank that operated in North Yemen before 1962 was the Saudi National Commercial Bank. The only currency was the Maria Theresa dollar (or *thaler* – the original form of the word 'dollar'), which was a silver coin introduced into the Middle East by Napoleon's 1798 conquest of Egypt. Being made of silver, it was universally acceptable; and it was minted in Austria from 1780 onwards – but always bearing the date 1780.[12] It was a completely unsatisfactory form of coinage; its value fluctuated with the world demand for silver – its average value was 80 cents – and its purchasing power within North Yemen varied both with the level of economic activity and with the availability of the imported coins, a factor made more unreliable by the frequency of hoarding. The Imam's administration was small, with minimal departmental divisions, and drawn mainly from Sada. There was no distinction between the Imam's private purse and the North Yemeni treasury, no cabinet and no legislative body. The law based itself on the traditional Moslem law, the *shari'ah*, backed by tribal custom. Public beheading and limb amputations were common punishments. The class structure followed simple lines. At the top was the Imam, and around 200,000 Sada, who owned much of the best land and controlled the administration; they comprised a closed group defined by their supposed descent from Mohammad. Next came the tribal leaders, the sheikhs, varying according to the strength and size of their tribes; many of them were the local administrators and tax collectors. Their position depended on their tribes, but was often hereditary; if loyal to him, the Imam would pay them subsidies to encourage them to stay that way. Below the sheikhs came the merchants and artisans in the cities; but most numerous were the mass of rural peasants – illiterate, sick, under-employed and sunk in a mire of tribal and religious mystification. At the very bottom were two small groups: slaves, mainly domestic servants for the rich; and an outcast group of around 50,000 *akhdam*, descendants of Ethiopian immigrants. It was a society overwhelmed with misery. In 1962 there were only fifteen doctors – all foreigners. There were 600 hospital beds in the whole country. Over 50 per cent of the population had some kind of venereal disease; over 80 per cent were suffering from trachoma. No money at all was spent on education by the state and less than 5 per cent of the children attended the traditional Koranic schools. There was not only no North Yemeni doctor, but there were no modern schools, no paved roads, no railways, no factories. The average per capita income was $70 a year. There was nothing romantic about it; it was a very horrible place.

The institution of the tribes had deep roots in Yemeni society, and since it was in no sense in decomposition, it was one of the major causes for the containment of social discontent among the oppressed peasantry in North Yemen. The instinct to revolt took the form of uprisings against the centre (over levies, taxes, produce) by whole tribes or of compensating for the poverty of one tribe by pillaging another. The men and women of the Yemeni countryside who suffered the misery of the Imamic system knew of no way out of this oppression.[13] Relations between tribes often took the form of loose confederations; and two notable Zeidi alliances, the Hashed and the Bakil, had considerable stability in the pre-1962 period. These inter-tribal alliances were shifting, as was the relation between tribes and the centre. The Imam was able to coerce tribes by arms or to induce them by bribes and concessions; if he appeared to be too generous or weak the tribes would disobey him, but if he was too bullying or too mean they might revolt all the more determinedly. Under the Hamid ad-Din the Imams tried to split the tribes and to win Zeidi loyalty by giving them privileges over the Shafeis, and on at least one famous occasion in 1948 the Imam allowed his Zeidi followers to loot the Shafei city of Sanaa.

Hamid ad-Din Rule of United North Yemen: 1918–62

Imamic incorporation of the tribes was completed two decades after the Turks withdrew from North Yemen. At first many of the tribes refused to accept the Zeidi Imam as North Yemen's ruler; after 1918 the Shafei Zaraniq tribes in the Tihama plain set up their own state and appealed to the League of Nations for recognition. But they and other recalcitrant tribes were crushed in a series of centralizing campaigns that lasted up to 1939. Most of these campaigns were carried out by Yahya's son Ahmad, a notoriously cruel commander who had a terrifying appearance because his eyes seemed to pop out of his head; such was his reputation that it was believed by many Yemenis he had deliberately cultivated this appearance as a young man by continuously throttling himself with a rope. Control of the subjected tribes was through nomination of headmen and tribal sheikhs; but another characteristic method was the taking of hostages, mainly the sons of sheikhs, and treating them well or badly according to the behaviour of their tribes. At the end of the unifying campaigns in 1939 it was estimated that Imam Yahya had around 4,000 hostages in his castles, and in 1955 there were believed to be around 2,000, in Ahmad's palace in Taiz and elsewhere. When Imam Ahmad went to Rome in 1959 for medical treatment he even took some of his hostages with him.

The Hamid ad-Din concentrated power in their own hands. Yahya put his sons in key positions and made special efforts to displace members of the al-Wazir family, Zeidis who had held the Imamate before his father. Considerable Zeidi opposition broke out in 1927 when Yahya nominated his son Ahmad to be his successor and so bluntly flouted the Zeidi principle about electing, or at least going through the motions of electing, an Imam. Yahya terrorized his opponents. The basis of government was a simple flow of decisions from the Imam and a flow of information and requests to him; under Imam Ahmad the traditional Moslem system of petitioning was supplemented by one modern addition, the telegram, which became a popular form of communication. Individual North Yemenis were able to cable

105

the Imam; and with no telephone and bad land communications it was a better medium of general contact than the letter. Under Ahmad the centralization of the state took on paranoid forms; he put much of the state treasury in secret hiding places and then killed the slaves who had transported it. He also put the army's munitions into secret arsenals to prevent the army from turning their guns against him. Tanks and planes imported from abroad were locked up and demobilized by having key parts removed; bullets and shells were issued in small amounts for specific campaigns.[14]

The army was divided, as in Saudi Arabia, into a crack royal corps derived from loyal tribes, and a regular army used for less sensitive activities. Both groups were drawn heavily from the Zeidi tribes, particularly from the Hashed confederation. The royal corps were used for crushing rebel tribes and for collecting taxes, the latter function being well expressed in their anthem the Samel, which contained the lines: 'We, the soldiers of the King, are stronger than all the peasants.'[15] A second army, the so-called regular army (*al-Jeish al-Nidhami*), was used for guarding the frontiers; when North Yemen wars ended in 1939, the army totalled around 25,000. The soldiers were badly armed and underpaid. Their officers were trained at a college near Sanaa; but for a period starting in 1934 some officers were sent to Iraq for training. This experiment came to an end when the officers returned with political ideas; and from then on foreign officers, Iraqi and then Egyptian, were brought to North Yemen instead. These imported officers brought in the same nationalist ideas, and were one of the factors contributing to the 1962 revolution.

Apart from domestic duties, these armies were deployed in the Imams' foreign wars. North Yemen's frontier with Saudi Arabia was ill-defined; and in 1934 the two countries fought over the possession of Asir, a province on North Yemen's north-west frontier. The Saudis made a two-pronged thrust into Yemen; one column under the future King Feisal stormed down the coast and captured Hodeida, while another under the future King Saud was blocked trying to advance through the north-east mountains. Yahya was crushed by the capture of Hodeida and abandoned Asir; and a Treaty of Moslem Friendship and Arab Fraternity was signed at Taif in Saudi Arabia on 20 May 1934. Under this agreement, the Saudis won control of Jizan, Asir and Najran for thirty years. From then on the two dynasties were close allies and the Saudis came to the aid of the Hamid ad-Din family whenever they were in danger – in 1948, 1955 and most of all from 1962 onwards. Given the expansionist tendencies of the Saudi regime, they might well have annexed North Yemen outright in 1934, had it not been for British opposition; as it was the Saudis were satisfied by their client relationship with the defeated Imam Yahya. Clashes with British imperialism continued in the South, where the British had been established since 1839. The Imam recognized neither the British position in the South, nor the boundary between the two areas that the Turks and the British had defined in 1914. From the time of the Turkish withdrawal he realized the British were his enemies. They had tried to prevent him seizing the Tihama plain and had given the port of Hodeida to the ruler of Asir. In 1921 Imam Yahya counter-attacked, took Hodeida and sought influence with the tribes around Aden being bribed and armed by the British. Boundary clashes continued during the 1920s; and in 1928 the RAF bombed Taiz, using warplanes against defenceless civilians as they were later to do in South Yemen.[16]

The Imam refused to capitulate until 1934 when during the Saudi assault he was forced to cover his southern flank; he then recognized the status quo along the frontier, while the British acknowledged him as Imam of North Yemen. Once the agreement was signed the British proceeded to violate it by signing new treaties with border tribes and strengthening their hold on the unadministered areas. Relations further deteriorated during the Second World War when Yahya opened relations with the Italians in Ethiopia; the British cut off supplies of kerosene to North Yemen, and Yahya stopped supplying *qat* to the South.

Under Imam Ahmad, after 1948, relations worsened, especially after the British developed a plan in 1950 for a Federation of South Arabian tribes. This represented a lessening of influence for the Imam. Many of these tribes were Shafei and traditionally

107

hostile to the Imam; but Ahmad sent money and arms across the border and occupied contested areas. In 1957 he even invited a group of foreign journalists to the North–South Yemen border to witness a bombardment of British positions. But he abandoned the campaign in 1959 when internal crises broke out. Although he posed as an anti-imperialist, Ahmad was incapable of winning support from the masses in the occupied South both because his own regime was backward and because he was clearly playing with the British and unable to launch a full assault on them. His claims to the South were dynastic and annexationist and when he thought it was convenient to do so, he dropped them. In the end it was the overthrow of the Imams, not their vacillating anti-imperialism, that laid the basis for the liberation of the South.

One consequence of the Imams' hostility to Britain was occasional relations with the Soviet Union. During Yahya's campaigns in the 1920s trade links were established; and in 1928 a ten-year Treaty of Commerce and Friendship was signed. A Soviet film unit visited Yemen in 1929; and medical supplies were sent; but by the mid 1930s these contacts had ceased and only one doctor remained. In the mid 1950s a similar process occurred. Ahmad's son al-Badr visited the communist countries and opened diplomatic relations with the USSR and the People's Republic of China; trade with Yemen and the provision of military supplies followed. But these exchanges depended on the Imam's relations with Egypt and deteriorated accordingly.[17]

The Internal Opposition

Throughout their rule both Yahya and Ahmad faced various oppositions. Tribal hostility to the new state did not cease until 1939, and during the Second World War further antagonism came from a group of exiles in Aden. Mainly Shafei merchants, they opposed the Imam's control of trade and his failure to provide a climate in which they could invest their profits. They called themselves the Free Yemenis; their leaders included Ahmad Mohammad Noman, from a family of hereditary Shafei sheikhs, and Mohammad Mahmud al-Zubayri, a Zeidi lawyer and poet from Sanaa. They wanted a number of straightforward reforms, including a constitutional Imamate and an economic climate favourable to reinvestment of capital – namely, no confiscations and no punitive taxation. Other people shared these views – displaced religious leaders, sacked administrators and dissident tribes. An attempt to kill Yahya in January 1948 was unsuccessful, but a month later they assassinated him outside Sanaa and proclaimed Abdullah al-Wazir Imam. But despite support from the Free Yemenis and army officers, al-Wazir's rule did not last. Yahya's son Ahmad, with Saudi support, swept out of the northern mountains, deposed the new Imam and sacked Sanaa. For the rest of his reign Imam Ahmad never returned to what he considered to be the guilty city.

After a period of repressive calm a new outburst came in 1955. An incident occurred in which peasants of the Hawhan tribe near Taiz attacked a group of tax collectors, killing three of them; the local army commander wanted to punish the peasants but Ahmad thought it better to let the matter drop. Enraged, the officer attacked Ahmad in his castle, and in Taiz a rival Hamid ad-Din prince, Abdullah, proclaimed himself Imam. Although opposition leaders began to make public statements, Ahmad was by no means defeated; once again the northern tribes were rallied, this time by his son al-Badr, and once rescue was on its way Ahmad burst out of his castle and routed his opponents.

Following this successful venture, al-Badr was given greater freedom, and was sent to Europe, the Soviet Union and the People's Republic of China. Under the influence of his reforming tendencies, and to forestall the growing pro-Egyptian nationalist opposition, Yemen moved into alliance with Egypt. Military and economic agreements were signed and in 1958 North Yemen joined Egypt and Syria to form the Union of Arab States. North Yemen was provided with a large number of Egyptian technicians and army officers; and in 1959, while Ahmad was in hospital in Rome, al-Badr, under the influence of his experiences in the outside world, introduced a series of reforms. To win the support of the army he raised their salaries by 25 per cent; and

109

he gave added subsidies to leaders of the Hashed and Bakil confederations to consolidate their loyalty, thereby upsetting the balance of bribery and terror on which Ahmad had relied. When the Imam returned in fit health at the end of the summer he made a wild attempt to undo al-Badr's changes. Reforming leaders were imprisoned, and Ahmad executed the sheikh of the Hashed confederation, Sheikh al-Ahmar, who refused to give back a subsidy paid to him earlier in the year by al-Badr.

Nevertheless Ahmad was unable to regain control; and in the last three years of his rule the multiple contradictions of North Yemeni society grew sharper. Ahmad himself was a sick man, dependent on morphine, which he tried to encourage his courtiers to take as well; he had fits of hallucination, when he would retire, charged with morphine, to a special chamber fitted out with coloured lights and toys where he would play alone. In the northern mountains tribal opposition had been increased by his treatment of Sheikh al-Ahmar; and his brother, Prince Hassan, was plotting from the distant safety of the Plaza Hotel in New York. Most importantly, a Nasserite opposition was calling for democratic and economic reforms and was released from temporizing when Ahmad broke with Egypt in 1961 and left the Union of Arab States, to which he had never in any real sense belonged. This schism reached a crisis in December when Ahmad read over the radio an anti-socialist poem he had written denouncing Nasser.[18] In reply Cairo radio broadcast speeches by Yemeni exiles from the Yemeni Union (*al-Ittihad al-Yamani*), a group including Free Yemenis and nationalists such as the Ba'athi Mohsen al-Aini, together with a Shafei merchant Abdul Rahman al-Beidhani, who was linked with the Egyptian regime through his marriage to the sister of Anwar es-Sadat.

The Imamate could not survive. It was exposed to the blast of Arab nationalism, beseiged internally by several groups of opponents and unable either to contain or to resolve the contradiction it had created. Ahmad was too sick to govern and al-Badr had no decisive power base; and, even if in better positions, neither could have checked the tide. Beneath the political convulsions the economy was deteriorating. The merchants had been turned into an opposition force by punitive taxation; under the Imamist regime capitalist development had no chance. North Yemen, whose main product was cereals, was a net importer by the early 1960s; coffee exports were down to a quarter of their 1942 level; cotton and wheat had also declined catastrophically. By imposing export taxes Ahmad actually discouraged the export of primary products. The Imam was blocking the political and economic development of North Yemen and trying hopelessly to isolate it from the world. The economic and political contradiction between the pre-capitalist enclave and the capitalist world had reached its point of culmination; and all possibilities within the Imamist regime had been exhausted.

Notes

1. Some of the information in these and the subsequent two chapters has been derived from conversations with Yemenis and from a reading of the available press and periodical materials. Of the books used, the following are the most important: Dr Said al-Attar, *Le Sous-développement économique et social du Yémen*, Algiers, 1964, an economic analysis of pre-1962 society; Sultan Ahmad Omar, *Nazra fi Tatawwor al-Mojtam'a al-Yamani* (*A Look at the Development of Yemeni Society*), Beirut, 1970, by a revolutionary militant who participated in the movements in both North and South Yemen; Manfred Wenner, *Modern Yemen: 1918–1966*, Baltimore, 1967, a scrupulous assembly of much of the known historical data on Yemen in this century. All three have bibliographies.

2. A reliable and easily available introduction to the history of the Arabs is Bernard Lewis, *The Arabs in History* (numerous reprints since 1950).

3. Al-Attar, op. cit., p. 73.

4. Eighty thousand Yemeni workers were employed in Aden port after the mid 1950s; several hundred thousand emigrated as construction workers to Saudi Arabia; and there were Yemeni trading communities along the African coast; and colonies of Yemenis in Britain (Cardiff, Birmingham, South Shields) and in the USA (Brooklyn, the Dearborn suburb of Chicago).

5. For a summary of the communist sects that split off from orthodox Islam in the eighth to tenth centuries see Lewis, op. cit., Chapter 6,'The Revolt of Islam'. These movements bore certain social and ideological similarities to the primitive communist sects that emerged in medieval Christianity.

6. Maxime Rodinson, *Islam and Capitalism*, London, 1974, is an invaluable guide to the structure of medieval Islamic society and to the way in

111

which a capitalist sector could survive without either succumbing to or transforming the predominantly pre-capitalist formation around it.

7. Omar, op. cit., p. 105.

8. ibid., p. 106.

9. Al-Attar, op. cit., p. 124.

10. In 1972 the YAR leadership called for an end to *qat* chewing; but it was unlikely to diminish markedly.

11. Al-Attar, op. cit., p. 193ff.

12. The Maria Theresa *thaler* went out of production in 1960.

13. There is so far as I know no adequate account of the working of the Yemeni tribal system. R. B. Sergeant, 'The Mountain Tribes of the Yemen', *Geographical Magazine*, 1942, gives some indications.

14. In this detail, as in many others, Ahmad bears a striking resemblance to Dr François Duvalier. ruler of Haiti from 1957 to his death in 1971. Like Ahmad, 'Papa Doc' also ruled his people by unharnessed terror and religious mystification, mixed with a truculent attitude to imperialism.

15. Al-Attar, op. cit., p. 81.

16. On the British use of air power in colonial Arabia see p. 188 n. 6.

17. Wenner, op. cit., pp. 155–6, 176–7.

18. 'Why do you fill the atmosphere with abuse? ... Why do you shout over the microphone with every discordant voice?' it asked. The poem went on to denounce as anti-Islamic the attempt to create equality between rich and poor and to take property from its owners without consent. Al-Attar, op. cit., pp. 83–4.

Chapter Four
Civil War and
Counter-Revolution

The September Revolution

Ahmad died, in his sleep, on 18 September 1962. Next day his son Mohammad al-Badr announced the news and was himself proclaimed Imam by the religious leaders of Sanaa, the *ulema*.[1] He at once took measures to forestall the different sources of opposition. To check the liberals he announced a programme of reform, abolishing some of the country's restrictive economic laws and releasing political prisoners; to check the northern tribes who had links with al-Badr's pro-American uncle, Hassan, the new Imam announced that despite his reforms he would rule North Yemen as his father and grandfather had done. These measures reflected no decisive policy. Imam al-Badr was personally and politically incapable of containing the contradictions inside Yemeni society. A reformed Imamate could not have carried through the capitalist transformation of North Yemen. Even had it so wished, it would have been unable to overcome traditional opposition to reform, besides which it represented a ruling class that was itself a major cause of North Yemen's condition.

Al-Badr knew his immediate opponents were in the army and took measures to win their loyalty; he raised their pay and appointed Abdullah as-Sallal, a known nationalist, as head of his bodyguard. Sallal was a Zeidi, the son of a blacksmith, who had been sent to Iraq with the first group of officers in 1934; after the 1948 coup he had been imprisoned for seven years. He had no loyalty to al-Badr and used his position to organize a coup. A separate group of Nasserite officers in the army had been planning a coup for late September and had been taken by surprise when Imam Ahmad died on the eighteenth. But when Sallal was appointed to his new post they contacted him, and allegedly to protect al-Badr's palace, Sallal brought tanks into Sanaa from Hodeida. On the evening of 26 September, while al-Badr was inside, the tanks shelled the palace and destroyed its upper storey; the plotters thought they had killed the Imam, and the next day, with Sanaa in their control, they proclaimed North Yemen the Yemen Arab Republic.

The Nasserite group that executed the coup was made up of members from a secret committee within the 400-strong officers' corps. Only eighty of them actually participated in the coup; and the rank and file of the army were locked into their barracks by the conspirators, who suspected their loyalties. One of the most active members of the group was a twenty-five-year-old lieutenant who had studied in Egypt, Ali Abdul al-Moghny. Other key officers were Abdallah Jezeilan, later Minister of Defence; and Abdul Latif Deifallah, later Minister of the Interior.[2] Sallal himself was not a member of the group, but he had his own conspiratorial relationship with certain tribes, and he agreed to work with the young officers. They had a reason for working with him, as he was a senior nationalist of some prestige and experience, and they agreed to give him the presidency of the Republic. Much has been made of the Egyptian role in this coup; but it was not its decisive cause. The nationalist officers were ideologically formed by Arab nationalism, and Egyptian officers brought to North Yemen had contributed to politicizing the officers' corps. The Egyptian chargé d'affaires in Sanaa, Abdul Wahhad, was in contact with Sallal and the officer group and had deviously warned al-Badr of an impending coup so as to encourage him to bring tanks from Hodeida to protect his palace. But the coup expressed the contradictions of North Yemeni society itself and its agents were Yemenis who reflected this; neither the contradictions nor the agents originated in Cairo.

Many sectors of North Yemeni society responded enthusiastically to the proclamation of the Republic. In Taiz a civilian people's committee took power when the news came of events in Sanaa. In Aden the North Yemeni migrant workers demonstrated in favour of the Republic. The Shafei merchants enthusiastically backed the YAR, as did the Free Yemenis in Cairo and Aden. Cheering crowds swept through Taiz, Sanaa and Hodeida. But support was not confined to the cities or just to Shafei areas as might have been expected. In the rural areas around Ibb peasants attacked sheikhs who were known for their cruelty and for having flogged peasants who did not pay their taxes. In the Zeidi mountains tribes that had been opposed to Imam Ahmad rallied to the YAR; the Hashed confederation, led by Abdullah al-Ahmar, proclaimed its support. Thousands of tribesmen swarmed into Sanaa with petitions to offer to fight for Sallal, although many may have had little idea of what Sallal or the Republic stood for.[3]

The coup was a direct if partial reflection of the crisis of North Yemeni society. It had been carried out by a section of the armed forces without the participation or prior knowledge of the popular masses or even of those sections of the intelligentsia and the commercial bourgeoisie who immediately supported it. It met with mass spontaneous approval in the towns, the Shafei areas, and some of the Zeidi hinterland; but it had powerful opponents and within its supporters there were many conflicts. The most fundamental political weakness was that although the masses backed the coup it was carried out by a small conspiratorial group who acted in lieu of mass organization; like the Egyptian officers led by Neguib and Nasser who overthrew Farouk in the 1952 Egyptian revolution, and like some nationalist military in Latin American countries, it was both a representative of the masses and a displacement of them, profoundly suspicious of the people and unwilling to organize, educate or rely on them. The North Yemeni masses lacked autonomous political organization or any coherent consciousness of their aims; but they supported the army, and the proclamation of the YAR was clearly in their interests.

September 1962 can be called a revolution. It was the YAR that introduced capitalism into North Yemen – opening it to the world market and unleashing the domestic bourgeoisie – and it destroyed the political rulers who had governed North Yemen up to that time. But different options faced the revolution, and the YAR was controlled from the beginning by army officers and their allies – the commercial class and tribal leaders who saw the overthrow of the Imam as an occasion to advance their own status. Subsequent events confirm this and developed the post-1962 Republic in a direction radically different from the popular transformation possible at the start. In 1962 North Yemen could either become a component of the capitalist world, with a pro-imperialist foreign policy and economic relations, and a capitalist ruling class and capitalist relations at home. Or it could defeat both the pro-Imamic forces and the rightist republicans, together with their foreign allies, and lay the basis for a socialist transformation of North Yemen without years of capitalism in between.[4] This depended on the strength both of the different forces in North Yemen and of external imperialist pressures; but also on the determination of forces that came from outside to help the Republic.

The first actions of the republicans were to form a cabinet composed of officers and Yemeni Union civilians and to enact a series of reforms: the Imamate was abolished by the very declaration of a Republic; slavery and the hostage system were outlawed; all the property and land of the Hamid ad-Din family were confiscated; many Sada and other administrators were put on trial and executed. The new government took measures to unblock the economy: a new currency was created to replace the Maria Theresa dollar; a Yemen Reconstruction and Development Bank was set up; exile capital was encouraged to return. No changes were made in the countryside except for the confiscation of the Imam's land. The defining characteristic of these reforms was that they encouraged the entry of capitalism into North Yemen, removing the obstacles for the domestic bourgeoisie and encouraging foreign capital.

The politicians around the leadership were a heterogeneous group. Sallal himself was a veteran anti-Imamist but lacked any precise power-base even in the army; he had no definite ideological orientation. Al-Beidhani, Sadat's brother-in-law, was a Nasserite intellectual, part of the civilian Yemeni Union who shared a common position, if a different origin, with the Nasserite army

116

officers. The third group consisted of some of the Free Yemenis and Shafei merchants who had allied to a limited degree with Nasserism in the late 1950s; they were ideologically independent of the Egyptians and later constituted the 'third force', also known as the 'Khamer group', who were played off by the Egyptians against Sallal. A fourth group comprised tribal leaders who supported the Republic for traditional reasons, knowing that patronizing the central government could advance their position; prominent among these were Sheikh Abdullah al-Ahmar of the Hashed, in the north, and Abdullah Tariq of the Morad tribe, near Marib in the east. Another group, numerically weak, but important politically, was the urban-based left-wing political element: the Popular Democratic Union, communists educated abroad who had supported the 'progressive role' of the Imam in the 1950s;[5] the Ba'athis, mainly Zeidis, followers of the party later in power in Syria and Iraq,[6] with Mohsen al-Aini their most prominent Yemeni leader; and the North Yemeni branch of the Nasserite Movement of Arab Nationalists (MAN), mainly Shafei and in charge of the only trades union in North Yemen, formed from workers building the US-financed road from Taiz to Sanaa.[7]

The Nasserite Intervention

The major threat facing the YAR was not, however, from the internal diversity of its support but from the external threat that consolidated in the first weeks after the coup of 26 September. Some tribes took the occasion of turmoil at the centre to break away altogether and proclaim their own local Imams. Others rallied to Prince Hassan, returned from New York via Saudi Arabia, who was believed to have reached an agreement with the US government about possible cooperation; but despite initial Republican claims it turned out that Imam al-Badr himself was still alive. After escaping from his palace he was sheltered during the first fortnight of October by some of the northern tribes; and Hassan and other claimants fell into line behind him. From October 1962 to the summer of 1968, and sporadically after that, the Imamist forces and the Republicans were locked in a civil war estimated to have killed up to 200,000 people – around 4 per cent of the North Yemeni population. Not only did this civil war preoccupy North Yemen, but it was transformed into an international clash through the intervention of imperialism and its allies on one side and Egypt and the Soviet Union on the other. Both internally and internationally the phrase 'civil war' conceals the fact that it was a war between two social systems within North and South Yemen; it was a war of intervention and repression on one side and a war to defeat these forces on the other. Yet although the YAR survived in name and the Imams never returned, the Republic that finally emerged in 1970 was a deformed relic of the 1962 republic, based on a coalition of rightist republicans and the main royalist factions minus the Imam's family. This degeneration of the Republic cannot just be ascribed to the internal weaknesses of the YAR, nor to the exhaustion of war, nor to the strength of the antirepublican forces. It was considerably assisted by the character of the Nasserite intervention.

Egypt and the communist countries immediately recognized the YAR and by 1 October, within a week of the coup, Egyptian paratroops and supplies were arriving at Hodeida to help quell tribal opposition. Regular troops followed, and by the end of the year Egypt had around 20,000 soldiers in North Yemen. The September revolution had come at a time when Egypt's foreign policy was on the defensive; the 1958 union of Egypt and Syria had fallen apart with Syria's secession in September 1961, and Saudi Arabia was now posing a right-wing threat to Nasserite nationalism. In 1965, when he was already negotiating to retreat, Nasser described the context within which the initial Egyptian intervention took place:

You know the circumstances in which the UAR decided to intervene militarily to help the people of Yemen. They followed the Shtaura conference held in August 1962 when the separatist forces in Syria aided by the reactionary, isolationist and defeated forces in the Arab world launched a violent psychological offensive against all the revolutionary forces in the Arab world. Suddenly, in this terrible atmosphere, the revolution exploded in one of the parts of the Arab world where it was least expected. The great meaning of this event is that it was not possible for any force whatever to suppress the legitimate aspiration of an Arab people to run its own life. Our attitude from the first was to give moral support to the Yemeni people and to allow it to assume its responsibilities.[8]

Nasserism expressed its policies in terms of the anti-imperialist struggle. Egypt was at that time embattled by world imperialism and threatened by Saudi Arabia; the North Yemeni revolution was a blow at these forces and in any case their intervention in North Yemen made it imperative to support the YAR against them. Nasserism did have an anti-imperialist content and, within its confines, was a positive force. But the anti-imperialism of the Egyptian militarized state was limited, bounded by the class interests of its rulers, and it ceased when these interests dictated compromise. In more material forms, Egypt's drive to unify the Arab world expressed the aspirations of its bourgeoisie and its private capitalist allies[9] to dominate the economies of the Arab world; and a foothold in North Yemen brought Egypt nearer the richest economic resource in the Arab world. Control of some or all oil would both provide the Arab nationalist movement with the surplus needed to transform the Arab world as a whole, and would give the Egyptian bourgeoisie the economic resources it required. Such an advance would have the added political effect of routing Saudi Arabia and jeopardizing the British imperialist position in South Yemen and the Gulf. Within Egypt itself the intervention was partially welcomed by the army, which had seen no active service since the 1956 attack by Britain, France and Israel; and which regarded the North Yemeni campaign as a warming up for the coming battle with Israel. It also served to boost the earnings, savings and therefore class mobility of Egyptian officers and soldiers; bonus pay for service in North Yemen ranged from an extra £2–3 per month to £20–30 per month for officers, and such extra earnings would assist soldiers, after leaving the army, to buy a shop, some land or a taxi and start up in business. Soldiers were also able to spend on consumer goods unavailable in Egypt but flooding into

North Yemen via Aden and Hodeida and which were readily available on the flourishing black market.

The Egyptian intervention spared the YAR from a probable rapid defeat by northern tribes; and the availability of Egyptian military and political support contributed to the launching in October 1963 of the struggle in South Yemen against the British. These were positive consequences of Nasserite policy. But, from the start, one aspect of the intervention limited its effectiveness and stifled the YAR. The Nasserite équipe in North Yemen dominated the YAR strategically and executively, and antagonized many YAR supporters within the government and the cities. It had a manipulative and bureaucratic way of handling Yemenis and clearly wanted to exclude them from important decisions. Moreover, while initial Egyptian support for the YAR derived from the relatively progressive anti-imperialist interests of the Egyptian ruling class, it was clear in 1964–5 that these interests would not benefit from continuing the war; it was a net political and economic drain on Egypt, and there was no prospect of overthrowing the Saudi regime. The Egyptians consequently started holding back the YAR and encouraged capitulation to the Imamist forces. After Egypt's defeat by Israel in 1967 Nasser abandoned the YAR altogether; and in return for this, a portion of the oil surplus which he may have hoped to appropriate through the YAR was now paid to Egypt directly by Saudi Arabia. The paradox of the Egyptian intervention is that it at once saved and destroyed the YAR. By treating the YAR leadership and the population as subordinates the Nasserites denied the YAR any political base; moreover they relied increasingly on republican tribes, whom they bribed with money and guns. At the end of the Egyptian intervention in 1967 these sheikhs, opportunist adherents to the Republic, formed the YAR's most powerful support. They were strong enough to make a deal with their royalist counterparts and together form the coalition that in 1970 brought 'peace' to Yemen. YAR supporters who opposed the arrangement were liquidated. Such was the result of Egypt's five-year intervention in North Yemen.

The Civil War: 1962–7

The history of the civil war, from its outbreak in September 1962 to the final ceasefire of June 1970, falls into three periods. The most intense fighting was in the time up to 1965 when both sides sought complete political and military victory. The period 1965–7 was one of military stalemate, reflected in attempted negotiation between Nasser and the Saudis and in the growth of the dissident republican 'third force'. This period ended with the Israeli defeat of Egypt in June 1967; the Egyptians subsequently departed and republican tribes crushed an attempt by the republican left to block agreement with the royalists. The war ended in 1970 with the formation of a royalist–republican cabinet and Saudi recognition of the YAR.

In the first weeks of the war the YAR consolidated its hold on the coastal areas and the royalists organized themselves in the mountains of the north. By the end of October the royalists had already gained a number of towns in the eastern hills, including Marib and Harib. The Egyptians had landed thousands of troops, and on the royalist side the Saudis and the British were sending in arms and money. In this early period the Egyptians thought they could crush the royalists in North Yemen and move on to smash the Saudi regime. In November 1962 they dropped arms inside Saudi Arabia and the Saudis claimed Nasser was planning to infiltrate Egyptian soldiers into Saudi Arabia disguised as pilgrims on their way to Mecca. But these were disorganized attempts; and when Sallal broadcast appeals for a united 'Republic of the Arabian Peninsula' the Nasserites forced him to stop using what they considered too radical a slogan. In January 1963 Egyptian planes bombed Saudi positions along the border area from which royalists were operating and in February, following a visit to Yemen by Field-Marshal Amer the commander of the Egyptian army, the first major offensive began. Five thousand troops set off on 18 February in what became known as the 'Ramadan Offensive': they swept east into the desert, then back westwards into royalist-held mountains. Marib and Harib, the royalist-held towns, were recaptured, and the Egyptians advanced some distance into the northern mountains. In reply the royalists enlisted further outside help – from Saudi Arabia, Britain, France and Israel, and especially from Saudi Arabia.[10]

Saudi Arabia provided most support, following a conference in Riyadh, the Saudi capital, between royalist leaders and King Feisal. By April 1963 the royalists had begun to win back territory: supply lines had improved and the Zeidi tribesmen, originally frightened by Egyptian planes, had now got used to this novel threat. The US was playing an ambiguous role, recognizing the YAR but sending jets to protect Saudi Arabia; through US pressure the United Nations organized a ceasefire that began on 30 April.[11] The Saudis agreed not to back the royalists; the Egyptians said they would stop attacking the royalists and the Saudis and would pull their troops out of Yemen altogether. In July a UN Yemeni Observation Mission, UNYOSM, went into operation along the Saudi–Yemeni border and in the ports and cities of the YAR. Even then some of the Egyptian leadership favoured a decorous capitulation. But by September fighting had begun again, UNYOSM was withdrawn, and the Saudis gave their support to the royalists in a better organized offensive culminating early in 1964. All the territory lost to the YAR in the Ramadan offensive was regained and some significant blows were inflicted on the Egyptians; royalists cut the roads linking Sanaa to Hodeida and to Taiz; they also captured a republican pay convoy carrying 180,000 Maria Theresa dollars to be used for bribing republican tribes; and they severely wounded the Egyptian commander-in-chief in Yemen, General Anwar al-Qadi.

Although able to recover terrain in the mountains the royalists could not dislodge the Egyptians from the cities and the plains; and in April 1964 Nasser paid his first visit to North Yemen in order to prepare a new Egyptian offensive. The aim of this campaign was not to finish off the royalists, but to inflict a defeat on them that would strengthen Nasser's bargaining position at the Second Arab Summit Conference, scheduled for September of that year. In June the Egyptians deployed 4,000 troops plus tribal forces of the Hashed federation in an attempt to dislodge the royalists from their northern strongholds; planes carried out raids on supply lines between Saudi Arabia and the Yemeni mountains. The campaign was a failure; in August heavy monsoon rains made it impossible for Egyptian armoured cars to advance; and the royalists were able to pick off their enemy's armour with newly acquired supplies of anti-tank weapons. Although Imam al-Badr was forced to flee from his headquarters, royalist supply lines remained intact. The Egyptians, thwarted of victory, now more than ever desired a compromise with the Saudis. At the September Arab summit Nasser and Feisal issued a joint appeal for a coalition government; and under this external pressure royalists and republicans met in October at Erkwit in the Sudan. The two sides agreed on a ceasefire and planned a National Congress to be attended by 169 tribal, religious and military leaders; but fighting began again at the end of the month and the congress never took place.

This time, in their second major offensive, the royalists went on to the attack, hoping to convince the Egyptians it was not worth holding on. 1965 was a disastrous year for the YAR; the royalists regained all the land they had lost in 1964 and recovered towns they had not held since the first Egyptian attack, the Ramadan offensive of early 1963. By early August 1965 the Imam's forces held about 50 per cent of North Yemeni territory.

The Egyptians were paying a large price for the war and it had become clear to them that their original objectives were inaccessible. They had failed to crush the royalists; the Saudis were secure; and with defeat and increasing losses the North Yemen war had become very unpopular in Egypt itself, where it was seen as a major cause of the economic difficulties the country faced in the mid 1960s. According to possibly unreliable western intelligence sources the Egyptians lost 15,195 men *killed* between October 1962 and June 1964 – an average of twenty-four per day and a staggeringly high rate.[12] The cost of the war in foreign exchange and diverted investment funds has not been assessed; but estimates of the daily cost from 1962–5 range from $500,000 to $1,000,000. By 1965 Egypt's foreign reserves were almost depleted and as tension with Israel rose, North Yemen,

123

for a time the front line of the Arab nationalist offensive, appeared more and more as a diversion.

Given the particular social character of the Egyptian regime, the North Yemen war was evidently no longer in the interest of the governing classes; but they failed to see that this very social character – bureaucratic and manipulative – was what weakened the YAR and made it politically and militarily less effective. From the first months the republican camp had begun to disintegrate. Three different trends had emerged. Sallal and the officers and administrators around him were the most loyally Nasserite, but opposed an abject surrender. The 'third force', comprised of former Free Yemenis, merchants and tribal leaders, wanted compromise and blamed the Egyptians for prolonging the war; they made contacts with some royalists and ceased to cooperate with the republican government. A third group criticized the Egyptians for their bureaucratic and self-defeating conduct of the war and their ill-concealed desire to reach a safe face-saving peace; this group, small at first, mainly included members of the MAN. Although the Nasserite al-Beidhani had resigned in protest at the UN ceasefire as early as 1963, the MAN cooperated with Egypt up to the Erkwit conference of October 1964. But when it was clear the Egyptians wanted to concede to the Saudis, the MAN went into opposition and were themselves subjected to increasing repression.

The 'third force' began to crystallize in 1964 and in December of that year two former Free Yemeni leaders, al-Zubayri and Noman, resigned from the YAR government; al-Zubayri set up his own reconciliationist party, the Party of God, while on the royalist side tribal leaders opposed to the unlimited power of the Hamid ad-Din started to talk about a 'constitutional Imamate', backed by a representative body of *ulema* and sheikhs. The 'third force' tried to rally both groups of dissidents, playing on anti-Egyptian feeling, invoking Islam and rallying all those who did not want the civil war to continue now that they themselves had strengthened their positions. Although at first the Egyptians ignored these dissidents, this was no longer possible when the 'third force' organized a conference at Khawlan in

March 1965 which was attended by many republican tribal leaders and which called for an Egyptian withdrawal. Al-Zubayri was soon assassinated, while on his way to Saudi Arabia; but the Egyptians had to placate the growing tribal opposition and they agreed to Noman becoming Prime Minister. He called a larger tribal conference, this time at Khamer, lasting from 30 April to 5 May. It was attended by 4,000 tribesmen and called again for an Egyptian withdrawal and negotiations with the royalists. This was a provocation to the Nasserites; Noman was sacked and went into exile, and the Egyptians decided they would have to take the initiative themselves in peace moves. In August 1965 Nasser flew to Jeddah in Saudi Arabia and met with Feisal in an attempt to reach a peace settlement. In return for a Saudi promise to stop aiding the royalists Nasser agreed to withdraw his troops gradually from North Yemen. Yemeni tribal, religious and military leaders were to meet at Haradh on 23 November to organize a plebiscite on Yemen's future.

This arrangement, which was also reputed to contain un-published agreements limiting the anti-British struggle in South Yemen, was made without consulting the YAR leadership. President Sallal at once protested and flew to Cairo; the Nasserite response was to lock him up and prevent him returning to North Yemen, a characteristic bureaucratic manoeuvre.[13] Instead of Sallal the Egyptians installed General Hassan al-Amri as the Yemeni leader; and they also urged their followers to attend the Haradh conference. The conference did take place, but it broke down because the royalists tried to insist on the return of the Hamid ad-Din family; a demand unacceptable to even the most vacillating republicans. But although this was the issue on which the conference formally broke, it reflected a deeper division, if not between Egypt and Saudi Arabia, than at least between the two North Yemeni factions, who could still not agree on the division of peacetime power. So the war went on. Egyptian relations with Saudi Arabia quickly soured, particularly as the Saudis, backed by the US and Iran, undertook an international offensive against Arab nationalism and tried to organize a counter-revolutionary alliance of states called the 'Islamic

Pact'. Inside North Yemen the Egyptians gave up their attempted reconquest of the royalist lands, and withdrew to a triangle bounded by Sanaa, Taiz and Hodeida, where they pursued a cautious policy that became known as the 'long breath'.

The towns of the north and north-west were now in royalist hands, and the Egyptians lost much tribal backing; in so far as they did attack royalist territory it was from the air.[14] Inside the YAR camp the Egyptians juggled with different factions. General Hassan al-Amri – commander of the army – emerged as an autonomous force with a base among Zeidi officers and close tribal ties; al-Amri edged closer to the 'third force' tribes, and in August 1966 the Egyptians released Sallal from arrest in Cairo. When Sallal arrived at Sanaa airport al-Amri tried to stop him getting out; but Egyptian troops intervened; and when al-Amri flew to Cairo to deliver his protest the Nasserites locked him up instead. It was a political mess; furthermore militarily the Egyptians were hemmed into their defensive triangle. They launched a wave of arrests and trials and executed several members of the Khamer groups as well as members of the anti-capitulationist left; in the absence of any policy for offence or face-saving retreat the Egyptians were determined to crush all opposition with the YAR itself.

Republican Tribalism[15]

The Egyptians destroyed any chance the YAR had of strengthening itself and developing a capable North Yemeni state at the centre. The main consequence of their intervention was that they strengthened the centrifugal forces, the tribal leaders, who came to represent the most powerful force in North Yemen. These were precisely the elements who went to make up the 'third force'; namely those who refused to wage an all-out attack on the royalists, and who, once consolidated, were enthusiastically calling on the Egyptians to depart. The standard western interpretation of the North Yemeni war is that the YAR relied on the Egyptians for its very existence and that the Egyptians were reluctant to allow North Yemenis to run their own affairs and find peace. *In fact the Republic remained weak and got weaker precisely because the Egyptians stifled it. And the forces who called on the Egyptians to leave owed their vitality to the way in which the Egyptians had run the war.* The war was concluded by the republican tribalist forces whom the Egyptians had subsidized and who then turned the country into a Saudi satellite.

Militarily the Egyptians were unable to cope with North Yemeni conditions. Many of the soldiers came from the Nile delta and had never seen or coped with mountain conditions before; given the parasitic and authoritarian character of the Egyptian army, staffwork was weak and officer–men relations were often bad. Corruption, of a kind prevalent in Egypt and expressively demonstrated in the 1967 war with Israel, also undermined the army's morale; by 1964 it was a defensive army, predictable and vulnerable. In what was no doubt an exaggeration royalists used to say that they knew they could always attack on Thursday evenings because they knew the troops would be listening nostalgically to the weekly radio broadcast of Egypt's favourite singer Umm Kalthoum.[16] The horrible massacres which befell many of the soldiers in the mountain terrain did nothing to improve army morale, and after a time Egyptian local commanders, following orders from above or out of timidity, established their own ties with local royalists: they signed truces, negotiated safe conducts, transferred supplies. They fought the war throughout as foreign invaders rather than as allies of the young Republic. This was clearest from their treatment of the North Yemeni army. In so far as they used North Yemeni forces at all they relied more on tribal forces than on the central army. It is true that in 1962 the central army was ill equipped and undermanned and that it had suffered heavy losses in the first weeks of fighting. But the Egyptians did nothing to remedy this. North Yemeni officers sent abroad for training in the Soviet Union were put into desk jobs on return and not allowed to fight. In 1964 when Sallal flew to Moscow to obtain an independent supply of military support the Egyptians got the Russians to cancel the agreement. In 1966 al-Amri flew to Cairo to see Kosygin, then in Egypt on a visit, hoping to persuade the Soviet leader to activate the 1964 agreement; but the Egyptians would not let al-Amri see Kosygin. When al-Amri ordered some armoured cars from the German Democratic Republic he was forced to cancel the agreement after the Egyptians told him they themselves would take charge of the cars when they arrived.

Politically, a similar control was enforced. Every North Yemeni government had to accept Egyptian orders; and ministries were controlled and often largely staffed by Egyptians. The opponents of Egyptian rule were dealt with in a number of ways – expulsion, defamation, detention in Cairo and sometimes execution. The Nasserites treated the problem of political organization as they had treated it in Egypt itself. They constantly invoked *al-Jamahir*, the masses, and used to mobilize cheering crowds, to whom they handed out banners, to celebrate actions by the government. But they were terrified of allowing the same *Jamahir* to express their own views, and were especially afraid of any real mass organization. The various post-1952 Egyptian mass organizations – the Liberation Rally, the National Union and then the Arab Socialist Union – were all created from above and allowed no autonomy to the base; the same applied in North Yemen. It was only in 1965 – three years after the Imam was ousted – that the first political organization, the Popular Revolutionary Organization, was set up. It held its only congress in January 1967. By contrast to this manipulative effort, the Egyptians did on one occasion try to mobilize mass support by importing 100 Shafei *ulema* from Egypt to deliver pro-Egyptian sermons in the mosques of Sanaa and Taiz. The tribal leaders were the one Yemeni force that did grow in strength. Once the Imam had disappeared the tribal sheikhs were able to exert their autonomy; added to this were the bribes and arms they received in the civil war, together with the fact that although these sheikhs were pre-capitalist elements they were able to benefit from the introduction of capitalism into North Yemen by trade and the black market. When the Saudi and Egyptian subsidies dried up they were partly replaced by foreign aid. A major instance was the case of Sheikh Naji bin Ali al-Gadr, who became paramount chief of the Bakil confederation during the civil war. In 1962 he was sheikh of the al-Aroush, one of the six tribes of the Khawlan area, and had only 120 armed men at his disposal. When the revolution broke out he declared his support for the royalists and received arms and money from the Sharif of Beihan, a British client in South Yemen through whom the British and the Saudis funnelled supplies. But in February 1963 al-Gadr had a secret meeting with Egyptian Field-Marshal Amer; the latter gave him 2,000 rifles, 800,000 Maria Theresa dollars and an ample supply of ammunition in return for which he was to bring the tribes of the Khawlan into the republican camp. He then handed over part of the arms and money to the royalists and kept the rest for himself. Six months later he went to Riyadh, in Saudi Arabia, and asked King Feisal for more arms, since his tribe occupied a strategic position on the routes linking the royalist bases in Najran to Sanaa. With more arms and money he was able to increase his influence among the tribes until in 1964 he was elected paramount chief of the Bakil federation, with 12,000 men under his command. He told *Le Monde* correspondent Eric Rouleau in 1967:

'At the moment I receive subsidies from King Feisal, from Sharif Hussein of Beihan, and from our sovereign (may God grant him a long life!), the Imam al-Badr. The latter has also authorized me to accept money from any foreign power willing to support our cause.'[17] In 1967 he was rich enough to send his nephew to London for medical treatment and to maintain his 12,000-strong private army – twice the size of the North Yemeni regular army. He never broke his contacts with either the republicans or the royalists, and although he leaned towards the latter he preserved his commercial interests in the area administered by the YAR.

The leader of the other main confederation, the Hashed, was Sheikh Abdullah al-Ahmar; he leant towards the YAR but also played at being neutral, and emerged in time as the most powerful republican sheikh of all. His armed men played a supporting role in the 1963 Ramadan offensive and in the summer campaign of 1964, and for a time he served as Minister of the Interior and Tribal Affairs in the republican government. In 1964 sections of his federation defected to the royalists after his release of hostages from their leading families; and in 1965 after the fall of the Noman government he went into temporary exile, adopting a position of hostility to the Egyptians and Sallal. This profitable oscillation was described by a correspondent of *The Times* who visited a royalist camp in Saudi Arabia and found the dynamics of tribal loyalty in full swing: 'Stories circulate of tribesmen pledging themselves to the royalists, receiving rifles and selling them to the republicans; and soldiers have been heard joking that they are "royalist" by day and "republican" by night.'[18]

In the political and military stalemate from 1965 to 1967, these enriched and revitalized sheikhs gathered influence and waited for the Egyptians to go. In June 1967 Israel inflicted a major defeat on Egypt; and the loss of Suez Canal revenues made Egypt dependent on subsidies from Saudi Arabia and Kuwait totalling £110 million a year. In return Nasser agreed, at the August 1967 Khartoum conference of Arab leaders, to pull all his troops out of North Yemen by the beginning of December. Sallal opposed the deal and refused to cooperate with a three-man commission on North Yemen set up by the Khartoum conference. When the commission arrived in North Yemen on 3 October angry crowds attacked it and over thirty Egyptians were killed. But Sallal had no independent base, and not only the Egyptians but also al-Amri and the 'third force' were conspiring against him and were all allowed by Nasser to return to Yemen from exile or detention abroad. The end came in November; Sallal left Yemen to attend the Fiftieth Anniversary Celebration of the Russian Revolution in Moscow, was deposed in his absence on 5 November and went into exile in Iraq.

The Siege of Sanaa and the Emergence of the Left

The government that replaced Sallal included the 'third force' leaders, Noman and al-Iryani, with al-Amri in a key position as head of the army. The republican tribalists had triumphed; Sallal and the Egyptians had left. But despite this they still had to face one final royalist onslaught as a group of militant royalists, headed by the Imam's cousin Mohammad bin Hussein, decided that this was the time for one last attempt to sweep the board. The Egyptians had gone and the YAR appeared in disarray after the coup of 5 November; there was less reason to compromise than ever before, and even if the offensive failed it would strengthen the royalist position in future negotiations. Mohammad bin Hussein rallied his forces to capture Sanaa, arousing memories of the 1948 sacking of the city by Zeidi tribes under Imam Ahmad. He said that he had 5,000 trained troops in the hills outside Sanaa and another 50,000 tribesmen at his disposal near by. On 1 December he closed all the roads out of Sanaa and encircled the city with its 3,000 armed defenders inside. However, he lost the initiative within a few weeks. As it was Ramadan the royalists were not too active in the first weeks of the siege and this gave the YAR time to bring in support; al-Amri flew in to head the defenders, and the Soviet Union carried out a massive airlift of supplies from Russia via Egypt. In January 600 volunteers arrived from the NLF in South Yemen, bringing additional arms and ammunition, while NLF and YAR forces in the border area of Beihan collaborated in a joint anti-royalist campaign.

Al-Amri took command in Sanaa and handed out weapons to the population, which formed into a Popular Resistance Force, PRF. Several thousand civilians were armed in this way, and they controlled defence within the town while the 3,000-strong regular army occupied surrounding areas, particularly the strategic point of Jabal Nuqum overlooking the town. In January the royalists made in vain three attempts to break in; and as their initial optimism died down many of the royalist tribesmen drifted away. The Saudis, who had covertly supported the siege in violation of their Khartoum agreement with Nasser, also eased their support. On 8 February 1968 the siege was lifted when a relief column, actively supported by Chinese engineers who repaired the bridges on the road, broke through from Hodeida.

No sooner had the siege of Sanaa ended than the republicans split into two opposed camps: the republican tribalists led by al-Amri and the sheikhs, and the anti-capitulationist left who had emerged in the siege to fill the political vacuum left by the Egyptian departure. This new group of militants was based on the old MAN in North Yemen, allied to sections of the other parties. The communists, the PDU, had worked with Sallal and the Egyptians and had not played a significant role; the Ba'ath had also played a small part and by comparison with its other anti-Nasserite sections elsewhere in the Arab world had moved to the right – its leader al-Aini became Prime Minister in the government that took over on 5 November. The MAN, meanwhile, had a more positive history. After the September 1962 revolution they had opened a cultural club[19] in Taiz and had expanded the trades unions from their original base among the road workers. In 1963 they founded the General Union of Taiz Workers; and this became the General Union of Yemeni Workers, which was recognized in 1965 by the Arab Confederation of Trades Unions. Within the YAR-controlled area there was a certain amount of economic development – factories, port expansion – and the MAN built its organization among the thousands of newly created proletarians who worked in these projects; in the urban areas they also had support from shopkeepers and intellectuals. The North Yemen MAN broke with the Egyptians after the Erkwit conference of 1964; and as a result MAN members began to be dismissed from the administration and lost their control of the YAR radio station. Their club in Taiz was closed down; and on 26 September 1966 three of their trade union members were killed by Egyptian soldiers who attacked an MAN march commemorating the fourth anniversary of the overthrow of the Imam. In October 1967 it was the MAN who organized the anti-Nasserite demonstrations that greeted the 'peace' commission sent to Yemen by the Khartoum conference.

This radicalization of the North Yemen MAN was related to developments elsewhere in the organization, especially in the Gulf and among Palestinians; but North Yemen anticipated the break with Nasserism among MAN supporters in general; in 1964, when the North Yemeni MAN started to oppose Egyptian policies in Yemen, the MAN centre in Beirut, through its weekly *al-Horria*, was still talking of the 'progressive role' of the

Nasserite intervention. Working underground, the MAN won support because it was a defender of the YAR and criticized Egypt's smothering of local forces; and in the siege of Sanaa it was able to man the PRF because it stepped into a breach left by Egyptian blockage of the development of a regular Yemeni army. The PRF spread during the Sanaa siege to Taiz, Hodeida and smaller towns and comprised a hastily created people's militia organized by arming civilians on a clear political issue: defending the Republic. Most leading government officials and top army officers had left Sanaa itself; and the PRF recruited from unionized factory workers, and from shopkeepers and intellectuals; but the MAN also had a substantial following among junior military cadets at the Sanaa military academy and among the key sections of the regular army, the paratroops and the commandos, defending the surrounding hills. It won this support by its self-reliant and militant defence of the Republic.[20]

By the end of the siege, in February, the MAN led a considerable political movement opposed to compromise with the royalists. The demands of the PRF and of the MAN army officers included the following: rejection of the Khartoum conference resolutions and of attempts to compromise with the royalists; the building of a strong central army to form the military basis of the republic; the extension and strengthening of the people's militia, the PRF; and equality of Shafei and Zeidi in the YAR government. The MAN was simultaneously building an organization in some areas of the countryside, where they won support for their opposition to the republican tribalists. Peasant leagues (*Lejan Fellahia*) were set up in the countryside of the Shafei south, around Taiz, Ibb and Radah. These leagues were an important development; the YAR had passed no land reform, except for confiscating the Imam's land, since to do more would have antagonized the sheikhs and other landowners on whom the Egyptians were relying. The organization of the peasantry was therefore a direct threat to the republican tribalists. The leagues were only organized in a minority of areas and were still in an early stage of development. They demanded reforms which, though elementary, nevertheless struck at the basis of republican tribalist power: the extortionary powers of lawyers should be ended by getting the state to settle all disputes between peasants free of charge; in rural areas, schools should be built; roads, hospitals and drinking water systems should be built; there should be a development of a patriotic and revolutionary consciousness; cooperatives should be established; there should be a General Yemeni Union of Small and Landless Peasants; and the political, economic and administrative power of the sheikhs and other big landowners should be stopped.[21]

In the Riyashi and Hubaishia areas peasant leagues arrested landlords and declared that the power of the sheikhs had ended; in the Abus area sheikhs were forced to give up their positions and had to sign documents of resignation. These measures hit at the two linked powers of the rural oppressors – land ownership and tax collection.

Thermidor

It was clear to al-Amri and the sheikhs that these developments had to be stopped, both to reassure the royalists, with whom they were now able to reach an agreement, and to preserve their own military and social position. Although al-Amri had been instrumental in creating the P R F during the Sanaa siege he soon decided to do away with it now that there was no longer a major royalist threat. After the siege was lifted in February 1968, Sanaa was commanded by Abdul Raqib Wahhab, a leader of commandos, and advocate of a strong central army, for which he recruited with the object of strengthening the state and replacing the private armies of the larger sheikhs. Other officers did likewise elsewhere. The first clash soon transpired; a Soviet ship was expected at Hodeida on 22 March with arms including fifty tanks; and al-Amri had announced that these weapons would be distributed to the private armies of the sheikhs.

The P R F and Abdul Raqib Wahhab opposed al-Amri; they wanted the shipment to go to the regular army. The people's militia and the left-wing army sealed off Hodeida three days before the ship was due; but al-Amri, who was in Cairo on his way to

Peking, hurried back and mobilized the tribes to counter-attack. His main support came from Sheikh Sinan Abu Luhun, leader of the Nehm tribe, a tribal republican supporter and the father-in-law of Ba'athi leader Mohsen al-Aini. Al-Amri had the left outnumbered and after massing his forces outside Hodeida he marched in. The PRF based on the port workers' union resisted and their headquarters was destroyed; al-Amri won the day and the PRF in Hodeida was crushed. A supporting move in Sanaa by Abdul Raqib Wahhab was stopped when tribes under Sheikh Abdullah al-Ahmar invaded. In South Yemen there was a parallel development when the right-wing NLF leader Qahtan ash-Shaabi struck against the leaders of the NLF left on 20 March – although the degree of coordination between the two moves is unclear.

Whatever the degree of cooperation the 'March events' marked a setback for the left in both North and South Yemen and the rightist leadership in the North were encouraged by this coincidence to push ahead with their counter-revolution. The left tried to re-form politically and in June the ex-MAN cadres met to produce a new organization. They decided to break all ties with the MAN centre in Beirut, to constitute themselves as the Revolutionary Democratic Party (*al-Hizb al-Thawri al-Dimoqrati*) and to launch a political and military attack on the republican tribalists. In common with the other 'left' sections of the MAN they proclaimed their ideology not as nationalism but 'Marxism–Leninism'. They declared support for the left NLF in South Yemen, who were fighting Qahtan ash-Shaabi, and called for a united struggle. A central committee of eleven members was elected. The party was, however, on the defensive, particularly as its predominantly urban base limited its strength in the countryside and this base had in any case been hard hit by al-Amri and his sheikh allies. Although it had mass support, it probably had only a few hundred cadres and, though the alliance with the militant young officers in the army was instinctively strong, there was no tight organizational coordination.

Al-Amri and the sheikhs met in July at Abs to decide on their next moves. All left officers were to be purged from the army;

135

the PRF was to be liquidated; 'subversive ideas' (*al-Afkar al-Mokharreba*) – left-wing books and magazines – were to be banned. The conference called for a 'popular army', a euphemism for an army of tribal forces commanded by their separate sheikhs. After the conference al-Amri sacked Salam al-Razihi, the chief of staff, and replaced him by one of his followers, Abdul Latif Deifallah. He then dismissed the chief of the artillery and one of the heroes of the Sanaa defence, Ali Mothanna. The commanders of the commandos (Abdul Raqib Wahhab), of the infantry (Major Farhan) and of the paratroops (Major Naji) then demanded Mothanna's reinstatement; the left controlled some sections of the army and was prepared to fight. Al-Amri deployed the standard North Yemeni defence: he brought in the tribes to surround Sanaa; heavy fighting broke out on 23 August and lasted for three days. Over 300 people were killed, and although many of the victims were al-Amri's tribesmen shot while storming buildings controlled by junior officers, victory was in the hands of the right. The PRF and the peasant leagues were dissolved; and while Abdul Raqib Wahhab and twenty-one other officers were exiled to Algeria, hundreds of trades unionists and other militants fled to Aden.[22]

Four months later, in December 1968, Abdul Raqib Wahhab returned to Yemen via Aden and started to call for the release of officers and trades unionists imprisoned during the August battle in Sanaa. Al-Amri responded by sending a platoon of men who shelled Abdul Raqib Wahhab's house, killing him in the process; it was then announced that Abdul Raqib Wahhab had been plotting to assassinate President al-Iryani. The army was purged again and resistance ceased for a time. The unions and the Revolutionary Democratic Party were banned; and although some of the non-military militants had opposed the fierce resistance policies of the young officers and had considered the left's position too weak, they were obviously unable to avoid al-Amri's onslaught when it came. The only protests that were heard on the death of Abdul Raqib Wahhab were from North Yemenis abroad. In Cairo 300 North Yemeni students occupied the YAR embassy, denouncing 'the conspiracy between certain leading circles in Sanaa and the royalists aimed at making Yemen an Islamic state, which would preserve the name of the Republic, but abandon the principles of the revolution'. They were correct in their description of what al-Amri and the sheikhs were doing.

The defeat of the left in 1968, particularly of the militia and the junior officers, repeated a pattern often seen in other revolutions: in the first phases of the struggle the masses are armed and defend themselves, waging their own battles. But a new state, once consolidated, seeks to disarm the people, take initiative from them and incorporate guerrillas and irregulars into the new regular army. This was the core of Bonapartism in its original form in France; it was equally clearly so in Egypt where the army was the key to the regime's parasitic operation (jobs, privilege) and mystification of the people and where nothing angered the regime more than the call for a popular militia. Further cases in point are the rapid attempts by Mujibur Rahman in Bangladesh to disarm the Bengali guerrillas in 1972 and the refusal of the 'left nationalist' Torres regime in Bolivia to arm the masses there in 1971. In all cases the question is posed whether a new popular military apparatus is to be formed or whether the old state apparatus or a conservative replica of it is to survive. In the case of North Yemen, where the republican right opposed even a regular army of any size, the clash was bound to come.[23] Once the left had been crushed, at the start of 1969, al-Amri and the sheikhs were secure within the YAR and began to negotiate a final rapprochement with the royalists. More and more tribes were defecting to the YAR and the Saudis agreed to stop backing the Imam provided the YAR held down the left and swung its foreign policy to the right. The Saudis wanted North Yemen to be an 'Islamic state', a phrase that summed up their positions of domestic repression and mystification and loyalty to the dictates of the Saudi state itself. To meet these demands al-Amri set up a National Assembly of religious and tribal leaders, of whom thirty were 'elected' and fifteen nominated, with twelve seats for delegates from the South, which were never occupied. All parties were banned. 'A political party too often works for the interests of the party and not for the country as a whole,' al-Amri

137

said[24] – unlike tribes, no doubt. In foreign policy North Yemen swung enthusiastically to the right and had the distinction of being the first country in the world to break off diplomatic relations with the German Democratic Republic and then establish them with the German Federal Republic. As relations with Saudi Arabia improved, relations with South Yemen deteriorated; and when the left-wing NLF came to power in June 1969 and ousted Qahtan ash-Shaabi the two Yemens were on collision course.

The war ended in 1970. There appeared to be difficulties at the beginning of the year when last-ditch royalists attacked the historic Zeidi town of Sada in the far north; but reconciliation was reached at a twenty-two-nation Islamic Conference held in Jeddah during March. Al-Aini headed the delegation from North Yemen and on 28 March he reached an agreement with Saudi King Feisal; there would be an end to polemics, a final ceasefire and no more Saudi subsidies to the royalists. In May the National Assembly was expanded from forty-five to sixty-three seats to include eighteen royalists; and royalist ministers were brought into a new coalition government. Only the Hamid ad-Din family were banned from returning. In July diplomatic relations were established between the YAR and Saudi Arabia and regular commercial flights began between the two countries. Al-Amri and the sheikhs were now secure and Saudi Arabia was pleased to patronize the tamed Republic. The London *Economist* hailed the end of the civil war as 'the best news to come out of the Arab world for many a month'.[25] But the last word must be with the port workers of Hodeida: in May when they heard of the formation of the coalition government they went on strike to protest and to denounce the agreement with Saudi Arabia. They were only halted when al-Amri's forces had killed six of them during a demonstration.[26] They knew that the Republic had survived only in name.

Notes

1. This account of the coup itself is based on Wenner and al-Attar, op. cit., and from Dana Adams Schmidt, *Yemen: The Unknown War*, London, 1968, by the *New York Times* correspondent who covered the war from both camps. An excellent account of the coup and the first weeks of the YAR is Eric Rouleau, 'Le Yémen violé par le siècle', a series published in *Le Monde*, December 1962.

2. Al-Moghny was killed fighting the royalists a few weeks later. Deifallah was a key agent of Hassan al-Amri in the 1968 counter-revolution, and was Minister of Communications in the 1971 al-Aini cabinet, the first stable cabinet after the peace agreements.

3. A story told about this period, and also told about Iraq after its July 1958 proclamation of the Republic, is that tribesmen came to town hoping to see the beautiful young woman called 'Jumhouria' who had suddenly appeared – *Jumhouria* (a feminine noun) being the Arabic for republic. Although this is a story that is told by urban intellectuals and may reflect their anti-tribal bias rather than historical fact, it illustrates the confusion of the time. Foreign observers also found it hard to make out what was going on. 'The oddest feature of the situation is Australian recognition of the revolutionary government. There is speculation whether this foreshadows Australians chewing qat or Yemenis playing cricket', wrote Kim Philby in the *Observer*, 22 October 1962. Philby, son of the English explorer of Saudi Arabia St John Philby, was for thirty years a determined and successful infiltrator of the British intelligence system, during which time he carried out important tasks for the USSR. He was *Observer* correspondent in the Middle East until 1963. His father's life and times are retailed in *Philby of Arabia*, by Elisabeth Monroe, London, 1973. While the elder Philby was an original and idiosyncratic explorer of the peninsula, his voluminous writings add little to our understanding of it.

4. The experience of the Russian and Chinese revolutions has shown that it is not necessary for societies to pass through the different historical stages of socio-economic development before starting to build socialism. A revolutionary movement, led by the most advanced sections of the population, can carry out the tasks of the uncompleted pre-socialist stages. In both Russia and China, though to different extents, this involved liquidating the remnants of pre-capitalism in the countryside and carrying out primitive accumulation, i.e. industrialization. In both countries, too, the central state had to unify a country containing many regional and ethnic differences. Yemen was a society far more backward than either Russia or China, and in addition to the tasks carried out by the revolutions in Russia and China the Yemeni revolution would have had to combat the institutions of tribalism, sedentarizing the few nomads, destroying the powers of the sheikhs, combating particularist ideology. This would have taken time but given

correct leadership it could have been carried through. The example of Albania, where tribal divisions were extremely strong and where socialism has had a short but intense history, is relevant in this respect.

5. The PDU in Aden adopted a similar position; at this time the communists supported the idea of Yemeni unity, and hence had a unified party for North and South.

6. On the history of the Ba'ath party see Kamel Abu Jaber, *The Arab Ba'ath Socialist Party*, Syracuse, 1966. The main components of Ba'ath ideology were anti-imperialism, anti-communism and a belief in Arab unity. Its confused mélange of political themes has found its most successful supporters among the military of Syria and Iraq. The Ba'ath were in power from 1963 in Syria; and in Iraq after a brief spate in 1963 they regained power in 1968. Their ferocious anti-communism and distrust of the masses makes them analogous to Nasserism as a form of petty-bourgeois nationalism, although their relations with Nasserism have tended to be bad. Both forces exhibited the same demagogic trends and the same inability to confront the tasks facing the Arab peoples.

7. For the MAN see p. 40.

8. Speech of 25 November 1965.

9. Despite the nationalizations of 1957–63 private business remained strong in Egypt, and after the June War of 1967 there was a progressive trend to denationalization. Restrictions on Egyptian capitalists were often not applied to their activities abroad. For example the construction firm Othman Ahmad Othaan, founded in 1950, were taken under state control, but the Othman family were allowed to retain 50 per cent of the share capital; they were responsible for the engineering work on the Aswan Dam, and at the height of operations were employing 36,000 men. In 1964 their *foreign operations* were denationalized, and under a separate title, 'Arab Contractors', they were active in the Gulf.

10. See p. 152.

11. There is an exposition of US policy in John Badeau, *The American Approach to the Arab World*, New York, 1968, Chapter 7, 'Yemen – A Case Study'. Badeau was US Ambassador to Cairo at the time. Arthur Schlesinger gives the following account:

'Kennedy, fearful that the civil war in Yemen would lead to a larger war between Egypt and Saudi Arabia – a conflict which might involve the United States because of our interests in Saudi oil – decided to accept the revolutionary regime in the hope that it could stabilize the situation in Yemen and begin the job of modernizing that fifteenth-century country ... the Yemen affair dominated American relations with Egypt in 1963 and interrupted Kennedy's effort to turn Egyptian energies inward.'*

*A. Schlesinger, *A Thousand Days*, London, 1965, p. 452.

12. Schmidt, op. cit., p. 234. Schmidt states that these are the official Egyptian figures. By official estimations, more than 11,000 Egyptians were killed in the Israeli attack of June 1967. These figures illustrate the enormous

140

cost paid by the Egyptian workers and peasants for the errors of their leadership.

13. The Nasserite regime consistently used its intelligence services, the *mokhabarat*, for internal and pan-Arab political activity. The devious factional style of politics this gave rise to, and the cat-and-mouse game played with political opponents, were marks of the regime; it affected the treatment of communist opponents inside Egypt, as well as the treatment of Palestinians, Yemenis and other militants who had dealings with Cairo.

14. Egypt was constantly accused by the imperialist press at this time of using poison gas in North Yemen; some instances of this were authenticated, and the use of such methods did nothing to win support for the YAR among the masses. However the outcry in the western press was of a bogus kind, since these same papers were silent about the horrendous massacres being committed at that time (1965–7) in Vietnam by the United States. The campaign waged by the *Daily Telegraph* and its penumbra of Conservative MPs in Britain was noteworthy in this respect.

15. The term used by the North Yemeni left wing is 'republican feudalism'. I have not used this term here since its use of 'feudalism' is the political one common on the left to describe any pre-capitalist mode of production which is based on some kind of agrarian production. Feudalism is also a specific type of pre-capitalist mode – one of many – and it is in this restricted sense that the word is used in this book.

16. Many of the stories told about Egyptians in Yemen (after 1962), Syria (after 1958) or in Libya (since 1969) reflect the hostility felt by the people there for the bureaucratic methods of Egyptian advisers and politicians. This anti-Egyptian feeling often takes a somewhat racist form which is common in the Arab world.

17. This account is based on Schmidt, op. cit., pp. 170–71, and Eric Rouleau, 'L'or du cheikh Ghader', *Le Monde*, 12 May 1967. The sheikh met his end in 1972 leading tribesmen in an attack against the frontiers of the People's Democratic Republic of Yemen.

18. *The Times*, 16 February 1966. This practice of switching sides was even reflected in the emergence of two Arabic words for 'to go republican' and 'to go royalist' – *tajamhara* and *tamallaka*.

19. In the Middle East, as in nineteenth-century Europe, cultural clubs often form the context for political activities; this is both because overt political organizations are banned and because in a nationalist movement culture and politics are linked in a direct way.

20. An interesting analysis of the social formation of the resistance movement was given by the commander of the royalist siege of Sanaa: 'These men of the special republican brigades were poor men, recently returned from abroad. For years they had worked as labourers in Djibouti, in Kuwait or elsewhere. They had lost their tribal roots, they no longer respected their relations, and had no family or clan to take refuge with if things went badly for them. They had nothing to lose and knew they were

in a losing situation. So they fought like lions.' Claude Deffarge and Gordian Troeller, *Yémen 62–69*, Paris, 1969, p. 263.

21. Sultan Omar, op. cit., pp. 193–4.

22. This account of the 1968 events is taken mainly from conversations with participants. The *Neue Zürcher Zeitung*, 13 October 1968, published a long account from its Beirut correspondent Arnold Hottinger based on material in the Lebanese daily *al-Nahar*. *Al-Horria*, 31 March 1969, 4 and 11 August 1969, provides the left's analysis of the events.

23. Al-Amri's conduct in 1968 is in many respects analogous to that of Chiang Kai-shek, who massacred the communists in Shanghai and Canton in 1927.

24. *Keesing's Contemporary Archives*, p. 23680A.

25. *Economist*, 23 May 1970.

26. *Le Monde*, 19 May 1970.

Chapter Five
The Counter-Revolutionary State

The Peacetime Regime: Collusion and Repression

The Saudi–Yemeni agreements of March and July 1970 signalled
the end of armed conflict between the two rival sections of the
North Yemeni ruling class, and laid the basis for the future political
development of Yemeni society. The royalists had failed to
capture the Republic from without; the siege of Sanaa had marked
their last attempt. On the other hand, the republican right had
no desire to continue fighting the royalists and had purged those
who opposed a capitulationist peace. Both sides had now im-
plemented the policies they wanted and were prepared to cooperate and compete within new institutional limits. In May
1970 six royalist ministers had been included in the YAR
cabinet and in September a draft constitution was announced for
'discussion' in the country. This 'discussion' resulted in further
right-wing alterations to the draft, and the proclamation of a
radical new constitution in Aden in November only encouraged
the counter-revolutionaries in the North to make their own as
different as possible. The YAR constitution was unveiled on
28 December 1970 and manifestly expressed the distribution of
political power. Elections were to be held within three months
to choose 159 members of a Consultative Council (*Majles
ash-Shura*); the President would nominate a further twenty
members, bringing the total to 179. These elections were to be
'indirect', with each village choosing nominees who would then
'elect' the representatives in the Council. This method of
'election' was clearly little more than a means of ensuring that
the sheikhs and rich farmers in each area would send their men to
Sanaa. The nomination by the President of twenty extra members
was justified on the grounds that this would enable the President
to put into the Council those urban-based educated intellectuals

143

who might not be included were they to depend on a village vote. The Consultative Council was to be the supreme legislative body and would replace the sixty-eight-member provisional National Assembly set up under al-Amri in 1969. The council would then elect a five-man Republican Council which would itself nominate the Prime Minister. All motions in the Consultative Council would require at least thirty of the 179 votes in order to be discussed at all, and would require a two-thirds majority in order to be passed. There could be no clearer indication of the regime's determination to keep the centre as weak as possible, making all central decisions dependent on a tribal compromise and leaving power in the villages for lack of a centre capable of acting. Equally clear was the constitution's ban on political parties. Al-Aini stated that political parties 'might reopen differences in our country. We have tribes and we do not have political maturity. Our people are not ready to practise party politics.'[1] Al-Iryani, on the other hand, was more forthright in giving his reasons for the ban on parties: 'People import political ideas from outside the country,'[2] he said. In effect the ban was a way of preventing development of any non-tribal and non-confessional organization; the sheikhs and religious leaders had their own traditional forms of organization and did not need parties to mobilize support. Far from being afraid to reopen past differences they were intent on preserving them as the basis of their strength.

The 'elections' were held from 27 February to 18 March 1971 and the old National Assembly and Presidential Council were dissolved in April. Sheikh Abdullah al-Ahmar became leader of the Consultative Council and al-Iryani remained as YAR President. It was the same regime as before, and it did not take long for familiar contradictions to reappear. Peace had brought extra power at the centre to the sheikhs but had taken away the basis of their livelihood – the subsidies paid by Saudi Arabia and Egypt to keep their loyalty during the war. They had only one place to turn to in order to get their money and turn they did – to the central budget; their only other means of obtaining the money was to foster a war with the People's Republic in Aden and receive Saudi subsidies for their efforts in this direction.

The first cabinet under the new constitution was formed on 3 May 1971, with Ahmad Noman as Prime Minister, in what was believed to be a compromise between al-Amri, who remained head of the army, and al-Aini, who was sent off as ambassador to Paris. Three and a half months later, on 20 July, Noman resigned; in a radio broadcast and a resignation letter he blamed his decision on the impossibility of running a government while tribal leaders claimed so much of the budget. He pointed out that the YAR was £75 million in debt and that the current budget deficit was £6 million out of a total expenditure of £13 million. Noman allegedly intended cutting subsidies to the tribes and proposed also cutting the regular army; but he was unable to handle the tribes and had to desist.[3] A month of haggling followed and on 26 August al-Amri became Prime Minister once again.

He was initially popular with the tribes and tried to make himself more so by yet another purge, this time of a group of Soviet-trained officers who were arrested while coming out of the Russian embassy in Sanaa; and to win extra Saudi backing he included in his cabinet as Foreign Minister Abdullah al-Asnaj, former leader in the South of the FLOSY party and a determined enemy of the ruling NLF. Although seats for 'Southern' delegates had been kept empty in the 1969–71 National Assembly, and there was considerable rhetoric about 'Yemeni unity', this was the first time representatives of the Southern opposition had been included in the cabinet of the YAR; and it reflected a further worsening of relations between the two states. With all these factors in his favour al-Amri appeared to be in a position to consolidate power as he wanted. Yet as it turned out he lasted barely a week. By 2 September he had flown to protracted exile in Beirut.[4] It appears that he tried to act, as Noman had, to control the tribes – and was intending to dissolve the Consultative Council elected five months before. With his departure it was time to summon al-Aini back from Paris; and on 18 September 1970 he formed his fourth cabinet, and the twenty-first since the September 1962 revolution. His tenure of office was more successful than Noman's and al-Amri; and he was able to balance the rival factions until late 1972.

The Administration and the Economy

The society over which al-Aini presided was markedly different
from the Imamic Yemen that existed before September 1962.
Although pre-capitalist forces predominated, some changes had
occurred; for although radical transformation had been excluded,
a new ruling class existed which was different from the old. It was
solidly linked through Saudi Arabia, and more directly, to
imperialism both in the administration and in the economy.
Before 1962 the Imam and the Sada had dominated the administration; they had now been eliminated from power, and in
the first weeks of the Republic many of the Sada had been
executed. The new members of the administration were Shafei
urban intellectuals or nominees of the tribal leaders. At the same
time its function had changed. Formerly it was a relatively com-
pact adjunct to the Imam's autocracy; now it had become a
sprawling parasitic institution, absorbing, together with tribal
subsidies, much of the budget, and living off the country's small
economic surplus and the available foreign aid. One estimate says
that in 1968-9 there were 13,500 officials – excluding bank
officials and members of the armed forces. An instance of what
happened to funds intended for civil service projects was that
of the moneys allocated for land reclamation between 1963 and
1966. Enough money was made available to recover 750,000
acres; but only 20,000 were in fact reclaimed.[5]

The economy had undergone a parallel transformation.
North Yemen had been opened up to western capital and the
bases of an infrastructure had been laid; there were new buildings
in the towns, the port of Hodeida had been expanded and there
were new roads and a telephone system. In 1972 it was estimated
that two million North Yemenis were employed in agriculture;
400,000 were in commerce; 42,000 were in services and 8,000
were in industry;[6] this was not a reversal of the pre-1962 picture
but it did reflect a change, and one likely to continue. Under
the Republic, agrarian production had to some extent changed.
In 1963 YAR had reduced the *zakat* tax, making the peasant
less at the mercy of the tax collector and the sheikh. Despite the

meagre results of land reclamation, some model farms and cooperatives had been set up, although these remained under the control of local sheikhs. Some merchant capital moved into cotton production; but the one big company set up jointly by private capital and the Y A R, the Makha company, was a failure and had to be bought out by the state in 1967. What was most important was that apart from confiscation of the Imam's lands in 1962 there had been no land reform and the total potential of Yemeni agriculture had not been developed; according to one estimate only 40 per cent of the cultivable 500,000 hectares was being farmed in 1972, and of this only 4 per cent was under irrigation. Such was the damage wrought by the war and three years of drought (1967–9) that in 1970 many died in a famine before minimal food supplies were organized.

The effects of this opening up to the world were most felt in the towns. At the end of the war there were estimated to be 120,000 people in Sanaa, 90,000 in Hodeida and 80,000 in Taiz. In all there were now sixty-four industrial enterprises in the country, of which twenty-one were state owned. These included eighteen producing building materials, thirteen producing electricity, nine producing food and seven classified as 'light industry'. Only two employed more than fifty people and one of these was the Chinese-built textile plant in Sanaa.[7] While these enterprises were built mainly with foreign capital, from the west and east, North Yemeni capital continued to concentrate on commerce, especially as a growing percentage of the Y A R's trade had been diverted from Aden to Hodeida. This was due partly to the deterioration of relations with the South, and partly to the flight to the Y A R of Adeni merchant firms nationalized in November 1969; it was also made possible by a Russian-backed expansion of the port facilities at Hodeida, which was able to handle 305,000 tons by 1970 compared to 79,000 tons in 1967.

The merchants who controlled and expanded North Yemeni trade were mainly Shafei who had been in exile or suppressed under the Imam; and their central concern was to establish themselves as a comprador bourgeoisie, having, that is, a mono-poly of imported western goods yielding a significant profit.

In 1969 they pressed for and won the opening of diplomatic relations with West German y. A black market grew, as did the trade deficit and the Yemeni rial sunk from 6·60 South Yemeni shillings in 1964 to 1·20 shillings in 1970. Foreign trade was catastrophic; in 1967 the trade deficit was 75 per cent, but in 1970–71 it rose to over 90 per cent: exports totalled 13·5 million rials, and imports totalled 174·5 million rials, giving a deficit of 161 million rials. This crisis could not be attributed to the strains of war, but to the heady expansion of peace; a fact confirmed by the composition of the import bill, 78·5 million rials of which went on importing foodstuffs, and another 11 million rials on importing cigarettes – all of wh ich Yemen could have produced itself. Foreign trade was as before the September 1962 revolution; the country was exporting primary products in order to import *more* primary products.[8]

Table 7
North Yemeni Exports July 1970–June 1971

Commodity	Value in rials
Coffee	5,742,059
Qat	3,530,327
Rock salt	2,120,980
Hides and skins	1,170,013
Cement	343,200
Potatoes	281,099
Small freshwater fish	136,489
Grapes	42,095
Dates	37,659
Tobacco	20,200
Ghee	19,687
Others	54,165
Total	13,497,973

These budgetary and foreign trade deficits made the YAR dependent on aid from the governments and financial institutions of the capitalist west. A welcome inflow of capital also came,

Table 8 North Yemeni Imports July 1970–June 1971

	Rials
Foodstuffs	78,700,473
Refreshments	17,607,433
Raw materials	9,080,499
Chemicals	7,130,887
Manufactured foods	32,551,256
Machinery	13,601,960
Transport equipment	11,080,076
Textiles	4,809,129
Total	174,561,713

however, from Yemeni émigrés living abroad – believed to total 1·5 million, of whom 1 million were in Saudi Arabia. The YAR's economic prospects for the 1970s were undeniably stark. Foreign aid would continue to cover the deficits in return for compliance by the YAR in international matters; and the agricultural richness of the country, however under-exploited, would be capable of preventing large-scale starvation. But unless oil or some other mineral was discovered in quantity the ruling class would run North Yemen as a permanently subordinated and impoverished extension of the world market; the country's agricultural and industrial potential would only be developed by a political leadership markedly different from the one established in the wake of the civil war. It was this latter perspective that the foreign powers dominating and financing North Yemen wanted to suppress. Having fought an eight-year interventionist war and having now successfully crippled the YAR itself they were resolved that North Yemen would not pose a threat to their interests again.

Saudi Arabia's Satellite

Saudi Arabia was the main agent of the political and economic subordination of the YAR to the west, a more efficient and nuanced agent than any western power directly intervening could have been. Saudi Arabia also employed the YAR in its own counter-revolutionary campaigns within the peninsula and exploited it economically through the large force of North Yemeni migrant labour working in Saudi cities. The Wahhabi state established by Ibn Saud in 1926 had laid claim to the whole peninsula and had always tried to intervene in other states, except where blocked by their main rivals, the British. In 1934 the Saudis had defeated the Imam of the Yemen in a full-scale war in which they had laid the basis for deep Yemeni resentment by annexing the three provinces. In the internal North Yemeni crises of 1948 and 1955 the Saudis had intervened to save the Hamid ad-Din family from domestic threats. When the September 1962 revolution occurred in North Yemen it did not take long for the Saudis to reactivate their interventionist campaign, and throughout the civil war they provided the main logistical, financial and material support to the Imam's forces. Training camps were established at the border towns of Jizan and Najran, and the Imam's men were able to use Saudi facilities in every way; despite frequent clashes between the Saudis and various quarrelsome Hamid ad-Din princes, aid continued with interruptions to flow via the Governor of Najran until the 1970 settlement. This Saudi support was not based on any specific love for the Imam, but rather on a fear of the threat that the YAR posed to stability inside Saudi Arabia and to the – well-founded – fear that revolutionary action could spread from North Yemen into other areas of the peninsula. Hence in 1970, when it was clear that a subsidized republic could be no threat, the Saudis abandoned the Imam and his family. There was persistent disagreement between the YAR and the Saudis about whether the Yemeni state should be officially called an 'Islamic state' (*Doula Islamia*), but the content of the settlement was clear.

The international function of the YAR was twofold. First, by preserving its stable republican tribalist regime it provided a safe flank for Saudi Arabia. Equally importantly, it provided a base for action against the revolutionary government in Aden which the Saudis refused to recognize and which they were intent on overthrowing. Saudi subsidies to the YAR state and YAR sheikhs were paralleled by payments to anti-communist exiles from Aden based in the North who were recruited into a number of organizations designed to invade the South and there constitute a pro-Saudi regime. There were disagreements among these Saudi clients about whether the best solution was to annex South Yemeni to the YAR under the slogan of 'Yemeni unity' or whether it was better to try to set up a separate pro-Saudi government in the South made up of elements that had fled from the South in 1967–9. These political and strategic considerations were what dominated Saudi relations with the YAR. Economic relations were far less important. Trade between the two countries was very small; official figures for 1970–71 state that only 152,000 out of the YAR's total of 13·5 million rials' exports went to Saudi Arabia, and only 1·3 million of her 174·6 million rials' imports were of Saudi origin. No doubt such trade could increase in the future; and the Saudis were indeed exploiting the YAR through its migrant labour force; but although few figures are available it is probable that the net flow of capital was from the Saudis to the Yemenis in return for definite political benefits and for the future political and economic 'stability' that these promised. The official Saudi figure for direct aid to the YAR budget in the year March 1973–March 1974 was 80 million Saudi rials – but this omitted the numerous covert subsidies paid to sheikhs.

Relations with the capitalist west coincided with Saudi policies. The money paid by Saudi Arabia to the YAR came from oil revenues – the counter-revolutionary 'stability' of the YAR was of direct interest to the American oil companies pillaging the Gulf. Within a week of Saudi recognition of the YAR in July 1970 Britain and France, who for eight years had covertly supported the Imam, also recognized the Republic. Relations with the Federal Republic of Germany had already been opened in 1969 when the YAR broke relations with the German Democratic Republic, making itself the first country ever to do so. As a result of these exchanges foreign aid began to return to Yemen; and a law was passed in 1970 to encourage foreign investment.[9] One country with a special relationship to North Yemen was Iran; the Shah had sent his own covert aid to the royalists in the mid 1960s and withheld recognition of the YAR till July 1970. Seeing the strategic importance of North Yemen, Iran then began to supply military advisers, trained YAR pilots for three years in Iran and also provided technical assistance in setting up YAR television.

Britain and France provided aid through an operation in which they 'turned a blind eye' to the activity of supposedly private entrepreneurs. For the British there were two main forms of support. One was the channelling of supplies through the Sharif of Beihan, whose South Yemeni state bordered the North, and through whom men and weapons were sent until 1967. The second means was through a group of former British officers with close connections within the Conservative party. These included Lieutenant-Colonel Neil 'Billy' MacLean, M.P., who visited royalist Yemen on several occasions, and Colonel David Stirling, founder of the Special Air Services regiment. Through their coordination British advisers served in the royalist zone from 1963 to 1967 running the radio network and carrying out sabotage activities.[10] French mercenaries, in simultaneous co-operation and rivalry with the British, also served in North Yemen, among them such veterans of French colonial wars as Colonel Roger Faulques. The Israeli intervention was more covert. An Imamist delegate visited Israel in March 1963 to ask, without success, for long-term help, but it is known that un-marked Israeli planes made about fifteen flights from Djibouti to drop arms over royalist areas in the period 1962–3.

Relations with the United States took longer to consolidate, although the concrete interests of the US were well cared for by Saudi Arabia, herself a subordinate ally of Washington. The US had opened diplomatic relations with North Yemen in 1946, but had broken them in 1948 on the death of Yahya and had not renewed them till 1950. In the early 1950s Yemeni appeals for aid went unheard; and it was only when Soviet aid appeared in 1957 that the US became interested. Allen Dulles, head of the CIA, appeared before the US Chamber of Commerce in Washington in 1958 to document Soviet penetration of the Yemen; and the first US aid arrived in January 1959 in the shape of food supplies.[11] When the 1962 revolution occurred the US was under the Kennedy administration; and some leading State Department officials saw support for non-communist nationalists, rather than support for inefficient conservatives, as the best means of defeating revolution. In the Arab world this took the form of a friendly attitude towards Nasser's Egypt. The US recognized the YAR in December 1962, partly to keep Nasser's sympathy and partly because they saw the best way to protect Saudi Arabia and the US interests there was to work on Nasser for a compromise ceasefire. This arrangement was what finally did come to protect US–Saudi interests; but it was not concluded for another eight years. Immediately after US recognition of the YAR Egyptian planes attacked Saudi Arabia; and in January 1963, in an operation unequivocally entitled 'Operation Hard Surface', eight US jets were dispatched from Germany to signify, and if necessary provide, US support for the Saudi government; a US destroyer and paratroops were also sent. The US then sent out Ellsworth Bunker, later to organize the US invasion of Santo Domingo in 1965 and to serve as US proconsul in Saigon from 1968, to negotiate a ceasefire between Egypt and the Saudis, and between the factions in North Yemen. The ceasefire lasted for a time; but when it broke down the US adopted a more nakedly pro-Saudi policy.[12]

At this time Soviet influence on Egypt and the YAR was clearly stronger; and as relations between the US and Egypt deteriorated and as Johnson abandoned the 'moderate' stance affected by the Kennedy administration, US influence in the YAR declined to a minimum. By 1966–7 the US was quietly supporting Saudi policies of countering Egypt with an 'Islamic Pact'; and when the Arab–Israeli war broke out in June 1967 the YAR severed relations with Washington. From then on the initiative was left with the Saudis, and the US had no reason to feel any threat from the YAR as the rapprochement between the two North Yemeni sides continued. The general pretence of hostility to the US affected by many Arab governments in order to posture as 'anti-imperialist' may well explain the delay with which the YAR and the US rebuilt their ties, for it was only in July 1972

153

that diplomatic relations were restored. US Secretary of State Rogers flew in a special plane from Ceylon for a day-long visit in which relations were formally re-established. In a speech to the Commonwealth Club in San Francisco on 18 July he reported on his trip in a semi-travelogue vein. The tone did not however conceal the political considerations lying behind his visit, at a time when the US was increasing its influence throughout the Middle East and the Gulf:

... with Yemen, a beautiful republic on the Arabian peninsula, we had had no diplomatic relations since 1967; my visit to Yemen's mountain capital of Sanaa was the occasion for their re-establishment and for underscoring the importance we attach to maintaining good relations with all Arab countries.

That visit to Yemen was also a useful reminder of the importance of all the world's nations. We flew into the capital of this remote and poor country in gathering darkness – to land on a runway with no lights or navigational aids of any kind. At that moment it may have seemed difficult – particularly for our pilot – to think of Yemen as a significant factor in world affairs. And yet it is – with an important geographical position on the oil-rich Arabian peninsula and with the largest population on the peninsula. We value the positive step Yemen has taken in welcoming an American Embassy back to Sanaa. And we hope that other Arab countries which have been estranged from us since the Arab–Israeli conflict will consider similar steps.

Rogers visited Sanaa on 2 July 1972. On 18 July Sadat announced that all Soviet military advisers had been ordered out of Egypt, thus handing the US on a plate the best diplomatic present they could have imagined. When Rogers spoke about 'other Arab countries' in his San Francisco speech he was pointing out that the recognition by North Yemen and his trip there were part of the general anti-Soviet campaign being waged by the US at that time, both in regard to the Arab–Israeli question and in the peninsula where the US had developed its military and diplomatic position following the partial British withdrawal at the end of 1971.

Relations with the Communist Countries

Although this internal and international swing to the right after 1967 did not lead to any immediate change in the YAR's relations to the communist states, it did do so in time. The Soviet Union had had ties with Imam Yahya in the 1920s and with Imam Ahmad in the 1950s: on both occasions they supported the Imams as anti-imperialists, not because they had illusions about the social character of the rulers but because these harassed the British in Aden.[13] From 1962 onwards they supported the YAR and became the main source of financial and military aid during the civil war. The YAR leaders often complained that the Nasserites blocked direct communication with Moscow and that arms and material were being stolen en route. Sallal in 1964 and al-Amri in 1966 made attempts to acquire and direct independent supply of arms from the Russians but the Egyptians were able to stop them. When Nasser pulled out in November 1967 and the royalists besieged Sanaa, the Russians mounted a vital airlift to Sanaa and contributed to withstanding the attack. When the fighting ended they continued to support the YAR with military and economic aid; but as the Arab world in general and the YAR in particular moved to the right in 1971–2 the position of their 100-odd military advisers in the North and of their diplomatic staff became weaker. They were also heavily committed to the government of the People's Republic in the South, and clearly made this their priority. They had seen their aims in the YAR in terms of helping to defeat the royalists but also in terms of strategic interests; and they had built the airport at Sanaa and expanded the port at Hodeida at least partly with these considerations in mind. For example, had the airport at Sanaa been ready in January 1964 they might have been able to airlift troops to the eastern Congo to rebuff the imperialist attack on Stanleyville; but while these facilities would always be convenient they became less so once the Russians had acquired a secure position in the South. In October 1972 al-Aini stated that the Soviet Union had provided no arms or spare parts for three

155

years. As a result, the YAR army was re-equipped with US equipment and uniforms channelled from Saudi Arabia, and YAR officers were sent to Iran, the US and West Germany for training. Some Russian spare parts were allegedly obtained by a devious ploy: Israel sold some of the material she had captured in the 1967 war to Iran who then shipped them to Hodeida. But this source was clearly not enough.

The People's Republic of China played a less important military role than the Soviet Union; but the Chinese were popular in North Yemen because, unlike the Russians and expatriate westerners, they lived like the people, in poor conditions, and worked extremely hard. Like the Soviet Union, the PRC had recognized Imam Ahmad for straightforward strategic reasons; but they too had given full support to the YAR from the beginning. The main Chinese projects were the textile factory in Sanaa and the road linking Sanaa to Hodeida; throughout the war they continued working on the road and such was their popularity that they were never attacked by the royalists who might have been expected to be hostile to them. Their direct political influence on the masses was slight; the left-wing opposition was influenced, like the MAN throughout the Arab world, by China; but there was no direct contact within North Yemen itself and the Chinese confined themselves to their popular aid projects. In 1972, when Soviet influence in the YAR was waning, there appeared to be no such decrease in Sino–Yemeni friendship; and China continued to regard the YAR as an ally in its global strategy. A delegation headed by al-Aini visited China from 16 to 27 July. Chou En-lai spoke at a banquet welcoming the delegation: 'Yemen is a country with a tradition of opposing imperialism; and its people are an industrious and brave people who waged valiant and undaunted struggles for a long time against imperialist and feudal rule and oppression before finally winning national independence and liberation,'[14] he said. Later a new aid agreement was signed granting the YAR £8·5 million in economic and technical aid; and in a joint communiqué the two sides expressed common positions on a number of major issues – Palestine, the five principles of co-existence, Vietnam – but without any mention of politics in the Arabian peninsula itself.[15] The Chinese later adopted a neutral position in the inter-Yemeni war of 1972.

The Strategic Importance of the North Yemeni Revolution

Ten years after the revolution of September 1962 the YAR was a solid member of the imperialist camp, despite its friendly relations with China and its verbal espousal of anti-imperialist positions. But despite this negative conclusion, a general assessment of the revolution has to take other factors into consideration. On the international scale the North Yemeni revolution had two positive consequences. First, it was an anti-imperialist event of great importance for the revolutionary movement in the peninsula as a whole. It undermined the British position in South Yemen and led directly to the launching of guerrilla war in the Radfan mountains against the British in October 1963. This in turn contributed to the launching of guerrilla war in the Dhofar province of the Sultanate of Oman in June 1965. A whole series of outbreaks and plots inside Saudi Arabia also followed from the North Yemeni revolution. On logical grounds it might be questioned how the 1962 revolution could be anti-imperialist if the Imam himself was likewise inclined. Clearly, given the possibilities before 1962, the Imam's truculent if feeble clashes with the British were more positive than his acting as a docile client; but once a more radical challenge to the British was possible, the Imam was no longer progressive. The second positive consequence of the North Yemeni revolution was its partial discrediting, in the mid 1960s, of Nasserite nationalism. North Yemen played its part in this process both because local Nasserite groups developed by conflict with the Egyptian military and intelligence men, and because within Egypt and the Arab world it was clear that the tremendous sufferings and cost of the Egyptian campaign had led not to victory but to compromise and retreat. Within Egypt a militant if small opposition had emerged out of this crisis and in the peninsula the NLF in People's Yemen and the Popular Front in Oman had evolved

157

out of the Yemeni experience and its consequences into independent and revolutionary political organizations.

Internally the North Yemeni revolution had an ambiguous character. The Egyptian intervention, initially progressive and later negative, saved the YAR from extinction and a restoration of the Hamid ad-Din dynasty. What it later encouraged was the negative side of the 1962 revolution itself; it had been brought about by a coalition of merchants, who wanted to bring North Yemen into the world market, and officers, who wanted to bring her into Arab politics, together with tribal leaders who wanted to gain power at the expense of the centre. The Egyptians did not create this second tribal component but they strengthened it so that the YAR, instead of pursuing a more radical and continuing change, underwent minimal changes before settling into its present counter-revolutionary mould. The international clash, between Egypt and Saudi Arabia, and between the west and the communist world, was superimposed on the domestic North Yemeni conflict and further strengthened the backward elements both within the YAR itself and outside of it, in the royalist camp. But there were progressive consequences. The Imam and the Sada were driven out; and North Yemen was opened to western capital, a positive step compared to the pre-capitalist night that had hung over the country for so long.

The post-1970 regime also contained its own instabilities, which placed a continuous strain upon the compromise settlement. North Yemen was part of a larger unit, the Yemen as a whole; and its internal politics could not be isolated from occurrences in the revolutionary South. This was clear not only to Yemenis, but also to Saudi Arabia, which tried to use the North to fight the South. In 1972 this led to a new situation in the YAR. On the one hand, pro-Southern guerrillas had revived opposition to the regime; a new Organization of Yemeni Resisters and the old Revolutionary Democratic Party both began attacks on unpopular sheikhs and developed underground political activity in the rural areas. The government replied by destroying villages and by wide-ranging arrests in the towns. On the other hand, in September 1972 the Saudis organized counter-revolutionary exiles in the North to attack the South. After around two weeks of war, the two Yemeni states surprisingly agreed to a peace settlement and signed an agreement unifying them as a single Yemeni state.

This sudden re-emergence of the Yemeni unity issue opened a new political front. Saudi Arabia and its client sheikhs in the North opposed the unity agreement, and Prime Minister al-Aini was forced to resign. The new al-Hajari government was quick to reassure Saudi Arabia and agreed to waive the YAR's claim to the three Yemeni provinces annexed in 1933 and which, under the 1934 Treaty of Taif, were due for return to North Yemen forty years later. However impossible the joining of state to state may have been, unity was immensely popular in both North and South, and the Saudi opposition had the effect of creating a strong Yemeni nationalist trend opposed to the intervention of the Riyadh regime and the power of the pro-Saudi sheikhs in the North. The dynamic of the 1962 revolution was thereby able to re-emerge via the unity question. Apart from it being positive that Yemen be united, it also became clear that the movement for unity could rally a strong anti-feudalist and anti-Saudi front in the North.

Throughout the period after the unity agreement YAR politics was dominated by two conflicts: one was within the regime – between the outspoken pro-Saudi group around al-Hajari and the relatively independent line represented by President al-Iryani; the other was between the regime as a whole and its militant opponents in the junior ranks of the armed forces and in the underground guerrilla groups. Between May and October 1973 over forty people were officially executed for 'subversion', and the unity talks with the PDRY did not progress (see page 257). In the summer of 1973 al-Iryani went into a temporary and calculated exile in Syria in protest at the policies of al-Hajari, and in the late autumn al-Hajari was replaced by a less pro-Saudi premier, the former foreign minister Hassan Makki. Yet, despite these real differences within the ruling group, thousands of prisoners remained in gaol and the power of the sheikhs was not seriously challenged. The struggle within the North was predominantly political, with a subordinate military aspect; at the same time it was part of a struggle being fought at a pan-Yemeni level – in the North, in the South, and in the three 'occupied' provinces. The 1962 revolution had taken place in unfavourable international circumstances and in a country where much of the population, in the Zeidi areas of the north, were still dominated by tribal ideology and institutions. Any revolution in the North would have to confront these forces and the international allies who used and supported them. At the same time the North was inextricably linked to the South, and had both affected the revolution there and in turn been affected by it. By a process of delayed interaction, the North Yemeni revolution was continuing to affect and to be affected by the revolutionary movement in the Arabian peninsula as a whole.

Notes

1. *The Times*, 6 January 1971.

2. *The Times*, 13 January 1971. The full text of the constitution is in the *Middle East Journal*, Vol. 25, No. 3, summer 1971. Its Islamic character is emphasized throughout; in the opening quotes from the Koran, in the reintroduction of the *zakat* tax (Article 135), in the defence of *waqf* land (Article 136) and in the derivation of all laws from the Moslem *shariah* (Article 3). All of these have been abolished by the Aden government; and all were abolished in Turkey in the secular reforms carried out by Kemal Ataturk in the 1920s.

3. The budget deficit rose from 56·98 million rials in 1967–8 to 59·94 million rials in 1968–9 to 77·14 million rials in 1969–70, with military expenditure rising in the same period from 34·69 million rials to 49·70 million rials to 71·70 million rials. (Economist Intelligence Unit, *Quarterly Economic Review* Annual Supplement, 1972.) It can be seen that the budget deficit rose with the amount of military expenditure, and that this military expenditure grew greater the less fighting there was. By comparison, in the period 1969–70, 9·62 million rials were spent on health and 6·88 million rials on education, one quarter of the amount allocated to 'defence'.

4. *New York Times*, 6 September 1971.

5. Sultan Omar, op. cit., p. 133. Citing the *Official Revolutionary Gazette*, No. 664, 14 October 1964, pp. 153–4, Omar gives the number of officials as 13,525, of which 775 had the rank of 'minister' (*wazir*), 171 the rank of general director (*modir am*) and 1,419 the rank of section chief (*rais qesm*).

6. Economist Intelligence Unit, *Quarterly Economic Review* Annual Supplement, 1972.

7. ibid.

8. *Foreign Trade Statistics for the Yemeni Arab Republic for the Fiscal Year 1970/71*: Yemen Currency Board Research Department number 2, Sanaa, 1971.

9. Until 1970 over three-quarters of the total foreign aid, excluding Egyptian aid, came from the Soviet Union and the People's Republic of China. Since then the Y A R has become more reliant on the west; in 1970 it joined the I M F, the I B R D (the 'World Bank') and the I D A. I M F aid has since followed, as well as aid from official Arab sources – Kuwait, Saudi Arabia, Abu Dhabi, Libya. Of the western capitalist nations, West Germany has given the most (£8·2 million by August 1971). The U S agreed to resume distribution of aid after relations were reopened in July 1972; Britain and France have so far given small amounts.

10. When *Le Monde* correspondent Eric Rouleau visited the royalists in 1967 he found British mercenaries paid by 'a mysterious centre in London, which is called by the elliptical name of the Organisation. This is supposed to be run by . . . Colonel Stirling and Major Brooke'. When Rouleau asked a tribal leader about one British mercenary he was told: 'He is one of the many British historians who are enquiring from us about contemporary events in the Yemen' (*Le Monde*, 16 May 1967). In a later article in the *Sunday Times* (18 January 1970) it was reported that Stirling had put a plan to the Saudis in 1967 offering a 'task force' to carry out sabotage in Yemen which would have 'access to the S A S Regiment of the British army'. An account of the Yemen operation by ex-S A S officer Colonel 'Jim' Johnson, later a City businessman, appeared in the *Daily Telegraph*, 4, 5 and 6 February 1970, with the opening headline 'Second "Lawrence" Foiled Nasser's Army in Yemen'. This British operation could never have been carried out without official support and it had many ramifications. Stirling himself set up a firm named Watchguard (International) Ltd to supply Asian and African rulers with military advisers, and in 1970 was involved in an abortive attempt to oust Libyan ruler Gaddafi (see Patrick Seale and Maureen McGonville, *The Hilton Assignment*, London, 1973). Stirling also had interests in Iran via another firm, Television International Enterprises. One of the other two directors of Watchguard was Richard Helier Cristin, a lawyer who was also a director of Chant Investments Ltd, a Jersey-based firm controlled by Stirling's friend Geoffrey Edwards; Edwards was the man who sold £160 million of British aircraft and missiles to Saudi Arabia in 1966 (see p. 89). Involved in the Yemen operation were former British army officers who had been, or were to be, involved in the Sultanate of Oman; these included Colonel David Smiley, Major John Cooper and Major David Bayley.

11. Wenner, op. cit., pp. 169–71, 177–82, 201ff.

12. See page 122.
13. See Stephen Page, *The U S S R and Arabia*, London, 1971.
14. *Peking Review*, No. 29, 21 July 1972.
15. *Peking Review*, No. 31, 4 August 1972.

Part Three
South Yemen

Chapter Six
South Yemen
Under British Rule

Imperial Strategy and Uneven Development

Britain occupied South Yemen in the early nineteenth century for
strategic considerations, and these concerns were dominant in
British policy right up until 1966 when the decision to withdraw
was announced. A century before the British invaded, Aden and
its hinterland had been part of a united Yemen. But in 1728 the
local administrator and client of the Yemeni Imam, the Sultan
of Lahej, revolted and more of the Southern area broke away.
By the time the British took Aden, South Yemen had split up
into numerous small sultanates and other states. Although the
British certainly encouraged and solidified the division between
North and South Yemen, it is historically incorrect to state, as
some Yemeni nationalists have done, that the division was
created by imperialism. Britain utilized a pre-existing division.

Original British interest in the area dated from the Napoleonic
wars as part of Britain's world-wide counter-revolutionary
campaign at that time; Britain occupied Aden as it also seized
Ceylon and South Africa – to forestall French influence – and
Britain saw Aden, as it saw the Gulf, in terms of protecting the
approaches to India. Although the British occupation of Aden
was transitory, this concern for India reappeared in the 1830s, to
prompt renewed interest in Arabia. The armies of the Egyptian
ruler Mohammad Ali were advancing through the peninsula into
North Yemen; and the aggressive British Foreign Secretary,
Palmerston, whose hatred of Mohammad Ali was similar to
Eden's hatred for Nasser, regarded British interests as being in
danger. In addition, the ruler of Aden, the Sultan of Lahej,
decided in 1837 to break off relations with Britain and briefly
detained a marauding British ship. It was also around this time
that Britain was introducing steamships into the Indian Ocean
and these ships needed a coaling station on the way. For these

reasons the British sent a force from Bombay to seize the port of Aden.[1] Aden is the best natural port in the Arabian peninsula and the Red Sea, and has always played an important part in the area's trade. When the Red Sea has prospered Aden has prospered, and under the pre-Islamic empires, the early Moslem empires and the British, the city flourished. But as trade has declined, Aden has fallen too. When Marco Polo visited it in 1276 he found it had a population of 80,000 with 360 mosques. After the Portuguese and the Dutch had discovered the Cape Route to the Far East and the Turks captured Egypt, the region's trade declined in the seventeenth century, and when the British attacked in 1839 Aden's population had fallen to 500.

The port was occupied in January 1839 against the resistance of the local population. A year later Britain forced another strategic port to join her empire when she launched her campaign of aggression against China in the first so-called Opium War and annexed Hong Hong. But unlike Hong Kong, which was a gateway to markets, Aden was occupied uniquely for its strategic position.

When the Suez Canal was opened in 1869 Aden port revived its historic prosperity; but it flourished entirely on the basis of stimuli external to the area and the hinterland behind Aden was never developed. For political reasons this was encouraged by the British, who wanted a secure tribal buffer zone to protect the important port. South Yemen as a whole therefore developed in a spectacularly uneven way, both politically and economically, and this irregular development later became the determinant factor in the area's politics. The British tried to encourage it and fostered the tribal rulers of the hinterland, hoping to use them to hold down the increasingly turbulent port. It was eventually this apparently 'stable' hinterland which rose in revolt, and by ejecting Britain's tribal clients undermined the basis of colonialism in the area. British penetration of the hinterland from Aden began in the 1870s when the Turks reoccupied North Yemen, and the British started to sign so-called 'protection' treaties with hinterland rulers to keep Turkish influence at bay; these sheikhs agreed to obey the British in return for arms and money.[2]

In the western region, known as the 'Western Protectorate', the process of signing these treaties lasted until 1954 by which time over ninety collaborationist agreements had been made. These treaties fossilized tribal divisions and froze relations within the tribes by strengthening the sheikhs with recognition and subsidies. After the 1934 agreement with North Yemen Imam, the British went a stage further and signed a series of 'advisory' treaties designed to amalgamate these ninety units into larger states. In the end they were left with seventeen, which were then urged to form a South Arabian Federation.[3]

Because of the east's distance British contacts with the area grew slower than in the west. There had been a treaty with the Mukalla-based Sultan of Quaiti in 1888 and one with the Sultan of Kathiri in 1918; but it was not until 1934 that the British took the zone into their full control.[4] A British envoy was sent to the area, which at the time was divided into around 2,000 warring factions.[5] He was able, by a series of negotiations, to mediate in many of these disputes, and signed a total of 1,400 treaties with eastern tribes. British control and that of the half-dozen major sultans was thereby strengthened, and the British signed with them a number of new 'advisory' treaties. The major reason for this initiative in the east was the British fear of Italian fascist influence; the Italians were entrenched in Somalia, across the sea, and had contact with certain Hadrami sheikhs. But their influence never posed a serious threat to the British in South Yemen, and the integration of the Hadramaut and Mahra into the Protectorate system also accorded with the deeper logic of British policy in the area.

By the 1950s Britain had consolidated its hold over the whole of South Yemen, an area of 112,000 square miles with an estimated population of 1·5 million. There were three separate administrative units: Aden Colony, the Western Protectorate and the Eastern Protectorate. While Aden was ruled by a governor the hinterland was administered through a system known as 'indirect rule'.

The British pretended not to be responsible for the internal affairs of the sultans and amirs of the Protectorates; that they could merely 'advise', 'protect' and so on. This was a gross ideological distortion of the situation, but it was functional to Britain's interests. Imperialist control was facilitated by the use of local collaborators. Britain intervened in tribal affairs, attacking and deposing rulers when it needed to and when its clients rebelled. But apart from such interventions, the alliance of colonial power in Aden and sultanic rule in the mountains was a stable and convenient means of protecting the approaches to Aden without deploying a substantial political or military apparatus, and, except for bribes and arms, without expenditure. By hiding behind the myths of 'indirect rule' the British also had an excuse for doing nothing to alter the oppressive social relations that prevailed in the mountains, or to assist the population in any form of economic development. While actively preserving the sultanic regimes in the mountains, they pretended that they could not intervene to develop the area as this would prejudice the autonomy of the sheikhs.[6]

The Port of Aden

The British developed Aden as a staging post to India, a line that included Gibraltar, Malta, Cyprus and the Suez Canal.[7] In 1853, only fourteen years after they had annexed it, they made Aden into a free port; then in 1869 the opening of the Suez Canal reversed the historical decline begun three centuries before. By 1900 the population had grown to 44,000; and during the post-1945 boom it rose from 80,516 in 1946 to 138,400 in 1955; to an estimated 225,000 by 1964; and to probably over 250,000 by 1967. The only full census, that of 1955, showed the diverse origins of the people who had made up this increase in population. These ethnic divisions were reflected in social divisions and in residence patterns. The Europeans living at Steamer Point and Khormaksar were in undisputed political control until the 1955 elections when they co-opted some Arab merchants into their system. The Indians were merchants and civil servants favoured by the British and, as in the Gulf and East Africa, were uneasily sandwiched between the colonial power and the local population.

168

Table 9

Adeni Population 1955		Percentage of Total
Adeni Arabs	36,910	26·7
Other South Yemenis	18,881	13·7
North Yemenis	48,088	34·8
Indians	15,817	11·4
Somalis	10,611	7·7
Europeans	4,484	3·2
Jews	831	0·6
Others	2,608	1·9
Total	138,230	

Source: Aden Census Report, 1955.

The North Yemenis living in Crater and Sheikh Othman were migrant labourers from North Yemen, employed in the port and construction, and ferociously excluded from all political decisions by the British, who tried to split them from their fellow Yemenis of the South. The Somalis had come across the few miles of sea from Africa and were the most oppressed section of the population, living in shanty towns on the sides of the hills in Crater and doing the most menial jobs. There had been a Jewish community of 7,300 in 1946; these had been concentrated in commerce and did not work in the administration. The majority emigrated to Israel after communal riots in 1947–8.

Aden derived its prosperity from four sources: from entrepot trade with North Yemen and the South Yemeni hinterland; from bunkering and shopping facilities for passing ships; from industry and from the British base. Until 1961, when the port at Hodeida was expanded, 80 per cent of North Yemen's trade passed through Aden. In addition to this Aden was by far the most important port in the South, with only Mukalla in the east taking likewise a significant amount of trade. The largest item in both imports and exports was petroleum and petroleum products – imported for the refinery and then exported straight or sold to ships visiting the port. But other imports, around 60 per cent, included food, tobacco, raw materials and some machinery and manufactured goods. Exports, apart from

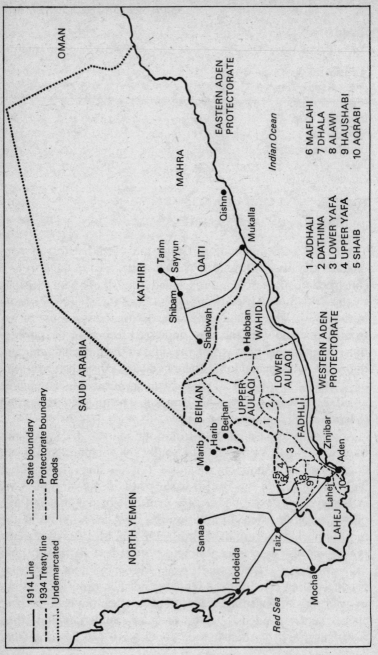

Map 5   South Yemen under the British

petroleum products, were port services, skins and hides. Very little of the trade with the South went to areas outside Aden.[8]

The free port status imposed on Aden tied it by its prosperity to the outside world. Because there were no import duties it was difficult for local industry to develop. And this dependence was reinforced by the fact that trade and finance were controlled by foreign capital, much of whose profits were repatriated. British colonial banks were dominant – the British Bank of the Middle East, the Eastern Bank, National and Grindlays and the Chartered Bank; what others existed were controlled by Jordanians (the Arab Bank) and south Asians (the Bank of India and the Habib Bank of Pakistan). Trade was tightly controlled by the expatriate firms of A. Besse & Co. and Luke Thomas, who shared the insurance business with the local branches of North American and British concerns.

These financial and trading interests dominated the port, in liaison with the refinery facilities opened by BP in 1954. After 1956 the average yearly number of ships visiting the port was 5,450, of which some were transport ships using the refuelling facilities, while others were passenger ships on the Asia–Europe run. A total of 200,000 transit passengers and 27,000 tourists a year visited Aden and shopped in the duty-free shops clustered around the passenger piers at Tawahi or 'Steamer Point'. By 1964 Aden had the fourth largest bunkering trade in the world, less only than London, Liverpool and New York. This dependence on trade had negative effects on Aden by limiting economic activity to services, and also made the port dependent on Red Sea shipping and hence on the political situation around the Suez Canal. The cycle of prosperity and decline that the area had encountered before with changes in Red Sea trade could now take place within a matter of weeks – as it did in 1956–7 after Suez and again after the June War of 1967. In 1956–7 the monthly shipping average fell from 454 vessels a month to 277 in November 1956 and to 93 in February 1957, the lowest it reached; in the period after the June War of 1967 the monthly average fell from 450 to 140. These figures, however, understate the damage from such closures. First, virtually all passenger lines were diverted round the Cape, and the shopping areas of Aden were especially hit. Secondly, even those transport ships that continued to come tended to be of a smaller kind specializing in trade in that part of the Indian Ocean.

Most of local industry was not directly dependent on the port's shipping, but its main component, the refinery, was so; besides which, its industrial development was typical of any colonial country. Up to the early 1950s the main industrial activities in Aden had been the manufacture of salt and fish processing, but in 1952 BP began to build an oil refinery on the west side of Aden bay, at Bureika ('Little Aden'). The construction, at a cost of £45 million, took two years and employed 10,000 local workers and 2,500 specialists. In 1954, when it was completed it had a permanent staff of over 2,000 workers. The refinery was originally built to replace the BP refinery in Abadan, Iran, which Mosadeq nationalized in 1951. Most of its oil came from Kuwait, where production was increased in 1951–3 to compensate for the loss of oil from Iran. But when Abadan began operating again in 1954, Aden had acquired a market of its own; its original capacity, 5 million tons a year, was later increased and by April 1966 it could handle 8·3 million tons a year, although it did not operate at full capacity. Sixty per cent of its products were re-exported to Red Sea ports and East and South Africa; 37 per cent were sold locally to shipping companies at special prices; and only 3 per cent were absorbed by the local market. The refinery was the basis of local production; it provided 10 per cent of the GDP, 20 per cent of industrial employment and (from exported products plus bunkering income) 75 per cent of export earnings.

Other industries were less significant. There were some soft drinks factories, with a total output of 50 million bottles in 1965; a small ship-building and ship-repair industry; and in the hinterland two cotton ginneries and a tuna-processing plant. The main industrial activity apart from operating the refinery was construction, which provided per 7 cent of GDP and 50 per cent of industrial employment. Speculative housing development boomed in the decade after 1956, when the British decided to make Aden a major base and moved in thousands of troops.[9]

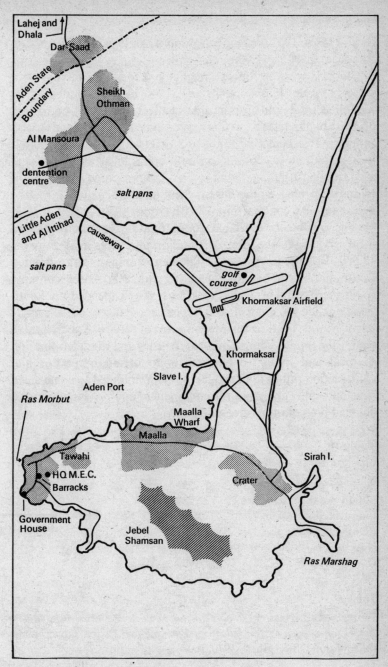

Map 6 Aden under the British

From 1947 to 1962 the number of those employed in construction rose from 1,900 to 12,700.

The base was the fourth category of economic activity, after entrepot trade, bunkering facilities and industry. Much of its economic inputs and outputs did not affect Aden at all, consisting of British purchasers buying goods and services from British suppliers. But there were points of contact with the local economy: local labour, local contractors and some local materials were used in constructing facilities for the increased numbers of military. In 1960–64 the British spent an average of £11 million a year on new construction. British troops spent a part of their income on locally available goods (mainly imported) and on local services. Of the total £8·7 million purchases in 1965 by the 17,000 British servicemen and their families, an estimated £2·1 million could be classed as being within the Adeni economy.

All these activities were precarious; they depended on conditions outside the control of the local population, and all, apart from the industrial sector, were a form of service. The free trade status, the foreign control of local industry and the determination of local and foreign entrepreneurs to invest in services and construction rather than production all reinforced this one-sided development. The figures for employment and production give a detailed presentation of conditions.

Table 10
Employment in Aden 1965

Port	7,555
Building and construction	12,789
Industrial undertakings	13,301
Retail and wholesale trade	10,714
Government, police and army	18,231
Domestic service	17,000
Others	1,385
Total	80,975

Source: M. S. Hassan, *Report to the People's Republic of Southern Yemen on Guidelines for Industrial Planning and Policy*, Government Information Office, Aden, 1970, p. 6.

Table 11

GDP and GNP for South Yemen 1965[10]

	GNP	GDP
Base	10	10
Refinery	3·5	9
Bunkering and petroleum distribution	2	2·5
Tourism	0·3	0·5
Shipping services	4	5
Wholesale and retail trade	8	13
Banks	1·3	1·6
Other industry	3	3
Agriculture	7	7
Local government	25	10
Construction	2	2
Transport	1·5	2
Ownership of dwellings	2	2
Services	7	7
Emigrant remittances	5	–
Total	82	74

Source: as for Table 10, p. 4.

The picture shows an extremely distorted economy, more dependent on external forces and even less capable of an internally generated dynamism than most 'service-orientated' colonial economies elsewhere in the world. Aden, unlike Hong Kong or Havana or Colombo, did not even exist as the parasitic intermediary between a plundering imperialist country and a populous colonial victim exporting raw materials or drawing in imports from abroad. Nor did its local bourgeoisie develop the most minimal industrializing activities, given the pressure of the 'free port' and of colonial rule, and given the fact that Aden business was in the hands of foreigners. The Adeni bourgeoisie was a uniquely comprador class. The Aden Port Trust established in 1889 to run the port exemplified this. Until the mid 1960s it was run by British and Indian businessmen; only in August 1967, three months before independence, did it acquire an Arab chairman; and up to that time no Arab port pilots had been trained. The surplus accumulated in the Trust's reserve fund was spent exclusively on port facilities and was never used to broaden the economic base of the Colony as a whole; what was not spent by the Trust was held in a growing pile of idle capital. Profits from other activities, the refinery, the shopping centre and commercial services, flowed overseas. The banks controlling finance did not invest in industry or agriculture; speculative housing was the main productive activity.

Repression and Poverty in the Hinterland

The boom in Aden had only a limited effect on the tribal areas, due to the fact that the Aden growth was generated externally and its profits went abroad. But the insulation of Aden also reflected a political decision by the British to keep the tribal areas as unchanged as possible. This was the key to the uneven development of the area. If the economic changes in Aden had affected the hinterland's structure, the political stability and the buffer zone that Britain wanted among the tribes might have been undermined. If all the workers brought into Aden had come from up country and not from Somalia and North Yemen, or if the British had educated local Yemenis to do the jobs they had trained Europeans and southern Asians to do, the sultans and sheikhs of the hinterland would have been unable to retain complete control. Instead the British deliberately fostered a dichotomy within the economy and society of the South, so as to preserve imperialist control.

In the hinterland the main economic activity was agriculture. About 0·5 per cent of the total land area, 300,000 acres, was cultivated, although it was estimated that up to 1.5 million acres were potentially cultivable. All cultivation depended on some kind of irrigation whether perennial, by wells, or seasonal, by using flood waters during certain periods of the year. The main crops were cotton, tobacco, vegetables, fruits and cereals; but although agriculture provided two thirds of all employment in South Yemen it produced only £7 million, less than 10 per cent out of a total GNP of £74 million. Throughout the British occupation there were only two development projects of any significance: both produced cotton; one in Abyan, the other in Lahej. The British introduced cotton into Abyan in 1940 as an insurance in case other sources were cut off by the war; and after 1947 production was raised to make up for what independent India began to retain. They provided an initial grant of £10,000, and at first 700 acres were placed under irrigation. In 1947 a Cotton Board was set up to manage the area, but although it purported to be controlled by the local producers it was in fact run by the local sultan and by the rulers, who controlled the country up-stream from which the flood waters came. In 1949–50 a cotton ginnery was built at Zinjibar, the capital of Abyan province, and by the mid 1960s over 50,000 acres had been irrigated. In 1957 a similar though smaller project was begun in Lahej, north of Aden, and by 1962 cotton alone made up 56 per cent of the Protectorates' exports.

Some livestock was raised; but the land was poor and this never provided much income; in 1961 there were estimated to be a million sheep and goats, 68,000 cattle and 80,000 camels in the hinterland, yet many of these were undernourished. All the skins and hides were processed abroad. Another 10,500 people were estimated to be employed in fishing, out of Aden, Mukalla and smaller ports; but there were only 170 boats with engines and a few hundred more with outboard motors. The majority of fishing boats were canoes and local round-bottomed craft called *sambuq*.[11] Oil might have become a major source of income; in the 1950s a subsidiary of the Iraq Petroleum Company carried out exploration in the Hadramaut, and in the 1960s a subsidiary of Standard Oil of Indiana was granted the same concession. Some oil was found, but the companies declared it unavailable in commercial quantities and said production would be uneconomical given the cost of transporting oil from the desert interior over the mountains to the sea. There was no doubt that the exploration drives were hampered by quarrels between the sultans of Quaiti and Kathiri, each of whom hoped to appropriate as much future income as possible; these disputes discouraged imperialist firms from going further although the failure to

177

discover large quantities soon after independence showed the problems were not only political.

The tribes of South Yemen were predominantly settled, with only a 10–15 percentage of nomads, and were mainly Sunni Moslems of the Shafei affiliation, like the inhabitants of the southern and coastal sections of North Yemen; like their northern fellow-Shafei they were distrustful of the Zeidi Imams, who longed to reunite Yemen under their rule. But there did exist a definite consciousness of a common Yemeni culture, exemplified in such things as chewing *qat* and the wearing of the *futa*, a kind of Yemeni kilt, by a sense of a past political unity, and structured by economic ties and the common movements of individuals and families within the greater Yemeni area. When Southern tribes wanted to resist the British they were often able to get support, military and financial, from the Imam.

Because there was no Imam in the South the local tribal leaders and the Sada had in some ways greater individual power than in the North; the strength of the sheikhs was confirmed by the series of direct treaties between these local rulers and the British. Sheikhs received not only recognition and a promise of support in times of crisis, but the money and guns to consolidate their position. Some of these tribal leaders were landowners; in nomadic times the land had been held collectively by the tribes but, with settlement, land was broken up into estates owned by tribal leaders and into small individual plots. In the state of Lahej the Sultan was the biggest landowner in the whole of South Yemen; 50,000 acres – one sixth of cultivated land – was owned by the sultans, while another 100,000 acres were owned by tribal chiefs. In the more remote parts of the country tribal chiefs were economically undistinguished, and just as wretchedly poor as the rest of the tribe. In Dathina and in parts of the Yafai area no rulers were acknowledged, perhaps partly due to remnants there of the primitive communist Qarmati belief. Most cultivators worked land that belonged to the whole tribe but to which they had a particular long-standing title. Throughout the area the sultans and sheikhs were flanked by the Sada; whereas in the North these putative descendants of Mohammad were Zeidi, in the South they were Shafei and in the absence of even a minimal state structure they performed a number of necessary social functions off which they lived and which they monopolized; they acted as lawyers interpreting the *shariah*, as money-lenders, as arbitrators in disputes and often but not necessarily as landowners. Some of these Seyyid families, such as the Jifri family from Yeshbum in the Aulaqi area or the Attas family from Hureidha in the Hadramaut, produced intellectuals who participated in the political struggles of the 1950s and 1960s, the former for the pro-Saudi South Arabian League, the latter for the revolutionary NLF.

The social organization of the Eastern Protectorate was distinct from that of the Western, and the consciousness there was as much of being a distinct entity, the Hadramaut, as of being part of a semi-historical greater Yemen.[12] The east was divided into the coastal towns, the greatest being Mukalla, and the fertile valley of the interior; in between lay the dry, windswept mountains known as the *jol*. In the interior, irrigation supported a subsistence agriculture of dates and cereals. Fish were brought from the coast over the *jol* in caravans and used as fertilizers and as fodder for animals; the control of transport between the coast and the interior, through ownership of camels and through taxation, was a source of revenue for some tribes. The Hadramaut had traditionally prospered on the incense trade, producing incense itself and acting as an entrepot area for incense coming from Dhofar farther to the east. In the Moslem Middle Ages many Hadrami families had emigrated as merchants or scholars to other parts of the Moslem world; Ibn Khaldun, the prominent Moslem social thinker born in Tunis around 1332, came from a family of Hadrami émigrés. Many Hadramis emigrated and traded in East Africa and the Indian Ocean; and in the twentieth century a Hadrami community of up to 300,000 worked as traders in Indonesia, and as property owners in Singapore. In the historical Hadramaut the income from foreign sales of incense had supported considerable building, and the long-standing

179

relationship of the area to the outside world gave it a greater international consciousness and stronger emphasis on education than the isolated hinterland of the western areas.

The influx of wealth from the East Indies in the twentieth century led to the building of many palaces up to eight storeys high in the towns of the interior like Tarim and Seiyyun, and cars and other luxury items were introduced in the 1930s. But the availability of wealth discordant with local productive forces had disruptive effects on the Hadrami economy; agriculture broke down as the population came to rely on imported rice rather than on local crops; and the increase in wealth exacerbated conflicts between tribes. The tall houses built in the valley were like the tower dwellings of medieval Italy – designed to impress in peacetime and to act as fortresses during civil war. In the 1930s factional conflict had escalated dangerously in parts of the Hadramaut, with some families having been stuck in their towers for decades and rivals poisoning each other's date trees with kerosene. The introduction of modern firearms accentuated the conflicts.

Although the British-directed peace reduced this conflict there was a new crisis in the Hadramaut when the Japanese invasion of the East Indies cut off the supplies of money on which the area had relied. In 1943 and 1946 there was famine in the Hadramaut. Later another crisis broke when camel-owners clashed with the government because trucks had begun to displace them in the transport business. An effort was made to revive local agriculture from its decline in the 1920s and after the war the remittances from the East Indies flowed again. But despite irrigation development after 1945 the Hadramaut's dependence on the income from abroad kept its prosperity precarious.

One area in the east distinct from the Hadramaut was the 20,000-square-mile Mahra area, between the Hadramaut and the Omani boundary. Formally ruled by the Sultan of Socotra, who remained on Socotra island, Mahra was the most impoverished area of all in South Yemen, with almost no agriculture and some minimal fishing and livestock rearing.[13] The British set up only a low-level administration in the area and were prepared to leave it alone as long as no other outside force appeared to be gaining ground there.

In comparison to British or French colonialism elsewhere, the dominant characteristic of colonialism in the South Yemeni hinterland was its restricted nature; economically and politically the British impinged only minimally. Their only motive was to prevent any force hostile to the base and the British presence from gaining a foothold in the area. The very state apparatus was skeletal – military control by plane, absence of any infrastructural or social service development till the final decade, manipulation of existing rulers as the main form of politics. Yet even this meagre colonial regime had its effects on the social system. The support for specific tribal leaders altered the balance of power within tribes and between tribes. The drift of peasants to Aden and foreign work encouraged some South Yemenis to liberate themselves from tribal ideology. And especially in the Hadramaut the introduction of money, and of motor transport, began to undermine the previously stable subsistence economy. This was the social and economic basis for the political upheavals that would sweep the old regime away.

The Federation of South Arabia

Until 1927 South Yemen was ruled from India, but in that year the hinterland was placed directly under the London administration, and Aden itself followed suit in 1937. The myth remained, however, that Aden was administered directly as a Colony with a Governor, while the hinterland was administered 'indirectly' through the two Protectorates. Until the 1950s the British were content to rule these different areas distinctly and not to manoeuvre them into any unified state. There was no mention of granting independence to South Yemen, and it was realized that colonial 'stability' gained from the fragmentation of the area.

This distinction between the *forms* of imperialist control reflected no substantive difference in the *degree of power* exercised by the British over Aden and the interior, but did reflect different political instruments and the different economic evolutions of the two zones. It was only in 1963 that the two were brought together. In Aden the first British reform came in 1947 when they set up a Legislative Council; half its members were *ex officio* and the other half were nominated by the Governor. It was a reflection of the dominant European merchant interests; in case of difficulty the Governor had control of the agenda and he was not bound by the decisions of the Council. In 1955 when Arab nationalism was already strong in the Middle East the British made a token gesture, allowing four out of the eighteen council seats to be contested in the election; but the only party to accept this token and participate was the Aden Association, the political expression of the pro-British merchants. No real attempt was made to democratize the government of Aden, and there was no move to Arabize the civil service. The Governor of Aden from 1950 to 1956, Tom Hickinbotham, was unequivocally opposed to any such concessions and believed that the presence of any opposition on the Council would lead to 'a deterioration in security'.[14] His memoirs state his belief about Aden that 'security will remain and be maintained as long as Great Britain remains great'.[15] This bland view of the situation was official British policy at the time, and was eloquently expressed by the then Minister with responsibility for the the colonies, Lord Lloyd, who visited Aden in May 1956. While gesturing toward the interests of the local people, or at least sections of them, Lloyd made it quite clear that Aden was now to play an important role in British imperial strategy:

There has been much speculation recently about the political future of the Colony of Aden. Such speculation, if unrelated to practical possibilities, is harmful to the commercial interests of the Colony upon which the prosperity and, indeed, the whole livelihood of the people depends; if carried to undue lengths it can easily divert into unfruitful channels energies which might be better exerted in the pursuit of reasonable aspirations ... I should like you to understand that for the forseeable future it would not be reasonable or sensible, or indeed in the interests of the Colony's inhabitants, for them to aspire to any aim beyond that of a considerable degree of internal self-government.

Therefore, whilst I have indicated the type of constitutional advance to which the people in this Colony may legitimately aspire, Her Majesty's Government wish to make it clear that the importance of Aden both strategically and economically within the Commonwealth is such that they cannot foresee the possibility of any fundamental relaxation of their responsibilities for the Colony.[16]

The British view of Aden in the mid-1950s reflected both the situation in the Middle East and the global realignment of British policies. In 1948 the British had left Palestine, up to then the major base area in the Middle East. They had built up the base in the Suez Canal Zone, but that had come under attack from Egyptian nationalists and had been abandoned, amid much protest from the Conservative party right, in 1954. After the disastrous invasion of Egypt in 1956 British defence policy was revised and found its new expression in the 1957 Defence White Paper. This laid emphasis on bases east of Suez and in East Africa and in 1960 Aden replaced Cyprus as the Headquarters of Middle East Command; the British backing of Kuwait in 1961 reinforced these views on Aden and when the British pulled out of their bases in East Africa at the end of 1963 more troops were deployed in Aden. The policies for the 1960s had been clearly laid down in the 1962 Defence White Paper, entitled *The Next Five Years.* This stated that Britain would continue to back the sultans and other rulers in South Yemen and in the Gulf and that the Aden base would be the *permanent* headquarters of this operation; together with the United Kingdom itself and Singapore, Aden was to be one of the three key points in Britain's global military deployment.[17]

As they wanted to retain Aden for these strategic and economic reasons, the British tried to mould a local political arrangement that would deflect liberal criticism and forge a regime of collaborationist Arab clients capable of holding down any nationalist threat. The formula was simple: to unite Aden and the hinterland in a federation so that the military base could remain in Aden while the hinterland provided the conservative political weight needed to protect British interests. The first discussions of a federation had taken place around 1950, but neither the

183

British nor the sultans were enthusiastic until they saw that the nationalist danger was growing. The anti-imperialist wave that shook the Arab world including Aden in 1956 after Suez, and the Egyptian and Soviet influence in North Yemen, frightened the imperialists and their clients: in February 1959 a 'Federation of Amirates of the South' was formed by six states from the Western Protectorate. Ten other states had joined by the end of 1961, and one more in June 1964, leaving only one of the seventeen western states outside; in the east the two major sultanates, the Quaiti and the Kathiri, stayed out hoping to find an economic base for a separate independence in oil.[18]

There were contradictions in the hinterland that impeded the formation of this federation. Rival tribal leaders were reluctant to work together, and larger states objected to formal equality with smaller ones. Some state leaders opposed the Federation out of a real or assumed nationalism, which led to a clash with the British. In 1958, for example, Sultan Ali Abdul Karim of Lahej was deposed by the British, who then coerced the family council there into appointing a more docile successor. Similar depositions took place elsewhere in South Yemen, as they did later in the Gulf (Abu Dhabi 1966, Oman 1970) when the British found the pliant myths of 'indirect rule' too restrictive. But the principal contradiction in the hinterland was neither between the rulers themselves nor between the rulers and the British, but between the rulers and the British on the one hand, and the South Yemeni people on the other. That contradiction, which came to destroy the Federation, exploded later. The most dangerous immediate problem the British faced was that of getting Aden into the Federation; and the Adeni bourgeois, whom the British wanted to use, were cautious about allying with the sheikhs of the interior.

A first move towards welding Aden to the hinterland, which coincided with the formation of the Federation in the interior, was a bogus liberalization of the Adeni election laws in January 1959. For the first time the elected members, of whom there were twelve, would outnumber the *ex officio* and nominated members, of whom there were respectively five and six. But the powers of the Legislative Council were not changed; and only 21,500 out of the total population of 180,000 could vote. All North Yemenis were excluded because they would have backed the nationalists. This gerrymander was made possible by allowing the vote only to those who were born in Aden or were British subjects or British-protected subjects who had lived in the colony for seven out of the past ten years. This enfranchised Yemenis from the South, all English residents, and the Indians and Somalis in Aden. But it disenfranchised all North Yemenis – over a third of the population. The nationalists boycotted the 1959 elections because these were restricted; and only 27 per cent of the eligible electorate took part, putting mainly pro-imperialists into the Council. But the British pushed on with their attempt to forge the Aden–tribal union. The wave of nationalist strikes that shook the Colony from 1958 to 1960 was temporarily crushed; and prolonged negotiations sought a constitution to satisfy Adeni merchants and the sheikhs. Nevertheless the British were only able to impose their policy by reverting to further uneasy manipulations. The original Legislative Council vote on 26 September 1962 took place with the majority of the *elected* members absent – that is to say, it was passed by the *ex officio* and nominated members (mainly British and South Asians) plus a few particularly submissive Adeni bourgeois, who did not even represent a majority of the people elected in 1959. In addition the haggling over the future took so long that the Council's life had to be extended beyond the statutory limit of January 1963 in order to 'pass' the final agreement, bringing into existence the new Federation of South Arabia.

Two features of the new Federation marked it out for defeat. It was an overtly British fabrication, dependent for its existence on the imperial power. British imperialism has often tried to use federations to bolster its residual imperial ambitions and weak local clients; in the West Indies, in the Central African Federation, in the Malaysian Federation these attempts were all defeated by the artificiality of the British administrative creations and their inability to resolve internal splits or defeat nationalist forces. In South Yemen the artificiality and dependence were clear; in the 1963 agreement Britain gave no date for independence, and reserved the right to remove Aden or any part of it from the Federation if this was considered necessary to Britain's global defence. The base was to remain and Britain was to maintain so-called 'security' for the foreseeable future. The Federation was also disastrously dependent on Britain financially. Aden was a free port, so there were no excise taxes to be collected there; in the interior the merger of the states had removed the tolls on which many sultans had relied. As has been shown, productive forces were undeveloped. The only available source of income, given the British failure to encourage economic change beneficial to the South Yemeni people, was the British government. The state apparatus of around 6,000 civil servants and a similar number of locally recruited military were entirely dependent on the British. British expenditure on development of the area had always been minimal.[19] Up to 1940 not a penny had been spent on the hinterland, and what followed was a mean trickle allocated to projects like cotton-growing which served Britain's imperial interests. Between 1946 and 1960 only £1·4 million was spent on hinterland development and even in the final period 1965–8 only £7 million was spent. Before 1939 the British had spent £100,000 a year on bribing hinterland chiefs, and after 1950 this went up to £800,000; but even in 1967, when the British departed, the country had only fourteen tar-macked miles of road outside Aden, three Yemeni doctors and 950 hospital beds. Educational facilities hardly existed outside Aden. In the final period of their occupation the British did make increasing payments to the Federal budget; but this was for so-called 'defence' – that is, political repression and stabilization. Between 1963–4 and 1967–8 military expenditure rose from £3·6 million to £13·9 million in an attempt to suppress nationalism.

The nationalist movement was the second weakness of the Federation, and ultimately destroyed it. From 1956 onwards demonstrations and strikes rocked British confidence and undermined the service economy. The British response from 1960 onwards was to attack the trades unions and disenfranchise much of the population. At the same time they hoped to use the apparently 'stable' hinterland to counterbalance the rebellious port of Aden. Neither policy succeeded. In Aden itself the political opposition grew in strength and received an additional boost from the revolution in North Yemen on 26 September 1962, a day after the bogus vote in the Adeni Legislative Council in favour of Aden joining the Federation. The clash escalated, until from 1965 to 1967 urban guerrilla war gripped the town. But what totally undermined the British plan was that the revolutionary movement also grew in the hinterland, attacking not only the British but also the sultans who were discredited for their subservience to the British.

The very Federation designed to use the 'stable' sultans to crush Aden was the structure that undermined their stability. In 1963–4 the outbreak of guerrilla war in the Radfan mountains signalled the start of the armed revolution. Then in 1967 the collapse of sultanic power in the hinterland destroyed the Federation. The NLF fought in Aden, had consolidated in the hinterland, 'unsophisticated' and 'simple' as the British liked to describe it, and were carried to power in a liberated South Yemen.

Notes

1. There are two rich sources of information on South Yemen which have been used extensively in this chapter. One is M. S. al-Habashi, *Aden*, Algiers, 1964; and the other is the British Naval Intelligence handbook *Western Arabia and the Red Sea*, London, 1946. The British deliberately discouraged study of South Yemen; but several Governors and High Commissioners have penned their apologias: Tom Hickinbotham, *Aden*, London, 1958; Charles Johnston, *The View From Steamer Point*, London, 1964; Kennedy Trevaskis, *Shades of Amber*, London, 1968; Humphrey Trevelyan, *The Middle East in Revolution*, London, 1970. The rising panic evident in these titles is itself a commentary on events. David Holden, *Farewell to Arabia*, London, 1966, has good descriptive chapters on the area, and Tom Little, *South Arabia*, London, 1968, gives a British account of the Federation and the nationalist struggle.

2. The hypocrisy of the British was such that they constantly railed at the Imam of Yemen or the Saudi leaders for 'bribing' and 'suborning' sheikhs, while they claimed they were perfectly entitled to 'assist' Britain's 'friends' in the tribal areas. On the one occasion when the sheikhs were in need of protection, during the Turkish advance on Aden in the First World War, the British abandoned them and fled to Aden.

3. Trevaskis, op. cit., gives an account of the early years of the Federation and of conditions in the hinterland. An account of one specific region is found in A. M. A. Maktari, *Water Rights and Irrigation Practices in Lahej*, New York, 1972.

4. Later, in the 1940s and 1950s, there were border clashes with North Yemenis and with Saudi-supported U S exploration teams interested in the Hadramaut.

5. The best account of this action is that of the envoy himself, Harold Ingrams, in *Arabia and the Isles*, London, 1966. See also Ingram's *A Report on the Economic and Political Condition of the Hadramaut*, London, 1937.

6. A key weapon in control of the interior was the use of air power. *From 1927 to 1957 Aden and the interior were under the control of the Royal Air Force, not the army as might have been expected*. The British first used air power to quell peasants in Iraq during the 1920 insurrection; and they used it extensively in Somalia and the 'North-west' frontier with Afghanistan. In 1928 they bombed Taiz in Yemen to terrorize the Yemeni government into submission. British apologetic works, e.g. Little, op. cit., pp. 40ff, are full of praise for this system of collective punishment. A world that has been shocked by the use of air power in Vietnam on a vastly greater scale might remember that it was the British who in the 1920s pioneered the use of unchallenged planes against colonial peoples.

7. The French communist novelist Paul Nizan, who lived in Aden in the 1920s, reflected, on seeing warships in Aden harbour on their way to protect European interests in China during 1926–7: 'Aden is a crossroads of several sea routes staked out by lighthouses and little islands bristling with cannon; it is one of the links in the long chain that maintains the profits of London businessmen around the world. A port of call full of murderous symbols, a companion piece to Gibraltar.' (*Aden, Arabie*, New York, 1968, p. 109.)

8. There was a constant deficit on foreign trade which grew from £7·3 million in 1955 to £34 million in 1966. It was covered by British funds and émigré remittances.

9. Total troop figures rose from a few hundred in the 1940s to over 17,000 in the mid 1960s.

10. These figures include the hinterland; but the only non-Adeni component is agriculture.

11. The most common fish are tunny, sardines, anchovies, kingfish and Indian mackerel.

12. On the Hadramaut see Ingrams, op. cit.; Freya Stark, *The Southern Gates of Arabia*, London, 1936; and an important analytic book, Abdalla S. Bujra, *The Politics of Stratification: A Study of Political Change in a South Arabian Town*, London, 1971.

13. The island of Socotra, 1,400 square miles, lies 150 miles off the tip of the East African horn. The population number around 12,000 and live off herding and fishing. Until the seventeenth century Socotra was, as a result

of Ethiopian influence, a Christian island. It has a lush climate, and its people are ethnically and linguistically similar to the people of Mahra and Dhofar.

14. Hickinbotham, op. cit., p. 39.

15. ibid., p. 25. The following excerpt from p. 111 of Hickinbotham's musings may illustrate his *Weltanschauung*:

'Progress throughout the area would have been more speedy and more spectacular if it had been possible to observe the old proverb in our dealings with some of the Rulers that "to spare the rod is to spoil the child". Children some of them were, and Teddy Boys were not lacking among their subjects, and while I agree that it is better whenever possible to lead children, there are times when even the most amiable child must be corrected in its own interest, and I have never faltered in my opinion that an ash plant, properly applied, is one of the few things that is effective in dealing with young thugs in this or any other country.' Elsewhere Hickinbotham tells us that hinterland Arabs are 'never familiar and never presume' (p. 3).

16. Little, op. cit., pp. 34–5.

17. Gillian King, see *Imperial Outpost – Aden*, London, 1964, in which the author discusses the strategic background to the Aden base. See also Phillip Darby, *British Defence Policy East of Suez 1947–1968*, London, 1973, Chapters 3 and 4.

18. The six original members of the Federation were: Dhala, Audhali, Upper Aulaqi sheikhdom, Beihan, Fadhli and Lower Yafai. Ten others joined by the end of 1961: Lahej, Lower Aulaqi, Aqrabi, Dathina, Wahidi, Haushabi, Alawi, Muflahi and Shuaibi. Only Wahidi was from the East. Upper Aulaqi sultanate joined in June 1964, leaving only Upper Yafai outside.

19. Apologists for British neglect tend to invoke the so-called 'British tax-payer', i.e. considerations of economy. Tens of millions of pounds were spent on grandiose imperial expansion in Aden in the early 1960s without anyone caring for the British tax-payer, who was then told it would have to be abandoned. There was subsequently a similar occurrence in the Gulf.

Chapter Seven
The Liberation Movement
1953–67

Pre-Nationalist Resistance and the First Political Groups

The history of South Yemeni opposition to the British begins with the history of British rule itself. When in 1838 the British first tried to occupy Aden they met with fierce resistance by 1,000 local warriors along fortified shores; and it was only with reinforcements from India and after three days of fighting that they managed to land. During the nineteenth and twentieth centuries tribes on several occasions resisted British expansion inland, but without success. They were usually led by sheikhs who were not prepared to wage all-out war, and who wanted to strengthen their bargaining position with a power whose rule they in the end accepted. They were often manipulated from North Yemen – by the Turks up to 1918, and then by the Imams. Moreover these tribal risings were usually limited to specific tribes and had no Yemeni orientation. They were waged without modern military technique or modern weapons. The ideology of this resistance was that of loyalty to a traditional order, one that offered no positive prospects for the people of the South and that rejected positive aspects of imperialist rule that later movements incorporated within their own programmes.

An anti-imperialist movement that went beyond traditional tribal resistance only arose once nationalism had become a force elsewhere in the colonial world and once South Yemen had become affected by capitalist change.[1] The places in which non-tribal political groups first arose were Aden and the Hadramaut, the two areas most connected to the outside world. But because they were anomalous islands within the pre-capitalist sea of South Yemen the movements that arose there reflected the interests of these areas in contradistinction to the rest of the South; they took the form of specifically Hadrami and Adeni

190

groups. Because they reflected the ideas of merchants and intellectuals, they opposed the political autocracy of the sheikhs and sultans, and the anti-capitalist economic power that these represented. But this was to seek to split off these areas from the rest of the South, since under British rule there was little prospect of general capitalist development of the whole area.

The first nationalists were Hadrami émigrés in Indonesia and Britain; the former were influenced by the Indonesian nationalism that grew in the 1920s and under the Japanese occupation; the latter were less militant, but absorbed ideas of organization and reform from the British Labour party. As early as 1927 a congress of returned Hadrami exiles met in Mukalla and appealed, without success, to the Quaiti and Kathiri sultans to convoke a national assembly and unify their two states. Similar meetings took place in Singapore; and in 1939 an Indonesian Hadrami Reform Committee appealed to the British with equally little success to recognize the unity and independence of the Hadramaut; after the Second World War destroyed the basis of Hadrami prosperity, the remittances from abroad, many more Hadramis returned and tried to pressure the sultans.

The Adeni political movement grew in the context of Aden's economic expansion after 1945. Cultural and political clubs were set up and the newly founded Arabic language press began the discussion of reforms – including ideas of nationalism, the status of women and the need for education. The Hadramis were influential in this; so too were the merchant exiles from North Yemen, the Free Yemenis. The influence of Arab nationalism as found elsewhere in the Middle East was less strong, and only became powerful in 1956. The Adeni Association, founded in 1950, was the first political group; it called for Aden for the Adenese, and for cooperation with the British in constitutional reform and eventual independence, possibly within the Commonwealth.[2] It was backed by Adeni merchants, some Arab but many of Indian origin, and was hostile to the sultans of the interior and to the Imam of North Yemen, whom it saw as inimical to merchant interests. Through its press, owned by the group's founder Mohammad Ali Luqman, it appealed to the British for concessions, and it contested the first elections to the Legislative Council, those of 1955.

A more radical perspective was opened up by the group around the magazine *an-Nahda* (*Renaissance*),[3] founded in 1952. It wanted to unify the South into a single state, breaking down the difference between Aden and the hinterland and abolishing the powers of the sultans; it also called for unification of the South with the North. Instead of traditional rule it demanded local assemblies with a federal capital in Aden. These demands went too far for the British, who opposed reforms that might undermine the powers of the sultans and were at that time in favour of keeping Aden and the hinterland separate. In 1953 *an-Nahda* was banned; but in 1954 the same group produced a new magazine entitled *al-Fajr* (*Dawn*). *Al-Fajr* likewise called for internal unity of the South and for the union of the South with the North; and it revealed the existence of a political group supporting these aims: the Union of the Sons of the South, later better known as the South Arabian League. This group included some Arab merchants in Aden who had ties with Yemen and the hinterland, as well as hinterland notables like the Seyyid al-Jifri family, who were rivals of the sultans. In 1955 the Union joined with other groups to oppose the elections the British were holding in Aden. Their coalition, the United Na ional Front, called for universal suffrage, a unitary state in the South, and British withdrawal. It demanded unity with the North, although it envisaged maintaining two separate Yemeni states until the Imams had been ousted. The trades unions backed the UNF and met hostility from the British, who were for the first time faced with an opposition that they could not quell and which directly challenged their position.[4]

Proletarian Opposition in Aden

The situation in South Yemen was transformed in the mid 1950s by the emergence of the Adeni trade union movement, the most militant of its kind the Arab world has yet seen. As tens of thousands of workers migrated to Aden from the southern hinterland and from the North, opposition developed on a totally new class basis. At the same time the victories of Arab nationalism in Egypt and the start of the war in Algeria generated for the first time a pan-Arab political consciousness in the South which linked with the spontaneous Yemeni nationalism already present. The working and living conditions of the newly arrived workers reinforced this radicalization; the disorientation experienced by peasants newly arrived in a large city was aggravated by inflation, a housing shortage and exploitation of migrant labour by middlemen. Anti-Yemeni discrimination, institutionalized by Britain in elections, in employment policies, in education and in residence permits (by harassment and deportations) also fuelled radical opposition.

At first the workers organized in clubs and groups of tribal origin; and this division was reinforced by the policy of Adeni firms, who often restricted employment to men of a specific tribe. The first ideological task of the trade union movement was therefore to organize workers on the basis of a national, non-tribal, identity as Yemenis and of a class identity as workers. Although unions had been legalized in Aden in 1942, the first union actually established was that of the eleven Europeans employed as pilots in the port. But in 1953 workers in the base formed the Forces Civilian Employees Association; and the employees of Aden Airways soon followed; by December 1956 twenty-one unions were registered with the government, with a declared membership of over 20,000 people. This growth was all the more striking since it proved impossible to mobilize the more than 15,000 Yemenis employed as domestic servants. Because there was next to no skilled Arab labour there were no craft unions, and union organization was based on individual plants; but these were in no sense 'company unions' in the sense of puppet unions set up by the employers and of a kind found elsewhere in British colonies. In March 1956 the Aden Trades Union Congress (in Arabic *al-Motammar al-Ummali*: The Workers' Congress) was founded; as its English title suggests, it was influenced by the British trades union movement, with whom it maintained close contacts. But the dynamic of the A T U C came above all from its role as an organizer of the workers around labour demands and a nationalist position.[5] In July 1956 Egypt nationalized the Suez Canal, and in October it was attacked by Britain, France and Israel. The Adeni working class, already militant in their own demands, rallied to the support of Nasserism in this the hour of its greatest triumph. The first strikes took place in March when in a five-week period over 7,000 men came out in thirty-three separate strikes. They were protesting at the dismissal of fellow workers by colonial employers and demanded changes in their working conditions. In June–July and again in August–December up to 18,000 workers came out on strike in a series of actions protesting local issues and in solidarity with Egypt. Such was the British fear of the nationalist masses in Aden that when the British navy captured the *Damietta*, an Egyptian warship, they were too frightened to bring the POWs to Aden and instead dumped them on Djibouti, the French colony across the Red Sea.

A Commission of Inquiry on labour conditions set up by the colonial authorities in 1956 made a predictable attack on the nationalist UNF whom it accused of injecting the strikes with nationalist politics. But the Commission also highlighted the specific local issues that had sparked the actions: the importation of foreign labour from other British colonies, which was a means of dividing workers in Aden, and the employment of workers through parasitic middlemen, the *moqaddam*. These issues were merely aspects of the general exploitation and repression of the recently created working class, which continued in new forms and became sharper as the trades union movement grew stronger. The British were at first taken by surprise, but as 1956 progressed they hoped to stave off the masses with concessions.[6] Only one firm, Luke Thomas, refused to negotiate and preferred to lose business rather than submit. As a result of these negotiations, and the Commission, the authorities introduced reforms; the working week was fixed at forty-eight hours, the minimum wage was raised and some employers agreed to paid holidays. For the first time a minimal social security system was initiated by a few employers.

The other side of the British response was an outburst of repression which led to the 1960 Labour Ordinance. In 1956 the first serious clashes took place in Aden between the masses and the authorities, and in August of that year the British banned SAL leader Mohammad Ali al-Jifri from the Colony. Further clashes occurred during the Suez invasion; but the closure of the Canal lowered the level of economic activity in Aden; and in 1957 the unions were less active. Many workers returned temporarily to their villages until business resumed. Proletarian action began again in 1958, once more combining specific labour demands with nationalist protest. The main provocation was the British importation into the Colony of non-Yemeni labour; immigrants from Somalia or India received civic rights, while workers from North Yemen were deprived of civic rights and frequently deported. Improvement in relations between North Yemen and Egypt and the influx of Russian weapons into the North also fuelled anti-British militancy, and the desire for Yemeni unity, however difficult this appeared. A series of strikes and bomb explosions in March 1958 led to the arrest on political charges – of 'subversive activity' – of the Assistant General Secretary of the ATUC and other officials and in May a state of emergency was declared. Aden was preparing for new elections, and, as in 1955, the blatant rigging of the electoral roll had crystallized political opposition by linking the condition and composition of the working class to the wider issues of national and political independence. The British were trying to crush the movement – after the May arrests the ATUC journal *al-Amel* (*The Worker*) was banned, only to reappear as *al-Ummal* (*The Workers*); but despite a ban on strikes the Port Trust Employees Union struck in January 1959 and were followed later in the year by the BP workers. The strike in the refinery paralysed the port for thirty-four days, and the authorities claimed there had been eighty-four separate strikes by the end of the year. In 1960 there was no let-up; after the BP employers, backed by the colonial authorities, refused to negotiate with the union a new strike by 2,000 workers paralysed the port for another ten weeks.[7]

195

This militancy proved too much for the imperialists. As long as the refinery was paralysed the port was losing £10,000 a day in lost services as ships stopped for fuel at Djibouti or elsewhere. In August 1960 a new Industrial Relations Ordinance was brought in to quell the unions. It imposed compulsory arbitration before any strike and set up an Industrial Court to settle disputes. The Ordinance was forced through the puppet legislature by the Minister of Labour, Hassan al-Bayoomi, and for a time Adeni merchant capital was reassured.

It was becoming ever more important to quell the workers, for political and strategic reasons, quite apart from the economic vulnerability of the port itself. The British had wanted to keep Aden separate from the hinterland – this was one reason why they had suppressed the *an-Nahda* group in 1953. But as their thinking on this changed, after 1956, they realized that they needed a Federation of the two. The prosperous port was necessary to them to subsidize the hinterland, while they needed the hinterland to ensure traditional political control of the port. This decision to join the sultans and the port provoked a split within the Adeni merchants: in 1958 the Aden Association divided. One group, led by Luqman and his son, re-emerged as the People's Constitutional Congress; it still advocated an Adeni separatism and was supported by the big commercial houses and by Adenis of non-Arab origin. The Luqman group did not deny the eventual possibility of federation with the hinterland, but insisted at that time on the great economic and political differences between the two zones. The other faction, led by Bayoomi, constituted the United National Party; and it was they who spearheaded the discussion that brought Aden into the Federation in 1962. They wanted economic support from Britain and a special status for Aden within the Federation; but they were aware of the political dangers if the two parts remained separated. Supporters of this faction included local businesses that stood to gain from British contracts under long-term economic and military development.

The proposed Federation provoked armed opposition in the hinterland itself. The Imam of North Yemen, backed by Egypt and the USSR, encouraged this development, since the Federation would weaken his influence in the South. The opposition of the 1950s was a precursor of the guerrilla war of the 1960s, and bequeathed a considerable experience; but it retained many traditional tribal forms of revolt. It was transitional, combining the old tribal resistance with influences from the nationalist movement. The Imam's conduct, too, exemplified this transitional quality; he undeniably aroused the Southern people with his calls for Yemeni unity and his attacks on the British; but he was aiming to extend his own autocracy and was in the end bought off by the British as his father had been before him.

The first rural outbreaks came in 1954–5 with a series of risings in which the British-created Tribal Levies, a mercenary armed force, were destroyed by mutinies. In 1957 tribesmen with arms and money from North Yemen struck out in Beihan and Yafai and harassed the British in a campaign more serious than any they had so far encountered:

The situation was far more menacing than any within our past experience. The rebels were more numerous, better armed, and more widely deployed; in Dhala and Fadhli they were threatening havoc to districts which had been administered and developed; in Radfan they controlled the only road to Dhala; and to the east of Abyan they straddled the only trade route linking Audhali and Dathina with Aden. And all this was happening at a time when British prestige was at its lowest following the fiasco of Suez . . .[8]

These risings, quite apart from their effects in the hinterland, put the whole Federation in question and also encouraged the opposition in Aden. But their leaders vacillated and the British succeeded in containing them. By 1959–60, once the Imam had been persuaded to quieten his backing and once he had fallen out with Egypt, this movement subsided. A more serious threat came from the SAL, the first nationalist party to have any influence in the hinterland. It was strongest in Fadhli and Lahej, and its main activists were the Sultan of Lahej and the al-Jifri brothers. In 1957–8 the chief administrator of Abyan in Fadhli state, Mohammad bin Aidrus, clashed with the British over the control of the irrigation system there, and managed to wage

197

a campaign of harassment for several months after expropriating £10,000 from the state treasury and swinging the Tribal Guards to his side. In Lahej the Sultan, whom the British had installed after deposing his homicidal brother in 1952, had started to militate against the Federation and had invited Mohammad Ali al-Jifri to Lahej after his expulsion from Aden in 1956. They published and plotted in Lahej against the Federation plan, but were limited by their class interests. They could not conceive of a struggle that would mobilize the population and they were opposed to Yemeni unity. In 1958 the British deposed the Sultan without difficulty, exiling him and the al-Jifri brothers to Cairo. There the latter were both supported by Egyptian patronage, until 1962–3 when they moved their base to Saudi Arabia and turned the S A L into an appendage of Saudi intervention.

If these activities in the hinterland merely bothered the imperialists they had the historical merit of preparing the ground for the emergence of a revolutionary guerrilla movement. But the initiative in the anti-imperialist struggle remained throughout the 1950s and up to 1963 in Aden. Just as the trades union movement had mobilized to oppose the 1955 and 1959 elections, so it now mobilized in opposition to the merger of Aden and the hinterland. The first general strike after the 1960 Labour Ordinance was held in July 1962 to protest the terms of the agreement reached in London between Bayoomi's U N P and the sultans; the British were too afraid of possible repercussions to try to stop the strike and the demonstrations. The A T U C had formed the new People's Socialist Party to replace the old U N F; and as the date for the Legislative Council's ratification of the agreement drew near the P S P campaign grew stronger.

On 24 September 1962 the Legislative Council was to meet to debate the London agreement. The Legislative Council building was a converted Methodist Chapel atop a hill in the Crater district of Aden, an ugly and alien symbol brooding uneasily over the predominantly Moslem town beneath. Soon after dawn on the twenty-fourth crowds began to gather at the foot of the hill and the whole of the Aden police force, plus three platoons of British infantry, had to ring the hill. As pressure built up the police attacked with tear gas and bullets to drive back the tens of thousands of workers who had encircled the building, outnumbering several times over the tiny electorate who had voted for the members up in the Assembly. One person was killed and five wounded in the subsequent demonstrating, but the debate proceeded in the Assembly. On 26 September 1962 the Aden Assembly voted through the deal, uniting Aden to the hinterland in the Federation. What no one in Aden knew was that in North Yemen on the very same night of 26 September a squad of tanks was rumbling into Sanaa to depose the Imam. On the morning of 27 September the people of South Yemen awoke to hear that the Republic had been proclaimed in the North. The Legislative Assembly vote had come only just in time. As the then British Governor of Aden was later to write: 'If the Yemeni revolution had come one day earlier, or the Legislative Council vote one day later, I feel pretty certain that the London Agreement would never have obtained the support of a majority of local members.'[9]

As it was the vote on the London Agreement was in several ways undemocratic: the electoral roll had included only 21,000 of the approximately 180,000 population – excluding all women and all Yemenis from the North; only 27 per cent of *that* electorate had voted in the 1959 election; and the majority of the elected members had walked out of the Assembly before the vote was taken. The agreement was ratified by a 'majority' made up of the nominated members plus the rump of those 'elected', and the British had prolonged the life of the Assembly for a year in order to ensure passage of the plan.

Already enraged by this kind of electoral manipulation, the Southern masses were further mobilized by news of the revolution in the North. On 28 September, a day after the news came through, the PSP organized a mass demonstration in support of the North. The meeting sent greetings to the YAR and called for the unification of the North and South, a goal now more practicable given the removal of the Imams. Four ATUC leaders of northern origin (including Mohsen al-Aini) went North to take up cabinet posts; thousands of other exiles, including many merchants, packed their belongings and set off back home. Although strikes were illegal the A T U C called for a strike on 22 October: the British hit back with deportations and refused to reverse these decisions in the face of further P S P protests. This led on 18–19 November to a general strike. As a result, Aden was now plunged into mass proletarian protest of the kind that had taken place in 1956 and 1958–60.

The British were quick to see the danger posed by the Y A R to their hold on the South. They responded by hardening their line in the South, and, after some indecision, by conspiring to destroy the Republic in the North. The British Labour Party and a number of Adeni ministers wanted to delay the merger of Aden and the hinterland because of the changes in the North; they argued, correctly as it turned out, that the forced merger was further weakened by the overthrow of the Imam. But the British government, with Colonial Minister Duncan Sandys in command, decided to continue, and the merger was ratified by the British parliament on 13 November. Aden then joined the Federation in January 1963 and Bayoomi cooperated with the British in a clampdown in the port. The British brought in as the new police chief Nigel Morris, former head of security in Malaya during the counter-revolution there.[10] Pro-Y A R activities were attacked. Al-Asnaj, the A T U C leader, and his deputy al-Qadi were imprisoned on trumped-up charges and opposition papers and banners were banned. Pictures of Nasser and Sallal, the Y A R President, were forbidden. In January 1963 the Adeni Legislative Council passed special anti-Y A R laws, making it an offence to serve in foreign armies and to assert that the South Arabian Federation was part of any other state. Since thousands of Yemenis had gone North in the first weeks to defend the Republic against the royalists, and since the basis of Yemeni unity was the joining of North and South, the import of these laws was blatant. In April when a U N Commission on Aden tried to enter the country the British simply refused to let them in.

The other side to British policy was their attack on the North.[11] Duncan Sandys was again the leader of this counter-offensive. Once it became clear, in mid October, that the royalists existed as a force, the British and their local clients decided to send support. Sharif Hussein, the ruler of Beihan, on the border of royalist-held territory, sent munitions into North Yemen and acted as the conduit for British and Saudi supplies. Yet, although the Conservative party right wing knew what to do, other sections of the British government were confused, and wanted to imitate the USA in granting the YAR recognition in order to lever out the Egyptians. It took the British until February 1963 to decide that they would not recognize the YAR, and to pull out the diplomatic representatives left over from the time of the Imam. From then onwards the British were committed to fighting the YAR as an extension of their colonial policy in the South.

The Creation of the National Liberation Front

At first the main support to the resistance in the South was the YAR's mere existence rather than concrete aid. As long as the British prevaricated the YAR was unsure what position to take on the South beyond general evocations of Yemeni unity. The YAR leaders calculated that to get British recognition would block off the flow of weapons and money through Beihan into the royalist areas, and for some months they refused to give full support to the movement in the South.[12] When interviewed on 31 October 1962 YAR President Sallal stated: 'we have no intention of getting involved' (in Aden), and although later in 1962 some YAR leaders attacked the British the definitive YAR position of support for the South only emerged *after* the UK had decided to back the royalists in February 1963. Here, as later, Nasserite and YAR support for the revolution in the South was conditional, and not one of full solidarity; as the struggle progressed the confusions and vacillations of Nasserite policy in the North were reproduced in a different way and with different results in, and in relation to, the South.

What changed the anti-British nationalist movement was the strategic development of the civil war in the North. After the Egyptian–YAR offensive of February–March 1963 the royalists reorganized, and by April were regaining territory; despite the uneasy cease-fire that lasted to September the Saudis and the British kept up their supplies to the royalists and in September fighting began again with a royalist offensive that lasted until early 1964. It was clear that flanking support in the South would be of great assistance to the hard-pressed Republic. If it succeeded in defeating the British or disrupting supplies through Beihan that would be excellent; if it did not it could still harass the British and strengthen the bargaining hand of the Nasserites in the event of a future negotiation. The difficulty was that the existing dominant political organizations were the PSP and the ATUC which were confined to Aden and were limited by experience and ideology to peaceful struggle and a political solution to the problems of the South. Effective as they could be through mass mobilization they could not hit Britain very hard in the hinterland, which was where the battle needed to be waged. The strategic needs and opportunities of the nationalist movement in the South had gone beyond the abilities of the PSP. It was in this situation that a new organization, the National Liberation Front, emerged to take the initiative.

The NLF was formed by militants from the South who had gone to the YAR after September 1962.[13] They included tribal leaders who supported the Republic, army officers who had been serving as mercenaries in Saudi Arabia and the Gulf, workers from Aden and the Gulf, intellectuals from the hinterland who had been studying in Aden, as well as militants who had rushed to the North in October and November to participate in the first battles for the defence of the Republic. The Front was what its name said – a nationalist front. Neither in its organization nor in its ideology did it in any way at this time approach the model of a socialist political party, nor did it claim to; and right into the post-independence period it was several times nearly destroyed by destructive factionalism. It differed from the NLF of South Vietnam, for example, in having a looser structure and no strong Marxist–Leninist group at its centre. It differed, too, from the Algerian FLN in that among other things it was forced into a violent clash with Nasserism that determined much of its later development, and in that after independence it officially proclaimed itself an adherent of Marxism-Leninism.

The most important component of the Front was the South Yemeni branch of the MAN, founded, like the branches in North Yemen and the Gulf, in the 1950s. All these branches reflected and participated in the general evolution of the MAN from enthusiastic Nasserism in the 1950s to a criticism of Nasserism and an organizational break with it in the late 1960s.[14] The South Yemeni MAN had its main base among workers and students who had migrated to Aden both from the North and from the Southern hinterland, in contrast to the ATUC, which was based predominantly among workers from the North. One of the first MAN cells in the South was in the important secondary school, Aden College, where the future Prime Minister Mohammad Ali Haitham, the future foreign Minister Ali al-Beedh, and many other future NLF militants were students. These workers and students who formed the MAN in Aden had kept their ties with the Southern hinterland – precisely what the ATUC lacked – and of the nine other smaller groups who went to make up the NLF many were the expressions of hinterland interests. The Yafai Reform Front and the Mahra Youth Organization speak for themselves, as does the Formation of the Tribes (*Tashkil al-Qabail*). The other groups were: the Nasserite Front, the Secret Organization of Free Officers and Soldiers (ex-Yemeni mercenaries in the Saudi army), the Revolutionary Organization of the Free Men of Occupied South Yemen, the Patriotic Front, the Adeni Revolutionary Vanguard and the Revolutionary Organization of the Youth of Occupied South Yemen.

These exiled militants began to meet and organize in 1963 and the first news of the NLF was broadcast from the North in June that year, as Nasser and Sallal were issuing a joint communiqué in Cairo in which they supported 'the right of the Yemeni people – in the Northern part of the country as well as in the Southern part – to freedom and unity'. According to statements from Sanaa tribesmen, sheikhs and army deserters from the South had offered to support the YAR by armed struggle in the South. An early June congress of these people had founded the NLF and on 16 June there had been a meeting of pro-YAR Southerners in the office of Qahtan ash-Shaabi, an adviser on South Yemen affairs in the YAR government. Ash-Shaabi had been in the SAL in the 1950s and came from Lahej; although he had not attended the founding conference, as an experienced handler of Arab diplomatic and exile politics he was to play a key role in the history of the NLF and in its relations with the Arab states. His cousin, Feisal ash-Shaabi, at that time a civil servant in Aden, was to play an equally important role, and through his paper *ath-Thawri* (*The Revolutionary*) published in Aden, he greeted the founding of the NLF. So little did the British know about what was going on that they did not even ban the organization until June 1965.

Although the NLF was divided along several lines from the start it presented a relatively unified political front to the world, and its political statements over the initial years show a distinct political stance. Though events would outstrip these statements, and even reveal them as unrepresentative of contemporary NLF opinion, they demonstrate nevertheless the two positions on which the NLF differed from previous groups and which were to be the basis of its victory: *armed struggle* and *mobilization in the hinterland*. An early political statement issued by Sanaa radio on 28 July 1963 announced the foundation of the NLF and provided a critique of existing political organizations:

Our aspiration in the occupied Yemeni South has now entered a phase which demands a fundamental change in the methods of the struggle to win complete independence and to overcome imperialism. The weakest point is the lack of coordination in the struggle in the Yemeni South as a whole. The major reason for this is the lack of a common command for national action in Aden and the Amirates. Another reason lies in the circumstance that the majority of the political organizations limit their activity to Aden. They meet together merely for common opposition; but some political rulers have not been able to raise themselves above narrow party interests to the level of national responsibility.[15]

Later statements amplified these initial positions. In May 1964, just when the British were trying to get the sultans and the Adeni politicians to London for another conference, the NLF issued a detailed text listing its political positions:

1. The sultans and ministers in the South do not represent the people and do not have the right to speak in its name. They are agents of imperialism and traitors to the just Southern cause.
2. The people of the South therefore recognize none of the treaties agreed to by them with England, and will not be bound by them.
3. The National Liberation Front for Occupied South Yemen, which is now waging armed struggle against the English occupation troops in Radfan, adh-Dhali and Haushabi, which represents all the forces of the struggling people of the South and which has always believed in armed struggle as the solution to the problems of the South, presents the following demands of the people: (a) guarantee of the right to self-determination; (b) complete evacuation of the South through the liquidation of all land, sea and air bases and the liberation of the country.
4. The Liberation Front states as spokesman of the people that it will never abandon these aims and that it will continue its struggle until victory.

A year later at the First Congress of NLF, held at Taiz on 22–25 June 1965, the NLF's ideology received its first full-scale public statement in the National Charter adopted there. Although written by a right-wing NLF leader, Salem Zain, and although later repudiated as incorrect, the Charter was more radical than the Nasserite Charter of the Arab Socialist Union, adopted in Egypt in 1963. It criticized the previous political leadership in the South for their policies, and hailed the September 1962 revolution in Yemen:

The revolution of 26 September in North Yemen, by destroying the yoke of servitude imposed on our people by the reactionary Hamid ad-Din family for several centuries, which paralysed its energy and maintained iti n a deplorable state of underdevelopment, backwardness and misery, created a base and a natural ally for the national revolutionary movement. This revolution aroused an indescribably militant enthusiasm among the popular masses of the South and this led numerous groups to rush to the aid of the revolution and to carry arms to protect it against the reactionary imperialist plots.

The revolution of 26 September created conditions that were eminently favourable to the revolutionary upsurge in the South and came at a critical moment, marked by the attempts of the reactionary imperialist forces to isolate the liberating nationalist forces, especially after the Syrian–Egyptian split of 1961. From the national point of view it allows the nationalist revolutionary forces embodied by the United Arab Republic to manifest their presence in the whole Arabian peninsula, a region that was previously closed to them. The presence of the UAR forces in Yemen, to defend the gains of the revolution, will upset the situation in the region and create the conditions favourable for revolutionary energy in the South, marked by the insurrection of 14 October 1963.

The Charter hailed the UAR in vibrant tones as the leader of Arab nationalism. But the MAN in North Yemen had already clashed with the Egyptians in 1964 when it became clear the Egyptians wanted to end the war and two months after the First Congress of the NLF Nasser and King Feisal of Saudi Arabia were to meet and reach a compromise which included, so the NLF stated, secret clauses on the South. Certain differences with Nasserism are already clear from the Charter. It denies any progressive role to the national bourgeoisie, and points out the need to transform the national revolution into a social one:

The armed insurrection which has swept the South as an expression of the will of our Arab people and as the fundamental means of popular resistance to the colonialist presences, its interests, its bases, and its institutions of exploitation, does not only aim to expel the colonialists from the area. This revolutionary movement is the expression of a global conception of life which aims basically at the radical transformation of the social reality created by colonialism through all its concepts, values and social relations, which are founded on exploitation and tyranny, and to determine the type of life to which our people aspires and the type of relations which it wants to see installed on the local, regional, national and international levels.

The Charter also insisted on the need to organize 'a popular revolutionary army according to modern norms so that it will be able to protect the gains and objectives of the revolution'. This was a clear rejection of the kind of mercenary tribal army on which opposition in the hinterland had historically depended;

but a 'popular revolutionary army' was also quite distinct from the kind of parasitic professional army on which Egyptian society was based and which was all too evident in North Yemen.

Guerrilla War in the Mountains

The pro-YAR anti-British military campaign began in the summer of 1963; in July there was fighting in Upper Yafai, led by pro-YAR sheikhs, and the authorities had to send in British troops. At the end of August a second revolt broke out in Haushabi. These two groups were led by sheikhs who rallied to the defence of the North but were outside the NLF. The NLF's campaign began officially in October in the mountains of Radfan in the southern part of the Amirate of Dhala, just to the east of the strategic road linking Aden to the Yemeni border near Qataba. The first attacks on 14 October are taken by the NLF as the date on which the nationalist revolution began, and Ali Antar, NLF military commander in Radfan, became head of the Front's whole military structure.

The population of the Radfan area numbered around 50,000 and were mainly peasants living off the annual crop of *dhura* (millet) and off their herds; they were officially under the control of the Amir of Dhala, but he was not an elected tribal ruler and the then Amir was an ardent supporter of the British; Dhala had been one of the founding members of the Federation in 1959. The area was of traditional strategic importance, being on the main lines to Yemen, and both the Turks and the Imams had in the past mobilized anti-British tribes there. In 1905 the area had been witness to a militant Islamic preacher, known as *al-Majnoun* (*the Madman*), who had called on the peasants to fight the irreligious British – a type of anti-imperialism frequent elsewhere in the Moslem world but rare in South Yemen. In the mid 1950s there had been fighting along the Dhala road, during the risings against the Federation. Even on the admission of the British the Radfanis 'made excellent guerrillas':

They were usually good natural shots with wonderful powers of observation; they thus made fine snipers, for they knew just where to look for targets. They could conceal themselves perfectly, and also used to place marks in the ground, so as to know the range exactly. Being accustomed to carrying out lightning raids and ambushes, they could move far and fast across the mountains and were thus an elusive enemy. They were also extremely courageous, as was shown by their capacity to fight on in the face of heavy artillery and air attack.[16]

For the first three months of the campaign, up to December 1963, they were able to block the road to Dhala; and it was only in January 1964 that the first British attempt was made to dislodge them. A force of the Federal Reserve Army, with British officers and RAF support, launched a campaign entitled 'Operation Nutcracker'. According to the British Commander the aim was 'to carry out a demonstration of force in the area of Radfan, with a view to compelling the withdrawal from the area of twelve named dissidents, and convincing the tribesmen that the Government had the ability and will to enter Radfan as and when it felt inclined'.[17]

'Nutcracker' was a failure. The British were constrained internally by the fact that they doubted the loyalty of much of their mercenary FRA forces, and were afraid to commit too many of them in too major an operation. Another problem was the absence of any information about the forces opposed to them. 'A major problem (which was to recur throughout the campaign) was the lack of any specific reliable *intelligence* about the enemy – where they were, what their organization was, what their aims or objectives might be, or indeed, who they were.'[18] The major weakness in British strategy, and one which was to mark all their subsequent campaigns, was that they did not realize they were up against a new type of enemy with a new kind of strategy. It was always possible for the British, given sufficient troop concentrations and air support, to penetrate a specific area. The aim of the guerrilla was not primarily to *hold* territory. They certainly aimed to inflict as high a cost as possible on imperialist troops wanting to penetrate the mountains, but they were more concerned to harass the enemy, overextend him and weaken him politically.

Federal troops were successfully installed in two Radfan valleys in January, in Wadi Rabwa and Wadi Taym; but these were isolated garrisons, supplied from the air, and they came under increasingly heavy guerrilla attacks. In March they were withdrawn, and the British decided to go ahead with a more extensive plan, using British troops and coercing the population of Radfan to flee from their areas. In the same month there were clashes along the border of Beihan and the RAF had bombed the YAR town of Harib; the royalists were in retreat and it was essential to ensure the safety of their supply lines. The second Radfan offensive was then launched. Its political aim was to prevent the revolt from spreading, to 'reassert our authority' and to stop attacks on the Dhala road. The military aim was vaguely defined as 'to end the operations of dissidents in the defined area'.

Originally this second Radfan offensive was designed to last three weeks and to consist of a helicopter-borne assault into the Radfani interior; but it became clear that the British had no intelligence and did not know where it might be safe to land; and the plan was scrapped. A second overland attack came on 30 April; but the NLF ambushed the British troops, members of the counter-insurgency Special Air Services group, and this advance was also blocked. The British then decided they needed more troops: 2,000 men were flown out from England, amid much patriotic noise, and a new advance got under way in May, this time aiming to intimidate the Radfanis into submission, and provoke them into a head-on fight in order to inflict heavy casualties. Although one British writer later complained that they only had a 6:1 advantage over the guerrillas instead of the 10:1 advantage normally prescribed for counter-insurgency operations,[19] the British were finally able to seize certain points within the Radfan mountains, culminating in the capture of the mountain peak of Jabal Horria on 11 June.

The counter-insurgency campaign illustrated developments in British military tactics that were later seen more dramatically in Dhofar. The Radfan campaign was the first that British troops had fought in mountain conditions since the war to crush the Korean revolution in 1950–53. It was the first time the British in the Middle East had used helicopters in tactical assaults of this kind. It was also the first time the Centurion 105 tanks had been used in battle – the next time they were used in the Middle East was by the Israelis in 1967. Of equal importance, and relevant both to their later Gulf policy and to US policy in Vietnam, is that the imperialists were caught between using the local puppet troops, who were unreliable, and using their own troops, which exposed the political nature of the war.

The most important counter-insurgency aspect of the war was the British attack on the civilian population, again repeated in Dhofar. 'Denying an area to the enemy' became a disguise for driving out the whole population. Air control was traditionally part of British policy and they decided in April 1964 to prevent the Radfanis from sowing their spring crop when the early rains came in May. This crop was the economic basis for the region. In their assault the British drove them out, using 1,000-pound bombs to destroy villages and fields. The British terrorized the population by dropping leaflets telling them to clear out, and then coming in and blasting the area. Tens of thousands of peasants had to flee to North Yemen. The British made no attempt to conceal this, describing in bland tones what they were trying to do.

Under 'proscription' the inhabitants all had to leave their homes and move out of the area until further notice, a hardship which it was hoped would persuade them of the foolishness of continuing to support the rebels.[20]

When questioned in the London Parliament, the British Minister of Defence was even more explicit about what they were trying to do:

Mr Warbey asked the Secretary of State for Defence for what reasons he authorized the burning of food stocks in Radfan villages and the expulsion of the tribesmen and their families from the lands just prior to the sowing season. Mr Thorneycroft: 'We are dealing with rebels, armed, equipped and incited from the Yemen. We can and do use military action in certain areas, but in others it is better to deny the area to them. It is inevitable that crops should suffer and food stocks be destroyed in the process of excluding the rebels from their settled area. We shall, of course, ensure that when these people submit to authority, they will not go short of food.[21]

When some press reports criticized this the lesson which the British drew was that when attacking the civilian population there should be no one around to see it. Just as later, with the cases of brutality in Aden, the Colonial authorities flatly refused to admit that they could be at fault. But they realized that world-wide criticism did not do any good. The British High Commissioner in Aden reflected that 'it was the publicity which did the damage'.[22] Again the lesson for Dhofar was obvious: keep it quiet.

The British campaign had taken six months, instead of the quick operation originally planned with 'Nutcracker'. Even the big offensive with British troops had lasted three months, instead of the planned three weeks, and had only then got under way when an extra 2,000 troops had been brought in to join the original 1,000. The British all along misunderstood the situation, thinking they were up against an old-style tribal resistance that could be frightened and shamed into submission. They did not realize that their enemy was quite different, had a correct grasp of the relations involved, and saw the Radfan movement in terms of wider political and military strategy. Mere penetration of Radfan valleys and the establishment of small garrisons on the sides of hills was not going to stop the N L F. The rapid collapse of the hinterland sultans and amirs in the summer of 1967 (see p. 230) came as a surprise to the British; yet it had been prepared over nearly four years of N L F activity, by the combination of military and political struggle that began in Radfan in October 1963.

Guerrilla War in Aden

Through Radfan the N L F had initiated the armed revolution in the South. It enabled them to demonstrate the possibility of guerrilla action, and to escalate the anti-British struggle to a new stage. The campaign in the countryside was not only of concrete assistance to the YAR, but also exposed the British in the South and undermined the political hold of the sultans in the hinterland. From Radfan, the struggle spread to other areas. By September 1964 there were four distinct areas of NLF guerrilla activity in Radfan, adh-Dhali, along the 'central Front' of Dathina-Audhali-Fadhli, and in Haushabi. In none of these was there a militarily contested liberated area, but the colonial state had been weak here and was unable to prevent the guerrilla operations from continuing, or to prevent the NLF from building its political organization. The complete collapse of the state and of the sultans in the mountains in the summer of 1967 was the fruit of these four years of work in the hinterland. British policy had been one of using the 'stable' tribal areas to tranquillize the militant workers of Aden. Suddenly the rural areas were aflame and acting as a catalyst on the town.

The NLF had two fundamental aims: to force the British to withdraw and abandon the base, and to undermine the new Federal state. It was obvious that once the armed struggle had got under way in the hinterland it had to move to Aden itself. There had been bombing and shooting incidents during the strikes of the 1950s, and in December 1963 a PSP cell within Aden Airways, including Khalifa Abdullah Hassan al-Khalifa, had tried to assassinate the High Commissioner Trevaskis while he was on the airport tarmac about to embark for England. But when the NLF launched its urban guerrilla war in August 1964 this was distinct from these previous military incidents in the town: it formed part of a struggle in both town *and* country, and it saw the use of urban guerrilla actions within the context of a wider politico-military strategy. The attacks on British troops and installations, the assassination of British officials and of their South Yemeni agents, were the military means of carrying this strategy to fruition. The British response to the armed struggle was at once stubborn and short-sighted. They knew nothing about the enemy, could not find out, and tried at each stage to save what they could. In June–July 1964 there was yet another conference in London at which for the first time a date was set for independence – 1968. But the London authorities still clung to their determination to maintain the base after then;

the final communiqué avoided demands for universal suffrage by saying that there would be 'direct elections as and when practicable'. In October 1964 new elections in Aden were held – after being postponed to enable the British to force through the merger. The nationalists had complained that the electoral roll in 1959 had been discriminatory, by excluding North Yemenis while including migrant labour from Somalia and southern Asia. The British response to the demand that the roll be made broader was to make it narrower: from 21,000 in 1959 it was now lowered to 9,000, while the population over the same period had risen from around 180,000 to around 220,000. It was not surprising that the P S P and the N L F called on Adenis to boycott the polls.[23]

The day before the Aden elections the British had had their own elections and the new Labour government had come into power. As had happened on previous occasions in British history the advent of the social-democratic party to power had encouraged illusions of radical reform both at home and abroad. In the case of Aden it took a few months before it was clear that the new British regime was as chauvinist as the old, although more aware of objective difficulties and more able to put on a conciliatory face. The new Labour Ministers stated openly that they intended to support the Federation and to hold the base; but in spite of this hopes in Aden remained high. In early December Colonial Minister Greenwood flew to Aden to try and soften the colonial regime and split the nationalist forces. The South Arabian old-timer Trevaskis was replaced as High Commissioner by Sir Richard Turnbull, who had been one of the leaders of the anti-guerrilla operations in Kenya. The Labour Minister also urged the Federal ministers to agree to a unitary state, in which their own power would be less.[24] In March 1965 the British went a stage further and appointed a right-wing nationalist, Abdul Makawi, as Aden's Prime Minister. Makawi was an agile politician who had joined up with the P S P. The British hoped that through him they could get the 'moderate' wing of the nationalist movement into discussions with the Federal ministers – hence the concession of making the state a unitary one. But the situation was past repair: caught between the intransigence of the British

213

who insisted on backing the Federation, and the militancy of the nationalist movement, Makawi had no role to play, and in September 1965 Turnbull dismissed him and suspended the Aden constitution, imposing direct rule.

The British and their clients were now more isolated than ever, and it was not long before the Federal ministers were struck by another blow as the Labour regime tried to salvage the situation. In February 1966, without any warning, the British announced in their Defence White Paper that they were to abandon the base: 'South Arabia is due to become independent in 1968, and we do not think it appropriate that we should maintain defence facilities there after that happens. We therefore intend to withdraw our forces from the Aden base at that time.' The sultans and Amirs who had sided with imperialism for decades on the assumption that British troops would protect them were now to be left on their own. The Conservatives in Britain, with Duncan Sandys leading the charge, were outraged at this 'betrayal'. But for South Yemen it was excellent. It was the traitors who had now been betrayed. The British had come to realize that the base was uneconomical and redundant in the context of a global military retrenchment; but they still wanted to preserve the Federal government, because of their othe₁ interests in the Gulf. As was later to be proven, a militant South Yemen would threaten the oil interests in the Gulf. So although they intended to leave they still wanted to hand over to a 'responsible' government; and they remained in South Yemen with 17,000 troops for another twenty-one months, killing and being killed to try to save their puppet Federation from collapse.

British figures show a steady rise in guerrilla actions in Aden from 1964 onwards: from 36 in 1964, to 286 in 1965, to 510 in 1966 and up to around 2,900 by the end of October 1967.[25] The counter-insurgency operation in Aden town followed standard repressive lines, of the kind prefigured in the towns of Cyprus and later to be developed to a much higher degree in Belfast and Derry. However they could not win for the simple reason that only a minority of people in South Yemen wanted them to stay, and, once they had said they would not keep the base, even this narrow support fell apart. Their 'internal security' operations centred on inspection and raids. It was relatively easy to control Crater since it could only be entered through narrow passes, but Sheikh Othman and Maala were more difficult, and the populated areas were even less easy to insulate than the Bogside and the Falls Road in northern Ireland. An indication of the low level of success of the British can be gained from the experience of one regiment: operating in Crater between February and September 1965 it searched 35,000 Arabs and 8,000 vehicles for a total yield of twelve grenades, six pistols, and some oddments.[26] It was clearly impossible to control the flow of weapons. In direct contrast to India, which the British tried to keep 'clean' of weapons, the Aden authorities had in the past bought the loyalty of sheikhs by giving them presents of weapons. The hills were full of them. In addition the YAR provided a plentiful supply. Women played a supporting role by smuggling arms in; camels, cars, and fishing vessels were also used. The NLF penetration of the Federal Army and of the police meant that they could bring in material in Federal military vehicles as well as get supplies from British stores. When the British tried to win the support of the local army and police by giving them more responsibilities, including inspection, this opened up a further breach in the system.

Torture: Brutality and In-depth Interrogation

As in Radfan the British were faced with the solid hostility of the masses. The 'total lack of any information from the local populace'[27] was the subject of much lamentation by the British, who ascribed it to 'nationalist intimidation'. By 1966 the whole of the Arab Special Branch had been assassinated. The only way they could get information was through interrogation, which from 1964 was carried out at the Joint Interrogation Centre at Fort Morbut, in the Tawahi military complex. 'Suspects'– that is, anyone the British army happened to decide to seize on – were taken there before being thrown into al-Mansoura prison or being deported to North Yemen as 'undesirables'. Under the state of emergency proclaimed in December 1963 and the imposition of direct rule in September 1965 the British were enabled to arrest, hold and mistreat. As early as January 1965 the pro-British Adeni Minister of Security, Hussein Ali Bayoomi, admitted that he knew of cases of subjects being tortured, and reports of brutality increased as the months went by. As in Northern Ireland it was in the interrogation centre (Fort Morbut/Hollywood Barracks) that the brutality took place and before the detainees were sent on to the regular prisons (al-Mansoura/Crumlin Road).

One British soldier who served in Aden in 1964 and 1965 later described what he had observed while working in the Joint Message Centre, a communications office within the Fort Morbut military complex, about twenty yards from the Joint Interrogation Centre. He had occasion to notice what was happening both while doing patrol duties in the area and because the Corporals' Club where he spent his evening overlooked the Joint Interrogation Centre.

Nearly every night after the state of emergency was declared and after a lot of suspects were being taken in, we used to hear, sitting in our Corporals' Club drinking, a lot of screaming and shouting; really disturbing screaming, as if it was associated with someone being hurt. This came from the Interrogation Centre and it was a common thing for us to just laugh and joke about it. 'There's another cunt getting fucking done in.' Then this would be supported in the morning, I can remember one particular guy from the . . . Regiment – who was a boxer for them. And he used to come in and boast in the morning. He used to come and say, 'Yeah, we thumped this wog last night and he's really screaming.' And he'd just boast about it and brag about it as if he'd done a great job.

On one occasion this soldier witnessed an incident which he later detailed in a letter sent to the *Sunday Times*.

I was in Fort Morbut on guard duty. At about mid-afternoon I heard screaming coming from the direction of the interrogation centre. Through our Guard Room window I watched three soldiers from a famous infantry regiment in — drag out an Adeni detainee into the exercise yard. There was blood coming from the man's mouth and he was dressed only in a loin cloth round his waist. The three soldiers, standing about five yards apart began, in turn, to hit the Adeni. The first soldier was using a five-foot-long broom handle and beating the man about the head and prodding him in his midriff and genitals. He was then passed to the second soldier who hit him with a tin mug commonly used by the Infantry. The third used his fists. The unfortunate wretch fell unconscious twice. He was then revived with a fire hose only to be beaten again. This was the only act of brutality I witnessed but you can be assured many more took place.[28]

The British handled this issue in their usual manner. One response was a prior self-righteousness which enabled them to dismiss all accusations as slander. ' . . . Any charges made by our enemies (and regrettably by some of our own countrymen) that the Security Forces resorted to unwarranted force while keeping the peace in Aden, are totally unjustified and false'.[29] To maintain this position they refused to allow foreign observers to interview detainees in al-Mansoura: the International Red Cross were refused in 1965 and 1966 and an observer from Amnesty International was similarly blocked. When the latter produced a report in September 1966 detailing criticism of the British, a wave of chauvinist protest broke in the British legislature and press, just as in 1971 when Amnesty International published an analogous report on Northern Ireland. In both these cases the British government replied by appointing inquiries to be conducted by men of their own choosing (Bowen/Compton) and by deflecting criticism with an official smoke screen. The Bowen Commission which reported on Aden did find that there had been 'irregularities' and quoted reports from medical officers at al-Mansoura specifying damage (e.g. pierced eardrums) found on detainees coming from the Joint Interrogation Centre. But by the time the report had appeared the public furore had died down and the British were able to ride the criticism relatively unscathed.[30]

There was another more subtle reason why the use of torture in South Yemen was not revealed. Brutality of the kind mentioned so far is only one kind of torture; in 'modernized' police forces 'traditional' techniques such as beating are being displaced by more scientific methods – either the use of more precise instruments (most noticeably electrodes and the injection of drugs) or the use of psychological disorientation techniques. The purpose of the latter is to break the victim down by destroying resistance and by encouraging loss of awareness of the outside world. These techniques were used in Aden but this use was concealed at the time because the British Army, the Yemeni victims and the protesting international organizations all, for different reasons, concentrated on debating the use of the 'traditional' methods. However, following the use of disorientation techniques in Northern Ireland in 1971 an official British investigation confirmed the use by the British Army special interrogation units of techniques such as 'wall-standing, hooding, noise, bread and water diet and deprivation of sleep'. It went on:

They have been developed since the War to deal with a number of situations involving internal security. Some or all have played an important part in counter-insurgency operations in Palestine, Malaya, Kenya and Cyprus and more recently in the British Cameroons (1960–61), Brunei (1963), British Guiana (1964), Aden (1964–7), Borneo/Malaysia (1965–6), the Persian Gulf (1970–71) and in Northern Ireland (1971).[31]

The minority report by Lord Gardiner, attached to this investigation, expanded on the question. The techniques, it stated, 'had been used in Aden, although, surprisingly, it does not appear from the report of Mr Roderic Bowen Q.C. (Cmnd. 3165 of 1966) that he ever discovered that these interrogation procedures were used there'. The minority report also states that '. . . the procedures are illegal by the law of England and the law of Northern Ireland. We have seen the Constitution of Aden and the relevant Statutory Instruments and Regulations relating to Aden and the same applies to Aden law.' The perpetrators of both kinds of torture – 'traditional' beating and 'modern' disorientation – were never brought to justice. The use of the former was concealed by an official whitewash; the use of the latter escaped attention mainly because it left few signs, and because those concerned were culturally predisposed to pay attention only to the more spectacular (and probably inefficient) forms of brutality. The reason the British Army used the more antiquated form of torture in addition to the disorientation techniques was probably that there was a shortage of skilled interrogators when the large-scale torture of 'suspects' began in 1965.

FLOSY and the Nasserite Regime

The nationalist organization developed against this background of imperialist retreat and rising mass militancy. In the last two years the movement was split between two rivals – the NLF, and the less militant FLOSY, which was led by al-Asnaj and Makawi. Al-Asnaj's PSP at first opposed the armed struggle launched by the NLF and for two years, up till the middle of 1965 and the break with the British Labour Party, al-Asnaj denounced those who wanted to turn Aden into 'a second Congo'. He remained an advocate of the peaceful road, and criticized the PSP minority group led by Khalifa who had nearly succeeded in assassinating the High Commissioner at Aden airport in December 1963. He went to London in June 1964 for the Lancaster House constitutional conference, although he was not able to attend the sessions; and he used this opportunity to renew his contacts with the Labour party. When Labour was elected in October 1964 al-Asnaj saw his chance. The right-wing turn of the PSP after 1962 had won to it many Adenis who, like Makawi, had previously thought it too militant; and since the British were in retreat it was also obvious to even the most backward political leaders in the South that they ought to change sides. It was only late in 1965, after all his reformist efforts had failed, that al-Asnaj was prepared to support armed struggle. Right up until his final defeat in November 1967 he saw it as a secondary adjunct to his political campaign which he continued to wage through contacts with the Federal ministers, appeals to the UN[32] and machinations with the Egyptians.

This vacillation on the question of revolutionary struggle undermined the PSP's hold on the Adeni working class. However confused its leadership had been, up to 1962 it had mobilized and led the people in a series of important struggles. Its general loyalty to Nasserism was an adequate basis for political action in an era when Nasserism had no direct role in the Yemens, and when Arab nationalism was at the zenith of its success. As the limits of Nasserism became clearer, and especially so in North Yemen, this PSP stand became weaker. And it was made more so by the fact that the PSP continued to rely for its victory on winning Egyptian backing: it counted as much on the Nasserite apparatus in the North as it did on the masses in the South. The NLF, by contrast, while allying with and using the Nasserite apparatus, relied primarily on the armed struggle in the South.

The NLF itself underwent a gradual radicalization after 1963, as a new group of militants, known as the 'secondary leadership', emerged in the struggle. A number of factors led to this. The development of an armed struggle in the mountains and in Aden exposed the limits of previous nationalist thought. It had forced the militants to develop their theoretical understanding and study the literature of Marxists (Mao, the Vietnamese) who had experienced |these problems before. The technical fact that the leading cadres had to spend long periods hiding in Aden enabled them to study and develop. The gradual cooling of Egyptian enthusiasm and the vagaries of Nasserite control also forced the cadres to develop theories of political, military and financial self-reliance. In addition to these specific factors, radicalization of the MAN throughout the Arab world, and the international political climate in the mid 1960s (rise of the Vietnamese struggle, the great proletarian cultural revolution in China, the prestige of Cuba) reinforced this trend. The secret visit to China by a group of cadres early in 1967 was also a source of inspiration.

The radicalization of the NLF was greatly encouraged politically by the small communist group operating in Aden, the Popular Democratic Union. The PDU had always supported armed struggle, and its ideological and organizational experience was at the disposal of the young NLF cadres. It was led by Abdullah Badheeb an ATUC founder. The PDU trades union militants cooperated with the NLF, thus provoking the bitter hatred of FLOSY; in 1966 FLOSY assassins killed the leading PDU trades unionist, Abdullah Abd al Majid Salafi, as he was leaving his home for work; and in January 1967 they blew up the PDU press because the communist paper, *al-Amal* (*Labour*), had criticized FLOSY policies.

The first members to be dropped from the NLF comprised a number of tribal leaders who had joined the front in 1963. They were expelled for having a mercenary attitude to the struggle – not unlike that of some republican sheikhs in the North. After being excluded they remained in Taiz and were occasionally used by the Nasserites for diversionary initiatives. The major division between the leadership and the militant cadres opened up in 1964–5. The NLF remained tied to the pan-Arab MAN up to 1968 and in 1964 it sent representatives to an important MAN congress in Beirut. The conference divided between a rightist group led by George Habbash and Hani al-Hindi and a more militant group, critical of Nasserism, led by Mohsen Ibrahim. The NLF delegation, headed by Qahtan ash-Shaabi, sided with Habbash; but the MAN delegation from the YAR sided with the left wing in their criticism of Nasser; and in this they were later backed by the secondary NLF cadres who were unrepresented at the conference.

The NLF division was based on questions of ideology and of organization: the former included the party's relation to Nasserism, and the question of Marxism, which the secondary cadres had begun to study; the organizational question concerned relations with the Egyptians, that between the external leaders in Taiz and Cairo and the cadres inside the South, and the question of what bond there was to be between the NLF and the people. Qahtan ash-Shaabi and his group had a clear idea of what they wanted: a relatively close relation to Nasserite ideology and to the Nasserite apparatus, strongly authoritarian and paternalistic relations within the NLF and a mobilizing relation to the masses, who were nevertheless not to be given too much power. This policy deliberately tried to keep the internal cadres ignorant of what was happening outside.

The First Congress, held in Taiz in June 1965, was dominated by this Nasserite group. The eight-man Politburo elected by the Congress reflected their control; likewise the Charter adopted at the conference. Yet two months later, after Nasser's Jiddah meeting with Saudi King Feisal, it became clear that the Egyptians wanted to play down the struggle in the South; a concession they could make to the Saudis was that the Nasserites in the South would agree to a compromise with the Federal ministers and the British. The Jiddah agreement was not carried out at the appointed time – it broke down in the North – and the Egyptian plan for the South accordingly did not take shape; but the Nasserites wanted to unify the different South Yemen organizations, to reassert their control over the struggle. As early as July 1964, on his return from lobbying Harold Wilson in London, al-Asnaj held merger discussions in Cairo, attended by the PSP and the SAL; but the NLF refused to attend. In March 1965 a second PSP–SAL conference was held in Cairo, where the Kuwaitis were offering £80,000 if the groups could unite. But despite Egyptian pressure the NLF would not go along with this – Qahtan was afraid of losing his autonomy. The NLF remained apart when the PSP and the SAL merged in May 1965 to form OLOS – the Organization for the Liberation of the Occupied South (*Monadhamat Tahrir al-Junoub al-Muhtall*).

OLOS was not a viable guerrilla organization. It had been set up as a rival to the NLF and had little of the latter's mass support, especially in the countryside. The class forces supporting it comprised the anti-British sultans and Sada in the hinterland and the nationalist bourgeois and some of the unions in Aden. It depended for its survival on Egyptian money and arms, and it was founded at a time when the other extension of the PSP, Makawi, had been appointed Prime Minister of Aden. The NLF base inside the country knew this, and insisted that OLOS was a creation of the Nasserite regime and not of the South Yemeni masses. Meanwhile Asnaj's old base inside Aden was falling away. In the trades unions a new grouping headed by the oil worker's union, and including workers in the Coca Cola factory and in some other manufacturing plants, were backing the NLF. The oil workers were led by Mahmud Ushaish, the future Economics Minister. An NLF Arab women's association was for the first time organizing women, and female students, bringing them out of the homes in which they were trapped, and encouraging them to take up an autonomous political role within the struggle.[33] The NLF had strong organizations in the secondary and primary schools and in the mercenary army and police. These groups were calling explicitly for a 'proletarian' politics by late 1965, and they sent a delegation to Taiz to query the leadership's position. A list of thirty-eight questions was posed, in which the Nasserite aspects of the Charter were criticized; they demanded the holding of a Second Congress to rectify the mistakes of the first. After weeks of discussion it was agreed that the Second Congress be held on 23 January 1966.

But before this could take place the Egyptians pulled off a coup. Three of the eight Politburo members (Taha Moqbel, Salem Zain, Ali Salami) flew to Cairo and there announced, on 13 January 1966, that the NLF had agreed to join with OLOS. The pro-Saudi SAL broke away to the right and the new organization, linking NLF and PSP, was to be called FLOSY – the Front for the Liberation of Occupied South Yemen (*Jabhat Tahrir Junoub al-Yaman al-Muhtall*). At first the NLF cadres inside the South refused to have anything to do with it. They were not willing to meet with FLOSY people, and there was no cooperation on the ground. But the Egyptians plotted to overcome this. From January 1966 their media ascribed all actions in the South to FLOSY, refusing to mention the NLF at all; and this fantasy continued up to the autumn of 1967.

To force through the merger they mobilized the MAN leaders and brought them to Taiz to persuade the NLF: George Habbash, Mohsen Ibrahim and Hani al-Hindi were flown down. The MAN centre in Beirut were still with Nasser: they had expressed support for the Jiddah agreement and the founding of FLOSY. But the MAN branch in North Yemen knew better, and they opposed the centre's line. They supported the NLF cadres, and advanced a four-point position: 1. That the difference between FLOSY and the NLF was a class difference; the former representing the sultans and the Aden bourgeoisie, the latter the workers, the peasants and the progressive sections of the petty bourgeoisie. 2. This being the case, there could be no cooperation between them. 3. That the NLF leaders should leave Taiz and return to the struggle in the South. 4. That the NLF should start political education and cadre training to strengthen their operations.

After two months of discussions in Taiz, the NLF cadres, with the support of Mohsen Ibrahim, rejected union with FLOSY. The Egyptians then invited the NLF leaders to Cairo, where on the pretext of further discussions they detained them. According to one account the Egyptian intelligence chief, Salah Nasr, was particularly insistent that the NLF should stop talking about 'Marxism-Leninism'.[34] In August, after months of further wrangling, a new 'agreement' was announced. Under this 'Alexandria Agreement' the NLF was to join FLOSY and was to surrender its heavy armaments to the FLOSY military command, which was in practice dominated by sheikhs. According to the official reports this agreement had been signed by Qahtan ash-Shaabi, Feisal ash-Shaabi and Abdul Fatah Ismail. Conditions inside the South precluded such a deal. After the NLF leadership was spirited off to Cairo in March 1966 the militants inside the South had become self-reliant and had taken the opportunity to develop their own organization. Up to then the groups in the South had been linked to Taiz, but had been relatively isolated from each other. The Southern groups now overcame this isolation. They also began to raise their own financial support. 'Ali Antar', in Radfan organized supplies and money to be sent from the population who supported the NLF in the Northern border areas of Ibb and Rada. In Aden the first political education courses were held,[35] on the initiative of two leading political cadres: 'Moqbel' (Ali Saleh Abbadh), a trades unionist from Abyan, and Abdullah al-Khamri, the future Minister of Culture and a leading NLF theoretician. Under pressure from these cadres a Second Congress was finally held in June, at Jibla in the North. The Congress expelled from the NLF the three Politburo members who had carried out the January coup and set up FLOSY; it also expelled Qahtan ash-Shaabi and his cousin Feisal, whom it considered responsible for the way the matters had been handled. A new eleven-man General

Command was elected to replace the old Politburo. It reflected the new cadres who had arisen inside the N L F. It included Abdul Fatah Ismail, a schoolteacher who had migrated from the North in his teens and was now the overall commander of political and military activity in Aden; Mohammad Ali Haitham, a cadre from Dathina involved in work among junior army officers, many of whom were from that area; 'Salmin' (Salem Robea Ali), a military leader in Radfan; 'Ali Antar', the commander of the Radfan forces; and Ali al-Beedh, a militant in the Hadramaut. After independence they were all prominent figures.

This Second Congress was held while some N L F leaders were still in Egypt; a fact that made possible the announcement, two months later, of the pro-F L O S Y Alexandria Agreement. However, after their return to Taiz in September a plenary meeting took place of all N L F political and military leaders. The N L F clearly had to reject the Alexandria Agreement, which amounted to dissolving the Front and relying on Egyptian diplomacy for a peaceful settlement in the South. The lead was taken by the military commanders 'Salmin' and 'Ali Antar', with the support of North Yemeni M A N, who also participated. It was decided to hold a Third Congress to consolidate the new line. Pressure built up. In October, on the third anniversary of the outbreak of war in Radfan, the whole of the Aden N L F – the Women's Organization, the Student Organization, the N L F unions, the military wing – announced that they would split the N L F unless the ties with F L O S Y were formally broken. A preparatory committee for the Third N L F Congress laid down a plan for the break. F L O S Y, they argued, was a backward bourgeois ally unable to carry out the national liberation struggle. Since breaking with it would involve losing all Egyptian finance, the N L F would have to expropriate money from the bourgeois through raids on banks and jewellers, and through political contributions.[36]

This programme was carried by Congress at its meeting in November in the North Yemeni town of Khamer. The Third Congress also saw the reintegration into the N L F of the Qahtan group, though not of the three rightists who had set up F L O S Y.

Ten people were added to the eleven elected to the General Command at the Second Congress; although this new ten included 'Ali Antar', 'Moqbel', Mahmud Ushaish, Feisal al-Attas and 'Faris' (Sultan Omar), it also included Qahtan and Feisal ash-Shaabi. The old paternalistic and semi-Nasserite group were back inside. Moreover the Congress decided to increase cooperation with sympathizers in the army and the police; the effect of this move, however necessary, was to open the Front to further right-wing influence. The inner-organization strugglewas by no means over.

The Victory of the NLF

When the NLF broke with FLOSY in November 1966, a clash between the two was inevitable. Since the Egyptians controlled all information about the struggle in the South, the world did not know what was taking place, except for occasional FLOSY attacks on 'separatists' and 'British agents' who were 'trying to weaken and divide the revolution'. On four distinct occasions in 1967 (January, June, September, November) there were serious cases of fighting between the two, with FLOSY deploying its own new military group, PORF (Popular Organization of Revolutionary Forces), against the NLF. The Egyptians went on ascribing all anti-British actions to FLOSY and denying the NLF existed. Ultimately a group came to power that Cairo pretended had not existed and the Egyptian-backed organization was not to be seen.

In January 1967 the NLF called for a general strike on the anniversary of the original 1839 British attack on Aden. This was opposed by FLOSY. They denounced 'a group which has deviated from the revolutionary unanimity and the method of armed struggle which the Front believes to be the only way of liberating the South'.[37] The Qahtan group within the NLF were also prevaricating and Qahtan himself was back in Cairo discussing reunification. But 'Moqbel' and Khamri pressed ahead with the strike and three successful days ensued of mass demonstrations and strikes. FLOSY took this occasion to attack the

N L F and to blow up the press of the communist paper *al-Amal*. But so powerful was the mass showing that over Cairo radio F L O S Y hailed the demonstrations as proof of their own following in the South. In February and March similar incidents occurred as the N L F demonstrated the power of its mass organization in Aden.

In 1966 and the first months of 1967 the British tried to salvage what they could. Their decision of February 1966 to withdraw had been dictated by considerations of global strategy, and not by a direct menace to their base itself. On the other hand they retained an interest in ensuring that a pro-imperialist Federal government should remain in power after independence, and they continued to work towards this end. They were unable to get the Eastern Sultanates into the Federation, and their invitation to the S A L leaders to come back was useless since the S A L was completely discredited. So they hoped that some more concessions might do the trick. A hurried 'Arabization' of the civil service and the army was taking place, and in 1967 they began to hand over security duties to the Federal Regular Army and to the police. They also raised the pay of the officers and men so that it was possible for the last British commander of the F R A, Jack Dye, to boast that after Kuwait his men were the best paid in the peninsula. These moves were designed to bolster the Federation by widening its political base a little and by encouraging the state apparatus to see itself as having a distinct interest binding it to imperialism; it was obvious that if the civil servants and army officers were to continue to earn their high salaries after independence, they would have to get the moneys from Britain.

As 1967 went by the British appeared to concede some ground. In March they brought forward the date for withdrawal to November of the same year. In April the U N, who were refused entry in the past, were invited to Aden in the forlorn hope that they would create agreement between the Federal ministers and the 'moderate' nationalists. In May Turnbull was replaced as High Commissioner by Sir Humphrey Trevelyan, a former British ambassador to Moscow and Cairo. Trevelyan states in his

227

memoirs that he had two aims: 'to evacuate the British forces and their stores in peace'; and 'if possible, to leave behind an independent government which could ensure peace and stability'.[38] But although Trevelyan himself had a shrewd appreciation of how weak the British and Federal position was, officials in London seem to have had a different idea. Having failed to get what they wanted through concessions, the Labour government decided on one last lurch to the right. In this they were encouraged by King Feisal of Saudi Arabia who visited London at the end of May; in his memoirs Harold Wilson describes the situation:

King Feisal of Saudi Arabia was still in London, expressing his concern about our proposed evacuation of Aden and South Arabia. On the Friday, 19th May, we had long talks in which he gravely urged us not only to leave military units in the area but to accept a binding military commitment to use them to defend the new South-Arabian state against attack or infiltration from U A R-inspired Arab nationalism ... Unless we held firm in Southern Arabia, the Gulf would be subverted within months.[39]

The British must have taken this to heart, and may well have been further encouraged by Egypt's defeat in the June 1967 War with Israel, which clearly weakened Nasser's position in North Yemen and lessened the chance of a continued threat to the Federation from that quarter. The result was a startling turnaround: on 20 June Foreign Secretary George Brown announced in the British parliament that after all Britain was to provide naval and air backing for the country for at least six months after independence; the date for withdrawal was pushed back to 9 January 1968 and Britain was to give another £10 million in military aid.

This was a complete volte-face. Conservative ex-Colonial Minister Duncan Sandys, who had been braying for over a year about how Labour had betrayed the Federal sultans, said that when listening to Brown speaking he could have been listening to himself.[40] But the very day that Brown was playing Britain's last colonial card in London the N L F in South Yemen had gone on to the final offensive. British troops had been pulling out of the hinterland since April and on 20 June the Radfani guerrillas emerged from the mountains, seized the capital of the Dhala Amirate and confined the Amir in his own prison. In the next two months the whole of the hinterland was to fall. Of more importance was that on the very same day the British had been forced to evacuate Crater and leave it in the hands of the NLF. This occupation of Crater was to last for thirteen days and was to symbolize the headlong retreat of the imperialists.

For some weeks the NLF military liaison group, including 'Moqbel', 'Salmin' (who had come down from Radfan) and al-Khamri, had been in touch with junior officers in the FRA. These officers wanted to know what policy to pursue as the British pulled out of the hinterland, because the senior officers were close to the Federal government and the British had been trying to induce them to constitute a 'third force', between the NLF and the British Army. On 1 June the FRA was renamed the South Arabian army and it acquired its first Arab commanding officer, Colonel Nasser Bureik al-Aulaqi, a nominee whom the Federal Ministers wanted. Nasser Bureik was extremely un-popular among the junior officers; a group of them who protested were suspended on 16 June. As a result the army revolted with NLF support: on 20 June the police and army in Crater mutin-ied and attacked the British troops there. The British suddenly realized that their last credible instrument, the SAA, could collapse; and if they forcibly reoccupied Crater it might well disintegrate. To preserve it they held back and for thirteen days Crater was governed by the NLF. They released several hundred people from prison, gutted the Legislative Assembly building, and carried out propaganda among the population. Villas belonging to British officers were distributed to the people.

The rising in Crater was felt throughout the Arab world. For South Yemen Crater was the historic centre of Aden and its occupation, however short-term, was of immense psychological importance. In the Arab world the rising was greeted with exceptional delight, as it was the first piece of good news after the crushing Israeli victory eleven days beforehand.[41] Inside South Yemen the defeat of Egypt had the effect of further discrediting the Egyptians, however much people sympathized with them, and of increasing loyalty to the NLF. FLOSY was claiming over Cairo radio that it was still the 'sole representative' of the South Yemeni people, and inside Crater PORF gunmen assassinated a number of NLF cadres. But for the first time FLOSY militants began to come over to the NLF and the actions of Makawi and al-Asnaj in Cairo and New York seemed increasingly irrelevant.

Although the British were able to re-enter Crater in July,[42] they were engaged only in a holding operation. Events in the hinterland were moving fast, and in August the British awoke to discover that the Federation had been simply swept away in an amazing wave of NLF seizures of power. After 'Ali Antar' and his men had seized Dhala in June they sent the arms they had captured to NLF militants elsewhere. After Dhala, Lower Yafai and Audhali fell. On 13 August the NLF announced that they had arrested the ruler of the Muflahi sheikhdom and had forced the deputy leader of Lahej to flee to Aden. On 14 August they staged an 'armed demonstration' in Dathina, drove out the local sheikh and released the prisoners. On 27 August they entered Zinjibar in the Fadhli Sultanate and established their headquarters there, thirty miles from Aden. By the end of the month only one Federal ruler remained on South Yemeni soil (he was in Aden) and the NLF was in command of twelve states. In September they continued. On 3 September the ruler of Beihan crossed into Saudi Arabia; the NLF then occupied his state, released all prisoners and set up an administrative committee. On 17 September the sultans of Kathiri and Quaiti arrived at Mukalla on a Saudi Arabian ship and were prevented from landing by soldiers who told them they supported the revolution. The sultans went back to Saudi Arabia. In October the NLF announced that it had captured the easternmost Sultanate of Mahra and arrested its ruler, Sultan Abdullah bin Ashur bin Afrir. The last seizure of power came on 29 November, hours before independence, when a squad of NLF militants landed on the island of Socotra and claimed it for the revolution.[43]

FLOSY tried to stem this wave. It was claiming over Cairo

radio that the seizure of power all over the South was its own, and it was itself in control of three states: Wahidi, the upper Aulaqi sheikhdom and the upper Aulaqi Sultanate. In September sections of the South Arabian Army, led by Aulaqi officers, left Aden to try to join FLOSY elements in these areas, but turned back short of their destination and the states later fell to the NLF. The biggest FLOSY counter-offensive came in Lahej. They had over 1,000 armed men encamped near Taiz, with UAR support; when it became clear that FLOSY were losing out they tried to launch a conventional military invasion of the South, thrusting down the eighty-mile road through Lahej to Aden to link up with anti-NLF sections of the South Arabian army. On 16 August they announced that they had seized a customs post at Kirish, just inside South Yemeni territory, and in the North they made an arrest of NLF leaders. Although blocked for a time at Kirish, FLOSY built up its forces and in early September in the village of Dar Saad just outside Aden serious fighting broke out. The SAA stepped in and imposed a truce, but PORF then tried to arrest NLF cadres in Sheikh Othman and further fighting ensued.

FLOSY, as always, was equally active on the diplomatic front. The NLF had set up headquarters in Zinjibar and claimed to be the legitimate government of the South. FLOSY, with Egyptian backing, was making a similar claim for itself. But the NLF were again divided, and Qahtan and his group were prepared to compromise; in discussions in Cairo FLOSY and the right wing of the NLF agreed on a cease-fire and on the holding of talks to discuss a coalition government. This was announced on 25 September by Makawi and Feisal ash-Shaabi, who regretted the fighting between their forces that had taken place in Aden, Lahej and Dhala.

The NLF militants refused to accept this, so long as the FLOSY leaders were still intent on altogether crushing the NLF. When the 25 September compromise was announced al-Khamri flew to Beirut where, together with Abdul Fatah Ismail, he denounced it. The old General Command of the NLF had been dissolved but Qahtan and his men consistently refused to hold the Fourth Congress, which the militants insisted be held *before* independence to discuss the politics of the new state. The anti-Qahtan forces constituted a new provisional General Command which included Ushaish, the trades union leader, 'Moqbel', al-Khamri, 'Faris', Ali al-Beedh and a newly arrived left-wing cadre, 'Hassan Ali' (Abdullah al-Ashtal).

The British had long since seen that the Federal government was no more. At the end of August the chairman of the Federal cabinet, Sheikh Ali Musaid al-Babakri, declared: 'it is a people's revolution and we cannot oppose it'. On 5 September Trevelyan broadcast to the South Yemeni people stating that the Federation had broken down and he was prepared to negotiate with the nationalists. The British government still wanted to prevent the NLF from seizing power on its own, and Trevelyan in his memoirs hints that he was very much impeded by the anti-NLF position being taken in London.[44] The British still hoped the army might dominate the situation; and the negotiations at the Arab League would have provided the civil adjunct to this. But the army was too politicized to play this role. It did step in and play a neutral role in Dar Saad. But when it occupied Little Aden after the British pulled out they handed the area over to the NLF. Throughout October the situation remained unclear, and on 1 November there were more reports of a Qahtan–FLOSY agreement. But on 2 November, while George Brown, assuming such a deal was possible, was announcing details to Parliament of the British withdrawal, 500 heavily armed FLOSY men launched their final attack in Sheikh Othman. In five days of heavy fighting probably over 100 people were killed and over 300 wounded; but in the end the SAA moved in, forced FLOSY out of their positions, and on 7 November announced that it supported the NLF.

From then on the path was clear. Britain announced that 'South Arabia' would become independent on 30 November. On 21 November negotiations began in Geneva, and continued till the morning of 29 November. Apart from agreeing to establish full diplomatic relations, the two sides found little common ground and the British, mean as ever, reneged on their aid commitments. The original £60 million was whittled down to £12 million amid mutterings from the British about their financial difficulties (sterling had just been devalued). They complained, more relevantly, about how the 'British public' (i.e. the Wilson government) could not be expected to give aid to people who had been attacking the British army until a month before. All British troops were out on 29 November and at midnight on the night of 29–30 November 1967 the People's Republic of South Yemen was born. One hundred and twenty-eight years of British rule had come to an end.

The South Yemeni victory was the only one in British colonial history which inflicted a defeat of this kind on the British Army and the British state. In southern Ireland, Cyprus and Kenya, where nationalists had won independence after military struggles, the British withdrawal had been preceded by lengthy negotiations and the regimes that came to power soon harmonized their relations with London. In South Yemen, the British refused to recognize the N L F until within ten days of their final departure, and the post-independence regime, far from abandoning the anti-imperialist struggle, proclaimed its intention to expel Britain from the whole of the peninsula. In the Arab world, the South Yemeni struggle is equalled only by that of Algeria, where a guerrilla war that was longer in its duration (eight years as opposed to four) and many times bloodier in its conduct, forced a French withdrawal. On a global scale, the South Yemeni struggle bears some similarities to that in Cuba. In both countries the guerrilla movement was begun by a non-Communist grouping, which only later declared an adherence to Marxism. In both, the struggle was brief enough to leave predominantly intact the social and ideological system created by colonialism; in both too, the economy was badly hit by the break with the world-capitalist market; as a consequence tens of thousands of irate class enemies fled to vengeful exile in Taiz and Miami. Both had to some extent slipped through the net of world counter-revolution – in Cuba because the USA had underestimated the revolutionary movement, in South Yemen because the British were intent on leaving the base anyway, and because they were fixated by the danger of 'Nasser'. Both states established themselves as base areas for the revolutionary movement in their neighbouring continents, and both were quickly subjected to the belated fury of the imperialist powers.

Notes

1. For the pre-1963 history of the nationalist movement I have drawn on the already mentioned works by al-Habashi and Omar, on Little, and on two informative articles: T. Bernier, 'Naissance d'un nationalisme arabe à Aden', *L'Afrique et L'Asie*, No. 44, 1958; and D. C. Watt, 'Labour Relations and Trades Unionism in Aden, 1952–60', *Middle East Journal*, No. 16, 1962.

2. It is a sign of the strength of pan-Arab feeling, even in the most pro-western parts of the Arab world, that none of the eleven Arab states that Britain has ruled ever joined the Commonwealth. This includes such regimes as Farouk's Egypt, Nuri Said's Iraq and Hashemite Jordan. By contrast many purportedly 'progressive' African and Asian states continue to shore up British imperialism by remaining inside this body.

3. The title *an-Nahda* was given to the revival of interest in the Arabic language and in Arab history and culture during the nineteenth century which contributed to the development of Arab nationalism itself.

4. Little, op. cit., p. 32, writes that '... it (the UNF) was regarded by the government and the Aden Association as an irresponsible rabble'. Among its founders the UNF included Sheikhan al-Habshi, a Hadrami lawyer who was believed to have been a member of the Indonesian Communist party, but who later led the SAL in its pro-Saudi phase; Aidrous al-Hamid, a journalist who produced *al-Fajr* with the help of Egyptian subsidies; and Seyyid Abdullah al-Jifri, who had studied in Britain and in Egypt and was later one of the SAL leaders in the period after 1964. A more radical trend was represented by some of the younger members: Abdullah al-Asnaj, future head of the ATUC; Abdullah Badheeb, South Yemen's first Marxist; and Ahmad Mohammad Noman, a liberal from North Yemen whom the British deported in 1960 to assuage the Imam, and who was later YAR Prime Minister.

5. The issue central to trades unionism in advanced capitalist countries of *politicizing* a trades union movement which is militant on *economic* questions alone did not arise in Aden. From the start the unions were intensely politicized and often struck for purely political reasons.

6. Trevaskis, op. cit., p. 156, writes:
'There was, at first, reason, perhaps, for taking a tolerant view of the wild-cat strikes which crippled Aden over and over again. Trades Unionism was adolescent and exuberant and many employers were still embalmed in

old-fashioned attitudes. One had to expect growing pains. Given time, it was thought trade unionists would become more responsible and employers more liberal and then, eventually, Aden would bask in the warmth of industrial peace. But peace had not come ...'

7. See Watts, op. cit., for an account of these actions.

8. Trevaskis, op. cit., p. 106.

9. Sir Charles Johnston, *The View from Steamer Point*, London, 1964, pp. 124–5. Johnston gives an interesting account of his state of mind at this time:

'One of the worst things for me personally about the autumn crisis was the feeling that I was myself responsible for a sudden worsening of conditions which might well lose us Aden. I never doubted that our policy was right, and deep within myself I knew that all would turn out well in the end. But there were a few days when the normal smooth surface of life in Aden looked particularly hollow to my eyes. At breakfast on the terrace, I watched the big ships coming in, picking up their pilots, hooting to their tugs exactly as if nothing was wrong. How much longer can this normal appearance go on for, I asked myself? How soon will the ghastly secret be out?'

He was nervous about going to Khormaksar Races in case he would be ostracized by other British officials who might blame him for the crisis.

'When they came up and talked and joked in an absolutely normal way, as if nothing was wrong, I was astonished and overjoyed. For those in the inner circle this was an act, just as much as it was for me. They knew it, and I knew it, and the thought of our being in the act together brought me a feeling of solidarity and comfort.'* Had he not been right he would have been paranoid.

* Op. cit., pp. 127–9.

10. Morris had been Commissioner of Police in Singapore during the Malayan counter-revolution and had also served in Hong Kong. After Aden he served in the Caribbean until 1968 when he retired and became the London representative of an Anglo-Caribbean property company, Intercontinental Bahama Realty.

11. See p. 161. The conventional British claim is that they only turned against the YAR when the latter threatened the situation in the South. This is not the case, as is demonstrated by the *Observer*'s Foreign Editor Robert Stephens in his *Nasser*, London, 1971, p. 395.

12. Since British accounts of this period are especially unreliable I have relied on the excellent documentation of Jens Plass and Ulrich Gehrke in *Die Aden-Grenze in der Südarabienfrage (1900–1967)*, Opladen, West Germany, 1967. In general this work is an important antidote to conventional British accounts, Stephens excepted.

13. The NLF was originally known as the National Liberation Front for Occupied South Yemen (*al-Jabha al-Qaumia li-Tahrir al-Junoub al-Yamani al-Muhtall*). It is conventionally known in English as the NLF and in Arabic as *al-Jabha al-Qaumia* (the National Front); its later rival FLOSY

was usually referred to as *Jabhat at-Tahrir* (The Liberation Front). For the history of the N L F I have used three main sources: material provided by Abdullah al-Khamri from two long interviews with Fawwaz Trabulsi and myself; Sultan Omar's work on Yemen, pp. 234ff., and Jean-Pierre Viennot, 'Aden, de la lutte pour la libération à l'indépendance', *Orient*, Vol. 14, 1970.

14. See p. 40.

15. Plass and Gehrke, op. cit., pp. 214–15.

16. Julian Paget, *Last Post; Aden 1964–67*, London, 1969, p. 41. Paget's work gives the British military account of the last four years.

17. ibid., p. 47.

18. ibid., p. 57.

19. ibid., p. 108.

20. ibid., p. 71n.

21. *Hansard*, 10 June 1964.

22. Trevaskis, op. cit., p. 208.

23. The British claimed that because of the high poll – 75 per cent, as they said – their policies had been vindicated. This myopia was soon dispelled.

24. Greenwood refused to allow the U N to supervise general elections, saying that Britain had ensured conditions for free elections in Malta and Guyana and could do so in Aden.

25. Paget, op. cit., p. 264. A total of fifty-seven British military were killed and 651 wounded over the same period; British estimates state that 290 local people were killed and 922 wounded; 240 of these were in the last year, and include F L O S Y – N L F casualties. These figures apply only to Aden. Comparable figures for Northern Ireland in 1969–72 were 146 British military and fifty-seven local military killed; 470 Irish civilians killed in the same period.

26. Paget, op. cit., p. 146n.

27. Paget, op. cit., p. 129. See all p. 149ff.

28. 'Did the Special Branch Torture Corporal Lennox?' in *7 Days*, No. 12, 19–25 January 1972. *7 Days* was a weekly news magazine, of which the author was the foreign editor, which ceased publication in May 1972. The British soldier in question, George Lennox, states that after protesting about the Aden atrocities to the *Sunday Times* in October 1966 he was detained and tortured by plain clothes British officials in June 1967 and then expelled from the army. George Lennox's allegations about beatings and his report of what happened in June 1967 are similar to the report of Captain Ernest Law. Law was a British officer who while 100 per cent healthy was expelled from the army 'on medical grounds' after protesting at the beating of detainees in Kenya; he was then illegally imprisoned for five months himself in Kenya after asking for assisted repatriation. See Peter Benenson, 'Five Months Without Trial', in *Gangrene*, London, 1959.

29. Paget, op. cit., p. 157. For an analogous self-righteousness over army conduct in Northern Ireland see 'Anti-Army campaign condemned by minister', *The Times*, 1 December 1972.

30. On British policies on interrogation see Peter Deeley, *Beyond Breaking Point*, London, 1971. The Amnesty report by Dr Salahdin Rastgeldi, a lawyer of Kurdish origin living in Sweden, appeared in September 1966. It is in many respects similar to Amnesty's 'Report of an Enquiry into Allegations of Ill-Treatment in Northern Ireland' published in 1971. The British government's own investigation, by Roderick Bowen Q C, *Procedures for the Arrest, Interrogation and Detention of Suspected Terrorists in Aden*, was published in November 1966. This report did 'recommend' that the conduct of three unnamed civilian interrogators formerly employed at Fort Morbut should be investigated. It was later reported that an internal inquiry on this was taking place (*Sunday Times*, 12 February 1967), but the interrogators had long since been moved elsewhere and neither Bowen nor his nominators (the Foreign Office) pressed the matter. By a series of blocking manoeuvres and procrastinating concessions the British authorities had killed the protests, in an exemplary Whitehall cover-up operation.

31. *Report of the Committee of Privy Counsellors Appointed to Consider Authorized Procedures for the Interrogation of Persons Suspected of Terrorism*, Chairman: Lord Parker of Waddington, Cmnd. 4901, March 1972, p. 3. The quotes from Lord Gardiner's minority report are in ibid. pp. 12, 14. It is relevant to draw attention to the phrase 'the Persian Gulf (1970–71)': Officially, the British Army was not involved in any active campaigning there, and there was no armed opposition campaign. Where in the Persian Gulf was this torture being used? In 1972 the Ministry of Defence refused to answer a highly placed Labour Party official who questioned them on this point; but the answer is obvious – it was in Oman, where the Whitehall authorities were concealing the involvement of British troops (see p. 356).

32. On 11 December 1963 the U N General Assembly passed a motion calling on Britain to withdraw from her base, repeal her repressive measures and allow self-determination through the holding of general elections. This motion and subsequent U N initiatives helped to harass the British; but U N activity also enabled the P S P leadership to gain publicity through purely diplomatic manoeuvrings. As the anti-Portuguese guerrillas have shown, the U N can be used for revolutionary purposes; but the N L F were always wary of it, and rightly refused to be trapped by an organization that is essentially the defender of great-power interests. The Vietnamese N L F took a similar stand.

33. See Omar, op. cit., 'The Struggle of the Yemeni Woman', pp. 227–9.

34. Omar, op. cit., p. 252. Salah Nasr was the archetypal Nasserite organizational man, particularly detested by militants in the Yemens and the Gulf. Despite his anti-communist position he was arrested and imprisoned by Sadat in 1971.

35. The N L F had originally kept quite distinct its political and military wings, a form of division not found in organizations like the South Vietnamese N L F, or in P F L O A G where the political wing commands the military. The distinction is found in other nationalist Arab guerrilla groups

and prevails in the Irish Republican movement, through the distinction Sinn Fein–IRA.

36. According to al-Khamri the NLF raised 5 million shillings (= £250,000) through robberies, from the Eastern Bank in Sheikh Othman, Crater and Mukalla, and from jewelleries in Sheikh Othman.

37. Cairo Radio, 20 January 1967.

38. *The Middle East in Revolution*, p. 211.

39. Harold Wilson, *The Labour Government: 1964–70*, London, 1971, p. 396.

40. Trevaskis, op. cit., p. 242.

41. Voice of the Arabs, Cairo's pan-Arab station, excelled itself:

'Britain will not remain in the south. The darkness of the bitterest enemy of Arabism and Islam will lift from the south of the Arabian peninsula, from the land of the Arabian peninsula, the land of Mohammad, may the blessing of God be upon him ... The British imperialists are at their wits end in the south; anguish has befallen them without their knowing its coming; the revolution has come from an unexpected quarter, from the men of the Federal Army ... The *mujahidin* in the south have dispersed Brown's dreams and stupidities. They have given their silencing reply to his statements.'*

* Voice of the Arabs, 20 June 1967.

42. As if the stage was not crowded enough, a new and extraordinary figure appeared in the shape of Lieutenant-Colonel Colin Mitchell, commander of the Argyll and Sutherland Highlanders who were garrisoning Crater. 'Mad Mitch', as he became known, was a surreal relic of Britain's colonial past; a crazed fusion of the Celtic madman, belligerent imperialist and cantankerous military commander. His memoirs, *Having Been a Soldier*, London, 1969, tend to berate the 'squeamish politicians', 'prowling journalists' and 'white Arabs' (liberal English) who got in his way. Mitchell tried to spread the rumour in Crater 'that we were wild Bedouin tribesmen from the Scottish Highlands who could get very rough if provoked'.

43. In an interview with the author in December 1972 Denis Healey, Labour Minister of Defence from 1964 to 1970, said that there were two things which had surprised even the best-informed British people about Aden. One was what he termed 'the appearance of the Provisionals', that is of people 'fully committed to violence'; the other was the disappearance 'overnight' of the sheikhs and sultans of the interior whom everyone on the left and right had thought to be so secure.

44. *The Middle East in Revolution*, p. 258. Trevelyan comments on the British refusal to support the hinterland rulers: 'We had to stick to the decision to withdraw. We were not going to create a little Vietnam'; ibid., p. 243.

Chapter Eight
The People's Democratic Republic of Yemen

A Perilous Beginning

The People's Republic of South Yemen emerged into a world where danger confronted it from every direction. The already meagre basis of the economy had been undermined in the last six months before independence: the closure of the Suez Canal in June cut the port of Aden's trade by 75 per cent; the British evacuation of the base threw over 20,000 people out of work; and the British betrayal of their aid commitments deprived the state of 60 per cent of its income. A political furore raged above this fractured economic base. The state apparatus which imperialism had bequeathed to the PRSY was riddled with tribal and political factionalism, and despite the army's last-minute support for the NLF its loyalty to the new regime was uncertain. Moreover within the NLF the factional fighting that had gone on since 1965 was intensified by the many extra problems faced once the NLF had come so suddenly to power. Beyond the boundaries of the new state, and leagued with elements within, a host of enemies marshalled their forces to crush the revolutionary state: the ousted FLOSY and SAL nationalists, and the right wing of the republican regime in North Yemen, together with Saudi Arabia and the Sultanate of Oman, were all determined to sabotage the PRSY. In this they were joined by Britain and the US, who soon realized that now it had come to power the NLF would pose an even greater threat to their interests in the area.[1]

These immediate difficulties were superimposed on the long-term problems that the independent republic had inherited from the sultanic and colonial regime. The guerrilla movement had lasted for a relatively short time – four years, compared to the decades of the Chinese or Vietnamese revolutions. Despite the ferocity and intelligence of the struggle, therefore, the social and

239

ideological structures of Yemeni society had been only superficially altered, and much of the country had been hardly affected at all. The country's economic backwardness, division and poverty remained. Per capita income stood at around £40 p.a.

This meant that although the NLF had wide support among workers and peasants, the social and economic transformation remained to be carried out after the successful national revolution. The NLF had been changed in its four years of struggle but it remained a predominantly nationalist organization with a loose structure, relying on conspiratorial work as well as on mass support. The 'left' within it had still to be proven in the conditions of an independent state. Moreover outside South Yemen a number of factors de-limited the state's future; they included the evolution of politics in the rest of the Middle East, particularly in the Gulf; and the policies of the Soviet Union and China, the countries on whose support South Yemen relied. Whatever the intentions of the South Yemeni leadership, their freedom of action was conditioned by considerable problems both internally and without.

The state's establishment went smoothly. The first twelve-man cabinet was announced on 1 December; Qahtan ash-Shaabi became President, Prime Minister and Supreme Commander of the armed forces.[2]

In his first official statement as President he laid down the policies of the new government. The 'socialist revolution' would now start; the PRSY would work closely with North Yemen and would pursue a policy of 'positive neutralism'; the PRSY would support the revolutionary movements in Palestine and the Gulf. Since the Federal government had been abolished, the General Command of the NLF would act as supreme legislative body until the establishment of a new legislature; the old state divisions were abolished and the country was divided into six Governorates,[3] corresponding to the combat areas set up during the guerrilla struggle. The government's initial economic policy called for developing agricultural and industrial production. In his opening speech Qahtan had already denounced the British for betrayal of their aid commitments. But the PRSY opened diplomatic relations with Britain, and despite last-ditch Arab League manoeuvrings the NLF was finally accepted by the Arab governments. Even Syria, which until mid November had denounced the NLF as British agents and compared them to the Saigon regime, by 4 December had fallen in line. Later in the month the PRSY was admitted to the Arab League as the 'fourteenth Arab state' and subsequently to the United Nations.

The regime was quickly faced witn the problem of restructuring the state: the NLF had to take over; having done so, it found itself in a position to transform the colonial state that the British had set up. The state was a privileged and a tribalized structure, and relatively weak outside Aden and the richer parts of the country (Lahej, Abyan, Mukalla). Revolutionizing it meant purging it politically, changing its social role and extending state power to the whole of the PRSY's area. Within the NLF transformation of the state became the major issue. It was a question of whether to work with it and accept its existing character, which was President ash-Shaabi's position, or destroy it and replace it with a popular state, as the NLF left argued, explicitly basing their positions on Lenin's *State and Revolution*,[4] which underlined the need for a revolution to smash the pre-existing structure and build popular state institutions.

As the British, in June 1967, pulled back from the hinterland into Aden and their core base around Tawahi, the NLF had set up embryonic state structures: popular committees, a popular guard (*al-Haras ash-Shaabi*) and administrative groups formed from NLF cadres and members of the colonial state administration. In many parts of the country where the state had hardly existed the NLF set up state structures for the first time. By mid November Aden radio was broadcasting NLF decrees, and threatening to punish those who attacked property of Yemeni or foreign residents.[5] By the time 'independence' actually came on 30 November the NLF had been administering parts of the country for several months, and had had their own underground administrative structures for several years. This meant that even before they had begun to purge the state apparatus, the old colonial system was flanked by the cadres and partisans of the

241

N L F itself. The N L F left urged the creation of a new state. The old army and civil service should be abolished and new structures built on the basis of N L F partisans. They suggested cutting the civil service by over a half to 3,000. In addition to the regular army there should be a militia of 100,000 to 150,000 armed men and women, to defend the revolution internally and against foreign attacks. The basis of political power should be popular committees in each village which would elect members to the highest legislature, the Supreme People's Council.[6] A radical economic policy should be put through: there should be a low limit on land ownership, and foreign capital should be nationalized.

This line was opposed by Qahtan and his group who commanded the N L F in Aden; the left were influential in Aden but had to contend with Qahtan's close ties to the colonial army. The left's main stronghold was in the Hadramaut, where there had been less actual fighting than in the west but where many left-wing militants were active. By August 1967 they had control of the Hadramaut and their weekly journal *ash-Sharara* (*Spark*) later made their policy explicit:

Making the socialist revolution means transforming existing social relations and installing revolutionary social relations, in other words destroying the old state apparatus and building an entirely new one in its place . . . Shouts of indignation will rise from the ranks of the worried and hesitant petty bourgeoisie: but where are the competent personnel? By 'competent personnel' they mean people with university degrees. Our reply is straightforward: what we need are not bourgeois competences but devoted workers. The great historical experience of the workers' councils is there to prove that the working class can govern themselves without difficulty, without bureaucracy and without bourgeois 'competences'.[7]

N L F partisans were mixed with former members of the Hadrami Bedouin Legion in a new regular army; two brigades of militia, The First of May and Che Guevara, were formed. In Mukalla a 'people's congress' was reportedly convened, as the first of many created to form throughout the Hadramaut the 'state of workers and poor peasants'. A Land Committee was set up to expropriate

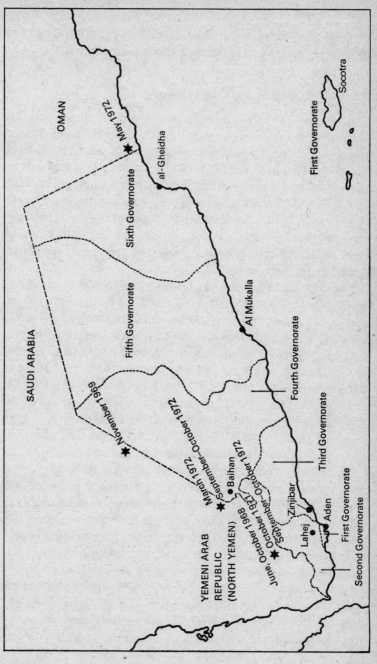

Map 7 The People's Democratic Republic of Yemen ★Indicates major border clashes

SAUDI ARABIA

OMAN

May 1972 ★

al-Gheidha ●

Sixth Governorate

Fifth Governorate

Al Mukalla ●

Fourth Governorate

First Governorate

Socotra

November 1969

March 1972–October 1972

★

September–October 1972

★ ● Baihan

September, October 1971 October 1972

Zinjibar ●

June, October 1968

★

● Lahej

Aden ●

Third Governorate

First Governorate

Second Governorate

YEMENI ARAB REPUBLIC (NORTH YEMEN)

all landlords, and the local NLF called for the nationalization of all capital, foreign and national, without compensation.[8]

The Fourth Congress and Qahtan's Autocracy

The policies of the Hadramaut NLF, even if they were often little more than intentions, were in direct opposition to those of the Aden leadership. But attempts by NLF Secretary-General Feisal ash-Shaabi to discipline the Hadrami section met with no success, and were partly undermined by pro-Hadramaut elements in Aden itself. A leading figure in the Aden disputes was Minister of Defence Ali al-Beedh, himself a Hadrami by origin; in February he outflanked Qahtan and the army by dismissing the twenty-eight British officers still serving with the army, because he suspected their loyalty to the NLF.

The clash came to a head at the Fourth Congress of the NLF, which met in Zinjibar, near Aden, on 2–8 March 1968. The left had insisted that this meet *before* independence to lay down policies for the new government. But when it met *after* independence the Qahtan's group was strengthened by the tactical backing of the colonial army; despite protests from the left, army officers who were not NLF members attended the Zinjibar debates. The left's position was most clearly expressed in the programmatic speech by Abdul Fatah Ismail entitled 'The non-capitalist path of development'.[9] Abdul Fatah Ismail argued that the key question was the class character of the state, which in South Yemen could be ruled by the petty bourgeoisie or by the revolutionary forces – the workers, poor peasants and partisans. The petty bourgeoisie was unable in this epoch of world history to fight imperialism and to carry through necessary economic and social development against the opposition of imperialism; namely, a free economy, agrarian development, industrialization. He ranged back over the historical failures of the petty bourgeoisie in the European revolutions of 1848 and 1870, and he ascribed the collapse of the Second International in 1914 to its dominance by petty-bourgeois elements. Abdul Fatah also attacked the role of the petty bourgeoisie in Ghana and Indonesia, where the regimes of Nkrumah and Sukarno had recently been overthrown; he then criticized the governments of Egypt, Algeria, Syria and Iraq.

The compromising petty-bourgeois leadership in the epoch of imperialism is even more dangerous for the national popular democratic revolution than the explicit counter-revolutionary policies of the semi-feudal, semi-bourgeois alliance.

In Arab countries like Egypt the petty bourgeoisie had masked its dictatorship as 'socialism'. The same danger could now be seen in South Yemen, where a 'pathetic phraseological socialism' dominated the N L F. Revolutionary partisans and cadres were being pushed out and the institutions forged in struggle were being destroyed. The petty bourgeoisie had no role to play, and there was a *fortiori* none for the national bourgeoisie. The old state machine had to be smashed. The country should be flooded with revolutionary literature to help build the new culture; flanked by the militia of 100,000 to 150,000 people, all power should be given to the councils of 'workers, poor peasants and partisans' and to the Supreme People's Council.

This was a speech of a kind rarely heard in the Arab world. Abdul Fatah Ismail was partly influenced by the critique of 'petty-bourgeois nationalism' developed in opposition to Nasserism. But the positions and examples adopted were resolutely international, rather than conventionally Arab nationalist. Some positions formally adopted were extremely radical beside those of comparable revolutionary movements. In contrast to, for example, Chinese positions, the N L F left wing refused to divide the revolution into specific 'stages', and their revolutionary bloc was far more restricted; whereas the Chinese stated that the four basic forces of the Chinese revolution were the workers, peasants, revolutionary intelligentsia and petty bourgeoisie, under the leadership of the workers, the South Yemenis included only the workers, poor peasants and partisans. The most common serious criticism of the line was that it was verbally radical, was ultra-left, and was the product more of a rhetorical and transient militancy than of a deep and permanent break with the N L F's past. The failure of the N L F to implement its left-wing programme after 1969 has certainly given strength to this argument.

The counter-arguments of the Qahtan group are exemplified in an official statement issued some time after the Fourth Congress.[10] It attacks the 'infantile leftism' of their opponents and singles out what they regard as the number one error: the belief in conflict between classes and in imposing a dictatorship of one class rather than working for harmony between them. This amounted to an exposition of one of Nasserism's central theses: that one defining characteristic of 'Arab socialism' is its disbelief in class conflict. Qahtan and his group attacked the left for criticizing other 'brother' Arab countries, and castigated them as alien to 'South Yemeni reality':

They have passed lightly over realities and objective circumstances, as a result of their own conception of the NLF, which consists in jumping over all the stages of objective scientific evolution and in making the NLF into the party of a single class, whereas the National Charter specifies it as a popular coalition grouping all the labouring forces. They have considered our society as similar to European societies of the nineteenth century, thereby appearing to ignore all the fundamental differences of religion, history, tradition, customs and economics.

The Fourth Congress overwhelmingly supported the left, and the newly elected forty-one-man General Command reflected this. The Congress defined the NLF as 'a revolutionary organization which represents the interests of the workers, peasants, soldiers and revolutionary intellectuals and adopts scientific socialism as its method of analysis and practice'. Membership of the NLF was restricted to people from these four groups. The NLF had to carry out cadre formation and ideological training. The government was instructed to put through revolutionary measures: immediate creation of popular councils, agrarian reform, nationalization of foreign capital, a purge of the army and the administration and a programme of mass education. The left having won this victory at the NLF level, it was clear that they would come into conflict with opposing forces outside the NLF. Furthermore, control by the NLF itself of the country as a whole was unsure; the left's victory at the Fourth Congress had not ensured implementation of their decisions. Their militancy was restricted by their limited power. During the Congress leading officers had been carrying out propaganda in the armed forces denouncing 'communist influence'; and when the Congress ended on 8 March they decided to stage a coup. The moment for action came on 19 March 1968 when the N L F cadres in Aden were holding a mass meeting in support of the Fourth Congress decisions. Army elements broke the meeting up, and next day, 20 March, they arrested eight leading N L F cadres. These moves were objectively also in the interests of the Qahtan group; but Qahtan was unable to let matters develop because a series of demonstrations broke out in Aden, Jaar, Yafia and the Hadramaut.

Qahtan ordered the release of the imprisoned cadres in support of the imprisoned left leaders, calling the army move 'sincere, but in error'. He also ordered the arrest of army conspirators. To further boost his radical image he rushed through a hurriedly prepared land reform act, under which confiscated lands were parcelled out to N L F partisans. Nevertheless the army had dealt a severe blow to the left, who were now excluded from leading positions both in the Aden party and in the government. The Fourth Congress decisions remained a dead letter; there were further arrests, and many cadres fled from Aden to the hinterland and to North Yemen. In the Hadramaut the left-wing cadres dug in, and a *de facto* secession took place as relations between Aden and Mukalla were broken. According to some Hadrami militants 'U S imperialism had seized power in Aden': the U S military attaché, Dale Perry, had been advising the army before the coup, and the petty-bourgeois line of Qahtan constituted the Aden government as objective allies of the U S.

While much of the left was in disarray, one group decided to launch a second guerrilla war, this time against the Aden government. The plan was to weaken the government by undermining its hold on the lower echelons of the army, and then to stage simultaneous uprisings in different parts of the country. The Aden government railed at 'pro-Chinese extremists and secessionists' in the Hadramaut. The plans for the uprising only partially materialized; on 14 May armed groups seized the towns of Jaar and Abyan, near Aden, and the Hadramaut supported them. But the planned rising in Aden, to be led by 'Ali Antar', the leader of Radfan, did not take place. The army remained firm. In early June the Aden government counter-attacked and reoccupied Jaar, Abyan and the Hadramaut. Many NLF cadres were killed, and some fled to North Yemen; Ali al-Beedh, who had fled from Aden to Mukalla after the coup of 20 March, was reported to have been captured.

No sooner had Qahtan's group imposed its power on the left than it was faced with an equally serious challenge from the right, in the shape of defections and attacks by supporters of the defunct pro-British Federation. All the leading Federal leaders had fled by the summer of 1967 and some had been tried *in absentia* and sentenced to death for treason. But they had found support in Saudi Arabia, and the republican regime in the North had also begun to give them shelter after its shift to the right in early 1968. From the middle of 1968 both Saudi Arabia and North Yemen were bases for border attacks on the PRSY. The first clashes had taken place in February 1968, when the exiled ruler of Beihan launched a foray from Saudi Arabia, just when the Sultan of Muscat's army was apparently menacing the PRSY's eastern border. In June 1968 the clashes became more dangerous: Saudi-supported tribes in the Second and Fourth Governorates revolted and occupied the town of Said, and the Aulaqi areas, of which Said was the capital; at the same time right-wing forces revolted in Radfan, with support from counter-revolutionaries in North Yemen. By mid July FLOSY and SAL forces, ex-nationalists who had been discredited in the liberation struggle, had poured across the borders into the South, and on 2 August the commander of the PRSY's security forces, Colonel Abdullah Salih Sabah al-Aulaqi, defected to North Yemen with 200 of his men and their armoured cars. Many of these army defectors were Aulaqis who refused to fight their fellow tribesmen in the rebellious areas.

Despite these blows, parts of the PRSY army held firm and were joined by partisans of the NLF struggle. By mid August 1968 the Aden government had recaptured Said and crushed the rebellion. According to the government 109 rebels had been killed and sixty-eight captured. The government's position now appeared stronger. Threats from both left and right had been met; the NLF and its parallel organizations were in decline; Egypt was giving considerable diplomatic backing to Qahtan's policies. The remnants of the colonial state were also reconciled to the NLF: 'The army now calls the political tune, a point President al-Shaabi now evidently appreciates,' wrote one western observer.[11]

The appearance of stability was deceptive. Counter-revolutionary attacks on the Fourth Governorate – Beihan – began again in October and November 1968, and by early 1969 the North Yemeni government were encouraging plots among exiled FLOSY elements in the North against the PRSY. Exiled sultans attacked again from Saudi Arabia in March 1969. The internal economic situation was precarious, and the state machine's unreliability and his own hostility towards the NLF left Qahtan little political support. He needed the NLF militants he had ousted. For the defeated left this all presented a new opportunity; it was clear to them after the defeat of the May 1968 insurrection that a 'second guerrilla war' was no longer possible. Some left-wing elements remained inside the Aden government; some were in prison; some were in exile. Abdul Fatah Ismail, who had been convalescing in Bulgaria for some months, returned to the Middle East in August and after urging renewed guerrilla struggle decided that this was pointless. Instead he and the other left-wing leaders argued that the left should seek a new accommodation with Qahtan and work to overthrow him from within the government.

The 'Corrective Move' of June 1969

The defeat of Qahtan, when it came, was brought about by an internal dispute in which the left formed a tactical alliance with others of his opponents. Both the means of ousting the right-wing leadership, and the alliance involved, produced obstacles to the implementation of the left's programme. In late 1968 and early 1969 the left began to regroup within the regime, exploiting the difficulties created by Qahtan's autocratic and short-sighted policies. Under pressure, Qahtan agreed in April 1969 to give up the post of Prime Minister, but he insisted on appointing in his stead his equally unpopular cousin, Feisal ash-Shaabi, already Secretary-General of the N L F. The issue causing sharpest disagreement did not directly exemplify the political divisions between Qahtan and the left, but was nonetheless useful to the left. This was the question of control of the armed forces. The Minister of the Interior, Mohammad Ali Haitham, had been responsible for liaison with junior officers during the liberation struggle; many of these were Dathinis, like Haitham himself; and as Minister of the Interior, Haitham was able to lessen Qahtan's control of the army's lower echelons. In June the clash came to a head. On the sixteenth Qahtan tried to dismiss Haitham but was blocked by the N L F, strengthened now by the return of the left. Four days of dispute followed; but Qahtan now faced an opposition he could not control. On 22 June his resignation was announced, together with that of Feisal ash-Shaabi. A new collective leadership comprising a five-man presidential council took over the functions Qahtan had exercised.

The new leadership was drawn from the N L F's 'secondary leadership'; they represented the policies the left had advanced in factional disputes dating from 1965. The new President and chairman of the presidential council was Salem Robea Ali, a foremost military leader in the liberation period, an organizer of the Crater and May 1968 uprisings against Qahtan; Haitham, the new Prime Minister, Abdul Fatah Ismail, the new N L F General Secretary, Ali Nasser, the new Defence Minister, and Mohammad Saleh Aulaqi made up the five-man collective leadership. The new cabinet included other left-wing leaders. In an official statement on 22 June the N L F General Command attacked the 'tendencies towards individualism and personal power' of the previous leadership; the latter had 'diverted the revolution from its true path and by alienating the creative forces of society and by weakening the N L F's potential have exposed the revolution to innumerable internal dangers and difficulties and have completely paralysed its natural development, in the way this was conceived of by all devoted militants'. The General Command subsequently stated that the 'corrective move' of 22 June was needed to rid the party of the opportunists and petty bourgeois who had seized control of it. It was now possible to test the radical resolutions voted by the Fourth Congress that Qahtan had so far blocked.

Politics: The New Constitution and the Fifth Congress

One major policy, formerly advanced in opposition by the left leadership, was that of politically revitalizing the country, by building democratic institutions and mobilizing the people. Since independence no political institutions had been created to replace the defunct legislature of Aden and the Federation; officially the supreme legislative body had been the N L F General Command, but this had atrophied under Qahtan, and real power had come to rest with the group around the former President. In December 1969 the General Command announced that a constitution for the P R S Y would be formulated in the next year. In the summer and autumn of 1970 the draft was circulated throughout the country, and in November 1970, on the third anniversary of independence, the new constitution was announced.

The name of the country was changed from People's Republic of South Yemen to People's Democratic Republic of Yemen. The omission of the word 'South' reflected the fact that the N L F did not think of Yemeni unity in terms of unifying the two Yemeni states, but regarded itself alone as the legitimate state of the whole Yemen. The inclusion of the word 'Democratic' reflected a new analysis on the part of the N L F leaders as to which phase of the revolution they considered they were in. Full legislative powers were to be vested in the Supreme People's Council, a new 101-member body. Eighty-six of these members were to be chosen by local councils in general elections; the other fifteen were to be elected by the trades union movement. Within the eighty-six, a special quota was reserved for the women's organization, although women were free to stand for direct election as well. However the basic structure of popular councils throughout the country stipulated by the Fourth Congress of March 1968 did not yet exist, and this meant that the eighty-six members of the first 'provisional' Supreme People's Council were nominated by the NLF and not elected. This 'provisional' Council was to remain in power till the establishment of popular councils made general elections possible.

The first session of the Supreme People's Council met in August 1971, but mainly as a ratifying body only, without an independent or diverse political will. It elected Abdul Fatah Ismail to be its Speaker, and unanimously agreed to changes in both govern-ment and party leaderships. Since the 'corrective move', NLF control of the state had been strengthened: 'Ali Antar', former commander of NLF military operations against the British, became commander of the armed forces in December 1969; and Mohammad Saleh Yafai, known as 'Motiah', was made Minister of the Interior. In the August 1971 changes to the Supreme People's Council, the former Minister of Defence, Ali Nasser, became Prime Minister, replacing Haitham.[12] In a parallel de-cision the Supreme People's Council elected a new ten-man committee to direct the NLF. Whereas the new state's constitu-tional institutions developed slowly and at a pace directed from above, the NLF, while not officially calling itself a 'party', was becoming transformed, in the period after the 'corrective move', into a broader mass organization. The new leadership stressed the need to broaden its political following and strengthen ties with the people. Frequent appeals to exiled nationalists were made by the Aden authorities, and after 1969 many hundreds of former FLOSY supporters did return. At the same time the NLF developed closer ties with the two other left-wing organiza-tions in South Yemen: the communists and the Ba'ath. In De-cember 1969 Abdullah Badheeb, a communist, and Anis Yahya, a Ba'athi, joined the government, and discussions on uniting these organizations produced, in 1972, the merger of the communists with the NLF.

In the trades union movement the NLF had acquired a certain base during the last two years of struggle, and by August 1967 it was supported by the majority of the Adeni trades unions. After independence the old Aden Trades Union Congress had been transformed into the General Union of Yemeni Workers; whereas the old AT U C had been confined, as its name stated, to Aden, the G U Y W had branches throughout the country, and by 1972 its membership was estimated at 45,000 – almost double that of the old A T U C. The major problem facing the trades union movement was the dispersal of its old base by the collapse of the Adeni economy. Over 80,000 people were reported to have left Aden in 1967–8 to find work elsewhere (in the Gulf, and East Africa), and up to 20,000 of those who remained were unemployed; the general fall in demand hit all sections of the economy, and surplus capacity increased. To this blow was added the problem that historically the majority of the Adeni proletariat had supported F L O S Y. Although most of the unions swung behind the N L F before independence, political loyalties in parts of the movement and the economic deprivation that hit the Adeni proletariat at independence generated considerable anti-N L F feeling. This was exacerbated by periodic heavy-handed N L F intervention in trades union affairs. The N L F also set up a number of other mass organizations. In the period before independence the women's struggle had been confined to Aden and had been based on two forms of activity: involving women in the political struggle, through women's demonstrations and through underground work in support of the revolutionary movement; and activity against the imprisonment of women in the family and in their houses, and in favour of legal equality for women and equality in education. In February 1968 a new General Union of Yemeni Women was founded, with branches in the rural areas as well as the towns. Women were for the first time trained to form part of the militia, and in 1971–2 mass women's demonstrations took place in the rural areas in opposition to the wearing of the veil, for long a symbol of traditionalist Islamic oppression of women. The Women's Union was given the power to adjudicate divorce proceedings. The call for the freeing of women from traditional social structures during the liberation struggle had been bitterly denounced by the chief religious leader of Aden; in the post-independence period this campaign, as part of the social transformation of the country, was allied to the trades union and student organization. A new divorce law, modelled on the secular legislation of Tunisia, was introduced in 1974 to terminate polygamy and equalize divorce conditions.

Throughout the ideological apparatus, some changes were made while old cultural forms remained. All existing papers, which had been controlled by the Adeni bourgeois and Federal officials, were banned soon after independence, and a new revolutionary press was founded. But bad land communications and low literacy made Aden radio the main source of information; in 1973 the circulation of the only daily, *14 October*, was just 6,000.[13] The regime undertook to spread primary schools throughout the country, with the aim of ensuring compulsory education for boys and girls by 1981. At the end of 1973 there were 477 primary schools, 56 intermediate and 11 secondary schools with a total enrolment of around 100,000 – double the amount in school in 1967.

This cultural policy also had definite limits, reflecting both political and technical conditions within the Republic. The lack of resources made impossible the creation of the necessary television and cinema materials; instead, these were imported, mainly from Egypt. Consequently non-revolutionary cultural traits already engrained in the population were reinforced. Contrary to what their enemies proclaimed, the Aden authorities did not attack religion, although they did confront cultural forms associated with religion, such as the oppression of women. Religion continued to be practised in the Republic; it formed part of the school curriculum and religious holidays were officially observed.

One area of considerable political activity was the armed forces. Here political change took two forms: the purging of officers and men believed to support opponents of the regime; and the army's ideological transformation through different admission and education policies. The former armed forces were not completely dissolved, as the left wing of the NLF had once demanded, following Lenin; many of its members were expelled, but some were retained and these were joined by former members of the

NLF guerrilla organizations. The army was then thrown open to individuals from all parts of South Yemen, in contrast to the restricted entry practised by the British, and commissars in each unit carried out political education. To underline this new political character, the army was organized to work on projects related to the people, building schools, roads and irrigation projects. The NLF stated that instead of trying to insulate the army from politics, it was trying to revolutionize the army and render it a political force.

The new orientation of the post-1969 political line was confirmed at the Fifth Congress of the NLF, which met in Madinat ash-Shaab in March 1973. It was a different NLF from the one that met in Zinjibar in March 1968. Qahtan and his group had been expelled in 1970 for conspiracy, and even though other differences remained, the Congress was the first one not dominated by the old conflict between the factions of the left and right. Unlike all previous Congresses this one was preceded by several weeks' discussion among local NLF branches of the resolutions and reports to be submitted. The country's political atmosphere had been charged for months with a series of pro-NLF peasant and worker risings demanding democratic control of production. *Le Monde* correspondent Eric Rouleau, attending the Congress, described the scene as the 170 delegates arrived:[14]

Aden had been filled for days with demonstrating workers and peasants; crowds of militants chanting 'Long Live Marxism-Leninism' greeted the delegates. The average age of the delegates was between twenty and thirty – most of them from poor backgrounds – and many were hardly able to read or write; but despite the difficulties involved the sessions were long, serious and highly politicized.

In his opening address Abdul Fatah Ismail stressed the difficulties which the NLF faced in changing from a guerrilla organization to the agent of social transformation:

No one can belittle our brief and modest experience gained in the struggle for power under the feudalist and colonialist regime and in shouldering the tasks and burdens of progressive authority. The problem is that we dreamt of building a new society and everything appeared

255

to us to be simple and clear. But as usual reality is harder to understand and more complicated than we imagined. We had to fight both great historical problems and the day-to-day tasks, during the stage of national liberation and the burdens of struggle, and then during the period when we had taken over power. We had to go through a series of new and extremely difficult attempts ... The NLF is changing its status from being a mass organization destroying everything set up by the feudalist and colonialist regimes and leading the broad mass through the national liberation stage into being a leading force in society directly responsible for authority, drawing up programmes for the broadest masses ...

The documents of the Fifth Congress differed in several respects from those of the Fourth. While continued emphasis was laid on the role of the masses and on the need to strengthen the NLF organization, the NLF was now prepared to grant a certain role to 'sections' of the petty bourgeoisie, a class that was no longer denounced as a whole. This appeared to coincide with recent official policies of encouraging the national bourgeoisie to play a definite, if subordinate, role in the 'national democratic' phase of the revolution. In foreign policy too, it was noticeable that attacks on the 'petty-bourgeois' Arab regimes had ceased. In themselves, these changes could have been defended as reflecting a more realistic assessment of the South Yemeni revolution's current capabilities. More serious was the government's reluctance to construct the mass organizations it had called for when in opposition to Qahtan, and which, three and even four years after the 'corrective move', were still mere projects. A real political test of the South Yemeni leadership remained whether it could give content to the democratic slogans of the earlier period, or whether power would remain concentrated at the summit.

Mobilizing in the Hinterland

One area of undoubted political achievement was the countryside. Despite the past prosperity of Aden and the presence there of the state and NLF organizational centres, most of South

Yemen had remained rural, pre-capitalist and based on a subsistence economy. If the leading role in the revolution had been assigned to both workers and peasants, it was the latter who numerically predominated. Revolution in the hinterland was a strategic imperative. Social revolution in the countryside involved an attack both on the tribal structures and on those exploitative productive systems that still prevailed. Tribalism divided groups of peasants from each other and reinforced the ignorance that prevented improvements in health and agricultural technique; it thus impeded the social development of South Yemen. But in addition it reinforced the class structure of the hinterland, by forcing the peasant to rely on his tribal ruler, sultans and sheikh. It blinded him to the common interest that linked him to other tribes and to the division of interest between him and his own tribal oppressors. The straightforward class relations that prevailed – share-cropping, tenancy and slave ties – provided a more unmystified parallel to these tribal institutions.

Both tribal and class structures had been somewhat weakened by the guerrilla struggle, but the liberation movement had fought for only four years, and the NLF had been at the beginning a coalition that included tribal formations. Although NLF militants later stressed the 'backwardness' of South Yemeni society they tended to mean by this only the predominance of the petty bourgeoisie; the problems of South Yemen society were almost universally ascribed to the influence of this and other retrograde *classes* and less emphasis was laid on other retarding forces. In fact tribalism also remained powerful in the hinterland after 1967. In the remoter parts of the Fifth and Sixth Governorates in particular traditional forms of authority prevailed; tribes obeyed if they thought the state was strong, and disobeyed if they thought it was weak. In the army tribal divisions were accentuated by Saudi interferences. Furthermore, President Qahtan ash-Shaabi had a 'tribal' approach to political problems; not only did he handle intra-NLF factions like the quarrelling factions of a tribal federation, but he also worked out solutions to national problems by playing tribes off against each other.

The first anti-tribal measures were those of the national struggle itself. Yemeni nationalism and Arab nationalism stressed a unity that transcended tribal divisions, and the N L F struggle was the first one that encompassed the whole of South Yemen in a single coordinated movement. After taking power the N L F divided the country up into six Governorates, thereby abolishing the prevailing state divisions which corresponded to, and thereby reinforced, tribal lines. A more radical blow was struck through the enforcement of non-tribal law. Tribal conflicts were centred around real conflicts over issues of economic scarcity – water rights, grazing rights and caravan tolls. Conflicts between tribes were handled by vengeance and prolonged by feuds. Such law as existed was *urf*, traditional tribal law. The N L F set itself up as a supra-tribal institution which would remove these spurs to tribalism. In January 1968 the government decreed a 'General Truce Among the Tribes' to run for an initial five years. Revenge of all kinds was outlawed. All pre-existing feuds were declared in suspense, and the government undertook to punish anyone in the rural areas committing murder.[15] In 1970 rural (i.e. tribal) murder became a capital offence and the government began a stronger attack on tribalism at the ideological level by banning all tribal associations and clubs in the First Governorate.

The attack on tribal structures and consciousness could never succeed on its own, without elimination of the factors that sustained them: the rural class system and the poverty and ignorance that went with it. The anti-tribal and democratic campaigns are necessarily intertwined.

The rural oppressors had been ousted in the nationalist struggle but this had been mainly because of their character as traitors – that is, opponents of the nationalist movement and allies of the British – and not because of their class role. The task of rural revolution still had to be carried out, and this, because of conditions in South Yemen, differed from analogous campaigns elsewhere. In most countries land reform consists of redistributing existing land to peasants, either in plots or in forms of collective ownership. In South Yemen this was one aspect of the problem: up to 150,000 of the 300,000 acres could be so redistributed. But this only made available 0·3 of an acre per person, far too little to meet the people's needs. It was, therefore, necessary to increase the amount of cultivable land and to improve the techniques used to cultivate this land. In order to perform these tasks peasants had to be mobilized on a massive scale and land had to be redistributed along democratic lines.

The original land reform was decreed in late March 1968 by Qahtan ash-Shaabi, partly to counterbalance his attack on the NLF left. All lands of sultans, amirs and sheikhs who had worked with the British were confiscated without compensation. The upper limit was twenty-five acres of irrigated land per person and fifty acres of unirrigated land. Lands in excess of this were to be redistributed to NLF partisans and poor peasants in amounts of 3·5 acres of irrigated land and 6–10 of unirrigated.

The left opposed this reform. First, they argued that the land was being distributed in excessively large amounts – they wanted a five-acre limit on unirrigated land. Secondly, they said that the peasants who worked the land should receive it first. And, most importantly, the land which had been taken over should be grouped into cooperatives and not split up among individual peasants. The effect of Qahtan's land reform was, they argued, to create a class of rich peasants, *kulaks*, in the countryside: the big landowners had been weakened, but the poor peasants were still just as poor. This, they pointed out, was what had happened in Egypt.

When the left came to power in June 1969 they decided to restrict the operation of this reform but they did not abolish private ownership of land. They pointed out that some NLF partisans living in Aden had even stayed in the town and lived off the rent they got for leasing out their newly acquired lands. In December 1970 a second land reform was passed: this revoked the March 1968 law, and lowered the limits on land from fifty to forty acres for unirrigated land and from twenty-five to twenty acres for irrigated land. This limit applied to families, whereas the previous law had only applied to individuals, and different members of a single family had often divided excess family lands up between them.

Whereas the 1968 law gave priority to NLF partisans the 1970 law gave priority to those who tilled the land, and laid emphasis on grouping these peasants into cooperatives. In itself this law would have constituted a decree from above to be administered by government and party officials but its nature was transformed by the fact that it coincided with a popular mobilization, in the form of *intifadhat* or insurrections, which swept South Yemen in 1970–71. These provided the political basis for carrying out the rural transformation legally laid down in the December 1970 land reform act.

The first *intifadha* predated but anticipated the land reform act: in October 1970 hundreds of poor peasants in the Batis region of the Third Governorate, armed with forks and scythes, occupied the lands and houses of the landowners, arrested them and set up a popular committee to administer their assets. The lands were then distributed in 3–5 acre lumps and grouped in a cooperative. In November 1970 peasants with N L F backing went on to the attack in the Fourth Governorate, where under the 1968 law only 294 acres had so far been distributed; the rest had been parcelled out by landowners and merchants to their associates and had thus slipped under the minimum requirements.

An N L F militant later described how the peasants were helped to rise:

We persuaded the peasants that the exploiters would never change and that they had to act. They took their hatchets and sickles and immediately arrested all the sheikhs, sada and other feudalists – eighty-two in all. The population were stupefied. They thought that these people were untouchable and that whoever lifted a hand against them would die on the spot. When they saw that the lords remained in prison and that the town was not struck by any cataclysm all tongues were loosened and all the other peasants joined those who had taken part in the risings and came into the peasant leagues. There are now five Peasant Defence Leagues in the province. It was important that the peasants themselves took the people to prison. Some were armed, but we did not distribute arms because we were afraid of a massacre.[16]

Similar risings followed in other provinces. As President Salem Robea Ali put it:

... the land does not give itself away. It has to be taken. The NLF encouraged the *intifadhat* and other popular revolts, because revolutionary violence is the only way to produce a definite break between the large landlords and the workers ... This policy also had some major consequences: the peasants, fishermen, and workers have set up militia to defend, arms in their hands, both their social gains and the popular power that made them possible.[17]

By March 1972, fifteen months after the second land reform act, twenty-one cooperatives and twenty-four state farms had been set up. There were several hundred families in each. The process of creating rich peasants, begun by Qahtan, had been reversed. 'We want progressively to transform the small peasants into agricultural workers,' Salem Robea stated.[18]

The Economic Front: Austerity and Self-Reliance

The rural transformation programme was part of the general economic transformation which began at independence. The economic outlook was extremely grim: on top of the poverty of colonial society had come the collapse of the Adeni economy when it lost its three main sources of revenue – the port, the base and the British subsidies. Between 1966 and 1968 the country had an estimated *negative* growth rate of 10–15 per cent bringing its 1968 GNP down to £53 million, i.e. a per capita income of £34.

An economic report prepared in 1968 stated what had to be done:

On the one hand there is the need to counteract the depression created by the abnormal fall in income and employment and the budgetary deficit; and on the other hand there is the long term problem of developing the productive sectors of agriculture and industry so as to transform the 'service economy' into a national economy.[19]

South Yemen, unlike Cuba or Chile, had no sugar or copper, no source of income, to seize from foreign capitalists.

The first steps had to be austerity measures; income could only be raised in a longer period. In February 1968 the basic

261

salaries of all government employees, civil and military, were cut by amounts ranging from 60 per cent for those earning over £200 a month to 6 per cent for those earning between £23·5 and £25 a month. In June 1968 a comparable measure was applied to the private sector: a special tax was levied on all wages and salaries in the private sector ranging from 47·5 per cent for those earning over £250 a month to 5 per cent for those earning £25 a month. In both the public and private sectors those earning under £23·5 were not affected. Further measures to increase government revenue followed: in December 1970, as part of the drive to establish national control of the economy, Aden's free port status was abolished; with the exception of goods for tourists and goods in transit, imports were to be taxed and this was to raise £5 million a year. In 1971–2, as the *intifadhat* spread to Aden, the NLF encouraged calls for wage cuts in addition to those of 1968. In August 1972, after seven days of demonstrations in Aden, all wages in state enterprises were cut by one third.

In the last five years before independence more than 60 per cent of all revenue had come from British aid. Suddenly this was cut off: from an original pre-independence offer of £60 million the British lowered their offer to £12 million and in the end, after much haggling, reluctantly parted with £3 million after independence. Aid from other sources took time to materialize: by March 1972 amounts of around £25 million had been promised by both Russia and China, and smaller amounts had been given by the German Democratic Republic, North Korea, Kuwait and Algeria. But the major source of revenue had to come from inside; between 1966–7 and 1968–9 direct taxes rose from 7·7 per cent of the budget to 24 per cent; in the same period indirect taxes rose from 10·1 per cent to 29·2 per cent. British aid, just for the record, sank from 70 per cent to zero.

These austerity measures taken by the government enabled it to cut the large budget deficit that had faced it at independence and which was one of the many barbed legacies of British colonialism.

Similar rigid control enabled the government to cut deficits on foreign trade and in the Aden port. The foreign trade deficit was

Table 12

The South Yemeni Budget (£ million)

Year	Revenue	Expenditure	Deficit
1963–4	3·4	8·2	4·8
1964–5	3·7	10·8	7·1
1965–6	4·1	13·7	9·6
1966–7	4·4	17·2	12·8
1967–8	4·8	25·2	20·4
1968–9	7·0	16·0	9·0
1969–70	11·0	16·0	5·0
1970–71	13·5	18·5	5·0

Sources: up to 1967–8 from Ministry of Economy, Commerce and Planning, 'The Problems Facing the Emergent State of the People's Republic of Southern Yemen', Aden, 1968, p. 23. For the last three years from the Economist Intelligence Unit, *Quarterly Economic Reviews*.

a legacy of imperialism, and was a flagrant example of the colonial character of the economy; by 1971 it was coming under control.

Table 13

The Foreign Trade of South Yemen (£ million)

Year	Imports	Exports	Deficit
1964	107·5	66·8	40·7
1965	101·9	67·9	34·8
1966	72·2	50·5	21·7
1967	106·1	74·3	31·8
1968	84·5	45·8	38·7
1969	90·9	59·8	31·1
1970	83·8	60·7	23·1
1971	64·7	53·1	11·6

Sources: up to 1967 Ministry of Economy, Commerce and Planning, Central Statistical Office, Aden, statement of 18 February 1969; for 1968–71 Economist Intelligence Unit, 'The Arabian Peninsula: Sheikhdoms and Republics', *Quarterly Economic Reviews*, Annual Supplement, 1972.

The port's deficit was of a different kind; it had been caused by the closure of the Suez Canal and had not existed before 1967. But as a result of the Canal closure bunkering revenue fell from 33 per cent of the country's exports to 7 per cent, port revenue dropped by over a half and by 1967–8 the port had a deficit of £493,000 out of total expenditure of £1.5 million. Strong control enabled the port to cut its expenditure to around £800,000 by 1969–70 and to generate a small surplus.

The end of foreign control of the economy was a priority after the June 1969 'corrective move'. In July 1969 a new investment ordinance specified that 75 per cent of all employees of foreign firms had to be South Yemenis, and that after five years one half of the senior staff had to be so too. In November 1969 a major nationalization law was passed: all banks, insurance companies, trading houses and petrol distributors were nationalized – in all around forty firms. In 1970 the South Yemeni dinar broke all links with the pound sterling, to which it had been tied. The ending of the free port status and the nationalization of all soft drinks factories in 1972 strengthened government control. But the largest foreign-owned enterprise in the country, the BP refinery, remained unnationalized. It had been running at a loss since 1967 and, without finding oil on its territory, South Yemen could not have obtained oil for refining had it ousted BP altogether.

These nationalizations gave the government strategic control of the economy, and the austerity measures squeezed what small surplus there was out of the impoverished country. The long-term economic transformation, ending the dependence on services and increasing income, was found to be a difficult process. The public sector set up by the nationalizations of 1969 showed a surplus of £1·25 million in its first year of operation and in 1971 the first development plan was announced. Over three years £40.7 million were to be spent; half of this was to come from foreign sources. £9·9 million was to go to raising industrial production, including the expansion of eight existing plants and the installation of thirty new ones. Excluding the refinery this would raise industrial production by 150 per cent. Another £10.5 million was to raise agricultural production: with rises in productivity and an 8 per cent rise in the cultivable area, crop output would rise by 26 per cent and livestock by 20 per cent. South Yemeni fishing, tapping one of the richest fishing grounds in the world, would rise by 35 per cent. By 1974 fish were expected to replace cotton as the main export. The greatest hope of all was that South Yemen would discover oil, but efforts by a joint Algerian–South Yemen exploration company had not produced significant results by the end of 1972. In the absence of any such bonanza the economic development of South Yemen was bound to be long and hard.[20]

The People's Republic Under Siege

South Yemen's foreign policy was characterized by a militant internationalism, especially after the 'corrective move' of June 1969. At one level this reflected a deep political commitment to support other struggling movements who were carrying through the policies for which the NLF itself had fought. At another level it reflected the concrete needs of the South Yemeni revolution itself which had been born amid a world of enemies and which had common interests with anti-imperialist forces elsewhere.

Diplomatic relations with the USA were broken off altogether in October 1969 in protest at US citizens being allowed to serve in the Israeli army. Relations were formally established with the Democratic Republic of Vietnam and with the Provisional Revolutionary Government of South Vietnam; and in time close ties grew with Cuba and with the Democratic Republic of North Korea. It was obvious that People's Yemen stood firmly on the side of the communist world, and that the economic aid which it needed had to come from there. The Soviet Union and China had provided around £25 million each by March 1972 – the Soviets in aid to the army and the fishing industry, the Chinese in medical aid and in a road project linking Aden to the Hadramaut. But despite this general support the PDRY stood to the left of both these major powers on a number of key issues. Both Russia and China opened diplomatic ties to the states of the lower

Gulf whom the PDRY at first refused to recognize and whom it tried to exclude from the Arab League and the United Nations.[21] On Palestine, the PDRY opposed the UN resolution of November 1967 which the Soviet Union had sponsored, and the NLF's initial criticism of the 'petty-bourgeois' character of such states as Egypt and Algeria contrasted with the favourable official Soviet characterization of them.[22] On the other hand the PDRY did not regard the Soviet Union as a 'social imperialist' country, as the Chinese maintained, and it therefore held that the United States remained the number one enemy of the peoples of the world. In addition to the above there were other differences. The Chinese support for the Nimeri government in the Sudan after the July 1971 massacre of the Communist party leaders contrasted with PDRY solidarity with the murdered revolutionaries. Like the Vietnamese, the PDRY refused to be drawn into Sino–Soviet polemics, but, like the Vietnamese too, the South Yemeni revolutionaries felt the negative consequences both of the rivalry between the two communist states and of the separate détentes which both were seeking with the USA.

The PDRY stood far to the left of any other Arab government, particularly in their tense and principled relations to the chloroforming institutions of inter-Arab politics such as the Arab League. Their experience with inter-Arab politics before independence had been bitter. The most immediate enemies they now faced were other Arab states, and their solidarity with anti-imperialist forces all over the world and their refusal to accept the mystifications of 'Arab socialism' were unique. They were often accused of being 'outside Arabism' and anti-Islamic. They were the first Arab state to recognize Bangladesh – in explicit rejection of the reactionary 'Moslem solidarity' which tied the other states to Pakistan. On Palestine they consistently supported the guerrilla organizations and, while having special relations with the PDFLP, gave what support they could to the guerrilla movement as a whole.

The most immediate fronts for the PDRY were those to the north-west, north and north-east – the Red Sea, North Yemen, the Gulf. In order to meet these threats its army was increased from around 6,000 in 1967 to 14,000 in 1972, and was re-equipped by Soviet supplies. Across the narrow mouth of the Red Sea lay enemies: Ethiopia, a single-mindedly pro-US regime which was suppressing the people of Eritrea;[23] and Djibouti, a French Aden which had been used, among other things, to fly supplies to the North Yemeni royalists. The PDRY commanded the island of Perim in the Bab al-Mandeb straits; and this gave it a potential stranglehold on shipping up the Red Sea; even without the opening of the Suez Canal the Red Sea was coveted by western interests because of rich mineral deposits just off the coast of the YAR. Moreover from 1970 tankers were ferrying oil from Iran to the Israeli port of Eilat at the top of the Red Sea for use in Israel or shipment to the Mediterranean, and in early 1973 it was reported that Israel had established commando units on Ethiopian islands near the Bab al-Mandeb straits.[24] During the fourth Arab–Israeli War in October-November 1973 the Bab al-Mandeb straits were blocked to Israeli shipping, and the PDRY artillery on Perim Island was instrumental in this. Ships of the US Seventh Fleet were moved nearer the straits, and jets from a US aircraft carrier buzzed planes preparing to land at Aden airport. But there was no direct clash involving either US or Israeli shipping. Ethiopia also broke off diplomatic relations with Israel during the October War; this was dictated by the mounting internal crisis within Ethiopia, and did not end the close economic and political cooperation between the two regimes.

On the north-east flank the PDRY had a common border with the Southern, Dhofar, province of the Sultanate of Oman; even before independence support was given by the NLF to the Omani guerrillas; and after independence the full support of the South Yemeni state was at the disposal of the Gulf revolution. The PDRY was always clear that the enemies it faced were the same as those faced by the peoples of the Gulf – Iran, Saudi Arabia, Britain and the US. In 1971 they refused to recognize the puppet states granted 'independence' by Britain (although they failed in their campaign to exclude them from international organizations) and they kept up a barrage of political attacks on

267

the pro-imperialist forces in the region. For this reason the PDRY was in a state of permanent hostility with both its north-eastern neighbours; along the fifty-mile frontier with Oman, and along the 300-mile frontier with Saudi Arabia. Border clashes were frequent, and in May 1972 Omani forces made an air and ground attack on guerrilla positions inside the PDRY.

Saudi Arabia had been an active if inefficient patron of the south Arabian sultans during the pre-independence period, and after November 1967 these exiled counter-revolutionaries were able to use Saudi facilities to carry on their campaign: they acquired a radio station, Radio Free Yemeni South, in 1970 when it was no longer being used by the North Yemeni royalists, and were allowed to use facilities at ash-Sharura, a desert camp on the Yemeni border, 400 miles north-east of Aden. The biggest clash came in November 1969 when Saudi troops backed by Lightning jets attacked the Yemeni border post at al-Wadiah, thirty miles south of ash-Sharura. Since then Saudi forces, and the pro-Sultan 'Army of Deliverance', have been probing and harassing in the desert area. If the PDRY found oil in the region, Saudi attacks could be expected to increase; and, in the event of an all-out attack, Saudi forces would try to push through the Fifth Governorate of the PDRY to the sea, cutting Dhofar off from the rest of South Yemen and giving Saudi Arabia direct access to the Indian Ocean.

After initial optimism, relations with North Yemen deteriorated. Yemeni unity had been urged by all Yemeni nationalists, both North and South, all, that is, except the South Arabian League. The arguments derived from common culture, common Yemeni consciousness, economic complementarity and a real, if intermittent, historical unity. The nationalists were right to claim that there was a Yemeni nation; but to blame the division just on the presence of imperialism was incorrect. By 1967–8 the two states represented quite distinct class interests, had quite different international alignments and represented contradictory social formations. Imperialism, ably assisted by Saudi Arabia – who backed the North – exploited the situation. The massacre of the left in the North in 1968 and the advent of the NLF left to power in the South in 1969 ended hopes of immediate unity and in September 1972 full-scale war broke out as Saudi-supported Southern exiles and Northern tribesmen tried to invade the South. The main organization behind this was a United National Front of South Yemen headed by ex-FLOSY leaders al-Asnaj and Makawi. They received backing from Saudi Arabia and from Libya, who were in competition for influence in the area, and were covertly supported by the United States.

Their invasion attempt was stopped within a week, and after several partial cease-fires a final cease-fire between the two Yemens was signed in Cairo on 28 October 1972. The cease-fire agreement was accompanied by a shock – the surprise announcement that the two states would merge to form one Yemeni state within a year; this was solemnized a month later when presidents al-Iryani and Salem Robea Ali met in Libya.[25] In the short term this agreement had definite advantages for both governments: it enabled the PDRY to disperse the hostile forces on its boundaries, and to weaken Saudi influence in the area, as well as to win influence by championing Yemeni unity. On the other hand the central government in the North was able to increase its influence at the expense of the tribal leaders whom the Saudis were supporting; while the tribal leaders wanted war with the South, the central government did not. Not surprisingly Radio Free Yemeni South denounced the deal as a communist plot and the Saudis were angry.[26] The North–South committees, set up under the 1972 agreements, continued to meet in 1973; but, while there was agreement on economic and cultural matters, there was stalemate in the constitutional committee where the affair of the three Yemeni provinces under Saudi administration was discussed. At the Algiers summit of non-aligned countries in September 1973 Presidents Salem Robea Ali and al-Iryani agreed to postpone formal unification indefinitely, although certain forms of economic cooperation between the two governments appeared to be increasing. While Yemeni unity remained a policy that united anti-imperialists in North and South real unity between the two states was impossible given the different social systems in the two parts.

South Yemen

From Aden to the Gulf

After 1967 the PDRY became the main supporter of the revolutionary movement in the Arab peninsula as a whole, and – like Russia, China, Vietnam and Cuba after their revolutions – it had to face the determined hostility of imperialism and imperialism's clients in the surrounding area. It overcame its short-term problems; but the political nature of the South Yemeni revolution, of the NLF and of the social transformation in the PDRY depended in the long run on developments outside as well as inside the boundaries of the People's Republic.

The NLF's achievements were considerable: it had, in the period 1963–7, swept out the British and the local elements who were tied to them – the sultans and the Adeni bourgeoisie. In the post-1967 period it had carried this process further by mobilizing the rural and urban masses, by initiating a self-reliant development programme, and by destroying the grip foreign capital had on the economy. The NLF itself had changed both its ideology and its organization; from being a nationalist group loosely structured around a set of general demands it had become much more firmly organized and had built stronger ties with the population; its ideology had moved to the left, because of the influence of objective forces, and because of the substantial influence of Marxism within the organization.

At the same time, the South Yemen revolution faced some major obstacles, both inside and outside the country. The central internal problem concerned the character of the South Yemeni state, and of the NLF's role. Survival was the first concern of the state and the NLF, and this conflicted in direct ways with the realization of a democratic, political life within the Republic. The need for mass democratic institutions, within the party and within the state, had been one of the cornerstones of the 'left's' critique of Qahtan. Yet when the 'left' itself came to power it proved unwilling to actualize its previous slogans. One factor impeding them was the constant threat of foreign attack and internal disruption by counter-revolutionaries. Another was the lack of political cadres and the continuance among the masses of pre-revolutionary ideas and practices. The continuing economic difficulties of the Republic also made the building of a party and of mass democratic institutions more difficult. But the failure to build these led inevitably to the growth of other forms of centralized political control in which the armed forces and the top leadership substituted for the democratic interrelationship of government and people.

These factors constituted objective constraints upon the South Yemeni revolution. Its ability to overcome them depended on the continuation inside and outside South Yemen of the revolutionary movement: the building of revolutionary institutions inside the PDRY formed the one sure internal guarantee of future independent politics. But the fate of the PDRY itself depended to a considerable extent on the development of the revolution elsewhere – in North Yemen and in the Gulf.[27] On its own the state would face a very hard and delimited future: for economic, psychological and military reasons it needed a breakthrough elsewhere. While the PDRY was the first liberated state in Arabia, its fate was directly tied to the fate of the revolution in the rest of the peninsula.

Notes

1. The account of events up to 1970 is based on discussions with NLF members during a visit by Fawwaz Trabulsi and myself to Aden. This includes information given in talks by Abdul Fatah Ismail, Mohammad Ali Haitham, Ali al-Beedh, Abdullah al-Khamri, Abdullah Badheeb and Feisal al-Attas. I have used press reports and government publications for additional and later information, as well as material gathered on a second visit in 1973. For a vivid account of the PDRY in 1972 see Joe Stork, 'Socialist Revolution in Arabia: A Report from the People's Democratic Republic of Yemen', MERIP Reports, No. 15, March 1973.

2. Qahtan argued before independence that the NLF had to appoint him President because he was the only member of the leadership over forty, and the PRSY would not command respect in the world if its head of state was too young.

3. The six Governorates, *mohafazat*, had formed the basis of the NLF's underground structure from 1963 onwards.

4. A major analysis of this period is Nayyef Hawatmeh's *Azmat ath-Thawrah fi Yaman al-Junoub* (*The Crisis of the Revolution in South Yemen*),

Beirut, 1969. Hawatmeh, a leader of the left current within the MAN, visited Aden in early 1968 and attended the Fourth Congress of the NLF. His analysis centres on the dangers of the 'petty bourgeoisie' controlling the state and on the need to smash the state apparatus. His book provoked a reply by Feisal ash-Shaabi, leader of the NLF right, entitled *Kaif Nafham ath-Thawrah fi Yaman al-Junub* (*How We Understand the Revolution in South Yemen*), Beirut, 1969. Abdul Fatah Ismail was falsely named as one of the authors of this apologetic tract.

5. An Aden radio broadcast on 16 November stressed that the British were hated 'not for their race or for being soldiers but as colonialist usurpers and imperialists dominating the country.'

6. The theory of this form of popular democracy was based on the Bolshevik model of *soviets*.

7. *Ash-Sharara*, Mukalla, March 1968.

8. Hawatmeh, op. cit., pp. 71ff., gives a formal if idealized account of the Hadrami experience to March 1968.

9. Full text of this and other Fourth Congress documents and resolutions in Hawatmeh, op. cit. Extracts from these in *Orient*, Paris, Vol. 14, 1970. A German translation of Abdul Fatah Ismail's speech is in Bassam Tibi, ed., *Die arabische Linke*, Frankfurt am Main, 1969, pp. 138–58. The description 'non-capitalist path of development' is a misnomer, since what it referred to was the *socialist* path of development; the conception of the 'non-capitalist path' had been produced by apologists for *capitalist* states in the third world who pretended to be socialist (Egypt, Ghana, etc.).

10. General Command statement of 14 May 1968.

11. Economist Intelligence Unit, *Quarterly Economic Reviews*, 'Arabian Peninsula and Jordan', No. 4, 1968, p. 19.

12. Although Haitham had been one of the leaders of the 'corrective move' he had had disagreements with the left leaders, especially over the army and relations with Egypt.

13. Apart from the daily *14 October* the following weeklies were published: *Saut al-Ummal* (*Voice of the Workers*) for the trade unions; *ath-Thawri* (*The Revolutionary*), the NLF's theoretical weekly; *al-Jundi* (*The Soldier*), the army weekly; *al-Haras* (*The Guard*), for police and security forces; *al-Hejma* (*The Attack*) and *ath-Thaqafa al-Jadida* (*New Culture*) were periodicals for cultural workers.

14. 'L'Étoile Rouge sur le Yémen du Sud', Part 1, 'Les guerrilleros au pouvoir', *Le Monde*, 27 May 1972. This series of four consecutive articles gives an excellent impression of the PDRY in early 1972.

15. In the *Ministerial Resolution Supplement to the Official Gazette*, No. 33, 18 July 1968, the preamble to the General Truce gives an interesting illustration of the kind of appeal being made to the tribes:

'As the common interest necessitates the maintenance of peace and security among citizens throughout the Republic, and in confirmation of the tribal truce decisions taken by the local commands of the National Liberation Front in all six Governorates, and in view of the need for everyone to contribute towards building up an honourable social and economic future for this new-born Republic, it is resolved as follows ...'

16. Claude Deffarge and Gordian Troeller, 'Sud-Yémen: Une Révolution Menacée?', *Le Monde Diplomatique*, April 1972, p. 6.

17. Rouleau, 'La révolution dans la révolution', op. cit., 28–9 May 1972.

18. ibid.

19. Dr Mohammad Salman Hassan, *Report to the People's Republic of Southern Yemen on Guidelines for Industrial Planning and Policy*, Aden, 1970; the report was presented in October 1968.

20. An interesting and sympathetic critique of the economic policies of the PDRY government is contained in René Lefort, 'Révolution au Sud-Yemen', *Le Monde Diplómatique*, February 1971. Lefort considers that the NLF for too long underestimated the role of the rural masses and had therefore not properly exploited rural resources; at the same time he argues that the nationalization measures were carried out over-hastily and had short-term negative effects on the economy.

21. When the Sultanate of Oman, a British colony in all but name, applied to the UN for admission in 1971 the only state to support the PDRY was Cuba, which abstained on the vote.

22. When in June 1970 the Conservative government came to power in Britain it orchestrated an anti-communist campaign distorting the significance of the Soviet naval presence in the Indian Ocean. It put out lies to the effect that there was a Russian harbour master in Aden and a Russian base on the PDRY island of Socotra. These assertions were duly repeated as fact by the collusive 'diplomatic correspondents' of the London press. On 30 December 1970 *The Times* diplomatic correspondent A. M. Rendel published an article entitled 'Importance of the Suez Canal to Russia', in which he alleged: 'There is a Soviet harbour master at Aden and the Russians appear to be developing facilities on the island of Socotra.' The article was obviously based on an 'unattributable' Foreign Office briefing. Unfortunately for Rendel, *The Times* had at that time a man in the PDRY, Nicholas Ashford, who reported that the harbour master at Aden was an Indian (31 December 1970) and that 'There is no Soviet base on the island of Socotra' (11 January 1971).

23. Since 1961 guerrillas in the Eritrean province of Ethiopia have been waging a guerrilla war under the leadership of the Eritrean Liberation Front. The closure of the Ethiopian–Sudan border to the guerrillas and the end of support by the People's Republic of China after Ethiopia recognized Peking have weakened their struggle; but it has continued none the less. See Fred Halliday, 'The Fighting in Eritrea', *New Left Review*, No. 67, May–June 1971.

24. *Time*, 19 March 1973. In June 1971 a naval commando of the PFLP attacked the tanker *Coral Sea* which was transporting 65,000 tons of Iranian petrol to Eilat. The guerrillas set out from South Yemeni territory

but followed the tanker up the Red Sea, and after attacking it were forced to land on North Yemeni shores. In a spectacular illustration of the shared interests of Israel, Iran and Arab reaction, the YAR authorities arrested the Palestinian militants. The Eilat pipeline, opened in 1970 and costing £48 million, was carrying 35 million tons of oil in 1973. Much of this was ferried semi-clandestinely by tankers using faked records, but was an open secret in Middle East oil circles. For an early exposé see 'Mystery of the Disappearing Tankers', *Sunday Times*, 13 December 1970.

25. According to the 28 October 1972 agreement unity was to take place within a year, but the November agreement made no mention of a time limit. According to the latter the single state was to be called the Yemeni Republic; its capital was to be Sanaa, Islam was to be its religion and the state was to aim 'at achieving socialism which is inspired by the legacy of Arab Islam, its humanitarian values and the circumstances of Yemeni society'.

26. According to Radio Free Yemeni South (29 November 1972), 'This unity is merely a superficial and hurried measure to achieve the so-called dispersion of concentrations, the reopening of the border and the exporting of international violence to the north'. It also alleged (1 December 1972) that 'the Yemeni people raised a clamour because it described the crimes, atheism and anarchism of the regime in Aden and its usurpation of land and money as gains . . .'

27. The development of ties with nationalist forces in North Yemen represented an important second line of attack for the PDRY, as strategically necessary as the advance of the revolution in Oman. One summary captures the thinking behind this: 'The government officials and the National Front cadre I spoke with stressed repeatedly that the dangers of this course of coupling their progressive but still very new political and economic structures with the much larger but much more backward political economy of the North were outweighed only by the longer-run danger of not seizing this opportunity. The future of revolutionary socialism, they maintain, cannot rest on its isolated presence at the tip of the Peninsula. The historic and organic unity of Yemen can provide the necessary base. If I could distil this strategy into a slogan, it would be: Socialism in one country, perhaps; socialism in half a country, no chance at all', Joe Stork, op. cit., p. 25.

Part Four
Oman

Chapter Nine
The Sultanate of Oman –
A British Colony

From Empire to Isolation

From the mid-nineteenth century Oman has been under British domination.[1] Yet, like the hinterland of South Yemen, its importance was strategic, not intrinsic. Oman was not developed economically, it was a static and safe link between South Yemen and the colonies in the lower Gulf. In the period after 1945 this policy began to encounter serious opposition, as the political and economic changes in the Gulf and Aden undermined the basis of colonial power in Oman. The very instability of these other areas made Oman's role as a tranquil buffer ever more important, but imperialism and its clients in Oman were unable to contain the contradictions. In 1957 an insurrection broke out in the Omani interior and was only put down two years later by British troop reinforcements. In 1965 guerrilla war broke out in the province of Dhofar, and quickly developed into a full-scale people's war. Oman, which had been the most backward and static part of the whole peninsula, had become the focal point of the anti-imperialist movement in Arabia.

The Sultanate occupies the territory in between South Yemen and the Gulf, 82,000 square miles that stretch along the Indian Ocean and the Gulf of Oman to the east and north, with the sands of the empty quarter of Saudi Arabia on the west and a common frontier with South Yemen in the south-west. The Sultanate is made up of two distinct parts: there is the north-east area, which consists of a fertile coastal zone and its mountainous interior, dominated by the 10,000-foot plateau of the Green Mountain. In previous epochs this area was known as Oman; but the name is now applied to the whole Sultanate. To the south-west, across 500 miles of desert, lies a quite distinct area, the mountainous southern province of Dhofar, which was annexed to the Sultanate in the 1880s. Estimates of the population range from 500,000 to 1,500,000, and, as most of the country is barren and waterless, the people cluster around the ports and the scattered fertile areas. Until 1970 the Omani economy was of a very primitive kind; fishing was common along the coasts, and dates and limes were grown for export on the fertile Batinah plain, north-west of Muscat. Subsistence agriculture was carried out in the interior on the patches of fertile land irrigated by wells or underground canals. The peasants lived in a state of almost complete economic autarky, trading a few animals or agricultural products for arms, rice and cloth brought up from the coast. There was only one road, along the Batinah coast, and no industry of any kind. Foreign trade was a trickle of primary products and of a few necessary manufactured imports like cement and cotton goods.

If North Yemen was regarded as an isolated Arabian country, a Middle Eastern Tibet, Oman was so cut off from the outside world that no one even noticed it was isolated; until 1970 it was ultra-Tibet. Society was organized along the tribal lines found elsewhere but, in Oman, the ideological expression of tribal differences was often more fierce than elsewhere. Within each tribe there was some social differentiation and in the towns of the interior, such as Nizwa, poorer tribesmen worked on the plots of richer ones. As in North Yemen the position of tribal leaders was sometimes conditional on the support of their tribesmen, and their position was maintained through the services they performed – settling disputes and dealing with outsiders. The country was ruled by these sheikhs who maintained an oscillating relationship with the central power, the Sultan of Muscat. The Sultan when strong was able to appoint governors to rule the areas of the interior, but when weak he was content to allow these tribal areas to rule themselves on condition that they did not actually challenge his position as Sultan.

The present tribal shape of Oman was formed by a series of immigrations which took place before and after the advent of Islam. Tribes migrated from Yemen and from the northern parts of the Gulf and settled on the fertile coasts and mountains of Oman. The present division of the country into about 200 tribes derives from this era, and many of the tribes trace their origins to named ancestors who came from a particular part of Yemen. In the seventh century, when the Islamic empire was established, Oman became a part of it, and fell under the domination of the imperial capitals, Damascus and Baghdad. This rule was never strong and Oman quickly regained its independence. This independence was expressed in Ibadhism, one of the most militant versions of unorthodox Islam. Ibadhism was fiercely loyal to the specific injunctions of the Koran, and was intensely hostile to non-Moslems; the only leader they acknowledged was the Imam, the religious and political head chosen by the elders of the tribes. Like the Zeidism of North Yemen, this anti-centralizing ideology and the institution of Imam corresponded to the needs of a tribal society, hostile to rule from an imperial capital, where power was exercised by a coalition of powerful tribal leaders.[2]

Ibadhism was brought to Oman from Iraq in the eighth century and by around 850, less than two centuries after its original conversion to Islam, Oman had broken away from the Islamic empire and had constituted its independence around the Imamate. From the ninth century until the sixteenth this arrangement prevailed: several invading forces tried to win over Omani tribes or to occupy the ports, but the Omani Imamate remained in control and was able to reassert itself.

The centre of Imamic power lay in the interior, around the Green Mountain and the towns of Nizwa and Rostaq. The coast was less important, but depended for its prosperity on the trade between the Indian Ocean and the states further up the Gulf. This predominance of the mountain over the coast was upset by the penetration of western shipping to the area in the early sixteenth century. In 1507 the Portuguese, who had sailed around the Cape of Good Hope, captured the port of Muscat. They dominated the Gulf for over a century and, as the trading economy grew, Muscat became a link between the Persian and Ottoman empires to the north, and India, the Far East and Europe. The Portuguese built two large forts at Muscat, which still dominate the port, and the fort at Jalali is still the main prison of the Omani Sultans.

When, in the seventeenth century, the British displaced the Portuguese and the Dutch as the dominant sea power in the area, the Omanis were able to reassert themselves; and in 1650 an indigenous Omani army recaptured Muscat. This time the weight of the Omani state lay on the coast, and for two centuries Muscat was the capital of a flourishing commercial empire. The Yaruba family, who led the capture of Muscat from the Portuguese, founded a new dynasty with Muscat as the capital and by 1700 they had built the largest fleet of any non-European state active in the Indian Ocean. Their power stretched down the coast of Africa where they appropriated former Portuguese colonies, and by 1730 they had occupied Mogadishu (now capital of Somalia), Mombasa and the islands of Zanzibar and Pemba.[3]

At first the main challenge to the Yaruba Sultans came from inside Oman, from the tribes of the interior whose former dominance had now been displaced by the prosperity of the coast. Civil war broke out in the early eighteenth century and two tribal confederations, the Hinnawi and the Ghafiri, united the 200 tribes of the interior and challenged the coast. The Yaruba in Muscat were defeated by this internal opposition, and their place was taken by a new dynasty, which exploited the wars in order to seize power on the coast. Once established, this new dynasty, the Al Bu Said, was just as opposed to the tribes of the interior as the Yaruba had been, but allowed a division of authority to take place. For the first time political and religious power were separated. The office of Imam was to remain with the tribes of the interior, but his non-religious powers were to be limited. The main political power was to be with the Sultan of Muscat, who was to control the Omani empire.

Under the Al Bu Said dynasty the Sultan's trade monopolies and taxes on trade provided ample revenue. The only town in the interior to pay any taxes was Nizwa.[4] Muscat had a low 5 per cent import tax and it prospered as the major trade entrepot in the whole Gulf with an excellent all-weather harbour. It controlled the slave trade from Africa and was a political force in the

Indian Ocean as a whole. In the nineteenth century economically important sultans of Muscat were in diplomatic contact with western powers. Napoleon wrote a personal letter to the Sultan, trying to enlist his support for the planned French invasion of India, and the British were in treaty relations with him from 1798 onwards. In 1833 the USA signed its first ever treaty with an Arab state when it entered into relations with the Sultan of Muscat.

But imperialism was destroying all rival economies and political forces in the colonial world and the Omani economy was bound to be overwhelmed like the artisan economies of Egypt and India and the agricultural economies of Africa and the Americas. The basis of Omani prosperity was the slave trade which Britain had begun to suppress;[5] by the mid 1850s 80 per cent of the slave trade had been stopped. In 1856 the richest source of income, Zanzibar, was split off from Oman when the reigning Sultan Said died, and the empire was divided between his two sons. Although Oman received an annual subsidy from Britain after 1866, the economy was undermined by the loss of the African colonies.[6] In 1862 the arrival of steamships in the Gulf removed the trade of Muscat's fleet, and rival ports soon predominated. The advent of cheaper manufactured textiles also threw local artisans out of work and foreign, mainly Indian, merchants gained control of the area's commerce. The coastal economy around Muscat collapsed. In a twenty-year period, between the 1850s and the 1870s, the population of Muscat fell from 55,000 to 8,000; the number of ships visiting the port declined, and an increasing number were foreign-owned. Trade fell in 1874–5 to £426,000, a quarter of its level in the 1830s.[7]

The destruction of the Omani empire and of the commercial economy had three important consequences which, taken together, defined the history of the country for the next century. The first was that Oman was plunged into an economic depression which severed its connections with the outside world, depopulated the coastal towns and drove most of its impoverished inhabitants back to a near-subsistence economy. Later writers tend to state that Oman *never* developed. This is false: *Oman did not remain stuck in the Middle Ages; it was driven back into the Middle Ages by the advance of modern capitalism.* Unlike North Yemen, which had never developed and which, for internal reasons, had contracted, Oman had been forced backwards. Its underdevelopment was induced.[8]

The second consequence of the end of empire was that the conflict between the coast and the mountainous interior became more pronounced. As long as the empire had prospered the sultans of Muscat had not needed to raise taxes in the interior, excise taxes had been low, and Omanis from the interior who had emigrated to African colonies sent money, goods and slaves back to their relatives. The prosperity of the coast had sustained demand for the interior's few products. When the Omani empire collapsed in the 1860s the tribes of the interior no longer saw rule from Muscat as beneficial to them, and they decided either to impose their rule on the coast, as had been the case before the sixteenth century, or to break away from a regime that brought them no benefits. This hostility to the coast and to the outside world found expression in a militant Ibadhism which called for stricter observance of Islam.[9] The office of Imam, which had been moribund for some decades, was revived, and an anti-coastal alliance was formed under the leadership of the al-Harithi tribe. In 1868 this alliance swept out of the mountains, down to the coast, and captured Muscat. Foreign merchants were driven out, coffee shops – a symbol of alien 'corruption' – were closed and the literal interpretation of the Koran was imposed. But this conservative restoration was totally unable to grapple with the economic and social problems that confronted Oman and was equally unable to face up to the force that had destroyed the Omani empire, British imperialism.

In 1871 Britain invaded Muscat and restored the Sultan to power, thus establishing Oman as a *de facto* British colony. This situation lasted for the next hundred years. The imposition of British colonial rule was the third consequence of the collapse of the Omani empire.

A Very Simple Form of Colonialism

The British have never admitted that Oman was a colony and have always tried to mask the nature of their control. One standard way has been to state that Oman is an independent country which Britain 'advises' and 'assists' under treaty obligations. But this is often hard to sustain as British military might upholds the Sultan, British advisers run his government and, until 1967, British money made up over half of his revenue. A less mendacious ploy is to say that the relationship between Britain and the Sultan is 'very complicated' and that only 'experts', 'Arabists' or whoever fully understand it; Britain's spokesmen do not accept that Oman is a colony, yet 'we' seem to be very deeply involved. This is a 'mystery' and attempts to clarify it are lost in the sands of the desert. This is all evasion. It is power, not treaties, that determines history. Only writers blinded by a fog of legalism and imperialist ideology can doubt that Oman has been a *de facto* British colony in that the regime depended on Britain, and Britain imposed its will when it wanted to. The pretence of Omani 'independence', like the 'complexity' of the relationship, is meant to hide what is in fact a pellucid arrangement. Britain supports the Sultan and has told him what to do when it needed to; otherwise it has allowed him to rule as he likes, provided he keeps Oman tranquil and defends British strategic interests. The Sultans are British collaborators.

The first official relations between Britain and Muscat were opened in 1798 when Britain tried to secure the Sultan's support against France. The French threat never materialized, but, throughout the nineteenth and twentieth centuries, British policy was to keep control of the Sultan in order to prevent any other imperialist power (French, Russian, Turkish) from gaining a foothold there. Britain also benefited from the destruction of the Omani merchant fleet and the division of the Omani empire, because this gave British subjects an added advantage, and the reduction of Omani power also ensured the 'safety' i.e. unbridled predominance of British traders in the Gulf. Another concern of the British was that the Sultan might be overthrown from within; and this problem highlighted one of the contradictions of imperial rule: while Britain benefited from the destruction of the Omani empire and brought it about, this end of empire weakened the sultans internally and necessitated greater British intervention. *The advent of imperialism both exacerbated the conflict between the Omani interior and the coast and prevented it from being resolved.*

The full-scale uprising of 1868 and the fall of Muscat to the tribes of the interior began a long series of British interventions in defence of their client sultans. After the restoration of the Sultan in 1871, when all-out colonial control began, there were further clashes in 1877 and 1883 when British warships shelled and drove off tribesmen who were attacking Muscat. From 1866 onwards the British paid the Sultan an annual subsidy from the Indian treasury and he was able to use this gold to bribe certain key tribes. In 1886 the British went a stage further and gave a formal guarantee to 'uphold Sayyid Turki in repelling unprovoked aggression during his lifetime'.[10] In 1891 Turki's son, Sultan Feisal, was forced to sign a treaty which included a secret guarantee binding him not to alienate any of his territory to a third power.

Sultan Feisal tried and failed to weaken British control. In 1895 the British refused to support him in the face of an al-Harithi attack on Muscat and they only agreed to restore him on condition that he accepted their orders. Later he tried to grant bunkering rights to France, but at a time when Britain and France were quarrelling in Africa (Muscat was called 'a second Fashoda') this French intrusion into the Gulf was blocked. No one at that time had any doubt about the nature of the ties linking Oman and Britain.[11] When Lord Curzon, viceroy of India, visited Muscat in 1903 he praised the Sultan for his behaviour which was, he said, like that of 'a royal feudatory of the British Crown rather than that of an independent sovereign'.[12]

In the early twentieth century the conflict between the coast and the mountainous interior grew. In 1912 the British forced the Sultan to ban the import of arms into the Sultanate and the tribes of the interior took this, quite rightly, to be a means of controlling them and an index of the Sultan's capitulation to

1. *above* Sallal (centre, in uniform) and al-Beidhani (in light jacket) in Sanaa, shortly after the proclamation of the Republic in North Yemen in 1962

2. *right* Abdul Raquib Abdul Wahhab, Yemeni Republican commander, talks with his men during the siege of Sanaa, January 1968. Eleven months later he was assassinated by the North Yemeni government

3. *above left* Nasser and Feisal meet at Jiddah, August
1965. Although their agreement broke down after
these talks, they had paved the way for the long-term
Saudi-Egyptian alliance that followed the June War
of 1967

4. *left* British imperialism and its clients in South
Yemen: Commonwealth and Colonial Secretary
Duncan Sandys poses with ministers of the South
Arabian Federation in May 1964. With him, from the
left, are: Sheikh Mohammad al-Aulaqi, Sultan Ahmad
bin Abdullah al Fadhli, Sultan Fadhl bin Ali al Abdali,
Sir Kennedy Trevaskis and Abdurrahman Basendwah.
On the top right is Sharif Hussein of Beihan

5. *above* A British soldier kicks a demonstrator to the
ground during nationalist demonstrations in Crater,
1967

6. *above left* Members of the National Union of Yemeni Women, during a demonstration in August 1972 in support of women's emancipation and the ending of oppressive traditional practices

7. *left* US equipment captured by the PDRY after mercenary attacks from the Saudi frontier. The inscription on the truck reads: 'Army of National Deliverance, Hadramout and Mahra, South Arabia'

8. *above* Sultan Said bin Taimur visits London, 1961; and is greeted by Edward Heath, at that time a member of the British government

WELCOME TO
ROYAL AIR FORCE
SALALAH

9. *above* Salala air base in Dhofar; from this position
Sultan Qabus's air force flies missions against the
revolutionary forces. Official mythology has it that
Sultan's army and air force are independent of
British control

10. *above right* Young women receiving training in a
unit of the People's Liberation Army

11. *right* Children attending the Lenin School, Hauf

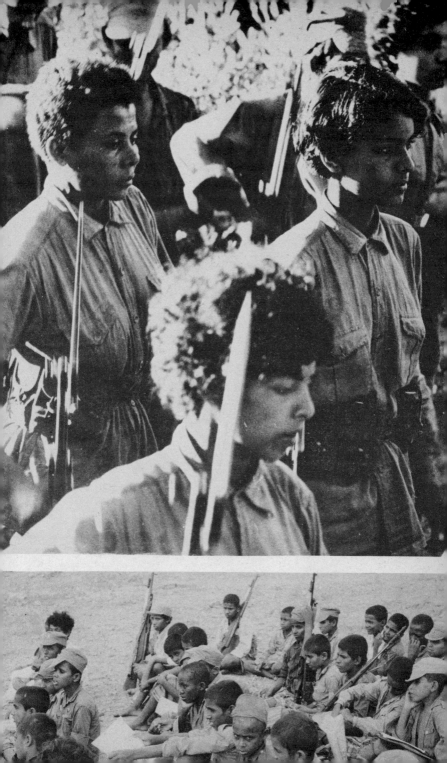

12. On a mountain trail in Dhofar, guerrillas examine one of the flares dropped by British planes as part of their counter-insurgency campaign

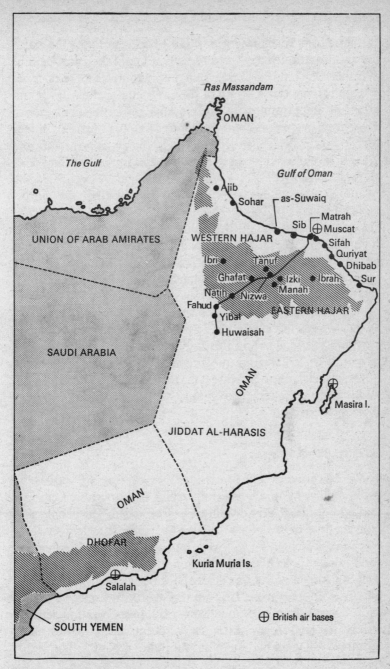

Map 8 The Sultanate of Oman

Britain. A new Imam emerged with the backing of both the major federations, the Hinnawi and the Ghafiri, and they put forward demands which mixed Ibadhi militancy with their more material economic interests: a lifting of the ban on importing slaves and arms; an imposition of a ban on tobacco and alcohol; and a lowering of customs taxes and of food and cloth prices. To counter this threat the British landed 700 Anglo-Indian troops at Muscat and for several years there was a stalemate. But in 1920 an agreement, the Treaty of Sib, was worked out and this regulated the relations between the coast and the interior until the British violated it in the 1950s.

Under the Sib Treaty the Sultan granted control of justice, trade and administration to the people of the Omani interior, and limited his taxation of the interior's exports; for their part the tribes agreed not to attack the Sultan's position.[13] It was a rational arrangement from the point of view of British imperialism: it had its collaborator Sultan on the coast, and the tribes were left to do as they wished in the interior. In effect it amounted to a *de facto* partition of the area and this lasted as long as it suited British interests. In the interior the Imam ruled in alliance with the powerful tribal rulers. In Muscat the British financed, administered and armed the Sultan. The country as a whole was as pacific as Britain required.

Sultan Said bin Taimur

The balance worked out in the 1920 Treaty of Sib settled the main conflict inside Oman, and British rule at Muscat ensured that no outside powers or influences intervened. The people who paid the price of this policy were the Omani workers and peasants who were prevented in every way from escaping from the wretched conditions in which Britain had imprisoned them. The chosen agent of British policy was Sultan Said bin Taimur, who ruled as Sultan of Muscat from 1932 until the British dismissed him in 1970. The results of their forty years of close cooperation between British imperialism and their Omani client were clear for all to see. In 1970 Oman had an infant mortality rate of 75 per cent.[14]

It had three small primary schools, one hospital, no press and a literacy rate of 5 per cent. One visitor to the hinterland in the 1950s reported that: 'in the villages of Oman there is often not a single healthy inhabitant in sight'.[15] Another expert who visited the area in 1958 was equally shocked: 'in twenty years' experience of most of the countries of the Middle East he had never seen a people so poverty-stricken or so debilitated with disease capable of treatment and cure.'[16] Trachoma, venereal disease and malnutrition were widespread.

Said bin Taimur was born in 1910, the grandson of the reigning ruler, Sultan Feisal. From 1922 to 1927 he went to school in India at the College of Princes at Ajmer, in Rajputana (now Rajasthan), where he learnt to speak Urdu and English. The British were grooming him to take over in Muscat, and in 1932 his father Taimur was deposed for financial incompetence that had been exacerbated by the world depression. In 1938 Said went on a world tour: in Washington he met Roosevelt and toured the headquarters of the F B I; he then went on to London. After 1945 he often spent his summers in England, and he was known to be capable of exercising a special charm over English colonial officials inclined anyway to fawn on royalty, who were delighted by quotes from Shakespeare and his apparent knowledge of the 'workings of the English mind'.

Said bin Taimur was one of the nastiest rulers the world has seen for a long time. His brutality affected both the way the country was ruled and the treatment he meted out to those individuals over whom he chose to exercise his powers. Under the guise of respecting Ibadhism a savage regime was upheld. Said's rule prevented Omanis from leaving the country; discouraged education and health services, and kept from the population a whole series of objects, including medicines, radios, spectacles, trousers, cigarettes and books. Even the oil prospecting companies were prevented from carrying out welfare programmes and they were discouraged from any but the most minimal contacts with the local people. In 1958 the British set up a Development Department to ward off criticism but Said prevented anything being done. 'I always felt he was not really interested in development,' his development adviser later wrote;[17] 'the Sultan was, I felt, half-hearted about plans for health, education, agriculture and so on.' On one occasion he told the adviser: 'This is why you lost India, because you educated the people.'[18] Just before he was ousted in 1970 he had decided to close the three existing primary schools in the country – because they had become 'centres of communism'.

Until the production of oil the total budget of the country was less than £2 million per year, and £1·5 of this was paid by Britain under the 1866 arrangement. This money was used entirely to preserve Said's rule, mainly by bribing sheikhs with 'annual subsidies'. In 1958 Said obtained £3 million from Pakistan by selling Gwadur, an Omani enclave on the Pakistani coast, and this money was put away in a Swiss bank.[19] In 1967 oil production began and revenues rose from £8 million in 1967 to £44 million in 1970. This too was put away and Omani reserves rose spectacularly to around £80 million. In a rare interview in 1966 he tried, preposterously, to present himself to the world as an enlightened if cautious despot:

The Sultan made it clear that the oil money would go for development. His present development department will be expanded to cope. He said he felt that in the interests of his deeply religious people changes should be gradual. He does not plan, at present, to borrow in advance of his oil revenue. The oil community with their modern ideas will be largely segregated from his people. From within, he told me, there is no agitation for change.[20]

The repressive laws and bans on movements were tightened after the rising of 1957–9 in Oman and from then on no one was allowed into the country. The last journalist permitted to visit the Omani interior was allowed in in 1962, and the only subsequent visits were stop-overs to interview the Sultan at his palace. Said administered the country through appointed governors, *walis*; but even after the reintegration of Oman in the 1950s large areas of the country were left under the autonomous control of the tribal rulers. As in Imamic North Yemen the main tax was the Muslim *zakat*, a percentage tax on agricultural produce, and the law administered was the *shariah*. The *walis* and sheikhs co-operated in extorting from, and terrorizing, the peasantry.

The judicial system was savage, and up to a year before Said was deposed he had authorized public executions. A British mercenary who visited the prison of al-Jalali, in Muscat, described his reactions:

I had no wish to repeat my excursion; I felt physically depressed and mentally sick. The ordinary prisoners were permanently shackled with ponderous iron bars between their ankles. The tiny water ration, in that steaming furnace, must have been a tantalising mockery. Most important prisoners were kept in perpetual solitary confinement.[21]

Sentences were unspecified, many people died in prisons and many others went mad. Said Masoud, a militant from Dhofar who spent the years 1965 to 1970 in Kut al-Jalali, told the author of the shackles, beating, hunger and stifling heat, and of how the Baluchi guards carried out the terrorizing orders of British officers. One man he personally knew who died in the prison was Salem Mohammad ar-Rokeishi, an Omani imprisoned during the Imamist uprising. On one occasion, when Said protested to a British officer about conditions, he was told he was lucky he was not in Saudi Arabia where he would have been shot on arrest.

Prisoners who had been in the al-Hosn prison in Salala told of similar conditions to those in al-Jalali, with hundreds of prisoners shackled together in dark rooms, without proper food or light or medical attention. Torture was also common: 'two days of the *maqtara* (the wheel) were generally enough, the governor genially informed me as he took charge of my prisoner; a week in extreme cases'.[22] It is not surprising that when the U N sent a representative to Oman in 1963 he was refused permission to visit Jalali prison.

Said had his own personal aberrations, which paralleled his public tyranny. In the 1950s when he lived in Muscat he used to make his slaves swim in the water underneath his balcony and then amuse himself by shooting at the fish around them. His 500 or so slaves, descendants of blacks imported from Africa, were kept tightly isolated from the rest of the population, and banned from marrying or even learning to read or write without his permission. When slaves began to evade control he even passed a law under which all people of African descent were classed as slaves.

In 1958 Said retired to Salala, a cooler palace, far from the more troubled atmosphere of Muscat, and there he disappeared from sight altogether. After an assassination attempt in 1966 many of his subjects believed him to be dead and even a slave who worked in his intelligence service inside the Salala palace did not know whether the Sultan was alive or not. According to the slave's account there was a special sealed-off section of the palace from which four chamberlains would emerge each day bringing orders which they alleged came from the Sultan.[23]

Said's voyeurism was put to private and public use. After he was ousted his palace was found to be equipped with two-way mirrors, and his obsession with telescopes was an added bane to the already harassed subjects. In the 1950s he often telephoned the British Consulate in Muscat, across the harbour, to complain if he saw anyone smoking on the veranda. When he moved camp to Salala the Sultan would order the arrest of anyone he could see disregarding regulations. One man in Salala built an outside lavatory on to his home and government officials arrived the next day to knock it down, saying that the Sultan had seen him contravening regulations.

His palace at Salala was a nightmarish place. He kept many of his slaves locked up there and used to enjoy beating them. A correspondent who visited Salala after Said's removal wrote:

Among 12 slaves presented to foreign journalists some had been forced, under pain of beating, not to speak. As a result they had become mutes. Others stood with their heads bowed and eyes fixed on the ground, their necks now paralysed. The slightest glance sideways resulted in a severe beating or imprisonment. Others had incurred physical deformity from similar cruelty.[24]

Said was also found to have 150 women locked away in his palace and it was known by some of his British aides that he had been assaulting young girls.

The Salala palace also contained a private arsenal: thirty-three tons of weapons valued at £1·5 million were found there. These included anti-tank weapons and rockets. So far as is known no one but Said was able to find his way around all the secret rooms and passages; even his one (acknowledged) son, Qabus bin Said, was locked away there when he returned from training in the British army in 1966; his father refused to see him for four years.

This regime of tyranny and sadism could never have survived without the active and consistent backing of the British government. Until 1967 Said derived over half his revenue from them. In the 1960s all but one of the Sultan's advisers were British; and they, although private citizens, could not have continued without official sanction. The only Omani minister was Ahmad bin Ibrahim, the Minister of the Interior, who administered the Omani interior when Said retired to Salala and who was sent orders by radio-telephone. The other advisers included Brigadier P. R. M. 'Pat' Waterfield who was Secretary of Defence, Major Dennison, the chief of Intelligence, and Major F. C. L. Chauncy, who became Chief Adviser in 1958 after being British Consul in Muscat for the eight years before that. In effect the country had no foreign relations; its affairs in London were handled by a trading firm of a discreet character called Kendall & Co., who also worked as 'purchasing agents' for other Middle Eastern regimes. When, in the 1960s, the question of Oman came up at the United Nations the Sultan 'requested' Britain to represent him there.

The most important form of support was military. From the 1870s onwards the sultans of Muscat only remained in existence with the help of British military backing. Up to the First World War this took the form of naval support and of troop detachments from India. In 1920 the British began to train the Muscat Levy Corps using British officers and arms and recruiting from Oman, Pakistani Baluchistan and Iran. During the Second World War the British built four airfields in the Sultanate as links in a chain between Europe, central Africa and the Far East that would have been of vital importance if Egypt had fallen to the Axis powers. These fields were at Salala, on the island of Masirah, and at Bait al-Falaj and Azaibah, near Muscat, and were capable of being alternatively used for internal repression. In the 1950s, when British troops and RAF planes participated in counter-insurgency operations, the British decided to formalize their relationship with Oman, and in 1958 the British and the Sultanate came to a 'public' agreement under which the Sultan 'leased' the island of Masirah to the British in return for military help.[25]

The British always maintained that 'the Sultanate of Muscat and Oman is a fully sovereign and independent state'.[26] This was an out-and-out lie, which all British governments, Conservative and Labour alike, chose to maintain because it suited British imperial interests. Although there were contradictions between Said and some British officials in the area, Oman was in fact a British colony; and precisely because they had always used the Sultans of Muscat to administer the country it was the task of the British to deal with any ensuing internal difficulties. The appalling misery of the Omani people, and the sadism, murder and torture of Said's regime were the responsibility of the British. The pretence of Omani 'sovereignty' was simply a guise to disassociate Britain from the horrible consequences of her policy. While the complicit British press acquiesced in this, such a device did not fool the Sultan's desperate subjects, who were ruled by British ministers and killed by British bombs.

Buraimi and the Green Mountain

The first serious challenge to this system came in the 1950s when Oman began to feel the tremors of change in the rest of the Gulf. Large-scale development of the oil industry in the Gulf began after 1945 and by the early 1950s the hunt was on for further supplies; demand was higher because of the imperialist invasion of Korea in June 1950 and supply had fallen because the largest refinery in the Middle East, at Abadan in Iran, had been nationalized in 1951. Whereas previously there had been no need to define boundaries too precisely in the Arabian interior, the development of oil-wells made it essential; and territorial disputes became inevitable. Areas formerly allowed to subsist in autonomous isolation, like the interior of Oman, became certain to suffer invasion in the search for further resources. It was this advance of capitalism that raised the first serious challenge to the British insulation of Oman.

In 1949 Saudi Arabia and Oman clashed over control of the oasis of Buraimi, a cluster of nine villages lying between the Omani interior and the lower Gulf coast. Buraimi was a transit station for the caravan trade between the Omani interior and the lower Gulf, and in the nineteenth century had been occupied several times by Saudi armies. From the early twentieth century the villages were administered by Muscat and the sheikhdom of Abu Dhabi. The Saudis wanted to control Buraimi because the American oil company operating in Saudi Arabia, A R A M C O, were prospecting for oil in the area; and in 1952 Saudi forces, transported and armed by A R A M C O, occupied the oasis. A R A M C O also helped the Saudis to prepare their legal claims. The Sultan of Muscat wanted to drive the Saudis out but the British held him back: 'We couldn't let them do it ... the Americans were so mixed up in it all,' a British diplomat later said.[27] In 1954 Saudis and the British submitted their documents to international arbitration; but the British failed to win satisfaction and a year later forcibly reoccupied the villages, using the Sultan's army and the Trucial Oman Scouts, a force they had set up in their lower Gulf colonies. This provoked a wave of inter-imperialist vituperation. The British, whose hold on much of Oman and South Yemen was maintained by 'annual subsidies' to sheikhs, protested self-righteously at the Saudis 'bribing' tribal leaders around Buraimi. American Secretary of State John Foster Dulles denounced 'British aggression' in Buraimi, but acquiesced in the move. After 1955 the Buraimi dispute was dormant: Muscat administered three villages, and Abu Dhabi six. The Saudis did not accept the outcome, but decided to leave matters as they stood.

The search for oil in the interior of Oman led to a more serious clash. From the Treaty of Sib in 1920 to the early 1950s the Sultan of Muscat had allowed the Omani interior to govern itself. It was ruled by the Imam, who administered courts and collected taxes. Imamate Oman had no diplomatic relations with any other country, but it was a quiet pre-capitalist enclave and no one disturbed it. A triumvirate ruled the area: the Imam Mohammad; Suleiman bin Himyar, the dominant figure on the Green Mountain; and Isa al-Harithi, ruler of the al-Sharqiya area to the south-east. When the Imam died, in 1954, Suleiman, who called himself 'Lord (*amir*) of the Green Mountain', formed an alliance with the ruler of the Bani Hina tribe, Ghalib bin Ali. Ghalib became the new Imam, while Ghalib's brother, Talib bin Ali, commanded considerable power in the area and was governor of the town of Rostaq.[28] This change in the ruling personnel of Imamate Oman took place at the same time that the British-run Petroleum Development Organization was sending its first exploration parties into the Omani interior. In the summer of 1954 PDO prospecting parties reached Fahud, in the desert behind the Green Mountain. Forces commanded by Talib bin Ali were stationed near by in the village of Ibri, and the Imamate's representatives pointed out that the PDO moves had violated the autonomy of Oman. The British decided the time had come to end the *modus vivendi* that had so far prevailed; the Omani interior had to be occupied. In September 1955 they entered Ibri and drove out Talib bin Ali's forces; in October they entered the town of Rostaq and in December they took Nizwa. To crown this occupation Sultan Said bin Taimur drove across the desert from Salala to pay the first visit to the area by a Sultan of Muscat for over a century. The major tribal leaders of the area came to pay him at least formal respects, and even Suleiman bin Himyar came down in an old American car from the Green Mountain to offer his loyalty. It seemed that under pressure from capitalist expansion Oman had been successfully occupied.[29]

This turned out to be false. The Saudis had used their occupation of Buraimi to send arms to the Imamate forces; and it was only after the British had first retaken Buraimi that they were able, in December 1955, to complete the occupation of Oman. Talib bin Ali subsequently went to Saudi Arabia, where he received support both from the Saudis and from ARAMCO, who were hoping to regain Buraimi and possibly to acquire concessions in the Omani interior. He raised a force of exiles, the Oman Liberation Army, and gained diplomatic backing from the Arab League. The Imam's representatives opened an office in Cairo and the cause of Oman was adopted by the Soviet bloc. In response to the occupation of Oman the Imamate's forces raised a set of formal demands: they wanted an independent Omani interior, and the withdrawal of all Muscati and British troops.

In 1957 the Omani interior rose against its occupation by imperialism. Arms and men had been smuggled in via landings on the Batinah coast; but the original plan for a coordinated rising in the al-Sharqiya and Green Mountain areas was not carried out. These areas had been from the eighteenth century the base of the two main forces in the tribal alliances that had come out of the mountains to attack Muscat. If they had acted together they could have cut the oil company's communications and marched on Muscat. The al-Sharqiya area rose prematurely in April 1957 and was quickly suppressed. This left the Green Mountain on its own, and in July 1957 Imamist forces, commanded by Talib bin Ali, attacked. In their biggest victory of the war they ambushed and routed the Oman Regiment of the Sultan's army in the foothills of the mountain. They then reoccupied Nizwa and Rostaq, whence they had been driven in 1955.

The British counter-attacked with two columns: one moved north-east from the desert and captured Nizwa; the other travelled south-west from Muscat up through the main mountain pass and joined the first column at the foot of the Green Mountain. On the mountain plateau, RAF planes destroyed the village of Tanuf where were situated the headquarters of Suleiman bin Himyar, and by the end of August 1957 the British had retaken all the mountain's foothills. The Omani rebels – estimated by the British to number 600 – held out on the plateau, and in late 1957 beat off an assault. British RAF planes bombed the plateau; and at the foot of the mountain were stationed three companies of Cameronian Highlanders, two troops of Ferret Scout cars, a regiment of the Sultan's army and a number of Trucial Oman Scouts. To prevent any further men or arms from getting through, British naval vessels were patrolling the coasts.

In January 1958 the British Minister of Defence Julian Amery visited Muscat to discuss a fresh assault on the mountain, but the Imamist forces were strengthened by the arrival of heavier weapons from Saudi Arabia, including powerful American mines and mortars; although the rebels were unable to launch a proper counter-offensive they harassed the British forces by mining their roads and staging occasional ambushes.

In late 1958 the British undertook a decisive campaign. The RAF stepped up their bombing of the plateau, destroying villages and irrigation works, in the kind of terrorist campaign later carried out in Radfan and Dhofar. A squadron of SAS – Britain's special counter-insurgency troops – were flown in from service in Malaya, but were unable to do the job and had to be joined by a second squadron. After weeks of prevarication, the British reached the plateau by scaling the mountain at night, and by the end of January 1959 the rising on the Green Mountain had ended.[30]

Although by 1959 active military resistance by Imamist forces had ceased, mine-laying continued into the early 1960s.[31] Contrary to their claims, the Imamists did not hold a liberated area in Oman after 1959, and their activities were mainly diplomatic. Imamist offices in Cairo and Baghdad put out political statements and the Imam Ghalib bin Ali was based in Dammam, Saudi Arabia, from where he continued to deny the legitimacy of the Muscati occupation.[32] From 1957 onwards the question of Oman was raised at the United Nations by the Arab states, and in 1963 a UN representative visited Oman to see whether an independent state did exist.[33] In December 1965 the UN General Assembly adopted a resolution on Oman, calling for an end to British domination which, the motion said, was preventing the Omani people from exercising their right to self-determination. As late as December 1970 the General Assembly adopted a similar motion by 70 votes to 17, with 22 abstentions.

An Omani revolutionary speaking in 1971 made the following evaluation of the 1957–9 rising:

The most important thing to say about Imam Ghalib's movement is that it represented a clash *within* the imperialist camp. It was a conflict between the Imam and Said bin Taimur, i.e. a conflict between an absolutist regime and a caricature of that obsolete regime, represented by the Imam himself. When we say that it is a conflict within the imperialist camp, we mean that behind Said bin Taimur and Imam Ghalib were Britain on the one hand and America and Saudi Arabia on the other. However, although the Imam's movement represented a clash within the imperialist camp, it did have sizeable mass support; the masses who supported the Imam supported him mainly as a patriotic reaction to the British occupation of the interior of Oman in 1954.[34]

The Imamist movement was incapable of leading a mass struggle against imperialism because of its own class interests and because it relied on a traditional tribal military system. It failed, and was discredited. The task of leading and freeing the people of Oman awaited a more determined revolutionary leadership.

Britain Stages a Coup

The Buraimi and Green Mountain campaigns were challenges which British imperialism was able to contain; but the forces that they expressed were not containable, and the pressure on Oman continued to build up. It was obvious to US imperialism, for example, that the kind of ultra-conservative regime they were backing in Saudi Arabia had to be changed; and in 1962 they encouraged the advent to power of King Feisal, whose reforms had a stabilizing effect. In South Yemen and the Gulf, the British likewise pursued a policy of modernization. Their attempt to impose a neo-colonial solution on the people of South Yemen was defeated. In their Gulf colonies they then hurriedly introduced reforms and decided to launch at the end of 1971 a neo-colonial Gulf state, the Union of Arab Amirates, and to withdraw their troops.

These developments had a double effect on Oman. The need for 'stability' and the fear of endangering British control by uncontrolled change made Oman's tranquillity more than ever essential to overall colonial strategy. However, it was clear that the regime in Oman would ultimately have to yield to economic and political pressures, and that the longer this was delayed the more uncontrollable the process of change might be. It would have been rational for British imperialism to have deposed Said in the early 1960s before the contradictions inside Oman became too acute. But many British officials in the area could not see this, and the colonial apparatus became increasingly divided on policy. The discovery of oil in the Omani interior was an important precipitant of change. In 1923 Sultan Taimur had undertaken not to grant oil rights to a foreign country without prior consent from the British government, and in 1924–5 a British team had made a first exploration. In 1937 Sultan Said signed an agreement with Petroleum Concessions Ltd, a subsidiary of the Iraq Petroleum Company, giving them rights to prospect in Oman; and this concession was later extended to include Dhofar. The activities of the IPC subsidiary Petroleum Development (Oman and Dhofar) were limited by the fact that the Sultan only controlled one third of Oman and it was not until the 1950s that a prospecting team, backed by a military guard, penetrated the desert areas behind the Green Mountain. This was the expedition that led to the revolt on the Green Mountain and ended the autonomy of Oman, but it had no concrete results for the oil company, and in 1960 all but one of the IPC constituents withdrew, leaving Petroleum Development owned 85 per cent by Shell and 15 per cent by the Gulbenkian interests. In 1967 one of the IPC constituents, the French-owned CFP, re-acquired 10 per cent of the Gulbenkian portion. Oil in commercial quantities was discovered in 1964 in the desert 150 miles inland from Muscat, and three operational wells were developed at Fahud, Natih and Yibal. An underground pipeline, 156 miles long, was built from Fahud to a terminal at Mina al-Fahal, just north of Muscat, after the oil company had reached a series of agreements with the mountain tribal leaders through whose territory the pipeline had to pass. Production was originally scheduled to start at the end of 1967, but when the Arab states temporarily cut off oil exports after the June 1967 Arab–Israeli war the Omani oil-wells were prematurely put into action to seize part of the empty market. The loss of supply from Nigeria during the Biafra war also spurred output. Production leapt forward and royalty payments to the Sultan rose from £8 million in 1967 to over £40 million in 1970.

However hard they tried, the British and the Sultan could not completely insulate Oman from the effects of oil development. Moreover, although all migration was banned, up to 15,000 Omanis had left their country to work in the oil-fields of the Gulf, and Omani merchants had moved to Dubai to escape the anti-commercial policies of the Sultan. The mass misery continued, but the official argument that Oman was poor no longer applied after 1967 when Said bin Taimur began to accumulate the foreign exchange from his oil revenues.

The most serious challenge to the British was first posed in 1965 when guerrilla war broke out in the southern, Dhofar, province of Oman. By 1969 all of Dhofar except for Salala and the plain around it had fallen, and guerrillas were shelling the RAF base and Said bin Taimur's palace. In June 1970 allies of the guerrillas in Dhofar attacked in the Green Mountain area, just a few miles from the PDO oil-fields. The war in Dhofar and its extension to the interior of Oman directly threatened the Sultanate of Oman and thence the whole of the Gulf.

Said bin Taimur's savage but inefficient autocracy was incapable of facing these problems; and even the most bemused British officials began to see the need for a change. While the guerrillas posed a revolutionary solution to Oman's difficulties, the British sought a way out which would safeguard their interests. In this their aims agreed with those of the reformist wing of the Al Bu Said dynasty, led by Tariq, who wanted to modernize the Omani regime. Initial British attempts to 'persuade' Said to change his policies were a failure. He was more than equal to the colonial officials sent down to Salala to see him; and he mixed old-style charm with warnings about the destabilizing effects of sudden change. The British Political Resident in the Gulf, Stewart Crawford, flew monthly to Salala, in an attempt to persuade the Sultan; it was even planned that Crawford and the chief British military commander in the Gulf should arrive on a battleship, dressed in full regalia, and should order the Sultan to leave.

This timid policy came to nothing and by 1969 it was clear that a more blunt approach was needed. The coup of 23 July 1970 was later presented to the Arab world as resembling the 23 July 1952 coup which brought the Nasserist regime to power in Egypt. It had little in common with this. In early 1970 the British press rumoured that either Said was willing to resign, or had been already overthrown,[35] and in April a Foreign Office official was heard to remark that 'the old boy' would soon have to go: 'We need an Omani Zaid to Said's Shakhbut,' he said.[36] The Omani Zaid was none other than Said bin Taimur's son, the wretched Qabus, incarcerated in Salala palace since his return in 1966 from military training in Britain.

The outbreak of guerrilla war in the Omani interior on 12 June 1970 spurred the Shell oil company to urge action on the part of the British. On 20 June a British general election brought the Heath government to power: possibly the Labour regime had been unwilling to risk a coup in the pre-election period in case things had gone wrong. A month after the election, on 23 July, Said bin Taimur was overthrown and was flown to England and exile.[37] Qabus became Sultan, the fourteenth of the Al Bu Said dynasty, and was 'recognized' by Britain on 29 July.

The 23 July coup was presented by the British government in a devious way. Supposedly Qabus and 'loyal Dhofaris' had taken over the palace and arrested Said on their own initiative. London 'heard about it' a few days later and at first 'awaited further developments'. Of course, said the Foreign Office, the British had had no part in the coup. 'Last night Whitehall denied that the British government had connived at the coup. The Foreign Office seemed genuinely short of information. But there was evident relief at Sultan Said's deposition,' one journalist wrote.[38] Other papers recounted how Said had become the 'despair' of his advisers and how 'the Foreign and Commonwealth office were discreetly tossing their hats into the air'.[39] It was obvious that the coup had been staged by Britain. The British officers in command in Oman later disclaimed responsibility, and Sir Geoffrey Arthur, the then British Political Resident in Bahrain, was wont to say that when the coup occurred he was in hospital far away. In the political circumstances in Oman no such event could have taken place without British foreknowledge and approval. Key posts in the armed forces were all held by British officers; and it was clear that the ousting of Said was beneficial and indeed essential to the stability of the Omani regime and of British interests.

In welcoming the new Sultan the British had the problem of denigrating Said to praise Qabus, while avoiding any suggestion of British responsibility for the deplorable state of affairs in Oman before the coup. 'Change at Last in Muscat' editorialized *The Times*,[40] a paper that had never pressed its complaints about conditions in Oman before the coup, and whose post-coup coverage exonerated the British from all responsibility for Oman's circumstances. Chaperoned and collusive correspondents were flown out by the British to Salala to see the situation and were shown mutilated slaves and told of all the crimes committed by Said. But no one asked *who* had sustained the Sultan or carried out Said's orders. It all seemed to have been done by nameless 'Arabs', or perhaps by *djinns*.

Capitalist Modernization

In his first weeks of rule Qabus presented himself as the champion of his people, come to rescue them from the tyranny of his father: 'I had to forget my personal relations because the question was bigger than father or son', he said. 'It is a nation at stake and I had to forget all my personal affection.'[41] A few days after the coup he flew to Muscat, which his father had not visited since 1958; he was greeted by a stage-managed popular reception which at least impressed the British correspondents brought in to witness it.[42] A number of changes quickly followed: Tariq bin Taimur, Qabus' uncle, returned from exile and became Prime Minister in the first new cabinet. Said's henchmen in Oman, Ahmad bin Ibrahim and Ahmad al-Harithi, were sacked. The most conservative English advisers, Chauncy and Waterfield, were packed off to retirement. Slaves were declared free. Some prisoners were released. A national newspaper *al-Watan* (*The Nation*) was brought out once a week – though somewhat outdated, as it was

301

printed in Beirut. Muscat and Salala radio stations were set up. A number of Omanis returned from abroad. Because of the weakness of the local bourgeoisie, foreign capital was encouraged to flow in. Oman started to set up diplomatic relations with other countries, and a proper embassy was opened in London.

The purpose of all this was not to bring democracy to Oman or to distribute wealth in the interests of the people. It was to stabilize the situation and check the tide of revolution. The politically crucial point was Dhofar, where an attempt in 1970 and early 1971 to bribe and divide the Dhofari people gave way in the autumn of 1971 to a full-scale military offensive. The counter-revolutionary crusade in Dhofar was the government's main preoccupation and used up over half of the oil revenues. The government consistently refused to reveal the expenses of the budget or to tell the Omani people how much was being used to murder and maim the inhabitants of Dhofar.

In Oman itself most emphasis was on economic development and the introduction of the most elementary institutions formerly blocked by Said. Out of a GNP of £60 million it produced £50 million. Agriculture contributed £8 million and fishing £2 million. The key to this development was oil: oil accounted for 95 per cent of the budget.

Table 14

Omani Oil Production

	(million barrels)	(£ million)
1967	20·9	1·4
1968	87·9	25·5
1969	119·7	38·5
1970	121·3	44·4
1971	107·9	47·7
1972	103·2	49·3
1973	106·2*	75·0*

*estimated

Although in late 1970 a fourth field began production at al-Huwaisah the overall picture was unfavourable. In 1972 known reserves were only 2,000 million tons – enough for only twenty years. Over-hasty production aimed at beating the Arab oil boycott in 1967 and making up for lost Nigerian sources had distorted the pressure of the wells and in 1971 production fell by 11·5 per cent.[43] PDO costs were high by Gulf standards – 54c a barrel – compared to 6–10c in Kuwait – and further exploration revealed no new commercial quantities. In 1968 PDO surrendered its concession off the northern Omani coast and it was taken up by a West German firm, Wintershall AG: but they too had no success and at the end of 1972 announced that they had suspended exploratory drilling. South of Ras al-Hadd the American oilman Wendell Philipps was awarded a 450-mile offshore concession in March 1971: but this was taken off him in the autumn and given to a rival consortium in February 1973 headed by Sun Oil of the US. Simultaneously a mineral exploration consortium, made up of Marshall Exploration Inc. of the USA and Prospection Ltd of Canada, were awarded a 54,500 square-kilometre concession in the area north-west of Muscat. Although the offshore oil consortium did not find reserves quickly, the mineral group did find large quantities of copper and other ores within a year of initiating activities.

The country's most important projects necessitated an infrastructure. A six-berth harbour at Matra called Port Qabus cost £22 million. This was carried out jointly by Hochtief, a German firm, and Six-Construct, who were Belgian. Another project was a 125-mile tarmacked road from Muscat along the Batinah coast to Sohar, laid at a cost of £17·2 million by Strabag AG, another West German firm. An international airport, with a 12,000-foot runway capable of taking 747s, was being built at Sib at an expense of £5·5 million. Long-term plans were announced to develop fishing and agriculture, the main sources of employment, and a basic welfare system was slowly worked out. In 1972 the government claimed to have 30,000 children in primary schools – i.e. 20 per cent of the total – and an additional 1,500 Omani students at school elsewhere in the Gulf. An initial health programme also got under way, with a few rudimentary hospitals and the beginnings of curative medicine. In order to cope with the rapid increase in the urban population, two new extensions to the Muscat-Matra area were being built: one at Ruwi, next to Muscat, and the other at Qurum, further away. The latter, designed to contain 400 dwellings and costing £8 million, is to be named Madinat Qabus (Qabus City). All of this 'developmental' expenditure was designed to offset popular hostility; but some of it had a more specifically counter-revolutionary purpose: at Sur, where the government suspected the local fishermen of having ties to PFLOAG, a new port was constructed. Whereas before the local people had beached their ships along the coast, they were now forced to moor them in the harbour, and were thereby subjected to a more efficient scrutiny.

Of an estimated 100,000 in the labour force most worked in the traditional sectors, agriculture and fishing:

Table 15

Estimated Employment 1971

Agriculture	63,000
Fishing	15,000
Fixed private employment (PDO, Shell markets, cable and wireless, banks, merchants)	4,140
Contractors	5,520
Government	2,860
Police	1,270
Military (includes many non-Omanis)	4,280
Small shopkeepers, servants, taxi-drivers, etc.	3,500
Omanis in employment	99,570
Foreigners	7,000
Omanis working outside Oman	15,000

Wage rates reflected the violent inequalities of this dependent society. In the capitalist sector PDO and other contractors employed over 5,500 people as stable employees, and of these 4,140 were Omanis, while a full 1,400 were foreigners. The income for the lowest unskilled sections varied from 22 to 36 rials a month, whereas those for the higher-level staff (drilling foremen, office administrators) went up to 162 rials per month; and those for senior staff were much more. Similarly, in the government, income varied from 15 rials a month for the lowest grade of boy sweeper up to over 500 rials a month for ministers and secretaries (£1·1 = 1 Omani rial).

Contradictions at every level soon began to reappear, and after the initial enthusiasm foreign observers began to criticize the way Qabus and his British backers were handling Oman's problems. The wasteful overproduction of Omani oil in the years after 1967 was one sign that Oman's economic development was directed by the interests of foreign capital and not by the long-term interests of the Omani people. This set the pattern for other wastage, such as Qabus' luxury palace, commissioned at a cost of around £2 million, and the Omani participation in the Gulf Aviation company. While the British complained of 'Lebanese carpet-baggers' come to make a quick profit, it was European capitalists, led by the British, who rushed in to corner the newly opened oil market. The Lebanese bourgeois paper *Le Commerce du Levant* aptly described the situation in a 1970 headline: 'O M A N: Bonnes perspectives pour les exporteurs occidentaux'.[44] Imports rose from £4 million in 1966 to over £55 million in 1972, with imports of cars and lorries alone rising by over 600 per cent and imports of electrical goods by 280 per cent. The British led this rush with a 27 per cent share of the import market, and it seemed that Oman's oil income was available for all the world to pillage. The *Financial Times* correspondent wrote: 'In such boom conditions it might be difficult for anyone with a modicum of common sense and experience of the market to fail.'[45]

Foreign capital held the country firmly in its grip. Only Sultan Qabus knew the real content of the private treaties with P D O. The main banks in Muscat and other towns were three British banks; and the British Bank of the Middle East ran the Oman currency board, and controlled 85 per cent of all banking. Foreign construction companies, British and German, were awarded huge contracts. The two big hotels opened to cater for visiting businessmen, the al-Falaj Hotel and the Matra Hotel, were foreign owned. This soon had effects at the political level.

Table 16

Imports, by Country of Origin, 1971

Sr. No.	Country	Value in Rials Saidi
1	United Kingdom	2,707,558
2	Gulf	2,457,255
3	Burma	1,097,536
4	India	971,405
5	Australia	969,852
6	Japan	847,003
7	Iran	801,501
8	Netherlands	498,337
9	People's Rep. of China	490,466
10	Pakistan	454,412
11	West Germany	352,661
12	Spain	196,149
13	Singapore	175,815
14	Kenya	164,380
15	South Africa	149,034
16	USSR	147,433
17	USA	134,671
18	Thailand	115,612
19	Liberia	111,131
20	Brazil	102,002
	Other	839,404
Total:		13,783,617

In January 1972 Prime Minister Tariq bin Taimur resigned, alleging that he had been prevented from carrying out his role because of the British hold on Oman. He said that as premier he had been excluded from any say in the three key fields of oil, finance and defence. Furthermore, Qabus had refused to reveal to him the agreement with PDO. The Sultan had also refused to introduce a parliament or constitution, on the grounds that there was no internal demand for them, just as his father had done before. The British Bank of the Middle East, Tariq alleged, had blocked his proposal for a national bank because this would have weakened their hold on the economy. At the end of 1972 Qabus had become not only Sultan, but also Prime Minister,

Minister of Finance, Minister of Defence and Minister of the Interior. 'Sultan Qabus who, on great occasions, likes to throw handfuls of silver coins from his balcony to the crowd of his subjects come to pay homage, is, similarly, faithful to tribal customs when he refuses to establish a state budget or to make it public. "Why should I do it," he told us, somewhat irritated by the question, "this is a technical problem on which the vast majority of our subjects understand absolutely nothing. We take decisions which are in the interest of the country and it would be better that they be not questioned by ignorant people . . ."'[46]

Anyone who might have been surprised that he could carry out these tasks all at once would soon find the answer: they were administered by British aides, who ran a secret government just below the surface of Omani affairs. At times this led to some embarrassment, as when Oman was unable to send its (British) Minister of Defence to Arab conferences to coordinate strategy on Palestine. So unconcerned was Qabus that in both 1971 and 1972 he spent over two months in Europe on holiday and in consultative visits to his patrons in London.[47] The response of the Omani people to the change of regime was not for long in doubt. The guerrilla actions of June 1970 were a major breakthrough even though the leaders of the guerrilla movement were arrested on 18 July 1970 in a police raid on a house in Matra. Their organization, the National Democratic Front for the Liberation of Oman and the Arab Gulf – NDFLOAG – continued with underground political work and in December 1971 they merged with the guerrillas in Dhofar in a common front – the Popular Front for the Liberation of Oman and the Arabian Gulf. The immediate results of the influx of foreign capital into Oman soon angered the population: inflation of around 25 per cent per annum, pillage of Oman's resources by foreign companies and a rush of foreign labour into the country led in September 1971 to a violent uprising in the towns of Muscat and Matra. On 1 September 1971 Omani workers attacked PDO loading installations at Matra to protest at the importation of Indian and Somali workers. Thousands of workers blocked the roads to the airport and shouted slogans denouncing the Minister of Labour,

Sheikh Abdullah at-Tai, and then marched on Qabus' palace, four miles away at Muscat. Police and troops ringed the palace, and dispersed the demonstrators. A state of emergency was declared, and flights in and out of the country were stopped.

In the interior, opposition began immediately after the British-engineered coup. In August 1970 workers at the Fahud oil-field went on strike. They wanted an eight-hour day, the right to organize unions, higher wages and equal rights for Omani and foreign workers. They patrolled the area with sticks and encountered the famed Texan oil-fire fighter Red Adair, who had been flown in with his team to check a blaze in the fields.[48] In towns of the interior – Nizwa, Rostaq and Ibri – the first strikes in Oman's history took place, and the prisons at Jalali fort in Muscat, and elsewhere, began again to fill up. Economic changes were inevitably bringing about the politicization of construction workers employed by foreign companies. A government-sponsored Association of Omani Women, designed to fight illiteracy among women, had to be suppressed when its leader, Awatef Arraimi, organized discussions on the traditional ways in which women in Omani society were controlled.[49] Omanis from the new schools were encouraged by their education to articulate opposition to the governments, and anti-imperialist demonstrations were staged by students. The opposition was often spontaneous and quickly suppressed, but it highlighted the continued refusal of the regime to slacken control over the Omani people. Oman remained under the control of British imperialism, and of the Al Bu Said client dynasty.

The establishment of foreign relations was an easy task, compared to the new regime's domestic problems. Qabus quickly established relations with the other Gulf rulers, and was welcomed to the Persepolis celebrations of the Shah of Iran in October 1971. The Shah, who was publicly worried about the Dhofar war, sent crack troops to aid the counter-insurgency effort and in December 1972 was reported to have been allowed to station troops on an Omani island at the mouth of the Gulf.[50] Other right-wing Arab regimes were also quick to welcome the change. Jordan sent military advisers; in 1972 Qabus visited Amman.

The most important rapprochement was that with Saudi Arabia, which still maintained its claim to the Buraimi oasis. Saudi-financed mercenaries arrived in early 1971 and after initial diplomatic coldness Saudi Arabia agreed to recognise the new Omani regime. In December 1971, Qabus paid a visit to the Saudi capital of Riyadh, as a result of which the Saudis promised military aid. In the long-term, there was also a possibility of a coordinated attack on the eastern provinces of the PDRY in order to block the supply lines to Dhofar.

The agreement with Saudi Arabia removed all obstacles to closer ties with the USA. The US government was willing to let Britain play the leading role in Oman, but took up a strong supporting position. On a visit to London, in June 1971, Qabus met representatives of the CIA who agreed to provide $150 million in counter-insurgency aid, routed through Saudi Arabia. In October 1971 Qabus entertained aboard his yacht a Mr Robert Anderson: Anderson had been 'Texan of the Year' in 1955, had been Secretary of the Treasury in 1957–61, and was the front-man for an elaborate deal involving the US government and US private capital – a deal that the British tried to stop. Anderson himself received a concession on all offshore and land areas not already ceded to PDO and Wintershall, including those taken from Wendell Philipps.[51] He also got mineral rights for the whole country, and was signed up to arrange a diplomatic service for Qabus in western Europe and North America. Most important was Qabus' agreement to contribute £2 million as a 51 per cent share in a joint US–Omani fishing firm in which Oman would join with Mardela International, a firm chaired by Charles Black, the husband of film star Shirley Temple. Both Black and Anderson were friends of President Nixon and according to military officials in Muscat and Washington the 'fishing' fleet would be a cover for naval surveillance by the US along the 1,000-mile Omani coast.[52]

While Britain still maintained her place in the Sultanate, the Arab League and the United Nations, which for years had denounced British colonization of Oman, betrayed their previous objections. Responsibility for this lay with leading Arab countries, all of whom except the P D R Y decided to admit Oman to the Arab League.[53] That done, in September 1971, the U N presented no problem. But although Oman now had the trappings of independence and was being subjected to a brutal and belated modernization, it remained a British colony, a country in which foreign control of the economy and the state overrode the interests of the people. Meanwhile a different path was being mapped out by the revolutionary movement centred in Dhofar.

Notes

1. I have used the name 'Oman' throughout this chapter, although until 1970 the country was officially called 'Muscat and Oman'. The pre-twentieth-century history of the country is found in S. B. Miles, *The Countries and Tribes of the Persian Gulf*, London, 1919, and in A. Wilson, *The Persian Gulf*, London, 1928.

2. See J. C. Wilkinson, 'The Origins of the Omani State', in Derek Hopwood, ed., *The Arabian Peninsula*, London, 1972. During the Imamist rising of 1957–9 its supporters claimed that the Imam was a democratically elected popular leader. This was no more than anti-imperialist piety, and no truer in the twentieth century than it was in the ninth.

3. See R. D. Bathurst, 'Maritime Trade and Imamate Government: Two Principal Themes in the History of Oman to 1728', in Hopwood, ed. op. cit. See also G. F. Hourani, *Arab Seafaring in the Indian Ocean*, Princeton, 1951.

4. J. R. Wellsted, *Travels in Arabia*, Vol. 1, London, 1838, p. 125. So far as is known, Wellsted, a British naval officer, was the first European ever to visit the Green Mountain.

5. Britain began to suppress the slave *trade* after 1830, out of both idealism and material interest; but she allowed the *ownership* of slaves to continue in her Arabian colonies. In the 1960s rulers in Oman and South Yemen were in possession of slaves. The British seemed not to care; they were more concerned about 'communists'. For an analysis of the economic motivation behind the curbing of the Omani slave trade in East Africa see Richard D. Wolff, 'British Imperialism and the East African Slave Trade', *Science and Society*, Winter 1972.

6. The Omani empire was divided up by the British under the Canning Award of 1861. Zanzibar was to pay Oman an annual subsidy of 40,000 Maria Theresa dollars, but she fell in arrears almost at once and the Indian government picked up the bill. At first it was £6,000 per annum; by 1967 it was £1·5 million. Zanzibar became a British protectorate in 1891; and in 1964, soon after independence, a nationalist revolution overthrew the

Al Bu Said Sultan of Zanzibar and the ruling Arab caste. The Zanzibari revolution had a negative political effect in Oman, where traditional anti-African sentiments remained. But it did lead to the return to Oman of Omanis with some education.

7. The best account of this period is R. G. Landen, *Oman Since 1856*, Princeton, 1967.

8. The theory of underdevelopment described by André Gunder Frank in 'The Development of Underdevelopment', *Monthly Review*, September 1966, and other works, certainly applies to Oman; how this pre-industrial capitalism could have developed into a modern form of capitalism is, however, hard to imagine.

9. European writers tend to regard militant religious movements in the third world as 'traditional'. In fact they are usually *modern* reactions to the violent irruption of an alien culture and economic system. While offering no viable solution to their believers, they nevertheless express a distorted anti-imperialism.

10. Landen, op. cit., p. 227.

11. Landen, op. cit., p. 224n, writes: '... all the viceroys of the 1890s asserted that the Gulf principalities – including that ruled by the Sultan at Masqat – were, in fact, if not according to strict treaty stipulations, British protectorates'. The main reason why the British did not formalize their colonial hold in a treaty was that this would have been an unnecessary provocation to the French. The British authorities in India were pressing for formalized dependency relations, but the Foreign Secretary in London, Lord Salisbury, had a more global perspective. See B. C. Busch, *Britain and the Persian Gulf: 1894–1914*, University of California Press, 1967, for a detailed study of inter-imperialist rivalry in the Gulf at this time and its local consequences.

12. Landen, op. cit., p. 267.

13. For the text of the Treaty of Sib see David Holden, *Farewell to Arabia*, London, 1966, pp. 249–50.

14. *Observer*, 16 August 1970.

15. Holden, op. cit., p. 236.

16. H. Boustead, *The Wind of Morning*, London, 1971, p. 219. Boustead had been a colonial administrator in the Sudan and in the Hadramaut; in his youth he had participated in Denikin's British-backed White attack on the Caucasus in 1919.

17. Boustead, op. cit., p. 222.

18. ibid., p. 223.

19. ibid., p. 222.

20. B B C interview with Brian Barran, 1966.

21. P. S. Allfree, *Warlords of Oman*, London, 1967, p. 164.

22. ibid., p. 161.

23. Author's interview with Amir Ali in the People's Liberation Army training camp, February 1970.

24. *The Times*, 3 August 1970.

25. See Appendix 3. Britain and Oman had also signed a 'Treaty of Friendship, Commerce and Navigation', Treaty Series, No. 44 [1952], Cmnd. 8633, to which Britain apologists often refer; the operative counter-revolutionary agreement was the 1958 exchange of letters. This 'exchange of letters' was, as is conventional in these matters, a public ratification of other secret agreements. The real basis of the British RAF position in Oman was laid down in two agreements on 'civil aviation', signed in 1934 and 1947 respectively. The former granted the British exclusive rights to establish airports and air services in Oman. The text of the British side is not available, but the Sultan's answer included the sentence: 'I accord permission to the military aircraft which are employed in the service of your Government to enjoy at all times priority in the use of the aerodromes and of the existing facilities'. The text of the 1947 agreement is in *State Papers*, Vol. 147, p. 928. A full list of all known treaties signed by Oman between 1798 and 1970 is given in Joachim Düster, 'Die Völkerrechtlichen Verträge des Sultanats Oman', *Verfassung und Recht in Ubersee*, Hamburg, No. 3, 1971.

26. Thus the junior Labour minister in the Ministry of Defence, Roy Hattersley, in the House of Commons, 25 March 1970.

27. James Morris, *Sultan in Oman*, London, 1957, p. 132. On the Buraimi crisis see Holden, op. cit., Chapter 15. A presentation of the British position can be found in J. B. Kelly, *Eastern Arabian Frontiers*, London, 1964.

28. Some British accounts of the Green Mountain revolt have appeared, all of them more or less suffused with imperialist distortion: P. S. Allfree, *Warlords of Oman*, London, 1967; A. Shepherd, *Arabian Adventure*, London, 1961; Colonel de C. Smiley, 'Muscat and Oman', *Royal United Services Institution Journal*, February 1960. Smiley, a veteran counter-revolutionary later active in North Yemen, took command of the Sultan's army in 1958. An Omani assessment of the period can be found in *al-Horria*, Beirut, 20 July 1970. An account of the 1957 part of the campaign is also given in *The History of the Cameronians*, Vol. 4, by John Baynes, London, 1971, pp. 102–26. Following this regiment's intervention, Sultan Said wrote a letter thanking one of the senior officers: 'The Sultans of Muscat have long experience of the fine traditions of Her Britannic Majesty's armed forces, and I have myself always had the warmest possible regard for them. The appearance, spirit and general bearing of the men have always made them readily popular among my people ...' he wrote, op. cit., p. 117.

29. Morris, op. cit., gives an enthusiastic account of the Sultan's trip across the desert.

30. Philip Warner, *The Special Air Service*, London, 1971, gives a self-congratulatory account of the SAS role, pp. 209–21. SAS returned to Oman during the 1960s for training exercises, and were sent into Radfan (pp. 209–11) and Dhofar (pp. 348, 358). See also Philip Darby, *British Defence Policy East of Suez 1947–1968*, London, 1973, pp. 130–33, for the implica-

tions for British military thinking of the Oman intervention. During the campaign in 1957 the British were worried lest the USA should adopt a hostile position. Macmillan, then Prime Minister, spent considerable effort in reassuring Eisenhower that the Oman operations were justified by their common interests. See *Riding the Storm*, by Harold Macmillan, London, 1971, pp. 270–77.

31. Although the British later accused the Imamists of blowing up the steamship *Dara*, these have always rejected responsibility for this tragic and curious incident. The *Dara*, en route from Bombay to Basra, was sunk by an explosion in the early morning of 1 April 1961. It was returning to Dubai harbour after prematurely leaving it on the previous day because of the danger of a severe storm; as the ship had pulled out in haste it still had on board the customs officials, porters and salesmen who had come aboard for the duration of the Dubai stop-over. Considerable dispute raged about the death toll in the Gulf but according to the official inquiry: 'It was not true that the *Dara* was carrying an over-complement of passengers' (*The Times*, 19 March 1962). Neither the firm involved, the British India Steam Navigation Company, nor the court actually undertook a public inquiry into this side of the matter; the official inquiry stated that 236 people had been drowned out of a total complement of 820 (*The Times*, 21 April 1962). At least five Arab divers later drowned while trying to recover objects from the wreck.

32. One means of asserting his legitimacy was to issue stamps purporting to be from the 'State of Oman' (in Arabic, *Dawlat Oman*). These were in fact printed in London and were distributed by pro-Imam Arab League countries, via a post-box in Amman, Jordan. The Imam gained considerable revenue by printing stamps which appealed to 'thematic' or 'topical' collectors, those who collect stamps by the subject-matter pictured on them. The Imam issues series on flowers, sports, nude women and other topics. A special *Journal of Arab Philately* surfaced in the USA in 1971, publicizing the (fake) stamp issues of the 'State of Oman', the 'State of Dhofar' (sic) and royalist Yemen. There is believed to be a very large market – 40–50 million – of topical collectors in Europe and the USA.

33. *Report of the Special Representative of the Secretary General on his Visit to Oman*, UN Document A/5562.

34. Author's interview with Talal Saad and Said Seif, *New Left Review*, No. 66, March–April 1971, p. 57. Said Seif is speaking.

35. The *Daily Telegraph*, 24 April 1970, hinted: 'If the Chinese-led intrusion of his southern provinces cannot be halted, the Sultan has intimated that he will leave his country to live in Europe.' The *Economist*, 18 July 1970, urged the British government to 'persuade [the Sultan] to go before it is too late for an alternative ruler to hold the country together'.

36. Shakhbut was the conservative ruler of Abu Dhabi whom the British threw out in 1965 and replaced by Zaid. See p. 464.

37. Said bin Taimur died in England on 19 October 1972. He had spent

his last two years in a London hotel room, with a handful of slaves and a colour TV set. *The Times* (23 October 1972) gave him an unctuous obituary: 'Unhappily, being a deeply religious man of a retiring and somewhat parsimonious disposition, he appeared chiefly concerned to conserve these resources and to keep his people insulated against the spread of modern ideas and developments', etc.

38. *Financial Times*, 27 July 1970.

39. *Guardian*, 27 July 1970.

40. *The Times*, 27 July 1970.

41. *The Times*, 1 August 1970.

42. 'It was like Wembley Cup-tie day, Epsom Downs on Derby Day, and a fairground fantasy, all in one,' wrote Arthur Chesworth in the *Daily Express*, 31 July 1970. Amid all the articles written after Said's overthrow one piece stands out from all the others; that of James Morris in the *Guardian* on 27 July. 'We shall see no more sultans like him,' Morris mused.

'I was one of those who, being only intermittently distressed by the political conditions of Oman, rather liked him. I liked his wary doe eyes and his gentle voice ... His face was a stylized face, with its fringed beard and its calculating mouth, and his supple but portly figure spoke of oiled baths, frankincense, and the more decorous pleasure of an abstemious harem.'

43. Pressure on oil deposits to make them rise to the surface can come by pumping gas into the reserves so that the oil gets lighter and rises; initially, petrol rises naturally to the surface once a hole is drilled.

44. *Le Commerce du Levant*, 17 October 1970.

45. *Financial Times*, 17 November 1972; special supplement on Oman.

46. *Le Monde*, 30–31 May 1971. For Tariq's views see *Frankfurte Allgemeine Zeitung*, 3 January 1972.

47. On his first visit to London after the coup, in 1971, he at first undertook to speak to the press; he then refused to do so, possibly as a result of the deteriorating situation in Muscat. About his only known action was a visit to the play *How the Other Half Loves*, with British Foreign Secretary Sir Alec Douglas-Home.

48. The fire, with flames rising 450 feet, was at the Yibal well; it cost PDO $50,000 a day.

49. *Saut ath-Thawra*, PFLOAG weekly, No. 27, 20 November 1972.

50. The island, Umm al-Ghanem, was next to the 800-square-mile, Omani-owned tip of Ras Massandam. See map, p. 463. In late 1973, when several thousand Iranian troops were dispatched to Dhofar, they were allowed to establish a base on the Kuria Muria island of Hallaniyah. The Kuria Murias, a group of five islands stretching fifty miles from east to west, were administered by Britain from 1854 until 1967. The South Yemeni government claimed that they had the right to exercise jurisdiction over them after independence, but the British government handed them instead to the Sultan of Oman. Hallaniyah, with a population estimated at 100, is the only one to be populated.

51. Philipps soon made up for his Omani losses by being awarded a concession for all the land and territorial waters of Haiti, the first case in history of such a total concession. He had been a defender of the former Sultan, and had had published two books (*Oman: A History*, London, 1967; and *Unknown Oman*, London, 1966), which contained fulsome tributes to the Al Bu Said dynasty. Philipps had first reached Oman as an archaeologist, and had patronized excavations in Dhofar; he had been granted the oil concession to Dhofar and later to the southern coastal stretch by Said bin Taimur. According to Richard O'Connor in *The Oil Barons*, London, 1972, p. 357: 'Wendell Philipps must be the champion royal favourite of all time' ... 'Certainly he is the only Arabist who got rich at the trade ...'

52. See 'Nixon goes fishing to beat spies', *Evening Standard*, 27 March 1972. See also *Financial Times*, 4 February 1972. When the author wrote an article detailing this deal for *Ramparts* magazine (October 1972) Black tried to deny his role: 'We hatch fish, unlike *Ramparts*, which hatches fishy rumours,' he told *San Francisco Chronicle* columnist Herb Caen (*San Francisco Chronicle*, 28 September 1972). For details of how the US money was 'laundered' through Saudi Arabia and of the CIA role, see 'Who Runs the Sultan of Oman?', *Economist Foreign Report*, 3 February 1972.

53. The Imam apparently refused to agree to the terms that were being imposed on him and remained in his Saudi exile; but the traditional interests of the Omani interior were well represented in the new regime, and the new Omani ambassador to Saudi Arabia was a nephew of the pre-1954 Imam.

Chapter Ten
Guerrilla War in Dhofar

To all those who Support the Communist Rebels in Western Dhofar

The Sultan's Armed Forces warn you:

We have built an important and strongly defended base on Sarfeet mountain. We are thereby able to control the watering places of Sarfeet. Our soldiers and army units are loyal and reliable; they have been ordered to kill every communist in the western region and they will carry out this order.

You will remember the recent bombardment of Akut. The time has now come to settle with you, and to settle for every shell you have released. Remember the fine people, whom you have executed in the west. For every one of them, several of you will die.

Do not be so blinkered as to think that the coming battles will take the form of small attacks or of reconnaissance expeditions. Our battle will be total and merciless and the fear of death will strike through the hearts of your leaders. Remember the operations we carried out a few months ago in the eastern region of Dhofar. During these operations we killed hundreds of communists and brought large areas under our control, as for example in Wadi Durjat, where the peace-loving civilians came to us and told us about the hiding places of the subversive atheists. Because these people were sinful and rejected Islam and everything that is holy, they conflicted with the peaceful civilians, just as they are now doing in western Dhofar. And now, atheists, your hour has struck. Military planes, cannons and automatic weapons are out hunting for you. Wherever you have crept, they will teach you a lesson and in the end will kill you all.

Your supplies and food are getting less, and they will soon all be used up thanks to our armed forces, which have cut you off from all reinforcements. You will soon die of thirst and hunger. Death is approaching, and there is only one way in which you can avoid further pain and annihilation: surrender to our troops and turn your back for ever on Godless communism. We will give you money, food and water and you can live again as good citizens under the banner of Islam and the protection of his Majesty, Sultan Qabus, who has led our country from backwardness to culture, civilization, progress and a better life. So, be reasonable and choose the right path: either an honourable life under Qabus, or death and decay with Godless communism.

ISLAM IS OUR PATH – FREEDOM IS OUR AIM

(Leaflet dropped by SOAF planes over western Dhofar, 1973)

Tropical Arabia

Dhofar, the Southern province of the Sultanate of Oman, is distinct from other parts of the Arabian peninsula, in its climate and in the character of its people.[1] It is a tropical area lying on the southern coast of the Arabian peninsula half-way between Aden at the south-west end and Muscat at the north-east. On one side it is flanked by the Mahra province of South Yemen, now the Sixth Governorate of the PDRY, and on the other it is separated from Oman by the 500-mile-wide Jaddat al-Harasi desert. The area of Dhofar is approximately 38,000 square miles, with a 200-mile coastline that stretches from the Kuria Muria Bay to Ras Darbat Ali, on the Yemeni border. A coastal mountain range rises to 4,500 feet and catches the monsoon rains between May and September. Annual rainfall in Dhofar is thirty inches; however towards either side of the area the average rainfall for the year is only three inches.

Dhofar's relatively heavy rainfall produces in the mountains a tropical forest and creates an area of vegetation extending up to 40 miles inland before the mountains taper off into the barren desert that stretches away to Saudi Arabia. The population of Dhofar, estimated at 150,000, inhabits this green strip, the mountains and the coastal plains. The most important of these is the Jurbaib plain, in the middle of Dhofar, forty miles long and up to ten miles wide. The capital, Salala, is sited here, with the adjacent villages of al-Husn, site of the prison and the Sultan's palace, and Umm al-Qawarif, the military base, to which is attached an RAF airfield. Farther to the east lie the towns of Mirbat, Taqa and Sadh, while to the west are situated Raysut, the only natural port in Dhofar, and the town of Rakhyut.

The economic and ethnic divisions of Dhofar largely correspond to differences between coast and mountain. On the coast the main activities are fishing, agriculture and trading. In the mountains the basis of the economy is pastoral farming – mainly of cows, but also of goats and camels – with a small amount of agriculture. The tropical mountains provide wild fruit (tamarinds, figs, pomegranates), and in previous centuries the mountains of Dhofar were the main producer of incense for India and the Mediterranean area.[2] The plains and hill areas have some limited interaction: the mountain people traded incense, ghee and cattle for foodstuffs (rice, tea, sugar, vegetables) and simple manufactured goods like cloth and utensils. A peculiarity of Dhofar is that during the monsoon months the cattle, who have to be kept alive on fodder, are fed dried sardines caught along the coast, and the stench of rotting fish is present everywhere in the caves and huts of the interior.[3]

While in the more remote past Dhofar traded principally with the Mediterranean, exporting incense, the main trading ties in recent centuries have been with India, particularly Bombay. Rice and cloth were formerly imported from this city, and Indian merchants had the management of Dhofar's trade. In return Dhofar exported ghee and incense. There was also some trade with Muscat and Aden. These ties have had an effect on the ethnic composition of Dhofar, whose population comprises a number of racial groups. Descendants of the original inhabitants are short, dark people, in appearance not unlike Ceylonese or Ethiopians, and akin to their immediate geographical neighbours in the Hadramaut and Mahra areas. The incense trade was traditionally in the hands of Hadrami emigrants, through whose country the caravans passed and who came to Dhofar to buy the product at source. In the nineteenth century Arabs from Oman ruled the country, bringing with them black slaves from Africa, who today make up a distinct section of the coastal population. Other trading groups, Persian and Indian, settled in the twentieth century.

The majority of the population are descendants of the original Dhofaris and inhabit the countryside and the mountains. They differ from the rest of the population of Oman in that they are Moslems of the Shafei Sunni group, as opposed to non-Sunni Ibadhi. But Islam's hold is relatively weak, in that Dhofar has remained isolated from most of Arab history and preserves some relics of the pre-Islamic religion that Mohammad tried to replace. Many tribesmen observe Islam only when they visit the coastal towns whereas in the mountains they practise pre-Islamic rites. Exorcism of evil spirits (*djinns* and *afreets*), blood sacrifices of animals and vaginal blowing of cows to induce milk are included in this religion together with numerous taboos concerning vegetation and animals. The Qara tribe, for example, refuse to use donkeys for transport or to eat hyenas, foxes, birds, chickens or eggs. Many tribesmen and women wear amulets, special rings and other talismans. Facial and bodily marks play an important role.

In addition to preserving this pre-Arabic religious culture, the original Dhofaris also speak a tongue that prevailed throughout southern Arabia before the spread of Arabic. This language closely resembles Arabic and is a descendant of the pre-Arabic Himyarite found on inscriptions through North and South Yemen. Its main characteristic is the lateral consonant '11', as found in Welsh ('Llewellyn'). It sounds jerkier than spoken Arabic, but shares with it many similarities, and speakers of the mountain language can learn Arabic with relative ease. The mountain language has never been written down and its main literary form is the epic poem, sung at night around the camp fires. All terms used to denote modern phenomena, such as 're-actionary' and 'imperialism' are taken over directly from Arabic.[4]

The mountain people live in the region's many limestone caves, in simple wattle and mud huts, and between monsoon periods they sometimes sleep in the open, with smouldering fires to counter the cold nights. Most have permanent dwelling places, but in the dry season they abandon a settled existence. The tribes on the edge of the desert are, by contrast, fully nomadic. Two tribal confederations dominate Dhofar: the Kathir and the Qara. The former derive from a tribe of the same name in Hadramaut, and are believed to have entered Dhofar in the fifteenth century; they inhabit the coast, the northern slopes of the mountains and the desert edges, and live mainly by pastoral farming and gathering incense.

The Qara inhabit the central mountain area of Dhofar – known as the Jabal Qara – and are the richest and most aristocratic of Dhofar's tribes. They have nine main divisions and fifteen subtribes with no stable leadership. They are possibly descended from Ethiopian Christians who conquered south Arabia before the coming of Islam, and have since ruled the Shahara tribesmen, adopting their tongue and customs, and holding them as a dispersed and subject federation of tribes who serve their Qara overlords. The Qara own most of the cattle, water sources and incense trees in Dhofar. As cattle-herding is the more prestigious activity they refrain from agriculture, even though they may lease out arable land to lower tribes. In western Dhofar, for example, the al-Mashayekh and Bait Issa sections of the Qara leased land to tribesmen of the Shahara and Mahra. In the same way the Qara leased incense trees to the lower tribes.

The Mahra tribes of Dhofar are an extension of tribes of the same name in the bordering areas of South Yemen. They displaced the Botahara tribesmen, pushing them eastwards so that today the latter are a tribe of poor fishermen on the edge of the Kuria Muria Bay. In the east, the Mahra are bedouins who pick incense during the harvest period; in the west they are herdsmen, while some live on the coast, working as sailors and fishermen. On the far east of Dhofar live another minority tribe, the Harasi, who have adopted many customs of the Arab bedouin, with whom they interact.

These ethnic divisions intersect with divisions of a social kind in an elementary social system. The surplus in Dhofari society still derives mainly from manual labour; there is no capital accumulation, little use of tools. While social divisions are limited they are nevertheless felt; the population of Dhofar is divided into those who work and those who live off the labour of others. The latter category includes merchants, administrators and some of the richer sheikhs. The country's workers comprise the herdsmen, slaves, fishermen, farmers and coolies.[5] Caste divisions correspond to this pattern. A small caste of Sada, Arabs claiming descent from the prophet Mohammad, make up the summit of the class structure. Then come the tribesmen of the Qara, Mahra and Kathir. Below the aristocratic tribesmen are the subjugated tribes – the Shahara and Botahara – while at the bottom come the Sultan's slaves. Relations between tribes are carefully structured and while cattle are owned by families rather than individuals, there were significant differences in the possession of cattle between and within sub-tribes. The social differentiation is preserved by restricting lower jobs to the lower castes, and by insisting that men pay their bride's father a bride-price (*mar*), so that men are prevented from marrying women from families superior to their own.[6]

Omani Colonization

The modern history of Dhofar dates from the nineteenth-century annexation of the area to the Sultanate of Oman. Only fragments are known of the country's previous history. The incense trade made Dhofar known to the ancient civilizations of the Mediterranean and the Bible mentions it, in Genesis 10, as 'Ophir'; thus, in order to control this important trade, the pre-Islamic Himyaritic kingdom of Yemen invaded Dhofar. Pre-Islamic ruins have been found in Dhofar, but the most extensive historical remains are in the ruined town of al-Balid near Salala and date from the eleventh and twelfth centuries, at which time Dhofar was ruled by an indigenous dynasty, the Minjuis. Both before this era and subsequently Dhofar was annexed to Oman and to

321

Yemen. In 1285 Marco Polo visited the 'city of Dulfar' (i.e. al-Balid), ruled at that time by the Sultan of Aden,[7] and in 1325 the Arab traveller Ibn Batuta stopped there. Both Marco Polo and Ibn Batuta reported considerable trading, including the exports to India of horses, a form of commerce that subsequently ceased.[8]

In the fourteenth century the autonomous kingdom of the Hadramaut apparently controlled Dhofar, and in the sixteenth and seventeenth centuries the Portuguese and the Turks tried without success to subdue the coastal towns. The next definite information is of the year 1806, when Dhofar was ruled by a slave-owning pirate, Sayyid Mohammad bin Aqil, who made the town of Salala his capital and defended it with a force of 500 slaves. Sayyid Mohammad, who tried at one stage to enlist Napoleon's patronage, clashed with Qara tribesmen seeking support from the Sultan of Muscat; and in 1829, when Qara assassinated Sayyid Mohammad at Mirbat, the Sultan sent a force to occupy Dhofar. The attempted annexation failed, Omani forces withdrew, and for a time, in the 1830s, Dhofar was ruled by Abdullah Lloreyd a former Dutch cabin-boy who had been taken prisoner by Sayyid Mohammad, and who had married an Arab woman and settled in Dhofar.[9] The Omani Sultans later claimed that Dhofar had paid tribute to Oman throughout the nineteenth century, but there is no evidence of this, and Omani control was only reasserted in the 1870s when Dhofar was taken over by a Sayyid Fadhl bin Alawi. Sayyid Fadhl had been active against the British in India, whence he had been expelled in 1852. Being of partly Hadrami descent he had returned to Arabia; and after spending some time in Mecca he had settled in 1875 in Salala and been accepted as a ruling figure mediating between the tribes. To consolidate his position he wrote to the Turkish government in Istanbul hoping to get their support in Dhofar. The Turks at this time could do little, being preoccupied in Bulgaria by their war with Tsarist Russia. In 1879 a group of pro-Omani Dhofar tribesmen drove out Sayyid Fadhl and the province came under the administration of a governor, or *wali*, acting for the Sultan of Muscat.[10]

The Sultan's annexation of Dhofar had the continued support of the British. In the same way, they gave him their backing nearer Muscat against the rebellious tribes of the interior. The majority of tribal leaders in Dhofar favoured independence, while two smaller groups favoured Fadhl and the Sultan of Muscat respectively. What counted was force, and in 1880 and 1883 the Omani army were able to hold on to the coastal plain in the face of risings by the Qara tribes, including the original pro-Muscat factions. In 1894–5 the English travellers Theodore Bent and his wife visited the interior of Dhofar, the first time any travellers, Arab or European, are known to have done so.[11] They met the *wali*, Suleiman bin Suwaylim, who lived at al-Hafa, near Salala, and observed Dhofar to be at peace. But soon after their departure there was an unprecedentedly large rising in which two of Suleiman's sons were killed and the Turkish flag was raised over Salala.

This brought the first direct British military intervention in Dhofar: two ships, the *Lawrence* and the *Cossack*, were sent to re-establish Omani rule and to drive out any Turkish influence that might threaten British hegemony in the area. Suleiman was reinstated with British support and consolidated the system of plunder of Dhofar that constituted the basic form of Omani rule. The annual *zakat* tax on Dhofar amounted to one Maria Theresa dollar for every five camels, one dollar for every ten cattle and one goat for every twenty goats. Most of this was paid in kind, transported to Bombay and there converted into cash; by 1895 Dhofar was supplying the Muscat treasury with MT $15,000. While Oman was a British colony, Dhofar was an Omani colony: the task of the governor at Salala was to carry out the simplest form of imperialist exploitation – plunder. Throughout the period of Omani rule Dhofar was never fully integrated into the Sultanate, and this colonial position *vis-à-vis* Oman was formalized in its title 'The Dependency of Dhofar'.

The governor exercised control by two means – tribal conflicts, and blockading the hinterland. If one tribe resisted taxation the governor was able to arouse other tribes against it, and starve it into submission by cutting off the rice and dried sardines needed in the hinterland. The tribes were overtaxed and resented what they regarded as alien Omani domination; but the blockade, their own division and collective punishment of offending tribes by the governor kept the colony under some kind of Omani rule.

Governor Suleiman was assassinated in 1907 and his place as governor was taken by Bakhit an-Nubi, a slave whom Suleiman had used as a deputy after the recapture of Salala from the tribes in 1896. Bakhit's tenure was marked by several risings, and in 1916 Sultan Taimur bin Feisal visited Salala to investigate the situation. A new governor, a Dhofari named Abdullah bin Suleiman, was appointed, and when he died in 1921 he, like Suleiman, was followed by a slave. The sultans of Muscat tried to cope with the series of tribal risings by signing treaties with the tribal leaders, but direct subjugation along traditional lines was more common.

In 1932 when Said bin Taimur deposed his father, he visited Dhofar and appointed as governor Sheikh Hamud bin Hamid al-Ghafari, who was to be governor of Dhofar for over three decades. As was traditional in Moslem countries the accession of a new monarch was followed by a survey of land and property for taxation purposes, and the 1932 survey remained the basis of all taxation in Dhofar until 1970. Under Sultan Said's rule Dhofar remained as it had been, except for two intrusions from the outside world. During the Second World War the British RAF built an airfield at Salala, bringing home more directly to the Dhofari people the presence of the imperial power that stood behind their own Omani oppressors. Then in 1948 the first PDO oil exploration team arrived, and although it did not find oil the US consortium that replaced them, Dhofar-Cities Services Petroleum, did make a strike at Marmul in 1957. This consortium, made up of Cities Services Company and the Richfield Oil Corporation, said that the oil was not in commercial quantities and in 1962 the concession was handed over to a new consortium, in which John W. Mecom combined with the Pure Oil Company; in 1965 they were joined by the Continental Oil Company. These independent oil companies had been excluded from other areas of the Middle East by the big firms, and hoped to compensate by finding oil in Dhofar, but in vain. Once the armed struggle began in 1965 their activities fell off: in the early days of the conflict an oil exploration truck was blown up by the guerrillas, and in 1969 Dhofar was handed back to PDO. In 1971, as part of the Sultan's rapprochement with the US, it was once again given to a US consortium.[12]

These outside intrusions were less important than the character of the regime imposed on Dhofar by Said bin Taimur. Said married a Dhofari woman, by whom he had one son – Qabus – and two daughters, and from 1958 onwards he lived permanently in the palace at al-Hosn, near Salala. The harsh regime that he imposed on the whole of Oman was particularly virulent in Dhofar itself, both because Said himself was there and because its colonial status had always made it more oppressively treated than the rest of Oman. Although foreigners visiting Dhofar reproduced the myths of the Al Bu Said regime,[13] the Dhofaris themselves had a different experience of their country. The only road in the country was the military highway through the mountains from Salala to Thamrit ('Midway'), and from there to Muscat. There was only one primary school, no medical facilities and no water or electricity even in the towns. In addition to the prevalence of slavery and the horrendous poverty of the people, Dhofar was hit by a continual series of new prohibitions:

Our attention has been drawn to the fact that some of the Sultanate's subjects have been wearing clothes other than those habitually worn in this country. We warn each and every one to conform to the traditional national costume and refrain from wearing any foreign dress from the day of the publication of this communiqué. Whoever defies this order will be prosecuted.[14]

Said's spies in Salala, energetically flanked by his own peerings through his telescope, terrorized the population. They were not allowed to smoke, ride bicycles, play football, open restaurants, trim their hair, wear shoes or possess radios. Emigration was strictly prohibited. The only person licensed to import medicine, or to ride a bicycle, was an Iranian quack and favourite of the Sultan's named Ahmad Shofiq.

No attempt was made to encourage or allow the development of the Dhofari economy, despite the potential wealth in the agricultural land on the Jurbaib plain, the cattle in the mountains, and the rich marine life in the seas. Taxation actively discouraged it. For every five goats, one had to be paid annually as tax; the same applied to camels, and for every ten cows the tax was one calf. Fishing was similarly suffocated: in the western part of Dhofar, until its liberation in 1968, fishermen had to pay 120 rials to the governor at Rakhyut for the right to fish during the three-month fishing season; for each additional month they had to pay seventy-five rials. This only covered fishing for sardines. Other fishing was taxed daily: the governor, or his agent, waited for the boats to return and then arbitrarily took a quantity of the catch in tax.[15] Other taxes were equally oppressive: in the 1960s import taxes in Dhofar were 300 per cent higher than in the rest of Oman, and the meagre ghee exports of the Dhofari economy were also taxed, at the rate of 20 per cent.

This system rested upon a very traditional form of repression: by keeping the people isolated from the world, by discouraging all economic prospects and by exacerbating conflicts between and within tribes Said hoped to keep the Dependency of Dhofar in static subjection. However, the system created its own contradictions. From the 1880s onwards the traditional cycle recurred of taxation–resistance–blockade–subjection–taxation. Said's attempted use of tribal intrigue undermined domination by the sheikhs and upset the structured balance between tribes; it thereby weakened the tribal system. Most important was the fact that grinding poverty forced Dhofari men to emigrate to find work in the Gulf and aroused the oppressed classes of the province to fight for a different regime.

The Dhofar Liberation Front

When the oil boom hit the Gulf in the 1950s thousands of Dhofari men emigrated via land and sea to this newly created source of employment. They undertook especially employments for which they were qualified by their strong mountain physique; like the North Yemenis who emigrated to Saudi Arabia they were concentrated in the construction business and the armed forces. At one time over an estimated quarter of the police force in Qatar and in Kuwait were of Dhofari origin. The emigrant Dhofaris sent home some of their wealth, when possible, and used to return during the monsoon period to assist with the harvest.

In the Gulf these workers came into contact with nationalist political movements – the Imam Ghalib's group and the Nasserite movement, which, in the Gulf as in South Yemen, was represented by the MAN. At the same time, tribal leaders in Dhofar, aware of the Imam's challenge in the interior of Oman to Sultan Said, entered into contact with Saudi Arabia and with the Imamist headquarters in Dammam. In 1962 a group of Dhofaris in the MAN joined with other exiles to form the Dhofar Liberation Front (*Jabhat Tahrir Dhofar*). They set up a cover organization, and under the guise of raising money to build mosques and help the poor, they recruited members, built up their finances and laid the bases of an organization inside the Sultanate of Oman. The aim of some Dhofari nationalists among the DLF leadership was the liberation of their region from domination by Oman. In the same way the Imam, to whom they were linked, wanted to set up a separate state in the Omani interior. The MAN in the Gulf had a different perspective: they were Nasserists, dominated by the strong right-wing branch of the MAN in Kuwait, and temporarily immune to left-wing tendencies becoming apparent in the Lebanese and Palestinian branches of the organization. Yet the Gulf MAN stood for a unified struggle against British imperialism and its local agents throughout the Gulf, and they were suspicious of, if not openly hostile to, the Imam.

Although the differences between the groups were indisputable, various factors did enable them to form an alliance. The most important was the development of the revolution in the Yemens – in the North in September 1962 and then, in October 1963, in the South. This showed the non-Nasserite Dhofari leaders that the Nasserites were prepared for armed struggle; and in 1964 the Dhofari branch of the MAN merged with the DLF. The MAN brought political expertise and contacts with the Egyptians; the DLF brought the organization to within Dhofar itself.

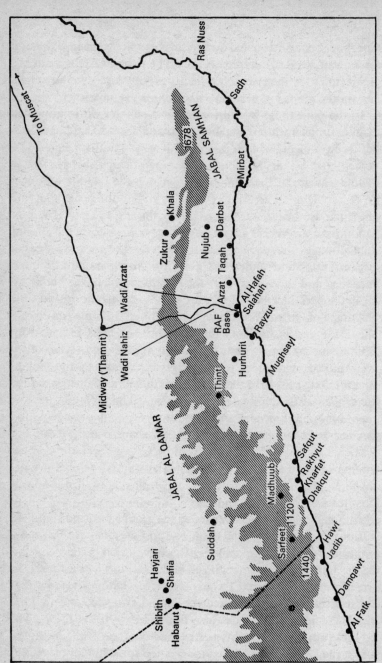

Map 9 Dhofar

These groups, now sharing the name D L F, were joined by a third, the Organization of Dhofari Soldiers, a loosely coordinated group of cells among Dhofari soldiers in S A F, the Saudi Arabian army, the Trucial Oman Scouts and the police forces of the Gulf.

The Dhofari M A N cadres who entered the D L F retained their own perspective on the future strategy of the revolution, but they broke their organizational ties with the pan-Arab M A N, and participated in the five-man executive committee set up to prepare for armed struggle. Another addition to the D L F was a leader of the Bait Kathir tribe named Musallim bin Nufl. Bin Nufl had been subsidized by Sultan Said, but in 1962 had turned against the Sultan and opened relations with the Imam and the Saudis. The oil wells found by the U S exploration team lay in Bait Kathir territory and Musallim bin Nufl, with Saudi encouragement, obviously wanted access to the riches kept from him by the restrictions of Omani colonialism.

The opening stages of the struggle were marked by setbacks. The U A R allowed the D L F to open an office in Cairo and until 1967 gave it a little military support. Iraq trained 160 cadres in 1964 and continued aid until 1968. But the Front had to rely on its own fund-raising and purchases to get most of the equipment it needed. In April and May 1965 over sixty of the D L F's militants were arrested in Muscat and Salala; and in May an Iranian naval patrol arrested a D L F arms ship on its way out of the Gulf.

In the face of these difficulties the Front's remaining militants withdrew from the towns and convened the D L F's First Congress in the Dhofari mountains; it met at Wadi al Kabir in central Dhofar on 1 June 1965 and elected an eighteen-man executive committee, which included Yusuf Alawi, the D L F representative in Cairo, and Mohammad Ahmad al-Ghassani, a native of Salala who had been working until recently for an oil company in the Gulf. Though these two militants came to represent the D L Fs two conflicting factions both originated from the pre-1964 D L F, and subsequent divisions were subordinated at this stage to the decision to launch an immediate armed struggle. While the spread of Nasserism through the Arab world influenced the D L F it was not the Nasserists but the tribesmen who dominated. Initially

329

they saw the Dhofar struggle as the latest in the long line of Dhofari risings against Omani colonialism.

Guerrilla War, Phase One: 1965–7

The D L F campaign to liberate Dhofar began after the First Congress, on 9 June 1965, with the ambush of a government patrol north-west of the Thamrit road, in which Said ar-Ruwai, the first D L F victim, was killed. The war that followed entered at least three stages. In its initial phase, from 1965 to 1967, fighting was concentrated in the central region of Dhofar around the Salala–Thamrit road, and mainly involved small hit-and-run actions. From 1967 to 1970 the guerrillas liberated the western and eastern sectors of Dhofar, and drove the Sultan's army into a tiny coastal enclave around Salala. In the third phase, beginning in 1970, the guerrillas escalated their struggle, in the face of a counter-insurgency offensive.

The guerrillas were a small group during the first phase. They depended at least in part on the inaccessibility of their terrain to escape from the S A F. The D L F attacked government posts at Taqa and Mirbat in the autumn of 1965, and in 1966 a series of battles took place in three valleys north-east of Salala – Wadi Nahiz, Wadi Jardom and Wadi Jarsis. The D L F were based in Arzuq and in the Amut and Hamrin valleys in central Dhofar, near the road where they ambushed a number of government convoys. A larger-scale confrontation occurred in July 1966 at Raydat al-Kala, where the D L F lost two men but blew up seven military vehicles, killed or wounded fifty-nine of the enemy and captured supplies of weapons. A broadcast over Cairo radio in March 1967 summed up the D L F's military tactics:

Their arms must be seized and used to arm and equip new units of the Liberation Army. Our aim in the liberation war must always be the enemy's rear. We should not engage in battles with him which he determines and the consequences of which he has already assessed and appraised ... Our war with colonialism, brother, is a long one. It is a war of life or death. The ideal military tactics of a people's war should be adopted: they are to hit and run.

The most spectacular DLF operation in this early stage was the attempted assassination on 26 April 1966 of Said Bin Taimur. Until 1964 the regular SAF had been excluded from Dhofar and the Sultan had relied on other armed groups – slaves; irregular soldiers, or *askaris*; and the Dhofar Force, based at Fort Arzat, north-east of Salala in the Jurbaib plain.[16] Some of the latter were Omanis, but others were Dhofaris, and contained a DLF cell. In April 1966 Sultan Said attended a farewell parade at Fort Arzat for the retiring SAF commander in Dhofar, a Pakistani who may have been called Major Mohammad Sakhi Raja. During troop inspection, Dhofari soldiers opened fire on the Sultan, wounding him and reportedly killing Major 'Raja'. A convoy of jeeps accelerated out of the compound bearing the wounded Said to safety; but from that date on he was never seen in public and many Dhofaris, including some who worked in his palace, believed him to be dead, particularly in view of the fact that the most convenient way for the British to run the country would be to execute their orders via a phantom Sultan.[17]

The reaction of the Dhofari population to the struggle was at first cautious. The tribesmen who fought initially were Dhofaris who had worked in the Gulf or came from the lower tribes.

All Dhofari tribes felt oppressed *as Dhofaris*, apart from a few sheikhs and spies who were on the Sultan's payroll. However it was the poorer elements of the al-Qara and the al-Kathir, and above all the Shahara, who were the first to rally to the call for armed struggle,

a guerrilla leader later stated.[18] Spies and government agents worked to divide the revolution and at times, especially in 1967, the guerrillas were on the defensive. On the other hand the DLF rising had differentiated itself from previous revolts by being above each particular tribe. One of the first acts of the Front was to divide Dhofar into three geographical units (West, Centre, East) in order to supersede definition by tribal area.[19]

The Sultan and the British responded by increasing the number of SAF in Dhofar to 1,000, although they still estimated DLF forces at under 100. After the April 1966 assassination attempt the Sultan excluded Dhofaris from his armed forces, but brought in recruits from loyal Omani tribes to patrol the Dhofar coastal zone. SAF missions tried with some success to 'search and destroy' DLF positions but collective punishment of rebelling areas only exacerbated Dhofari opposition. In early 1966 the British sealed off Salala with a barbed wire fence, harassing all Dhofaris who passed in and out, and trying to resurrect the economic blockade practised by previous Sultans in an attempt to starve the mountain people. In 1968 trading links with Aden were broken. These measures increased popular anger and the sense of trans-tribal unity: the mountain people suffered from the ban on trading with the coast, and many of the Salala population were forced to escape by sea, hanging on to rubber tyres and makeshift rafts till they reached the liberated areas. The other British policy was to cut the supply lines of the DLF. The overland route from Saudi Arabia appears to have been blocked from 1966, and bringing in arms by sea was also more difficult. The main source was now from captured arms and through South Yemen, where the NLF were able to pass quantities on to Dhofar. In October 1966 the British from South Yemen attacked and sealed the border village of Hauf, and arrested twenty-two Dhofaris, including – they claim – a former sergeant-major in the Dhofar Force. In 1967, however, the flow of arms and men from South Yemen increased and with the victory of the revolution in South Yemen the struggle entered a more militant phase.

Guerrilla War, Phase Two: 1968–70

1968 saw both political and military transformation of the struggle. The latter change resulted from transference of the war to the western sector, as the SAF tried to block supply lines from South Yemen. Yet this military shift would have been less important but for the political developments of that year. At the Second Congress of the DLF, held at Hamrin in central Dhofar in September 1968, the separatist and tribal leadership of the struggle was replaced. As the following chapter explains in detail the organization now aimed to liberate all of the Gulf from imperialism, and altered its name from the Dhofar Liberation Front to the Popular Front for the Liberation of the Occupied Arab Gulf (PFLOAG).[20] It declared as its guiding ideology adherence to 'scientific socialism' and committed itself to a programme of struggle against imperialism, neo-colonialism and the oligarchic regimes of the area.

Several factors contributed to this change: the establishment of the NLF government in South Yemen; the swing to right in the Arabian peninsula as Saudi Arabia and Egypt reached agreement and the Saudis were granted unchallenged supremacy; the British build-up in the Gulf following the flight from Aden; the radicalization of the MAN throughout the Arab world following the June War of 1967; and, above all, the pressure from within the revolutionary movement itself to replace the inadequate leaders and policies of the first two years.

The militants were acutely affected by international changes in the Middle East in 1967. The British retreat from Aden gave the DLF a secure ally on their south-western flank and for the first time provided a sure supply of food and equipment. The MAN inside the DLF were close allies of the left wing inside the South Yemeni NLF, and the predominance of the NLF left in the Hadramaut and Mahra was also of direct assistance.[21] The PRSY and the Sultanate of Oman clashed at the moment of South Yemeni independence when the British handed the Kuria Muria islands, up to then part of South Yemen, to the Sultan, and the next months saw Omani and Saudi forces probing on the PRSY's borders. Moreover while the Saudis had originally helped the DLF as part of their expansionist policies, the June 1967 War with Israel and the NLF victory in South Yemen swung Riyadh decisively behind the Sultan and the British.

The radicalization of the MAN throughout the Arab world became felt in Dhofar via the MAN in South Yemen, and – to a less extent – through the MAN in the Gulf. This process, embodied in the emergence of the Palestinian resistance, coincided with the internal difficulties of the DLF itself. It had relied on the Arab regimes for diplomatic support; yet after the June

War Egypt had fallen in line with Saudi Arabia and stopped its aid. The MAN had seen the Egyptian army incapable of facing up to the Israelis, and inside Dhofar it had been confronted by difficulties and defections, which had been discouraged only by Said bin Taimur's refusal to treat with the rebels. Supplying and administering a liberated area had also posed for the first time questions of politics and of the DLF's relation with the masses. The ideological changes at the Second Congress, and the many consequent decisions, resulted above all from this internal radicalization, which was reinforced by external change.

This political alteration coincided with an SAF assault on the western provinces of Dhofar. The October 1966 raid on Hauf had not stopped supplies coming through, and in 1967 the situation improved as Hadramaut and Mahra fell to the NLF. In response the British set up a line of positions along the northern edge of the popular area, with smaller points nearer the sea. In the west the centre of this line was at Madhoub (known to the British as DEFA) where an expeditionary force from the Muscat Regiment was stationed. From Madhoub and from lesser positions at Shagleet, Kharat and Janouk, SAF mercenaries with British officers tried to cut towards the coast and destroy supply lines. They were backed up by sea landings and by artillery attacks on the areas in between. A British officer seconded to the SAF has described the campaign in the western sector as he experienced it:

As it was Khareef (monsoon) time and the Jabal was blanketed in swirling mists and driving rain, the companies had pulled back on to the northern slopes of the Jabal on the edge of the desert area. I joined my company, which was over two days' journey from the next, in what we called the Western Approaches, the Mahri tribal territory bordering on South Yemen.

Things were quiet as the rebels were utilizing the heavy cover offered by the Khareef to move camel trains of weapons, ammunition and mines from their villages in South Yemen and I spent my first weeks on a series of patrols and ambushes designed to intercept the enemy supply routes ...

During my first month the area was so quiet that I stupidly began to believe that there were no rebel tribesmen around until I experienced my first taste of action in an area called Jaidrait, only a few miles from the South Yemen border. I was returning in landrovers with the reconnaissance platoon when we came under heavy automatic fire from an ambush position of some thirty rebels. My driver was hit by the first burst and the vehicle crashed into some bushes, throwing us out. Unfortunately the three soldiers in the back of the vehicle were all hit as they scrambled for cover. The ambush was well sited and less than one hundred yards away; but thick mist and bad visibility affected their aim. The rebels continued to fire for the next ten minutes until we managed to manoeuvre ourselves into a stronger position when they withdrew . . . The period directly after the monsoon showed that almost to a man the Qara tribesmen and most of the coastal Arabs were sympathetic to if not actually engaged in the struggle against the Sultan. Skirmishes became an almost daily occurrence, the Sultan's few mud forts in the coastal villages were frequently attacked, camps were mortared almost every evening and it was an impossible task to control this difficult area nearly the size of Wales. Water was very scarce, resupply became tremendously difficult, casualty evacuation was often by donkey, and, apart from containing the enemy, we were certainly not winning the war.

After the start of the guerrillas' 1968 autumn offensive this officer was evacuated from the desert position and was deployed for a landing on the coast at Dhalqut, just inside Dhofar near the South Yemen border:

The landing at Dhalqut was uneventful and on searching the village we found that all able-bodied men had taken to the hills. We then set about ferrying our stores ashore but in the middle of this we suddenly came under heavy and accurate automatic rifle and mortar fire from the thickly wooded and steep slopes above our camp from a force of about fifty rebels. We remained in this camp site for the next three days but constant enemy attacks proved that the position was untenable and after blowing up the village wells, we evacuated the camp during the hours of darkness and returned to Raysut. Once again we were forced to change our tactics and spent the next four months carrying out nocturnal seaborne raids on the coast of Dhofar from Ras Darbat Ali in the west, to the village of Sadh in the east.[22]

As this account suggests, the policy of blocking off the western border was a failure, and by the summer of 1969 the British had been forced to abandon the west altogether, and to fall back on the Salala area. Constant shelling of the British positions north of the mountains and counter-attacks on the coastal landings had defeated the SAF plan. In 1968 and early 1969 all the SAF positions except for Madhoub were abandoned; then the Front closed in and in June 1969 the SAF had to pull out of Madhoub as well. This left the only government forces in the coastal town of Rakhyut, which was the administrative, i.e. tax-collecting, centre of the western sector. On 23 August 1969 there was a particularly heavy monsoon storm, such that no air or sea support could be flown into Rakhyut by the SAF. The Front took this opportunity and attacked: Rakhyut fell and the Omani governor, Hamid bin Said, was captured with twenty-two of his men. Hamid bin Said was arrested, tried for being a British agent, convicted and shot. His men were released and allowed to return home or join the revolution. The western sector had been liberated.

The fall of Rakhyut ended the British attempt to isolate Dhofar from the victorious revolution in South Yemen, and it opened the way for an intensified political and military offensive throughout Dhofar. Fighting now concentrated on three targets, as the SAF fell back. These targets were: the Salala–Thamrit road – now renamed 'The Red Line', by PFLOAG; the Salala air base; and the eastern province. A PFLOAG military communiqué for the period between 12 November 1969 and 20 December 1969 details around sixty attacks along the Red Line and on Salala, in which an estimated 210 enemy soldiers were killed or wounded, and numerous Bedford trucks, artillery pieces, radio sets and SAF fortifications were destroyed. In February 1970 PFLOAG mortaring of the Salala base 'was so accurate that RAF officers at a mess party only narrowly escaped death';[23] as a result of this attack the British had to send in reinforcements of the RAF Regiment to man a twenty-four-hour radar and observation ring around the perimeter defences of the base.[24] In March PFLOAG pressure in the eastern sector of Dhofar was such that the SAF had to evacuate altogether when the easternmost coastal village of Sadh fell to PFLOAG forces. For the first time the British press now admitted the situation, that the guerrilla army 'now controls all of Dhofar except the desert and the narrow coastal plain where Salala and its airstrip are situated'.[25] A correspondent flown out in August 1970 described Salala as 'little more than a coastal enclave protected by a wall of barbed wire and a natural *cordon sanitaire* of open plain'.[26]

Inside the Western Sector

This was the situation when I first visited Dhofar with a group of Arab militants in February 1970.[27] In London it had been impossible to find out anything about the war, especially since there had been not a single press report from Salala over the whole five years of the war. Only a handful of observers had reported from the guerrilla side,[28] and there were rumours that heavy bombing and SAF attacks had destroyed the liberated areas. In Aden the representatives of PFLOAG assured us that the liberated area existed, and plans for our visit had been made.

One morning, at 4.30 a.m., we boarded the weekly DC–3 flight to al-Qeidha, the capital of the Sixth Governorate of the PDRY, which was about thirty miles from the Dhofar frontier. From there we moved east by jeep.

The first sight of the revolution was at the tiny village of al-Fitk where black Mahri fishermen ferried us in their unstable *sambuqs* out to sea to board the *Voice of the People* (*Saut ash-Shaab*), the guerrillas' only naval vessel: it had a machine-gun mounted in the front, and the PFLOAG flag on the mast. The crew of twelve, clothed in khaki gear, wearing Lenin and Mao badges, and armed with rifles and cartridge belts, welcomed us aboard, together with a sheep we had bought from shepherds as a meal. Although the *Voice of the People* was running arms and supplies into Dhofar – to Rakhyut and beyond – it was considered too dangerous for us to go in that way and it took us only as far as the Revolutionary Camp and the border town of Hauf. (Five months later, in July 1970, *Saut-ash Shaab* was sunk off Rakhyut by British planes and six of its twelve crew killed.) From Hauf we travelled by foot, over rough mountain terrain too wild to cross on donkeys or camels. The path through the mountains was so

337

narrow that it was often necessary to clamber off it to allow cattle and camel convoys to pass, and whenever a group of people was coming the other way our two parties would line up along the path and exchange greetings and information.[29] We were told that it would take two weeks of walking to reach the battle front along the Red Line – about 100 miles away – and that communications were so bad that it could take up to a month for news of a battle to travel from one end of Dhofar to the other. Wherever we went we were greeted with warmth and with intense questioning by the militants and population. We slept in the caves and wattle huts of the mountain people, and in the stone houses of Rakhyut, often under the same cover as the cattle and goats, whose noises throughout the night echoed round the dark rock caverns. Whereas the local population normally eat one meal a day, we were given endless cups of warm milk (camel, cow and goat), and goats and cows were killed and char-roasted over open fires. The main enemy was lack of energy, and the PFLOAG guides who accompanied us and carried double cargoes of luggage (theirs and ours) used to encourage us with the slogan: 'Exhaustion is a paper tiger' (*at-Taab Numurun min Warraq*).

The first village we came to was Dhalqut, scene of the 1968 SAF landings, and now deserted after successive air raids and shellings from the sea. Above the village in the hills from which the 1968 counter-attack had come was a detachment of the People's Liberation Army; soon after we arrived there was an alert, as to the east two Strikemaster jets from Salala came in over the mountains from the desert and dropped explosives on Rakhyut, several miles away. Simultaneously a Beaver reconnaissance plane out at sea came into view flying along the coast and a naval vessel of the Sultan's forces could be seen in the distance.

The PLA detachment went on to the alert, but the enemy forces withdrew and next day we continued our journey. We visited Rakhyut, which had fallen in the previous August and which was now almost deserted as a result of twice- or thrice-weekly air attacks. Many of the houses of the fishermen had been bombed and remnants of bombs lay in many parts of the town;

we also saw the former governor's residence, just to the east of the town, which was now a heap of rubble after being destroyed by PLA mortars. The PFLOAG flag flew over the town. In Rakhyut we met a PLA unit on its way from the eastern and central sectors to the Revolutionary Camp for training: it included sixteen new PLA recruits who had fought for two years in the militia and had been promoted last month to full membership of the PLA. The commander of this unit was Salem Ali who had been leading a platoon along the Red Line. He told of the most recent actions and of two ambushes in which he had taken part: one had caught an SAF unit trying to infiltrate the liberated areas from the desert, while another had attacked an enemy patrol coming up from the Salala base of Umm al-Qawarif to a well at Sahalmout. In the latter engagement the SAF had suffered twenty casualties.

Other fighters we met described the situation at the front line. They observed how the British officers hid in the midst of their troops to avoid being shot, and told of the last attack on Taqa. All PLA fighters and all civilians told of the air attacks on the liberated areas and on the herds, wells and houses of the inhabitants. The first people we met inside Dhofar were a group of thirty women and girls, aged between eight and forty, who were attending a literacy class conducted by a PFLOAG cadre. They were all refugees from the eastern and central regions whose livelihoods had been destroyed by SAF. Tufula from Kefkefout told how in 1966 the mercenary army had come and burnt all the cattle and houses in the village. Muna Musallim from Wadi Nahiz recounted how at the end of 1969 long-range SAF shelling of the area had killed all the cattle and camels in her village. Tuful Salem from the village of Bait Zerbeq told how in November 1969 the mercenary army had attacked at night, had shot a man, the father of seven children, who had come unarmed out of his house, and then burnt the 100-odd wattle huts in the village. Said Mahad described to us how the air force had bombarded the pastures and village around Iryash. Another woman asked why the Labour Government, which called itself socialist, was killing the peasants of Dhofar. 'You come from the country that is

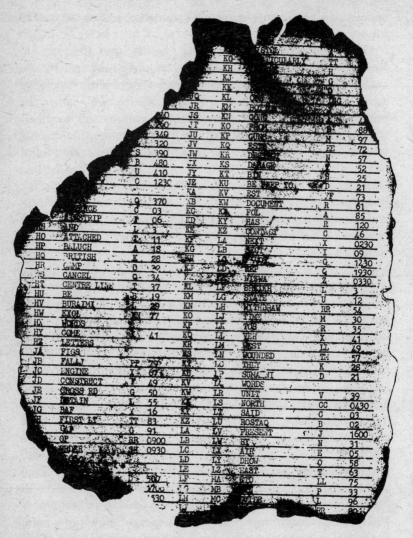

Figure One   British Code

oppressing us,' Tuful Salem said. 'Tell the British people what is happening here.'

After Rakhyut we walked into the mountains and reached the former British headquarters in the west, the position at Madhoub. Tens of deserted stone sangars and empty water barrels lay on the top of a hill; the unmarked grave of a dead Baluchi soldier lay near by; and there were hundreds of empty artillery crates marked 'Defence Department, Muscat'. One sangar stood out from the rest: its walls were thicker, the ground was smoother, and a small paved path led up to it. Inside lay the debris of imperialist officers: Yardley's shaving cream, beer cans, an old Sunday newspaper colour supplement, and the charred remains of the radio code which the British officers in their hurried retreat had failed to get rid of completely (see Figure One).

In February 1970 the western zone was free of SAF ground attacks, and the only harassment came from the air and the sea. The primary duty of PLA units in the zone was the defence of the liberated area of the vital supply routes that crossed the sector ferrying food, clothes and ammunition to the front and to the eastern sector. This involved constant reconnaissance, shore patrols and anti-aircraft defence, as well as arming and training the whole population for resistance to future attacks. We hardly saw a man capable of carrying weapons who was not in the PLA or in the militia; an increasing number had armed themselves following the decisions of the September 1968 Congress.

The western zone also served as a training and rest area for PLA fighters from the centre and the east; fresh recruits were sent there for political and military formations, and older cadres came for rest and to train the less experienced. At the central garrison of the western region around 100 members of the PLA were based. From there they undertook various missions, sometimes on the three-hour march to the edge of the desert where lay the ruins of a Provost plane shot down in the summer of 1969, sometimes to the coast to man the teams watching for infiltrators. Ali Mohsen, a member of the General Command of the PFLOAG, and an MAN militant of long political experience, explained to us the tasks of his garrison. He showed how the P L A make medicines out of the gums of trees and in the evening joined with the P L A members and the local inhabitants in singing Himyari songs around the camp-fire. The most popular song at this time had the self-explanatory refrain: 'from the mountains to the towns, from Dhofar to the Gulf'. Such was the military prepardness of the area that on one occasion the garrison had been put on full alert at the sighting of a suspected S A F patrol: it turned out to be our group returning from the inspection of Madhoub. On all occasions the author, the one European in the group, was accompanied by an armed guard who stood not more than five yards away – lest an over-vigilant P L A or militia member should decide to deal with a suspected British officer infiltrated into the liberated area.

In long discussions with members of the P L A, of the general population and of the P F L O A G General Command, the history and strategy of the revolution became clear. The turning point had been 1968, when the new leadership and ideology had been adopted and it had been decided to launch a political and social revolution inside the liberated areas. Wherever we went we saw people wearing Mao and Lenin badges, reading socialist works and discussing. Through the transistor radio the people were in touch with world events; while we were there Bertrand Russell died and this led to several discussions about his life and work, his pacifism and his later anti-imperialism. At the same time Wilson was on a visit to Washington – and this formed another topic of discussion. All sections of Dhofari society were found in the area: there were slaves who had escaped from Salala, sons of the richer families there, former shepherds and fishermen and many who had worked in the Gulf. Several members of the P L A had been mercenaries in the British armies of the Gulf. One told how he had been a policeman in Qatar, of the riot control routines he had been taught and of his role in suppressing the 1963 insurrection there. Another man knew three words of English, 'Good morning, Sir', a phrase he followed by a tense salute.

Dhofaris from the Salala area who had escaped to the mountains gave accounts of excessive taxation and low wages: Salem

Hassan, aged seventeen, worked as a fisherman at Salala for the three best months, and spent the rest of the time working as a labourer on government building projects. 'I was exploited to the utmost,' he said. 'Now I have regained my freedom.' Awad, a soldier in the central garrison in the west, had been a porter in the Umm al-Qawarif base and had escaped by sea. Awad had also been a cook in the British officer's mess, but in none of his jobs had he been properly able to live. 'I had no food and no clothes,' he said. 'My family was nearly starving.' Amir Ali, a former slave, had worked in the Sultan's palace as a scribe to the chief of the Sultan's intelligence service. He had escaped by sea late in 1969. One middle-aged man from Bait Handoub in the west had joined the DLF in 1966 'to retrieve pride and honour'. Another said that his motive was simply to avoid paying taxes. Both were in the militia. A man in the PLA who joined in 1968 admitted that he had joined because 'I heard of people fighting Said bin Taimur who came from Oman to dominate us'. He now insisted he could see that the real enemy was British imperialism. The influence of the Soviet Union and of China also contributed to this change. Dozens of militants had visited China and had been trained there; one man to whom we spoke praised the Chinese for their discipline and application, and remarked that he had been made to work very hard on his training course. His visit had also had a political impact: 'When I went there I was a nationalist,' he said. 'Now I am a Marxist–Leninist.'

Guerrilla War, Phase Three: 1970–72

The overall initiative which PFLOAG acquired in 1970 reduced the British to a defensive posture, which they were unable to hide. In May it was reported that 'a new serious Chinese threat to British oil interests in the Persian Gulf is causing grave concern at the Foreign Office'.[30] The guerrillas knew that their victories would provoke changes on the other side, and as early as May 1968 had outlined the form they would take: Said bin Taimur would be ousted in a coup; a new 'modernist' regime would be installed which would enter the Arab League and the UN, economic reforms would be promulgated and the country would be wrenched into line with the rest of the British-occupied Gulf. PFLOAG expected the change to come in 1968, yet it took two more years before the Whitehall-directed conspiracy got under way. Another mistake was that PFLOAG expected the British to compromise with the agile and capable Al Bu Said claimant, Tariq, who had been in exile for many years. Instead the British refused to trust Tariq (who was angling for ties to PFLOAG) and opted for his more pro-British and unimaginative nephew, Sultan Said's son Qabus.

Sultan Said was forced by the British to accept a number of changes as a result of the 1969–70 PFLOAG offensive: his long-standing Defence Secretary Brigadier Pat Waterfield was forced out in early 1970 and the new Secretary, Colonel Hugh Oldman, laid plans in April for an extra SAF force – the Jabal Regiment. But Said continued to hoard his thirty-three tons of weapons in his palace, and he offered the guerrillas only one choice: surrender or death. All this meant more trouble for the British: 'So far they've had it all their own way,' the Dhofar commander-in-chief later said. 'Sultan Said bin Taimur saw to that, and the war has changed from a rebellion against his style of government into a revolutionary struggle to change the whole fabric of society.'[31] When the guerrilla war spread from Dhofar to the Omani interior in June 1970 the British put their plan into execution and on 23 July 1970 the anti-Said coup took place. Like a latter-day Arabian Ngo Dinh Diem, Said bin Taimur was ousted by his erstwhile masters and disowned as a failure. One of the immediate consequences of the change was that the British Foreign Office altered its policy on Dhofar from one of silence to one of propaganda and lies. The May 1968 guerrilla analysis of the coming coup had stated: 'The duty of imperialist propaganda and information media would be to issue reports on the coup, give it special prominence, withhold reports on any counter-action and describe it as nationalist.'[32] And this is exactly what happened, over two years later. As has already been shown, one important task was that of covering up British responsibility for the crimes of Said's rule, and of disguising the fact that White-hall had directed the coup. But another key task was to reveal to the world the British story of the Dhofar war that had up to then been shrouded in silence. Whereas before July 1970 there had been probably a dozen or less mentions of the war in the British press and not more than five articles about it, now the well-oiled machine of briefings and background talks swung into operation.

In the dim ideological half-light inhabited by British official-dom, all revolutions are the work of 'foreigners' (in this case 'Chinese') and of their local agents, the small 'minority' or 'hard core' of 'fanatics' and 'communists'. According to this schema, the Dhofar war had been started by 'devout Moslems' who had then been thrown out in 1968 by an unrepresentative clique of 'Chinese-trained agents' who now 'held the jabal by terror'. Since this Manichaean world view is also that of much of the British press, the Foreign Office had no difficulty in getting its line repeated by the British journalists whom it flew out and who cooperated in the official disinformation campaign.

The most common allegation was that P F L O A G was advised by 'Chinese officers'. Ten, sometimes thirty, had been 'seen', although no evidence was ever produced.[33] Another frequent claim was that the guerrillas 'control three-quarters of Dhofar by terror'[34] – how else, after all, could they influence the people? The British intelligence man who briefed visiting journalists seemed particularly upset about the fact that women were playing an ever-growing role in the struggle and *The Times* reporter produced a ludicrous male chauvinist non-sequitur on this topic: 'There is also evidence that the guerrillas have begun to involve village women in their battle, and several cases of murder have been reported in the past three months.'[35] Later visitors to Salala were greeted with similar lies and a whole fabric of justification was woven to explain away the war in Dhofar.[36]

The British line on Dhofar was as dishonest as any other counter-insurgency apologia, but it fulfilled the limited function, of enabling the imperialist press to conceal the situation. No one asked how the 'hard core' communists were able to control the jabal 'by terror' if the much larger and better-equipped S A F had been unable to do so. Nor did any of the British journalists who inveighed without evidence against foreign – i.e. Chinese – influence in the Dhofari mountains question the more blatant foreign role played by the British on the side of the Sultan. None ever investigated P F L O A G allegations about terror bombing and shelling of the liberated areas, or about torture and illegal detention in the Sultanate's prisons. The press corps, whom Whitehall ushered in, manifested no critical abilities whatsoever.

The new regime's immediate steps aimed to split and deceive the Dhofari people and to undermine the revolution from within. Leaflets were dropped on the liberated areas urging the people to surrender; a radio station was started up in Salala; slaves were told they were free; and the £6 million Dhofar Development Plan got under way. In the government-held plain around Salala the authorities set up a model farm and introduced water pumps. As in the rest of Oman schools were opened, a health clinic and veterinary service got under way, and the more unnecessary restrictions of the old regime were ended. At Raysut a British construction company, Taylor Woodrow, undertook to expand the harbour, and the British Bank of the Middle East opened a branch in Salala town. Another British construction project, costed at £8 million, involved the development of Salala town. The Omani regime was hoping to encourage mountain Dhofaris to settle on the plain, in return for which they were given a house, a plot of land and a salary.

The British aim was to use the narrow social base for counter-revolution within Dhofari society to confuse the revolutionary forces. In the eastern sector they set about organizing a conspiracy. The east was the most populated part of the country, but had seen the least fighting; it was therefore the area where the traditional tribal system and the social forces of pro-imperialism were strongest. Furthermore, the new Sultan's mother was from a tribe in the east of Dhofar, and this gave the British a link with a number of sheikhs. Since the Second Congress of 1968 some sheikhs had crossed over to the British side where they were well rewarded with money, and the British hoped that the same manoeuvre would work in 1970.

In September of that year, two months after the coup, a group of tribal leaders in the east attacked P F L O A G. On 12 September they arrested approximately forty P L A and P F L O A G cadres with the intention of handing them over to the Sultan, together with the whole area. P F L O A G action prevented this; large numbers of P L A men were moved from the central sector to the east and by the end of the month the arrested cadres had been released. As a result more sheikhs and their men crossed over to the British side and were formed into counter-insurgency *firqas*. The conspiracy had been defeated and the British had been unable to exploit the revolution's weakness to penetrate the liberated areas.

P F L O A G rejected all the British-sponsored appeals for surrender and pointed out the significance of the coup and of the reforms in the Omani regime:

What happened in July 1970 was not unexpected; it was the result of a long-term plan, drawn up by British imperialism to contain, and then liquidate, the prevailing revolutionary trend. The overthrow of Said bin Taimur was part of a double plan. First there was the plan to set up the so-called 'Omani constitutional monarch', as had long been advocated by Tariq bin Taimur, Said's brother. The second plan was obviously that of the Union of Arab Amirates. Both were political fronts for British neo-colonialism in the area, in a desperate attempt to advance seemingly patriotic regimes.

There were two major reasons why the British were driven to replace Said bin with his son. This first was the success achieved by the revolution in Dhofar; this had begun to constitute a serious threat to the interests of imperialism in the whole area. The reactionary regime of Said bin Taimur had become incapable of coping with the rising tide of revolution in Dhofar. A second equally important cause was the beginning of armed struggle in Oman proper under the leadership of the National Democratic Front for the Liberation of Oman and the Arab Gulf. After Said's replacement, the British tried to undermine the revolution by a series of so-called reforms.[37]

P F L O A G's response was to escalate the struggle. With nearly all of Dhofar in their hold P F L O A G now aimed to cut the Red Line definitively and to destroy the four remaining British positions along the road. In constant shelling and ambushing throughout the autumn and winter of 1970 they repeated their success of 1968–9 in the western sector, and by May 1971 Haglit, the last S A F post on the road, had fallen. A British press report in the spring of 1971 reported that 'fighting is fiercer than at any time since the revolt began' and that P F L O A G 'mobility, equipment and tactical skill have all improved'.[38] By the summer of 1971, within a year of the overthrow of Said, the guerrillas had defeated every political aspect of the July coup and through their victory over the conspiracy had considerably strengthened their position.

Once the British plan had failed to divide the revolution by deceit, it was clear that they would build up for a military offensive. Although they began in 1970 to use Dhofari renegades as guides and as identifiers of P L A bases, they were unable for over a year to organize themselves properly or to stop P F L O A G moving in arms and food for the expected counter-offensive. The British considered the *firqas* to be unreliable – at best 'listless' and at worst 'treacherous'. In October 1971 the British finally launched a campaign against the eastern sector, entitled 'Operation Jaguar'. A reinforced Omani army, backed by British S A S counter-insurgency troops, attacked in the east, hoping to use their superior air and fire power to 'clear the jabal'. At the same time a string of positions was set up along the desert edge of the mountains, a 'Leopard Line', the purpose of which was to cut supplies of food and arms being sent to the eastern sector.

Fighting continued for over two months until in December the S A F offensive ground to a halt. Where they had applied heavy concentrations of fire-power, they had penetrated the mountain area and new positions were held with heavy defensive build-ups. The centre of the new British position in the east was at Khisoul, known to them as Madina al-Huq (City of Right), whence a 'pacification' programme was to be launched. But the overall initiative lay with the P L A and it responded, as in the west, by avoiding pitched battles, where necessary conceding territory and counter-attacking when the S A F set up fixed bases.

According to PFLOAG there were 290 engagements in the three months from 1 October 1971: 170 alone were in the east, 41 in the centre, 20 in the Ho Chi Minh area and 59 in the west. SAF lost 136 dead, while the guerrillas lost 31: in addition the imperialists lost two planes, one helicopter and several military vehicles. At the end of December 1971 a Dhofari militant reported as follows:

The situation in the liberated area of Dhofar is very good. The latest invasion of the eastern part of Dhofar by the British and the mercenaries has failed. Britain has lost many men and weapons, in particular from the commandos. Many mercenaries have also been killed and many British officers have been killed too; by the end of September seven British had been killed, and more have died since then. The British and Qabus were compelled to pull back the rest of their forces, and under the heavy attack of our comrades they had to abandon many of their positions – Dhaybdoot, Edot and others. The British and Qabus have learnt a hard lesson which they will never forget. Britain is now relying on her planes which are bombing the area no less than ten times a day. Their main targets are the inhabitants and their cattle and farms.

Due to this failure Britain has forced Qabus to go on a visit to Saudi Arabia where all differences have been settled. Saudi Arabia has now recognized the Qabus regime.

Our comrades are in control of everything. The latest news is that the mercenaries and the commandos are having a rest. We can assure you that a lot of British and Qabus' forces are now lying in hospital. And the government has now prevented the local inhabitants from receiving treatment in these hospitals.[39]

The poor results of Operation Jaguar had consequences beyond Dhofar. Tariq bin Taimur, who had been Prime Minister since the July 1970 coup, took this occasion to resign. In addition to his complaints about the British hold on the economy, he also denounced the British for military inefficiency and warned that if the Dhofar war continued to eat up Oman's revenues the needed modernization policy in Oman itself would collapse. This clash in Muscat coincided with some unwelcome publicity in London: despite tight controls, it became known in the Middle East that some SAS commandos had been killed by PFLOAG. The

Foreign Office was flushed out of its silence and forced to leak the news to the London press in order to pre-empt a larger dispute. For a week or so in early January the British press highlighted the British role in Oman and made a faint-hearted attempt to query some of the more blatant official evasions.[40]

The British responded to their setback in the east with a thrust at the west, and in the spring of 1972 they launched a second counter-insurgency campaign entitled 'Operation Simba'; the aim was to throttle PFLOAG supply lines, having failed to do so in 1968. 'The importance of the latest offensive close to the South Yemen border,' wrote *The Times*, 'is that, if successful, it will give the Sultan's forces virtual control of the guerrillas' lifeline from South Yemen.'[41] As in the previous campaign the SAF set up posts on the northern edge of the mountain and tried to cut through to the sea, but this attempt was accompanied by much fiercer attacks on South Yemen itself, including air attacks on the village of Hauf and on Habrout, and a land attack on Hauf at the end of May.

PFLOAG described Operation Simba as follows:

Since May 18 there has been renewed fighting between the British and the Sultanate's forces on the one side and the Democratic Yemeni forces on the other in which an estimated 300 troops have been brought by air and thrown against the Habrout base on the Omani side. Fighting is going on and the enemy have failed till now to avenge their failure, as the Omani Foreign Minister, Fahid bin Mahmoud, has clearly stated. On 25 May the RAF attacked Hauf throughout the day and did not spare any civilian targets: they bombed the school, the medical centre, the literacy centre, and the houses of the people. Five PLA and many women and children were killed, and 6 people were wounded. On the other hand two Strikemasters were shot down. Just before that, on 24 May, the enemy launched about 200 men by air against Khal-Arut, 10 miles north-east of Hauf; one group attacked into the Dhofar countryside, the other attacked the PDRY frontiers. The enemy is now in flight and has failed to accomplish the aim of his attack, which was to cut the Front's communications and transport and to establish a foothold in the western region of Dhofar and in the eastern region of the PDRY. We think that this is a prelude to a huge campaign which will be launched at the end of the monsoon. The aim of the present fighting is to deplete our resources (especially of ammunition and food) since supplies get scarce during the monsoon.[42]

By early June, when the monsoon had begun, the P L A held the initiative. The desert position of Thaqbeet, established in 1971 as a precursor to Operation Simba, was abandoned under P L A pressure in early May and within a month S A F were on the defensive.

Simba military post, balanced on four stone hills close to the Yemeni border, is held by one battalion, the Muscat Regiment, which will have to stay in it for the next five months ... Simba, as its 10 British officers see it, is a tiny bottle-neck holding back a tide of revolution from South Yemen ... But with the coming of the monsoon, for the first time the troops of Sultan Qabus bin Said are struggling to maintain their position against the rebels ... (whose) fire is intense and accurate producing 18 casualties in the past 12 days ... Constant patrolling is unpleasant and dangerous. Most of the troops are plainsmen, unhappy in the hills, and there is little doubt that without the British pilots and officers the war would fold up in a matter of days.[43]

The British, who had boasted earlier in the year that the eastern and central regions had been dominated, were now in for some surprises. In early June twelve British officers were injured when P L A men scored a direct hit on the officers' mess at Salala, and the wounded imperialists had to be flown out by special plane to Cyprus.[44] On 19 July P L A launched an attack on the eastern coastal town of Mirbat and held it for fourteen hours in the largest battle of the war, confounding the British and confirming that P F L O A G held the initiative.[45] In a subsequent four-hour occupation of the town of Taqa large quantities of food were seized and the merchants so deprived were paid in cash by the Front.

In the autumn of 1972 another S A F offensive loomed. P F L O A G warned of 'another October':

With our modest powers and abundant ability we are able and determined to stand bravely in the face of all these plans, and we are confident that this campaign, however great it is, can be replied to by us. This reply will not be through writing or through talk, but through the blood of our martyrs.[46]

In late September an attack came, at the same time as the counter-revolutionary invasion of South Yemen from North Yemen. On 23 September 1972 S A F forces, backed by helicopters and fighters, launched an attack on the eastern region of Dhofar: if nothing else, belying claims that the east had been crushed. On 26 September 1972 the Saudi-backed anti-communist invasion of the P D R Y was launched. This attack collapsed within two weeks and ended as an inspiring victory for the revolutionary forces in the peninsula as a whole. The S A F campaign in Dhofar also failed to achieve its objectives, and by early December the British were back on the defensive, holding out in mountain positions supplied uniquely by air, and indiscriminately attacking the liberated area in an attempt to smash the will of the people. The British had failed spectacularly to get the quick end to the war which they had so wanted, and P F L O A G, fighting a protracted war, had retained its domination of the liberated areas.

The Siege of Sarfeet

In April 1973, at the end of the 1972–3 dry season, I paid a second visit to the western liberated areas of Dhofar and saw units of the P L A besieging the British post at north Sarfeet, the only enemy position left in the western region from the previous offensives. Even before crossing the border I could see many changes compared to three years before: the South Yemeni villages in the Sixth Governorate were visibly more prosperous, with more running water, more housing, fuller shops and more extensively cultivated areas. The road east from al-Qeidha, which in 1970 had reached al-Fitk, now went as far as Damqut and was expected to reach Hauf in three to five years' time. The *sambuq* which now ferried visitors from Damqut to Hauf was fitted with an outboard motor – in 1970 the *sambuqs* had relied on primitive oars. The military events of the past year had left their mark on the border area. South Yemeni anti-aircraft positions were dotted around Hauf, and in the village itself P F L O A G members showed us the houses bombed in the attack of May 1972. The war a few miles away was always present; one could hear periodic artillery explosions, like distant thunder. On one moonless night there were flashes of light as ships of the Sultan's navy shone searchlights along the coast in search of boats ferrying arms and as the British at Sarfeet sent up flares and released shells.

The enemy position at Sarfeet was designed to blockade PFLOAG both by obstructing supply routes and by diverting energies and supplies that would otherwise be deployed farther east. Since their campaign in spring 1972 the British had claimed that the border was nearly sealed. The week after I crossed the border it was claimed that supply caravans 'have dwindled to about six camels a week, according to Omani intelligence'.[47] However, I was able to cross without difficulty and to reach the PLA position near the British at Sarfeet in about ten hours' walk. The mountain trails, as in 1970, were frequently clogged by caravans of twenty to thirty camels ferrying supplies. There was some random shelling by the British, and the white parachutes of fallen flares could be seen caught in trees. But the five-mile-wide 'neck' of the liberated areas was open and, although supplying now presented additional problems, the British and Omani claims were demonstrably false.

At the PLA post near Sarfeet Mohammad Hafiz, a local commander from Salala in his early twenties, explained the background to the siege. The British had been forced to abandon Thaqbeet and its outpost Kedbeet after heavy counter-attacks in the spring of 1972. They had then moved in from the desert and by air to set up about ten stone positions at north Sarfeet, on a rocky promontory 4,500 feet above the coastal hills, and about four miles from the PDRY border. At first they had tried to cut through the hills to the sea: in one fourteen-hour battle in Wadi Kohot below Sarfeet a Dhofari uncle of Sultan Qabus, Sheikh Mohammad Ahmad Hasheet, had been killed leading a group of Dhofari mercenaries together with British-officered SAF forces. By the late summer of 1972 all such expeditions had ceased and the enemy were trapped in their post. The use of loud-speaker equipment to harangue the population was stopped; and constant PFLOAG shelling had knocked out the landing strip used by Skyvan and Caribou planes, thereby forcing the British to rely uniquely on helicopter supplies, which came in nearly every day.

From a mountain top one and a half miles further inside Dhofar I witnessed a dawn attack by the PLA on the Sarfeet post. On the adjacent summit the low sangars of the SAF could be seen as the sunlight broke over them a few minutes before five. At three minutes past five the units of the PLA stationed nearer the post opened fire with mortars and machine-guns: black smoke from the mortar shells could be seen in and around the sangars, and after a few minutes the government position replied with their howitzers. The PLA unit I was with had a clear view of the whole operational field and was radioing coded directional instructions to the combat units nearer the enemy. After thirty-five minutes there was a distant roar as two Strikemaster jets flew in over the sea on an air strike from Salala. For around twenty minutes they circled the area rocketing and firing at suspected PLA positions, but without apparent success. As the ground fighting ceased they continued to circle before departing again for Salala. The PLA command assured me that there had been no casualties, and by 6.30 in the morning we had returned to the base camp.

A member of the PFLOAG leadership, Talal Saad, explained that in the 1972–3 dry season the enemy had reduced his activities. The ten or so positions which he held in the western and other regions were all, like the north Sarfeet position I had seen, under attack, and the enemy troops within them were unable to break out. While they expected a new offensive in the 1973–4 dry season along the lines of the 1971–2 attacks, they were confident of their overall position. The intervention of new foreign powers (Iran, Jordan, Saudi Arabia) in the war on the side of Qabus had certainly increased the difficulties of the revolutionary struggle; at the same time these interventions underlined and proved the revolutionary character of the war and the political character of the Omani regime as the servant of imperialist interests.

The greatest difficulty caused by the new counter-revolutionary strategy was the suffering inflicted on the population. In the border area I went through the civilian population were forced to live in the deeper caves, facing away from the normal lines of fire from the north Sarfeet position. Everybody one met had lost animals in the recent fighting; and many had lost members of their family. A growing number of refugees from the west and the central region had moved out of the combat zones and on to the Yemeni side of the border. In addition the economic blockade had led to intense malnutrition, especially in the east and the centre as a result of the cutting off of imports from the coast and the systematic SOAF burning of crops at harvest-time. Among the population as a whole, the consequences of malnutrition, tuberculosis and anaemia were increasing. While such developments only confirmed the people in their hatred of the British and of the Sultan, they imposed an extra burden on the revolution.

A different side of the war was portrayed by a Yemeni who had just joined the ranks of the guerrilla movement after deserting from SAF in early April. Twenty-one-year-old Corporal Mohammad Mananhi Amer had emigrated from Socotra to Saudi Arabia in 1968, and had worked in Dammam as a sweeper in an American restaurant for ARAMCO employees. In 1970 he had been forced, under threat of imprisonment, to join the Saudi Arabian army and had been sent, with eighty other press-ganged Socotrans, to the Saudi base at ash-Sharura, near the PDRY border. In early 1971, at a time when Saudi Arabia and Oman were still officially in conflict, the Socotran group had been sent from Sharura to Thamrit, in northern Dhofar, where they were told to await orders to participate in an attack on the PDRY. For two years they were then used in garrison duties inside Dhofar: they received Saudi pay but wore Omani uniforms. Amer showed me an Omani passport (No. 007796) which he had been issued for holiday trips to Dubai and Bahrain. As the man appointed to liaise between the Socotra group (known as Firqa

Socotra) and the British, he had been able to bring away sets of orders signed, in scraggly Arabic letters, by an English officer named 'Maknil'.

A British Laos

Mr William Wilson asked the Secretary of State for Defence how many British Servicemen are seconded to the Sultan of Oman for service with the army and navy of Oman.

Mr Ian Gilmour: One hundred and twenty-three.

Mr William Wilson asked the Secretary of State for Defence how many British Servicemen are in Oman but not seconded to the forces of the Sultan of Oman.

Mr Ian Gilmour: It is not our practice to disclose details of this kind.

Mr William Wilson asked the Secretary of State for Defence how many British Servicemen are engaged in the British Army Training Team.

Mr Ian Gilmour: It is not our practice to disclose details of this kind.

Mr William Wilson asked the Secretary of State for Defence how many British Servicemen, either seconded or under contract, have died in Oman in the last two years.

Mr Ian Gilmour: Three British Servicemen seconded to the Sultan of Oman have died in Oman in the last two years. Contract personnel are not serving members of Her Majesty's Forces and no figures are available.

(*Hansard*, 'Written Answers', 28 January 1974.)

No one involved doubted that in the early 1970s the Sultan's whole war effort depended on British support at the highest level. 'This war is British down to its desert boots,' one officer stated in 1972, and Sultan Qabus never tried to disguise his dependence on the imperialist masters who had placed him in power. British official comment on the war was always shrouded in lies: Oman was a 'sovereign' country, went the eternal refrain. The 1970 Defence White Paper gave the war a brief paragraph:

The Sultan of Muscat's armed forces, most of whose officers are British, have continued to be engaged in operations against the Dhofar rebels in the rugged hill country north of Salala. The Sultan has made awards for bravery to some British officers for their conduct in these operations.[48]

The 1971 White Paper was even less communicative about the army, although it did mention that the RAF had been involved in defending their base.

The blunt fact was that the British directed and commanded the war and all orders came from them. As the Sultan's Defence Secretary Oldman put it: 'Can you imagine a conflict between the Queen of England and the Sultan of Oman?'[49] The actual number of British personnel in Dhofar was a closely guarded secret; there were about 1,000 men by the end of 1972. Large numbers of British ground troops had still not been committed. However, as the command structure was run by the British, they kept overall control. Rather than being a Vietnam, involving large numbers of imperialist ground troops, it was a Laos, a counter-insurgency war run by the imperialist power through a puppet government and a puppet army with a disguised army of imperialist officers and advisers. As in Laos the actual numbers of men committed understated the strategic importance of the war for the relevant imperialist power. The situation was concealed partly by false distinctions between imperialist personnel. The British officially listed only one military category: serving personnel 'seconded' to the SAF and SOAF under the 1958 agreement. This omitted at least three other categories: British serving personnel in Oman who were not 'seconded' – RAF personnel manning and defending the Salala and Masirah bases; members of the British Army Training Team (BATT); and British officers no longer officially serving in the British Army. These distinctions were, as everyone knew, of no importance. The mercenaries, pompously styled 'contract officers', were, like US 'civilian' personnel in Laos and Vietnam, under the direct command of the official military structure and often members of semi-official mercenary outfits. The RAF personnel servicing and defending the Salala base were in every sense active since this was the combat base for S O A F operations. BATT was a disguised offensive course, and BATT members were involved in offensive operations. During the 1972 outcry over SAS deaths Whitehall purported that the SAS were only 'training' but would 'seek out realistic training conditions' and would 'defend themselves if fired upon'. The British even made great play of the distinction between being 'under the command of the British Army' and being 'under the command of the Sultan'. Since the Sultan himself was militarily under the command of the British this distinction, like the others, had no meaning.

The following table, divided into the different categories of British personnel in Oman, provides a partial guide to the British commitment:

Table 17

British Military Deployment in Oman

Category	1962[a]	March 1970	April 1971	November 1972
Seconded army officer	26	40[b]	49[e]	over 250[f]
Contract army officer	30	45[b]	71[e]	
Seconded pilots	10		60	
Contract pilots	?	?		
Seconded other ranks	?	7[b]	?	?
R A F Regiment	none	120[d]	?	?
Other R A F	?	?	hundreds	hundreds
B A T T	none	none	25[c]	100[c]

Source: (a) Report of the Special Representative of the Secretary General on His Visit to Oman, U N Document A/5562, paragraph 105; (b) Roy Hattersley, junior minister at the Ministry of Defence, in the House of Commons, 25 March 1970 – the figure for seconded officers included both army and air force; (c) unofficial press estimate; (d) *Daily Mail*, 17 March 1970, gave total R A F Regiment + other personnel at Salala; (e) *Economist*, 3 April 1971; (f) *Financial Times*, 15 November 1972.

While most of the contract and seconded officers were active in the field, some were also based in headquarters Dhofar, at

Umm al-Qawarif, while others were at SAF headquarters at Bait al-Falaj, near Muscat. The top officers were all seconded. The Sultan's Defence Secretary, Colonel Hugh Oldman, had been commander of the army in the early 1960s and was the overall military boss in the Sultanate. His closest colleague was the commander-in-chief SAF, who from 1970 to 1972 was a Brigadier John Graham, subsequently replaced by Brigadier Tim Creasy. The commander-in-chief in Dhofar was a Colonel Teddy Turnhill; and in October 1972 his place was taken by a Brigadier Jack Fletcher. Some of the people involved were long-term fixtures in the Sultanate: the head of the intelligence service, Major Dennison, first came to Oman in the 1950s and had built up the intelligence system under his command with District Intelligence Officers (DIOs) at every main military post. In 1972 the Dhofar DIO, Major Jack Sullivan, was the only man in the whole apparatus who spoke the language of the Dhofari mountain people. Many of the lower-ranking British personnel had long histories of counter-revolutionary activity to their name. The head of the Dhofar gendarmerie, Major Ray Barker-Scofield, told a television interviewer in 1972 how Dhofar was the last place in the world 'where an Englishman is still called sahib'. 'I am a mercenary and a professional soldier and I've done twenty-five years abroad in such places as India, Burma, South Africa, Egypt, Somalia, Mogadishu, Libya and Germany. This is my profession. Basically I am on the market,' he said. Some mercenaries, such as Captain Spike Powell, had fought in Katanga against the UN; others, such as David Bayley and John Cooper, had fought with the royalists in North Yemen. For many British adventurers it was an occasion to amass large savings tax-free; for others it was the only place left in the world where an old-style British colonial war could be fought.[50]

The expansion of the British presence in Dhofar was accompanied by overall expansion of the SAF and SOAF. Up to 1970 the SAF had totalled about 2,500 men, consisting of the Muscat Regiment, the Northern Frontier Regiment and the Desert Regiment. After 1970 these were augmented by the Jabal Regiment and the numbers of each were raised so that by the end of 1973

SAF reached an estimated 12,500. While recruitment in Oman rose slowly, the majority of the infantry and nearly all trained personnel, such as scribes and signal operators, were still mercenaries from Pakistani Baluchistan.[51] SOAF had been founded in 1959 after the Green Mountain rising, and had acquired twelve BAC–167 Strikemaster fighters in 1969 as the main attack force against the liberated areas. In the subsequent years SOAF acquired twelve Hawker Hunter planes, at least nine Skyvan short-takeoff transport planes, and twelve helicopters for frontline use. Even the rudimentary navy was expanded for counter-infiltration work and a special naval flagship was ordered from Brooke Marine Ltd of Lowestoft, England.

While British personnel commanded these revamped forces, other nations also participated. Australians and Rhodesians flew with the SOAF. Pakistan, which had supported the Sultan of Muscat before 1970, had around 100 officers in Dhofar by the end of 1972. India began to train the navy. Iran, worried by the example of Dhofar, sent helicopter crews and later troops. Jordan supplied intelligence officers and helped to train Omani officers; and as a token of its concern, appointed as ambassador to Oman in October 1972 a former army chief of staff, Mohammad Khalil Abd ad-Dayim. Saudi Arabia, which at first held back, was reported in December 1972 to have agreed to provide military aid valued at £6 million. The long-term coincidence of Saudi and Omani aims in harassing the PDRY was bound in time to have its effect.

Overall British strategy in Dhofar was guided by counter-insurgency principles evolved over a century of colonial repression. Many of these principles had been pioneered in nineteenth-century wars against a diversity of foes (Zulus, Afghans, Boers, Irish, Sudanese) and in the inter-war period air power had been developed as an economic means of administrative violence. In the post-1945 period the British even produced a version of counter-insurgency theory which they applied in a new round of wars (Greece, Malaya, Kenya, Cyprus, Oman, South Yemen) and which their less experienced US and Portuguese allies used in building up their own apparatus of colonial intervention.[52]

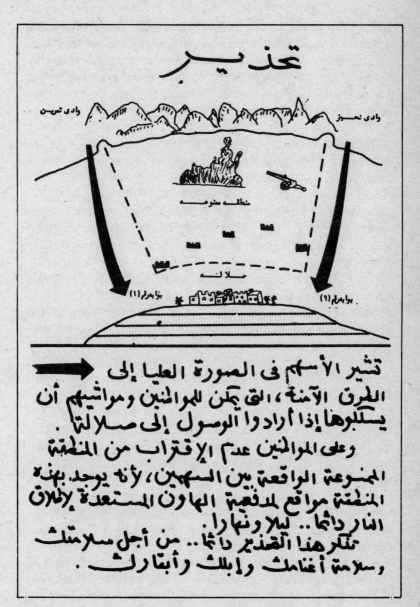

Figure Two   Leaflet dropped Over Central Dhofar in 1973

Translation: **WARNING**
The arrows in the picture above indicate the safe routes which citizens and their families may use if they wish to get to Salala. Citizens must not approach from the forbidden area between the two arrows, as there are field guns in this area always ready to fire, day or night. Keep this warning in mind, for your safety and the safety of your sheep, camels and cattle.

Counter-insurgency 'theory' has three functions. Like all ideology it is designed to enable its practitioner to master the world; and its simultaneous object is also to present a false picture of the world; it is necessarily both true and false. Yet these two elements, though static, yield a third dynamic component: the ideology falsely describes the real in order to translate it into the imagined form. It provides a guide, and disguise, for the transformation of what does not exist into what the agent wants to exist. Counter-insurgency practice in Dhofar and in Indo-China exhibits all these aspects. The long-term aim of the war is to destroy **PFLOAG** and the **PLA** and all resistance to the government, and thereby to eliminate a threat to Britain's strategic interests. This involves measures directly in line with counter-insurgent theory: cutting supply lines, engaging the enemy in battle, setting up secure zones and communications. What the theory cannot admit is that the enemy have the support of the population and that the theory's aim necessitates destruction of the population as a whole. This is where the deceit comes in. The enemy are just a 'hard-core' minority who rule the mountains 'by terror'. The British on the other hand are providing air and land support for 'Dhofari nationalists'. The problem is that there is no hard core – the oppressed majority of the people support the revolution and the so-called 'majority' are a small pro-imperialist sector kept by the British in Salala. The military operations are in fact a campaign of terror, which is served by the pacification programme. The British have from the beginning waged a savage attack on the population as a whole. The account of coastal raids by a British officer in 1968 leaves no doubt about this:

'We also burnt down rebel villages and shot their goats and cows,' he writes. 'Any enemy corpses we recovered were propped up in a corner of the Salala *suq* (market) as a salutary lesson to any would-be freedom fighters.'[53]

The same officer describes too how they blew up wells during the attack on the west in 1968.

Following the build-up of S O A F in 1969 the main form of terror became air attacks and long-range artillery bombardment. Again the so-called 'hard core' were not in the forefront of British minds: their aim was clearly to drive the resisting population into the desert or onto the Salala plain, where they could be controlled. Like 'resettlement' in Vietnam, the pretence that the population was being 'protected' or 'assisted' disguised an all-out campaign of coercion, of distorting reality to fit a repressive schema. Some British officers made no pretence of doing anything else:

It is very different, for example, from northern Ireland where I was this time last year, for a number of reasons. Firstly, here you know exactly who you are fighting because the only people in this area – there are no civilians – are all enemy. Therefore one can get on with doing the job, mortaring the area and returning small arms without worrying about hurting innocent people. This is of course completely different from northern Ireland where your hands are tied because of civilians.[54]

The murderous policy had its dynamic element. By bombing and shelling the liberated areas the British forced the population to move out and to flee to safer areas. The British poisoned and blew up wells, burnt villages, set crops and food stores on fire, shot herds, and cut off food supplies. This policy, already consistently applied in Radfan, was one of all-out attack on the population who supported the revolution. It was the truth that lay behind the talk put about by the British and Qabus of the 'hard core' and of 'economic development'.

The British could conceal but not alter the fact that their war in Dhofar was putting a severe strain on their overall post-colonial strategy in the area. By the end of 1972 some British officials responsible for the area had even begun to regret that they had

363

ever decided to oust Said bin Taimur. Britain had so far avoided some of the problems of colonial war: Dhofar was almost unknown in Britain; there had not been any significant number of British casualties; and there was no movement of opposition of the kind that had existed over Algeria or Vietnam.[55] On the other hand the war in Dhofar was using up an ever larger amount of the Omani budget – taking 12 million rials in 1970, 16·3 million rials in 1971 and 30 million rials in 1972.[56] The British could not let Qabus simply dump Dhofar and retreat to Oman proper since that would have been a crushing political defeat. Nor could Britain herself abandon Qabus since the ever-growing importance of Gulf oil made political stability in the area greatly to be desired.

The Iranian Intervention

It was in this situation that the Shah of Iran sent several thousand troops into Oman in December 1973. Recent events in the Middle East had encouraged this development: the rise in oil prices gave Sultan Qabus greater financial freedom, and the leading Arab governments were less likely to protest at events in Oman because they were preoccupied by developments on the oil and Israel fronts. Although the Iranian intervention modified the pre-existing *British* monopoly of control at Muscat, it nevertheless fulfilled two functions for Britain. First, it committed large numbers of well-armed and well-trained counter-insurgency troops, without incurring the political problems that would have followed from sending in the British Army. Second, it carried through the policy of post-colonial partnership that had been evolving with Iran and Saudi Arabia since 1971. The Iranian regime also derived concrete benefits: it was able to increase its influence on the Arabian side of the peninsula at the expense of Saudi Arabia, and was able to train its crack repressive troops in conditions that might prove useful in the event of further rural guerrilla outbreaks at home.

The Iranian regime had made no secret of its concern about 'security' in Oman. The occupation of the three Arab-administered islands (in 1971), and the deployment of a small helicopter squadron in Dhofar (in 1972), were part of the Tehran regime's expansionist policy. The Shah himself was direct:

Take the Dhofar rebellion in Oman. If it ever succeeded, just try to imagine what we could be faced with in Muscat, the capital, right in front of the Strait of Hormuz. At first a few rifles. And then naval guns and missiles. It's a familiar pattern. I cannot tolerate subversive activities – and by that I mean anything that is imposed from the outside . . . They [Oman] asked for our help and we sent it.[57]

The Iranian force sent to Oman attacked on 20 December 1973; one force hit north from Salala into the central region, the other hit south from the desert into the mountains. Using helicopter gunships they established themselves in about six positions along the Red Line, in an attempt to re-open the road and to prevent supplies from reaching the eastern region by cutting Dhofar in two. After about a month of heavy fighting, during which the Iranians lost an estimated 200 men killed, the road was still not open. PFLOAG sources reported that, although the enemy were able to move some heavily guarded convoys along the road, none of these convoys passed through without suffering damage, and the road was still unusable for ferrying supplies. The Iranians were held down in defensive positions, as SAF were in Sarfeet, and supply lines with the east remained intact.

The real purpose of the Iranian attack was diplomatic. Their main *fear* was that there would be an increase in Arab nationalist protest, and for this reason the Iranian presence was concealed. Iranian troops were kept off the streets of Salala and Muscat, and the Iranian soldiers were billeted on the almost uninhabited Kuria Muria island of Hallaniyah. Omani military communiqués mentioned only their own forces, and when PFLOAG announced the news of the Iranian presence Muscat, London and Tehran joined in a chorus of denial.[58] It was only in early February that the Shah admitted what he had been doing: claiming that his men had 'won battle honours in clearing the road from Dhofar to Salala and Muscat' [*sic*], he tried to vilify PFLOAG as being 'the forces of subversion, destruction, chaos and murder'.[59] While Libya and Iraq protested at the intervention, and while the Soviet Union stepped up its criticisms of the Shah, the major Arab states tried to avoid commenting, and participated covertly in the Muscat-Tehran manoeuvre. The official Iranian daily paper *Etela'at* stated that the purpose of the Iranian invasion was 'to force the rebel leaders and their friends to accept the peace offer made by the Muscat government',[60] and in early March the Arab League set up a mediating team (Tunisia, Algeria, Kuwait, Egypt, Syria) to reconcile the PDRY (and thereby PFLOAG) with the Omani Sultanate.

PFLOAG's response to this, as it had been to an earlier Kuwaiti attempt in mid-1973, was to state the conditions for negotiation being possible: 'the cancellation of both secret and public agreements with Britain, Iran and Jordan; the elimination of bases; the expulsion of Iranian forces from Omani territories; the establishing of a national and democratic regime; the provision of political and personal liberties; the adoption of a national economic policy; and adherence to an international policy of non-alignment.'[61]

PFLOAG did not consider that they could win by a purely military victory, nor did they present themselves as the only nationalist force in Oman. As long as the Omani regime remained dominated by foreign powers, and allowed foreign troops to fight in Oman, PFLOAG would continue its struggle, by both political and military means.

Notes

1. Most of the information in this chapter was acquired from interviews and discussions during visits to Dhofar in February 1970 and April 1973. Impressions of Dhofar can be found in the works of four visitors who travelled in Dhofar before the revolution: J. T. and M. V. A. Bent, *Southern Arabia*, London, 1900; Wilfred Thesiger, *Arabian Sands*, London, 1968; Bertram Thomas, *Arabia Felix: Across the Empty Quarter of Arabia*, London, 1932; and Wendell Philipps, *Unknown Oman*, London, 1966.

2. Philipps, op. cit., pp. 179ff., discusses this trade and gives a map of the different land and sea export routes. Camoens in *The Lusiads* (10, line 716) writes: 'Over Dhofar's plain the richest incense breathes.'

3. Ibn Batuta, the medieval Arab traveller, writes of Dhofar: 'Most of the fish are of the kind called sardines, which are extremely fat in that country. A curious fact is that these sardines are the sole food of their beasts and flocks, a thing I have seen nowhere else.' *The Travels of Ibn Batuta*, Vol. 2 ed., Hamilton Gibb, Cambridge, 1962, p. 383.

4. The Arabic word for 'an item of news' is *khabar*, the Dhofari *khubur*; the Arabic expression for welcome is *ahlan wa sahlan*, the Dhofari *hai wa sehla*. Bertram Thomas discusses the language in *Four Strange Tongues from South Arabia*, London, 1937; but the only disciplined philological account so far produced is that by an imperial Austrian expedition who took a Dhofari-speaker back to Vienna with them. See N. Rhodokanakis, *Der vulgärarabische Dialekt im Dhofar (Zfar)*, 2 vols., Vienna, 1908 and 1911.

5. It is an index of the hold of Anglo-Indian imperial culture on Dhofar that the word 'coolie' is commonly used by the local population.

6. On the role of the bride-price see p. 392.

7. *The Travels of Marco Polo*, Everyman Edition, London, 1967, pp. 404–5.

8. *The Travels of Ibn Batuta*, Cambridge, 1962, pp. 382–91.

9. 'Abdullah Lloreyd' was originally John Herman Poll, a Dutch cabinboy on the U S spice-ship *Essex*, from Salem, New Hampshire, which had picked up thirty crew members at Hodeida in the Red Sea. All the crew members were working for Sayyid Mohammad Aqil and massacred the whites. The young Poll was the only survivor of the attack.

10. The history of the annexation of Dhofar is found in J. G. Lorimer, *Gazetteer of the Persian Gulf*, Vol. 1, India, 1915, pp. 589–601.

11. See Bent, op. cit., pp. 227–76. Bent saw the political situation clearly: 'Unquestionably, our own Political Agent may be said to be the ruler in Muscat and his authority is generally backed by the presence of a gun-boat', (p. 60).

12. The concession was given to Wendell Philipps by Sultan Said, as related in Philipps, op. cit. pp. 240–47. Philipps then organized other companies to carry out exploratory work.

13. As, for example, travel-writer James Morris: 'Dhofar was a little backward Paradise on the sea-shore, and the Sultan (who ran it like a private estate) did not want to see it contaminated,' *Sultan in Oman*, p. 31. Wendell Philipps was not far behind: 'Today Dhofar enjoys peace and prosperity with friendly, relaxed, unafraid people. It is immediately apparent to all upon arrival that the Sultan treats Dhofar as his own personal Royal domain,' op. cit., p. 202.

14. *Dirasa Tahhiliya An al-Wadh al-Ijtimaia fi Mantaqat Dhofar* (*An Analytical Study of the Social Situation in the Dhofar Province*), P F L O A G publications, n.d., p. 15.

15. As told by fishermen from Dhalqut and Rakhyut, interviewed by the author, 1970.

16. The commander of the Dhofar Force in 1958 was a Major St John B. Armitage, who had previously served with the British Military Mission in Saudi Arabia and with the Arab Legion in Jordan under Glubb Pasha.

17. There was some mention of the incident in the British press. See *The Times*, 29 April 1966. Several participants in the attempt are now in the liberated areas.

18. In an interview with the author, February 1970.

19. In 1970 a fourth division, the Ho Chi Minh or al-Mummar region, was designated in between the central and western parts.

20. The 'Occupied Arab Gulf' designated Trucial Oman, Qatar and Bahrain.

21. On one occasion an NLF spokesman in Hadramaut spoke of Dhofar as part of 'natural Yemen', implying that it was possible that the PRSY would annex Dhofar if it could. This was immediately denied in Aden and has never been raised again. Although Dhofar has linguistic and ethnic ties with Mahra and Hadramaut, it is politically part of Oman and the Gulf and the form of oppression it experiences is a result of the form imperialist interests assume in the Gulf.

22. Captain N. G. R. Hepworth, 'The Unknown War' in *The White Horse and Fleur de Lys*, journal of the King's Regiment, Vol. VI, No. 6, Winter 1970. Another British account of the 1968–9 western campaign can be found in Sir Ranulph Fiennes, 'Where British Soldiers Still Die Under a Foreign Flag', *Observer* Colour Supplement, 6 June 1971.

23. *Sunday Times*, 15 February 1970.

24. *Daily Mail*, 17 March 1970.

25. *Sunday Times*, 15 February 1970.

26. *The Times*, 3 August 1970.

27. My three companions were: Fawwaz Trabulsi, Lebanese militant and correspondent of the Beirut weekly *al-Horria*; Abdullah al-Ashtal, former member of the General Command of the South Yemeni NLF, a militant in the anti-rightist movement of 1968 and later PDRY Ambassador to the UN; and Watheq al-Shikly, South Yemeni journalist and later editor of the Aden daily *14 October*.

28. The first foreign observer to visit liberated Dhofar was a French militant, Jean-Cyrille Godefroy, who travelled into the eastern region in 1968. In 1969 the French orientalist and Marxist Jean-Pierre Viennot and the journalists Gordian Troeller and Claude Daffarge visited the western sector. Two *Hsinhua* correspondents also travelled to the centre region in 1969 and a further visit by Chinese correspondents was made in 1970. Since our first visit there have been further visits by journalists to the western region; but the only people to go farther have been the Chinese and a film team, Heini Srour and Michel Humeaux, in 1971.

29. Among the bedouin of the desert, and in Dhofar, greetings take the form of a set of insistent questions – 'How are you?' asked in several different ways, 'What news is there?', etc.

30. *Daily Telegraph*, 29 April 1970.

31. Colonel Teddy Turnhill in *The Times*, 3 August 1970.

32. *BBC Summary of World Broadcasts*, Part 4, The Middle East and North Africa, ME/2767, 9 May 1968. The statement was broadcast by Damascus Radio.

33. The 'Chinese officers' story was accepted by, among others, *The Times* (3 August 1970), the *Guardian* (3 August 1970), the *Daily Express* (29 July 1970), the *Daily Telegraph* (23 April 1971) and the *Observer Foreign News Service* (12 August 1970). When we were in Dhofar we saw no Chinese officers, heard no mention of them and saw no reason why they should be there; the PLA has plenty of military cadres trained by the British in the TOS and elsewhere; and other PLA cadres have been to China for training. On the other hand the two Chinese journalists who visited Dhofar in 1969 made no secret of their visit, to which people in Dhofar often alluded. See 'Excellent Situation in Dhofar Area Armed Struggle', *Peking Review*, No. 49, 1969; and 'Dhofar Liberation Army Fighters and People Warmly Love Mao Tse-tung Thought', *Peking Review*, No. 4, 1970. So pervasive was this myth about mysterious Chinese that even Whitehall officials purported to believe it. A Foreign Office official to whom I spoke in 1971 said: '*Well* – how many Chinese *did* you see?'

34. *The Times* and the *Guardian*, 3 August 1970, uncritically produced almost identical, although unattributed, paragraphs from the British briefing official.

35. *The Times*, ibid.

36. A 'background information' statement on Dhofar issued by Qabus in September 1972 said that 'more moderate rebels' had come to oppose extremists who 'sought to deprive them of their traditional religious, social and cultural way of life'. An Omani regime advertisement in the *Financial Times*, 17 November 1972, maundered on about 'disgruntled, misguided youths' and a 'calculated, Communist inspired movement which proposes to crush existing democratic forms of government in the Gulf'. It did not elaborate on what the 'existing democratic forms' were.

37. Talal Saad, member of General Command of PFLOAG, in February 1971. Interview originally published in *New Left Review*, No. 66, March–April 1971.

38. *Economist*, 3 April 1971.

39. Letter to the author, 27 December 1971.

40. The original story was printed by *Daily Telegraph* defence correspondent R. H. Greenfield on 1 January 1972: 'Despite their official role as a training detachment, there is a strong suspicion in some quarters that the SAS are in fact fighting actively against the guerrillas. Local rulers are sensitive to accusations that they are receiving "colonialist" assistance.' Other characteristic timid headlines were 'UK fighting secret Gulf war?' (*Observer*, 9 January 1972); 'Is Dhofar Britain's hush-hush war?' (*Sunday Times*, 9 January 1972) and 'Not as Good as it Looks' (the *Economist*,

8 January 1972). The author attended the regular 12.30 Foreign Office news briefing on 4 January, when some non-British diplomatic correspondents tried to probe a bit deeper, but were deflected with the usual FO bromides: 'The SAS of course take action to defend themselves ...' 'We do not normally give information on troop dispositions ...', etc. Heavier questioning was stopped with a braying 'You're barking up the wrong tree' from a more senior official on the sidelines. The meeting was enlivened by evident official discomfort at the truculence of Maltese premier Dom Mintoff, who at that time was demanding higher rent for NATO use of his island's harbour.

41. *The Times*, 12 May 1972.

42. Letter to the author, 31 May 1972.

43. *Sunday Times*, 25 June 1972.

44. *Daily Express*, 15 June 1972, which reported hospital officials at Akrotiri, Cyprus, as saying: 'This is very hush hush. We have been told not to say anything.'

45. PFLOAG lost thirty dead and twelve captured in the attack on Mirbat, according to the detailed account of the battle issued later. Some prisoners were taken in chains to Salala and there beaten and humiliated in public by British officers.

46. 'Are we on the Threshold of a new October?', *Red Line*, PFLOAG weekly, No. 19, 25 September 1972.

47. 'Oman Cuts Rebel Arms Supplies', *Daily Telegraph*, 3 May 1973.

48. *Statement on the Defence Estimates*, 1970 (Cmnd. 4290), Chapter II, section 25; and *Statement on the Defence Estimates*, 1971 (Cmnd. 4592), Chapter II, sections 71 and 72. See also the 1973 *Statement* (Cmnd. 5,231), Chapter II, Section 34, and *Hansard*, 30 April 1974

49. *Le Monde*, 27–8 May 1971.

50. The *Sunday Times* of 25 June 1972 gave the following figures: pilots, as flight lieutenants, get £5,000 a year (£4,455 if unmarried).Contract captains get £3,665, majors £4,471. There is no income tax; and the officers, while on service, have no living expenses. Another report (*Sunday Times*, 16 July 1972) stated that the London Ministry of Defence hires seconded majors out at £9,000 a year while the majors themselves, who are still paid by the MoD, get only between £3,449 and £3,949. This money, which is being stolen from the Omani people, is used to pay their enemies.

51. Baluchistan is an area now divided up between Iran and Pakistan. Its population of around 2 million speak Baluchi, a language close to Persian (*farsi*) and to Urdu, and are mainly tribal herdsmen living on the dry plateau that stretches from the Kirman desert in Iran to the borders of Sind and Punjab. They form an oppressed minority within both Iran and Pakistan, and mercenary service is a traditional means of earning the income which their own area cannot provide. In 1972–3 a low-level armed rebellion broke out against the Pakistan regime. A small group of Baluchis emigrated to

Russia in the nineteenth century and since 1928 have been organized in stock-rearing *kolkhozes* in Turkmenistan.

52. U S, Vietnamese and Thai troops were trained in the late 1960s at the British Jungle Warfare School at Kota Tinggi in Malaya; see *Far Eastern Economic Review*, 11 September 1971, p. 19. One of the leading British counter-insurgency experts, Sir Robert Thompson, advised the Nixon régime in Vietnam for several years. The later exponents of these theories also applied them to conditions in Ireland and possible 'civil strife' inside England itself, as in *Low-Intensity Operations* by Brigadier Frank Kitson, London, 1971.

53. Hepworth, op. cit., p. 25.

54. Captain Julian Lancaster on Thames Television's *This Week* programme, 28 December 1972. S O A F pilots on the programme made such remarks as: 'It is just an experience you can't find anywhere else', 'they started it, we didn't' and 'you never see what is on the ground; you may see something move but you have no idea what it is'.

55. There are no official figures on British casualties in Oman, neither of seconded personnel nor of any other kind. P F L O A G claims to have killed an officer named 'Carter' in Wadi Nahiz in 1966; and *The Times* (25 May 1966) reported the death of a contract officer. Yet on 3 August 1970 it stated that 'none of the 35 seconded British officers and 60 others on contract to the Sultan's forces' had been killed. The *Observer* (8 June 1971) reported that one S A S man had been shot by an Omani soldier in 1970 and that two other British officers had been killed in ambushes. On 22 July 1971 the *Daily Telegraph* reported the death of a Captain M. R. A. Campbell; and the *Economist* of 7 August 1971 reported two deaths in the past year. In January 1972 two S A S deaths, Sergeant John Moore and Trooper Christopher Loid, were confirmed; in the London Parliament (24 January 1972) the junior Foreign Office minister Lord Balniel told M.P. Andrew Faulds that three seconded and three contract officers had recently been killed. A reporter in Muscat in the spring reported seeing a fresh grave marked 'captain R. H. Jones born 1947; died 1972'; and *The Times* of 12 May 1972 reported the death of S A S Trooper M. J. Martin, saying that the total number of British military killed to date was seven. A low estimate would be that around twenty British personnel of all kinds had died in Dhofar by the end of 1972.

56. *Financial Times*, 5 November 1972.

57. *Newsweek*, 21 May 1973.

58. When the author phoned the press attaché at the Iranian Embassy in London, Mr Ali Mohammad Shapurian, in early January 1974, Shapurian denied that there were any Iranian troops in Oman – the accusation was 'old hat' he said. Similar veracity was attached to the question of whether the Shah's troops were using the R A F base at Salala. The Minister of Defence, Ian Gilmour, answered 'No' when asked by William Wilson M P whether 'any of the facilities of British bases in Oman have been made

available for Iranian forces' (*Hansard*, 'Written Answers', 28 January 1974). Yet there was no other base they could possibly have been using, and Qabus himself confirmed that the Iranians were using the Salala base, in an interview with the Beirut weekly *al-Hawadeth* (8 February 1974).

59. *Daily Telegraph*, 7 February 1974.

60. *Etela'at*, 10 February 1974.

61. *S W B*, 3 April 1974.

Chapter Eleven
The Popular Front for the
Liberation of Oman and the Arab Gulf

DLF Ideology

The ideological transformation of the Dhofari guerrilla movement was clearly reflected in the different statements it issued from
1965 onwards.[1] The proclamation made after the First Congress
of June 1965 and which was immediately followed by the first
attacks was based on the DLF's current leaders' mixture of
Dhofari separatism and partial Nasserism. It stated their position
with eloquence:

> Arab people of Dhofar! A revolutionary vanguard has emerged from
> among you and, believing in God and country, has taken upon itself
> the task of liberating this country from the rule of the despotic Al Bu
> Said Sultan whose dynasty has been identified with the hordes of the
> British imperialist occupation. Brothers! This people has long and
> bitterly suffered from dispersion, unemployment, poverty, illiteracy and
> disease – these pernicious weapons introduced under the protection of
> the bayonets of British imperialism, and used against the Dhofaris
> by the government of the Sultans of Muscat.
> Arab people of Dhofar! You bear witness to this state of affairs
> and have all suffered from this absurd policy. God has wished us life
> and they wish us death. But the will of God is the will of Right which
> should prevail over this part of the great Arab fatherland ...

This appeal expressed a hybrid ideology, in which Arab nationalism and support for the struggles in other Arab countries were
the means of articulating resistance by an oppressed and non-
Arabic-speaking group within an autocratic Arab state. The
DLF correctly regarded the Al Bu Said dynasty as local agents
of British imperialism in Oman, although in diagnosing the
oppression of Dhofar it laid less stress on British imperialism
and more on the sultans of Muscat. The crux of the ambiguity
concerned Dhofar's identity and the scope of its liberation

struggle. On the one hand, its location between South Yemen and the Gulf laid it open to influence by both areas; on the other hand it was treated as an Omani colony. Dhofar was tied to the Sultanate of Oman by being ruled from there, while at the same time it was separated from Oman by its colonial status, its social distinctiveness and 500 miles of desert. But the Dhofar area could not become part of its south-west neighbour: though it had common characteristics with South Yemen and was affected by the liberation struggle there, it never regarded itself as part of South Yemen; and the dominant political experience of many Dhofaris had been their period as émigré workers in the Gulf.

The DLF never resolved this question and the June 1965 communiqué demonstrated the ambiguities involved. The statement emphasizes throughout that Dhofar's national identity is as part of the Arab nation. There were three reasons for this. By stressing that they were Arabs, the Dhofaris wished to assert their equality with Omanis who traditionally had regarded them as inferior. This meant that the DLF, although it was the liberation movement of an oppressed region, had decided not to glorify its own differences and its own past, but to assimilate itself to the dominant culture in the Arab world which was also that of Dhofar's oppressors.[2] The DLF also wished to stress its support for the liberation movement in the whole Arab world and reject the possibility of the Dhofari struggle being used by imperialism. A third reason for stressing the Arab character of Dhofar was that it would counter-balance the separatism implicit in the DLF's title.

The DLF at the same time identified Dhofar with 'South Yemen and the Gulf', a more restricted area than the Arab world as a whole. Because they were unable to stress one at the expense of the other, the DLF placed themselves at the centre of an imaginary region defined by both, and since the more traditional elements in the DLF were incapable of formulating an appeal specifically to the Omani people, they tried by referring to the 'Gulf' to avoid having to talk about Oman in particular. One of the first responses of Said bin Taimur to the Dhofar rising was to portray it to the Omani tribes as a rebellion against them by Dhofari tribes; and he tried to rally the former to fight in Dhofar. But the D L F could not handle this directly; a Dhofari spokesman commenting in November 1965 on this 'tribal' interpretation could only reply by calling for the unity of all revolutionary forces in the area.[3]

Dhofar's identity being thus ambiguously phrased, the scope of the struggle remained obscure. The original statement denounced the Al Bu Said dynasty, but the movement's aims were not made clear, and the communiqué merely said that the D L F would fight until 'the flag of freedom flies high in the sky of our beloved Dhofar'. Its concluding slogan, 'Long Live Dhofar, Arab and Free', managed to evade altogether the question of objectives. This imprecision enabled 'separatists' and 'nationalists' to coexist within a single Front; the former refused to see the Dhofari movement within the context of the Sultanate as a whole, possibly encouraged by the fact that the Imamist movement had only recently challenged the integrity of the Omani state. The latter refused to agree to an explicit Dhofari separatism which could have led to the call for an autonomous Dhofari state analogous to the Imamist call for an autonomous state of the Omani interior.

Over the next two years the D L F continued to avoid committing the struggle either to being that of an oppressed minority within the Sultanate or to being the first stage in a general struggle to liberate the whole of Oman or the Gulf. The change in the Front's ideology finally resolved these problems; Dhofar was definitively part of the Gulf, and its struggle was to initiate liberation of the rest of the Gulf. The defeat of the Arab states in June 1967 and the revolution's victory in South Yemen symptomatize the external developments leading to this conclusion. Meanwhile, difficulties within Dhofar discredited the D L F's previous leadership and brought the former M A N group to the fore. This change came about through the ex-M A N's appreciation of changes within the Dhofar revolution. The effect of these alterations and of the June 1967 defeat were clearly signified by the Front's attitude to the conventional nationalism of Egypt. Just before the Arab–Israeli war Yusuf Alawi, the

Nasserist D L F spokesman based in Cairo, broadcast to Dhofar in straight Nasserist terms:

> Free brothers, the decisive battle of the Arab nation is being embodied today in the vanguard of the army of Arabism advancing in Sinai, the heroes of Arabism, the officers and men of the U A R who are standing with determination, firmness and faith in the face of the Zionist and imperialist enemy, at the front ready to fight the decisive battle with Zionism and imperialism for the purpose of liberating Palestine, the heroic Arab land . . .

> Free Heroes in the mountains of al-Qara and Qarm, brave soldiers of the Dhofar Liberation Army, you have taught British imperialism sharp lessons, today is the day of Arabism. It is the day of vengeance for our free martyrs . . . This is our chance for revenge on the criminal Zionists and on their masters, the British and the Americans. Let it be the day of revenge. God is greatest. Long live Arabism victorious. Victory is for us. Death to the imperialists and Zionists.[4]

Ten days later the Egyptian army had been destroyed in Sinai and the impact of the defeat was being felt throughout the Arab world. The defeat broke D L F subjection to the Egyptian state and coincided with the build-up of the British position in the Gulf, in the Bahrain and Sharjah bases. Clearly, therefore, the D L F had a double impulsion to escalate their struggle: to compensate for the defeat in Sinai, and to counter the imperialist build-up in the Gulf. This change even received short-lived encouragement from Egypt, which saw the Adeni 20 June rising in Crater and the possibility of intensified fighting in Oman both as ways of hitting back at the victorious imperialists.

In July 1967 the D L F was already appealing for renewed efforts: 'Brother Dhofaris, free men of the Dhofar Liberation Army, the present circumstances through which the Arab homeland is passing require greater sacrifices', it said.[5] And in August, Voice of the Arabs appealed to all Dhofaris, to 'our men, women, children, old men, peasants, workers, students and intellectuals' to participate. 'The Arab nation is calling on the free Arabs of Dhofar to prepare themselves to fight, and to take part, with determination and using every available means.'[6]

In September the weekly D L F broadcast was given not, as

usual, by Yusuf Alawi, the D L F representative in Cairo, but by Mohammad Ahmad al-Ghassani, one of the leaders of the militant Arab nationalist faction within the D L F who opposed the narrower separatism represented by Alawi. While hinting at the D L F's difficulties from the British blockade of supply lines in the western sector of Dhofar, al-Ghassani went beyond Dhofari's militancy and appealed to all people of the Gulf to support Dhofar:

Arab people in Muscat, Nizwah, Sharjah, Dubai, Bahrain and all parts of the Gulf, the D L F is calling you, the liberation revolution in Dhofar is your revolution, it is your hope. British imperialism and its agents, the Sultans of Muscat, are trying to strike at your revolution in Dhofar. They are trying to stifle your human voice coming from the valleys and mountains of Dhofar.[7]

By 1968 the Front saw itself clearly as part of the struggle throughout the Gulf, and at the same time had broken with the Nasserism of before June 1967. There could be no sharper indication of the change than the difference between the proclamation of May 1967 on the 'vanguard of the Arab army advancing in Sinai', and the following evaluation:

The defeat of 5 June 1967 has concretely proved the failure of the policies of the Arab regimes on both the ideological and strategic levels. Those policies have now become totally discredited in the eyes of the toiling masses. However, we should not simply dismiss them verbally or by bureaucratic decision but rather try to understand the objective conditions that led to the emergence of the Palestine liberation movement ... The military defeat initiated debates within the ranks of the revolutionary forces in the Arab world as it did among those most directly hit by the imperialist Zionist aggression. Those forces submitted themselves to thorough self-criticism and some petty-bourgeois organisations collapsed under the strain.[8] This debate was bound to reach the Arab Gulf where the Dhofar revolution carried its own self-criticism and decided to extend its activities to all the areas of the Gulf, emphasizing that the victory of the revolution essentially depends on the level of social consciousness achieved by the masses.[9]

The Second Congress

The Second Congress of the DLF met at Hamrin in central Dhofar between 1 and 20 September 1968. It was attended by approximately sixty-five delegates from the DLF, the Dhofar Liberation Army, the militia and the Front's underground organization in the Gulf. Only three of the eighteen DLF leaders elected in 1965 were re-elected, and a new twenty-five member General Command was formed, with Mohammad Ahmad al-Ghassani as secretary. Some of the old leaders agreed to the change, while others including Yusuf Alawi and Musallim bin Nufl broke away and continued to call themselves the Dhofar Liberation Front. This latter rump, who represented Dhofari pro-imperialism, later went over to the British, and worked with them against the revolution, falsely claiming that the 1968 Congress had been a coup by a 'Chinese-trained hard core', who had ousted the 'devout Moslems' of the DLF.[10]

The Second Congress carried reappraisal of the Front's experience in every field – theoretical, organizational, strategic and political. A majority adopted the thesis presented by the left: the crisis of the guerrilla struggle in Dhofar was due to the DLF's incorrect isolationist strategy, and the absence of a revolutionary theory and revolutionary party capable of leading the struggle. The solution was to adopt 'scientific socialism' and to build a revolutionary organization, launching a social revolution in the liberated areas and tying the Dhofar revolution to the struggle in the Gulf and the world-wide combat against imperialism, reaction and their allies.

The official communiqué issued after the Congress began by analysing 'negative factors' that had affected the Dhofar struggle: these included rivalry between Arab states, 'the ideological confusion which has characterized the Arab revolution in its struggle for liberation' and 'the presence of bourgeois forces in the leadership of the Arab national democratic liberation movement'. The struggle had also had to face its enemies – Arab reaction, the British and the Imam of Oman.

The Congress took three 'strategic' decisions: 'to adopt

organized revolutionary violence' as the sole means of struggle; to change the name of the Dhofar Liberation Front to the Popular Front for the Liberation of the Occupied Arab Gulf and 'adopt a comprehensive revolutionary strategy for the whole of the occupied Arab Gulf by linking the struggle in Dhofar with the mass struggle in the Gulf – this being the fine destiny of the revolution in Dhofar'; and 'to work towards the unification of the revolutionary weapon of the popular masses in the occupied Arab Gulf as the sound and revolutionary prelude to the unity of the area itself'.[11] It attacked the Imam of Oman, the UAA and all who 'raise fake revolutionary slogans'; and it expressed its support for the struggles in Palestine, in Rhodesia and against racial oppression in the USA.

PFLOAG's understanding of 'scientific socialism' was expounded in a 'national charter' elaborated at the Congress and in a number of theoretical texts published later in the Front's journal. The charter began by stressing the social determinants of the Dhofar struggle:

The revolution of 9 June 1965 is an inevitable result of the class and social contradictions between the oppressed masses on the one hand and the feudal rulers and the various capitalist forces on the other. It will not stop whatever the sacrifices until the will of the masses, that is of those who have a real stake in the revolution, is victorious.

This emphasis was in marked contrast both to the 1965 analysis, in which the DLF had characterized its enemy as 'despotic' and 'corrupt' without any precise class definitions. It was also an implicit critique of the Imam's Green Mountain movement which had been curtailed once the tribal leaders felt it was no longer in their interests to continue the fight.

The charter highlighted the role of South Yemen in having 'prepared the favourable conditions for a similar revolution' in Dhofar and in proving the imminence of victory for the 'armed popular revolution' in the Gulf. Dhofar forms an 'intermediary link' between Yemen and the Gulf, but as in 1965, Oman, which linked Dhofar and the Gulf, was not explicitly mentioned. In the Gulf the need was for a movement led by 'workers, poor peasants, soldiers and revolutionary intellectuals', i.e. those whose interests were realized in fighting imperialism, and who rejected the feudal and bourgeois leadership that had dominated the movement up to then. Similarly, in the Arab world, the masses had to throw off petty-bourgeois leadership, which was rendered incapable of liberating them by 'its ideological obscurantism and middle-of-the-road policies, as has been amply demonstrated by the doomed defeat of June 1967'.

The aim of the revolution was establishment of a democratic and socialist society, necessitating both liquidation of the imperialist military and economic presence, and control of the means of production by the working class. The Front conceded some importance to the economy's private sector but asserted that the public sector must dominate. There had to be industrialization, agrarian reform, encouragement of local trade and the building of an economic infrastructure. The revolution must free slaves, end the oppression of women, develop health and education and encourage trades union activity.

Statements published in 1969 provided further exposition of the Front's new political positions. In an article entitled 'What Do We Understand By "Scientific Socialism"?'[12] the Front argues that there can be only one socialism, that socialism does not allow of local or ethical variations. This is based on the inevitability of class struggle, the need for the abolition of private ownership of the means of production, the need for the seizure of power from the ruling class and the recognition that it is the working class who make history. The bourgeoisie have carried through the national democratic revolution in the advanced capitalist countries; but in the colonial world they have not and cannot, and this necessitates 'permanent or uninterrupted revolution'. The colonial countries will not go through a bourgeois stage, and the tasks of the bourgeois revolution will be carried out by the working class. This seizure of power by the working class will be followed by the dictatorship of the proletariat, which will inflict decisive blows on the defeated ruling classes. The revolution must also include the socialist transformation of agriculture 'by modernization and collectivization, the only way

380

to end the contradictions between peasants and workers, between villages and towns, and to raise the standard of living of the countryside, to that of the towns'.

In another equally lucid statement entitled 'The World Working Class and the 1st May Festival' the Front described the situations of the working class in three areas of the world – in 'the countries of the socialist camp', in the advanced capitalist countries, and in the Arab world. The working class in the first area had the duty to give all possible aid to the struggles in capitalist and colonial countries. The working class in the capitalist countries had to reject the myth that there could be a 'peaceful transition to socialism' and support colonial victims of oppression by capitalist countries. The article, following Lenin's *Imperialism*, argues that a section of the working class have become a 'labour aristocracy', bribed by the profits of imperialism, and that this has weakened the working class in the advanced capitalist countries. If the colonial revolution by its triumph was able to weaken imperialism and lessen its profits, this would directly assist the anti-capitalist struggle.

For this reason, one can say that the revolutionary movement in the advanced capitalist countries will remain a myth as long as the struggles of the workers in Europe and in North America against the capitalist system are not closely united against imperialism and world capitalism with those of the hundreds of millions of oppressed people in the colonies.[13]

The working class in the Arab world had still to accomplish the national democratic revolution, which required a protracted armed struggle against imperialism, colonialism and Arab reaction.

The decisions of the Second Congress were followed by a campaign of mass education throughout Dhofar, in which the teaching of literacy and of the Arabic language went together with political education. The Front distributed as widely as it could Arabic translations of revolutionary classics – Lenin's *State and Revolution* and *Imperialism*, Marx's and Engels's *The Communist Manifesto* and writings of Mao, Stalin, Ho Chi Minh and Che Guevara. These, with texts from the Palestinian PDFLP, formed part of the political education programme taught to all cadres and provided the basis of discussions and lectures. At the Revolutionary Camp where PLA cadres were trained, this course was divided into three parts. The first consisted of PFLOAG's own major texts: the charter, the 'Analysis of the Social Structure of the Dhofar Province', 'Women and the Revolution in the Gulf'[14] and studies of the national-liberation and workers' movements in the Gulf. This involved study of Nasserism and analogous groups such as the Ba'ath, as well as of the history of the Arab communist parties. The second part of the course consisted of the major Marxist texts already mentioned, which could be studied in more or less detail depending on the time available.

Both these sections presupposed a relatively high degree of literacy and of political reading, which only about 10 per cent of the people in Dhofar possessed, and for this reason PFLOAG evolved an introductory course in political education designed to make the basic revolutionary concepts accessible to the people as a whole. This course, in twenty-five sections, constituted the basic educational material, and was transmitted throughout Dhofar. Its four main headings were: the Formation of the Revolutionary Militant; Organizational Principles; Principles of Marxism-Leninism; and Internationalism, National Liberation and Class Struggle.

PFLOAG Theory

This theoretical change in the Front and the education campaign launched after 1968 were an attempt to bring socialist ideas to one of the most isolated parts of the colonial world and to apply to a society that had only the elementary forms of division of labour and of property relations a theory which began as a study of the capitalist mode of production in industrial Europe. The application of Marxism-Leninism to such non-industrial societies as China and Vietnam by the respective Communist parties had long since demonstrated that the liberation of those countries could only be achieved by mass movements armed with revolutionary Marxism. In a world dominated by imperialism most bourgeoisies in non-industrial society were unable to carry through economic and social tasks. Yet at the same time the anti-imperialist struggle required the uniting of as broad a front as possible against the common enemy, including many who did not necessarily support socialist theories as such.[15]

The revolutionary movement in Oman differed from those in China and Vietnam in at least two respects. While the Dhofari revolutionary movement confronted imperialist military and economic aggression as China and Vietnam had done, Dhofari society was far less developed than either of these – in particular, it had not produced any comparable landowning class or a comprador bourgeoisie. It is true that a comprador class had evolved in the Gulf, and that capitalist exploitation was flourishing in the oil industry. But this had only made the coastal and oil-producing areas of the Gulf socially quite different from Dhofar, to whom they had never approximated even in pre-capitalist times.

A second difference was that socialist ideas had been brought to China and Vietnam by Communist parties, constituent members of the Third International whose leading cadres had often been trained in or influenced by the Soviet Union in the 1920s and 1930s. These parties were bound by strict Comintern discipline and by strong links to the Comintern centre in Moscow. It is true that one of the achievements of Mao Tse-tung, both theoretically and politically, was to wage an independent struggle, in China, but the existence of the Third International and of its influence – especially in the early 1920s – had an important effect on these parties, the Chinese included. The forces that transformed the DLF into PFLOAG were independent of these influences; the process was more autonomous and did not produce a Communist party. The specifically Gulf–Oman radicalization was also influenced by events in South Yemen and by radicalization of the MAN centred in Beirut; by a crisis, that is, *within* Arab nationalism.

The DLF was dominated until 1968 by a nationalist ideology and a militarist view of guerrilla struggle. At the Second Congress, however, it abruptly proclaimed adherence to 'scientific socialism'. Two concepts to which P F L O A G most adheres illustrate very sharply the birth of new ideas from the failure of the old. One, the concept of 'organized revolutionary violence', derives directly from the failure of the previously dominant form of violence, that is, tribal violence. This, by implication, is unorganized and non-revolutionary; it is also spontaneous, widespread and often heroic – as in the Green Mountain and many Dhofari tribal risings. But it relied on individual heroism and a mystique of the gun, not on a theoretical grasp of the struggle, particularly the need for mass organization. In 1967 D L F spokesman Yusuf Alawi stated: 'Freedom as the free know it depends on how thick the smoke of bullets, bazookas and grenades is.'[16] By 1970 their position was distinct:

We are never in favour of saying that violence has the ability to achieve everything. But we are bound to call for revolutionary violence as a means of implanting the revolutionary spirit in the masses. In our view the criteria of revolutionary violence can be summarised in two organically interlinked points: revolutionary consciousness and revolutionary organization.[17]

Also crucial is the concept of a clear class leadership for the revolutionary movement in the Gulf, led by the workers and peasants. Just as the concept of different practice and theory resulted from internal failure of the D L F within Dhofar, so external weaknesses of the revolutionary movement in the Gulf, its divisions and compromises, had led it to abandon the classless Utopia of the hitherto prevailing form of bourgeois nationalism.[18] This change was impelled by national, not class, failure; the Arab armies had claimed to justify their privileges and policies on the grounds that they could defeat Israel – and in June 1967 they failed: the same Arab regimes, whose allies included Saudi Arabia and Kuwait, claimed to defend 'the Arabism of the Gulf', yet they were in fact collaborators of the oil companies and of western imperialism. Moreover the unofficial nationalist groups that had emerged in the peninsula during and after 1956 had been contained. The reason for this was that they were usually restricted to specific states (e.g. Bahrain) and to reformist policies. If they did use force (as in Saudi Arabia), it took the form of individual attacks divorced from political mobilization of the people.

The development by PFLOAG of new policies and of a new theory of the revolution involved uniting as large a following as possible, while at the same time insisting on its own analysis and introducing new concepts into the revolutionary struggle. This was a problem faced by all revolutionary movements; the theoretical turmoil of 1968 had given PFLOAG a new world view, yet the population to whom it appealed had experienced the conditions leading to this change of theory – the crisis of anti-imperialism in the Gulf and in the Arab world as a whole – in a more spontaneous and sporadic way. Immediately after the Second Congress PFLOAG declared that it, as a Front, was 'Marxist-Leninist' and insisted on its members' acceptance of 'Marxism-Leninism'. Yet this inevitably limited its political appeal; the NLF of South Vietnam, however influenced by Marxism, had never adopted such a position and had a much broader political and mass base. Similarly, in the Gulf it seemed to the Front that imperialist unity could be countered only by a more open approach, and this decision is reflected by the documents of the Third Congress of July 1971 and of the Ahlish Unification Congress of December 1971. The insistence on 'Marxism-Leninism' was toned down. Instead of defining imperialism in purely class terms, as immediately after 1968, PFLOAG saw imperialism as having both a class *and* a national aspect; its national democratic programme formed a basis for uniting non-Marxists, nationalists and anti-imperialists of many kinds. After 1967 rhetorical leftism and infatuation with the revolutionary phrase had often led to defeat, both in the Arab world and beyond. The radicalized anti-imperialist movement in the Gulf hoped to avoid this through a revolutionary strategy consonant with their opposition and their own capabilities.

Mass Education

To PFLOAG the revolution's social and military tasks are of equal respective importance and are the concrete expression of its

385

revolutionary theory. To quote Tuful Said, a woman refugee from the eastern sector whom I met in the western sector in February 1970: 'Here we are fighting on two fronts. The first front, that of revolutionary violence and armed struggle, is the easiest. The second and most difficult one is where we fight against illiteracy, ignorance and backwardness.' A number of measures resulted from the Second Congress. Slavery was abolished. Education classes in politics and literacy were set up throughout the liberated area. For the first time young children received primary education; and in 1970 a Lenin School was set up just inside the PDRY. In addition to learning history, mathematics, politics and languages, the children shared the tasks of the camp – cooking, cleaning and guard-duty – and had group discussions on the tasks they had to perform. Many of these children had spent weeks walking through the dangerous central zone, and some had seen PLA cadres die while ensuring that the road ahead was clear. One visitor to the Lenin School in 1971 was told by a young boy how he had come to the school to study so that he could go back to the fighting areas and teach his other comrades.[19] Such was the demand for education that in April 1972 PFLOAG also set up the 9 June School, to which the older children were sent. By early 1973 850 children attended the two schools: since there were only twelve teachers for both, older students from the 9 June School shared in teaching the younger ones in the Lenin School, and all students participated in camp duties of guarding, cleaning and cooking. At this stage 25 per cent of the students were women. The schools aimed to fulfil two functions: to educate the children to understand the revolution, and to teach them basic technical skills. Military training formed an integral part of the curriculum.

The most important educational and training institution was the Revolution Camp, established after 1968 as part of the Second Congress Programme. When we visited the camp in 1970 there were fifty-two young men and eighteen young women; the women were the first squad to attend and the number of women relative to men has subsequently increased. There were five cadres in charge of training: the camp leader was Omar, a participant in the first attack of June 1965. He was supported by two military cadres, Huda, the women's political commissar, the daughter of a prosperous businessman in the Gulf and a former student at the American University of Beirut; and Abdul Aziz Abdurrahman, the son of a Moslem judge (*qadi*) from Salala, who had studied in Kuwait and in Egypt.

The day at the camp began at dawn, around 5.00 a.m., when members arose, assembled in the central part and saluted the PFLOAG flag. After breakfast, in cooking which the whole camp participated, there were usually four hours of military training, on the theory and practice of guerrilla warfare in the mountain areas and in towns, and the use of weapons and explosives. After lunch there was a literacy class, followed by two more hours of military training, until it was time for supper at sunset around 5.00 p.m. After supper were four hours of political education, following the condensed twenty-five point course prepared for basic political instruction.

For the militants in the camp and for people in the liberated areas a basic text was Mao Tse-tung's selected quotations. The reason for this was not China's training of guerrillas or support for the revolution – Chinese aid to Pakistan has not made Punjabi peasants read Mao's works, any more than Russian aid to Egypt has led the peasants of the Nile delta to read Lenin.

The popularity of Mao's works is due to the fact that they were written for a situation similar to that of Dhofar – for a newly literate peasantry suddenly wrenched into a guerrilla war, having to administer a liberated area and fight a protracted war against an imperialist enemy. The ferocious insistence of Mao on personal self-sacrifice is immediately communicable to a Dhofari militant living in the horrendous conditions of the mountains where British rockets and bombs may hit him at any time. It is through day-to-day experience of the war 'on both fronts' that general truths become accessible.

The Emancipation of Women

Since 1968 the Front has made the emancipation of women one of its priorities: a document listing the social achievements of the revolution gives 'the emancipation of women' as one of the social tasks confronted by the revolution, together with mass education, the abolition of slavery and the attack on tribalism. 'The revolution,' it says,

has worked to solve the causes and results of women's condition, out of a belief that woman is a human being equal to man. There must be no privileges between one sex and another. The revolution places men and women on an equal footing both in regard to their rights and in regard to their duties ... The energy of woman has begun to mobilize in our country and has begun to shake off all the symptoms which made her out to be stupid, a condition under which she suffered for long centuries. In brief, she is joining men in all fields of the revolution.

As this quotation suggests, the emancipation of women is still to be fulfilled and is not something that P F L O A G pretends can take place at once. One basis of their policy is that women suffer a double oppression – as victims of an oppressive social system and as victims of men. 'We suffered from four sultans,' several women told a visitor in 1971. 'We had the political sultan – the Sultan of Muscat; the tribal Sultan – the sheikh; the religious sultan – the Imam; and the family sultan – the father, brother and husband.' This emphasis on the specific of the oppression of women *as women* is elucidated in a theoretical document 'Women and the Revolution in the Gulf':

If we name a human being in whom, in all class societies, all forms of oppression and exploitation are centred, that being is woman. Woman is not the only example of someone who suffers from the economic structure in a class society. We can point to other victims of suffering and exploitation by capitalism: workers suffer, and farmers do too. But a woman-worker or a woman-farmer in addition to her sufferings under the relations of feudalist or capitalist production also suffers from her position inside marriage and in the family she was in before that. Moreover, she suffers from the oppression of society in general, since society imposes on her traditions and old customs which paralyse her activity and deprive her of the sensation of being a human being.[20]

The analysis argues that women nevertheless participate in the revolution more readily in Dhofar than elsewhere because they are somewhat less persecuted than women in the Gulf. In Dhofar, women have preserved some of the autonomy that disappears with development of the division of labour and of property relations: women within marriages possess cattle, and are often the owners of the family's means of livelihood; women can divorce easily and remarry, without being stigmatized; women participate in work, travel freely without their husbands and are not socially segregated. By comparison with more evolved Moslem society elsewhere, these are definite advantages, and are attributed by the Front to the relatively limited class differentiations in the Dhofari hills:

Such a conclusion is in conformity with, and confirms, the correctness of the Marxist theory according to which the persecution of woman and the deterioration in her condition are a result of the development of the division of labour and of the development of property relations.[21]

However, this relationship to men is only more free by comparison with oppression elsewhere – and the task of emancipating women remains. Women remained excluded from education, and had no access to learning through emigration to work in the Gulf. Women's divorce rights were less than those of men and their first marriage, though not subsequent ones, was often arranged between the father and the prospective husband. Polygamy was still practised by men who could afford it and the violent superstitious practice of female circumcision (clitorectomy) remained. While development of property relations intensified their exploitation, women were oppressed *as women* in Dhofari society *despite* the relatively low level of property differentiation.

The participation of women in the revolution was encouraged by the fact that from the start women had spontaneously joined the men and supported them in the battle, and in so doing had somewhat weakened their oppression. According to the PFLOAG analysis women responded more favourably than

men to the outbreak of the struggle and rallied more spontaneously. This soon clashed, however, with social relations.
Women began to keep food in reserve for fighters who might
arrive unexpectedly; husbands often opposed this and the women
were forced to hoard the food secretly. Secondly, women wanted
to leave their parents or husbands in order to work on the battle
front. The case of one woman named Aziza is illustrative: her
husband objected to her participation in political activity, but
she left home and after walking for several days reached the
training camp and volunteered for service in the women's section.
Her husband followed her and demanded that his wife be returned to him. PFLOAG refused on the grounds that Aziza
had freely decided to join the PLA.

Inside PFLOAG women are organized in cells, where they
carry out political education and literacy work. One way of
teaching literacy is through the 'alphabet of the revolution':
T for *tabaqa* (class), M for *mujtama* (society), F for *fellah*
(peasant) and so on. At the Revolution Camp in 1970 two young
members of the women's training group, Tufula, aged fifteen, and
Amina, aged twelve, gave a vivid account of the life they had left
and of their experiences after joining the revolution:[22]

Q. Why are you fighting and supporting the revolution?

Tufula: Because British imperialism is killing our men and
women. We are fighting to get them out.

Q. What did your family do?

Tufula: My family are shepherds in the western province and
I used to work with them. For three months of the year we
grew crops, and for the rest of the time we were nomads, herding
our flocks. I never went to school or learnt to read. I joined the
Front two years ago, and my parents tried to stop me. I felt I
should join my comrades.

Amina: I lived in Salala, the capital, and you can't escape by
land as it is surrounded by a big fence. So I escaped by sea with
my brother. That was last September.

Q. Why did you run away?

Amina: Because of imperialism. My father was a poor farmer;
he got four or five rupees a day. We were very poor. So my

brother got an old car-tyre and we swam in the sea for eight hours till we reached the coastline controlled by the Front.

Q. Weren't you cold and frightened? Could you swim?

Amina: I couldn't swim well, and we got very cold and hungry and thirsty. But it is better to die in the sea than be captured by the British.

Q. Who thought of escaping, you or your brother?

Amina: Everyone thinks of escaping.

Q. What is life like in Salala? Have you seen British officers or the Sultan?

Amina: Sometimes I'd see British officers out shopping, but they generally stay in their base. I've never seen the Sultan; he is dead, though agents say he is alive.

Q. How did you hear about the Front in Salala?

Amina: People found leaflets against the Sultan. They said: 'This is good and so is the revolution.'

Q. Tufula – since joining the Front what have you done?

Tufula: Well, at first I was in the militia, the Popular Guard, and then I took part in defending Shahbout when the enemy attacked it in the summer of 1969. The battle lasted for twenty-four hours and I carried water to the fighters at the front. I think that I was the first woman in the western area who joined the army.

Q. When did you learn to speak Arabic?

Tufula: The Front taught me, and I learnt from working with comrades in the Front. But it is still difficult.

Q. What have you learnt from the Front since you fled, Amina?

Amina: I've learnt literacy, politics and revolution.

Q. Do you ever miss your parents?

Amina: I don't think about my parents, I think about the revolution ...

Q. What do you think of the relations between men and women and the system of marriage contracts here?

Tufula: It is a pity to ask something from a person if you are going to marry him. If I want a man I'll marry him because I want to and he won't have to buy me. Anyway, there is no difference between men and women, and I've seen that I can do the same as they do. Before the revolution women used to be bought and sold and dispensed with like animals. Now they know their rights and take part in the struggle along with everyone else.

Q. What do you think of Islam? Are you religious?

Tufula: I live in a society of people who pray and I am one of them.

Q. Do you find that men resist the equality of women and hang on to their old ideas? What about marriage here?

Tufula: Marriage has to come after the revolution as it might slow down our work during the struggle. We are fighting here in Dhofar, and Dhofar is part of the Gulf. There is a problem about women participating since their families usually resist and some people say that if women join the British will come and take them and kill them. But people are getting over this . . .

It was the aim of P F L O A G to extend the women's movement to the whole of the Gulf, as an autonomous element of the revolutionary movement as a whole. Huda, the women's political commissar, explained it as follows:

In the rest of the Gulf, a lot of work is needed to make women aware of their duties and to convince them of the need to join the political struggle. The gravest error committed by the previous political movements under bourgeois and petty-bourgeois leadership was, from this point of view, their total disregard for the woman question. The new national liberation platform in the Gulf, inspired by Marxism-Leninism, must fill this gap. And the minimum demands that should be incorporated in it are: the ban on polygamy, equal right of divorce for women and the abolition of the bride-price.

In Dhofar polygamy and unequal divorce were stopped after 1968. Then the bride-price was lowered to a token level in 1970; and the women's platoon at the Revolutionary Camp demanded its abolition. The General Command then issued a statement in September 1970 that said that the purpose of this measure was to 'allow men and women to choose freely their partners without compulsion or intervention from any third party'. This was the first such measure passed anywhere in the Arab world and threatened a cornerstone of the traditional system. In a society between whose members there is little material distinction and where social relations are structured more by tradition than by control of the means of production the bride-price was one of the bases of power, both of men over women and of older men – fathers – over young men – prospective husbands. In so far as wealth did vary between tribes the bride-price ensured that men from lower tribes, such as the Shahara, did not marry women from superior tribes such as the Bait Kathir or the Qara. The bride-price thereby not only transformed women into cattle; it also acted as a lock on the traditional social system as a whole. And its virtual abolition was one extra blow by PFLOAG on 'the second front'.

The War on Tribalism

Until 1965 Dhofari society was structured by tribal divisions. The attack on these has been a central feature of revolutionary social policy. Said Masoud, a militant who from 1965 to 1970 was in Jalali prison, told the author that the most striking change he noticed on his return was the diminishing of tribalism. PFLOAG has not tried to hide the prevalence of tribalism in Dhofar, and its analyses of the past return time and again to the wasteful and divisive effects of inter-tribal feuding and oppression within the tribes.

The sultans reinforced the institution of tribalism by keeping Dhofar isolated and by politically manipulating it; and since 1965 the British, too, have made use of tribalism, in order to divide the revolution. Tribalism

contributed to the division of the people and was a source of real hatred and anger among the masses, leading to tribal conflicts and wars and to the prevalence of revenge as well as to other social problems such as marriage conflicts. The revolution has laid down a revolutionary and decisive solution to all such issues. It has banned revenge, and intervened to solve many tribal problems. The revolution has succeeded in turning men from blind allegiance to their tribe into a sound revolutionary allegiance to the revolution.[23]

As was demonstrated in Albania during the Second World War, in South Yemen in 1963–7 and in the Portuguese colonies in Africa, the experience of colonialist war can give a sense of common identity to tribes that were previously dispersed. Moreover, as in the case of North and South Yemenis employed in Aden, the experience of working in the Gulf had loosened tribal ideology among Dhofaris. Yet in Dhofar itself a conscious campaign was necessary, hitting both at tribal consciousness and at the institutions that sustained it. One of the bases of the tribal system was the constant feuding over land and water rights. After 1968 the Front began to collectivize land, and the Third Congress of 1971 declared all land in the liberated areas to be collective property. This then made it possible to develop agriculture and to win the tribes from their previous semi-nomadic reliance on their herds. This sedentarization not only made possible full exploitation of the natural wealth of Dhofar but also countered the economic blockade imposed by the British to starve the revolution of the food and fodder it had traditionally imported from the coast. In 1970 the settling of tribes in the western region was going ahead, but it met several problems. Ali Mohsen, a member of the P F L O A G General Command, attributed the resistance of tribesmen to several reasons. They had formerly been nomads to escape taxation, to avoid feudal adversaries and to maintain their traditional ownership of cattle as a sign of honour. Such was the survival of these prejudices that herdsmen felt demeaned by physical labour.

This sedentarization was a slow process, involving the setting up of cooperatives on the village level. Whereas the pre-existing village remained the unit of production, social relations changed; most of the crop would be consumed by the village – there was no sheikh to take a portion as his due – P F L O A G would buy the needed surplus for cash.[24] The peasants were encouraged to develop agriculture by innovations which P F L O A G introduced: pumps, new wells, irrigation, and the minimum tools. Agricultural committees in each province distributed seeds. A model farm was set up in 1970 where groups of twenty cadres a time were given three-month courses in agrarian technique;

and a road was built through the mountains from the PDRY border towards the Red Line to facilitate the movement of food and other supplies. The specific agent for fighting tribalism was the Committee for the Solution of Popular Problems (*Lajnat Tasfiah al-Mashakil ash-Shaabia*). Three of these, one in each sector, were set up after 1968, with the task of settling disputes involving tribal feuds, divorce and personal conflicts. Each acted as a roaming judiciary which travelled through the liberated areas. In 1971 they were replaced by Popular Councils. Tribal murders committed before September 1968 were settled by the payment of a compensation by the killer's family to the family of the victim. Killings after September 1968 were punishable by death. Executions of such killers and of people convicted of treason are published in documents which set out the reasons for the measures taken. Other cases are settled collectively; on one occasion a former tribal leader hit a woman at a well near Dhalqut because she 'dared' to water her cattle before his. The man was arrested by the local PLA. He was then taken to the scene of his crime, where the woman related what had happened. The Committee then pointed out the incident's political lesson: all citizens have equal rights over land and water. In the end the local people attending the trial decided to pardon the sheikh, since it was his first offence.

These reforms in the liberated areas are constantly denounced by Sultan Qabus and the British as 'alien' impositions on the 'traditional' life of the people of Dhofar. There could be no clearer instance of one aspect of imperialism in Arabia – the reinforcement of ignorance, disease, poverty, tribalism and the oppression of women. Another favourite ploy of the British is to accuse PFLOAG of being 'atheists' in the hope of antagonizing the population. In fact, however, in religious terms PFLOAG is open to all, including religious leaders. Its own teachings are secular, but people in the liberated areas are free to engage in religious practices and visibly do so; and religious believers are encouraged to see that there is no contradiction between anti-imperialism and a belief in Islam.

This latter argument has helped unmask a number of imperial-

395

ist agents who have tried to combat the revolutionary movement in the name of Islam. In Rakhyut a sheikh we met in 1970 expounded the absence of contradiction between socialism and Islam: 'The book of God commands us to observe equality and achieve justice and to wrench right from the oppressor and give it to the oppressed. I see no contradiction between socialism and Islam.' When asked whether he supported the Islamic Pact between Moslem nations advocated by King Feisal of Saudi Arabia he expressed his position without any ambiguity: 'Feisal is Johnson's ass,' he said.[25]

We do not think much of him. After the Arab defeat of 1967 he sent 12,000 soldiers to fight the Moslems in North Yemen. We do not recognize the Islamic Pact because it comes from an authority which does not itself recognize any God or religion – the authority of Sultans, Amirs and Kings, who are but the stooges of their imperialist masters and do not serve any religion, country or society.

Sheikh Ali was not disturbed either by the aid received from the Soviet Union and China:

We are willing to accept arms from any source, provided there are no strings attached to it, and to the exclusion of arms from the imperialist camp – unless they are arms we ourselves capture. The socialist camp does not pose any conditions on any Front fighting for the liberation of an oppressed people. We welcome armed struggle and scientific socialism. May the People's Liberation Army be victorious, by the will of God.

He himself had been the imam of a mosque in Rakhyut, from 1960 to 1966, when he had quarrelled with the local governor and had had to leave. In 1969, after the liberation of Rakhyut, he had returned and had made speeches in the town mosque denouncing imperialism and supporting the armed struggle. To escape British bombing he moved to a cave with his wife, her mother and his child, and lived off the fees paid to him for performing religious rights and off his own goats. His last request to us was that we should relay his greetings 'to all the comrades in the socialist camp'.

One aspect of conditions in pre-revolutionary Dhofar was the absence of any medical facilities. The prevalent ignorance was compounded by Said bin Taimur's ban on the import of medicine, and the casualties and food shortages caused by the guerrilla struggle itself increased the burden on the people. In 1970 PFLOAG acquired its first medical personnel: three men who had spent one year studying to be medical orderlies at the Republic Hospital (formerly Queen Elizabeth Hospital) in Aden. They set up makeshift medical centres in each region and did what little they could for those who could reach them. In 1972 the first hospital was established just inside the PDRY frontier, named after Mohammad Habkook, a central command member killed in July 1970 in the sinking of the ship *Saut ash-Shaab*. But within a few months the hospital had been attacked by SOAF planes. A new, makeshift hospital was built on the beach farther inside the PDRY. When I visited it in April 1973 there were about fifty people there: forty civilians from the western region, and some military, living in a cluster of huts and caves. The doctor, Marwan abu Hakim, a Syrian who had joined the revolution through the PDFLP, explained that the only patients who could reach the hospital were those from the western region – the one area of Dhofar least affected by malnutrition and wounds received in battle. He mostly treated tuberculosis and anaemia, both of which had increased since the struggle began; other perennial Dhofar diseases, including rheumatic problems, remained widespread; and there were also a few cases of leprosy. Doctor Marwan stressed that their minimal supply of medicines had led to a policy of curing a few patients properly rather than trying to spread wider their facilities. Given appalling conditions and minimal communications, there was little that one doctor could do, and the medical teams at the hospital were facing many problems: they had no refrigeration with which to keep medicines, and they could rarely get to seriously wounded cadres before it was too late. When asked how long he would stay, Doctor Marwan replied: 'Until victory.'

Oman and the Gulf

The overall strategic aim of PFLOAG has been fixed since 1968; it comprises the extension of revolutionary struggle from Dhofar to Oman, the lower Gulf, Bahrain and Qatar. The revolution in Southern Oman is regarded as resolved to assist the revolutionary movements throughout those areas, which PFLOAG considers a natural unit with Dhofar artificially divided by British intrigue and the conflicts of local rulers. Moreover, the revolution in Dhofar cannot in the long run survive without the overthrow of these regimes, given the latter's determination to crush all revolutionary movements, whether in the PDRY or Dhofar.

The main means towards PFLOAG's objective is people's war; and the Third Congress has stated that 'protracted, stubborn people's struggle is the only way to liberate the Gulf'. But it also stressed that 'other means of struggle' were possible and that the conflict should be undertaken in the towns as well as in the mountains. The 'national united front' of anti-imperialist groups coordinated on a 'national democratic programme' was the political key envisaged by PFLOAG for extending the struggle, and the Third Congress of PFLOAG, held in Rakhyut in June 1971, produced a twenty-nine-point programme as the basis for such a front.[26]

Active anti-imperialism in the Gulf was represented by former MAN branches and other Nasserites, and groups of communists and Ba'thists. All were potential candidates for the front.

PFLOAG itself had two quite dissimilar areas – Oman and the coastal areas of the Gulf – in which to apply its policies, and its strategy varied in each. Oman was the transition area between Dhofar and the Gulf, and PFLOAG there entered into cooperation with the former local MAN branch, now known as the Popular Revolutionary Movement. In June 1970 an extension of the PRM, entitled the National Democratic Front for the Liberation of Oman and the Arab Gulf, launched armed struggle in the Green Mountain area, bringing the war into the Omani interior. A PRM militant speaking in February 1971 analysed the situation:

The British and their local agents consider the interior of Oman to be the safe rear for defending the coastal Oman area and the other oil-producing states. The revolutionary movement starts from the same premiss. Britain's safe rear area can be turned against it. In addition Oman's geographic nature, its social composition and the politics of its people make it suitable to revolutionary work.[27]

Unfortunately for the revolutionary movement a series of errors committed by the NDFLOAG led to the arrest of its leading cadres on 18 July 1970 in the coastal town of Matra. The British realized that they were faced with a well-organized threat.

The spread of the revolutionary struggle was interrupted by the arrests and the temporary confusion created by the anti-Said bin Taimur coup; but it was soon consolidated by the new situation in Oman. Strikes in the new oil-fields and mass demonstrations in Muscat in September 1971 showed the extent of popular opposition to the government, and at the end of 1972 the British announced that they had arrested over one hundred people in several Omani towns.[28] At the same time, the NDFLOAG tightened its links to PFLOAG. In December 1970 the two Fronts issued a joint statement analysing the causes of the coup of July 1970 and the shift to neo-colonial forms of rule in the Gulf as a whole. They pointed out that these changes reflected the attempt by imperialism to contain the advancing revolution. In December 1971 the two Fronts met again, to discuss the national democratic programme elaborated at PFLOAG's Third Congress. As a result of these discussions, which were held at Ahlish in liberated Dhofar, the two Fronts merged into a common organization: the Popular Front for the Liberation of Oman and the Arab Gulf.

The establishment of this united Front was an important step forward, which had only been taken when the preconditions were fulfilled. It was conspicuous that the 1968 PFLOAG title had omitted the word 'Oman', and that the armed struggle had been started in Oman in 1970 by the NDFLOAG – a different group from the organization fighting in Dhofar. This omission was despite the fact that the Green Mountain and Dhofar were both inside the boundaries of the Sultanate of Oman. This separation within the struggle resulted from suspicion between the masses in each area. At first the Dhofari population regarded the Omanis as colonizers, while most Omanis had originally a chauvinist attitude to the subject Dhofaris. This mutual hostility was a classic result of the way in which the British and the Al Bu Said sultans had balkanized the area and accentuated existing distinctions so as to facilitate their own control.

The PFLOAG Third Congress led to other ties with Gulf groups and to a broadening of the Front's political appeal. In November 1972 PFLOAG held talks with another Omani anti-imperialist group, the Arab Workers Party in Oman. This had been the Omani branch of the MAN right wing and had confined itself to the Sultanate.[29] After the 1972 meeting the two Fronts also agreed to coordinate on the basis of the national democratic working plan. In the same month PFLOAG and anti-imperialists from Bahrain, Kuwait, Saudi Arabia and the PDRY issued a joint declaration. The coherence with which PFLOAG saw the situation in the Gulf is shown in its August 1972 analysis, entitled 'The Enemy Plan and How We Fight It'.[30] In this, PFLOAG asserted that the united anti-imperialist Front was the only possible reply to imperialist strategy in the area. The USA, acting through Saudi Arabia and Iran, was trying to re-stabilize the situation: Saudi Arabia was attacking the PDRY, while Iran was arming itself and seizing islands to police the Gulf. Jordan had also been recruited and the smaller Gulf states were selling themselves to the highest bidder. The united front, with the PDRY and Dhofar as its base, was the answer to cooperation among the counter-revolutionary enemy.

PFLOAG did not limit its ties to those with groups in the Gulf. In its statement in June 1970 on the fifth anniversary of the outbreak of the Dhofar struggle it pointed out that the principal enemy of the peoples of the world was US imperialism, and appealed to the peoples of Iran and of Britain to join with them in a common struggle against oppression by the number one imperialist power. Its appeals to the Iranian people led Arab regimes to accuse it of regarding Arabs and Iranians as equals. PFLOAG has consistently supported the revolutionary movement in Palestine, North Yemen and Eritrea, and in September 1972 liberated Dhofar was visited by a delegation from the NLF of South Vietnam, as a result of which the two Fronts issued a statement of mutual support.[31]

PFLOAG's relations with states, as distinct from other organizations, have changed with the movement's general evolution since 1965. Relations with Egypt have deteriorated; in 1968 PFLOAG spokesmen were taken off Cairo's Voice of the Arabs radio programme for the peninsula, and in 1972 the PFLOAG office in Cairo was closed down. Saudi Arabia cut off aid soon after 1965, when it realized it was not dealing with a movement like that of the Imam. On the other hand, PFLOAG defined its main enemies – imperialism, Arab reaction and Iran – and tried to win as much support from other states as possible. This meant that where a state was hostile to them on the basis of false information or Qabusite propaganda, the PFLOAG leadership worked patiently to change this state's position. Relations with Libya were improved in this way, and in late 1973 PFLOAG was able to open an office in Tripoli. Relations with Iraq also improved: the Iraqi governments had played a certain role in Gulf politics during the 1960s, but despite a radicalization within the Iraqi Ba'ath, differences subsisted. In time, however, the Baghdad government increased its political support for PFLOAG and provided valuable propaganda assistance in spreading news of Oman throughout the Middle East.

The main supporter of PFLOAG has been the PDRY, which since independence in 1967 has provided both political and material backing. Other principal supporters have been the communist states. Relations with the People's Republic of China were consolidated in 1968. The Soviet Union was at first reluctant to support the revolutionaries; and this problem was only overcome after the visit to Dhofar in 1970 of Soviet journalists and in 1971 of a PFLOAG delegation to the Soviet Union. PFLOAG cadres have visited the Soviet Union and People's China for training, and both states have provided support of all kinds. Confronted with accusations of being 'pro-Chinese' or 'pro-Soviet' and of being agents of foreign governments,

PFLOAG has always replied that its task is making revolution in the Gulf. Its relations to other movements and states are governed by their position on revolution in the Gulf. They have also stressed their own self-reliance and their refusal to side in Sino–Soviet polemics. Like the Vietnamese, PFLOAG has called on the Soviet Union and the People's Republic of China to resolve their differences; at the same time its relations with them have been friendly and conducted in a spirit of internationalism. The foundation of PFLOAG's policies remained the masses in Oman and the Gulf. The revolution in Dhofar provided hope and inspiration for those still under imperialist rule, and pointed the way to a different future. While imperialism, Arab reaction and Iran were hoping to serve their own interests at the expense of the peoples of the area, PFLOAG was pioneering a path based on anti-imperialism and democracy.

Notes

1. In the pre-1968 period the main sources for DLF statements are the Kuwaiti weekly *at-Talia* and the *BBC Summary of World Broadcasts*, Section 4, 'The Middle East and North Africa'. Later the Beirut MAN weekly *al-Horria* published DLF and PFLOAG statements. In 1968 PFLOAG began to publish a monthly, *Saut ash-Shaab* (*The Voice of the People*); in June 1970 a new enlarged monthly entitled *9 June* appeared. In June 1972 *9 June* went weekly under the title *al-Khatt al-Ahmar* (*The Red Line*); and in November 1972 this weekly's title became *Saut ath-Thawra* (*The Voice of the Revolution*). In addition to these, PFLOAG also published individual statements on major events. All monthlies and weeklies contained detailed military communiqués on PFLOAG actions, including enemy and PLA casualties. The analysis of PFLOAG's thinking contained in this chapter would have been impossible without the painstaking exposition given by many PFLOAG members, including General Command members Talal Saad and Mohammad Ahmad al-Ghassani, as well as by political commissars Huda, Abdul Aziz and many other militants.

2. This refusal to glorify Dhofari culture and the distinctive language of Dhofar contrasts with the diversionary obsession with language found in many bourgeois nationalist movements – e.g., in Ireland and Yugoslavia.

3. *at-Talia*, No. 155, Kuwait, 17 November 1965.

4. *SWB*, 25 May 1967. The talk was actually broadcast on 23 May.

5. *SWB*, 27 July 1967.

6. *SWB*, 17 August 1967.

7. *SWB*, 14 September 1967.

8. This is a reference to the MAN, whose pan-Arab organization broke up in 1968.

9. Proclamation on the fourth anniversary of the Dhofar revolution, in *al-Horria*, No. 470, 30 June 1969. *9 June*, No. 5, dated October 1970, printed a cautious obituary on 'Gamal Abd al-Nasser, the Arab mass leader' in which it recorded his positive anti-imperialist achievements, and emphasized that the national democratic tasks of freedom and democracy still remained to be accomplished. Compared to the crescendo of confused and uncritical eulogy that swept the Arab world at the time it was a strikingly unenthusiastic text. On the other hand PFLOAG has never criticized Nasser personally.

10. The proclamation on the fifth anniversary of the outbreak of the revolution, dated 9 June 1970, stated that 'after the Hamrin conference it was inevitable that numerous opportunistic elements would collapse, since they were permeated by an attitude of superiority towards the oppressed masses, and of tribal, strictly regionalist and fanatical concepts at the national and religious level; it was moreover necessary to purge the ranks of the revolution of these parasites who had joined the revolution at the beginning, so that the working masses would be able to participate in commanding the revolution.'

11. Communiqué published at the end of the Second Congress.

12. In *Saut ash-Shaab*, No. 9, January 1969.

13. In *Saut ash-Shaab*, No. 13, May 1969.

14. See pp. 388 ff.

15. For documentation of debates on these questions see Stuart Schram and Hélène Carrère d'Encausse, *Marxism and Asia*, London, 1969.

16. *SWB*, 26 October 1967.

17. From 'Women and the Revolution in the Gulf', *9 June*, No. 3, August 1970.

18. On the Marxist theory of the nation and its inadequacies, see Horace B. Davies, *Marxism and the National Question*, New York, 1968. The basic theory used by Marxists has remained that evolved by Lenin and Stalin, which are inadequate for societies where the national question had a character distinct from that prevailing in Europe or Russia in the earlier twentieth century.

19. *Afrique-Asia*, No. 21, 8–21 January 1973. I am grateful to Heini Srour, who visited and filmed the liberated zone in 1971, for her description of the Lenin School.

20. 'Women and the Revolution in the Gulf', *9 June*, No. 3, 1970.

21. The Front's analysis is in conformity with Engels in *The Origin of the Family, Private Property and the State*, Marx and Engels, *Selected Works*, Vol. 2, Moscow, 1958.

22. In 1971, following this interview, Tufula was killed in a British bombing raid and Amina was seriously wounded in the back.

23. P F L O A G document 'Achievements on the Road of the Revolution', n.d.

24. Despite the relatively isolated character of Dhofari society, cash had permeated it and the Front encouraged this process. When we were in western Dhofar in 1970 P F L O A G officials responsible for transporting our bags and film equipment hired transport (camels and donkeys) from local people and paid cash for them.

25. In fact Nixon had been U S president since January 1969, but the point remained equally valid.

26. See Appendix 4 (a), p. 531.

27. Said Seif in an interview with the author, February 1971.

28. *The Times*, 17 January 1973.

29. In 1970 the Popular Front for the Liberation of Palestine, led by Dr George Habbash, began to build up a pan-Arab party, the Arab Workers Party. In an interview with the author in February 1971 the editor of the P F L P weekly *al-Hadaf*, Ghassan Kannafani, praised the political developments in South Yemen and Dhofar but was concerned about the future: 'Given the importance of oil, this revolution is not going to be left alone. The more the revolution in South Yemen and Dhofar advances, the more pressure the imperialists will put on it, militarily and politically.' Kannafani was murdered in Beirut in July 1972 when a booby-trap exploded in his car. On the Omani section of the Arab Workers Party see the interview with one of their representatives in *al-Ittihad*, Kuwait, No. 53, October 1972.

30. *The Red Line*, No. 13, 15 August 1972.

31. The N L F delegation consisted of Vo Dang Gieng, member of the N L F Central Committee; Duc San Tam, member of the N L F Afro-Asian Solidarity Committee; and Nguyen Dinh Ka, member of the editorial board of the N L F weekly *South Vietnam in Struggle*.

Part Five
The Gulf

Chapter Twelve
Oil and Exploitation

The Domination of the Monopolies

The oil crises of 1973–4 have proved the importance of oil to the world economy. Annual world production has risen from 20 million tons in 1900 to 2,400 million tons in 1972. By the 1960s it had overtaken coal as an energy source and had come to supply more than half the energy needs of the industrialized capitalist world. Despite the advance of other potential sources like nuclear energy oil seemed likely to remain the major supplier of energy, at least until after the year 2000. The scale on which oil was produced had made it a major constituent of the capitalist market. It accounted for 10 per cent of the value of world trade and 50 per cent of world shipping tonnage. It made up 30 per cent of total US foreign assets and 60 per cent of its income from the colonial world. On the basis of estimating companies by their sales, six of the top thirteen world businesses in 1972 were oil companies. In the US the five major oil concerns came among the twelve leading companies; in Britain the two largest companies were Shell and BP. For all these enterprises the Gulf had a special importance. By the late 1960s it provided 30 per cent of total world production yet it contained at least 65 per cent of all known reserves. This meant that the subsequent strategic dependence of capitalist economies on the Gulf was bound to increase. Barring the unexpected discovery of a substitute for oil or the equally improbable finding of other oil sources, the Gulf was to be the main source for the increased oil demands made in the last three decades of the twentieth century. Such dependence confirmed imperialist determination to maintain its hold.

Since the 1920s the world petroleum industry has been dominated by seven large firms.[1] Between them these concerns have controlled the three main processes of production, refining and

Table 18

The Major Oil Companies

Firm	Sales* (1972)	Assets (1972)	Employees (1972)	Profits† (1972)	Profits† (1973)
Exxon	18·7	20·3	143,000	1,532	2,440
Shell	12·7	19·7	185,000	704	1,780
Mobil	8·2	8·6	75,300	574	843
Texaco	7·5	10·9	75,200	889	1,292
Gulf	5·9	9·5	57,200	197	800
B P	5·2	7·9	70,600	178	803
Socal	5·1	7·5	42,500	547	844

* in $ billions
† in $ millions

Source: *Fortune*, 1972; *Financial Times*, 13 May 1974.

marketing; as late as 1968 they controlled 77·9 per cent of world production, 60·9 per cent of refining and 55·6 per cent of world marketing facilities. Five of these firms are North American: Standard Oil of New Jersey (Exxon),[2] Standard Oil of California (Socal), Texaco, (Mexican) Gulf and Mobil; the two others are British (BP) and Anglo-Dutch (Shell). The French Compagnie Française des Pétroles (which sells *Total*), has also had a share of political power, although its economic strength has been some-what less. Despite competition, the major oil companies have handled their activities in relative harmony, knowing that their plunder and their exclusion of smaller rivals are secured by mutual adjustment. The ownership pattern of the major Gulf consortia, as demonstrated in Chart 1, illustrates this cooperation.

The record of these companies is one of unrelenting aggression both against producer and consumer countries. In 1917, when the Bolshevik Revolution nationalized foreign oil companies in the Caucasus (then the world's second largest oil-producing area), Standard Oil of New Jersey and Shell subsidized the counter-revolutionary separatist regimes in the area, and the British government sent a military expedition which occupied the fields for two years. When this outright aggression was ended

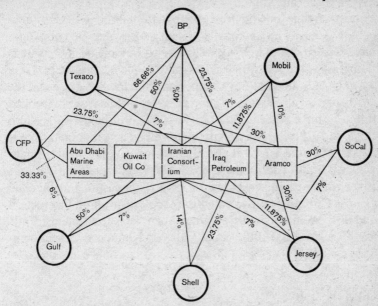

Chart Ownership Links between the Major International Oil Companies (including Compagnie Française des Pétroles) and the Major Crude-oil Producing Companies in the Middle East, 1966.

Source: Penrose, *The Large International Firm in Developing Countries*, 1968, p. 151.

the oil companies enforced a world-wide boycott of Russian oil. The next major clash came in 1938 when Mexico nationalized her oil. Jersey, Shell, Socal and Sinclair tried with another boycott to bring Mexico to its knees. They failed. In 1948 the Acción Democrática government in Venezuela was toppled for proposing nationalization. In 1951, when Iran nationalized its oil, BP launched another boycott campaign, sabotaged the Iranian economy and mobilized the British and US governments in support. This international plot succeeded, and in August 1953, Mosadeq fell from power. The CIA operative who organized the August 1953 coup, Kermit Roosevelt, became vice-president of the Gulf Oil Company in 1960. The Iraqi nationalization of 1961 was met by IPC counter-measures including the refusal to increase production; and the Algerian and Libyan nationalizations of 1970–71 led to company law suits throughout the world

409

against anyone buying from them nationalized oil. Consumer countries have had an equally violent experience. Oil companies have refused them a choice of where to buy oil on the grounds that this would stop the sale of oil at inflated prices. In 1960, when Cuba wanted to buy cheaper oil from the Soviet Union, the US broke off all relations. In the same year India was bludgeoned into refusing a Soviet offer of oil at 20 per cent below the western price. In 1962, when Ceylon nationalized oil distribution facilities, the US Congress passed the Hickenlooper Amendment, under which US aid would be cut off to states nationalizing US property without compensation. In 1969 the measure was invoked against Peru and Bolivia when they took over all oil production and distribution facilities, an amendment later used against Chile when it expropriated the equally vicious Kennecott copper company and ITT.

Oil in the Gulf

It has been known for millennia that oil exists in the Gulf area. The classical writer Plutarch wrote that 'the territory of Babylonia is full of underground fire' and once production of oil by modern methods began in the 1850s it was only a matter of time before this form of technological exploitation was initiated in the Middle East. The first Gulf oil concession was extorted from Iran in 1901, and the first oil in commercial quantities was discovered at Masjed-i-Suleiman in southern Iran in 1908.[3] At that time the USA and Russia were the main world producers and demand was a fraction of what it was later to become. But the British were quick to see the strategic significance of Gulf oil and to consolidate their hold on known resources. In 1913 the British Admiralty, headed by Winston Churchill, ordered the navy to replace coal by oil as fuel; in order to ensure future supplies the British state acquired a controlling interest in the Anglo-Persian Oil Company and allocated itself two directors, with veto powers, on the APOC board.[4] In a parallel pre-emptive move they coerced their Gulf colonies into agreeing not to grant any exploration rights to non-British companies without

410

prior British consent. Capitulationist agreements to this effect were signed by Kuwait in 1913, by Bahrain in 1914 and by the lower Gulf states and Oman in the 1920s.

When the First World War realigned the capitalist powers in the Middle East, the question of oil became an issue of inter-imperialist conflict. In 1912 the Turks had granted a western consortium concession rights in Iraq; after the war the British and French companies in the consortium expelled the representative of their defeated German rival, the Deutsche Bank, and tried to monopolize the Iraqi concession area. They forced their newly created Iraqi client monarch to confirm the concession previously extracted from the Turks, and hoped to prevent their new imperialist rival, the USA, from gaining a foothold. But North America's more vigorous capitalism had already begun its displacement of European forerunners and eventually two US firms, Standard Oil of New Jersey and Socony-Mobil, acquired a joint 23·75 per cent share in the Iraq Petroleum Company; CFP, BP, and Shell all held their own 23·75 per cent shares and the remaining 5 per cent went to the entrepreneur Gulbenkian, who had helped negotiate the deal with the Turks in 1912.

With a successful compromise in Iraq, the internationally dominant firms set up the instruments for joint pillage of the world's oil. The first part of this was the 'Red Line' agreement to curtail *competition* within a certain area: in October 1927 the French presented a map to the negotiation teams with a Red Line drawn around the area to be included in the deal. This included all the Arabian peninsula, minus Kuwait, as well as Iraq, Syria, Jordan and Turkey. A year later, in September 1928, the major companies reached a second agreement, this time on *pricing*. They agreed to combine interests and share facilities, and to fix all prices for sale outside the cartel at the level prevailing in the US ports on the Gulf of Mexico. All oil was to be priced at this level plus the cost equivalent to that of transportation to its destination from the Gulf of Mexico. The result was that a client in India or East Africa who received cheap oil direct from the Gulf would be paying a grossly inflated price both for the cost of producing the oil and for the transportation. This system lasted till

411

1944, and the companies prospered. In the 1930s the US moved farther into the Arabian peninsula. Ibn Saud, the new monarch of Saudi Arabia, granted a concession in 1933 to Standard Oil of California for the whole of 'eastern Saudi Arabia' and in 1938 oil was discovered in commercial quantities. Production began a year later and the concession was altered so that Socal was joined by a consortium of other US firms who went to make up ARAMCO – the Arabian American Oil Company: Socal, Jersey and Texaco each got 30 per cent and the remaining 10 per cent went to Mobil. In Bahrain the British were forced by pressure from the State Department to allow operation by US firms. Socal and Texaco set up the Bahrain Petroleum Company with a 50 per cent interest each; and to get around the 1914 UK–Bahrain treaty, Bapco was registered in Canada as a separate company. This did not deceive anyone, but it enabled the British to claim that the 1914 treaty had not been broken. Production of Bahrain oil began in 1934 and a refinery was built to process oil both from local wells and pumped by underground pipeline from near-by Saudi Arabia.

In Kuwait as in Bahrain American interests were obstinately opposed by the British. Originally BP and Gulf had presented rival bids to the ruler of Kuwait, but their respective governments later agreed to a compromise and in 1933 the two companies agreed to enter a 50–50 consortium, the Kuwait Oil Company. KOC signed a deal with Kuwait in 1934 and oil was discovered in 1938; but the absence of port facilities and the outbreak of the Second World War ensured that production did not begin until 1946. Once it did, the increase in output was spectacular: in the period 1950–53, when Iranian production was cut off, Kuwaiti production was increased, to fill the gap, from 17 million tons in 1950 to 46·9 million in 1954. Kuwait became the largest producer in the Gulf, only being outstripped by Saudi Arabia in 1966.

The Gulf boomed after the Second World War. Its major beneficiaries were firms already established in Saudi Arabia, Kuwait, Iraq and – initially – Iran. The rise in world demand was met largely by the Gulf; Saudi production rose from 0·5 million long tons in 1939 to 25·9 million long tons in 1950, and over the same period Iranian production rose from 9·6 million long tons to 31·8 million tons. Production also spread to areas previously untouched and to the lower Gulf. The Neutral Zone between Kuwait and Saudi Arabia was handed in 1949 to Getty Oil and the Aminoil consortium.[5] In Qatar IPC had a concession where oil was found before the Second World War. Production only began in 1949, but the rise in volume was spectacular and quickly overtook that of Qatar's neighbour Bahrain. In 1964 Shell, which had an interest on land through its share in IPC, began producing oil from wells off Qatar's shore. In Abu Dhabi two consortia had interests: the Abu Dhabi Petroleum Company, a subsidiary of IPC; and Abu Dhabi Marine Areas, a firm in which BP held two thirds and CFP one third. Production off shore began in 1962, and on shore in 1963; by 1966 Abu Dhabi was the largest producer state among Britain's Gulf colonies. The only other lower Gulf state to produce was Dubai, where Dubai Marine Areas discovered commercial quantities of oil in 1966 and began production in 1969. Dubai Marine Areas was a broader consortium than many others; BP held 33¾ per cent, CFP 16½ per cent, Continental Oil 35 per cent, Deutsche Erdöl AG 10 per cent and Sun Oil 5 per cent. Consortia were also at work in the five other coastal Omani states; but by the end of 1972 none of these had begun production.

The increase in Gulf oil production after the Second World War began to affect the position of the long-established firms, as they began to be challenged both by new rival firms and local nationalist forces. The first major crisis broke in Iran in 1951 when the nationalist premier, Mosadeq, nationalized his country's supplies of oil and expropriated the Anglo-Iranian Oil Company. The imperialist firms answered with an attempt to sabotage the Iranian economy; and after Mosadeq's ousting, in August 1953, the Shah and the oil companies came to a new agreement. AIOC, now renamed BP, lost its monopoly in Iran and had to enter a new consortium into which US firms had elbowed their way; BP now held 40 per cent, a group of US majors got 40 per cent, Shell received 14 per cent and CFP got 6 per cent.

A new arrangement followed the post-Mosadeq settlement in

413

Table 19

Crude Oil Production
(million metric tons)

	1938	1969	1970	1971	1970–71 percentage change
Iran	10·4	168·2	191·7	227·0	18·4
Saudi Arabia	0·1	148·8	176·9	222·0	25·5
Kuwait	–	129·6	137·4	145·0	5·5
Iraq	4·4	74·7	76·6	83·0	8·4
Abu Dhabi	–	28·8	33·3	44·5	33·7
Neutral Zone	–	23·5	26·7	26·4	− 1·2
Qatar	–	17·3	17·3	20·0	− 15·9
Libya	–	149·1	159·2	132·0	17·1
Algeria	–	43·8	47·3	36·5	− 22·8
Egypt	0·2	15·5*	20·9*	21·0*	–
Oman	–	16·1	17·2	14·7	− 14·4
Syria	–	3·2	4·4	6·5	33·1
Dubai	–	0·5	4·3	6·5	33·7
Tunisia	–	3·7	4·1	4·2	1·2
Bahrain	1·1	3·8	3·8	3·8	–
Turkey	–	3·6	3·5	3·3	− 6·0
Israel	–	0·1	0·08	0·07	− 12·0
Morocco	–	0·0	0·05	0·02	− 60·0
M.E. Total	16·2	829·8	924·5	996·4	7·8
M.E. percentage World Total	7·7	38·9	39·6	40·4	0·8
Venezuela	28·1	187·6	193·2	184·0	− 4·8
Nigeria	–	27·3	53·4	74·0	38·5
Indonesia	7·4	36·7	42·1	44·0	4·5
U.S.A.	170·0	526·2	533·6	532·0	− 0·3
U.S.S.R.	37·7	333·3	353·3	378·0	7·0
Canada	0·9	62·8	63·7	77·0	20·0
Mexico	5·5	23·7	25·0	28·0	12·0
Argentina	2·4	18·6	20·5	22·0	10·0
Trinidad and Tobago	2·4	8·2	7·3	7·3	–
World total	280·5	2,134·5	2,336·2	2,464·7	5·5

*includes ouput of Israeli-occupied Sinai

Source: *The Middle East and North Africa 1972–3.*

Iran. It involved partnership of several concerns with the National Iranian Oil Company, a state enterprise set up by Mosadeq but used for different purposes by the Shah. In 1957 the Italian state company ENI set up a joint company with the NIOC through its subsidiary AGIP. Under this arrangement the Italian company was to pay the whole of the exploration cost. If oil was found – and it later was – AGIP was to be repaid 50 per cent of the initial cost; it would also receive half the oil, paying taxes on it of 50 per cent, and would sell the other half for NIOC. In effect this gave the Iranian government a 75–25 share of the profits. It was a breakthrough in the kind of deal being signed in the area; Iran went on to make similar arrangements with Standard Oil of Indiana and with Shell, while Saudi Arabia and Kuwait achieved comparable bargains on a smaller scale.

The next nationalization crisis in the Gulf took place in Iraq. The IPC had two fellow businesses owned by the same consortium: the Basra Petroleum Company and the Mosul Petroleum Company. In all, these concerns had a 160,000-square-mile concession. But they developed only a very small part of it; and in 1961 the government of General Qasim passed 'Law 80', which expropriated 99·5 per cent of the whole concession area. The land nationalized in 1961 included the North Rumaila fields, which belonged to IPC; and it took until 1967 for IPC and the Iraqi government to come to a partial agreement. They clashed again in 1972 when the IPC cut back its oil exports to the Mediterranean; production fell by 28 per cent in the first four months of 1972 but the IPC refused to satisfy the Iraqi government; its Kirkuk fields were nationalized, on 1 June 1972, by 'Law 69', and a legal battle broke out. While Iraq was able to sign an agreement in 1972 with the Soviet Union for the sale of oil from the North Rumaila field, it was still forced to negotiate with the IPC for lack of an outlet for the oil it had nationalized. In March 1973 IPC and the Iraq government finally reached an agreement; outstanding claims were settled and IPC retained control of the Basra field in return for a commitment to increase production to 80 million tons a year by 1976. Conflicts of this kind, between long-established firms and local governments,

Table 20

Major Oil Companies in the Gulf 1971
(million metric tons)

OPEC States	Esso	Shell	BP	Gulf	Texaco	Socal	Mobil	CFP	Others	Total
Iran	14·5	29·1	83·8	14·5	14·5	14·5	14·5	12·5	26·3	227·0
Saudi Arabia	66·6	–	–	–	66·6	66·6	22·2	–	–	222·0
Kuwait	–	–	72·5	72·5	–	–	–	–	–	145·0
Iraq	9·8	19·7	19·7	–	–	–	9·8	19·7	4·3	83·0
Abu Dhabi	3·25	6·5	17·8	–	–	–	3·25	12·2	1·4*	44·5
Partitioned Zone	–	–	–	–	–	–	–	–	26·4	26·4
Qatar	1·1	12·5	2·4	–	–	–	1·1	2·4	0·5*	20·0
Total	95·2	67·8	196·2	87·0	81·1	81·1	50·8	46·8	58·9	–

* Represents 5 per cent Gulbenkian interest marketed by major partners in IPC, ADPC and QPC. In practice these figures can be counted as part of the major companies' production share.

Source: as for Table 19.

provided the opportunity for other firms to enter. Areas previously unallocated, or withdrawn from the original concession-aires, were made over by local governments in new agreements with Japanese interests and US 'independents'. A number of existing owners also sold off some of their concessions to new firms; in January 1973 BP announced that it was going to sell 45 per cent of its interest in Abu Dhabi Marine Areas, for the sum of £330 million. Despite these changes, however, the eight majors retained their dominant hold.

Price Rises and Participation

The major change for the dominant eight firms derived not from a challenge by rival capitalist firms, but from adjustment to a new system of partnership with local governments. Before 1945 the oil companies had paid the governments a concession sum (£10,000 to Iran under the 1901 deal, £400,000 to Iraq in 1927, £50,000 to Saudi Arabia in 1933), and a royalty of four gold shillings per ton of oil produced. Otherwise they were free to do as they wanted. They were untaxed; they had huge areas of concession at their disposal; they staffed their firms with foreign nationals; and they exerted direct political power in the producer countries. This ceased to be the case after 1945, when, as a result of a similar change in Venezuela, companies agreed to pay the local governments 50 per cent of profits. This 50–50 arrangement was introduced in Saudi Arabia, Iraq and Kuwait and, in a variant form, in Iran. Here profits were defined by deducting the production cost per barrel from what was known as the 'posted price', an artificially invented gauge designed for tax reference purposes.

This still gave the companies enormous advantages. They were able to fix the posted price well below the real price they received. American firms were also able to deduct taxes paid to Middle Eastern governments from taxes raised in the US.[6] In addition the companies were effectively able to avoid their original royalty payments by deducting royalties from the profits on which the 50–50 deal was based. The local governments began,

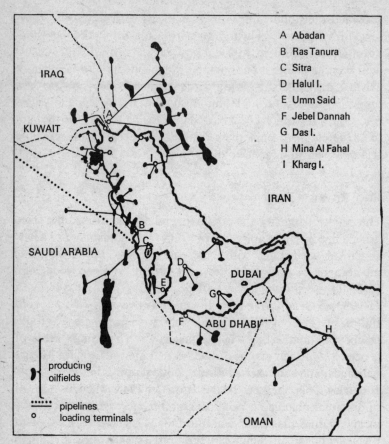

A Abadan
B Ras Tanura
C Sitra
D Halul I.
E Umm Said
F Jebel Dannah
G Das I.
H Mina Al Fahal
I Kharg I.

IRAQ

KUWAIT

SAUDI ARABIA

IRAN

DUBAI

ABU DHABI

OMAN

producing
oilfields

•••••• pipelines
○ loading terminals

Map 10 Oil Production in the Gulf

in time, to negotiate for adjustments in this system. In 1960 the Organization of Petroleum Exporting Countries was founded to counter the continued drop in posted prices, which the companies had been justifying in the name of an 'oil glut' – created by themselves – and by the mid 60s O P E C was able to check this decline.[7] In 1964 and 1968 the companies agreed to a system known as 'royalty expensing', whereby royalties were deducted, as expenses, from total income, rather than from profits.

The next stage came in 1970–71, when the O P E C countries negotiated collectively in Tehran for increases in the posted price and for guaranteed rises in subsequent years. A price increase won by Libya demonstrated the weakness of the companies and encouraged the Gulf states. The Shah of Iran had been negotiating similar one-year deals since 1967 and in February 1971 a delegation from Iran, Iraq and Saudi Arabia reached an agreement on behalf of all Gulf countries. The posted price rose from \$1·79 per barrel to \$2·17 and was to continue rising by 2·5 per cent and 5 c. for each successive year up to and including 1975. In return, the governments agreed to make no more price demands, even if other exporters – for example, in North Africa – did manage to get higher prices. The Tehran agreement cost the companies an extra \$3,000 million in 1971 alone, and the cost of the 1971–5 rises was estimated at another \$2,000 million for each further year. Meanwhile, in August 1971, Nixon devalued the dollar and the producer countries demanded a rise in the posted price to compensate for the fall in value of the amounts agreed to in Tehran. In January 1972 a new round of talks in Geneva raised posted prices in the Gulf by an immediate 8·49 per cent, to counteract the U S devaluation. After the second U S devaluation of early 1973, prices were raised by a further 11·9 per cent.[8] However, these price rises were still only adjustments to the classic concession system, and would have left overall power in the hands of the big companies, whose internal financial arrangements and executive decisions were still made in secret.

In 1972 O P E C went a stage further than its previous demands, and began to negotiate for *participation* in the running of the oil industry in their own states. Up to then the national oil companies of Iran, Iraq, Kuwait, Saudi Arabia and Abu Dhabi had signed some deals with oil companies, while the big concessions had remained untouched. In February 1971 Algeria had nationalized C F P and E R A P, the two French firms that dominated its economy, and after negotiations had taken a 51 per cent share in their operations. In October 1972 the Gulf states of Saudi Arabia, Kuwait, Abu Dhabi and Qatar negotiated a similar arrangement with the oil companies operating in the Gulf. Government companies were to get an immediate 20 per cent share in local operations; this was to rise to 25 per cent in 1975, by 5 per cent in each successive year, and in 1983 local participation was to be 51 per cent. Each government was to reach a separate agreement with its local concessionaires on the compensation to be paid and on the price at which the companies would buy back the oil – called 'participation crude' – from national enterprises.

All of these changes appeared timid after the unprecedented upheavals of 1973. The Arab oil embargo and the simultaneous price rises produced international results of a kind never seen before in such a transparent and universal form: the fragile international monetary system, which had limped through various crises without throwing off the Bretton Woods structure, was brought to a new head; inter-imperialist contradictions, especially between the U S and the E E C, were inflamed by divergent policies towards the Arab world; within the major capitalist states class conflict and economic recession, already increasing, were further exacerbated by the shortages and price rises – a blunt demonstration of the fact that the prosperity and inter-class peace of the developed world was historically based on obtaining raw materials at prices below their market value. Most important of all, the crisis of 1973 represented an enormous shift of wealth, and reflected a parallel shift of power, between the advanced capitalist and oil-producing states.

Four different questions were involved: price, ownership, supply and the disposal of revenue. Although the changing nature of each question coincided with the October Arab–Israeli war, the tendency and rationale behind each change derived from economic factors, and the Arab–Israeli war merely precipitated and accentuated processes that were inherent in the logic of capitalist competition. First, price: the producer states realized by mid-1973 that they held a monopoly and could force the price of oil up. The emergence of the 'energy crisis' in early 1973 proved as much. As a consequence, the price of oil was raised in October to $5·09 per barrel and in December to $11·65 per barrel, in effect quadrupling the price of oil from its earlier level and quadrupling the oil deficits of the advanced capitalist consumers. The income of Gulf states was therefore expected to rise from a pre-October estimate of $10,000 million to a post-December estimate of $40,000 million. It is evident that the motivation if not the timing behind these price rises was independent of the Arab–Israeli dispute, because in early 1974, when Saudi Arabia was organizing a *moratorium* on price rises, the Shah of Iran was calling for a further *increase*. Despite the differences, all oil producers insisted that the price for oil find its 'market level'.

The question of ownership was again one where economic rationale predominated. The 1972 participation agreements were not ratified by the governments that signed them: it was soon apparent that they represented ineffective holding operations by oil companies that should have had nothing to fear by allowing a wholly new system to come into operation. The sharpened political climate of 1973 put an end to the 'ownership' illusion; as a result, the governments of Kuwait, Saudi Arabia, Qatar and Abu Dhabi took majority holdings in the oil production of their own states, and in return guaranteed the oil companies what they most needed – supply. Here again, the Arab–Israeli question was secondary, since the Iranians had already negotiated such an agreement earlier in the year. Within the third question, of supply, there *was* a political aspect: the ban on oil exports to the U S and Holland, and the 25 per cent reduction in oil output were part of an Arab attempt to exert pressure on Israel. But the reduction also had an economic basis: that it was irrational for states that were unable to absorb their revenues to produce above a certain level. For Iran, Algeria and Iraq conservation was not important, but for Saudi Arabia and the smaller Gulf states it was. Nevertheless, despite this materialist reason for limiting supplies, the restrictions on oil production were lifted in early 1974 – long before the Israelis had fulfilled the original conditions for the oil boycott being ended. It seemed that the Egyptians and the Saudis, who had negotiated the lifting of the Arab oil ban, were worried lest their action do permanent damage to the advanced capitalist economies, and were prepared to override their own interests in order to reassure and reinforce their allies in Washington, Tokyo and the capitals of western Europe. This judgement applied above all to the question of disposing of oil reserves. Those countries unable to invest and spend their new revenues showed no reluctance to dispose of them within the structures of a capitalist world that was now willing, after an initial surprise and reluctance, to welcome its new partners into a restabilized system. The price rises certainly represented a massive shift in economic power: the $500,000 million expected to flow to the Middle East producers in the following decade equalled three times the capitalization of the City of London and 5/8 that of Wall Street. As the authoritative *Middle East Economic Digest* put it: '. . . the oil producers of the Middle East are on the whole a force for economic stability once their interests and their paramount importance in today's world are recognized'.

Imperialist Profits and the Energy Crisis

The events of 1972 and 1973 were seen in many parts of the world as a great victory for the countries of the Middle East and a defeat for the major imperialist powers – a view expressed not only by the Gulf countries, but also by the oil companies themselves. Conversely, some revolutionary critics thought it made no difference at all and that the Gulf countries merely remained straightforwardly neo-colonial clients of imperialism. Neither of these analyses was accurate. The price rises and the ownership agreements certainly represented substantial changes in the allocation of the surplus gained from selling oil, and oil products, in the advanced capitalist countries. They involved a new political role for producer states. But this was not an anti-imperialist victory; it was a change that could well stabilize the capitalist system as a whole and accentuate the oppression of the people of the oil-producing countries in particular. To show this it is necessary to examine the different ways in which imperialism benefits from the pillage of Gulf oil. In the boom period from 1945 to the mid 1960s, imperialist profits from the Gulf came in the simplest way. Gulf oil was cheap, but was sold at a high price. Geological differences made the cost of extracting oil vary enormously: in the Gulf the price per barrel ranged from 5–6c. in Kuwait to 35c. for offshore drilling at Dubai. Venezuelan oil cost between 50c. and $1 a barrel; while in the U S or the North Sea a barrel costs $3 or more. In 1972 investment per barrel a day of production capacity was $100 on shore in the Gulf and $2,000–$2,500 off the Scottish coast. The cost of transporting oil by tanker and refining it does not vary; hence the profit from oil derives mainly from the gap between its production cost and the price at which it is sold.[9] Estimations of profit from Gulf oil have to be rough since the oil companies themselves do not reveal figures; but one calculation for the period up to 1960 gives a picture of how operations worked.[10] According to this estimate the average price of Gulf crude was a third the price of Venezuelan crude during the period 1948–60, and was therefore even less that of US crude. To calculate profitability, gross income was divided by net assets; this indicated that in the period 1948–60 oil companies in the Gulf enjoyed an average rate of return on capital of 111 per cent. When royalty and tax payments to host governments were deducted the rates of return were still high: from 61 per cent in 1948–9 they rose to 72 per cent in 1958–60, giving an average return of 67 per cent. The comparable figure over the same period for Venezuela was 21 per cent and in the US the rate of return dropped from 16 per cent in 1948–9 to 9·6 per cent in 1958–9.

This cheapness enabled imperialist firms to import low-cost oil and save their own country foreign exchange. When the Suez Canal closures cut off Gulf oil in 1956 and 1967 Britain had to buy oil from Venezuela and its import bill greatly increased. The 1967 closure thus contributed to devaluation of sterling in

November of that year. But Britain, the US and France also benefited directly from the profitability of Gulf oil in that it very much increased invisible earnings by their oil firms overseas. These companies were registered in specific countries but produced, refined and sold their oil elsewhere: ARAMCO, for example, was an all-American consortium; but in 1965 only 9·7 per cent of its production went to North America; 43·7 per cent was sold in Europe, 32·8 per cent in Asia, 6 per cent in South America, 4·6 per cent in Australia and 3·2 per cent in Africa. Since the US produced most of its own oil, other American countries operating in the Gulf had a similar system; and both Mobil and Socal got 50 per cent of their profit from Gulf sales; the British and French firms, too, had a sales network far beyond their own boundaries.

Estimates of direct benefit through profit flows from the Gulf to the imperialist metropolises are again hard to come by. Shell and BP were estimated in the 1950s and early 1960s to produce a third of British income from overseas investment at a time when nearly all their crude came from the Gulf. Their relative contribution subsequently declined to a fifth, but they remained Britain's number one invisible earners; and Gulf operations alone were estimated to bring in £200 million a year. In 1967 a British government White Paper estimated that 40 per cent of the import costs of oil were offset by British oil company earnings. Figures for the US also give a clear picture: in 1968 US oil firms in the Gulf and Libya together earned around $1·3 billion; of this only $263 million was reinvested, leaving over $1 billion to be repatriated to the USA. According to one estimate, in 1966 oil accounted for 30 per cent of all US foreign investment, and for 60 per cent of all profits from the developing world. While the latter figure did include Venezuela, the Gulf share must have been nonetheless very high. These profits moved back to the metropolitan countries were available either to bolster more costly oil production elsewhere or for general expansion of the capitalist economy by 'diversification' of the oil companies into other fields.[11]

The price increases of the 1960s and the subsequent participation agreements changed this original system of pillage; a larger share of the profit went not to the oil company but to the producer governments. But even though the companies had to pay more and lost some control, they did gain security of supply. Moreover, price rises were passed on to consumers, and Gulf rises made operations in high cost areas, like the North Sea, more profitable. Nor did these changes take money from the capitalist west to give to the Middle East instead. The extra moneys and power acquired by Gulf countries were indeed diverted through Riyadh, Tehran or Kuwait; but they found their way back to the west nonetheless. The most obvious means was the purchase by Gulf countries of western goods; lacking productive capacity themselves, these countries spent their extra money on the products of Europe and North America. Luxury goods, manufactured imports of all kinds and of course weapons were the means by which the moneys lost to the oil companies were paid back to the imperialist countries. The rise in Gulf incomes led to a rush of carpet-baggers and sharks of all kinds, hoping to siphon off the newly granted riches of the Gulf countries. The profits from oil went to construction firms, Lockheed and the British Aircraft Corporation, rather than uniquely to Shell and Standard Oil of New Jersey. The overall result still benefited the capitalist economies of the west. Gulf oil was no longer so cheap for the oil companies but the increase in cost represented not a rise in the money needed for investment, but a change in the size and allocation of the surplus. During the crisis of late 1973 the major oil companies all complained about the deleterious effects of the rise in posted prices; yet their price increases at the petrol pump more than covered this, and profits for 1973 showed unprecedented increases. Exxon's rose to $2,440 million, a rise of 59 per cent on 1972; Texaco's rose by 45 per cent, Mobil's by 47 per cent, Gulf's by 60 per cent, Socal's by 40 per cent, Shell's by 28 per cent. It was a changed world, but they were hardly bankrupt or even short of cash.

The producer countries helped in several other ways to re-cycle profits back to the imperialist west. In the 1950s and 1960s Gulf countries were encouraged by the workings of the 'sterling area' to bank their unspent revenues in Britain as 'sterling balances', thus bolstering the faltering British imperialist financial system with added deposits. Private Gulf investors were also encouraged to bank in London. Although figures for such investment were kept a close secret by both public and private investors, some indications emerged. In 1967 Kuwait was estimated to have a total of £979 million invested in London:[12] £311 million came from the government's International Reserves, £48 million from the Currency Board and the Kuwait Fund for Arab Economic Development, £190 million was from the four Kuwaiti commercial banks and £430 million was from private Kuwaiti investors. Middle Eastern sterling balances – deposits, that is, with the Bank of England – rose from £286 million in 1962 to £534 million in 1971, and despite the rundown of the sterling area after 1968 unspent revenues continued to flow into London. With official British gold and foreign currency reserves at around £1,000 million in the 1960s, Kuwait alone could have bankrupted Britain by pulling out its public and private deposits; and even the withdrawal of the sterling balances could have crippled Britain's foreign exchange position.[13] Projections for the rest of the 1970s, made in early 1973, outlined a dramatic increase in this form of capital flow. With estimated Gulf oil income at $400 billions between 1973 and 1980, it was reckoned that only $200 billion of this would be spent on purchases and local investment. The remainder would be diverted back to the west, to be banked as reserves or invested in capitalist enterprises.[14] It was reckoned that Saudi Arabia alone, with up to $200 billion, would have larger reserves than the totals of the US and Japan combined. Such a prospect aroused intense fears in the minds of western financiers; when the dollar was forced by speculation to devalue, in February 1973, 'Arab' money was blamed for this development – without evidence – and the possibility of a future wrecking operation was raised. The Arab states themselves were quick to reassure their western debtors that they had no such intentions in mind. As revenues rose, the Gulf countries increasingly poured funds directly into investments in the capitalist west, where profits were often more readily available. Given the enormous revenues of these Middle Eastern states, it was quite possible that around the year A.D. 2500, when Gulf oil had run out, some of the former oil-producing countries, without major productive resources, would be able to live easily of earnings from investments in more productive countries. Saudi Arabian revenues were paid into accounts run by Chase Manhattan and Morgan Guaranty, while Abu Dhabi's long-term investments were handled by London-based William Glynn & Co. 'Down-stream' investment was encouraged by the oil companies and part of the Saudi proposal to boost its production for the US in the 1970s involved the investment by Saudi Arabia of 20 per cent of its revenues in the US. These developments were accompanied by the growth of joint banking ventures linking Arab, European and other consortia.[15]

In addition to locating their revenues in the west, these Gulf countries also began to spend in other ways that had a stabilizing effect on capitalism. In the Middle East itself several Gulf states actively aided imperialism by subsidizing pro-western regimes: Saudi Arabia poured money into Jordan and Lebanon, as well as aiding the military campaigns of counter-revolutionaries in North Yemen and in Oman; Kuwait spread the funds of her Kuwait Fund for Arab Economic Development throughout the Arab world, and shored up shaky regimes in the lower Gulf; and Iran and Saudi Arabia both used their moneys to build up powerful military machines designed to crush any revolutionary threat. The counter-revolutionary war of the Sultan of Oman depended entirely on his oil revenues.

The overriding reason for the oil companies' agreement to grant ownership to the producer countries was the 'energy crisis' that became suddenly apparent in the industrialized countries in the early 1970s. In 1970, world dependence on Gulf supplies was already marked; Europe imported 50 per cent of its oil from the Gulf, Britain over 55 per cent[16] and Japan 85 per cent. The US war effort in Indo-China depended almost entirely on Gulf oil (mainly Iranian and Saudi) for its fuel needs. But the world's reliance on the Gulf was bound to increase, since, while it supplied around 35 per cent of world production it contained

Table 21

Oil in the Middle East and North Africa
Proven Reserves
(million tons)

	End 1971	World percentage
Saudi Arabia	19,904	23·0
Kuwait	9,044*	10·5
Iran	7,602	9·0
Iraq	4,903	5·5
Partitioned Zone	3,336	4·0
Abu Dhabi	2,596	3·0
Qatar	822	1·0
Libya	3,425	4·0
Algeria	1,678	2·0
Syria	1,000	1·0
Oman	712	1·0
Egypt	547	0·75
Dubai	212	0·5
Bahrain	86	0·01
M.E. Total	56,059	66·0
Venezuela	1,904	2·25
Nigeria	1,600	2·0
Indonesia	1,425	1·5
USA	5,900	7·0
Soviet Area	13,400	16·0
Canada	1,300	1·5
Argentina	342	0·5
Mexico	616	1·0
Trinidad and Tobago	70	0·01
North Sea	405	0·5
World Total	85,442	+1% over 1970

* No official estimates have been released. The government commissioned a survey after suggestions in the National Assembly that Kuwait's reserves may only total 3,000 million tons.

Source: as for Table 19.

over 60 per cent of known reserves. With world oil consumption expected to double between 1970 and 1980 from around 40 million barrels a day to 80–100 million, the only place where the oil could come from was the Gulf.

The 'energy crisis' had significant variations in different countries. Japan, which had to import all its oil, tried to diversify its supplies by exploration in South-East Asia and by imports from China and the Soviet Union.[17] Europe developed new oil- and gas-fields in the North Sea, and estimates of their daily output ranged from 1 million to 3 million barrels a day, with total reserves estimated at between 3,000 million and 5,000 million barrels.[18] European consumption of oil in 1972 was around 15 million barrels a day and by the mid 1980s was likely to rise to 23 million, so although the North Sea fields were a significant economic development and a definite saving on Europe's foreign exchange, they were able, at best, to supply 12 per cent of Europe's future needs. Even if, as appeared likely, the oil companies were deliberately understating their reserves, North Sea production could only meet a fraction of the increase in Europe's demand.

For the USA, the situation was more serious. With 6 per cent of the world's population, it consumed 33 per cent of the world's energy. It had historically provided nearly all its own oil, and in 1959 the Eisenhower administration had fixed imports of oil by sea – that is, excluding Canada – at 12·8 per cent of domestic production. This protection of more expensive domestic producers was combined with other devices which *in toto* were estimated to loot US purchasers of $3·5 billion a year.[19] In the early 1970s this situation deteriorated rapidly, and in 1972–3 the US experienced fuel shortages. Production levelled off in the USA, and began to decline while demand rose. In 1972 demand increased by 7 per cent from around 16·5 million barrels a day, as US production fell by 1 per cent to 9·5 million barrels a day. With demand expected to continue rising at around 5 per cent a year, the existing 5,700 million tons of reserves, including those in Alaska, would last only another seven or eight years.

New deposits were found in Alaska, and once the 789-mile

Alyeska pipeline came into operation this oil, too, would be available for U S consumption.[20] Moreover, the higher the cost of Middle Eastern oil and the higher the price at the gas station itself, the more it was possible for companies to extract oil from high-cost wells and offshore deposits previously ruled out as too expensive. Official alarm at the 'energy crisis' was certainly in part an orchestrated attempt by the oil companies and the U S government to justify a rise in oil prices, together with other changes, including possible rationing and the encouragement of substitutes such as coal and nuclear energy. But a problem did remain, in that by 1985 the U S might have to import up to half of its fuel. In 1970, when Nixon started to relax the 1959 import quota system, it had a fuel balance of trade deficit of around $2,000 million; the National Petroleum Council calculated that by 1985 this deficit could have risen to $30,000 million – up to twelve times the size of the U S balance of payments deficit in 1972.[21] Following the oil embargo of 1973–4 the U S government declared its intention of counteracting its dependence on foreign petroleum sources. Added research into alternative sources of energy, and extraction of oil from sources made more attractive by the rise in posted prices, were the two means explored. Nevertheless, whatever the long-run contribution of Gulf oil to the U S economy's energy supplies, the dependence was bound to increase – both in terms of imports of crude and processed petroleum, and in terms of the contribution made by U S oil companies to the overall profit picture of North American capitalism.

Class Formation in the Producer States

Politically, the 1973 'energy crisis' and oil embargo intensified imperialist commitment to their junior allies in the Middle East and aroused anxiety as to how these allies might use their new power. The governments of the Gulf had become of vital importance to the stability of the whole capitalist system and were receiving every support that Europe, Japan and the U S could give them. Increased revenues were part of this support, making the Gulf states recipients of enormous sums that both stabilized their own domestic situations and helped increase the circulation of money throughout the capitalist world.

Table 22

Government Oil Revenues
(million US dollars)

	1962	1964	1966	1968	1970	1973*	1974*
Iran	334	470	593	817	1,076	3,885	14,930
Saudi Arabia	415	561	777	966	1,200	4,915	19,400
Kuwait	526	655	707	766	897	7,945	7,945
Iraq	267	353	394	476	513		
Abu Dhabi	3	12	100	153	231	1,035	4,800
Qatar	56	66	92	110	122		
Libya	39	197	476	952	1,295		
Algeria	n.a.	n.a.	145	200	280		

* Estimated. In 1971 posted prices and tax rates were increased in the Tehran, Tripoli and Baghdad agreements.

Source: as for Table 19; *The Times*, 30 January 1974.

It appeared that in the years between 1973 and 1980 these revenues would rise much higher and that an estimated $400 billion would flow into the Gulf states. Even by 1970 these countries had been transformed by the increase in their revenues. For some, oil constituted not only the sole source of foreign exchange and of government revenue, but also well over 90 per cent of the GDP.[22] Even in such states as Iraq, Iran and Saudi Arabia, which had sizeable populations, oil was by far the main origin of wealth and likely to remain so. Diversification projects were certainly under way, but these countries had little immediate incentive to reduce their dependence on oil; even Bahrain, whose reserves were likely to last only until around 1990, was dependent on oil and gas piped from Saudi Arabia. The barrenness of the land and the absence of any comparable source of income made other economic activities unattractive to the ruling groups in most of these countries.

The social effects of oil varied. In Iran and Iraq the existing royalist military regimes, the Pahlavis and the Hashemites, had used oil to suppress their predominantly agricultural peoples and build parasitic state structures; when the Iraqi monarchy was overthrown, in 1958, the subsequent nationalist military juntas continued to use oil revenues as the economic basis for their rule and differed from similar équipes in Syria and Egypt only in the origin of their income. In some Gulf states – Kuwait, Bahrain, Dubai – the ruling families had long based their prosperity on trade and control of pearling, and they used their sudden rise in income to diversify their dependence without interrupting control, except by incorporating other merchants into the state. In other states, such as Qatar and Abu Dhabi, the ruling families had been extremely poor and without any commercial role; for them the change was even greater and in both cases – in Abu Dhabi in 1966, and in Qatar in 1972 – these retentive rulers were replaced, with imperialist encouragement, by more expansive members of their family. In Saudi Arabia, which differed from all the aforesaid states, oil revenues went into the pockets of a family who ruled a vast desert kingdom and whose pre-oil power had rested on military dominance over nomadic tribes and scattered and impoverished peasantry.

The production of oil comprised a relatively isolated sector within these countries' economies; the capital came from abroad, and until the 1970s most of the profits went abroad too; labour was mostly imported, and as a further safety measure, even the unskilled workers were brought in from outside. Production companies often went so far as to bring in food and water through separate concessions; and little was done to diminish the insulation of the oil economy from the pre-industrial agrarian, desert or coastal economies of the producer states.

Since oil production is itself a capital-intensive operation, the actual employment of local labour in the oil industry is far less than the importance of oil for the economies as a whole. Oil exploration involves negotiations with local populations; the construction of oil installations and pipelines and loading areas also employs some unskilled labour. But the oil proletariat created by the boom has always formed a minority of the working population; and as capital intensity grew, actual employment fell. Industrial employment was low in these countries, and most of the working class were employed in services and in construction. This, together with the ethnic divisions within the working class and the absence of trades union traditions, made them more vulnerable to repression and control. Whereas in Aden the newly created working class in the 1950s was relatively homogeneous (North and South Yemeni) and could strike at the centre of the Colony's economy (the port), and was also being mobilized by Arab nationalism against British imperialism, none of these favourable conditions existed in the oil-producing states. From the start, the growth of the oil industry led to an influx of labour. This took two forms: the first was the flow to Arab Gulf states of migrant labourers who came to work in construction and other menial jobs, either where labour was short, in Abu Dhabi and Qatar, or where the local population were acquiring a privileged and parasitic position, as in Kuwait. These migrants came from the Yemens, Oman, Iran, Iraq, Pakistan, India and farther afield. Their immigration was favoured by the companies, who saw in them a more controllable labour force than the local population. The second kind of immigration was the importation by the companies of 'skilled' personnel, whom

Table 23

Employment in the Oil Industry (approx.)

Country	1957	1970	Total employment 1970
Saudi Arabia	20,000	15,000	1,200,000
Iran	48,000	40,000	7,000,000
Iraq	15,000		
Kuwait	8,000	7,500	200,000
Bahrain	8,500	4,300	60,300
Qatar	4,500		
Oman	–	4,000	100,000

Sources: *Middle East Journal*, Spring 1958 for 1957 figures on employment; *The Middle East and North Africa 1972–3* for 1970 figures.

they claimed could not be found locally. This often masked a preference for imported personnel and the initial refusal to train local people for fear that they would then demand control.[23] Senior personnel throughout the oil industry continued to be recruited from Europe and North America.

The proportion and origin of the migrant labour varied. In Saudi Arabia they were mostly North Yemenis, numbering possibly as many as 400,000, and concentrated in construction. In Kuwait immigrants officially outnumbered Kuwaitis by 387,000 to 346,000 in the 1970 census. The official figures understated the situation, and the disproportion continued to increase; around 50,000 of the workers in Kuwait were Palestinians employed in white-collar jobs; but many were Iraqis, Iranians, Omanis and south Asians, living in appalling squalor. In Bahrain the 1970 census showed nearly 20 per cent of the population to be non-Bahrainis: 15,000 were from south Asia, 10,000 were Omanis and 5,000 were Iranians. In Qatar, Abu Dhabi and Dubai the population rose by immigration so rapidly in the late 1960s, that the numbers of immigrants were almost impossible to calculate, amounting in the latter two to a possible 75 per cent of the population. All these states gave exclusive privileges to their own nationals and practised maltreatment and arbitrary expulsion of the migrant workers. All the states also favoured Arab as opposed to non-Arab immigrants, in an attempt to preserve their 'Arabism'.[24]

The oil revenues both accentuated differences in wealth within the Gulf countries and created a proletariat, however small it might at first have been. At the same time they developed the base of the ruling groups and the determination of imperialism to support these regimes. Expanded state structures gave salaries, if not employment, to thousands. Oil accentuated class differences within the countries and the importance of these differences for the world. In all Gulf countries trades unions were ruthlessly suppressed and a succession of strikes from the 1940s onwards led to arrests, murders, deportations and exile. In all these countries, too, the oil companies worked hand in hand with the regime to crush any independent workers' movement and through their own imperialist governments gave military aid and advice to the newly enriched local rulers.

The task that confronted the working classes of these states, both in the oil-fields and other new industries and in the long-existing peasantry, was that of wresting control of oil from their oppressors – the local regimes and the imperialist oil companies. This was a democratic and a national task, but it was one that could only be achieved through a socialist struggle, since the producer bourgeoisies were tied to imperialism, and the pre-bourgeois regime in Saudi Arabia was even less capable of breaking its ties with the west or of establishing democracy. So far, changes in price and ownership had involved incorporation of local rulers into world capitalism.

Notes

1. For general accounts of the oil industry see Christopher Tugendhat, *Oil: The Biggest Business*, London, 1968; and Peter R. Odell, *Oil and World Power*, London, 1970. An earlier, brilliant assault on the oil companies is found in Harvey O'Connor, *World Crisis in Oil*, London, 1962. The manoeuvrings of oil companies inside the US are documented in Robert Engler, *The Politics of Oil*, Chicago, 1967, while the monopolies' bullying of oil-consuming countries is analysed in Michael Tanzer, *The Political Economy of International Oil and the Underdeveloped Countries*, London, 1969.

2. The Standard Oil Trust was established by the Rockefellers in 1882 but dissolved under anti-trust legislation in 1911. Since then its largest component, Standard Oil of New Jersey, has operated under a number of names; it was most commonly known as 'Esso' (i.e. 'SO'); but because of anti-trust limitations it also marketed in parts of the US as Humble Oil. In the early 1970s it tried to get one unified brand name and fixed on the word 'Enco' until it discovered that this was the Japanese for a stalled car. In the end it came up with 'Exxon'.

3. The history of Middle Eastern oil is documented in detail in S. H. Longrigg, *Oil in the Middle East*, third edition, London, 1968. Harvey O'Connor, op. cit., provides the political dimension that Longrigg omits.

4. In 1933 Persia became known officially as Iran; hence the APOC became the AIOC. After Mosadeq nationalized AIOC in 1951 it changed its name to British Petroleum – BP. The French CFP has a similar structure to BP: 40 per cent of its shares are held by the French government which thereby occupies a commanding position.

5. The 2,000-square-mile Neutral Zone was demarcated in 1922 by

Kuwait and Saudi Arabia. The Aminoil (American Independent Oil Company) consortium contained the following US firms: Philipps Petroleum 37·34 per cent, Signal Oil and Gas Company 33·57 per cent, Ashland Oil and Refining 14·13 per cent and five others with smaller shares.

6. For example, in 1956 when ARAMCO grossed $749 million it paid Saudi Arabia $80 million in royalties and $200 million in tax for the 360 million barrels of crude produced. The royalty was deducted from ARAMCO's taxable income obligations to the US, while the tax was a foreign tax credit set directly against the amount due as American income tax. ARAMCO paid no US taxes in its Arabian venture, while retaining $280 million as its reward. Engler, op. cit., p. 224.

7. OPEC's original members were Iran, Venezuela, Saudi Arabia, Kuwait and Iraq. Others joined later: Qatar (1961), Libya and Indonesia (1962), Abu Dhabi (1967), Algeria (1969), Nigeria (1971) and Trinidad and Tobago (1972). The criterion for admission was that countries export a minimum of 20 million tons per annum.

8. In 1972 tax calculations on a standard barrel of Gulf oil being exported by ARAMCO were as follows: ARAMCO deducted 11c. production costs and a 12·5 per cent royalty of $0·297 from the posted price of $2·373, giving company profits of $1·966. This was taxed at 55 per cent, giving Saudi Arabia $1·081 and the company $0·885; with the royalty and tax added together Saudi Arabia got a total of $1·378.

9. Other super-profits come from shipping: the tanker owners did extremely well in the years after 1967 when demand rose unexpectedly high and the Suez Canal was closed. In 1969 for example Onassis made an estimated $4·2 million by leasing a single 200,000-ton tanker to Shell for a trip between the Gulf and Europe: this one voyage paid for around one third of the ship's total cost of $13 million. See 'The Lush Era of the Tanker Tycoons', *Newsweek*, 19 October 1970.

10. Charles Issawi and Mohammad Yeganeh, *The Economics of Middle Eastern Oil*, London, 1962, Chapter 5, ' Returns on Investment'. For a later estimate based on a different method see Zuheyr Mikdashi, 'The Profitability of Middle East Oil Ventures, a Historical Approach' in M. A. Cook, ed., *Studies in the Economic History of the Middle East*, London, 1970.

11. The Chairman of Gulf, speaking in 1955 to a US Senate Committee, stated:

'Kuwait does give Gulf remarkable profits. Against those profits which we have been able to retain in the company, we have put quite a number, hundreds of millions of dollars, into exploration here in the US and into the development of our reserves which would not have been possible for us to do but for our income from out there.'

Quoted in Edith Penrose, *The Large International Firm in Developing Countries*, London, 1968, p. 120.

12. *The Times*, 7 June 1967.

13. Another British colony in Asia, Hong Kong, played a similar role

and held an estimated £750 million in sterling balances in London. See *Hong Kong: Britian's Last Colonial Stronghold*, issued by the Association for Radical East Asian Studies, London, in 1972. At times this system backfired; as in 1957, when speculative money poured out of the imperialist net through the so-called 'Kuwait Gap'. In general the sterling area acted for twenty years as a form of coercion that greatly cushioned the post-war collapse of British imperialism.

14. Only about 15 per cent of the price purchasers actually paid at petrol pumps in Europe or North America ended up in the producer countries; and most of that went to governments. One estimate stated that in 1972 $113 billion were paid by consumers for oil. Of this only $17 billion reached the producer countries, and of this $15 billion went to the governments, $1 billion to the workers and $1 billion to local contractors. Of the remaining $96 billion, $28 billion went in taxes, another $28 billion in profits to the companies, while $18 billion went to employees and $22 billion to furnishers of services. See *Le Monde*, 14 November 1972, quoting U S economist Victor Perlo. In early 1974, when petrol cost 50p a gallon in Britain, only 20 per cent of this went to the producer countries: 22.5p – i.e. 45 per cent – went in tax to the U K government, another 22 per cent went to the oil company, and the rest to the retailer.

15. Details of the different kinds of banking arrangement are given in 'Floating on Oil: A World Money Survey', the *Economist*, 23–9 March, 1974. While Arab oil-producers had till then relied on pre-existing banks and currencies, it was only a matter of time before they launched their own currency, a pan-Arab *dinar* or *rial*, to take its place beside the yen, Mark and dollar.

16. In 1970 Britain imported the following percentages of its oil from the Gulf: Kuwait 25 per cent, Saudi Arabia 13·6 per cent, Iran 8·5 per cent, Iraq 4·1 per cent, Qatar 3·5 per cent, and Abu Dhabi 2·1 per cent – a total of 56·8 per cent. The rest came from Libya, Nigeria and Venezuela.

17. Japanese imports, 85 per cent of Gulf origin, were expected to rise from 2·87 million barrels a day in 1969 to 8 million by 1980. On the Japanese recapture of South-east Asia in the search for markets and raw materials see Gavan McCormack and Jon Halliday, *Japanese Imperialism Today*, London, 1973. Japanese investment in Gulf exploration took place through the following companies: Arabian Oil (the Neutral Zone); Abu Dhabi Oil (offshore); Middle East Oil (Abu Dhabi, land); Qatar Oil (offshore); Iran Oil (land); and Joint Oil Development (Abu Dhabi, land). The total capital invested was 55 million yen, of which 25 million was in Arabian Oil.

18. *The Times*, 20 October 1972, special supplement on the North Sea.

19. *Fortune*, April 1965. The chief items in this system were: (a) a 27·5 per cent depletion allowance tax discount; (b) limitation of oil production in the name of 'conservation'; (c) the oil import quota system which in effect gave the oil companies a Federal subsidy as large as the difference between the banned foreign oil and their own more expensive supply.

20. Estimated volume of Alaskan production once the pipeline got going was 2 million barrels a day – less than 10 per cent of future U S needs. For several years the Alyeska pipeline was blocked by political opponents. The oil companies in the U S came under considerable attack in the late 1960s and early 1970s from a variety of critics, ranging from Weathermen who bombed the New York offices of companies such as Standard Oil of New Jersey (November 1969) and Mobil Oil (March 1970) to conservationists distressed about 'ecology'. Following the oil crisis of late 1973, oil companies were accused by irate Congressmen of deliberately withholding supplies from the U S market in order to push up prices, and of encouraging the producers to raise the posted price.

21. The 'energy crisis' was in one sense a faked-up panic: the U S had enough coal to last it 500 years and enough shale oil to last 35–120 years. The crisis was one of price, not of supply. See 'America's Energy Crisis', *Newsweek*, 22 January 1973. For an analysis of the implications of the rise in oil revenues see 'How the Arabs plan to spend their riches', the *Economist*, 5 May 1973.

22. In some countries such as Kuwait, Qatar and Abu Dhabi oil accounted for almost all of revenue and foreign exchange, and for most of production.

23. 'On the occasion of at least one recent oil company strike, it was discovered that among the instigators had been local employees whom the company had provided with a college education. Results such as these are likely to dampen oilmen's enthusiasm for higher education abroad at company expense.' From David Finnie, 'Recruitment and Training of Labor. The Middle East Oil Industry', *Middle East Journal*, Spring 1958, p. 143. Education policies changed in the 1960s in accordance with the overall concession of more power to selected local personnel.

24. Arab nationalist analyses of the migrant labour question have often slid into chauvinism when discussing non-Arab workers in the Gulf. The movement of the impoverished Pakistani and Iranian immigrants into Arab countries has been bogusly seen as part of a 'plot' by these countries to colonize Arab territory as the Zionists colonized Israel. This argument is a dangerous misconception which assists the ruling classes and the oil monopolies by dividing the working class. The Iranian and Pakistani regimes have a form of colonialist activity quite distinct from Zionism; the latter worked by territorial expansion and the displacement of the local population; the former works through political and economic patronage of the existing, i.e. Arab, ruling classes. The agents of Iranian expansionism are not the migrant Iranian proletariat but the Arab rulers of Bahrain, Sharjah and Oman who are supported by Iran and execute Tehran's policies. The workings of the capitalist market, not some grand design, force workers to migrate. It is class not nation that forms the counter-revolutionary alliance.

Chapter Thirteen
The Smaller States of the Gulf

The Establishment of British Hegemony

British domination of the waters and shores of the Gulf lasted over one hundred and fifty years, from the early decades of the nineteenth century until Britain's official and, indeed, partially real, withdrawal at the end of 1971. The core of British control was in ten small coastal states directly held as a result of conquest and treaty. These were: Kuwait, at the head of the Gulf; Bahrain, a group of islands off the Arabian coast; the peninsula of Qatar; and the seven entities of the lower Gulf to which the British refer as the 'Trucial States'.[1] At the same time influence extended into the larger states bordering the Gulf: to Iran, including in partic- ular the southern areas near the Gulf; to Iraq, which Britain dominated through Arab clients from the time of Turkey's retreat in the First World War up to the republican rising of 1958; and to the Arabian interior – where its power was real, if somewhat less – until the 1930s when its role in the area was displaced by that of the United States. Since the First World War oil has been the Gulf's main interest. Yet the discovery and ex- ploitation of this enormous economic attraction took place within a political structure that long predated them. British ships had frequented the Gulf since the sixteenth century, and in the seven- teenth century had helped to drive out the Portuguese. British naval and commercial influence in the area had expanded from the direction of India, and in the nineteenth century direct control was imposed. Napoleon's plan of an attack through Egypt had provoked British anxiety about the Gulf, as it did about Muscat and Aden; and concern grew further as the power of the local Arab fleets challenged British naval supremacy and the advance of trade by British subjects.

Although there was little cultivable land along the coast, there

439

were tens of villages in between Ras Massandam and Bahrain from which fishing, pearling and trade were carried out. In the late eighteenth century the chief of these villages were Ras al-Khaimah and Sharjah, ruled by the Qawasim tribe, who in 1800 reportedly had a fleet of sixty-three large vessels, smaller boats numbering 800, and up to 19,000 men. In the eighteenth century, the Qawasim and other local Arab traders had benefited from the weakening of the Persian and Ottoman states. Their growth posed a commercial threat which the British could not tolerate. The British decided to crush their rivalry, branding them as 'pirates', a term they applied to any fleet in the Indian Ocean – except, of course, that of the British – which challenged other fleets by force.[2] In the course of the early nineteenth century, the Arab fleets detained British ships that had tried to break into areas traditionally outside British control. The Arab sailors did not accept British intervention peacefully. Consequently, the British, under the rubric of stopping 'piracy', had an excuse for imposing a military solution without pretence of negotiation or peaceful competition. In 1807 a combined British and Muscati force attacked the Arab-occupied island of Quishn off the Iranian coast; and in 1809 the Governor of Bombay sent a naval force to crush Ras al-Khaimah. In 1819 and 1820 British naval forces returned to attack and burn down Ras al-Khaimah and other coastal towns, together with their fleets. Local tribal leaders were forced to sign a 'General Treaty of Peace With the Arab Tribes', in which they renounced attacks on British-protected ships. In 1835 they had to sign a temporary truce renouncing attacks on each other; and in 1853 this was turned into a permanent maritime truce, with Britain as the 'guaranteeing power'.

These early treaties made the Gulf safe for British traders and enhanced the security of India. British influence was subsequently increased by a new set of local political treaties. The first of these was with the al-Khalifa family, rulers of the islands of Bahrain, who had moved there from the mainland in the eighteenth century.[3] In 1861 the Sheikh signed a 'Protectorate Treaty' with the British in which he 'accepted' British support against external aggression and agreed to give Britain jurisdiction over her subjects living in Bahrain. In 1880 and 1892 these ties were strengthened by two 'Exclusive Agreements'; under the latter the Sheikh, Isa bin Ali al-Khalifa, gave Britain further powers by agreeing to the following terms:

— 1st. That I will on no account enter into any agreement or correspondence with any Power other than the British Government.
— 2nd. That without the assent of the British Government I will not consent to the residence within my territory of the Agent of any other Government.
— 3rd. That I will on no account cede, sell, or mortgage or otherwise give for occupation any part of my territory save to the British Government.[4]

This Exclusive Agreement of 1892 with Bahrain formed the model for treaties with seven other tribal leaders along the coast whom Britain later forced to make similar agreements. These states included the defeated naval powers of the area, Ras al-Khaimah and Sharjah, and five smaller entities. These chiefs were assured of British backing in return for accepting imperial control. After the annexation of the Trucial States and Bahrain was completed, in the 1890s, two other states were added to the British realm. Kuwait, a prosperous trading port at the top of the Gulf, owed nominal allegiance to the Ottoman empire; and to counter this the ruling as-Sabah family turned to Britain. The Kuwaiti ruler Sheikh Mobarak, who came to power in 1896 by murdering his two brothers, wanted independence from the Turks; and the British were alarmed at the prospect of German and Turkish influence in the Gulf being increased by the building of the proposed Berlin–Baghdad railway. In 1899 the British signed a treaty with Mobarak in which he gave them an exclusive presence in Kuwait in return for £15,000 a year. The Turks protested, but got no redress. The other later British acquisition was Qatar, an arid peninsula between Bahrain and the Trucial States which was ruled by the ath-Thani family and had been a dependency of Bahrain's in the early part of the nineteenth century. From 1871 to 1916 it fell under formal and effective Turkish rule; when the First World War drove out the Turks, the British coerced the Qataris into signing a submissive treaty with them.

The 1916 treaty with Qatar marked the limit of Britain's formal territorial annexations in the Gulf; a century had elapsed since the first truce imposed upon Ras al-Khaimah and Sharjah in 1819. The system Britain applied in these states was similar to that in Oman and in South Yemen, and has given rise to the same fictions:

At no time, however, has Britain held sovereign rights over any of the sheikhdoms though treaty relations as explained above go back as far as 1820. The British government does not interfere in the internal affairs of the various States except that jurisdiction over certain classes of foreigners is in the hands of the Political Agents.[5]

This was no more realistic an analysis of the Gulf than elsewhere. Britain did not interfere in local internal affairs because it neither wanted nor needed to. The form of colonialism that prevailed in the area was one of prevention and exclusion just as it was in the rest of the peninsula. When Britain did want to interfere and when the development of the oil economy necessitated it, the form of colonialism changed.

The main agents of British policy were the colonial administrators sent to the Gulf who, under the Indian system, took the name of 'Political Resident' and subordinate 'Political Agents'. The Resident was until 1947 based in Bushire on the Iranian side; he then moved to Bahrain and remained there until 1971. The function of Agents gradually expanded as economic conditions changed. Their role up to the First World War consisted of 'keeping the peace', limiting the slave trade and keeping out rival foreign powers – Russians, French, Germans and Turks. After the war Britain acquired control of Iraq, where it put down a popular rising in 1920 and installed as king the Hashemite prince Feisal. This monarchy remained until 1958 and, supported by strong man Nuri Said, ensured that no threat came from Iraq to Britain's interests in the Gulf. With the faint echoes of capitalist development beginning to be heard in the distance, the British decided to reinforce their hold by a series of additional treaties. From the 1920s, local rulers were coerced into agreeing not to give oil concessions to foreign firms without British consent;

and British banks were given special privileges; for example, in 1942 the British Bank of the Middle East was given an exclusive concession for Kuwait, under which all other foreign banks were excluded. The Indian rupee was the currency used in the Gulf, thus ensuring another means of British influence. Although oil began to be produced in Bahrain in 1934, the Gulf states remained almost completely stagnant until after the Second World War. The British dominated political life; where it was not their official representatives who held sway, unofficial 'advisers' played a powerful role, as, for example, Sir Charles Belgrave, the man who 'advised' and in effect ruled Bahrain from 1926 to 1956.[6] The 'non-interference' myth never deluded the people of the Gulf. The British presence was in itself an obvious interference. It kept the existing ruling families in power; and enforced, and in some cases created, differences between areas that had previously enjoyed more fluid interaction. In particular it cut off the coast of Oman from the Omani interior. It ensured that any development of the oil industry remained under the control of imperialist firms, who siphoned off their profits. Moreover, when their collaborators rebelled and it became necessary the British did interfere: for example in 1923 they sent the Political Resident and two warships to Bahrain and deposed the ruling Sheikh Isa.[7] Consequently when oil did begin to flow the British had their clients in position waiting to guarantee continued imperialist domination.

Kuwait: The New Slavery

Britain's interests in the Gulf after 1945 were both strategic and economic. The British wanted to ensure exclusion of foreign and hostile powers, together with continuation of the benefits from Gulf oil that the boom promised – cheap crude supplies, growing export markets, revenues invested in London, British ownership of local resources. It was never a prior necessity that these interests be guaranteed by overt political control; and in the two and a half decades after 1945 the ten states that Britain ruled were all accorded a formal independence. The reasons were many: Britain was globally in retreat and unable to intervene and finance interventions in the way she had done up to then; India became independent in 1947 and this lessened British concern with the Gulf as an area of strategic importance; the Gulf states themselves became richer and more exposed to Arab nationalism. A new kind of relationship was needed to link the industrialized west, and Britain in particular, to the oil-rich mini-states.

The first Gulf state which Britain formally relinquished was Kuwait. The population there had risen from 75,000 in 1937 to 740,000 in 1971. Oil production had begun in 1946 and had had a spectacular increase, with the result that by the late 1960s Kuwait had the third largest output in the Middle East. B P had a 50 per cent interest in Kuwait's oil industry, and the K O C had been the main beneficiary of the Iranian oil crisis of 1951–3. As Iranian output was boycotted by B P and as all other purchasers were forced to accept this boycott, B P raised its Kuwaiti output in order to make up for the loss in Iran. In 1971 Kuwait's oil production of 145 million tons was third only to that of Iran and Saudi Arabia throughout the Middle East, and it possessed 10 per cent of all known world reserves.

Table 24

Kuwaiti Oil Production

million metric tons

1950	17·3
1955	54·9
1960	81·7
1970	137·4
1971	145·0

As far as the British were concerned, the situation inside Kuwait was excellent. The ruling as-Sabah family kept the population firmly under control and dispensed some of their money in welfare payments to Kuwaiti citizens. Restrictive nationality laws prevented others from joining in. All education, at home or abroad, became free for Kuwaitis. Medical care was likewise

444

available without charge. All native inhabitants were entitled to housing, and a system of favourable low-income housing was instituted for poorer Kuwaitis. Kuwait city itself was almost completely rebuilt, and the old wall around the city broken through. In Kuwait there were no income taxes, local telephone calls were free, and petrol cost a quarter of what it did in Europe. Such were the consequences of this system that the many remaining Kuwaiti bedouin received the material benefits of this system but chose to remain with their tents and flocks in the desert for most of the year; their free houses in town were rented at great expense to foreigners, and when the summer became too hot they departed for holidays in cooler climates.[8]

The state of Kuwait was eminently stable, and the as-Sabah family were able custodians of Anglo–US interests. There was no danger in abrogating the existing agreements between Kuwait and Britain. In the late 1950s an additional reason for change was that Arab nationalism was on the offensive; the Suez attack had been made, and diplomatically defeated, in 1956, and in 1958 Iraq, Kuwait's northern neighbour, had been the scene of a republican military coup that had overthrown Nuri Said and the ruling pro-British monarchy. Kuwait was therefore granted independence, in 1961.

The real character of Kuwaiti independence was put to the test almost immediately after the British had handed over sovereignty, in July 1961. The Iraqi government, under General Qasim, announced that Kuwait formed part of Iraq and should be annexed to it accordingly. Within days British troops had been airlifted back into the country and were retained there until Qasim had been pressured into silence by Arab diplomatic forces. Iraq never gave up its formal claim, and until 1971 the British kept forces in Bahrain and a 'tank stockpile' in Kuwait under an Anglo–Kuwaiti defence agreement. After 1971, when Bahrain became independent, the Kuwaitis stationed planes there to avoid a possible Iraqi surprise attack, and Saudi guarantees replaced British ones. The independent state of Kuwait displayed a political character, both internally and externally, that must have delighted

445

its imperial masters. Behind the official propaganda about 'miracles' and a Gulf El Dorado, it was a viciously reactionary state with an untarnished record as a supporter of imperialist interests. Kuwait affairs remained under the grip of the as-Sabah family and its close allies. In 1971, for example, it was calculated that 90 per cent of all Kuwaiti investment abroad was controlled by a mere eighteen families. Kuwaiti citizens were certainly given considerable material privileges; and a political life of a kind was allowed. In the decade after the British departure there were three general elections for the fifty-member National Assembly: in January 1963, January 1967 and January 1971. Yet this Assembly had little real power, and in the 1967 elections vote-rigging and discrimination were practised quite openly. The opposition, led by Dr Ahmad al-Khatib of the M A N, continued to call for internal and external reforms. Following the signature of the oil participation agreement in late 1972, the Khatib group succeeded in having the National Assembly refuse to ratify this. But the demand for full Kuwaiti ownership at once was no more radical than similar demands being made in Iran and Saudi Arabia, and in no way challenged the ties between the as-Sabah clique and imperialism. Had it done so, it is unlikely that the Assembly's debates would have been allowed to have effect.[9]

The key to the oppressive internal structure of Kuwaiti society was the fact that almost all physical labour and many white-collar jobs were carried out by non-Kuwaitis, who formed a deprived proletariat within Kuwaiti society. What distinguished this body of migrant labour from similar forces elsewhere in the Gulf and in Europe was that by the late 1960s they formed the majority of the population. According to the April 1970 census the total population of Kuwait was 733,000; of these 346,000 were Kuwaitis and 387,000 were foreigners. This ratio understated the predominance of the foreign community in the labour force, since a far higher percentage of the foreigners were male migrant workers without children, wives or other dependants, whereas the Kuwaiti figures included all of these. According to the 1970 census there were 417,000 males as compared to 316,000 females – 100,000 more men, that is, than women. Around 80

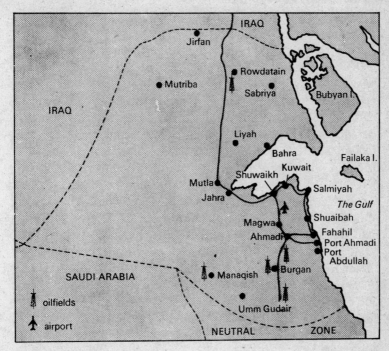

Map 11   Kuwait

per cent of the total labour force were immigrants, from surrounding sources of cheap labour – Iraq, Iran, Oman, the
Yemens, Pakistan and India. Unlike the Kuwaitis, they had none
of the benefits of the welfare state. The better educated Palestinians were at an advantage; but all had to pay for schooling and
medical care; many of the manual workers received minimal
payment and because of the high cost of these services were further discouraged from bringing in their families. Many, too,
had entered Kuwait without the correct papers; they had had to
bribe an official to get in, and were then tied to paying him a
percentage of their earnings to prevent him from having them
expelled. An upper limit of 10 per cent was placed on the number
of immigrant Arabs who could attend school. However, private
schooling cost from six to seven and a half Kuwaiti dinars a
month, with the result that the children of, for example, poor
Omani immigrants received no education at all. From the middle
1960s private doctors reaped enormous profits from the deprivation of the immigrant working class. In housing there was similar
discrimination; foreigners were not allowed to own houses, and
migrant workers were not provided with proper housing. The
result was that Kuwaitis often rented their government-given
houses at exorbitant rates to those foreigners who could pay;
while the poor lived in shanty towns which the Kuwait city
authorities ensured were placed away from main arterial roads
and the sight of possible observers.[10]

In some professions, such as the hotel trade and teaching, there
were next to no Kuwaitis at all. In government jobs, on the other
hand, Kuwaitis held numerous sinecures in inflated ministries,
and excluded all foreigners from 'jobs' they never performed. Of
the total Kuwaiti population in 1970, probably up to 100,000
were bedouin who remained outside capitalist employment. The
total of Kuwaitis in employment – that is, the least privileged
citizens – was estimated in 1970 at 43,000; of these 36,000 were
white-collar employees of some kind, with only 7,000 classifiable
as labourers. The first 6,000 of these were paid an average of KD
180 a month, the middle 30,000 received KD80 a month, and the
bottom 7,000 received around KD55 a month. The average

monthly wage of the immigrant worker was KD18–20 (1973: £1 = KD0·67).

While class differences existed within native Kuwaiti society, the major difference throughout the system was that between Kuwaiti citizens as a whole and the oppressed imported proletariat who performed menial labour, or worked in other physical jobs and in the services sector. Non-Kuwaitis were excluded from trades unions: they were not allowed to join Kuwaiti unions, nor were they allowed to form their own.

Table 25

Estimated Employment 1966

	Number	Percentage Distribution
Agriculture and fishing	3,146	1·7
Quarrying and mining	6,992	3·7
Manufacturing industry	17,933	9·7
Building and construction	30,867	16·6
Electricity and water	7,257	3·9
Commerce	23,045	12·4
Transportation, communication and storage	11,128	6·0
Services	85,219	46·0
Total	185,587	100·0

Source: *Middle East and North Africa 1972–3*, p. 472.

While political opposition among native Kuwaitis was restricted, political activity among foreigners was completely banned. Arrest and deportation without any restraint was common. During the 1960s only one strike occurred in Kuwait – in January 1969, for twenty-four hours, among the oil workers (mainly Kuwaitis). The oil company was reported to have lost £2 million through that stoppage of one day. Other political activity was also sporadic: a series of bomb explosions around the same time, in January 1969, in protest at the rigged elections two years before, was a unique and unrepeated development.[11] Kuwait's economy

The Gulf

continued to rest on oil despite gestures at diversification and the creation of an industrial area, at Shuaiba, south of Kuwait city. In 1970 oil provided 57 per cent of total output and 92 per cent of government revenue, while providing only 3·3 per cent of employment.

Table 26

Kuwaiti GDP 1969–70 Total KD983 million

	percentage
Agriculture, fishing	0·5
Oil	56·6
Manufacturing	3·7
Construction	4·0
Services	7·4
Electricity, gas, water	3·7
Transportation and communication	3·6
Wholesale and retail trade	8·6
Banking, insurance and finance	1·8
Ownership of dwellings	4·5
Public administration and defence	5·6

Source: Economist Intelligence Unit, *Quarterly Economic Review, The Arabian Peninsula: Sheikhdoms and Republics*, Annual Supplement, 1972.

The result of this configuration has been that Kuwait has had enormous sums of spare cash, and these have formed the basis of its foreign policy. The ratio of savings to total income in the period 1965–70 was 50 per cent. This cash was deployed in numerous ways. The most prestigious channel was the Kuwait Fund for Arab Economic Development, which was established after the 1961 confrontation with Iraq as a means of paying for Kuwait's continued existence; in return for loans at minimal rates, the states of the Arab world were to recognize Kuwait and ensure that Iraq did not attack. In 1971, with a capital of KD68 million and reserves of KD10 million the loan situation was as follows:

Table 27

Kuwait Fund for Arab Economic Development
Distribution of Loans on 31 March 1971

Country	Total in KD millions	percentage
Algeria	10·00	12·3
Bahrain	2·00	2·5
Iraq	3·00	3·7
Jordan	7·50	9·3
Lebanon	2·84	3·5
Morocco	10·05	12·4
North Yemen	0·89	1·1
Sudan	13·77	17·0
Syria	3·00	3·7
Tunisia	14·50	17·9
Egypt	13·30	16·4
Total	80·85	100·0

Source: Kuwait Fund for Arab Economic Development, Ninth Annual Report, 1970–71.

The Kuwait government provided funds to Egypt and Jordan after the 1967 War and to Egypt in 1973; ostensibly these funds were to fight the enemy, but in fact they served to stabilize these two regimes. Both Kuwaiti government and private moneys were deployed in investment throughout the Arab world and the western capitalist nations. The Kuwait Investment Company, 50 per cent of whose capital was government-owned, specialized in investing Kuwaiti money in Europe and North America and played an important part in the Eurodollar market, with an investment at the end of 1970 estimated at $75–100 million. Two US broking firms, Clarke Dodge and Merrill Lynch, had offices in Kuwait for funnelling funds onto the New York market, while a London affiliate of the Commercial Bank of Kuwait – the United Bank of Kuwait – specialized in deploying cash onto the British capital market. In addition to the Commercial Bank, four other banks of mixed Kuwaiti and western composition performed analogous functions. These were: the National Bank of

451

Kuwait, the Gulf Bank and the Bank of Kuwait and the Middle East, all of which involved some British participation; and the al-Ahli Bank of Kuwait, which included French capital. A further government-run organization, the Kuwait Foreign Trading Contracting and Investment Company, was active in banks in Britain and the Lebanon, and financed loans to companies in the U S, Europe, the Philippines and Mexico.

Acceleration of this trend was inevitable as Kuwait acquired increasing revenues in the 1970s and 1980s. No imperialist could have hoped for a better arrangement as the oil continued to flow and growing revenues returned rapidly to the capital-hungry industrialized countries. On occasion the Kuwaitis did do badly; they lost an estimated £30 million in the collapse of the Beirut-based Intra Bank in 1966, and Kuwait investors were prominent among the victims of the I O S and Gramco affairs. In general, however, the Kuwaiti ruling clique and the western capitalist regimes had an excellent relationship. In the Gulf, the Middle East and the capital markets of the west, Kuwait played an important and growing counter-revolutionary role. Its internal reliance on a class of imported helots was mirrored by its international role as a steward of capital.

The National Liberation Movement in Bahrain

The conditions that enabled Britain to forge a different relationship to Kuwait in 1961 did not prevail in the rest of the Gulf colonies. In 1960 only two states were producing oil: Bahrain had begun to do so in 1934 and Qatar in 1949. The other mini-states were still extremely poor and the internal political conditions were difficult for imperialism to control. If Gulf oil was to be safe the collaborationist ruling families needed British military and politicals upport throughout the foreseeable future. There was also a strategic military reason for the British remaining in the lower Gulf: they needed to retain their bases at Bahrain and Sharjah in the interests of their policy east of Suez; and since 1947 U S ships had also used the naval facilities at al-Jufair in Bahrain. Not only were these positions part of a global network; but they also had a local use: they formed part of the basis for a possible future defence of Kuwait, and were links in the chain of imperial communication that stretched from Cyprus to Singapore and Hong Kong. During the suppression of the guerrilla movement in Borneo in 1961–5, Bahrain had been expanded to handle a rise in military traffic, and this same base was equipped to deploy air and land forces northwards to Kuwait and eastwards to the 'Trucial States' and the Sultanate of Oman.

The most highly evolved of the nine lower Gulf states was Bahrain, an archipelago of thirty-three islands, of which two (Manama and Moharraq) were inhabited and a third (Jidda) was used as a prison. The total area was approximately 255 square miles and by 1971 the population was 216,800. Bahrain had long been a meeting place for traders and fishermen in the Gulf and many of its population traced their origins to neighbouring states. The Iranians had occupied Bahrain in the seventeenth and eighteenth centuries and a large number of Bahrainis were of distant Iranian origin; and although the ruling Arab family were Sunni Moslems, many inhabitants were Shia. In the 1970 census, 82·5 per cent of the population were stated to be Bahraini citizens; but there were no figures given on their Arab or Persian origin. Of the non-Bahraini population, Indians and Pakistanis totalled 15,000, Omanis 10,000 and Iranians 5,000.[12]

Bahrain is surrounded by shallow waters and has a climate not unlike that of the Caribbean; and it is physically less extreme than mainland Arabia. The traditional economy had been based on fishing, pearl diving and agriculture, in the fertile northern part of Manama island. However, the pearling was undermined in the 1930s by the importation of artificial Japanese pearls; and the Bahraini economy was only just saved by the discovery of oil. Bahrain's oil production was not large, and it was estimated that reserves would run out in 1990; but the country did have the largest refinery in the Middle East after Abadan and two thirds of its production came via an underwater pipeline from the oil-wells on the Saudi mainland; in 1971 the refinery produced 94 million barrels, of which 27·3 million were produced by the Bahrain Petroleum Company, the rest having been pumped over from Saudi Arabia. Socal and Texaco, co-owners of BAPCO, each owned a 30 per cent share in ARAMCO.

Because its oil production and revenue were less significant than in other states, Bahrain undertook considerable real diversification in the 1960s. In 1962 an expanded port was opened at Mina Sulman and a free zone was set up to encourage trade. Bahrain's largest industrial plant, the ALBA aluminium smelter, in which the government had a $27\frac{1}{2}$ per cent interest, began production in 1972; using gas from the local oil-field it was intended to produce up to 120,000 tons of aluminium a year from material imported from Australia.[13] Other projects included a satellite communications system, inaugurated in 1969 by a conversation between the Sheikh of Bahrain (in Bahrain) and the Duke of Edinburgh (in Windsor Castle), and a new £5 million terminal building at the airport, which had been specially expanded to catch the jumbo-jet traffic.[14] In Bahrain, as in Kuwait, the government used its oil revenues to create welfare facilities. Although poorer than its northern counterpart, Bahrain had a far more developed educational and medical system than any other state in the lower Gulf. In 1969 27 per cent of the budget was spent on education; 30,000 boys and 19,000 girls were receiving free education under this system, and Bahraini teachers and intellectuals were being deployed in the educational system growing lower down the Gulf.

As a result of widespread education and other oil-related development, Bahrain had a small and militant working class, which in the 1950s and 1960s was in the front line of struggle in the Gulf. Bahrain had a long tradition of opposition to British domination; its trading contacts, its relatively developed pearling and agricultural economy, and the Shia opposition to the al-Khalifa family all contributed to an anti-imperialist consciousness among the merchant community. In 1911 a group of merchants wanted to limit British influence and set up a committee to adjudicate pearling disputes. The leaders of this movement were deported to India. After the deposition of Sheikh Isa in 1923 British power was confirmed in the Bahrain Order in Council, which gave the British additional powers; and the arrival of

Table 25

Bahrain Employment in 1971

Agriculture and fishing	3,900
Mining and manufacturing	4,152
Oil	4,312
Public utilities	1,705
Construction	10,404
Wholesale, retail and catering	7,706
Transport and communications	7,743
Finance, business services, social services	13,182
Public administration and defence	5,206
Other	817
Total	60,301

Source: *The Middle East and North Africa 1972–3*, p. 203.

Belgrave as 'adviser' to the government in 1926 confirmed this trend. In 1938, after Arab nationalism had begun to affect the area, the first strike occurred; the demands raised were for local control of education, the right to organize trade unions, a legislative council, the replacement of the British 'Political Agent' and the expulsion of foreign workers from the Bahrain Petroleum Company. Three leaders were arrested and, as before, exiled.

In the post-war period this relatively mild form of protest gave way to a mass movement. The working class of Bahrain recognized that the oil economy and the welfare measures undertaken by the administration were progressive developments. They demanded more, however – political control in particular – and these demands clashed with the determination of the British to keep control. In 1953 rioting broke out between the two religious communities – the Sunni and the Shia – and it looked as if class conflict would degenerate into conflict between sects. But leaders of both groups called an anti-sectarian meeting in the village of Sanabis; and a joint 'Committee of National Unity' (*Lajnat al-Ittihad al-Watania*) was set up under the slogan 'No Sunnism and No Shi'ism From Now On'.

They were at first tolerated by the government, since they con-

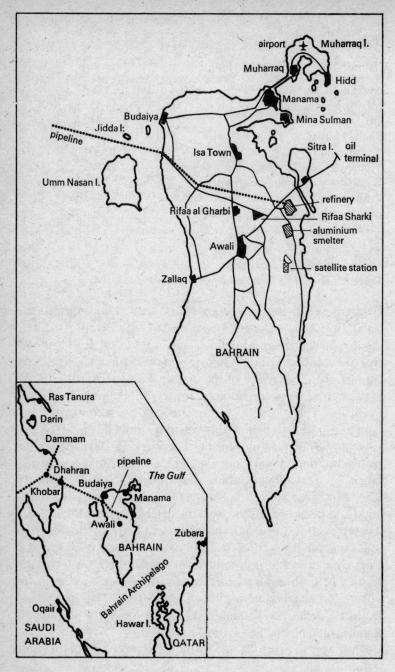

Map 12 Bahrain

fined themselves to peaceful protest. In March 1956, however, the situation changed; the dismissal of General Glubb by King Hussein of Jordan at that time led many Bahrainis to conclude that a similar move in Bahrain would not be amiss – namely, the dismissal of Belgrave. The occasion for a mass outburst came when the British Foreign Secretary arrived at Bahrain for a brief visit. Tens of thousands of demonstrators chanting 'Selwyn Go Home' swarmed out of Moharraq, the mainly Sunni town near the airport, and blocked the causeway linking Moharraq island to Manama, the site of the government buildings. Selwyn Lloyd was forced to cross the water by boat, the police attacked and a general strike followed. The leadership of the Committee of National Unity entered into negotiations with the government and for some months relative peace continued. But the Bahraini population refused to accept this truce, and in November 1956 mass demonstrations broke out again in protest at the Suez invasion. This time the government counter-attacked violently; the leaders of the Committee were tried by a tribunal (Belgrave and three members of the al-Khalifa family) and five of them were deported to the island of St Helena. The first wave of mass opposition in Bahrain had been broken.[15] Two consequences followed from the opposition of 1954–6. The British realized that Bahrain had a more advanced and therefore dangerous political character than any other Gulf colony. Because the oil revenue and level of production was so much lower than in Kuwait, they had been unable to turn the indigenous population into a parasitic class with an enslaved migrant proletariat underneath. Their response was intensified repression, and a tightening of control by the al-Khalifa family. The latter had moved out of their palace in Manama during the 1956 riots and had taken up permanent residence in the village of Rifaa al-Gharbi, which only they and their bedouin guards were permitted to inhabit. Nepotism was the key to stability; in 1958, out of 60 key posts in the government, 14 were held by al-Khalifa and 23 by British officials; in 1965, 25 out of the top 63 officials were al-Khalifa. The police and CID were built up with imported experts; in 1959, out of 739 police, only 202 were Bahrainis. 127 were North

Yemenis, 69 Iraqis, 61 Omanis and an equal number South Yemenis. Seventeen of the 29 officers were British and in 1965 six British women inspectresses were brought in. The chief CID men, three Cypriots known in Bahrain as 'Ben, Bob and Green', were especially loathed; the former two retired from service after being severely wounded by a bomb planted in Bob's car in 1966.

For the opposition the lesson of 1956 was that a peaceful movement led by bourgeois reformers would never succeed. Some of the leaders of the 1954–6 movement later joined the regime. The trades union movement, which worked underground, had a communist element, formed in the Bahrain National Liberation Front. The influence of the Nasserite MAN and of the Ba'ath was also felt. The first protests after 1956 were in 1962 when teachers in the secondary school struck and were arrested. In 1963 women participated in public opposition for the first time when they demonstrated in favour of the closer ties agreed on between Egypt, Syria and Iraq. The merchants who had worked in the 1954–6 movement took no part in this wave. The class character of the opposition had changed; and in March 1965 Bahrain was brought to a halt by a strike of BAPCO workers, in protest at BAPCO's dismissal of several hundred oil workers. This soon became a general strike, supported by students in the secondary schools. A Front of Progressive Forces (*Jabhat al-Quwat at-Taqaddumiyat*), which included communists and Ba'athis, raised new demands including and going beyond those of 1954–6: the cancellation of all dismissals, the recognition of the right to form unions; the right to hold political meetings and the lifting of the state of emergency in force since 1956; the freeing of all political prisoners and the sacking of UK and foreign employees.

These demonstrations were broken by the government's intervention, which led to more imprisonments and deportations. Saudi Arabia and Kuwait gave backing to the member of the ruling family, Sheikh Khalifa bin Sulman, who rushed to visit them; and Bahrain returned to the repressive peace of the previous ten years. Nevertheless British complacency had been dented.[16] They decided to strengthen the al-Khalifa still further and to pay an increase on the mere £450 per annum they had shelled out up to then. In May 1966 the *Economist* wrote, 'If the troops were not there the government would probably be overthrown, even if only temporarily'; but it continued to muse in that characteristic British way about imperialist control and its relationship to repression:

The extent to which the British can in fact influence Bahraini affairs is as vague as the whole British set-up in the Gulf. Earlier this month the ruler felt himself triumphantly vindicated in his suspicions of creeping democracy by the Kuwaiti government's sharp slapping down of people it felt were getting above themselves. And certainly the British have no sympathy with the notion of political organisations in Bahrain.[17]

As British troops pulled out of South Yemen and Aden in the autumn of 1967 Bahrain became the new centre of Britain's Middle East military command. For the al-Khalifa family this meant more importance in British eyes; and for the people of Bahrain it meant more repression. At the same time, international capital, which suddenly awoke to the new prospects for plunder, moved in force into Bahrain, to make use of it as a jumping-off point for penetration of the lower Gulf.

The Lower Gulf

No other Gulf states experienced political evolution comparable to that of Bahrain; all had a shorter experience of oil and none had even half of Bahrain's population. The only state to have anything like Bahrain's historical commercial ties with the rest of the world was Dubai, where a correspondingly outward-looking regime was in power. The first state after Bahrain to develop oil was Qatar, whose production quickly rose to outstrip Bahrain's; by 1971 Bahrain was producing only 3·8 million tons, while Qatar had an output of 20·0 million tons. As a result of this production the population of Qatar increased, from under 30,000 before oil to an estimated 112,000 in 1971. The British presence there was far less noticeable; there was no foreign

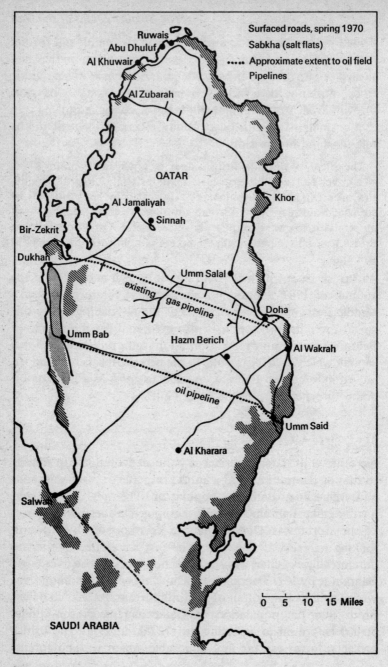

Map 13   Qatar

merchant community and no military base. The strict Moslem rule of the Wahhabi rulers added to the prevailing political oppression. Foreign employees of the oil company found 'drinking with natives', or in other ways loosening social restrictions, were expelled.

The ruling ath-Thani family were notorious throughout the Gulf as the meanest and most thuggish of all British clients.[18] They numbered in all about 12,000; and in 1970 they took between a third and a half of the oil revenues. At one time the ruler, Amir Ahmad, and his father Amir Ali, were reported to own 452 cars between the two of them. In his later period of rule Amir Ahmad decamped to Geneva and declined to return to Qatar even for the occasion of the accession of his country in 1971 to formal independence. For the population of Qatar there were none even of the modest welfare benefits available in Bahrain. In April 1963 there was a popular uprising in Qatar: one of the ruler's nephews, Abdul Rahman bin Mohammad bin Ali, opened fire on a group of Qataris who were celebrating the proposed union of Egypt, Syria and Iraq and who had blocked his car. A National Unity Front formed and demanded limitations on the power of the ath-Thani family, the establishment of a state budget and a representative council. The Front were strongest in the town of Khor on the north of the peninsula. The most vigorous members of the ath-Thani wanted to bombard the place; but a more cautious policy prevailed. In the end none of the Front's demands was met and the dark night of Wahhabi repression descended on the Qatari peninsula once again. It was 1970 before its government acquired a cabinet – seven out of ten were members of the ath-Thani family – and 1972 before it acquired a proper budget and a token assembly.

On the 'Trucial Coast' Britain had traditionally played a minimal role in the small and impoverished villages that stretched from Qatar to the mouth of the Gulf at Ras Massandam. This area had close historical links with Oman proper; and the very top of Ras Massandam was a detached part of the Omani Sultanate. Conditions in the other sheikhdoms were often fluid and it was only in 1952 that the British settled on the figure of

461

seven sheikhdoms out of all the possible contending numbers. The population of the area as a whole was probably less than 50,000 in the pre-oil era; and for some states the prosperity of the oil-producers remained a distant prospect. Even in 1972 only Abu Dhabi and Dubai were producing oil. Sharjah had made some money out of its military base; but the poverty of the others was extreme; and their main source of income was the sale of special postage stamps to European and North American collectors. One estimate of revenues for the five poorest sheikhdoms in 1964 gave the following picture: Sharjah £110,000; Ajman £24,000; Umm al-Qaiwain £32,000; Ras al-Khaimah £44,000; and Fujairah £25,000.[19]

In the early 1950s the British set up two minimal state institutions: a Trucial States Council and an armed force, the Trucial Oman Levies. The Council had no power and was merely a forum for sheikhs to meet in twice a year. A derisory Five-Year Plan was introduced in 1956–61; the British allocated to it the princely sum of £381,000 and even then only managed to spend £280,000. Neglect continued throughout the 1960s; by 1965 a Development Office had been set up; and over three and a half years the British put in £1 million, with smaller contributions from Qatar, Abu Dhabi and Bahrain. Less reticence was shown in the establishment of another main institution, the Trucial Oman Levies, a Gulf version of the Arab Legion. Originally a 500-man force with the task of patrolling the borders, it was recruited from men rejected by the Aden army: the first batch of these Arabian Black and Tans murdered their British officer and then sold their arms to the local tribesmen. New recruits were then brought in from Dhofar, from Oman and from the Bani Kaab tribe in the 'Trucial Oman' area. Their name was later changed to Trucial Oman Scouts, and they were thought to be in fit enough shape to be deployed at Buraimi (1952–5) and against the Imamist rebels in the Sultanate of Oman. The latter escapade was a failure, as many of the men sympathized with the rebels; and the T O S had to be replaced by British troops. They returned to duty in the lower Gulf and by 1970 had a force of 1,500; of these, 40 per cent were from 'Trucial Oman', 30 per cent from the Sultanate of

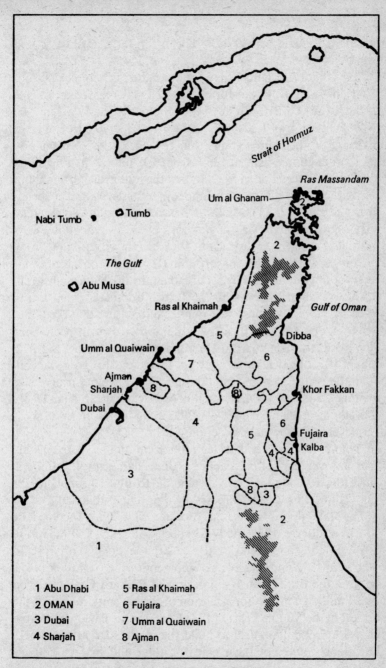

Strait of Hormuz

Ras Massandam

Um al Ghanam

Nabi Tumb •   ○ Tumb

The Gulf

○ Abu Musa

Ras al Khaimah

Gulf of Oman

Dibba

Umm al Quaiwain

Ajman
Sharjah

Dubai

Khor Fakkan

Fujaira
Kalba

1 Abu Dhabi
2 OMAN
3 Dubai
4 Sharjah

5 Ras al Khaimah
6 Fujaira
7 Umm al Quaiwain
8 Ajman

Map 14   Ras Massandam and the Strait of Hormuz

Oman and the other 30 per cent from India, Pakistan and Iran.[20]

Abu Dhabi and Dubai were the states that economic development conspicuously transformed. Abu Dhabi reproduced some of the features of Kuwait in an even more extreme form; in 1966 its population was 17,000; by 1972 it reached 70,000, the great majority of them immigrants. Oil revenues rose spectacularly after production began in 1962; from £35 million in 1967 to an estimated £200 million in 1972. At first the ruling Sheikh Shakhbut refused to part with any of his money; total development spending up to 1966 was £1·75 million. Abu Dhabi had no commercial past and Shakhbut was a stubborn conservative whose ways infuriated even the British. Until 1965 he refused to sign a 50–50 agreement with the oil consortium. He insisted on keeping his reserves in gold and on inspecting them in the bank each week. Such was his obsession with the British aristocracy that a firm of contractors, Paulings, were only able to ensure that Shakhbut would cooperate with them by appointing a British peer, Lord Brentford, to their board.[21] He hid himself on his yacht in Abu Dhabi harbour, where he kept his sheep and his gold bars. In 1966 the British deposed him and installed his more progressive brother Zaid.[22] Abu Dhabi then boomed; under an Abu Dhabi Development Plan for 1968–73 BD296 million were to be spent on developing the state's economy, with BD53·4 million going on communications and BD63 million on industry. Abu Dhabi had an even higher per capita income than Kuwait, although since the revenue was only beginning to filter through to the population, this was not necessarily a meaningful fact.

The state of Dubai began to produce oil in 1969. Income rose to £13 million in 1971 and was expected to reach £50 million in 1973. Boom conditions hit the town; the population rose to 80,000 in 1972 and massive development of the port took place. In 1967 the British construction firm of Richard Costain signed a £24 million contract for extension of the harbour, making it the largest in the Middle East; in 1973 Costain and Taylor Woodrow signed a £69 million deal to build the world's largest dry dock. Oil alone could not have paid for this; and in fact Dubai's prosperity mainly derived from its position as the main entrepot for trade on the lower Gulf. The increase in trade began in the late 1950s; imports rose from £3 million in 1958 to £8 million in 1963 and £41·7 million in 1967, and were expected to reach £200 million by the mid-1970s.

The number of banks operating there rose from one in 1963 to twelve in 1970. Much of the trade passed on to the other Trucial States and to the Omani interior; but the most prosperous trade of all was smuggling gold to India. In 1969 there was estimated to be around £2,600 million's worth of gold in private Indian possession, and demand continued to rise despite the imposition in 1947 of a government ban on imports. Kuwait, which once had dominated the trade, gave way to Dubai in the 1950s; and by 1970 250 tons of gold a year passed through, bringing Dubai an estimated trade of £80 million. Foreign speculators were active in this market. 'It must be emphasised', *The Times* wrote in 1969, 'that the London gold dealers and the merchants of Dubai are not breaking any laws. Indeed, the Dubai branch of a respected international bank, based in New York, is one of the major buyers of gold on behalf of the merchants.'[23] The bank in question, which *The Times* declined to name, was the First National City Bank, which together with the British Bank of the Middle East and London and Swiss bullion firms, used Dubai as a base for quick profits derived from sabotaging the Indian economy.

The British Withdrawal: 'We Got Out at the Right Time'

The 1960s and 1970s were bonanza time in the Gulf and British capital was using its privileged position to grab as much of the new oil revenues as it could. In 1971, the year of the British 'withdrawal', the UK still provided around 40 per cent of Oman's imports, 38 per cent of Qatar's, 31 per cent of Abu Dhabi's, 35 per cent of Dubai's and 11·5 per cent of Kuwait's. Moreover, despite the *relative* decline, the *absolute* figures were rising sharply.

The first major advantage that British capitalists had was

Table 29

British Exports to the Gulf States (£ million)

	1964	1966	1969	1972	1973
Kuwait	19·3	25·8	14·9	31·3	36·1
Bahrain	7·6	7·6	12·5	19·5	24·3
Qatar	2·7	3·3	5·8	12·8	19·4
Abu Dhabi	2·3	3·3	14·9	15·3	24·7
Dubai	3·3	2·8	13·3	15·8	24·7
Oman	1·6	3·1	5·3	17·2	22·2
Total	36·8	45·9	92·7	111·9	151·4

that they knew the area. Firms like the trading company Gray MacKenzie had been in the Gulf for decades, and several British banks had previously had a stranglehold on Gulf finance. The British Bank of the Middle East, the Eastern Bank, and National & Grindlays had between them a dominant position in the area where the assets of all banks together in 1968 came to an estimated £800 million.[24] British consultancy firms were also in the forefront, pushed hard, if unobtrusively, by government officials on the ground, and BOAC had a 23 per cent share in Gulf Aviation, the local airline. One particularly effective and devious British trading operation was carried out through a semi-official outfit known as the Crown Agents. This institution, dating from 1833, was a purchaser for 250 foreign buyers, including over seventy governments. It bought in Britain up to £100 million a year, and had up to £1,000 million of foreign cash in London for use in property and stock market speculation. It annually placed orders with around 15,000 British firms. One of its eight overseas offices was in Bahrain, and all the Gulf governments used it; since the Crown Agents published no accounts of what they purchased, precise figures on the amount of trade they collared for British firms cannot be given; but it can be assumed that they were an important channel for funnelling back oil revenues to Britain from the Gulf, whether for use as reserves banked in London or as payment for British exports.[25]

British capital reacted to the possibilities of Gulf riches with the expansion of the late 1960s in Abu Dhabi and Dubai and with the military build-up there after Britain withdrew from Aden. A stream of special supplements on the Gulf poured out of the bourgeois press in London and readers of *The Times* and the *Guardian* found the centres of their daily papers clogged with repetitious verbiage introducing them to Bahrain and Fujairah. The basis of these supplements was economic – 'excellent prospects for British trade' – but this material core was flanked on either side by ideology, in this case politics and folklore. The former stressed the 'maturity' and 'stability' of the states; the latter sweetened the pill with what are euphemistically referred to as 'travel pieces' – benign drivel about falconry, dhows, stamp-collecting and the threatened extinction of the Qatari oryx. It goes without saying that the true character of political life in the Gulf was not illuminated by these mercenary productions.[26]

The British military position in the Gulf came to prominence as the troops began to pull out of Aden in the middle of 1967. Fifteen million pounds were spent on expanding the infantry base at Sharjah and up to 7,000 troops moved to the two Gulf bases, more than doubling the original garrison. There were two infantry battalions, twenty-four fighters – two squadrons – a squadron of minesweepers, at least one frigate and squadrons of armoured cars. The rationale for this build-up was that Britain had a 'legitimate interest' in the affairs of the Gulf. The cost was £20 million a year; but given the £200 million a year that Britain gained from oil it was deemed to be worth it. In October 1967 the British Minister of Defence, Denis Healey, put forward a justification of the decision to stay:

If we could be certain of the stability of the government with which we made a commercial agreement on the basis of a common interest – fine; but the risk at the moment is that disorderly British departure before there is an alternative basis for stability in the area could lead to a prolonged conflict.[27]

Such was government concern that their position be understood that a junior minister at the Foreign Office, Goronwy Roberts, was sent out to the Gulf in November 1967 to reassure Her Majesty's protected rulers.

It all proved, in fact, to be a mistake. In January 1968, less than two months after HQ Middle East had moved from Aden to Bahrain, it was announced that Britain would withdraw all forces east of Suez 'by the end of 1971'. The same Labour minister was sent out to tell the Gulf rulers of the decision. The withdrawal from the Gulf was the cause of contradictions within the British state between the Ministry of Defence and the Foreign Office. The former, faced with the inexorable collapse of Britain's world position, had been pruning costs throughout the 1960s and had decided to fix defence spending at £2,000 million per annum. This had been their rationale for pulling out of Aden; and they had only agreed to go on sitting in the Gulf because of Foreign Office alarm at 'the security situation'. The 1968 decision had reflected this line from the Ministry of Defence and had been made more likely by two extra factors: the devaluation, in November 1967, of the pound (a move precipitated by the added cost of importing Gulf oil after the closure of the Suez Canal); and the end of 'confrontation' in Borneo after the counter-revolutionary overthrow of Sukarno in 1965. This meant that troops could be pulled out of Singapore, Britain's other main base east of Suez and for which the Gulf had been a necessary link.

The Conservative party opposition challenged the correctness of this decision and in 1969 their party leader, Edward Heath, visited the Gulf. On his return he intoned that 'the long stability which the Gulf has enjoyed is now at risk' and blamed the Labour party for creating 'uncertainty' by its withdrawal decision. But Heath did not commit himself to reversing the decision and merely said that the Conservatives, once re-elected, would consult with Britain's 'friends' in the area.[28] Conservative backbenchers did want Britain to reverse the situation and they, together with the Nixon Administration, tried to make it do so once the Conservatives had been re-elected, in June 1970. After some months of hesitation the Conservative government announced in March 1971 that the decision, once taken, could not be reversed; and the withdrawal went ahead.[29]

One of Britain's major worries with regard to its withdrawal was the Shah of Iran's claim to Bahrain, derived from the Iranian occupation of the seventeenth and eighteenth centuries and bolstered by spasmodic propaganda about Bahrain being Iran's 'fourteenth province'. As the Iranian student organization CIS stated, the claim 'was made at a time when the regime was in serious difficulty in the face of accusations of servitude to foreign interest and wanted to make political capital out of the Bahrain issue'.[30] As Britain announced her withdrawal plans the Shah increased his pressure.

He realized that the majority of the Bahraini people, even if of Iranian origin, did not wish to be annexed to Iran. His aim was to create a situation where he would appear to be making a concession, and then to gain other advantages in return for this alleged 'generosity'. In March 1970, after prolonged secret diplomacy the UN Secretary General sent a personal envoy, Signor Vittorio Winspeare Guiccardi, to 'consult' the people of Bahrain. Guiccardi concluded, as was correct, that the majority did not want to become part of Iran. As a result, the Shah renounced his claim and the British heaped praise on him for his magnanimity. The so-called consultation was in fact a means of legitimizing the al-Khalifa clique. Guiccardi never suggested an election or a referendum; such simple ways of ascertaining popular desires were inconceivable in Bahrain at that stage. Guiccardi reported to U Thant that he had based his consultations on 'a list, made available to you, of organizations and institutions in Bahrain, from which to select those bodies providing the best and fullest cross-section of opinion among the people of Bahrain'. A study of this 'list' reveals not a single trades union or political party. Nor does Guiccardi say *who* provided the list; and it can only be assumed that it was drawn up by Britain and the Shah.[31]

The Bahrain 'consultation' brought the Shah considerable benefits. Iran's political and economic ties with other Gulf states as well as Bahrain improved and Iranian capital started to move across the Gulf. A branch of the Iranian National Bank (Bank Melli) opened in Bahrain almost immediately. The Arab rulers felt that the ending of this dispute now opened the way to serious discussion of what to do when Britain withdrew. As was their wont, the British had proposed a 'Federation', a Union of Arab Amirates, and the nine states in question had first met in March 1968. At that time the Iranian claim to Bahrain and the possibility of a Conservative victory in Britain bringing a reversal of policy hindered discussions; and between October 1969 and November 1970 the Supreme Council of the nine did not meet at all. The meeting of October 1969 had broken up in disarray after two of the sheikhs had accused the British Political Agent at Abu Dhabi, James Treadwell, of trying to coerce the meeting.

The major sources of contention among the nine were representation and defence. Bahrain, with 40 per cent of the total population, wanted the supreme body of the Union to reflect the different populations of the states. This was opposed by Abu Dhabi, which was the richest of the nine. The defence problem was complicated by the fact that the TOS had 1,500 men, whereas four of the nine states had their own private armies. The largest of these, the Abu Dhabi Defence Force, had 4,000 men, and superior arms to the TOS; and although the other three, the Bahrain Defence Force, the Qatar Armed Forces and the Ras al-Khaimah Mobile Force, were smaller, they each reflected the desire of the local rulers to preserve a military apparatus of their own. A report on a common defence force was produced in 1969 by a Major-General Sir John Willoughby; but the sheikhs had little time for Willoughby or the other British agents in the colonial apparatus who were trying to get them to shelve their differences. It was hardly surprising that since the British had encouraged division in the area for so long it was not possible now for them to push their clients into a single entity. Once it was announced that Britain definitely would withdraw at the end of 1971, outside Arab states tried to intervene to push the nine together. Egypt had enthusiastically hailed the Union proposal as 'a victory of Arabism', as did another supp sedly anti-imperialist country, Iraq.[32] In early 1971 Kuwait and Saudi Arabia tried through joint manoeuvres to bring about a full union. The British special envoy to the Gulf, Sir William Luce, flew around the area lobbying rulers and interested parties.[33] All this was of no avail.

In the end three different entities appeared: an independent Bahrain, an independent Qatar, and an independent Union (*Ittihad*) of Arab Amirates, which later changed its name to the United (*Mottaheda*) Arab Amirates. In July 1971 six of the seven 'Trucial' states announced the formation of their federation. Ras al-Khaimah stayed out until 1972. In August Bahrain, and in September Qatar, became 'independent'. In December the U A A also acquired 'independence', and by the end of the year all three had been admitted to the Arab League and the United Nations.

One important issue remained unsettled until the end of November. Iran had laid claim not only to Bahrain, but also to three islands, two named Tumbs and one named Abu Musa. One Tumb was uninhabited; another had 100 inhabitants and Abu Musa had a population of 300; Abu Musa was administered by Sharjah, and the Tumbs by Ras al-Khaimah. Iran wanted these islands to ensure her naval domination of the Gulf, and tried to get the British envoy Luce to assist them in this. Iran succeeded with Sharjah; and her troops were allowed to occupy part of Abu Musa; in return the Shah agreed to pay the ruler of Sharjah an annual income of £1·5 million until his income from oil reached £3 million. The ruler of Ras al-Khaimah refused to be bought off in this way and Iranian forces occupied the Tumbs anyway, killing at least three local Arabs.

Despite this attack by Iran and the popular protests it provoked, relations between Iran and the Gulf states were not permanently damaged. Iran's domination of the Gulf was more effective through her influence over existing Arab rulers than through direct annexation. Like the British, the Iranians masked their hold by pretending not to interfere; by collaboration, not blatant occupation. For the Shah, as for the British and the Americans, the greatest fears were that the Gulf states would be 'destabilized', either through clashes between the major states in the area (Iran and Saudi Arabia) or through internal revolt. The former was precluded by a Saudi–Iranian détente; in the case of the latter the Shah and King Feisal were obviously determined to intervene. However, their concern at the possibility of revolt was shared by the Gulf rulers themselves, who continued to build up their armed forces.

The first years of formal 'independence' demonstrated the character of the British withdrawal and the new states. British officers continued to be seconded to the Union Defence Force (as the TOS was renamed) and British troops and ships paid 'visits' to their former haunts. The US facilities at Bahrain were also confirmed.[34] The foreign capitalist invasion of the nine states continued apace. Meanwhile in Bahrain there was a resurgence of the workers' movement; and in March 1972 and in September there was a general strike as workers at the Gulf Aviation construction sites at the airport struck and workers in Moharraq and Manama towns supported them.[35] As a result of these working-class protests and of considerable underground activity by PFLOAG cadres, several hundred people were arrested during late 1972 and early 1973; some were quickly released, others were held for months and subjected to psychological torture techniques of a kind recently acquired by police forces throughout the imperialist-dominated peninsula. As part of their attempt to deflect this opposition, the al-Khalifa held elections in December 1972 for an assembly to draw up a Constitution; and following the promulgation of a Constitution in June 1973, general elections were held in December of that year for a thirty-member assembly. However, the executive direction of the state remained outside the control of this assembly, and it also proved unable to check the power of the police force, which continued to be commanded by British officers. While the establishment of the assembly represented a change in Bahraini political life, control remained where it had been before.

Elsewhere repression continued. In Qatar there was a palace coup in February 1972 when Sheikh Kahlifa bin Hamad ath-Thani overthrew his cousin and announced that less of the state revenue would be spent on the ruling family. In the UAA there were several waves of arrests of workers, students and officers opposed to the government's pro-imperialist policies. In Sharjah there was an attempted coup by the former ruler,

Sheikh Saqr, whom the British had thrown out in 1965 because of his support for Nasserism. But despite the fact that the current ruler was killed, Saqr nonetheless failed. The British claimed that these countries were given 'independence' and insisted that no defence agreements had been signed with them. In fact close military ties remained, whatever the formal arrangements, and the British kept their staging post in Masirah. U S officials who were attacked in Congress because of American ties to Bahrain defended themselves by saying that the British had not really left and therefore the U S was not taking their place. There had certainly been a shift however, and British delight at the ease with which it was effected needs to be analysed. As would be expected, it was themselves, the Shah of Iran and the correctness of their own long-term policy that the British congratulated. The real reasons for the change, however, are different. The combination within the Gulf states of welfare programmes and repression was one factor that enabled a smooth transition. Another was the realization by Saudi Arabia and Iran that their long-term interests lay in cooperating to partition the area between them. One actor on the stage whom the British should have thanked was Israel; the defeat of Egypt in June 1967 drove Egypt into the arms of Saudi Arabia and thereby ensured Egyptian support for the British plan to set up its client states.

The most important cause of the transition's success was the fact that the local opposition was too weak to prevent it. With the exception of Bahrain, the working class was small, immigrant and of recent origin. The Gulf rulers and the British were worried by the example of Aden and by 1969 had realized the threat from Dhofar. The overthrow of Said bin Taimur in Oman in 1970 was a direct result of British apprehension about what might happen if the trend in Oman was not reversed. Yet the imperialists and their Arab clients still had the upper hand, and they were reinforced by the cooperation of Saudi Arabia and Iran. All saw that they had a common interest in preserving existing arrangements. The revolutionaries working in the Gulf states faced many problems: the towns were well policed and full of informers; the regimes were rich and any serious threat to them that did emerge would lead to an Iranian and Saudi intervention. It was difficult to conceive of a successful revolutionary seizure of power in one alone of the small coastal states. A revolution in Oman would make this more possible; and a significant change in Saudi Arabia or Iran would have a decisive influence. Despite the problems the future was open for a revolutionary movement, linked to the guerrillas in Dhofar, to overthrow the domination of the Gulf by imperialism and its local allies.

Notes

1. These states were referred to as 'Trucial' because of the truces Britain forced them to sign in the early nineteenth century. This denomination was a piece of imperialist nomenclature; in Arabic the area was known as '*sahel Oman*', 'the coast of Oman'.

2. The most comprehensive history of the Gulf is Sir Arnold T. Wilson, *The Persian Gulf*, London, 1928 and 1954. An account of events between 1950 and 1960 can be found in John Marlowe, *The Persian Gulf in the Twentieth Century*, London, 1962. For an Arab nationalist overview of the area see Sayyid Naufal, *al-Khalij al-Arabi* (*The Arabian Gulf*), Beirut, 1969. Naufal, an official of the Arab League, was one of the Egyptian officials responsible for formulating policy towards the Yemens and the Gulf.

3. For the history of Kuwait and Bahrain in the eighteenth century see Ahmad Abu Hakima, *History of Eastern Arabia*, Beirut, 1965.

4. C. U. Aitchison, *A Collection of Treaties, Engagements. and Sands Relating to India and Neighbouring Countries*, Delhi, 1933, p. 238. For considerable factual material on the area see M. J. Sadik and W. P. Snavely, *Bahrain, Qatar and the United Arab Amirates*, Lexington, 1972.

5. K. G. Fenelon, *The Trucial States*, Beirut, 1967, p. 12.

6. See Belgrave's autobiography *Personal Column*, London, 1960. The title of the book alludes to the fact that Belgrave acquired the job after answering an advertisement in the small ads section of *The Times*.

7. Ali Humeidan, *Les Princes de l'or noir*, Paris, 1968. Active British depositions in the 1960s fell into two categories; those of ultra-conservative rulers who had outlived their purpose (Abu Dhabi, 1966; Oman, 1970) and those of nationalist rulers who opposed British rule (Sharjah, 1965).

8. The analysis of Kuwait presented here owes much to the information provided to the author by Sami Nayis, editor of *at-Talia*, Kuwait, during the author's visit to Kuwait in February 1971.

9. The al-Khatib wing of the M A N had been criticized by the South Yemeni and Dhofar sections (the N L F and P F L O A G) for pursuing 'rightist policies'; and the peninsular M A N had split after a conference in Dubai in 1969. However the M A N weekly in Kuwait *at-Talia* (*The Vanguard*) was the one magazine in the Gulf which consistently publicized and sup-

ported the struggle in Dhofar. *At-Talia* was banned on several occasions by the Kuwait government.

10. These conditions were consistently exposed in *at-Talia*. For a conventional analysis see Ragae al Mallakh, *Economic Development and Regional Cooperation: Kuwait*, Chicago, 1968.

11. In 1970 seventeen people were sentenced to terms of between one and seven years' imprisonment for their alleged role in these bomb attacks; four other people were acquitted. All but one of the accused were Kuwaitis and included students, junior civil servants and oil workers. Several hundred non-Kuwaitis were deported after the bombings.

12. The best analysis of Bahrain is found in Ali Humeidan, op. cit., and in the unpublished doctoral thesis of Ali Hassan Taki, 'L'Évolution de la Société du Bahrain', presented to the Sorbonne in 1970. Humeidan and Taki formed part of a group of young Shia intellectuals, the first Bahrainis to acquire doctorates, who went to France and not Britain to study because of their admiration for the rationalism of the French Revolution. In Bahrain many of the aims of 1789 remain to be achieved.

13. The original components of A L B A were: the Bahrain state 27·5 per cent, the British Metal Corporation 25 per cent, Western Metal Corporation 12·5 per cent, Guinness Mahon 10·0 per cent and Aktiebolaget Elektrokoppar 25 per cent; later two new U S firms muscled in – General Cable Corporation acquiring 18 per cent and Boston Investments 10 per cent. The completion of the plant was delayed for several months because of strikes: the local contractor, al-Afu, was paying the workers 800–900 fils a day, while the contractors were paying him B D 4 per worker per day. (B D 1 = 1,000 fils.)

14. Similar developments took place at Qatar and Dubai. The Gulf states had some assets to offer international aviation – cheap petrol, uncrowded airspace and little likelihood of airports being closed because of states of emergency. Less desirable items picked up on Gulf stop-overs were hijackers and cholera. Stringent measures to exclude both had to be taken.

15. For the account of one of those deported to St Helena see *Min Bahrain il al-Manfa* (*From Bahrain to Exile*), Beirut, 1965.

16. See Patrick Seale, 'Riots Shatter Calm of Rule by Cocktail Party', the *Observer*, 28 March 1965. A 3,000-strong British civilian community lived in Bahrain in archaic colonial conditions. When rising local nationalism threatened to break into the exclusive Gymkhana Club the colonials changed the name to the British Club to keep out undesirable foreigners. 'It's quite a nice place, actually, rather like India used to be,' a British official told one U S reporter (*New York Times*, 14 April 1971).

17. *Economist*, 14 May 1966.

18. In 1972 a member of the ath-Thani family was involved in a diplomatic incident at London Airport when he was found to be transporting quantities of weaponry in his suitcase. Back in 1953, when the ruler of Qatar had been invited to the coronation of Elizabeth II, he had annoyed the

British by bringing his sheep with him to Beirut and then herding them on to the passenger liner that took him to Italy.

19. Donald Hawley, *The Trucial States*, London, 1970, p. 204. Hawley's work is the most comprehensive introduction to these states, where he himself was Political Agent from 1958 to 1961. In 1971 he was appointed British Ambassador to Muscat.

20. 'Scouts Help to Calm Hot Tempers', *The Times*, 3 March 1969.

21. See the account by Shakhbut's one-time development adviser Hugh Boustead in *The Wind of Morning*, Chapter 17, London, 1971.

22. During his reign Shakhbut was relatively unknown outside the Gulf; but in the year after his deposition he became a familiar figure on British cinema screens as the supposedly wise and generous hero of a *Look at Life* travelogue. This film was made before his overthrow.

23. *The Times*, 3 March 1969. The gold was flown to Dubai in 10-*tola* pieces, each weighing about 4 oz. From there it was shipped in fast launches to the coast off Bombay where Indian smugglers picked it up. See Timothy Green, *The World of Gold*, London, 1968, for details.

24. K. G. Fenelon, 'Banking in the Gulf', *The Banker*, October 1970. British banks operating in the Gulf made a practice of co-opting former imperialist administrators on to their boards. Humphrey Trevelyan, former ambassador to Iraq and last Governor of Aden, joined the board of the British Bank of the Middle East; Sir William Luce, Political Resident in the Gulf from 1960 to 1966, joined the board of the Eastern Bank and of Gray MacKenzie on his retirement.

25. For an excellent exposé of the Crown Agents and of their role in British capitalism see 'How the Crown Agents Manage Their £1,000m', in the *Guardian*, 5 August 1971. The Agents were the largest single force in the City of London after the Bank of England itself.

26. Since these supplements were financed by imperialist firms and client regimes who bought advertising space, they tended to reflect the common desiderata of these friendly forces. At times however, the system fell apart; on one occasion *The Times* had to delay a supplement on Saudi Arabia when it was discovered that none of the 'experts' had been there for several years; on another occasion the Sultanate of Oman blocked a supplement in the same paper which it said was too critical. The most entertaining idiocy of all was to be found in *The Times* special supplement on 'The Arab World' dated 7 March 1968. The front page carried a piece by the then Middle East correspondent Nicholas Herbert entitled 'Unity Frayed In Aftermath of War'. The back page carried what purported to be an Arabic translation of the same. The text was identical but the headline had been judiciously doctored to read '*wahda taqawim aqab al harb*' – 'Unity Raised Up In Aftermath of War'.

27. *The Times*, 3 October 1967. A major internal difficulty faced by the British military build-up in the Gulf was the state of morale of the troops sent there. Class differences were accentuated by the tensions within the

army; while the officers entertained themselves in 'North-West Frontier' conditions, the working-class rank and file detested their stay there. One member of the First Battalion the Queen's Own Regiment who deserted as a result of spending time in Bahrain later explained why:

'I spent my first five years in the army as a driver, driving the top brass all over the place. It was a cushy number and I was lucky to get away with it, but after a while I was sent to an island called Bahrain in the Middle East. It's just a fucking great oil field, nine months out there were just too much. You just go lame brain. We were supposed to be protecting the oil well. Can you imagine 20,000 servicemen protecting thirty square miles of sand dune?'*

* *International Idiot*, No. 3, March 1970.

28. Edward Heath, 'Back to the Gulf', *The Times*, 27 April 1969. According to this observer the Gulf should follow 'the example of Kuwait, not of Aden'.

29. The *Daily Telegraph* of 2 February 1971 carried protests from two Conservative MPs about the British withdrawal. John Biggs-Davison, a long-time supporter of Portugal and of the Smith regime in Rhodesia, wrote that 'No one with a knowledge of the Arab world could pin his faith to a union of emirates of local forces, even with British officers and NCOs.' Carol Mather, MP, warned that 'revolutionary regimes will quickly replace the existing rulers. The Russian fleet will lie at anchor in the Gulf.' Unfortunately such alarm was unfounded.

30. *UN Document S/9772*, para 5.

31. *Iran Report*, Vol. 1, No. 5, July–August 1966.

32. *Voice of the Arabs* declared on 17 March 1968 that 'there is no doubt that the creation of the Federation was a natural reply to the imperialist tune'. In February 1968 the Iraqi government declared that the UAA was 'a logical step ... adequate to confronting the covert and overt schemes against the Arab character of the Gulf and its nationalism'.

33. Sir William Luce was appointed Britain's special envoy to the Gulf when the Conservative government returned to power. His earlier views on the Gulf are found in 'Britain in the Persian Gulf', *The Round Table*, No. 277, July 1967.

34. Continued US use of the Bahrain base was agreed to in a deal on 13 December 1971. Later the Senate held hearings on the agreement and tried to block the deal; its motives were not anti-imperialism, merely the preservation of the honour of bourgeois democratic institutions. The Bahrain government pretended it had cancelled the agreement with the US during the 1973 Arab–Israeli war; but it transpired that they had only cancelled a fuelling agreement with the US navy, not the actual use of the al-Jufair facilities.

35. An account of the 1972 mass movement is found in *Dirasat Arabia (Arab Studies)*, Beirut, September 1972.

Chapter Fourteen
Iran

The Rise of the Pahlavi Regime

Iran, a non-Arab state facing the Arabian peninsula across the waters of the Gulf, has often played an important role in Arabia; and with the emergence in the 1960s of a strong and aggressive regime in that country, Iran came once again to have a considerable influence in the politics of the region.[1] Iranian history has seen a cycle of strong states with expansionist policies being succeeded by weak states that were overrun from without. The country has undergone domination by a long series of aggressors, including Alexander the Great, the first Arab caliphs, Genghis Khan and Tamburlane, down to twentieth-century imperialists such as Curzon, Churchill and Dulles. In both periods, both of strength and weakness, Iran's geographical position has played an important part. With a population of over 30 million, Iran occupies a massive bloc of 627,000 square miles at one of the cross-roads of the Eurasian land mass. On an east–west axis it lies between the Fertile Crescent – now Iraq, Syria and Jordan – and the Mediterranean on the west, and the central Asian steppes and India to the east. On a north–south axis it lies between Russia and the waters of the Gulf and the Indian Ocean. This nodal location has meant that whether Iran has been the victim or the aggressor its relations to neighbouring states have been a central aspect of its political life.

The states of pre-Islamic Iran, which lasted for a thousand years, were one of the glories of the ancient world. Iranian armies attacked Greece, fought the Romans and in the early centuries of the Christian era invaded and held parts of the Arabian peninsula.[2] When the Arab tribes expanded out of the peninsula in the seventh century A.D. Iran was converted to Islam and its language adopted the Arabic script; but Iranians soon began to exert a powerful influence within the Arab empires and as the Islamic world grew weaker Iran began to regain its former autonomy. From the tenth century onwards small breakaway states formed in parts of Iran; and in the early sixteenth century, just as the Ottoman Turks were establishing their new state on the ruins of the Arab and Byzantine empires in the west, Iran was reconstituted as an independent state by the Safavi dynasty. With the Safavis the Shi'a brand of Islam became dominant in Iran; Persian architecture reached its peak in the great mosques of Isfahan and Persian civilization spread south-east into what is now Pakistan and north India. Portuguese and British traders had contacts with the Safavis from the moment the Europeans rounded the Cape of Good Hope, and for two centuries capitalist Europe and merchant Iran had what appeared to be equal relations.

In the eighteenth century the Safavi dynasty was defeated; its place was later taken by a new regime, that of the Qajar who chose the village of Tehran as their capital.[3] By this time western imperialism was on the attack all over Asia; and Iran soon felt the encroachments of its two imperial neighbours. From the north, Tsarist Russia pressed down into the Caucasus and exerted a growing economic hold on the northern provinces of Iran. From the south-west the British, implanted in India, exerted their equally baneful influence. By the late nineteenth century Iran had become a semi-colony, a state formally independent but in fact controlled from outside by imperialist powers willing to preserve the existing archaic social and political apparatus for fear of losing control if it was destroyed.[4] In 1907 this situation was formalized in the Anglo-Russian Convention which divided Iran up into three respective spheres of influence; Russian in the north, British – with the oil concession area – in the south, and neutral in the middle. In the nineteenth century there had been several anti-imperialist movements in Iran; all had been dominated by religious mystifications and all were crushed. In 1905 a new opposition demanding constitutional reforms appeared at first to have a greater chance of success: Asia had just been shaken by the Japanese victory over Russia and anti-imperialist movements, from the Boxers in China to the first secular nationalists in Egypt, were raising the call for reform and independence. However, after four years of intense politics centred in Tehran, the 'Constitutional Revolution', as it was later known, foundered and stopped.

The First World War opened the possibility of a more radical breakthrough. Imperialist armies directly occupied the country. Anti-imperialist militants gathered in the north of Iran. Then in 1917 the great Bolshevik Revolution in Russia removed one of the underpinnings of Iran's semi-colonial system. Russian troops retreated, and the first Foreign Affairs Commissar, Leon Trotsky, renounced the imperialist treaties which Tsarist Russia and Britain had imposed on Iran. In the north a revolutionary situation prevailed. The province of Gilan, in the mountainous area near the Caspian Sea, had been severely disrupted by the spread of capitalist trading relations from Russia. There also existed a communist movement; up to 200,000 Iranians, many of them from Gilan, had worked in Russia's Caucasian oil-fields before the war, and had formed the first Iranian communist group, the *Hemmat*, as early as 1904. The defeat of the 'Constitutional Revolution' had led more Iranians to Bolshevism, and the Russian Communist party had played an important role in northern Iran. In 1909, for example, the Georgian militant Sergo Ordjonikidze carried out clandestine work in the area and in the same year, during a rebel defence of the town of Tabriz against a government siege, the Iranian artillery was commanded by a former gunner on the warship *Potemkin*.

Gilan was a centre of anti-imperialist activity; and once Tsarist Russia's hold had been broken, a coalition of nationalists and communists there set up an autonomous regime. They attacked British troops on the way to support the Whites in the Caucasus; and in 1920, when Bolshevik Russian troops landed at Enzeli on the Iranian shore of the Caspian, a Socialist Republic was declared in Gilan. However, the Gilan Republic had several weaknesses. There was division between nationalists and communists; the nationalist leader, Kuchik Khan, quarrelled with the more revolutionary leaders, Sultan Zade and Ehsanollah

Khan, who demanded radical social changes. Conditions in Gilan were also very different to those in the rest of Iran, and a revolutionary movement did not exist in the areas to the south. International politics also affected the republic in that its establishment had been made possible by the civil war raging in the Caucasus between the Whites and the Reds. The presence of Red troops in Gilan, which greatly helped the Gilanis, was an extension of this Russian civil war as much as it was an act of internationalist solidarity.[5]

The first months of 1921 placed the Gilan Republic on the defensive. The revolutionaries tried to liberate Tehran and failed. Kuchik Khan and the Bolsheviks had quarrelled: he objected to their land reforms, their closure of mosques and their call to women to unveil themselves; they were also the main force behind the Committee for the Liberation of Iran which organized the march on Tehran. In February 1921 there was a military coup in Tehran by an officer in the Cossack Brigade, Reza Khan. Reza Khan set about recentralizing the country. Russian forces then pulled out of Enzeli in response to the British withdrawing forces out of the south. Reza Khan at first entered into negotiations with the Gilani leaders and exploited the split between Kuchik Khan and the Bolsheviks. But in October 1921 he attacked Gilan with a refurbished army and the first socialist republic in Iran was brought to a bloody end.[6]

The regime established by Reza Khan after 1921 set up a strong central government backed by a relatively efficient army. Reza Khan adopted a mild anti-imperialist position and opposed the attempts of the then British Foreign Secretary, Lord Curzon, to turn Iran into a protectorate. He entered into relations with the Soviet Union and brought in some foreign advisers to train his army and modernize the country. Like Kemal Ataturk he was a determined nationalist, unable to carry out a thorough break with imperialism or to maximize economic progress, but nonetheless a more capable wielder of state power than the enfeebled dynasty that had preceded him.

Although he abolished the Qajar dynasty in 1925 he decided to found a new line. He crowned himself Shah and adopted the name of an ancient Persian language, Pahlavi. To compensate for the obviously parvenu character of this new royalty he encouraged the growth of a fake-nationalist culture, stressing the link between the glorious past of Cyrus and Xerxes and the excellence of the Pahlavi present. Foreign archaeologists were hired to dig up the buried treasures of Iranian greatness; and Iran was forced to adopt a special system of months and years different from any other country in the world. This ideology had a double function: it had the positive role of giving Iranians a sense of national identity and of solidifying the limited independence of the state; but it also set out to mystify the people with a cooked-up version of history and with monarchist cant, which reached new dimensions under the regime of his son.[7]

Reza Khan carried out a number of reforms; he won a slightly more favourable agreement from the Anglo-Iranian Oil Company in 1933; he built a railway system; and he set up the beginnings of an educational and medical system. As long as the foreign powers were favourable he was able to remain in power. In August 1941, however, Britain and Russia united in a military occupation of Iran in order to keep open Allied supply routes to Russia and to exclude the Germans from the area. Reza Khan was deported to exile and unhappy death in South Africa. Although his son Mohammad Reza Pahlavi became Shah, the regime was seriously weakened by inflation and food shortages and by the political upsurge in Iran that followed the Allied occupation. At this point Iran entered a new phase of internal conflict.

Communism and Nationalism

The Second World War provoked political upheavals throughout the globe; and in many countries Communist parties gained unprecedented strength through leading struggles in the tempestuous conditions of the global battle. This was true in countries under fascist occupation or fascist attack where the Communist parties were among the most effective leaders of the anti-fascist movement and where they were able to benefit from the enhanced prestige of the Soviet Union. This was true in eastern Europe (Albania, Yugoslavia, Poland, Czechoslovakia), in western Europe (France, Italy and Britain) and in several countries of the Far East (China, Vietnam, Korea). In countries under the domination of imperialist powers fighting on the Allied side the Communist parties had a completely different problem; their prime response to the weakened imperialist hold was to call for all-out defence of the Soviet Union and a halt to anti-imperialist struggle. This meant that in a situation of economic and political turmoil it was the nationalists and not the communists who were able to come forward as the apparent champions of the oppressed peoples; and they were able to do so all the more easily in that they expressed themselves in the idiom peculiar to that country.

During and after the Second World War, in India, in the Middle East and throughout Latin America the Communist parties were reduced to defensive positions while bourgeois nationalists had the field all to themselves. In different ways, but all benefiting from this open situation, a generation of nationalists used the weakening of the world imperialist system by the Second World War to mobilize support. Where the Communist parties were reduced to paralysis, Mahatma Ghandi, Gamal Abd al-Nasser and Juan Perón rode the popular wave.[8] This situation applied with variations to Iran. There the unique demand of loyalty to the Soviet Union was made more complicated by the fact that Soviet troops were actually on Iranian soil and the Soviet Union was demanding an oil concession in northern Iran from the Tehran government. The loosened political situation created by the occupation had enabled political parties to organize and a Communist party, the *Tudeh* (Masses) party, had grown in strength both in Tehran and the north and in the oil-fields of the south. But the *Tudeh* were forced to concede ground to their bourgeois rivals and, when the Shah's government manoeuvred the Red Army out of northern Iran at the end of 1946, official attacks on the left grew stronger.[9]

The biggest threat to the Shah came from the nationalists, led by an anti-imperialist landowner, Mohammad Mosadeq, who was calling for the nationalization of Iranian oil. Between 1915 and 1950 the A I O C had realized a profit of $613 million, while the Iranian government had received only $316 million. While *Tudeh* was confined by its ties to the U S S R, Mosadeq was immensely popular with the urban masses; and in 1951 he became prime minister and immediately nationalized the oil industry. The expropriated British launched a campaign against him; the social-imperialists of the Attlee government organized a world-wide embargo on Iranian oil,[10] and made a determined effort to bring down the Iranian nationalist regime. They had some success, in that the end of oil revenues brought problems to the Iranian economy. Moreover, Mosadeq had an unorganized political following; he was popular, and backed by the majority of Iranians; but his National Front consisted of a coalition of small groups and was not coherently organized. The only organized anti-imperialist force, the *Tudeh* party, at first opposed him; the party secretary Radmanesh told the Nineteenth Congress of the Communist party of the Soviet Union in early 1952 that Mosadeq was an American agent, trying to wrest Iranian oil from the British. It was only after the Shah and Qavam-es-Sultaneh had tried to oust Mosadeq in July 1952 that *Tudeh* suddenly switched and began to support Mosadeq's position.

By this time it was too late. The U S had at first taken a cautious stand and had hoped to use Mosadeq to weaken the British. Later the State Department became worried by the growth of the mass movement. In January 1953 the change of administration in Washington brought Eisenhower and Dulles into power. In terms of cold-war strategy Iran formed part of what the Americans called the 'northern tier' – the anti-Soviet front line running from Turkey through Iran to Pakistan. Dulles, with his aggressive global strategy, wanted to consolidate the U S position in these countries; and the decision was taken to overthrow Mosadeq. Mosadeq's bourgeois allies had started to desert him; and on 13 August 1953 the Shah, with U S guidance, staged a showdown, by signing an edict (*firman*) that dismissed Mosadeq. Mosadeq resisted and arrested the chief of the Shah's Imperial Guard. The Shah then fled to Baghdad and thence to Rome; and in Tehran there was an outburst of republican demonstrations. Meanwhile, in a Swiss ski resort Allen Dulles, head of the CIA, held a meeting with the Shah's twin sister Princess Ashraf and the US Ambassador to Iran, Loy Henderson. A Colonel Schwartzkopf, who had trained the Iranian police during the war, was dispatched to Tehran with $10 million in notes; and there, in cooperation with CIA chief in the area, Kermit Roosevelt, the anti-Mosadeq coup was organized. On 19 August two prongs of the counter-revolution went into operation. First, bribed crowds of prostitutes and thugs swarmed up from southern Tehran, led by a right-wing bazaar leader named Shaaban Jaafari;[11] then the army, led by pro-Shah General Fazlollah Zahedi, marched into Tehran. Mosadeq was arrested and the Shah restored. A bewildered and terrorized population was unable to resist, while many of those in organized political groups expected that the reinstated Shah would be unable to remain in office for long.

This coup, known in Iran by its Persian date 'the 28th Mordad', was organized in detail by the CIA and the US Military Assistance Mission in Iran. As the director of US military assistance later told the US Congress:

When this crisis came on and the thing was about to collapse, we violated our normal criteria and among other things we did, we provided the army immediately on an emergency basis, blankets, boots, uniforms, electric generators, and medical supplies that permitted and created an atmosphere in which they could support the Shah ... The guns that they had in their hands, the trucks that they rode in, the armored cars that they drove through the street, and the radio communications that permitted their control, were all furnished through the military defense assistance program ... had it not been for this program, a government unfriendly to the United States probably would now be in power.[12]

Another US commentator was even more straightforward: 'It is senseless as some observers have written, to say that the Iranians overthrew Mosadeq all by themselves. It was an American operation from beginning to end.'[13]

The 'White Revolution': Capitalist Development

After 1953 Iran went through two phases. The period from 1953 to 1960 was marked by severe repression and by the regime's continued political instability. The phase from 1961 began with a temporary revival of the nationalist movement, but was dominated by the regime's programme of reform, which initiated wide-ranging capitalist transformation and the conversion of Iran into one of the dozen most powerful states in the world. Politics appeared to be more docile and controlled, until 1971, when a new revolutionary opposition movement emerged from the movement of the previous two decades.

Since it was the USA that had put the Shah back in power it was not surprising that for the first time they acquired some ownership of Iranian oil. Formally, this remained nationalized, but a new consortium of companies was given the right to continue plundering in a manner similar to before. BP retained a 40 per cent share; Shell acquired 14 per cent; CFP got 6 per cent; and the remaining 40 per cent was shared out between the five US majors, with 7 per cent each, and a 5 per cent share for a group of minor US companies. The new agreement was to last until 1994. A company set up by Mosadeq, the National Iranian Oil Company, was to receive 50 per cent of the profits along the lines of the 50–50 agreements which Saudi Arabia and Kuwait had already signed. The US domination was confirmed even more intensively in the military sphere. In 1954 Iran joined the pro-western Baghdad Pact (later CENTO). The formal reason for this military strengthening was the threat of a 'Soviet invasion'. The real reason was internal repression. US aid which poured into Iran over the period 1953–60 enabled the Shah to expand his army from 120,000 men to 190,000, his air force from nothing to 8,000 and his navy from nothing to over 4,000. Military expenditure rose from 2.5 b. rials in 1953–4 to 14.2b. rials in 1960–61 to 23.9b. rials in 1966–7. Between 1950 and 1965, 2,000 Iranians were trained in the US. In Iran itself at least three US military groups operated: ARMISH – the United States Military Mission with the Imperial Iranian Army; MAAG the Military Assistance Advisory Group to Iran; and GEN-MISH – the United States Military Mission with the Imperial Iranian Gendarmerie.

Hubert Humphrey summed it up in 1960: 'Do you know what the head of the Iranian army told one of our people? He said the army was in good shape, thanks to US aid – it was now capable of coping with the civilian population.'[14]

In the whole period from 1946 to 1970 Iran was estimated to have received a total of $1,365·6 million in military aid, of which $830·4 million came under the Military Assistance Programme and another $504·1 million took the form of credit from the US government.

Table 30

US Military Aid to Iran under the Military Assistance Programme 1949–69

	$ million		$ million
1949–52	16·6	1963	70·1
1953–7	133·9	1964	27·3
1958	73·0	1965	49·9
1959	90·9	1966	93·5
1960	89·1	1967	75·3
1961	49·2	1968	85·8
1962	33·3	1969	50·9

Source: *The Arms Trade with the Third World*, Stockholm International Peace Research Institute, Stockholm, 1971, p. 146.

This sum represented roughly 7 per cent of all US aid to other countries under the military assistance programme.

The organization that ruled Tehran by martial law after the coup, the *Farmandar-i-Nizami*, set about tracking down the Shah's opponents; US advisers imported FBI methods; and the Iranian security forces were revamped in 1956 to form the now notorious secret police, the *Sazman-i-Etelaat va Amniyat-i-Keshvar*, or Organization of Information and Security of the Country, known by its initials SAVAK.

There were three sorts of opponent whom the newly reinstated regime had to crush. First, there were the nationalist supporters of Mosadeq. These were arrested and tried; Mosadeq himself was sentenced to three years in prison and then banished to his village,[15] while Fatemi, his Foreign Minister, was shot; the loose National Front was shattered. The second source of opposition came from anti-monarchist tribes, particularly the Quashqai, in southern Iran. Their flocks and villages were strafed and bombed and their leaders driven into exile. The *Tudeh* were a more serious case. They had a powerful apparatus inside the officer corps; it numbered up to 600 men and was headed by an ex-officer named Khosro Ruzbeh.

The civilian *Tudeh* were rounded up during late 1953 and 1954 and the government gained considerable profit from the surprise of their coup and from *Tudeh*'s underestimation of the new US–Shah alliance.[16] The military network was broken through torture and constant harassment; and in 1958 Khosro Ruzbeh himself was captured after a gun battle, tried and executed. By the late 1950s *Tudeh* leaders, exiled in Leipzig, announced to the world that they no longer possessed an organization within Iran itself.

As far as US imperialism was concerned, the situation in Iran seemed to have restabilized itself. The state had been strengthened and the enemy crushed. Change was now possible. In 1960 political controls were lessened and a timid opposition was allowed to contest the elections for the assembly in August 1960. So blatant was the government's rigging of these elections that the Shah had to cancel them, and a new government was brought in to reorganize the political set-up. Political opposition broke out in the university and in a number of professions, including the teachers; and in 1961 and 1962 the army invaded the university with the result that students were shot and arrested. The leadership of this new wave went to the National Front, which raised the slogan of 'restoring constitutional government' and called for the return of Mosadeq. The *Tudeh* party tried to join the National Front; but were rejected as being anti-nationalists and agents of the Soviet Union.

The initiative at this time lay with the Shah, who was able to

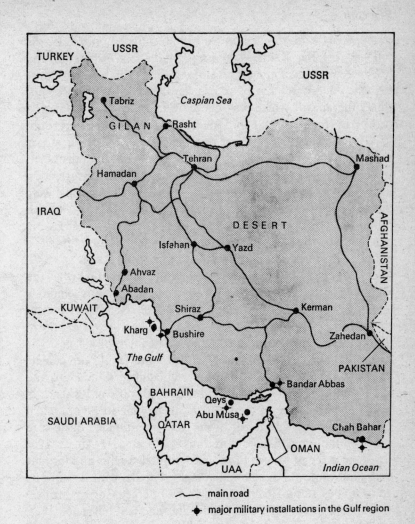

main road

◆ major military installations in the Gulf region

Map 15   Iran

outmanoeuvre his divided and uncertain opposition. Under the influence of the Kennedy administration in Washington and pressure for development at home the Tehran government launched a programme of reform entitled the 'White Revolution', the aim of which was allegedly to bring democracy and prosperity to Iran; and in January 1963 a rigged referendum validated the six principles of this 'revolution'.[17] Popular anger mixing revolutionary militancy and religious obscurantism continued to rise; and in June 1963 a full-scale popular insurrection took place in Tehran and its environs; thousands of people were gunned down in the streets, and the religious leader Ayatollah Khomeini was bundled off to exile in Turkey. Severe repression brought all opposition to an end and Iranian politics returned to a S A V A K-run peace comparable to that of the 1950s.

At first the key element in the White Revolution was the land redistribution. Up to 1962 Iran had been an overwhelmingly agricultural country, with around 50,000 villages; 70 per cent of the land was cultivated by share-croppers under a system known as *mozaree*, and some feudal families owned tens of villages. The biggest landowners of all had been the royal family, late-comers who had robbed other more traditional families in the 1920s and 1930s; but the Shah himself had begun to dispose of his lands in 1949. The first stage of land reform, from 1962 to 1964, limited ownership to one village per owner, and an estimated thirteen to fourteen thousand villages were thus reallocated. In August 1964 a second stage of reform introduced capitalist rents and farming techniques into the remaining villages. Parallel to this break-up of the old estates a Health Corps and a Literacy Corps were sent into the rural areas allegedly to educate and assist the people.[18]

This reform was accompanied by delirious propaganda in favour of the Shah and his 'wisdom'. It was pretended that the land reform showed the Shah's love for his people. In fact it showed the opposite – the people's hatred of the Shah, and his fear of them. As Ali Amini, the prime minister in 1962, remarked in defending the reforms: 'We must not allow the people's anger to rise. It would sweep us all away, the Shah and the Aminis.' Like many capitalist land reforms before it, such as Stolypin's reforms in Russia two years after the 1905 revolution, the main purpose of the land reform was political: to reduce tensions in the population, and to create a strong rural base for the regime.[19] Like the later 'Green Revolution' in India it tried to broaden the social base of the regime.

The land reform replaced pre-capitalist agrarian relations by a capitalist system. *Mozaree*, share-cropping, was replaced by rents. Those peasants who did receive land taken from the biggest owners were in general peasants who had been relatively well off before the reform. In 1967, at the end of the second phase of the reform, official figures showed that 786,715 peasants – around 20 per cent of the rural population – had become *owners*, but nearly twice that number – 1,223,968 – had become *leaseholders*. Many landowners were able to evade the reform provisions; the second phase allowed owners with 'mechanization' to retain more land; and many a rusty tool or tractor was produced to justify this claim. The cooperatives set up by the regime were in practice dominated by the rich peasants, who used them to control the marketing of others' produce.

Some Iranian revolutionaries at first argued that the land reform was a fake designed to deceive the Iranian people. This was clearly not the case; a real shift in class forces had taken place. The biggest and most backward landowners were weakened and then integrated into the new bureaucratic apparatus set up by the reform. Some peasants were co-opted into the system as owners; but many more saw the rate of exploitation rise as *mozaree* ties were replaced by rents to be paid in money. One consequence of this was the forced migration of rural population to the towns, where they formed a volatile and unemployed lumpenproletariat. Tehran's population rose from 1·5 million in 1963 to 3·3 million in 1973. But in the villages the Health and Literacy Corps provided the government with a bureaucratic apparatus through which to control the peasantry more easily. The distinguishing feature of this particular capitalist land reform was that other such reforms generally aimed not only to stabilize the political situation but also to generate an economic surplus from rural production that would facilitate the development of industry. In Iran the surplus came not from agriculture but from oil; and agrarian production actually fell behind the rise in population. In 1969 agrarian output rose by only 1·7 per cent, while the population rose by 3·2 per cent; and agriculture amounted for as little as 16 per cent while employing up to 45 per cent of the population. After ten years of White Revolution Iran had become a net importer of meat and cereals for the first time.

The rise in oil revenues formed the basis of Iran's growth rate, which in the middle and late 1960s was as high as 10 per cent. From 1967 onwards the Shah negotiated annual agreements with the oil consortium, guaranteeing rises in price and in Iranian output; and in February 1971 he patronized the Tehran talks between the OPEC Gulf states and the oil companies, which reached a comprehensive five-year deal on price and output figures. However, although in June 1972 he reached a further agreement with the Iranian consortium on long-term future co-operation, he was outdistanced by the Arab oil 'participation' agreement of October 1972. In January 1973, at the tenth anniversary celebrations of the White Revolution, he announced that new negotiations would be needed immediately to revise the concession. With planned investment for the 1973–8 five-year plan at $32,000 million, the annual production of oil would have to rise from its 1971 level of 222 million tons to around 400 million tons during the plan period. In May 1973 the oil companies agreed to terminate the 1954 agreement (scheduled to run till 1994) and to hand over ownership of its fields and of the refinery in return for twenty years' guaranteed supplies.

The economic growth actually carried out in the first decade of the White Revolution had two marked limitations. First, it was heavily concentrated in the services sector. Secondly, it was very much dependent on foreign capitalist penetration of Iran. The fastest growing sector of the Iranian economy was services, which in 1968–9 made up over 40 per cent of production. The industrial development carried out was often very inefficient; the two largest industrial projects, the gas trunk-lines to Russia and the Shahpur petro-chemical plant, both cost more than double the $500 million originally allocated to each. Most of the establishments listed as 'factories' were very small, employing an average of around four people, and were concentrated in the light industry zone.

Table 31

Factory Employment in Iran 1969

	Employees	Factories
Food manufacturing	127,877	21,564
Beverages	3,619	58
Tobacco	4,387	3
Textiles, carpets and gelims	204,706	42,849
Apparel, made up cloth	121,718	45,762
Wood and furnitures	34,613	13,333
Paper and cardboard	2,573	251
Printing and binding	8,230	1,054
Leather and hides	6,229	1,239
Rubber and rubber products	6,001	604
Chemicals	13,738	364
Non-metallic minerals	42,598	5,096
Petroleum	790	10
Basic metal	7,893	696
Metal products	70,811	23,930
Non-electrical machinery	6,378	5,037
Electrical machinery	18,068	70
Transport equipment	27,232	11,880
Other miscellaneous	17,925	7,183
Electric power	9,481	400
Total	734,867	181,383

Source: *The Middle East and North Africa 1972–3*, p. 313.

The foreign share of the economy developed apace despite the Shah's own rising revenues and his heady rhetoric about national independence. A special Centre for the Attraction and Protection of Foreign Industries – C A P F I – was set up for this purpose. The U S was the leading investor in this field. In April 1971, of the 119 foreign companies operating in Iran in fields other than oil, 32 were U S firms, 18 were West German and 14 British; but of the

493

total $350 million invested by foreign firms up to mid 1970 under the 1968–72 five-year plan, $215 million were US funds – i.e. US firms invested more per company in Iran and were more numerous over all. Whether American or not, all foreign firms were able to repatriate profits under the auspices of CAPFI; between 1965 and 1968 over 30 per cent of money invested in Iran through CAPFI left the country again as capital outflow to foreign firms.[20]

Another way of returning the surplus to the advanced capitalist countries was through military purchases. These escalated in the 1960s. In 1970 alone they rose by 50 per cent, and in 1972 came to $895 million, over a third of the budget – and dwarfed even those of Saudi Arabia. From 1961 the US gave less outright aid to third-world countries for military purposes, and such supplies were financed either through credit or through purchases by the countries themselves. Iran was in a position to meet both credit and outright purchase conditions; in the period 1962–8 US export sales to Iran were $515·4 million or 24 per cent of all US arms sales to the third world. Subsequent credits have included several hundred million dollars of Export-Import Bank credits for the purchase of Phantom F-4 jets, for re-equipping the army, for naval expansion in the Gulf. The British, too, provided extensive naval and land arms supplies, including 800 Chieftain tanks. In 1972 Iran's total foreign debt amounted to $12,232 million and over $200 million went on servicing the military part of it alone. In 1973 it announced a new $2,500 million arms agreement with the USA, and it was estimated that in 1973–4 Iran would spend more on arms than in the previous fifteen years. In 1972 Iran was estimated to have a total armed force of 191,000 and a defence budget of $915 million, which represented around 8 per cent of GNP. The army numbered 160,000 men, the navy 9,000 and the air force 22,000. The country possessed a vast arsenal of tanks, rockets, fighter-bombers and armed hovercraft, comprising by far the largest military power in the area. If up to 1961 the main purpose of the military supplies had been internal repression, the aim in the 1960s and 1970s was more strategic. The Shah propagated Iran's dominant role in the Gulf, once the British had left, and he built up his naval forces with the object of continued expansion into the Indian Ocean. In 1971 Iran occupied three islands, the two Tumbs and Abu Musa, in the mouth of the Gulf, and in 1972 the Sultan of Oman gave it the island of Umm al-Ghanem. The Shah stated flatly that Iran would not allow revolution on the Arab side of the Gulf. With one big $200 million naval base already established at Bandar Abbas, the Shah began construction of a second base outside the mouth of the Gulf, at Chah Bahar in Baluchistan, at a cost of $600 million. In 1972 he even announced that Iran had acquired naval facilities on the island of Mauritius, far out in the Indian Ocean; and he warned that in the event of rebellion in Pakistan, Iran would invade. When the Shah dispatched around 10,000 counter-insurgency troops to Oman in December 1973, this was the first time the Iranian army had fought a major campaign abroad since the bandit-turned-monarch Nadir Shah had invaded northern India and Oman in the early eighteenth century. The Iranian people, many of whom have a sharp sense of history, will recall the fate which befell Nadir Shah: 20,000 men lost their lives in Oman before the Iranian invaders were driven out. Then the monarch himself was assassinated by four of his army officers, who feared that the Shah's tyrannical practice might soon claim them as its victims.

The strengthening of Iran involved a change both in relations with Russia and with the imperialist powers. Although the Shah visited Moscow in 1956, relations with the Soviet Union in the 1950s were bad; and they only improved after the Shah's second visit to Moscow in 1965. In 1967 the Shah concluded a $110 million military purchase agreement; and this was followed by an economic treaty worth $280 million, under which the Russians would build a steel mill in Isfahan and Iranian gas would be piped to the Soviet Union. Around 1,500 Russian experts came to work in Iran; and when in 1972 the Shah paid a third visit to Moscow a further economic and cultural exchange agreement was signed. The imperialist countries at first viewed these ties with alarm; but it was soon clear that the Shah remained solidly in the western camp; and by 1970 Britain and the US were encouraging Iran to play an important role in the Gulf and Indian Ocean. More populous and capable than Saudi Arabia, Iran was allotted a key role in imperialist strategy. The *New York Times* summed it up in July 1971:

Acting with British–American blessings, Shah Mohammad Reza Pahlavi has accepted responsibility for the security of the Persian Gulf after Britain removes its protection and armed forces ... By 1975, when the present programme of military deliveries and training is completed, Iran is expected to be a major Middle Eastern power and an element of stability in the volatile Gulf region, American officials say.[21]

Nixon's visit to Tehran after his trip to Moscow in May 1972, and the appointment of former C I A chief Richard Helms as U S ambassador to Tehran, confirmed this support.

The New Opposition

The ideological component of the 'White Revolution' was the monarchist frenzy that the Shah tried to elicit from his people and from the rest of the world. He made no pretence of allowing any political freedom to his people and by 1973 had taken to lecturing western listeners about their 'softness' towards dissidents in their own country. Even loyal servants whose actions were popular, like the first agricultural reform minister, Arsanjani, and the mayor of Tehran, Nafici, were dismissed lest they lessen public concentration on the Shah. This megalomania reinforced the illusion that the Shah alone ruled the country, a version of events that masked the development under the Shah of a large ruling class in which remnants of the old and newly enriched elements united. Even the Iranian opposition appeared at times to be victims of this personalist mythology, failing to see the way in which the consolidation and subsequent expansion of the Pahlavi regime at the *political* level had been accompanied by class formation at the *socio-economic* level. The new ruling class depended partly on the expanded state apparatus (civil and military), the growth of Iranian commercial and industrial enterprise, however subsidiary, and the reorganized agrarian system. Its economic prosperity was visible for all to see; but it seemed to present no serious direct challenge to the Shah at the political level. It sheltered behind his dictatorship, and was accomplice to his terrorization of the people. Two puppet organizations, the *Iran Novin* (New Iran) and *Mardom* (People) parties, carried out a shadowy debate in the Iranian parliament and went through the motions of standing for election. This ventriloquy had little credibility. For example, despite government pressure, only at most 30 per cent of the people turned up in July 1971 for the elections. All premiers installed were chosen as loyal servants of the Shah himself.

Inside Iran, stringent measures were taken to preclude criticism of the Shah. Shakespeare plays that portrayed the murder of kings were banned lest the audience applaud. Parallel measures were taken abroad, where the gossip columns of western papers were fed with pap about the Shah and his wives; in the 1950s it was Queen Soraya and in the 1960s it was Queen Farah, but the message was the same trivialized smokescreen designed to hide the real situation in Iran. As the White Revolution progressed this operatic behaviour reached a new pitch. In 1967 the Shah had himself crowned king twenty-five years after his accession – it had been impossible to hold the celebration during the Second World War. In 1971 an even more grandiose project was executed, when up to $300 million was spent on celebrations of the 2,500th anniversary of the founding of the Iranian monarchy. Over seventy states were represented at the ceremony, which received world-wide publicity.

There were two other aspects of the 1971 celebrations that the Shah tried to hide. One was the fact that the 2,500th anniversary had in fact fallen in 1962, but because of the uncertain political situation nothing had been celebrated at that time. The other was that over 1,000 people were taken into detention by SAVAK in the months before the celebration in order to prevent any opposition. 1971 was marked by a much more important event for the Iranian people than the Shah's circus: it saw for the first time in a decade the emergence on a small scale of a revolutionary opposition. This new movement grew out of the defeat of the old.[22] The nationalist and communist movements that had grown up during the Second World War had become divided, and had paid the price of this in the bloody and passive defeat of August 1953. The *Tudeh* had then been too hostile to the nationalists and had been hampered by its ties to the Soviet Union. The nationalists had produced no strong political organization and had clung to parliamentary means of gaining and retaining power. In the relative relaxation of 1960–63 the *Tudeh* had followed after the nationalists, while the latter had reproduced in an even starker form the mistakes of the period before 1953. Their slogan, 'restoration of legitimate government', and their reformism were no match for the Shah and his manoeuvres. At the one permitted National Front congress, held in Tehran in 1962, a committee from Tehran university was defeated in calling for more vigorous activity and in opposing collaboration with the regime.

The opportunism of the old National Front leaders weakened its support; and in January 1963 the Shah went on to the attack with his capitalist reforms. A bewildered opposition denounced these as fake, tried to ask for more, and formed no coherent position on the religiously inclined rebels who flared up in Tehran and in the holy city of Qom. In June 1963, when thousands of workers and peasants rose in spontaneous opposition and were massacred, the vacillation and reformism of the National Front and their *Tudeh* trailers had been proven to many militants.

In the years after this second defeat the nuclei of a new, militant opposition began to reflect and to work. Some were former members of *Tudeh* or of the National Front; others were members of the university who had participated in the struggles of 1960–63. A powerful adjunct to this development inside Iran was the Confederation of Iranian Students, which operated in Europe and North America and which included all political tendencies within the 20,000 exiled student community who opposed the Shah. Other factors also assisted political clarification. The evolution of capitalist relations inside Iran increased the numbers of working class in the main urban centres. The growth of economic and military ties with the Soviet Union also enforced the need for self-reliance among the Iranian opposition. This was equally encouraged by the development of ties between the Shah and the People's Republic of China in 1971; and by the diplomatic praise granted to the regime by Chinese officials.[23] Another radicalizing factor was the growth of armed struggle in other parts of the colonial world: in Vietnam, in Palestine and in Latin America. In the Arab countries the Nasserists had initially benefited from the weakness of the Communist parties and had then given birth to a revolutionary current through their own degeneration; in Iran the discrediting of the *Tudeh* and then of the National Front combined with the world revolutionary upsurge of the late 1960s to produce the new opposition that broke out in 1971.

Although many distinct small groups made up this movement, they all had in common a recognition of the fact that armed struggle was a necessary form of political activity in Iran. Their disparities, meanwhile, were due more to diverse origins than to sectarian disagreement. One group which began in 1965 sent two of its militants to fight for a time with the Palestinian guerrillas; and in February 1971 it tried to start a guerrilla movement in the mountains north of Tehran. They attacked a police station at Siahkal on 8 February, but were quickly surrounded by hundreds of government troops backed by helicopters. Three were killed, twelve were arrested and later shot and the police later claimed to have captured another fifty. According to press reports the group had four components: a rural guerrilla section; an urban guerrilla section; a smuggling and munitions section; and a forgery section.

The Siahkal attack was the biggest guerrilla outbreak up to then: and despite their setback, the group that organized it continued their activities under a new name, the Guerrilla Organization of the Devotees of the People (*Chirikha–ye–Fedayi–i–Khalq*). Members of another organization, the 'Palestine Group', had been arrested in December 1970 while trying to escape from Iran over the Iraqi border to make their way to Jordan. At their trial, in January 1971, one of their members, Shokrallah Paknejad, described the political position he represented. 'I am a

Marxist-Leninist, and I am proud of my way of thinking,' he said.

I used to be a religious man, and in the course of social struggle, as a member of the Iran Nation party, which is a nationalist party, I joined the National Front. Later on, in due course, after long study and long analysis, and after having been arrested and imprisoned on several occasions, and after many political experiences, I reached the conclusion that the welfare of the Iranian people and the liberation of the whole of mankind can only be realized under the banner of Marxism-Leninism, that is, the ideology of the most deprived masses.

He made no secret of his support for the Palestinian people and of the inspiration provided for the militants in Iran by the Palestinian struggle. 'The Iranian ruling élite is putting on trial the solidarity of our people and that of the whole world with the people of Palestine, a solidarity for the liberation of that country from the yoke of imperialism and Zionism.'[24]

Information on the politics and actions of the guerrilla movement was fragmentary; and its members were both divided and at a relatively low level of action. In 1971 and 1972 at least four military leaders were assassinated; in April 1971 General Farsiu, the military prosecutor, was shot; and he was followed by General Sabet, commander of the gendarmerie in Kurdistan, by General Molavi, a SAVAK boss, and General Taheri, who had responsibility for the country's prisons. In 1971 guerrillas nearly succeeded in kidnapping US ambassador Douglas MacArthur II; and in 1972 they set off a number of bombs in solidarity with Vietnam during Nixon's twenty-four-hour visit. In May 1973 they shot a military adviser at the US embassy. Numerous armed clashes with police were reported both in Tehran itself and in other towns, as well as in different parts of the countryside.

The most significant parallel activity to these guerrilla actions was the sporadic strike activity of the developing working class. In May 1971 there was a particularly bloody clash at Karadj, twenty-five miles north of Tehran, when the police shot three workers as over 2,000 employees of a textile factory were trying to march to Tehran in support of wage demands. Other strikes were reported from the Ziba textile factory in Tehran around the

500

same time; but after 1953 protests and trades unions were banned; and there was no evidence of an organized relation between the small and secret guerrilla nuclei and the unorganized and oppressed working class.

The cost was also immense. The 60,000-man S A V A K staged a series of secret trials, marked by reported 'suicides', torture, harassment of lawyers and relatives and the rest. Numerous protests from abroad denounced the violent and unrestrained brutality of the police,[25] whom the Shah went out of his way to endorse. In the course of 1971 and 1972 an estimated 2,500 people were sent to jail; around sixty were executed and another sixty were killed in battle. The guerrillas were nevertheless able to derive internationalist inspiration from the struggles of other peoples. A member of a Marxist-Leninist group, the Organization of People's Combatants (*Mojahidin–i–Khalq*), told his judges in 1972:

During the present century 800 million Chinese and 200 million Russians have been freed. There is pandemonium in the Middle East and in Latin America. Today in Tehran they confiscate funds from the banks, while workers paralyse Spain. The end result will be the creation of a new society.

Yet while the courage and political stamina of the guerrillas was not in doubt the actions of 1971 and 1972 were only the first stages of a possible struggle. The Pahlavi regime was strong. They knew that guerrilla actions would not militarily weaken the regime; the purpose was political; the demonstration that the regime could be attacked and that the S A V A K's terror could be fought. As one cautious guerrilla writer put it in 1971:

No one can guarantee the final success of the present revolutionary movement in Iran. Nor can anyone foretell its immediate defeat under the severe blows that the brutal police apparatus is dealing it. Born out of the ruins of the Tudeh and Mosadeqist currents after the massacre of 1963 the present revolutionary movement, although still fragile, has a very good chance of success.[26]

Imperialism was for its part determined to prevent the Shah's regime from being overthrown. Not only was his oil important, but Iran's role in the Gulf and the Indian Ocean was increasingly vital. A special indication of Iran's importance came in November 1972 when, in company with South Korea and Taiwan, it sent F-5A fighters to the regime in Saigon to bolster it in the event of a US withdrawal.[27] As for the Iranian regime itself, it could certainly hold down the guerrillas at their level of activity reached in 1971 and 1972. Its long-term problems arose from the fact that economic changes it was putting through produced political strains that it could not necessarily meet and which might only be reduced by the end of the regime itself. It was a characteristic of Iran's development that the new capitalist ruling class was represented politically by the Shah and would be very much threatened if called upon in the Shah's absence to act politically. Increased awareness on the part of the peasantry and uncontrolled growth of the urban population combined with the socio-economic upsurges of the White Revolution to pose new contradictions. The guerrilla movement saw this and realized that their future lay in linking its armed nuclei to an organized working-class movement. The regime, with oil and astute political leadership, had a large room for manoeuvre. Yet any successful advances by revolutionaries in other near-by countries, and especially in the Gulf, would be of great assistance to the Iranian people.

Notes

1. Since 1933 the official title of the country is 'Iran'. The word 'Persia' is a corruption of the name for the southern province of Iran named Fars, which contains the ancient capital of Persepolis (known to Iranians as Takht-i-Jamshid, the Throne of Jamshid) and the town of Shiraz, where the classical Iranian poets Hafez and Saadi worked in the fourteenth and fifteenth centuries. The Iranians call their language *farsi* as a result of the importance of the Fars province in the genesis of the language and culture as a whole. Hence it is legitimate to call the language and culture 'Persian', while the country iself is best called 'Iran'.

2. This historical legacy is found in several Persian placenames in neighbouring Arab countries; e.g. Baghdad, the present capital of Iraq, and Rostaq, a town in the Omani interior. The history of Iranian conquest has left a residue of sometimes paranoid suspicion on the Arab side of the

Gulf and a rabid and arrogant anti-Arab chauvinism among the Iranian ruling class.

3. The founder of the Qajar dynasty was Agha Mohammad Khan, a eunuch whose cruelty is legendary in Iranian history. On the special Persian carpets which portray the heads of all the kings of Iran, Agha Mohammad is easily recognizable because he and the present Shah are the only two without beards.

4. For a detailed analysis of the concept of a semi-colony and of its application to Iran as well as its use by Mao in relation to China see Lucien Rey, 'Persia in Perspective', *New Left Review*, No. 20, Summer 1963. Rey's two articles, in *New Left Review* 19 and 20, provide an outstanding Marxist comprehension of Iran's history up to the launching of the White Revolution. Bahman Nirumand, *Iran: The New Imperialism in Action*, New York, 1969, gives an anti-imperialist analysis up to the start of the 'White Revolution'.

5. The general background to the Gilan Republic and to Soviet policy in this period can be found in E. H. Carr, *The Bolshevik Revolution*, Vol. 3, London, 1952. The general history of the Iranian communist movement is found in Sepehr Zabih, *The Communist Movement in Iran*, Berkeley, 1966. Zabih's account is a straightforward bourgeois one. A critical assessment of the history of the left from a Marxist position is found in A. P. Pouyan and M. Mani, *Iran: Three Essays on Imperialism, the Revolutionary Left and the Guerrilla Movement*, Florence, 1972. The latter work mentions an important Persian language source, for the Gilan period, E. Mirfakhrai, *Sardar Jangal, Mirza Kuchik Khan*, Tehran, 1965.

6. There are certain striking similarities between Gilan and Dhofar. Both are enclaves of tropical mountain in predominantly arid and flat terrain; in both the revolutionary movement began with an uneasy alliance of traditional tribal separatists and revolutionaries who had been radicalized by working in oil-fields elsewhere. The differences are, however, equally clear; in Gilan the revolutionaries were unable to dominate the situation; the Soviet Union stated that it was unable to play the supportive role which the PDRY plays for Dhofar; and the objective conditions in the rest of the target area (central and southern Iran, the Gulf states) were quite dissimilar. Most important of all is the fact that the Gilanis had no concept of protracted people's war.

7. On the Reza Khan period see Rey, op. cit., and A. Banani, *The Modernisation of Iran*, Stanford, 1962.

8. The aim of a revolutionary strategy in such countries should have been to support the anti-fascist struggle while simultaneously waging or preparing to wage an anti-imperialist struggle.

9. Until 1946 two pro-Soviet republics existed in Iranian Azerbaijan and in Kurdistan. Both were defeated when the Soviet Union pulled out, and the leaders were executed by the Tehran government. On the Kurdish experience see W. Eagleton, *The Kurdish Republic of 1946*, London, 1963.

The defeat of this republic led the way to the domination of the Kurdish struggle for national self-determination in Iran, Iraq and Turkey by more traditional nationalist elements.

10. Mosadeq in 1951 received the sour kind of torrential personal abuse which the British Foreign Office reserves for foreign statesmen who try to assert their nation's right to control their own economy. De Valera and the land annuities in 1932, Nasser and the Suez Canal in 1956 and Mintoff and the Valetta base in 1971 all provoked the same reaction, where dark hints about psychological 'instability' mixed with unreserved chauvinism. The Icelanders and their cod provoked the same response in 1972. A principled exception to this imperialism was the work of the British writer L. P. Elwell Sutton entitled *Persian Oil: A Study in Power Politics*, London, 1955.

11. Shaaban Jaafari was the head of a *zurkhane*, or 'strength house', a traditional kind of Iranian gymnasium given over to wrestling and juggling with heavy clubs. In the nineteenth century these had been the centre of progressive political opposition but had later become a recruiting ground for right-wing thugs. In the late 1960s the First National City Bank of New York chose Jaafari's *zurkhane* as the backdrop for an advertising photograph of its Tehran staff.

12. Major General George C. Stewart in 1954, quoted in Engler, *The Politics of Oil*, p. 206.

13. Andrew Tully, *C I A – The Inside Story*, London, 1962, p. 98. Chapter 7 gives a detailed account of the C I A's activities. See also the other classic work on the C I A, David Wise and Thomas B. Ross, *The Invisible Government*, London, 1964, pp. 108–12 for further details.

14. Quoted in David Horowitz, *From Yalta to Vietnam*, London, 1966, p. 190.

15. After his release from prison Mosadeq was banished to his estate at Ahmadabad where he lived in retirement. He died in hospital in Tehran in March 1967.

16. A former member of the *Tudeh* youth organization told the author of the following incident in which he participated. Such was the confidence of *Tudeh* after the August coup that they continued to hold fund-raising parties in private houses in Tehran. On one occasion in early 1954 up to 400 people were gathered at such a meeting, which was purporting to be a wedding party. At around 10.00 in the evening the police arrived, demanded to see the 'bride and groom', pointed out that it was not customary for guests at Iranian parties to pay for the food and promptly arrested everyone who was there. At first the imprisoned guests thought they had nothing to fear and it took several days of deprivation, followed by interrogation and escalating brutality, before they realized what had happened. This 'wedding party incident', well known in *Tudeh* circles, was one of the milestones in the government's breaking down of the party organization.

17. The six principles were later expanded to twelve. They were: land reform; nationalization of forests; granting of capital in state enterprises

as compensation to expropriated landlords; workers' participation in the profits of enterprises; granting women the vote; establishment of a literacy corps; a health corps; a rural development corps; judicial councils in villages; nationalization of water resources; urban and rural renovation; reform of the civil service and of education.

18. There does not, as yet, exist a systematic account of these economic and social changes. A concise background can be found in *Economic Development in Iran 1900–1970*, by Julian Bharier, London, 1971.

19. Two important and detailed works on land in Iran are: Anne Lambton, *Landlord and Peasant in Persia*, London, 1953, and her subsequent *Persian Land Reform 1962–66*, London, 1969. A Marxist critique of the land reform is found in Farhad Khamsi, 'Land Reform in Iran', *Monthly Review*, June 1969, and an excellent short piece by Paul Vieille, 'La réforme agraire a substitué le pouvoir d'une bureaucratie étatique à celui des féodaux', *Le Monde*, 27 January 1973.

20. The *Iran Almanac*, published annually in Tehran, gives a full list of foreign companies operating in Iran and of the repatriation of profits.

21. *New York Times*, 26 July 1971.

22. The best available source on the guerrillas is the work by A. P. Pouyan and M. Mani cited in note 5. Important documentary evidence is provided in the publications of the *Iranian Research and Publication Group*, London, 1972. For an important presentation of the guerrilla position see Ali-Akbar Safayi Farahani, 'What Every Revolutionary Must Know', Iran Research and Publication Group, London, 1973. Farahani wrote his text in 1970, participated in the Siahkal attack and was executed in March 1971. He had also worked with the Palestinian resistance.

23. In June 1973 Chinese Foreign Minister Chi Peng-fei visited Tehran. At a dinner given by Foreign Minister Khalatbari, Chi praised 'the vast struggle of the Third World's medium and small nations against imperialist aggression, subversion, domination and oppression' and then went on:

'Everyone's attention is now drawn to the situation in the Persian Gulf. Intensified expansionist activity, unwarranted use of influence and the struggle of some of the big powers have severely jeopardized the peace and security in this region. Iran is one of the important littoral states of the Persian Gulf. Your concern over the situation is natural and logical. We have consistently held that the affairs of one country must be managed by that country ... Iran and a number of other littoral states of the Persian Gulf believe that Persian Gulf affairs should be managed by the littoral states. They oppose outside interference. This is an equitable demand. We strongly support this. As the Shahenshah has said, the situation on the eastern and western sides of Iran is a very serious warning to Iran. Bearing in mind the situation created in this region, this country must strengthen its defence forces.' *S W B*, 18 June 1973.

24. Paknejad's final speech was published as a special pamphlet by the Confederation of Iranian Students.

25. In Britain Amnesty International issued numerous analyses and protests about the treatment of Iranian prisoners. In France a special committee for the defence of Iranian prisoners kept up a steady campaign. In Germany hostility to the Shah exploded during his visit to Berlin in June 1967 when one German student, Benno Ohnesorg, was killed and many others injured in demonstrations. Special squads of pro-Shah cheer-leaders, which the Germans call *Jubelperser*, were mobilized for such events.

26. Pouyan and Mani, op. cit., p. vi.

27. *International Herald Tribune*, 4 November 1972. On Iran's expansionist policies in the Gulf see Romhallah K. Ramazan, *The Persian Gulf: Iran's Role*, Charlottesville, 1972. An exposition of official Tehran thinking can be found in the two articles by R. M. Burrell on Iranian policy towards the Gulf and Indian Ocean, in *The Indian Ocean*, ed. Alvin J. Cottrell and R. M. Burrell, New York, 1972.

Part Six
Conclusion

Chapter Fifteen
Imperialist Strategy and Gulf Revolution

Imperialism in the 1970s

The history of the world over the past century has been that of two interrelated processes: the exploitative spread of capitalism from its places of greatest strength in Europe, North America and Japan to the rest of the world; and, in response to this, the rise of an anti-imperialist and socialist movement to challenge the capitalist mode of production. The history of the colonial world, and of the Middle East in particular, cannot be understood except n terms of these two general processes, and of the changes that have occurred within each. Whatever the specific phase of the battle between capitalism and socialism the general truth of their mutually contradictory character remains valid. On the very day after the signing of the Vietnam peace agreement Le Duc Tho, the North Vietnamese negotiator, reminded his audience that as long as there is imperialism there will be conflict and war.

In the decades following the Second World War imperialism went through a major transformation, partly forced upon it by the effects of the War and partly resulting from increased opportunities for capitalist development both in the industrialized countries and the colonial world. Politically this transformation took the form of decolonization: the handing of formal sovereignty to local governments and the withdrawal of direct and official imperialist responsibility for colonial countries. The economic concomitant of this was increased capitalist development of at least part of the colonial world; the growth of internal markets; the development of some manufacturing industries; the encouragement of capitalist agriculture and the increased penetration of these countries by foreign aid and private capital. Just as the members of the indigenous state began to play a larger political role as partners in this expanding system, so local state economic officials and private bourgeois now participated as a subordinate section of the imperialist economy. A third part of this transformation was military; whereas before, imperialist armies had played a direct role in stabilizing the colonial world, the trend was now towards a less visible imperialist presence. The imperialists retained key bases, provided aid and 'advisers', and remained ready to intervene when necessary; yet the front line of counter-revolutionary vigilance was now occupied by armies drawn from local recruits and at least partly commanded by local officers.[1]

This transition from direct to indirect control and, in some cases, to an interdependence did not necessarily involve an overall weakening of capitalist power. In so far as the economies of formerly backward countries expanded, the advanced capitalist countries were able to derive benefit from them; they acquired more raw materials, they controlled key sections of the new expanded financial and manufacturing sectors, and they had larger export markets. In return, they conceded greater political autonomy to the ruling classes in the formerly colonial states. The failure to accept this possibility has led to two complementary errors in revolutionary analyses of the post-colonial world. It was commonly asserted that political decolonization was a fraud, which in fact altered little or nothing of the previous colonial relationship; in some countries this was the case; and the category used to explain this, 'neo-colonialism', applied. But 'neo-colonialism' is a misnomer with regard to countries that have been subjected to intensified capitalist development, because it stresses the continuity rather than the difference. It asserts, falsely, that colonialism, i.e. direct control, is the only form imperialism can adopt; whereas colonialism is only one form of imperialism. Conversely, other revolutionaries argued that the economic development, and the larger margin of political and military autonomy found in post-colonial countries, signified a progressive anti-imperialist evolution. Both the Soviet Union and China argued versions of this theory. It rested on the same false premiss of the former argument: that imperialism allows only one relationship. The former argument maintained that since imperialism was dominant the relationship had not altered: the latter argued that since a new relationship had emerged imperialism and even capitalism had suffered a defeat. Neither of these positions was correct: the truth was that imperialism had taken a new form, distinct from the previous colonial model. The global expansion of capitalism was forced, and was able, to incorporate new junior partners into its system.

Capitalist Development in the Gulf

This transformation of imperialism was carried through in Arabia as in other areas of the colonial world. In the period between 1950 and 1970 the British decided to withdraw at least formally from South Yemen, Kuwait, Bahrain, Qatar and the 'Trucial' States. In Oman they also imposed a new 'moderate' regime and enlisted Arab states to participate in repression. In Iran and Saudi Arabia modernized versions of the ruling regimes were urged by the US to develop their economies and armies, and in response to internal and external forces took more vigorous independent political initiatives. Imperialism thus possessed a social base in these countries; and through this advantage, the advanced capitalist countries were able to begin a mutually advantageous and rapid development of the area.[2]

It was oil that provided the economic basis for this capitalist development. Unlike Egypt, India or Latin American countries, where the US urged a capitalist land reform, the surplus in Arabia did not have to come from a rationalized system of agriculture. In Iran, the one country where a large peasantry existed, a politically determined land reform was effected without generating a larger surplus. The available surplus from oil made foreign aid a negligible source of income; the indebtedness of the Gulf regimes resulted from overpurchasing and not from development loans. Industrialization also played a far smaller role than in other cases of capitalist development. The consequent economic boom attracted all kinds of capitalist interest, eager to share in the larger revenues. At the same time it created a larger political force, whose interests were tied to participation in world capitalism: in all these states the ruling families took first place in appropriating the surplus; but beneath them a growing class of state employees, comprador bourgeois and army officers were able to gain access to wealth and were consequently recruited to world capitalism. Over time, ruling *families* developed into ruling *classes*.

The existence of contradictions over oil and Israel between these expanding states and the advanced capitalist countries did not mean that they were anti-imperialist. Contradictions have always existed between and within capitalist states and ruling classes. Just as rival imperialism can clash over colonies, currency rates and inter-imperialist trade, so the oil companies and their patron governments can clash with Iran or Saudi Arabia without these latter intending to challenge the capitalist system as such. Similarly, Gulf holders of sterling and dollar reserves can, like any bourgeois investor, speculate on the weaknesses of advanced capitalist economies without this signifying that they are opposed to the system itself. There exists a hard dividing line between inter-imperialist and inter-capitalist contradictions on the one hand and contradictions between capitalism and socialism on the other. Local regimes and their apologists have tried to confuse this distinction in order to cast themselves in a spuriously anti-imperialist light. The crisis of late 1973 illustrated both the extent and the limits of the contradictions: the Arab oil producers were determined to exert diplomatic pressure on Israel, and to increase their economic advantages. But they were bargaining for a better position within the system and had no intention of undermining it.

Sub-Imperialism and Military Deployment

The continued and altered relationship between imperialism and Middle Eastern ruling classes is equally visible in the military field. The stability of the imperialist system in the area has rested on building up a set of intermediate capitalist states which are in general populous and strong enough to play a major regional role. These are sub-imperialist states, intermediaries in the

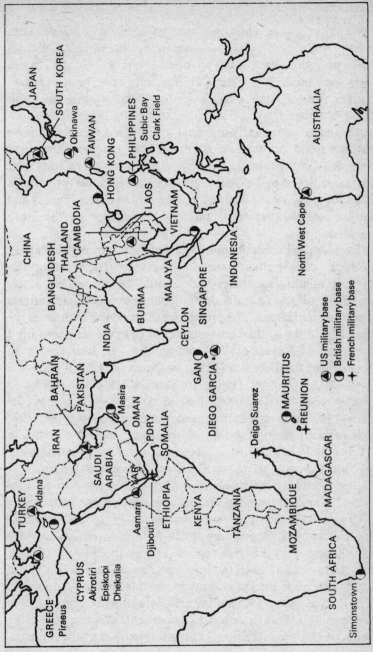

Map 16 Imperialist Military Deployment in the Middle East, Indian Ocean and Far East, 1973

exploitative whole. The armies and ruling classes of these states are the major agents of imperialism in the area, while imperialism itself maintains bases and provides covert aid. In the Middle East the countries which fulfil this role have been: Greece, Turkey, Iran, Pakistan, Saudi Arabia, Jordan, Israel and Ethiopia. Although Greece, Turkey, Pakistan and Ethiopia are non-Arab and geographically marginal to the Middle East they have formed stolid pro-western states on the periphery and have provided US imperialism with a low-level but vital military base for surveillance and possible penetration. Ethiopia provides a basis for guarding the Red Sea and the Indian Ocean. Turkey and Greece are the bases for military surveillance of the Arab countries.[3]

Despite their contradictions US and British imperialism have evolved a collaborative system in this respect. The two countries provide military assistance and advisers to pro-western states and have helped to train up the counter-revolutionary armies operating in the area. The present set of repressive regimes in the Gulf and in the Middle East would not be in existence but for a long line of British or US interventions: in Iran (1953), in Jordan and the Lebanon (1958), in Oman (in 1957–9 and 1965 onwards), in Kuwait (1961), in Bahrain (1956 and 1965), in North Yemen (1962–70) and in Saudi Arabia (1963). In both the June 1967 Arab–Israeli war and during the September 1970 war between King Hussein and the Palestinians US forces in Turkey and Germany were placed on the alert for possible deployment to support pro-US regimes (Israel and Jordan).

The strategic deployment of imperialism in the post-colonial period is evident from the line of bases which they retained after 1971 to bolster their pro-imperialist clients. In the north-west lay the US and British positions in the Mediterranean. At Asmara in Ethiopia the US retained an important NSA espionage establishment. In the Gulf, Britain had an air base on the island of Masira, while the US had use of naval facilities at Bahrain. In the Indian Ocean, where imperialist alarm at revolutionary movements and at an alleged 'Soviet' threat was evident, the British withdrawal from east of Suez was marked by the construction of a strong line of island bases linking Europe and the Gulf to imperialist positions in the Far East.[4] In the period after the announcement in January 1968 of the British withdrawal, several US spokesmen insisted that units of the Seventh Fleet would be moved west from duty in Indo-China to build up the US position in the Indian Ocean and in waters off the Arabian coast.[5]

In the Gulf itself both Britain and the US hoped to ensure stability through the alliance of Saudi Arabia and Iran, who would preside over a scene of post-colonial tranquillity. Speaking in January 1968 US Presidential adviser Eugene Rostow outlined US policy:

As to the Persian Gulf area, some very strong and quite active and stable states are interested in assuming responsibility for regional security ... Iran, Turkey, Pakistan, Saudi Arabia and Kuwait would certainly be a nucleus around which security arrangements could hopefully be built ...[6]

Similar perspectives were evident on the British side. An internal Conservative party document, written in February 1970 under the title *Defence Outside Nato*, hailed the newly reinforced 'Saudi–Iranian accord'.[7] Some sections of both the US and British states had hoped that the Conservative government elected in June 1970 would reverse the withdrawal decisions; but it was soon evident that a military deployment on the new model would be a more effective strategy. Even some low-level redeployment was questioned; British concern about Indian Ocean security and the need to arm South Africa was relatively short-lived; and the US government decision to continue the base at Bahrain met with serious Congressional opposition.[8]

A special role in this post-colonial system was played by the state of Israel, which had a specific role in the Middle East and a specific relationship to imperialism. Zionism was never simply a 'watchdog of imperialism'. It had always had a dual character; it was in origin an autonomous form of colonialism and had always retained its own interests; at the same time it had allied with imperialism as a junior and dependent partner and from the early 1950s was considered by US imperialism as a bulwark of

515

western interests in the Middle East. The state of Israel both served as an ally of imperialism and provoked contradictions for imperialism in the area. Its very presence both weakened Arab regimes (by demonstrating their incapacities) and gave these regimes eternal means of confusing class differences. Similarly its attacks on neighbouring Arab states (in 1956 and 1967) both constituted military attempts to destroy the achievements of the nationalist governments in Egypt and Syria and provoked intense anti-imperialist consciousness throughout the Arab world. While its indirect influence in Arabia was considerable – as via its defeat of Egypt – Israel's direct ability to intervene was limited; it did intervene, however, in North Yemen to support the royalists; and it maintained a military presence on the Ethiopian side of the Red Sea. It also had close economic ties with Iran. On the other hand the Israeli provocation to the Arab peoples was correctly seen by the oil companies as in some ways damaging to their interests, and this contradiction was reflected in political differences (between 'pro-Arab' and 'pro-Israel' groups) within Britain and the US.

Western Europe, Japan and the US realized their need for Gulf oil and this necessarily led them to deflect their policies away from Israel and towards the Arab states, especially after the 1973 Arab–Israeli war. This was a *real* problem for them, as the sharp disagreements between the US and the EEC countries on this topic showed. But this desire to placate the regimes in Riyadh and Kuwait also showed that Israel is not the main instrument of imperialist intervention in the Arabian peninsula: Israel is the main enemy of the people of Palestine, in the Gulf the main enemies of the people and the main allies of imperialism, are the Arab regimes themselves. They remain the guarantors of capitalist access to the region's oil, and there is little that Israel can do, militarily or otherwise, to protect European and US interests if they are further threatened.[9]

All of these intermediary imperialist clients had their main relationship with the United States, which was the undisputedly dominant imperialist power. It provided the bulk of the military support and controlled over half of all Middle East oil production.

By the 1960s the US had achieved a dominant position within imperialist control of the Middle East, parallel to the transition from direct to post-colonial control. Yet the other imperialisms remained influential; Britain in particular held on to much of its previous power. British–US relations in the Middle East had gone through a number of phases; up to the Second World War the US had minimal influence, except in Saudi Arabia. The period from the US entry into the war in 1941 to the proclamation of the Eisenhower Doctrine in 1957 was one of transition; it witnessed numerous Anglo–American contradictions in Saudi Arabia (1943–5), in Oman (1949–59), in Iran (1951–3) and over Suez (1956). Just as the Truman Doctrine had been proclaimed in 1947 to justify US replacement of the British in Greece and Turkey, so a decade later the Eisenhower Doctrine was proclaimed to mark the end of British political hegemony in the Middle East.

The British withdrawal from the peninsula spurred the US to increase its political and military role: in North Yemen, in Bahrain, in Oman the US acquired a position it had not previously held; in Saudi Arabia and Iran long-standing relationships were consolidated. Yet British imperialism retained considerable military and political influence in its former Gulf colonies, whose armies it officered and trained. Its economic record was even more favourable. Throughout the former colonial world the British had been in retreat politically but other sections of their imperial apparatus had remained intact and had grown with the growth of local economies. Although British domestic industry was weaker, the City of London and British financial institutions had continued to grow in strength, especially in the former colonies where British firms had retained an advantage. In four areas in particular, in the Caribbean, southern Africa, the Gulf and the Far East (i.e. Singapore and Hong Kong), British banks, consultancy firms and property and construction firms have enjoyed boom conditions.[10]

While US and British imperialisms remained dominant in the Gulf, their other fellow imperialisms also succeeded in gaining an economic grip on the growing Gulf economy. The French, whose constant and self-righteous berating of 'Anglo-Saxon' imperialism did not conceal the equally vicious character of French imperialism, maintained a share in oil production through C F P. French financial links with Gulf banks and French sales drives increased in the late 1960s; and A M X–30 amphibious tanks were sold to Saudi Arabia and Mirage jets to Kuwait and Abu Dhabi. This presence in the area represented a continuation of the long-standing French influence in the Middle East.[11] For the other three major imperialist powers, the defeated but revived bour-geoisies of the Axis powers, entry into the Gulf demanded a more disadvantageous competition. None was able to gain a significant hold on oil production and they had to remain in the position of being purchasers of crude from the major British and American firms. The Italians, through E N I, had concessions in Iran and Saudi Arabia; the Germans had concessions in Oman; and the Japanese had rights in Saudi Arabia, Abu Dhabi and the Neutral Zone. Their main hope for the future lay in signing agreements to buy crude oil from the national companies that were buying out the existing monopoly firms, as U S 'indepen-dents' were also doing. In the meantime their influence was at the level of providing goods and services; and in this sphere Japan-ese and German imperialism were able greatly to increase their share of Gulf markets.

The Role of the Communist States

The economic relationships of the peninsula and Gulf states with the communist countries were far less significant than those with capitalist states. The political ties established were more impor-tant; and the approach to the peninsula states formed part of the general foreign strategy of the Soviet Union and China. The most relevant and immediate difference between their actions lay not in their policies as such, but in the fact that the Soviet Union had the military and economic power to play an important role in the region in rivalling the west. The Soviet Union's role in the colon-ial world since the 1950s has led it both to support those states that were revolutionary (Cuba, Vietnam) and those where state bourgeoisies were establishing themselves under the guise of socialism (Egypt, India). This policy was not founded on un-wavering internationalism, yet it involved the maintenance of revolutionary states once these had come into existence. The same policy was applied to South Yemen after 1967 and in time considerable economic and military aid was available. In 1967 and 1968 the Russians also gave vital aid to the North Yemeni Republic. It gave backing to the anti-imperialist Ba'ath regime in Iraq. At the same time the Soviet Union entertained close re-lations with Iran and had contacts with several of the client pseudo-states of the Gulf – Kuwait, Bahrain and the UAA. Its policy was contradictory and refused to support consistently the anti-imperialist movement; while it aided South Yemen and gave belated support to the guerrilla movement in Oman, it also recognized the states whom these guerrillas were fighting and whose legitimacy was challenged by the PDRY. It played a definite, but limited, anti-imperialist role.

People's China differed in one important respect: in the 1960s the influence of Mao Tse-tung's theories had an important autonomous political effect for which the Soviet Union had no counterpart. In general China's foreign policy made the same ac-commodations. Like the Soviet Union, it gave much needed aid to the PDRY and supported the guerrilla movement in Oman; and at the same time it recognized, and thereby legitimized, the regimes challenged by the revolutionary movement. In the early 1970s China's foreign policy was governed by a general line of alliance with third-world governments against what it considered to be imperialist powers – the Soviet Union and the United States. It encouraged the divisive view that the Soviet Union was as or more dangerous than the US. In these terms it was essential to give support both to revolutionary movements and to govern-ments that opposed either of these 'imperialist' powers. The criterion of anti-imperialism was superficial and selective. Con-sequently China was inclined to characterize the Shah of Iran as anti-imperialist because of his price disputes with the oil companies. China also openly praised the Emperor of Ethiopia and gave support to the Nimeiry regime in the Sudan. In all these respects it differed from the local revolutionary movements, who were motivated not by a diplomatic concept of anti-imperialism, but by a class analysis of the regime in question.

The competitive polemical contradiction between the two Communist powers harmed the revolutionary movement in one respect; their common and separate détentes with imperialism harmed it in another, and posed a threat of even greater hindrance. Whereas in the late 1960s imperialist countries had been alarmed by Soviet and Chinese influence in the Middle East and the Indian Ocean, this apprehension declined markedly as the Kissinger–Nixon strategy got under way in the early 1970s. An early indication of the transition to collusion was the June 1970 Rogers Peace Plan, an attempt by the US, in alliance with the Soviet Union, to impose an unjust settlement on the Palestinian people. Part of the aim of this 'Peace Plan' was to enable the US to resolve the contradiction between its Israeli and oil-producing Arab clients. An analogous policy emerged in 1972–3, when the US alarm about oil supplies also led to a renewed diplomatic offensive. Following the October 1973 war, the Soviet Union almost abdicated its foreign policy role in the Middle East, in the face of Kissinger's energetic diplomacy and the accelerated swing of the Sadat regime to the right. Even the eternal dispute about Soviet naval influence in the Gulf and Indian Ocean was put to one side. The world-wide détente between the US and the communist powers was enabling imperialism to consolidate its counter-revolutionary position in the Middle East and, through great-power diplomacy, weaken the revolutionary movement.

The Autonomy of the Gulf Revolution

The imperialist strategy of crushing revolution and encouraging capitalist development operated at several levels, on each of which the revolutionary movement had to evolve its own response. This strategy was itself a response to the threats posed by the revolutionary movement throughout the world to the interests of imperialism. Within the Arabian peninsula its two principal aims were (a) to counter-attack the centres of revolutionary power – Dhofar and the People's Democratic Republic of

Yemen in the hope of insulating and then reversing the revolutionary movements, and (b) to ensure counter-revolutionary stability in existing capitalist states by the application of technically advanced means of repression, by military weight; and by political changes designed to broaden the social base of the existing regimes. On a broader international scale two further policies reinforced this peninsular strategy: (c) to build up the intermediate capitalist states as effective sub-imperialist guardians of counter-revolutionary stability; and (d) to evolve a divisive and minimally antagonistic relationship with the Soviet Union and China and thereby lessen their support of revolutionary movements.

Although some local conditions favoured the revolutionary struggle in Arabia, they did so at a time when the global trend was towards an at least temporary diplomatic détente and towards a consolidation of the post-colonial system. The continued escalation of popular struggle and inter-power contradiction presaged by the Vietnam War had given way to a new, more collaborative world approach. The effects of this on the Gulf, as on all other areas of revolutionary struggle, were negative. For the revolutionary movements of the Middle East, success was impossible without due emphasis on the autonomy of their struggle. This autonomy was not only strategically essential, but was also acknowledged by the counter-revolutionaries; the area was one where, both because of oil and because of the partially integrated character of peninsular politics, it was essential not merely to check but to reverse the anti-imperialist movement. In the case of Oman, because the Sultanate and its stability were essential to their Gulf strategy, the imperialists were forced to wage all-out war to try and destroy the liberated areas. At the same time they were forced to plan for the overthrow of the PDRY; the political interaction of the two Yemens was one reason for this; and the PDRY's internationalist support for the Gulf revolutionary movement meant that it was seen as a dangerous threat to imperialist interests.

The basic objectives of the revolutionary movement were defence of existing gains, and extension of the struggle through protracted political and military action. In South Yemen and Oman military defence of the liberated territories was accompanied by constant internal social and economic change – within the limits imposed by the poverty of these countries. In the areas of capitalist development – the Gulf states – the pro-imperialist regimes were forced to create ever larger working classes whose political consciousness they tried to anaesthetize by ethnic division; at the same time that they were carrying out economic transformation their political options were limited by the knowledge that a truly democratic system would place the power of the local ruling classes and of imperialism in jeopardy.

The importance of the Gulf to western imperialism guaranteed that the peoples of the area would only be victorious after a difficult and protracted struggle. There was no certainty that it would ever occur; no social system is ever necessarily overthrown. Revolution takes place only when favourable objective conditions combine with the intervention of a social agent capable of carrying through such a process. As the examples of the Chinese and Vietnamese revolutions had shown, such a revolution in a colonial or post-colonial state is possible under the guidance of flexible revolutionary politics and prolonged mass struggle. Other conditions in the world – the situation within the imperialist countries, the role of the communist states, the strength of anti-imperialist solidarity – help to determine the outcome. The only certainty is that imperialism will continue to intervene in the Arabian peninsula and to support the oppressive local regimes until the peoples of this area, united in and guided by revolutionary organizations, rise to assert their freedom.

Notes

1. For an early theorization see Hamza Alavi, 'Imperialism Old and New', *Socialist Register*, 1964. A detailed account of US imperialism's new military strategy is contained in Michael Klare, *War Without End*, New York, 1972.

2. An interesting index of a changed imperialist concern about the Gulf was found in the several seminars on the Gulf organized by pro-imperialist academic circles from 1968 onwards. Some of the earlier ones were obsessed

by the fear of a 'Russian threat' – as *The Gulf: Implications of British Withdrawal*, Washington, 1969. Later reports took a calmer view of the problem – see Elisabeth Monroe, *The Changing Balance of Power in the Persian Gulf*, New York, 1972.

3. The aid figures to these states tell their own tale; total US military aid to Near East and South Asian states in the period 1946–70 totalled $8,435·3 million. Of this $2,142·4 million went to Greece, $1,365·6 million went to Iran, $3,401·4 million went to Turkey. Jordan received $57·4 million, Pakistan $87·1 million and Saudi Arabia $35·7 million. Out of total US aid to all of Africa over the same period of $341·7 million, nearly a half, $166·1 million, went to Ethiopia.

4. The British line of bases to the east were Cyprus, Masira, Gan and Singapore. The US had immense air facilities in Turkey, its NSA base at Asmara in Ethiopia, its naval position in Bahrain and a base on the uninhabited island of Diego Garcia, begun in 1970 and opened in 1973 at a cost of $19 million. According to Admiral John S. McCain, US Commander-in-Chief, Pacific, 'As Malta is to the Mediterranean, Diego Garcia is to the Indian Ocean.' Klare, op. cit., p. 359. In early 1974 the Pentagon applied for a $29 million grant to expand the Diego Garcia base, and revealed that it might station F-111A bombers on the island. It was also planned to build naval facilities there too. Following international protests, the plan was temporarily withdrawn from public view.

5. Klare, op. cit., develops a general thesis about the spread of conflict westwards from Indo-China, in the chapter entitled 'The Great South Asian War'. The Indian Ocean was increasing in strategic significance; 15,000 ships a year passed around the Cape while the Suez Canal was closed; and these included all the oil tankers ferrying supplies to Europe; Soviet–US rivalry remained relatively strong in the area although the quantitative content of the Soviet naval presence was greatly exaggerated. Of more long-term significance was the fact that anti-imperialist movements had emerged all around the rim of the peninsula; in Ceylon (the 1971 armed insurrection); in Arabia (Oman and South Yemen); in Ethiopia (the Eritrean struggle); in Mozambique; and in Madagascar (the 1971 peasant rising in the southern Tular province). Even on some of the small islands, such as Mauritius and the French-occupied Comoros, anti-imperialist parties were organizing. See *The Indian Ocean: Its Political, Economic and Military Importance*, ed. Alvin J. Cottrell and R. M. Burrell, New York and London, 1972.

6. Voice of America, 19 January 1968.

7. 'Overseas Issues Facing the Next Conservative Government: Defence Outside NATO', Ref. CCOC 274, February 1970. This document, marked 'For private circulation: not for publication', was widely available in London, and considered counter-revolutionary perspectives in three sectors – the Gulf, South-East Asia and the Cape route.

8. See 'Executive Agreements with Portugal and Bahrain', *Hearings*

Conclusion

Before the Committee on Foreign Relations, United States Senate Ninety-Second Congress, Second Session on S. Res. 214. The chairman of the committee, William Fulbright, remarked, 'What is the reason for our presence there? It is so if anybody gets funny, we will come in' (p. 20). Later he proposed the more fashionable alternative: 'Why wouldn't it be wise to forget it and rely upon the Shah of Iran?' (p. 46).

9. The common assertion that Israel's function in the Middle East is *simply* that of guarding imperialist oil and strategic interests avoids the contradictory character of the Israeli role. In non-Arab Africa this is more directly that of a conduit for U S expertise and funds to pro-western regimes. See 'Israel: Imperialist Mission in Africa', *Tricontinental*, 15.

10. See the Association for Radical East Asian Studies, 'Hong Kong: Britain's Last Colonial Stronghold', London, 1972.

11. French imperialism had several military positions in the Indian Ocean area: in Djibouti, in the Comoros and at the naval base of Diégo-Suarez in northern Madagascar. In 1972 France had over 18,000 troops stationed abroad, and was actively engaged in Chad suppressing the liberation movement. Of particular relevance to Arabia was the French hold on Djibouti; this colony, known as the Territoire Français des Afars et des Issas (TFAI) and occupied by France in 1859, had an area of 8,500 square miles and a population of 137,000. Following mass demonstrations during De Gaulle's visit in 1966, a faked pro-French referendum was held on the lines the British had used in Aden – i.e. using a discriminatory electoral roll which excluded those of Issa origin. A special barrier of mines and barbed wire was set up outside Djibouti town to keep out 'illegal immigrants', and several people were killed by detonated mines. In 1972 the French set up their own bedouin army, the *Force Mobile de Protection et de Défense*, and increased their garrison to over 5,000 men. Pompidou's visit in January 1973 was the occasion for fascist declarations about the 'French' character of the zone. One of its main functions for France was that it served as the base for parent companies whose subsidiaries operated in Indo-China; these included CARIC, an auto-assembly subsidiary of Citroen, who assembled Dalat jeeps in Vietnam, and MICSA, a firm manufacturing cigarettes in Indo-China. French hypocrisy about being 'pro-Arab' carefully ignored the oppression practised in Djibouti, where Beau Geste held sway long after Lawrence and his epigones had been driven from the shores opposite.

Appendix One
Abbreviations

A D M A	Abu Dhabi Marine Areas
A D P C	Abu Dhabi Petroleum Company
A I O C	Anglo-Iranian Oil Company
A L B A	Aluminium Bahrain
A P O C	Anglo-Persian Oil Company
A R A M C O	Arabian American Oil Company
A T U C	Aden Trades Union Congress
B A C	British Aircraft Corporation
B A P C O	Bahrain Petroleum Company
B A T T	British Army Training Team
B P	British Petroleum
C F P	Compagnie Française des Pétroles
C I A	Central Intelligence Agency
D L F	Dhofar Liberation Front
F L O S Y	Front for the Liberation of Occupied South Yemen
F R A	Federal Regular Army
I P C	Iraq Petroleum Company
K O C	Kuwait Oil Company
M A N	Movement of Arab Nationalists
N D F L O A G	National Democratic Front for the Liberation of Oman and the Arab Gulf
N I O C	National Iranian Oil Company
N L F	National Liberation Front
N S A	National Security Agency
O L O S	Organization for the Liberation of the Occupied South
O P E C	Organization of Petroleum Exporting Countries
P D F L P	Popular Democratic Front for the Liberation of Palestine
P D O	Petroleum Development Oman
P D R Y	People's Democratic Republic of Yemen
P D U	People's Democratic Union

525

PFLOAG	Popular Front for the Liberation of the Occupied Arab Gulf (1968–71). Popular Front for the Liberation of Oman and the Arab Gulf (from 1971)
PFLP	Popular Front for the Liberation of Palestine
PORF	Popular Organization of Revolutionary Forces
PRF	Popular Resistance Forces
PRSY	People's Republic of South Yemen
PSP	People's Socialist Party
QPC	Qatar Petroleum Company
RAF	Royal Air Force
SAA	South Arabian Army
SAF	Sultan's Armed Forces
SAL	South Arabian League
SAS	Special Air Services
SOAF	Sultan of Oman's Air Force
SOCAL	Standard Oil of California
SWB	*BBC Summary of World Broadcasts*, Part 4
TOS	Trucial Oman Scouts
UAA	Union of Arab Amirates (1968–71); United Arab Amirates (from 1971)
UAE	see UAA
UAR	United Arab Republic
UNF	United National Front
UNP	United National Party
YAR	Yemeni Arab Republic

Appendix Two
Basic Data on Peninsular and Gulf States
(For oil statistics see pp. 432ff.)

Country	Capital	Area miles	Population	Armed forces 1971	Combat aircraft 1971
Iran	Tehran	627,000	32,000,000 (1972)	191,000	160
Iraq	Baghdad	169,240	8,500,000 (1972)	101,800	189
Saudi Arabia	Riyadh	927,000*	4,000,000*	40,500	71
Kuwait	Kuwait city	6,200	733,000 (1971)	9,200	30
Neutral Zone	–	3,560	–	–	–
Bahrain	Manama	255	216,000 (1970)	1,100	–
Qatar	Doha	4,000	112,000 (1970)	1,800	–
UAA		30,000	200,000 (1972)*	1,600	–
of which:					
Abu Dhabi	Abu Dhabi	26,000*	46,000 (1971)	7,000	12
Dubai	Dubai	1,500	80,000 (1972)	1,000	–
Sharjah	Sharjah	1,000	31,500 (1968)	–	–
Ras al-Khaimah	Ras al-Khaimah	650	24,500 (1968)	250	–
Fujairah	Fujairah	450	9,700 (1968)	–	–
Ajman	Ajman	100	4,200 (1968)	–	–

Appendix Two

Country	Capital	Area miles	Population	Armed forces 1971	Combat aircraft 1971
Umm al-Qaiwain	Umm al-Qaiwain	300	3,700 (1968)	–	–
Oman	Muscat	82,000	750,000 (1972)	10,000	15
South Yemen	Aden	112,000*	1,500,000 (1972)*	14,000	?
North Yemen	Sanaa	74,000	4,500,000 (1972)*	7,000	?

* These figures are particularly unreliable. Statistics on area are vitiated by the fact that the Saudis claim large parts of South Yemen and of Abu Dhabi. Population statistics are also variable: in the case of Saudi Arabia no reliable figures are available; in the smaller Gulf states immigration is so massive that figures change from month to month.

Sources: area, for all but Iran and Iraq, Derek Hopwood, ed., *The Arabian Peninsula*; for Iran and Iraq, *The Statesman's Year-Book 1965-66*; armed forces and combat aircraft, for all but the Yemens, *The Military Balance 1972-73*; population figures and armed forces of two Yemens from press reports.

Appendix Three

Exchange of Letters between the Government of the United Kingdom of Great Britain and Northern Ireland and the Sultan of Muscat and Oman concerning the Sultan's Armed Forces, Civil Aviation, Royal Air Force Facilities and Economic Development in Muscat and Oman

London, July 25, 1958

No. 1

The Secretary of State for Foreign Affairs to the Sultan of Muscat and Oman

Foreign Office, S.W.1,
My honoured and valued Friend, *July 25, 1958.*

With reference to the discussions which I have had the pleasure of holding with Your Highness in London, and following upon those which took place in Muscat between Your Highness and Mr Julian Amery in January, 1958, I have the honour to set out below my understanding of the agreement which has been reached between us.

In pursuance of the common interest of Your Highness and Her Majesty's Government in furthering the progress of the Sultanate of Muscat and Oman, Her Majesty's Government in the United Kingdom have agreed to extend assistance towards the strengthening of Your Highness's Army. Her Majesty's Government will also, at Your Highness's request, make available Regular officers on secondment from the British Army, who will, while serving in the Sultanate, form an integral part of Your Highness's Armed Forces. The terms and conditions of service of these seconded British officers have been agreed with Your Highness. Her Majesty's Government will also provide training facilities for members of Your Highness's Armed Forces and will make advice available on training and other matters as may be required by Your Highness.

Her Majesty's Government will also assist Your Highness in the establishment of an Air Force as an integral part of Your Highness's Armed Forces, and they will make available personnel to this Air Force.

Your Highness has approved the conclusion of an agreement for the extension of the present arrangements regarding civil aviation and the use by the Royal Air Force of the airfields at Salalah and Masirah.

We also discussed the economic and development problems of the Sultanate and Her Majesty's Government agreed to assist Your Highness in carrying out a civil development programme which will include the improvement of roads, medical and educational facilities and an agricultural research programme.

If your Majesty agrees that the foregoing correctly sets out the agreement reached between us I have the honour to suggest that this letter and Your Highness's reply should be regarded as constituting an Agreement between Your Highness and my Government.

I have the honour to be, with the highest consideration,

Your Highness's
sincere friend,
SELWYN LLOYD.

No. 2

The Sultan of Muscat and Oman to the Secretary of State for Foreign Affairs

Your Excellency, *London, July 25, 1958.*

We have received Your Excellency's letter of to-day's date, setting out the agreement which has been reached in discussions between ourself and Her Majesty's Government in the United Kingdom, and confirm that your letter and this reply should be regarded as constituting an agreement between us and your Government.

Your sincere friend,
SAID BIN TAIMUR.

Source: Treaty Series No. 28, 1958, Cmnd., 507.

Appendix Four

PFLOAG Documents

Section A. The National Democratic Working Plan, adopted at the Third Congress of the Popular Front for the Liberation of Oman and the Arabian Gulf, June 1971

When British imperialism took control of the territories of the Arab Gulf which stretch from Dhofar in the south to Kuwait in the north, it practised the worst kinds of annihilation and exploitation against our people. In spite of this, our people resisted the invasion of British imperialism very bravely, just as they had already resisted Portuguese and Dutch imperialism.

The main reason why the popular risings of the last century and a half failed was that they had a feudalist, tribal or bourgeois character. The leaders of these revolts betrayed our people and led their struggles along an incorrect and capitulationist path, in which they collaborated with the imperialists and reactionaries.

After a long series of combative experiences and of resistance to occupation, and through absorbing the great historical lessons won by our people from these experiences, which included realizing what the major weaknesses and setbacks were in addition to certain betrayals, our masses for the first time planned a correct and novel way forward. They set out on this road on 9 June 1965.

British imperialism was not content to impose control on our people, to install military bases in our country, to loot our resources and open up our lands and markets to Britain and other imperialist powers. It also split the area up politically into a large group of sultanates, sheikhdoms and other tenuous political entities. The aim of this was to weaken the area, separate the people off from each other and to create artificial conflicts and regional clashes so that it would be easy to control and exploit these areas for as long as possible.

The great growth of popular revolution in the south of the Gulf and the increase in popular hostility to imperialist control all over the area forced British imperialism to adopt a new colonialist policy. This involved modernizing the form imperialism took in the northern part of the Gulf, through evacuating some of its bases and troops from the northern area and granting these regions a fake and fictitious independence.

The United Arab Amirates, which Anglo-American imperialism in collaboration with local reaction is trying to establish, is in the interests of the imperialists and reactionaries, and is being set up against the will and the interests of the people. The people want to put an end to the division of the area and to turn the idea of unity into a reality.

The withdrawal of British troops from the northern part of the Gulf and the imperialist and reactionary plans which are directed by the US are only tactics by which, in different ways, they are trying to fortify their interests and weaken the national democratic movement in the Gulf . . .

The Enemies of the People and the National Classes

In our view society in the Arabian Gulf is a colonial society, semi-colonized in some areas, and semi-feudalist in others. For this reason the enemies of the people and of the revolution are imperialism, feudalism and all their collaborators. The comprador bourgeoisie collaborate with the feudalist forces; they help the representatives of feudalism to strengthen their dictatorship and exploitation of our people. They are therefore to be considered enemies of the people and of the revolution. The working class and the poor peasantry form the majority of the people. They make up eighty per cent of the total population and form the main group exploited by imperialism and feudalism. This means that these two classes form the driving political power of the revolution and the basis of the revolution. The petty bourgeoisie in the cities and in the countryside also suffer at the hands of the enemies of the revolution – of imperialism, feudalism and the comprador bourgeoisie. Therefore, the majority of the petty bourgeoisie can be included as part of the revolution.

The Importance of the Broad National Front

In order to face so many enemies, to conquer them and to be victorious all over the Gulf the masses must rise up against the imperialists and their puppets, the Amirs, sultans, feudalists and compradors. The other classes have a common interest in combating the enemies of the revolution and must unite in a wider front, which is an alliance between all patriotic classes and groups within the people.

We attach great importance to the establishment of a broad popular front all over the Gulf which is a precondition for conquering all the enemies of the people and defeating them. We also lay stress on the necessity of the revolution being led by the class which is in the majority and on the fact that this is a major condition of the realization of the

532

united front and the achievement of final victory. Through struggle we can unite as one block all anti-imperialist and anti-reactionary forces. Such a fighting bloc cannot be realized through compromises or an unclear political line.

Different Types of Struggle Against Imperialism and its Reactionary Allies

The Gulf revolution must be an armed struggle and the people must fight with all their revolutionary capacity to bring down the imperialist and reactionary powers. Without mobilizing all our forces we can never conquer and defeat any regime in any province of the Gulf and we can never protect our revolution. The enemy is certainly stronger than the exploited and unarmed people. But, equally certainly, this superiority is only temporary. We will successfully throw it out of gear, thanks to our revolutionary initiative and our determination to follow the path of protracted popular struggle, which is the only way to weaken the temporary superiority of the enemy. It is also the way to turn our temporary weakness successfully into an important force. Our determination with regard to the policy of armed struggle as a fundamental principle and as a strategy, and the necessity to use violence throughout the area, do not mean that we must give up other methods of struggle. Armed struggle can never be realized if it is not supported by other types of fighting. There are primary and secondary means of struggle and we must always apply both without confusion.

The imperialists and their allies, the local rulers and all reactionaries have concentrated their forces and activities in the cities. Therefore it is important for the revolution to direct its energies towards those villages where the population is most underdeveloped and to build up strong bases and revolutionary strongholds there. This does not mean that we leave the importance of the cities out of consideration. It is impossible for the revolution to exist and to triumph without receiving revolutionary support from the cities and without revolutionary activity spreading and including both the villages and the cities, where the enemy's military centres and bases are situated.

The Historical Character of the Revolution

What is the historical character of the revolution in the present situation? Since the enemies of the revolution are represented by imperialism, feudalism, and the comprador bourgeoisie:

Appendix Four

1. The revolution must be capable of crushing imperialism and achieving independence.

2. The revolution must also be thoroughly democratic and must be capable of crushing the allies of imperialism – tribalism, autocracy, feudalism and the comprador bourgeoisie. This means that the revolution in the Gulf is a national democratic revolution.

If we do not follow a clear line corresponding to the demands of popular democracy, the revolution will become stagnant and will be unable to win the national struggle. These two revolutionary tasks are tightly linked to each other.

Obviously the nature of revolutionary democracy is different from bourgeois democracy. Only the progressive forces can solve the democratic tasks of the revolution. The democracy for which the revolution is fighting and for which the masses are striving is certainly a democracy of a new kind. It is a new and revolutionary democracy.

The tasks and purposes of the national democratic revolution for which we must fight and on which the unity of all groups and national classes in the Gulf area are to be based are interpreted by the Popular Front for the Liberation of the Occupied Arab Gulf as follows.

The Tasks of the National Democratic Revolution

(a) The Local Dimension
1. The liberation of the area from all forms of colonialism and the realization of complete independence.
2. The eradication of all tribal and autocratic regimes.
3. The eradication of the division of the area and the realization of political unity
4. The eradication of all forms of feudalism.
5. The eradication of slavery and the abolition of all slave relations.
6. The establishment of a popular democratic authority.
7. The ending of exploitation by the comprador class.
8. The liquidation of all forms of foreign monopoly.
9. The liberation of the national market from all ties to the international capitalist market.
10. The building up of an independent national economy with an agricultural and a heavy industrial base.
11. The freeing and release of the energies of the masses who are the real beneficiaries of the revolution.
12. The mobilization of the people's resources politically and militarily.

13. The building up of a strong revolutionary army.

14. The eradication of differences in development between rural and urban areas.

15. The liberation of women from all forms of political, social and family oppression.

16. The attack on colonialist culture and the building of a revolutionary national culture.

17. The eradication of social injustice and the provision of a decent living for every citizen.

18. The combating of moral, administrative and political corruption.

19. The combating of poverty, illiteracy, disease and all forms of backwardness in society.

20. The guaranteeing of full rights for minorities and foreign communities.

21. The freedom of religious belief and affiliation.

(b) The Arab Dimension

22. Working towards the unity of progressive nationalist groups in the Arab world.

23. The effective participation in the Arab revolutionary movement in order to complete the tasks of the national democratic stage and to build up the united Arab socialist community.

24. The establishment of stronger relations between the masses of the Arab homeland who are the main force in the struggle now being waged between the Arab masses and the forces of colonialism, Zionism, and Arab reaction.

25. The exposure of reactionary Arab regimes which serve the forces of imperialism and Zionism.

26. The unification of the Palestinian nationalist organizations in the protracted popular struggle against Zionism and world imperialism and against their interests in the area, which is the correct way to liberate Palestine and destroy the presence of Zionism.

(c) The International Dimension

27. The consideration of the national democratic revolution in the Gulf as part of the international nationalist revolutionary movement.

28. The commitment of support to the struggles of oppressed peoples in the three continents of Asia, Africa and Latin America, who are waging a just struggle against the forces of colonialism and neo-colonialism and against racialist entities and movements in the world.

29. The participation with the international socialist and progressive

forces in their historic struggle against the forces of imperialism and world capitalism.

Section B. Declaration to the British people, February 1970

For over a century Britain has ruled the Arabian Gulf, first to protect the approaches to India, then to guard its oil interests. In the Gulf itself British rule has involved direct occupation of the area. In Muscat and Oman her rule has been indirect, through the local Sultan; he is formally independent but is in fact a British client, financed, armed and preserved by British power.

This British presence has led to the suppression of all movements that threaten Britain and her local servants, or that try to overcome the underdevelopment and misery of the people. The local people have been excluded from the politics of their country and the prisons of the Gulf are full of democrats who oppose this system. Britain has artificially preserved the separate units of the zone. In Oman there are no schools or medical services and the Sultan has over 5,000 private slaves to work his plantations and staff his bodyguard. This is the regime Britain is supporting.

Britain claims she will leave the Gulf in 1971. This is a fraud. Britain has grouped her client sheikhs into a Union of Arab Amirates which will pretend to be an independent state. Yet it will continue to protect British interests and it will be preserved by a mercenary army commanded and supplied by Britain. The sole aim of this army is 'internal security' – i.e. suppressing political opposition. Britain aims to continue her rule by proxy. Moreover in Muscat and Oman Britain's position will not alter at all since she claims that the Sultan is already independent. Her bases, planes and military personnel will remain there and will be ready to suppress any opposition.

In addition American imperialism is expanding its influence in the area and hopes to replace Britain as the dominant power. The reactionary monarchies of Iran and Saudi Arabia are being backed by America. all of them intent on controlling and suppressing the peoples of the Gulf.

Since 9 June 1965, we, the Popular Front for the Liberation of the Occupied Arab Gulf, have been fighting an armed struggle against British imperialism and her local clients, to liberate the whole of the Gulf from imperialism and oppression. In the Dhofar province of Oman we have liberated over two thirds of the territory and driven the British into a defensive position.

Using RAF planes and Pakistani mercenaries commanded by British officers, Britain has replied to military defeat by a brutal attack on the economic life of the liberated area. They have bombed and shelled our herds and the villages, pastures and wells where our people work. British officers have tortured prisoners and innocent citizens, and have personally ordered many of our villages to be burnt or bombed.

We are fighting against both national and class oppression; against the oppression of our nation by Britain and Iran, and against Saudi Arabia; and against the class oppression of the reactionary despots of the Gulf. We are also fighting on two fronts; a military fight against British intervention, and a social fight against the backwardness that imperialism has preserved in this area; that is against illiteracy, tribal division and the subjection of women. The liberation of Dhofar is only the first step to the liberation of the whole Gulf.

We demand the complete and immediate withdrawal of Britain from all areas of the Gulf, and the renunciation of all British defence ties with the sultans, sheikhs and Amirs she has been propping up for so long. We denounce both the Conservative and Labour parties for their identical policies of oppression in the area. Moreover we know that the British people have been kept in complete ignorance of these facts by a tight censorship and in particular by the refusal to permit independent observers to visit Dhofar.

Our struggle is part of a world-wide movement against imperialism and against exploitation by capital. We are one with the heroic people of Vietnam and with the people of Palestine and we stand with the peoples of Rhodesia and Northern Ireland who like us are fighting disguised forms of British colonial rule.

We appeal to all progressive forces in Britain to support our cause, and to oppose this savage and secret war being fought by Britain to protect her oil and her slave-owning Sultan. We shall continue our fight till the whole of the Gulf has been liberated and until British imperialism has been finally driven from the area. Long Live the Unity of the Anti-imperialist struggle in the World!

British and American Imperialism out of the Gulf!

Long Live the 9 June!

Source: The Popular Front for the Liberation of the Occupied Arab Gulf, Dhofar, 1970.

Appendix Five
Further Information

Readers wishing for further information on the revolutionary movement in the peninsula should write to PFLOAG at PO Box 5037, Maala, Aden, People's Democratic Republic of Yemen. PFLOAG issues a weekly magazine in English and Arabic editions and this carries full reports of the latest military events in Oman together with political analyses of latest events throughout the area. The Arabic weekly magazines *al-Horria* (PO Box 857, Beirut, Lebanon) and *at-Talia* (PO Box 1082, Kuwait) also contain sustained coverage of Gulf developments. Information is also available from support committees in some capitalist countries: in Britain – the Gulf Committee, c/o ICDP, 6 Endsleigh St, London W.C.1; in France – Comité de solidarité à la révolution Yémenite et aux mouvements de libération de la péninsule arabique, B.P. no. 20, Paris 14e; in Germany – Arbeitskreis Nahost/golf, 1 Berlin 30, Postfach 4048; in Denmark – Box 86, DK – 5800 Nyborg; USA – Gulf Solidarity, PO Box 40155, San Francisco, California 94140. The Confederation of Iranian Students can be reached via CIS(NU), 6 Frankfurt 16, Postfach 16247, West Germany.

The historical and background sources for the area have been covered in the notes. David Holden, *Farewell to Arabia*, London, 1966, gives the one general impression of the peninsula. On some subjects, such as North Yemen, oil and Iran, there exists a considerable literature; on others, such as South Yemen, Oman and Saudi Arabia, there is far less. Works of any serious analytic or theoretical character concerning the peninsula are few. Contemporary events are covered by a number of publications. The annual Europa year-book entitled *The Middle East and North Africa* and published in London every autumn contains detailed political and economic material, together with extensive statistical tables. The daily financial press in capitalist countries devotes some attention to Gulf developments, and there exists a more specialized weekly press devoted to the same topic: *Middle East Economic Digest* (London) and *Middle East Economic Survey* (Beirut) contain detailed weekly reports. The London-based Economist

Intelligence Unit publishes quarterly reports and an annual supplement on four relevant topics: *Iran, Middle East Oil, Saudi Arabia and Jordan* and *The Arabian Peninsula: Sheikhdoms and Republics*. An annual listing of manpower and armaments is given in the *Military Balance* published by the Institute of Strategic Studies in London. Political developments can be followed in the more informative western daily papers (especially *Le Monde*) and in the quarterly chronology printed in the *Middle East Journal* (Washington). The Beirut and local Arab daily papers are also selectively informative for those to whom they are accessible, and can be monitored via the London-based *Arab Report and Record*, and the Beirut-based weekly produced by *an-Nahar*. The best periodical analysis of the area's politics is to be found in the reports published by Middle East Research and Information Project, P O Box 48, Cambridge, Mass. 02138, U S A.

Governments and firms operating in the area publish some information. The Saudi Arabian Monetary Agency and the Bank Melli Iran are two central banks who do so. Oil, construction and financial companies also print material on their activities.

About the Author

FRED HALLIDAY was born in Dublin in 1946. He studied at Queen's College, Oxford, and the School of Oriental and African Studies, London, and worked on the staff of the periodicals *Black Dwarf* and *7 Days*. He has edited Isaac Deutscher's *Russia, China and the West 1953–1966*, and translated Karl Korsch's *Marxism and Philosophy*. He is a member of the editorial board of the *New Left Review* and lives in London.

VINTAGE BIOGRAPHY AND AUTOBIOGRAPHY

VINTAGE WORKS OF SCIENCE
AND PSYCHOLOGY

VINTAGE CRITICISM,
LITERATURE, MUSIC, AND ART

VINTAGE POLITICAL SCIENCE
AND SOCIAL CRITICISM